TETON SIOUX MUSIC

Da Capo Press Music Reprint Series

TETON SIOUX MUSIC

By Frances Densmore

DA CAPO PRESS · NEW YORK · 1972

Library of Congress Cataloging in Publication Data

Densmore, Frances, 1867-1957.
    Teton Sioux music.

    (Da Capo Press music reprint series)
    Reprint of the 1918 ed., which was issued as Bulletin
61 of Smithsonian Institution. Bureau of American
Ethnology.
    Bibliography: p.
    I. Indians of North America—Music. 2. Dakota
Indians. I. Title. II. Series: U.S. Bureau of
American Ethnology. Bulletin 61.
ML3557.D376   1972   784.7'51   72-1889
ISBN 0-306-70516-8

This Da Capo Press edition of *Teton Sioux Music* is an
unabridged republication of the first edition published
in Washington, D.C., in 1918 as Bulletin 61 of the
Bureau of American Ethnology, Smithsonian Institution.

Published by Da Capo Press, Inc.
A Subsidiary of Plenum Publishing Corporation
227 West 17th Street, New York, New York 10011

TETON SIOUX MUSIC

ŚIYA'KA

SMITHSONIAN INSTITUTION
BUREAU OF AMERICAN ETHNOLOGY
BULLETIN 61

TETON SIOUX MUSIC

BY

FRANCES DENSMORE

WASHINGTON
GOVERNMENT PRINTING OFFICE
1918

LETTER OF TRANSMITTAL

SMITHSONIAN INSTITUTION,
BUREAU OF AMERICAN ETHNOLOGY,
Washington, D. C., June 8, 1915.

SIR: I have the honor to submit herewith the manuscript of a memoir on Teton Sioux Music, by Frances Densmore, and to recommend its publication as a bulletin of the Bureau of American Ethnology.

Very respectfully,

F. W. HODGE,
Ethnologist-in-Charge.

Dr. CHARLES D. WALCOTT,
Secretary of the Smithsonian Institution.

III

FOREWORD

The analytical study of Indian music which the writer commenced among the Chippewa has been continued among the Sioux. Those familiar with the two books already published [1] will find no material change in method of treatment in the present volume. We have but passed from the land of pine forests and lakes to the broad plains where the buffalo came down from the north in the autumn and where war parties swept to and fro.

The present volume contains tabulated analyses of 600 songs, comprising the Chippewa songs previously published as well as the songs of the Teton Sioux. By means of these tables the songs of the two tribes can be compared in melodic and rhythmic peculiarities. In Bulletin 53 the Chippewa songs were grouped according to their use, and descriptive, as well as tabulated, analyses disclosed resemblances between certain groups of songs having the same mental concept. In the present memoir the comparison is based, not on the use, but on the age, of the songs, this series being divided for analysis into two groups, one comprising songs believed to be more than 50 years old and the other comprising songs of more recent origin. This analysis shows that the restrictions of civilization have had a definite effect on the structure of Sioux melodies.

In presenting Teton Sioux music the writer desires to acknowledge her appreciation of the valued assistance of her principal interpreter, Mr. Robert P. Higheagle, a member of the Sioux tribe and a graduate of Hampton Normal and Agricultural Institute as well as of the business department of Carnegie College. Mr. Higheagle's cooperation covered the entire period of collecting the Teton material and of preparing it for publication. To this work he brought a knowledge of Sioux life and character without which an interpretation of their deeper phases could not have been obtained. During Mr. Higheagle's absence it became necessary to employ occasionally other interpreters, whose aid is acknowledged in connection with the material which they interpreted. The principal assisting interpreter was Mrs. James McLaughlin, whose courtesy is gratefully acknowledged.

The writer desires also to express her appreciation of the assistance cordially extended by the members of the staff of the Bureau of American Ethnology and of the National Museum in their respective fields of research.

Frances Densmore.

[1] Chippewa Music, *Bulletin 45*, and Chippewa Music—II, *Bulletin 53*, of the Bureau of American Ethnology.

CONTENTS

ILLUSTRATIONS

LIST OF SONGS

1. Arranged in Order of Serial Numbers

songs used in ceremonies

Song of the Coming of the White Buffalo Maiden

XIV LIST OF SONGS placed above.

SONGS OF THE HEYO′KA

SONGS RECORDED AT SISSETON, S. DAK.

2. ARRANGED IN ORDER OF CATALOGUE NUMBERS

Cata-logue No.	Title of song	Name of singer	Serial No.	Page
450	"The many lands you fear"	Śiya′ka	8	109
451	Song of cutting the sacred pole	....do	11	113
452	Song of painting the sacred pole	....do	13	117
453	Opening song of the Sun dance (a)	....do	19	128
454	Song in honor of Two Bears	....do	188	453
455	"I fear not"	....do	185	449
456	"We are coming"	....do	5	105
457	Dancing song (e)	....do	33	146
458	....do. (f)	....do	34	147
459	....do. (g)	....do	35	148
460	Song in honor of Oni′han	....do	150	369
461	"A spirit has come"	....do	74	232
462	"Father, sing to me"	....do	73	230
463	"From whence the winds blow"	....do	75	233
464	"Something I foretold"	....do	76	234
465	Song concerning war paint	....do	138	353
466	"Tremble! O tribe of the enemy"	....do	139	354
467	"A root of herb"	....do	113	304
468	"Behold my horse!"	....do	140	355
469	Song to secure buffalo in time of famine	....do	183	445
470	"Chasing, they walked"	....do	112	303
471	"Something sacred I wear"	....do	105	295
472	"An eagle·nation is coming"	....do	55	193
473	Song of the crow and owl	....do	50	186
474	"Where the wind is blowing"	....do	51	187
475	Song of the buffalo hunt (a)	....do	180	440
476	....do. (b)	....do	181	441
477	"The White Horse Riders said this"	....do	224	502
478	"Take fresh courage"	....do	223	501
479	Opening song of the Sun dance (b)	Lone Man	20	129
480	Song of the departure of the young men	....do	9	110

2. Arranged in Order of Catalogue Numbers—Continued

Catalogue No.	Title of song	Name of singer	Serial No.	Page
481	Song of the return of the young men...	Lone Man......	10	112
482	Dancing song (c)........................	.....do........	31	145
483	"Wakaŋ'taŋka hears me"..............	.....do........	26	140
484	"I have conquered them"..............	.....do........	28	142
485	Dancing song (d).......................	.....do........	32	145
486	Song of victory over the sacred pole....	.....do........	12	115
487	Song of lamentation....................	.....do........	23	136
488	"With dauntless courage"..............	.....do........	7	108
489	"I sing for the animals"..............	.....do........	61	215
490	"My horse"...........................	.....do........	62	216
491	Song concerning a dream of the thunderbirds	.....do........	40	165
492	"The horsemen in the cloud"..........	.....do........	37	160
493	"Before the gathering of the clouds"...	.....do........	38	162
494	"A wind".............................	.....do........	41	168
495	"In a sacred manner I return"........	.....do........	42	169
496	Song in time of danger.................	.....do........	39	163
497	Song for securing fair weather..........	Red Bird......	4	99
498	Song of the Braves' dance..............	.....do........	6	107
499	Dancing song (a).......................	.....do........	29	143
500	Song of preparing the sacred place....	.....do........	17	123
501	Opening prayer of the Sun dance......	.....do........	21	130
502	Song at sunrise........................	.....do........	36	148
503	"Black face-paint he grants me"......	.....do........	27	141
504	Song concerning the sun and moon....	.....do........	25	139
505	Dancing song (b).......................	.....do........	30	144
506	Noon song.............................	.....do........	24	138
507	"Even the eagle dies".................	Eagle Shield...	164	394
508	"I took courage"......................	.....do........	165	395
509	Song of the Strong Heart society (a)....	.....do........	116	322
510	"Captives I am bringing"	.....do........	166	396
511	"Behold all these things"..............	.....do........	81	255
512	"We will eat".........................	.....do........	83	258
513	"These are good"......................	.....do........	84	259
514	"You will walk".......................	.....do........	85	260
515	"I am sitting"........................	.....do........	82	256
516	Song preceding treatment of fractures..	.....do........	86	262
517	An appeal to the bear..................	.....do........	87	263
518	Song of the bear......................	.....do........	88	264

2. Arranged in Order of Catalogue Numbers—Continued

2. Arranged in Order of Catalogue Numbers—Continued

Cata-logue No.	Title of song	Name of singer	Serial No.	Page
558	"A short time"	Gray Hawk....	231	509
559	Song of the moccasin game (d)	.....do.........	209	487
560	.....do.(c)	.....do.........	208	487
561	.....do.(e)	.....do.........	210	488
562	"He comes to attack"	Charging Thun-der.	58	197
563	"Worthy of reverence"	.....do.........	63	219
564	"A blacktail deer"	.....do.........	56	194
565	"From everywhere they come"	.....do.........	66	222
566	"A sacred stone nation is speaking"	.....do.........	64	220
567	"They move with a purpose"	.....do.........	65	221
568	Song of the old wolf	.....do.........	49	183
569	"I am walking"	.....do.........	1	67
570	Song of the young wolves	.....do.........	48	182
571	"The thunderbird nation"	.....do.........	43	171
572	Ceremonial song of the Miwa'tani society.	.....do.........	122	328
573	"My horse flies like a bird"	Brave Buffalo..	108	299
574	"Father, behold me"	Shooter........	71	228
575	"My life is such"	.....do......	106	296
576	"You should give up the warpath"	.....do.........	154	374
577	Song of the Buffalo society (c)	.....do.........	103	293
578	"Hence they come"	.....do.........	230	508
579	"I donated a horse"	.....do.........	229	507
580	Song of the Fox society (b)	.....do.........	115	317
581	"A bear said this"	.....do.........	57	196
582	"I was ordered to return"	.....do.........	72	229
583	"It is I, myself"	Swift Dog......	170	403
584	"Horses I seek"	.....do.........	171	404
585	"When I came you cried"	.....do.........	172	406
586	"I struck the enemy"	.....do.........	173	407
587	"I come after your horses"	.....do.........	174	409
588	"Two war parties"	.....do.........	175	410
589	"Sister, I bring you a horse"	.....do.........	176	411
590	Love song (a)	.....do.........	233	511
591	"He is again gone on the warpath"	.....do.........	153	371
592	Shuffling-feet dance (b)	Kills-at-Night..	202	479
593	"They are charging them"	.....do.........	195	473
594	Song of the grass dance (d)	.....do.........	197	475

2. Arranged in Order of Catalogue Numbers—Continued

Cata-logue No.	Title of song	Name of singer	Serial No.	Page
595	Song of the grass dance (c)............	Kills-at-Night..	198	476
596	....do.(a)	.....do.........	196	474
597	....do.(d)	.....do.........	199	476
598	Game song...........................	.....do.........	212	490
599	Song when a game is almost won......	.....do.........	213	490
600	Song of the shuffling-feet dance (a)	Kills-at-Night and wife.	201	478
601	Song of the night dance	.....do.........	203	480
602	"May you behold a sacred stone nation"	Brave Buffalo..	59	209
603	"The sunrise"........................	.....do.........	79	249
604	"When a horse neighs"...............	.....do.........	109	300
605	"Horses are coming".................	.....do.........	110	301
606	"A buffalo said to me"...............	.....do.........	44	174
607	"Owls hooting"......................	.....do.........	47	180
608	Weapon song........................	.....do.........	45	176
609	Song of the elks.....................	.....do.........	46	177
610	"Behold the dawn!"	.....do.........	80	250
611	"It is difficult"....................	Used-as-a-Shield	134	347
612	Song of Sitting Bull (a)	.....do.........	193	459
613	....do.(b)	.....do.........	194	460
614	"I wish to do my part"...............	.....do.........	186	450
615	"His customs I adopted"..............	.....do.........	187	451
616	"See my desire"......................	.....do.........	141	356
617	"The earth only endures".............	.....do.........	142	357
618	Song of victory......................	.....do.........	214	491
619	Begging song........................	.....do.........	205	483
620	Song of the maiden's leap.............	.....do.........	218	495
621	"Tell her"..........................	.....do.........	143	358
622	"An elk am I".......................	One Feather...	107	297
623	"May I be there"....................	.....do.........	156	382
624	"A prairie fire"....................	.....do.........	157	383
625	Song concerning Sitting Crow..........	.....do.........	158	384
626	"A spotted horse"....................	.....do.........	159	385
627	"Owls hoot at me"...................	.....do.........	160	386
628	Song after raising the sacred pole (a) ...	Red Weasel ...	14	119
629	....do.(b)	.....do.........	15	120
630	....do.(c)	.....do.........	16	121
631	Song of final visit to the vapor lodge	.....do.........	18	124
632	"In a sacred manner I live"	Bear Eagle.....	77	236

2. ARRANGED IN ORDER OF CATALOGUE NUMBERS—Continued

2. ARRANGED IN ORDER OF CATALOGUE NUMBERS—Continued

Cata-logue No.	Title of song	Name of singer	Serial No.	Page
671	"Two White Buffalo, take courage"...	Haka′la.......	225	503
672	"The tribe you help".................	.....do.........	226	504
673	Song in honor of Red Fish............	Red Fish.......	192	457
674	Song of healing.....................	Bear-with-White-Paw.	90	268
675	"The sacred stones come to see you"...	Chased-by-Bears.	60	212
676	Song of the warpath..................	Red Fox.......	155	378
677	Song of the Fox society (a)	Bear Soldier...	114	316
678	Song of the Ticketless society	Ćekpa′.........	237	515
679	Lullaby.............................	Yellow Hair....	217	493
680	Song of little girls' play (a)...........	.....do.........	215	492
681	.....do.(b)...........................	.....do.........	216	493
682	Begging song of the old women........	.....do.........	204	482
683	"They depend upon you"............	Silent Woman..	228	506
684	"Whenever the tribe assembles"......	.....do.........	227	505
685	"Learn the songs of victory"..........	.....do.........	149	368
686	Song concerning White Butterfly......	Mrs. Lawrence..	147	365
687	"He lies over there".................	.....do.........	148	366
688	"Wakaŋ′taŋka, pity me".............	White Robe....	22	135
689	"He is returning"...................	Earth-Medicine Woman.	146	364

NAMES OF SINGERS

STANDING ROCK RESERVATION

MEN

Number of songs	English name	Sioux name
29	Teal Duck	Śiya'ka [1]
20	Two Shields	Waha'ćuŋka-noŋ'pa
18	Lone Man	Iśna'la-wića'
18	Gray Hawk	Ćetaŋ'-hota
17	Eagle Shield	Waŋbli'-waha'ćuŋka
11	Charging Thunder	Wakiŋ'yan-wata'kpe
11	Used-as-a-Shield	Waha'ćaŋka-ya'pi
10	Brave Buffalo	Tataŋ'ka-ohi'tika
10	Red Bird	Zintka'la-lu'ta [2]
9	Shooter	Oku'te
9	Swift Dog	Śuŋ'ka-lu'zahaŋ
8	Kills-at-Night [3]	Haŋhe'-pikte
6	One Feather	Wi'yaka-waŋźi'la
4	Red Weasel	Ituŋ'kasaŋ-lu'ta
4	Bear Eagle	Mato'-waŋbli'
4	Old Buffalo	Tataŋk'-ehaŋ'ni
4	Shoots First	Toke'ya-wića'o
3	Jaw	Ćehu'pa
3	Weasel Bear	Ituŋ'-kasaŋ-mato'
3	One Buffalo	Tataŋ'ka-waŋźi'la
3	Dog Eagle	Śuŋ'ka-waŋbli'
2	Gray Whirlwind	Wamni'yomni-ho'ta
2	Many Wounds	Wopo'-tapi
2	Youngest Child	Haka'la
1	Red Fish	Hoġaŋ'-luta
1	Red Fox	Toka'la-lu'ta
1	Chased-by-Bears	Mato'-kuwa [4]
1	Bear Soldier	Mato'-aki'ćita [5]
1	Bear-with-White-Paw	Mato'nape'ska

[1] Died in March, 1913.
[2] Died in November, 1911.
[3] Kills-at-Night sang also two additional songs with his wife, Wita'hu.
[4] Died in February, 1915.
[5] Died in March, 1915.

WOMEN

Number of songs	English name	Sioux name
4	Yellow Hair..................	Paḣi′wiŋ
3	Silent Woman................	Ini′laöŋ′wiŋ
2	Mrs. Lawrence...............	Ćanku′lawiŋ
2	Woman's Neck [1]........	Wita′hu
1	White Robe..................	Taśi′naska′wiŋ
1	Earth-Medicine Woman.......	Maka′-peźu′tawiŋ

SISSETON RESERVATION (MEN)

4	Holy-Face Bear..............	Mato′-ite′-wakaŋ
3	Blue Cloud..................	Maḣpi′ya-to
2	Little Conjuror..............	Wakaŋ′-ćika′na
2	Moses Renville...............	
1	Twin.......................	Ćekpa′

[1] Sang with her husband, Kills-at-Night.

Total number of songs, 240.   Total number of singers, 40.

SPECIAL SIGNS USED IN TRANSCRIPTIONS OF SONGS

⌐‾‾‾‾‾‾‾‾‾‾‾¬ placed above the music indicates that the tones included within the bracket constitute a rhythmic unit.

+ placed above a note indicates that the tone is sung slightly less than a semitone higher than the diatonic pitch.

− placed above a note indicates that the tone is sung slightly less than a semitone lower than the diatonic pitch.

(· placed above a note indicates that the tone is prolonged slightly beyond the note value.

·) placed above a note indicates that the tone is given less than the note value.

Meaningless syllables are italicized.

Where no words are beneath the notes it is understood that meaningless syllables were used, except in songs whose words were sung too indistinctly for transcription, such instances being mentioned in the analysis.

PHONETIC KEY [1]

Vowels

The vowels are five in number. Each has but one sound except when followed by the nasal ŋ, which somewhat modifies it.

a has the sound of English *a* in *father*.

e has the sound of English *e* in *they*, or of *a* in *face*.

i has the sound of *i* in *marine*, or of *e* in *me*.

o has the sound of English *o* in *go, note*.

u has the sound of *u* in *rule*, or of *oo* in *food*.

Consonants

The consonants are 23 in number.

b has its common English sound.

ć is an aspirate with the sound of English *ch*, as in *chin*.

ç is an emphatic *ć*. It is formed by pronouncing *ć* with a strong pressure of the organs, followed by a sudden expulsion of the breath.

d has the common English sound.

g has the sound of *g* hard, as in *go*.

ġ represents a deep sonant guttural resembling the Arabic *ghain*.

h has the sound of *h* in English.

ḣ represents a strong surd guttural resembling the Arabic *kha*.

k has the same sound as in English.

ķ is an emphatic letter, bearing the same relation to *k* that *ć* does to *ç*. Formerly represented by *q*.

l has the common sound of this letter in English. It is peculiar to the Titoŋwaŋ dialect.

m has the same sound as in English.

n has the common sound of *n* in English.

ŋ denotes a nasal sound similar to the French *n* in *bon*, or the English *n* in *drink*.

p has the sound of English *v*. with slightly greater volume and stress.

s has the surd sound of English *s*, as in *say*.

ś is an aspirated *s*, having the sound of English *sh*, as in *shine*.

t is the same as in English with slightly greater volume.

w has the power of English *w*, as in *walk*.

y has the sound of English *y*, as in *yet*.

z has the sound of the common English *z*, as in *zebra*.

ź is an aspirated *z*, having the sound of the French *j*, or the English *s* in *pleasure*. Formerly represented by *j*.

---

[1] From Riggs, S. R., Grammar and Dictionary of the Dakota Language (*Smithsonian Contr. to Knowledge*, IV, pp. 3-4, Washington, 1852). See also "Siouan Dakota (Teton and Santee Dialects) with remarks on the Ponca and Winnebago," by Franz Boas and John R. Swanton, in Handbook of American Indian Languages, *Bull. 40, Bur. Amer. Ethn.*, pt. 1, pp. 875-965.

TETON SIOUX MUSIC

By FRANCES DENSMORE

INTRODUCTION

THE TETON SIOUX

A majority of the songs in this memoir were recorded among Indians belonging to the Teton division of the Dakota (Sioux) tribe, living on the Standing Rock Reservation in North and South Dakota. Songs were recorded also among the Sisseton and Wahpeton Sioux living at Sisseton, S. Dak.; 12 of these are included in this volume under the following numbers: 95, 96, 97, 189, 190, 234, 235, 236, 237, 238, 239, 240. Field work was begun in July, 1911, and continued until 1914, Mr. Robert P. Higheagle acting as principal interpreter at Standing Rock and revising the material collected at Sisseton, where a competent interpreter could not be secured. The words of the songs recorded at Standing Rock, with few exceptions, are in the Teton dialect, while those recorded among the Sisseton and Wahpeton Sioux are in the Santee dialect.

Before entering on a consideration of this material, the terms applied to the tribe and its various divisions will be briefly noted. "Dakota" is the word used by these Indians in speaking of themselves; this word means "leagued" or "allied" and is used also as an adjective, meaning "friendly." [1] The latter part of the word, meaning "friend," is pronounced *kola* by the Teton and *koda* by the Santee. The word "Sioux" was applied to the Dakota by Indians outside the tribe and by white men and has come to be the commonly accepted designation, even being extended to include cognate tribes known collectively as the "Siouan family." According to J. N. B. Hewitt the word "Sioux" is a French-Canadian abbreviation of the Chippewa diminutive form *Nadowe-is-iw-ŭg* (*nadowe*, 'an adder,' 'an enemy'; *is*, diminutive; *iw-ŭg*, 'they are'; hence, "they are the lesser enemies"). The Chippewa used this term to distinguish the Huron and Dakota from the Iroquois proper, whom they designated *Nadowe'wok*, 'the adders' or 'the enemies'. [2] A similar interpretation is given by Warren, the native historian of the Chippewa tribe. [3]

[1] Riggs, Stephen R., Grammar and Dictionary of the Dakota Language, in *Smithson. Contr.*, IV, pp. xv, 48, Washington, 1852.

[2] See Handbook of American Indians (*Bull. 30, Bur. Amer. Ethn.*), pt. 1, p. 376, 1907.

[3] Warren, William W., History of the Ojibways, in *Coll. Minn. Hist. Soc.*, vol. 5, p. 72, 1885

Riggs states [1] that the Dakota "sometimes speak of themselves as the 'Oćeti śakowiŋ,' *Seven Council fires.*" [2] This term referred to the seven principal divisions, which comprised the tribe or nation. Each of these was divided into numerous bands. The largest of these divisions was known as the Ti'toŋwaŋ, contracted to the word Teton. This division is said to have constituted more than half of the entire tribe and to have exceeded the others in wealth and physical development. They seem always to have lived west of the Missouri River. The four divisions of the tribe which lived east of the Missouri are now known collectively as the Santee. Riggs says: "These Mississippi and Minnesota Dakotas are called by those on the Missouri, Isanties, from 'isaŋati' or 'isaŋyati'; which name seems to have been given them from the fact that they once lived at Isaŋtamde, *Knife Lake,* one of those included under the denomination of Mille Lacs." [3] According to Riggs, these four divisions were the "Mdewakaŋtoŋwaŋs, Wahpekutes, Wahpetoŋwaŋs, and Sisitoŋwaŋs." Prior to the Indian outbreak in 1862 the home of these bands was in Minnesota. The two remaining divisions of the tribe are "the Ihaŋktoŋwaŋna and the Ihaŋtoŋwaŋs," the former living along the James River and in the vicinity of Devils Lake, and the latter west of the Missouri. Riggs states that "these two bands have usually been designated by travelers under the name of 'Yanctons.'" In the Dakota language, as spoken by these three large divisions of the tribe, there exist some differences, principally in the use of certain consonants. These differences are fully set forth by Riggs. [4] A simple illustration of one of these variations occurs in the tribal name, which is pronounced Dakota by the Santee and by the Yankton group, and Lakota by the Teton. Although the present memoir concerns chiefly the Teton group, the tribal name will be used in its commonly accepted form, Dakota. The words of the songs recorded by Teton are, however, given in the Teton dialect, while the Santee forms are used in the songs recorded by Santee.

The earliest definite reference to this people in history is found in the Jesuit Relations for 1640, in which they are called "Nadvesiv" (Nadowessioux). In the next century Col. George Croghan compiled "A List of the Different Nations and Tribes of Indians in the Northern District of North America, with the Number of Their Fighting Men." In this list the name appears as La Suil, and in a footnote the author says: "These are a nation of Indians settled southwest of Lake Superior (called by the French La Sue), who, by the best account that I could ever get from the French and Indians,

---

[1] In Grammar and Dictionary of the Dakota Language, op. cit., p. xv.

[2] See Dorsey, James Owen, Siouan Sociology, in *Fifteenth Rep. Bur. Ethn.*, pp. 215–222; articles *Dakota* and *Sioux*, in Handbook of American Indians; and Mooney, James, Siouan Tribes of the East, *Bull. 22, Bur. Amer. Ethn.*

[3] Op. cit., p. xvi.

[4] Ibid., pp. xvi, xvii.

are computed ten thousand fighting men." [1]   In 1804 this entry was
made in the Journal of the Lewis and Clark Expedition: "At 6 oC
in the evening we Seen 4 Indians . . . and three of them . . . belonged
to the Souix nation." [2]   But as white men came into closer contact
with this tribe they began to use the word used by the Indians
themselves.   Thus in the "Scientific Data accompanying the original journals of the Lewis and Clark Expedition," under the heading
"Ethnology," we find mention of the "Sieux or Dar-co-tars," with
an extensive description of the tribe, including a table of its subdivisions, which is probably the one sent by Clark to the Secretary of
War. [3]   Gradually the native name came into more general use, with
various modes of spelling, and in 1823 Major Long noted the "manners and customs of the Dacota Indians." [4]   However, the word
"Sioux" received the sanction of official usage in 1825, the statement
being made in a Government document of that year that "Returns
have been received from Gen. Clark and Gov. Cass, the commissioners appointed to mediate, at Prairie Du Chien, between the Sioux,
Sac, Fox, Iowa, Chippewa, Menomonei, and Winnebago Tribes and to
establish boundaries between them." [5]

On April 29, 1868, a treaty was made by the Government with the
Sioux and Arapaho Indians, which opens with the words: "From
this day forward all war between the parties to this agreement shall
forever cease.   The Government of the United States desires peace,
and its honor is hereby pledged to keep it.   The Indians desire peace,
and they now pledge their honor to maintain it." [6]   The Sioux Reservation established at that time comprised about 20,000,000 acres of
land, extending from the northern boundary of Nebraska to the
forty-sixth degree of north latitude, and from the eastern bank of the
Missouri River to the one hundred and fourth meridian of longitude. [7]
This was known as "the Great Sioux Reservation."   By the terms
of this treaty the Government placed agency buildings and schools
on the reservation, and provided that, under certain conditions, a
patent for 160 acres of land could be issued to an Indian, who would
thereby become a citizen of the United States.   The affairs of the
Indians were administered at seven agencies on this reservation, but
the Indians continued in large measure their old manner of life.

---

[1] Journal of Col. George Croghan, pp. 37–38; reprinted from Featherstonhaugh, in *Amer. Mo. Journ. Geol.*, Dec., 1831.

[2] Original Journals of the Lewis and Clark Expedition, 1804–1806, Reuben Gold Thwaites ed., VII, p. 61, New York, 1905.

[3] Ibid., VI, pp. 93–100.

[4] Keating, William H., Narrative of an Expedition to the Source of St. Peters River, under the Command of Maj. Stephen H. Long, I, p. 245, Philadelphia, 1824.

[5] McKenney, Thomas L., in documents accompanying the President's Message to Congress, Nineteenth Congress, First Session, No. 1, p. 90, 1825.

[6] Indian Laws and Treaties, compiled by Charles J. Kappler, vol. 2, pp. 770–75, Washington, D. C., 1903.

[7] The writer gratefully acknowledges the assistance of Maj. James McLaughlin, United States Indian Inspector, in preparing the following data concerning the Standing Rock Reservation. Major McLaughlin was Indian agent on this reservation from 1881 to 1895.

A part of the present Standing Rock Reservation (see pl. 2) was included in this territory, and an additional tract extending north to the Cannon Ball River was added by an Executive order dated March 16, 1875.[1] An agency near the present site of the Standing Rock Agency (Fort Yates, N. Dak.) was established July 4, 1873, and soon afterward a military post was established at that point.[2] Two companies of Infantry were stationed there, and this force was increased to five companies of Infantry and two troops of Cavalry during the Indian troubles of 1876. The original name "Standing Rock Cantonment" was changed to Fort Yates, and the post was continued until 1904.

The distinctively tribal life of the Teton Sioux may be said to have closed when the last Sun dance was held in 1881 and the last great buffalo hunt in 1882. A final hunt was held in November, 1883, and at that time the last buffalo were killed. Then followed a period of difficult adjustment on the part of the Indians, but Gall, Crow King, and others, who had been leaders in the tribal life, became also the leaders of their people in the adoption of farming and other pursuits recommended by the Government. The great change, however, did not come to the Indians until 1889, when the Great Sioux Reservation passed into history. In its place were established five reservations.[3] The boundaries of these reservations were determined by a commission of three, of which ex-Gov. Charles Foster, of Ohio, was chairman, his associates being Maj. George Crook, and Maj. William Warner. This commission went from one agency to another, holding councils with the Indians, who ceded about 9,000,000 acres of land to the Government at that time. A reference to the council which this commission held on the Standing Rock Reservation appears in the description of a song of Sitting Bull (No. 194). Shortly after the work of this commission was finished the boundaries of the several reservations were surveyed, and the various bands of Sioux were assigned to these reservations. After these agency rolls were completed it was expected that the Indians would not leave their reservations without passes from the agent. From that time until the present there has been a steady development of education among the Sioux in boarding and day schools, and also by means of practical instruction in the white man's manner of life.

---

[1] Indian Laws and Treaties, op. cit., vol. 1, p. 884.

[2] "There has been established by order of the War Department a military post at this agency of sufficient capacity for two companies of infantry."—Report of John Burke, United States Indian Agent, Standing Rock Reservation, in *Ind. Aff. Rep.* for 1875, p. 247.

[3] This was in accordance with an act of Congress dated March 2, 1889, entitled "An act to divide a portion of the reservation of the Sioux Nation of Indians in Dakota into separate reservations and to secure the relinquishment of the Indian title to the remainder, and for other purposes." Indian Laws and Treaties, op. cit., vol. 1, p. 328.

PRAIRIE

LOWLAND ALONG MISSOURI RIVER

VIEWS ON STANDING ROCK RESERVATION

Method of Work and of Analysis

The method of collecting the Sioux songs was similar to that used in connection with the Chippewa work.[1] Songs were recorded by means of the phonograph, and a transcription was made from the phonograph record, care being taken that the speed of the instrument was the same when recording the songs and when playing them for transcription. Ordinary musical notation is used for the transcription, with the addition of the special signs used in Bulletin 53.

The transcriptions of these songs should be understood as indicating the tones produced by the singers as nearly as it is possible to indicate them in a notation which is familiar by usage and therefore convenient for observation.[2]

As several hundred records were made, there were some accidental duplications of songs. In five instances (Nos. 125, 132, 133, 151, 173) these are transcribed, such being considered sufficient to show the slight differences which appear when a song is sung by several singers of equal ability, or at different times by the same singer. Other duplications examined by the writer show fewer points of difference than those which are transcribed. It occasionally happened that a song was known to have been imperfectly rendered, and in this case another record was made by a better singer, the second record being, of course, the only one taken into consideration. Indians distinguish clearly among good singers, indifferent singers, and totally unreliable singers. The writer has had experience with them all, and in the absence of information from the Indians, it is usually possible to distinguish them by comparing the several records of a song on the phonograph cylinders. As frequently noted in the descriptive analyses, the renditions of a song by a good singer are usually uniform in every respect. An effort was made to employ only the best singers. In selecting the principal singers, as well as informants, the writer ascertained a man's general reputation at the agency office and, in some cases, at the trader's store, as well as among his own people. In a few instances material which appeared to be interesting has been discarded because the informant was found to be unreliable. On one occasion a man was brought to the writer by an informant with whom she was acquainted. Mr. Higheagle was absent, but another interpreter was secured and data concerning the

---

[1] See Bulletins 45 and 53.

[2] Helmholtz, The Sensations of Tone (translated by A. J. Ellis), pt. 3, p. 260, London, 1885. Translator's footnote: "All these [scales] are merely the best representatives in European notation of the sensations produced by the scales on European ears."

Sun dance were recorded.   In a few days, on Mr. Higheagle's return, he said: "There is trouble among the Indians.   John Grass and other prominent men say they will have nothing more to do with the work if So-and-so is connected with it.   He killed a man, and his record in other matters is not good."   The matter was carefully considered, and the responsibility was placed on the man who introduced him. Finally all his material was expunged and the writer never saw him again.   Such precaution might not be necessary if this work concerned only the social songs, but all the old music is associated with things that lie very close to the heart of the Indian.

Throughout the work an effort was made to have the informants entirely at ease in discussing a subject, and never to allow the form of a question to suggest a possible answer.   Care was taken also to avoid an impression of seeking anything sensational or of tracing a similarity to the beliefs or traditions of the white race.   Indians become confused, even irritated, if questioned too closely, and for that reason it was often necessary to extend an investigation over several interviews, combining the data thus secured.   When this was done the result was translated to the Indian for criticism.

The method of analyzing the Sioux songs is the same as that used in the study of Chippewa songs.   The headings of the tables of analysis have not been changed, but a few subdivisions have been added.   For instance, in Tables 11 and 12 there is a separation of major and minor sixths and major and minor seconds, the last named being especially interesting, as it shows the minor second (semitone) to be used much less frequently than the major second (whole tone), a fact which has a direct bearing on the question whether Indians habitually and consciously use intervals smaller than those represented by the musical scale of the white race.

Except for the signs + and −, indicating that certain tones were sung slightly above or below pitch, there is no attempt at showing variations from what is known as the "piano scale."   It is, however, repeatedly noted in the descriptive analyses that intervals of the second and of the minor third were sung too small.   A similar reduction was not observed in the larger intervals.   In this connection the following statement by Prof. Max Meyer, of the University of Missouri, should be noted:

The result of our experiments [with Doctor Stumpf] made in Berlin was that the Major Third, Fifth, and Octave are preferred a little larger than theoretical intervals; the Minor Third, on the contrary, a little smaller. . . .   We may therefore state it as an established law that the smaller musical intervals are preferred diminished. . . . that the larger musical intervals are preferred enlarged. . . . and that the point where the curve of deviation passes zero, is situated between the Minor and Major Thirds.[1]

---

[1] Meyer, Max, Experimental Studies in the Psychology of Music, *American Journal of Psychology,* XIV, pp. 201–206, Worcester, Mass., July–Oct., 1903.

Many transcriptions represent the result of six or more readings of the phonograph cylinder, a considerable interval of time being allowed to elapse between these readings. It has been found that the final transcription is usually the simplest, as by repeated observations the ear eliminates bytones and the mannerisms of the singer. Thus in many instances it becomes possible to discern a rhythmic unit accurately repeated in every rendition of the song, when the melody seemed at first to be lacking in rhythmic form.

In the present series the final measure of a song is transcribed as a complete measure unless a repetition of the song begins without a break in the time. Such a repetition is indicated by the usual mark for repeat. It will be observed that in probably a majority of instances the time is unbroken during several renditions of a song. When a brief pause occurs in the melody it is usually filled with shrill cries and calls or words rapidly enunciated, accompanying which the drumbeat is continuous.

"Five-toned scales" are frequently mentioned in the descriptive analyses and also appear in the tabulated analyses. As stated in the author's previous works, the five-toned scales considered in these analyses are the five pentatonic scales according to Helmholtz, described by him as follows:

1. *The First Scale* without Third or Seventh. . . .
2. *To the Second Scale*, without Second or Sixth, belong most Scotch airs which have a minor character. . . .
3. *The Third Scale*, without Third and Sixth. . . .
4. *To the Fourth Scale*, without Fourth or Seventh, belong most Scotch airs which have the character of a major mode.
5. *The Fifth Scale*, without Second and Fifth.[1]

It may be needless to state that all these scales contain the same tones, the difference being in the keynote. The following examples are given for convenience of reference, the tones being the same in all:

First five-toned scale: Keynote G (sequence of tones G, A, C, D, E).
Second five-toned scale: Keynote A (sequence of tones A, C, D, E, G).
Third five-toned scale: Keynote D (sequence of tones D, E, G, A, C).
Fourth five-toned scale: Keynote C (sequence of tones C, D, E, G, A).
Fifth five-toned scale: Keynote E (sequence of tones E, G, A, C, D).

After a song is transcribed it is fully analyzed, the analyses being combined in the tables at the close of the various groups and later being incorporated in the tables on pages 12–21. Throughout the present work the repeated part of a song is not considered in computing the number of intervals which the melody contains. Such part often begins with the second or third measure, the opening measures taking the form of an introduction, a custom which was

---

[1] Helmholtz, H. L. F., The Sensations of Tone as a Physiological Basis for the Theory of Music (translated by A. J. Ellis), pp. 260, 261, 2d ed., London, 1885.

noted more frequently among the Chippewa than among the Sioux. Indian singers occasionally use much freedom in the arrangement of the phrases of a song in its repetition. It is therefore considered advisable to analyze only the direct and simplest rendition of a song. A "plot" of each melody is also made, as described and illustrated on pages 51–54.

The words of certain songs are in a "sacred (esoteric) language," which disguises their meaning. See words of Mĭde' songs in Bulletin 45; also footnote, page 120 of this work.

In the present volume the use of cross-references, which are found in Bulletin 53, is discontinued, and in their place will be found references to the analysis of the first song containing the peculiarity under consideration. Thus if a rest occurs in a song there will be found a reference to the analysis of song No. 79, which contains a list of all songs in which rests appear. The writer commends the use of the index of this book and of that of Bulletin 53 to those who wish to study the analyses closely. Songs can be traced also in the following manner: Let us suppose a reader is seeking songs from which the third tone of the octave is lacking. By consulting the index of Bulletin 53 a reference is found to page 5, on which the persistence of the third and fifth is considered; also, to the songs in both Bulletin 45 and Bulletin 53, from which the third is lacking. Full treatment of a peculiarity is usually given with the analysis of the first song in which it occurs, but in this instance it is given in connection with other peculiarities in Bulletin 53, song No. 53, page 140. It was there noted that more than one-half of the entire group were songs concerning or sung by women, but the proportion of women singers is much larger in the present series, while the proportion of songs lacking the third is much smaller (see analysis of song No. 22). Another method of tracing songs is by means of the tabulated analyses. Thus a student in search of songs from which the third tone of the octave is lacking would turn to Table 6, pages 21–23 of Bulletin 53, note the classes in which such songs are found, and trace them through the tabulated analyses of these several classes. This is the more interesting of the two methods, as it shows the frequency of its occurrence and also suggests a relation between the peculiarity under consideration and the class of the song in which it occurs. Having noted that the omission of the third occurs in only 3.5 per cent of the Chippewa songs, the student ascertains in the same way from the present work on Sioux songs that it is absent from only 5, less than 1 per cent of these songs. The tabulated, as well as the descriptive, analyses are intended to assist a careful, intelligent observation of Indian music. Both the means used and the results attained should be understood as anticipating a broader as well as a more intensive view of the subject when the study of Indian music shall have been more fully developed.

The purpose of the descriptive analysis following each song is to suggest a method of critically observing Indian music. No single analysis is intended to draw attention to every peculiarity of the song. One who becomes accustomed to a systematic observation of Indian songs may detect other peculiarities. It is possible that in some instances another keynote may be regarded as more satisfactory than the one which is designated. Some songs are so strictly harmonic in form that only one tone can be regarded as a keynote, but others are so freely melodic that they could be harmonized in more than one key. The melodies are regarded primarily as a succession of vocal sounds from which by the test of the ear the writer selects one which is reasonably satisfactory as a keynote. If more than one tone can be regarded as keynote, that one is selected which is simplest in its apparent key relation to the song as a whole. In two instances (Nos. 108, 166) the songs are classified as "irregular." The use of the term "key" throughout this work should be understood as a matter of convenience rather than as an indication that, in the opinion of the writer, there exists a fully established "key" in the sense of the term as used by musicians. It will be noted that in Table 1 the word "tonality" is used in preference to "key."

As an aid to the singing of these songs the writer would emphasize the importance of *rhythm*, suggesting toward this end that the rhythm of a song be mastered before the melody is played on a piano or other tuned instrument. Tap out the rhythm with a pencil, or, better still, master it *mentally*, then hum the song softly with intervals as nearly correct as possible. Play the song on a tuned instrument in order to test the intervals, but the song, regarded as a native melody, can best be reproduced vocally, either without accompaniment or (if the song is simply harmonic in form) with one or two chords to sustain the voice.

The musical customs of the Sioux do not differ materially from those of the Chippewa; for instance, there are the same reticence concerning old ceremonial and "medicine" songs, the same acknowledged ownership of personal songs, and the same custom of replacing in a war song the name of a half-forgotten hero with that of a new favorite. Among the Sioux, however, there seems to be more freedom in the rhythm of the drum. The Chippewa had drum-rhythms which were invariably used with certain classes of songs, but this feature seems to be more variable among the Sioux, except that the drum is always beaten in a rapid tremolo during "medicine" songs (as in the treatment of the sick), and also by a man when relating his dreams. The several drum-rhythms are shown in connection with their first occurrence, in Nos. 5, 6, 8, 12, 19, 64. In Nos. 12 and 13 the metric unit of drum and voice are in the ratio 2 to 1, suggesting points of coincidence, but the occasional prolonging or shortening of tones by the voice is such as to prevent a mechanical relation between the two. In many instances·the tempo of the drum appears entirely independent of that of the voice. The illustration on page 110 shows the seeming lack of relation between drum and voice in No. 8, but in this, as in the simple ratio, the slight variability of the voice should be taken into account. In No. 125 the drum was struck with a clearness which made it possible to transcribe its beats throughout the song. In this instance the drum and voice coincided on the first of the measure, but the drum-rhythm was broken. In a few songs the drum and voice were at variance during the song until the closing measures, in which they coincided. These were songs in which the drumbeat was in quarter-note values, and this "swinging together" of voice and drum is noted in the descriptive analyses.

At any gathering there is one man who acts as leader of the singers, who sit around the drum. The number at the drum varies with the size of the gathering; if a large number are dancing the singers sit as close as possible around the drum, each man beating the drum as he sings. Sometimes as many as 10 men can "sit at the drum." A singer of recognized ability may, if he likes, bring a decorated drumstick of his own, but the common custom is for the drummers to use ordinary drumsticks consisting of sticks wound at the end with cloth. If a singer at the drum becomes weary he lays down his drumstick, whereupon someone who has been dancing, or sitting with the spectators takes his place. It was said that "the leader starts every song, and if it is an easy song the others commence right away, but if it is new and hard they begin more carefully." Most of the songs may be sung an indefinite number of times, the leader giving a signal for the close by two sharp taps on the drum, after which the song is sung only once.

Sioux women usually sing with the men during the dancing songs; this is not the custom among the Chippewa. The Sioux women sit on the ground, forming a circle back of the drummers, and sing in a high falsetto, an octave above the men. In three instances (Nos. 201, 203, and a duplication of 173) the part sung by the women is shown in the transcription. Several other songs were recorded in this manner, but the transcription of each is from a subsequent rendition by a man singing alone.

Among the Sioux as well as among the Chippewa, variations in either time or intonation are found more often in unimportant than in important parts of a song.

It was said that there were "different ways of ending songs," and that "a man could tell the kind of song by the way it ended." The writer therefore sought more definite information on this point, consulting Used-as-a-Shield and other old-time singers. They said there were two ways, one being "to stop short" and the other "to let the tone die away gradually." On being asked which kinds of songs were ended in each of these ways they could not give a definite answer at once, and requested time to consider it. After several days they said that they had "tried over many old songs and found that they always stopped short when they sang such songs as the grass-dance, buffalo-dance, and Crow-owner's society songs," and that they "trailed off the tone" when singing war songs and similar songs.

Among the Sioux were found many songs which could be used on different occasions. Thus the songs in honor of a warrior could be sung when begging for food before his lodge, as well as at the victory dances and at meetings of societies. The songs of those who went to seek a suitable pole for the sun dance were used also by those who went to look for buffalo or for the enemy. Hence it did not seem appropriate to base a comparative study of these songs on their use, as was done with the Chippewa songs. A better basis for comparison seemed to be the age of the song, and accordingly the songs were divided into two groups, the first and larger comprising songs believed to be from 50 to 100 years old and the second those less than 50 years old. In addition to these comparative tables (pp. 12–21) the analyses at the close of each section are continued, for convenience of observation.

It is not so difficult to judge the age of a song as might be imagined. For instance, the last Sun dance was held more than 30 years ago, and a man who sang the ceremonial songs at that time said that he learned them when a young man from an aged man who was taught them in his youth. Such songs are undoubtedly more than a century old. In like manner, if a man about 70 years of age sings a song which he says that his father received in a dream when a youth and which he used in treating the sick, the song is evidently to be classed among the older songs. On the other hand, it is known that the Strong Heart society was organized among the Standing Rock Sioux only about 50 years ago, and that the White Horse Riders is a modern organization. The songs of both these societies are therefore comparatively modern songs, but the songs of the Miwa'tani are placed in the older group, as there was a certain ceremony connected with their initiation of new members, one of the ceremonial songs being preserved. The songs of the Crow-owners are also included with the older songs, as this was shown to be a society of more than 50 years standing, and only a few of its songs were remembered. Songs containing mention of a recent custom are manifestly modern.

TABULATED ANALYSIS OF 240 SIOUX SONGS

MELODIC ANALYSIS

TABLE 1.—TONALITY[1]

	Group I.[2] Old songs.		Group II.[3] Comparatively modern songs.		Total.	
	Number.	Per cent.	Number.	Per cent.	Number.	Per cent.
Major tonality	57	39	36	39	93	39
Minor tonality	88	60	57	61	145	60
Irregular	2	1	....	....	2	1
Total	147	....	93	....	240	....

[1] Since we are considering music of a period in which what we now designate *scales* and *keys* was not formulated, the terms "major tonality" and "minor tonality" are used in preference to the common terms "major key" and "minor key." *Tonality* is defined as "the quality and peculiarity of a tonal system" (Standard Dictionary, 1905 ed.), and *key* as "a scheme or system of notes or tones definitely related to each other" (The Oxford Dictionary, vol. 5, 1901).

[2] This group comprises songs a majority of which are believed to be 50 to 150 years old. (See p. 22.)

[3] This group comprises songs a majority of which are believed to be less than 50 years old. (See p. 23.)

TABLE 2.—FIRST NOTE OF SONG—ITS RELATION TO KEYNOTE

	Group I. Old songs.		Group II. Comparatively modern songs.		Total.	
	Number.	Per cent.	Number.	Per cent.	Number.	Per cent.
Beginning on the—						
Fourteenth	1	....	....	....	1	....
Twelfth	19	13	9	10	28	12
Eleventh	6	4	1	1	7	3
Tenth	15	10	8	8	23	10
Ninth	5	4	4	4	9	4
Octave	29	20	27	30	56	23
Seventh	1	....	....	....	1	....
Sixth [1]	2	1	1	1	3	1
Fifth [2]	45	31	24	25	69	29
Fourth [3]	2	1	1	1	3	1
Third [4]	10	7	8	8	18	8
Second [5]	1	....	2	1	3	1
Keynote	9	6	8	8	17	7
Irregular	2	1	....	....	2	1
Total	147	....	93	....	240	....

[1] Songs beginning on the submediant and having a compass of less than 13 tones.

[2] Songs beginning on the dominant and having a compass of less than 12 tones.

[3] Songs beginning on the subdominant and having a compass of less than 11 tones.

[4] Songs beginning on the mediant and having a compass of less than 10 tones.

[5] Songs beginning on the supertonic and having a compass of less than 9 tones.

MELODIC ANALYSIS—continued

TABLE 3.—LAST NOTE OF SONG—ITS RELATION TO KEYNOTE

	Group I. Old songs.		Group II. Comparatively modern songs.		Total.	
	Number.	Per cent.	Number.	Per cent.	Number.	Per cent.
Ending on the—						
Fifth	45	31	29	31	74	31
Third	21	14	14	15	35	15
Keynote	79	54	50	54	129	54
Irregular	2	1	....	....	2	1
Total	147	....	93	....	240	....

TABLE 4.—LAST NOTE OF SONG—ITS RELATION TO COMPASS OF SONG

	Group I. Old songs.		Group II. Comparatively modern songs.		Total.	
	Number.	Per cent.	Number.	Per cent.	Number.	Per cent.
Songs in which final tone is—						
Lowest tone in song	136	93	76	82	212	88
Highest tone in song	....	....	....	....	....	....
Immediately preceded by—						
Major third below	....	....	1	1	1	....
Minor third below	....	....	2	2	2	1
Whole tone below	2	2	5	5	7	3
Semitone below	2	2	1	1	3	1
Songs containing a fourth below the final tone	1	....	3	3	4	2
Songs containing a major third below the final tone	3	2	1	1	4	2
Songs containing a minor third below the final tone	1	....	4	4	5	2
Irregular	2	2	....	....	2	1
Total	147	....	93	....	240	....

TABLE 5.—NUMBER OF TONES COMPRISING COMPASS OF SONG

	Group I. Old songs.		Group II. Comparatively modern songs.		Total.	
	Number.	Per cent.	Number.	Per cent.	Number.	Per cent.
Compass of—						
Seventeen tones	1	....	2	2	3	1
Fourteen tones	4	3	1	1	5	2
Thirteen tones	11	8	6	6	17	7
Twelve tones	30	21	11	12	41	17
Eleven tones	6	4	3	3	9	4
Ten tones	24	16	15	16	39	16

MELODIC ANALYSIS—continued

TABLE 5.—NUMBER OF TONES COMPRISING COMPASS OF SONG—continued

	Group I. Old songs.		Group II. Comparatively modern songs.		Total.	
	Number.	Per cent.	Number.	Per cent.	Number.	Per cent.
Compass of—continued						
Nine tones	15	10	.13	14	28	12
Eight tones	49	33	34	37	83	35
Seven tones	3	2	1	1	4	2
Six tones	4	3	4	4	8	3
Five tones			1	1	1	
Four tones			2	2	2	1
Total	147		93		240	

TABLE 6.—TONE MATERIAL

	Group I. Old songs.		Group II. Comparatively modern songs.		Total.	
	Number.	Per cent.	Number.	Per cent.	Number.	Per cent.
First five-toned scale	1				1	
Second five-toned scale	16	11	15	16	31	13
Fourth five-toned scale	30	21	13	14	43	18
Major triad	1				1	
Major triad and seventh			1	1	1	
Major triad and sixth			4	4	4	2
Major triad and second	5	3	3	3	8	3
Minor triad	2	1			2	1
Minor triad and seventh	1				1	
Minor triad and fourth	17	12	13	14	30	12
Minor triad and second			1	1	1	
Octave complete	7	5	7	8	14	6
Octave complete except seventh	13	9	7	8	20	8
Octave complete except seventh and sixth	6	4	10	11	16	7
Octave complete except seventh, sixth, and fourth	1				1	
Octave complete except seventh, fifth, and second	1				1	
Octave complete except seventh and fourth [1]	2	1	3	3	5	2
Octave complete except seventh and third	1				1	
Octave complete except seventh and second	7	5	2	2	9	4
Octave complete except sixth	9	7	3	3	12	5
Octave complete except sixth and fourth	1		1	1	2	1

[1] These songs are minor in tonality, the mediant being a minor third above the tonic and the submediant a minor sixth above the tonic. In the fourth five-toned scale the seventh and fourth tones of the octave are likewise omitted, but the third and sixth intervals are major and the songs are major in tonality (see analysis of song No. 83, Bulletin 53).

MELODIC ANALYSIS—continued

TABLE 6.—TONE MATERIAL—continued

	Group I. Old songs.		Group II. Comparatively modern songs.		Total.	
	Number.	Per cent.	Number.	Per cent.	Number.	Per cent.
Octave complete except sixth and second.	3	2	1	1	4	2
Octave complete except sixth, fifth, and second	1	....	....	....	1	....
Octave complete except sixth and third...	1	....	....	....	1	....
Octave complete except fifth and second..	1	....	....	....	1	....
Octave complete except fourth	7	5	3	3	10	4
Octave complete except fourth and second.	2	1	1	1	3	1
Octave complete except third and second.	....	....	1	1	1	....
Octave complete except second	8	6	3	3	11	5
Minor third and fourth	....	....	1	1	1	....
First, fourth, and fifth tones	1	....	....	....	1	....
Other combinations of tones	2	1	....	....	2	1
Total	147	....	93	....	240	....

TABLE 7.—ACCIDENTALS

	Group I. Old songs.		Group II. Comparatively modern songs.		Total.	
	Number.	Per cent.	Number.	Per cent.	Number.	Per cent.
Songs containing—						
No accidentals	123	84	73	78	196	82
Seventh raised a semitone	4	3	6	6	10	4
Sixth raised a semitone	....	....	3	3	3	1
Sixth and third raised a semitone	....	....	1	1	1	....
Fourth raised a semitone	4	3	2	2	6	2
Second raised a semitone	2	1	1	1	3	1
Fourth and seventh raised a semitone.	1	....	....	....	1	....
Seventh lowered a semitone	1	....	2	2	3	1
Seventh and fourth lowered a semitone	1	....	....	....	1	....
Sixth lowered a semitone	4	3	1	1	5	2
Fourth lowered a semitone	2	1	1	1	3	1
Third lowered a semitone	2	1	1	1	3	1
Second lowered a semitone	1	....	1	1	2	1
Third and second lowered, and fourth raised a semitone	....	....	1	1	1	....
Irregular	2	1	....	....	2	1
Total	147	....	93	....	240	....

MELODIC ANALYSIS—continued

TABLE 8.—STRUCTURE

	Group I. Old songs.		Group II. Comparatively modern songs.		Total.	
	Number.	Per cent.	Number.	Per cent.	Number.	Per cent.
Melodic [1]	99	67	59	63	158	66
Melodic with harmonic framework [2]	28	19	19	21	47	20
Harmonic [3]	18	12	15	16	33	14
Irregular	2	1			2	1
Total	147		93		240	

[1] Songs are thus classified if contiguous accented tones do not bear a simple chord-relation to each other.
[2] Songs are thus classified if only a portion of the contiguous accented tones bear a simple chord-relation to each other.
[3] Songs are thus classified if contiguous accented tones bear a simple chord-relation to each other.

TABLE 9.—FIRST PROGRESSION—DOWNWARD AND UPWARD

	Group I. Old songs.		Group II. Comparatively modern songs.		Total.	
	Number.	Per cent.	Number.	Per cent.	Number.	Per cent.
Downward	106	72	59	63	165	69
Upward	41	28	34	37	75	31
Total	147		93		240	

TABLE 10.—TOTAL NUMBER OF PROGRESSIONS—DOWNWARD AND UPWARD

	Number.	Per cent.	Number.	Per cent.	Total.	Per cent.
Downward	2,821	63	1,830	64	4,651	63
Upward	1,624	37	1,050	36	2,674	37
Total	4,445		2,880		7,325	

TABLE 11.—INTERVALS IN DOWNWARD PROGRESSION

	Number.	Per cent.	Number.	Per cent.	Total.	Per cent.
Interval of a—						
Major sixth	1				1	
Minor sixth	5		1		6	
Fifth	18		8		26	1
Fourth	300	10	225	12	525	11
Major third	238	7	105	5	343	7
Minor third	831	29	565	30	1,396	30
Augmented second	2		3		5	
Major second	1,254	45	831	45	2,085	45
Minor second	172	7	92	5	264	6
Total	2,821		1,830		4,651	

MELODIC ANALYSIS—continued

Table 12.—INTERVALS IN UPWARD PROGRESSION

	Group I.		Group II.		Total.	
	Number.	Per cent.	Number.	Per cent.	Number.	Per cent.
Interval of a—						
Eleventh	1	....	....	....	1	....
Tenth	4	....	2	....	6	....
Ninth	3	....	3	....	6	....
Octave	32	2	31	3	63	2
Seventh	12	....	1	....	13	....
Major sixth	9	....	7	....	16	1
Minor sixth	23	1	7	....	30	1
Fifth	96	6	55	5	151	6
Fourth	238	14	184	18	422	16
Major third	174	11	97	10	271	10
Minor third	433	26	277	27	710	27
Major second	495	32	323	30	818	31
Minor second	104	6	63	6	167	6
Total	1,624	....	1,050	....	2,674	....

Table 13.—AVERAGE NUMBER OF SEMITONES IN AN INTERVAL

	Number of songs.	Number of intervals.	Number of semitones.	Average number of semitones in an interval.
Group I	147	4,445	12,864	2.89
Group II	93	2,880	8,558	2.97

Table 14.—KEY

	Group I.		Group II.		Total.	
	Number.	Per cent.	Number.	Per cent.	Number.	Per cent.
Key [1]—						
A major	10	7	2	1	12	5
A minor	8	6	7	7	15	6
B flat major	12	8	1	1	13	5
B flat minor	9	6	2	1	11	5
B major	6	4	5	5	11	5
B minor	9	6	7	7	16	7
C major	4	3	2	1	6	2
C minor	6	4	8	9	14	6
D flat major	4	3	1	1	5	2
C sharp minor	3	2	2	1	5	2
D major	5	3	6	6	11	5
D minor	10	7	5	5	15	6
E flat major	3	2	5	5	8	3
E flat minor	5	3	3	3	8	3
E major	1	....	6	6	7	3

[1] The term "key" is here used in its broad sense, as applicable to nonharmonic music, inclusive of modes.

MELODIC ANALYSIS—continued

TABLE 14.—KEY—continued

	Group I. Old songs.		Group II. Comparatively modern songs.		Total.	
	Number.	Per cent.	Number.	Per cent.	Number.	Per cent.
Key—continued						
E minor	3	2	5	5	8	3
F major	7	5	1	1	8	3
F minor	9	6	5	5	14	6
G flat major	2	2	1	1	3	1
F sharp major	1	....	....	....	1	....
F sharp minor	9	6	1	1	10	4
G major	6	4	4	4	10	4
G minor	8	6	9	10	17	7
A flat major	2	2	2	2	4	2
G sharp minor	3	2	3	3	6	2
Irregular	2	2	....	....	2	1
Total	147	....	93	....	240	....

TABLE 15.—PART OF MEASURE ON WHICH SONG BEGINS

	Group I. Old songs.		Group II. Comparatively modern songs.		Total.	
	Number.	Per cent.	Number.	Per cent.	Number.	Per cent.
Beginning on unaccented part of measure.	72	49	24	26	96	40
Beginning on accented part of measure....	75	51	69	74	144	60
Total	147	....	93	....	240	....

TABLE 16.—RHYTHM OF FIRST MEASURE

	Group I. Old songs.		Group II. Comparatively modern songs.		Total.	
	Number.	Per cent.	Number.	Per cent.	Number.	Per cent.
First measure in—						
2-4 time	83	56	59	63	142	59
3-4 time	60	41	34	37	94	39
4-8 time	3	2	....	....	3	1
5-8 time	1	1	....	....	1	1
Total	147	....	93	....	240	....

MELODIC ANALYSIS—continued

TABLE 17.—CHANGE OF TIME (MEASURE-LENGTHS)

	Group I. Old songs.		Group II. Comparatively modern songs.		Total.	
	Number.	Per cent.	Number.	Per cent.	Number.	Per cent.
Songs containing no change of time........	9	6	9	10	18	8
Songs containing a change of time.........	138	94	84	90	222	92
Total...............................	147	....	93	....	240	....

TABLE 18.—RHYTHM OF DRUM

	Group I. Old songs.		Group II. Comparatively modern songs.		Total.	
	Number.	Per cent.	Number.	Per cent.	Number.	Per cent.
Sixteenth notes unaccented [1].............	1	2	....	....	1	1
Eighth notes unaccented [2]................	26	43	16	26	42	34
Quarter notes unaccented [3]...............	16	27	28	45	44	36
Half notes unaccented [4]..................	2	3	....	....	2	2
Eighth notes accented in groups of two [5]..	4	7	7	11	11	9
Each beat preceded by an unaccented beat corresponding to third count of a triplet [6]................................	11	18	11	18	22	18
Drum not recorded [7].....................	87	....	31	....	118	....
Total...............................	147	....	93	....	240	....

[1] See No. 64.
[2] See No. 19.
[3] See No. 6.
[4] See No. 12.
[5] See No. 8.
[6] See No. 5.
[7] Excluded in computing percentage.

TABLE 19.—RHYTHMIC UNIT [1] OF SONG

	Group I. Old songs.		Group II. Comparatively modern songs.		Total.	
	Number.	Per cent.	Number.	Per cent.	Number.	Per cent.
Songs containing—						
No rhythmic unit.....................	48	33	23	25	71	29
One rhythmic unit....................	85	58	54	58	139	57
Two rhythmic units..................	12	8	13	14	25	10
Three rhythmic units.................	1	1	2	2	3	1
Four rhythmic units..................	1	1	....	....	1	....
Five rhythmic units..................	....	....	1	1	1	....
Total...............................	147	....	93	....	240	....

[1] For the purpose of this analysis a rhythmic unit is defined as a group of tones of various lengths, usually comprising more than one count of a measure, occurring more than twice in a song, and having an evident influence on the rhythm of the entire song.

MELODIC ANALYSIS—continued

TABLE 20.—METRIC UNIT OF VOICE (TEMPO)[1]

	Group I. Old songs.		Group II. Comparatively modern songs.		Total.	
	Number.	Per cent.	Number.	Per cent.	Number.	Per cent.
Metronome—						
48	1	....	....	....	1	....
52	3	2	....	.... ..	3	1
54	3	2	....	....	3	1
56	1	....	2	2	3	1
58	3	2	2	2	5	2
60	5	3	4	4	9	4
63	6	3	6	6	12	5
66	5	3	11	12	16	6
69	9	6	1	1	10	4
72	10	7	5	5	15	6
76	10	7	10	11	20	8
80	12	9	9	10	21	8
84	12	9	3	1	15	6
88	6	3	6	6	12	5
92	13	9	6	6	19	8
96	10	7	5	5	15	6
100	8	6	3	3	11	2
104	4	2	3	3	7	3
108	....	....	5	5	5	2
112	3	2	2	2	5	2
116	4	2	1	1	5	2
120	....	....	1	1	1	....
126	3	2	1	1	4	1
132	3	2	1	1	4	1
138	2	2	....	....	2	....
144	3	2	2	2	5	2
160	2	2	1	1	3	1
168	3	2	....	....	3	1
176	2	2	3	3	5	2
192	1	....	....	....	1	....
Total	147	....	93	....	240	....

[1] This refers only to the tempo in which a song begins. For a consideration of changes of tempo in these songs see analysis of song No. 5.

TABLE 21.—METRIC UNIT OF DRUM (TEMPO)

	Group I. Old songs.		Group II. Comparatively modern songs.		Total.	
	Number.	Per cent.	Number.	Per cent.	Number.	Per cent.
Metronome—						
56	....	....	2	3	2	2
60	....	....	4	6	4	3
63	1	2	3	5	4	3
66	....	....	5	8	5	4
69	1	2	....	....	1	....

MELODIC ANALYSIS—continued

TABLE 21.—METRIC UNIT OF DRUM (TEMPO)—continued

	Group I. Old songs.		Group II. Comparatively modern songs.		Total.	
	Number.	Per cent.	Number.	Per cent.	Number.	Per cent.
Metronome—continued						
72	3	5	2	2	5	4
76	3	5	4	6	7	6
80	4	7	7	11	11	9
84	1	2	4	6	5	4
88	5	8	5	8	10	8
92	6	10	3	5	9	8
96	7	11	4	6	11	9
100	2	3	3	5	5	4
104	3	5	4	6	7	6
108	....	....	5	8	5	4
112	1	2	1	2	2	2
116	3	5	2	3	5	4
120	2	3	....	....	2	2
126	1	2	....	....	1	....
132	4	7	....	....	4	3
138	4	7	....	....	4	3
144	2	3	1	2	3	2
152	2	3	....	....	2	2
160	3	5	....	....	3	2
168	2	3	....	....	5	4
176	....	....	3	5	....	....
Drum not recorded [1]	87	....	31	....	118	....
Total	147	....	93	....	240	....

TABLE 22.—COMPARISON OF METRIC UNIT OF VOICE AND DRUM (TEMPO)

	Group I. Old songs.		Group II. Comparatively modern songs.		Total.	
	Number.	Per cent.	Number.	Per cent.	Number.	Per cent.
Drum and voice having the same metric unit	29	48	47	76	76	62
Drum faster than voice	19	32	5	8	24	20
Drum slower than voice	12	20	10	16	22	18
Drum not recorded [1]	87	....	31	....	118	....
Total	147	....	93	....	210	....

[1] Excluded in computing percentage.

Comparison Between Old and Comparatively Modern Sioux Songs [1]

The songs comprised in the first group, almost without exception, were recorded by men 65 to 80 years of age. These men said they learned the songs or received them in dreams when they were young. A number of the songs comprised in the second group were also recorded by old men, but were said to be comparatively modern songs. The remaining songs were recorded by young men who now "sing at the drum" when the Sioux assemble. These songs represent a distinct phase of Sioux music, which should not be omitted from a general consideration of the subject.

Music may perhaps be said to be the last element of native culture remaining in favor among the Sioux. It is interesting to note that songs are being composed by them at the present time. Many of these are love songs, others are "praise songs" or songs of a general character. It is unnecessary to state that all are *social* songs, the use of songs for ceremony, war, societies, and the hunt having passed away. Many of the younger Indians among both Chippewa and Sioux find much pleasure in recording their songs on phonographs which they themselves possess. The writer was informed that among the Standing Rock Sioux' "an Indian who owns a phonograph usually has at least a hundred records of Indian songs. He and his friends make them and enjoy them much more than the commercial records. Some even make these records for sale among their people." The songs are usually recorded by several singers, while others at the same time give sharp yells or short exclamatory sentences. While such records are not adapted for the study of individual songs, they are an evidence of the Indian's continued pleasure in his music and of his readiness to adapt the means of civilization to an end which is purely native. Thus Red Fox caused a song to be composed in honor of Two White Buffalo, and, in order that the song might be accurately preserved, he requested that two phonographic records be made by the Indians who composed the song, these duplicate records to be kept in widely separated localities, so that, if accident befell one of them, the song would still be preserved in its original form. At a later date this song was recorded by the writer and appears as No. 222 of this volume.

Group I.—This group contains 147 songs believed to be from 50 to 150 years old, and comprises the following songs: (1) Ceremonial

---

[1] See p. 11.

songs used in the Huŋka and Spirit-keeping ceremonies and in the Sun dance;[1] (2) Songs concerning personal dreams;[2] (3) Songs concerning the sacred stones;[3] (4) Songs used in the treatment of the sick;[4] (5) Songs of the Dream societies named for animals,[5] consisting of men who had dreamed of the same animal. These societies were the Buffalo, Elk, and Horse societies. (6) A group of war songs which were believed to be more than 50 years old, including those of the Miwa'tani and Kaŋǵi'yuha societies.[6]

GROUP II. This group contains 93 songs, a majority of which are believed to be less than 50 years old, and comprises the following divisions: (1) Songs of those military societies which are comparatively recent among the Teton Sioux. These are the Fox, Strong Heart, and Badger societies, and the White Horse Riders. The fox, coyote, and wolf songs are so closely related that it is impossible to draw definite lines between them, but as a compromise the songs said to be Fox society or Coyote society songs are placed in this group, while the wolf songs (this being a common term for all war songs) are placed in the older group. In this division are included the incidental war songs and dancing songs used in the Sun dance, and those songs in honor of an individual which were sung to melodies of the military societies. This division comprises 32 songs.[7] (2) Songs of the buffalo hunt, together with council and Chief songs, one of the latter being sung at the Sun dance.[8] (3) All songs not otherwise classified. The first of these are three unclassified songs in the Sun dance—Song of Final Visit to the Vapor Lodge, Noon song, and Song concerning the Sun and Moon (Nos. 18, 24, 25). In this division are also the songs of various dances and games, those songs in honor of an individual which were sung to dance melodies, and the miscellaneous songs recorded at Sisseton, S. Dak.[9]

A comparison of the analyses of these two groups is shown in tables on the preceding pages. The percentage of major and minor songs is the same in the two groups, except that the older group contains two songs the keynote of which is so uncertain that they are classified as "irregular." The percentage of songs beginning on the twelfth and fifth is 44 in the older songs and 35 in the modern songs, but the proportion beginning on the octave is 10 per cent

[1] Nos. 1, 2, 3, 4, 11, 12, 13, 14, 15, 16, 17, 19, 20, 21, 36; total 15.

[2] Nos. 37–58, inclusive; total 22.

[3] Nos. 59–78, inclusive; total 20.

[4] Nos. 79–94, inclusive; total 16.

[5] Nos. 95–113, inclusive; total 19.

[6] Nos. 122–179, inclusive, except No. 178, which is a song of the Fox society, and is included in the second group.

[7] Nos. 6, 7, 8, 9, 10, 22, 23, 26, 27, 28, 29, 30, 31, 32, 33, 34, 35, 114, 115, 116, 117, 118, 119, 120, 121, 123, 124, 178, 223, 224, 225, 231; total, 32.

[8] Nos. 5, 180–194, inclusive; total, 16.

[9] Nos. 18, 24, 25, 196–240, inclusive, except Nos. 223, 224, 225, 231.

greater in the modern songs. Curiously, the percentage ending on the keynote and fifth is identical in the two groups. The modern songs show a smaller proportion of songs in which the final tone is the lowest in the song, the whole tone and the minor third below the final tone being used in several instances. The proportion of songs on the five-toned scales is 32 per cent in the older and 30 per cent in the more modern songs, while next in number are songs containing only the minor triad and fourth, which show a difference of but 2 per cent in the two groups. The first important point of difference is that the older songs show a much larger proportion having a range of 12 or more tones, the percentage having 10 tones being the same, the modern group has the larger percentage of songs which are harmonic in structure. This suggests less freedom in musical expression as the Indian feels himself coming under the restrictions of civilization and is of interest in that connection.

A larger proportion of accidentals is found in the newer songs, the tones most frequently affected being the sixth and seventh. In structure the modern group shows a larger proportion of harmonic songs, this feature being in accord with the stronger feeling for the octave as an initial tone and with the reduction of the compass of the songs. The modern group shows also a much smaller proportion of songs with the first progression downward, and we recall the steadily descending trend of melody as an acknowledged characteristic of primitive song. Yet in total number of progressions the proportion of ascending and descending intervals differs by only 1 per cent in the two groups. In the older songs the average number of intervals is 30, and in the more modern 31.3, a difference too slight to be of importance. The average interval in the modern songs is slightly the larger, but the difference is less than a tenth of a semitone. The smallest average interval (2.5 semitones) is that of the "buffalo hunt, council, and Chief song" group, while the largest (3.5 semitones) is that of the ceremonial songs. The key or pitch of the songs constitutes perhaps the least important of the tables; in this respect we note that the groups show no marked differences, the pitch of the song being somewhat a matter of adaptation to the compass of the singer's voice.

Table 15 shows a contrast which might be connected with the change from the older to the modern life of the Indians, the old songs having 51 per cent beginning on the accented part of the measure and the new songs having 74 per cent beginning on the accent. This suggests directness and the same psychological factor, which may account for the increase of songs harmonic in form. The newer group shows an increase in the proportion of songs which begin in 2–4 time and a slight decrease in the percentage of songs having a change of measure-lengths. Table 18 shows the newer songs to contain a decrease in those having the drumbeat in unaccented eighth-note values, in many instances approaching a tremolo, and a large increase in the proportion having the drumbeat in quarter-note values, this being a sharp, definite stroke and, of course, less rapid than the preceding. The proportion containing one rhythmic unit is the same in the two groups, but the newer songs show a large increase in the proportion having two or more rhythmic units, evidencing a development of the rhythmic sense. A comparison of the metric unit (tempo) of the voice shows no material differences, but in the following table is noted a decided decrease in the metric unit of the drum. Table 22 shows the percentage of old songs in which voice and drum have the same metric unit to be 48, and that of the new songs as 76, a difference of 58 per cent. This is the more interesting, as in this table the deduction of the songs recorded without drum causes the percentage to be reckoned on a total of 60 in the first and 62 in the second group.

Summarizing briefly the results of a comparison of the old and the more modern Sioux songs, we find in the percentages a reduction in the compass of the songs with an increase of harmonic form and of accidentals; a more direct attack (shown by the increase of songs beginning on the accented part of the measure) an increase of songs beginning in 2-4 time; and also in songs without a change in time. We find a change in the drumbeat from a rapid and somewhat tremolo beat to a quarter-note value, with a reduction in the tempo of the drum and an increase in the proportion of songs in which the tempo of voice and drum is the same. We note further a development of the rhythmic sense in song construction, shown by the increase in the number of songs having two or more rhythmic units. These contrasts between the two groups of songs may suggest a connection between the Indians' manner of life and the form of their musical expression, or they may be regarded as an effect of contact with the more conventional music of the white race. These and similar observations await further comparative study of Indian songs.

Tabulated Analysis of 600 Indian Songs (Chippewa and Sioux)

MELODIC ANALYSIS

Table 1a.—TONALITY [1]

	Chippewa songs.[2]		Sioux songs recorded by Chippewa.[3]		Sioux songs.		Total.	
	Number.	Per cent.	Number.	Per cent.	Number.	Per cent.	Number.	Per cent.
Major tonality.......	195	57	11	55	93	39	299	50
Minor tonality.......	142	42	9	45	145	60	296	49
Beginning major, ending minor..........	2	1	....	....	....	....	2	....
Beginning minor, ending major..........	1	....	....	....	....	....	1	....
Irregular..............	....	....	....	....	2	1	2	....
Total..........	340	....	20	....	240	....	600	....

[1] Since we are considering music of a period in which what we now designate *scales* and *keys* was not formulated, the terms "major tonality" and "minor tonality" are used in preference to the common terms "major key" and "minor key." (See p. 12.)

[2] See Bulletin 53, pp. 18–33.

[3] The songs comprised in this group are those of the Drum-presentation ceremony, analyzed on pp. 181–183 of Bulletin 53.

Table 2a.—FIRST NOTE OF SONG—ITS RELATION TO KEYNOTE

	Chippewa songs.		Sioux songs recorded by Chippewa.		Sioux songs.		Total.	
	Number.	Per cent.	Number.	Per cent.	Number.	Per cent.	Number.	Per cent.
Beginning on the—								
Fourteenth......	....	....	....	....	1	....	1	....
Thirteenth.......	4	1	....	....	....	....	4	....
Twelfth..........	105	31	2	10	28	12	135	23
Eleventh........	3	1	1	5	7	3	11	2
Tenth...........	24	7	2	10	23	10	49	8
Ninth...........	16	5	....	....	9	4	25	4
Octave..........	61	18	6	30	56	23	123	21
Seventh.........	6	2	1	5	1	....	8	1
Sixth...........	10	3	....	....	3	1	13	2
Fifth...........	72	21	3	15	69	29	144	24
Fourth..........	7	2	....	....	3	1	10	1
Third...........	10	3	2	10	18	8	30	5
Second..........	9	3	....	....	3	1	12	2
Keynote........	13	4	3	15	17	7	33	5
Irregular.............	....	....	....	....	2	1	2	....
Total..........	340	....	20	....	240	....	600	....

MELODIC ANALYSIS—continued

TABLE 3A.—LAST NOTE OF SONG—ITS RELATION TO KEYNOTE

	Chippewa songs.		Sioux songs recorded by Chippewa.		Sioux songs.		Total.	
	Number.	Per cent.	Number.	Per cent.	Number.	Per cent.	Number.	Per cent.
Ending on the—								
Fifth............	75	22	6	30	74	31	155	26
Third............	36	11	1	5	35	15	72	12
Keynote.........	229	67	13	65	129	54	371	61
Irregular............	....	....	....	....	2	1	2	....
Total..........	340	....	20	....	240	....	600	....

TABLE 4A.—LAST NOTE OF SONG—ITS RELATION TO COMPASS OF SONG

	Chippewa songs.		Sioux songs recorded by Chippewa.		Sioux songs.		Total.	
	Number.	Per cent.	Number.	Per cent.	Number.	Per cent.	Number.	Per cent.
Songs in which final tone is—								
Lowest tone in song............	307	90	18	90	212	88	537	90
Highest tone in song............	1	....					1	....
Immediately preceded by—								
Fifth below..	1	....					1	....
Fourth below	9	3	....	....	....	....	9	1
Major third below......	2	....			1	....	3	....
Minor third below......	7	2	....	....	2	1	9	1
Whole tone below......	5	2	....	....	7	3	12	2
Semitone below........	....	....	....	....	3	1	3	....
Whole tone below with fourth below in a previous measure........	1	....	....	....	....	....	1	....
Whole tone below with sixth below in a previous measure........	1	....	....	....	....	....	1	....
Songs containing a fourth below the final tone..........	3	1	....	....	4	2	7	1

MELODIC ANALYSIS—continued

TABLE 4A.—LAST NOTE OF SONG—ITS RELATION TO COMPASS OF SONG—continued

	Chippewa songs.		Sioux songs recorded by Chippewa.		Sioux songs.		Total.	
	Number.	Per cent.	Number.	Per cent.	Number.	Per cent.	Number.	Per cent.
Songs containing a major third below the final tone.......	....	....	....	....	4	2	4	1
Songs containing a minor third below the final tone.......	3	1	2	10	5	2	10	2
Irregular...........	....	....	....	....	2	1	2	....
Total.........	340	....	20	....	240	....	600	....

TABLE 5A.—NUMBER OF TONES COMPRISING COMPASS OF SONG

	Chippewa songs.		Sioux songs recorded by Chippewa.		Sioux songs.		Total.	
	Number.	Per cent.	Number.	Per cent.	Number.	Per cent.	Number.	Per cent.
Compass of—								
Seventeen tones..	....	....	....	....	3	1	3	....
Fourteen tones...	9	3	....	....	5	2	14	2
Thirteen tones...	29	8	....	....	17	7	46	8
Twelve tones.....	103	30	3	15	41	17	147	25
Eleven tones.....	31	9	5	25	9	4	45	8
Ten tones........	38	11	4	20	39	16	81	14
Nine tones.......	18	6	5	25	28	12	51	9
Eight tones......	71	21	2	10	83	35	156	25
Seven tones......	16	5	....	....	4	2	20	3
Six tones........	10	3	1	5	8	3	19	3
Five tones.......	13	4	....	....	1	....	14	2
Four tones.......	2	....	....	....	2	1	4	....
Total.........	340	....	20	....	240	....	600	....

TABLE 6A.—TONE MATERIAL

	Chippewa songs.		Sioux songs recorded by Chippewa.		Sioux songs.		Total.	
	Number.	Per cent.	Number.	Per cent.	Number.	Per cent.	Number.	Per cent.
First five-toned scale.	1	....	....	....	1	....	2	....
Second five-toned scale...............	40	12	3	15	31	13	74	12
Fourth five-toned scale...............	88	26	6	30	43	18	137	23
Fifth five-toned scale...............	2	....	....	....	....	....	2	....
Major triad...	4	1	....	....	1	....	5	1

MELODIC ANALYSIS—continued

TABLE 6A.—TONE MATERIAL—continued

	Chippewa songs.		Sioux songs recorded by Chippewa.		Sioux songs.		Total.	
	Number.	Per cent.	Number.	Per cent.	Number.	Per cent.	Number.	Per cent.
Major triad and seventh..............	1	....	....	....	1	....	2	....
Major triad and sixth.	42	12	....	....	4	2	46	8
Major triad and fourth.............	2	....	....	....	....	....	2	....
Major triad and second..............	3	1	....	....	8	3	11	2
Minor triad.........	1	....	....	....	2	1	3	....
Minor triad and seventh..............	3	1	....	....	1	....	4	1
Minor triad and sixth.	6	2	....	....	....	....	6	1
Minor triad and fourth.............	18	6	1	5	30	12	49	8
Minor triad and second..............	1	....	....	....	1	....	2	....
Octave complete.....	19	6	2	10	14	6	35	6
Octave complete except seventh.......	32	9	2	10	20	8	54	9
Octave complete except seventh and sixth..............	6	2	....	....	16	7	22	4
Octave complete except seventh, sixth, and fourth.........	....	....	....	....	1	....	1	....
Octave complete except seventh, fifth, and second........	....	....	....	....	1	....	1	....
Octave complete except seventh and fourth [1]............	4	1	....	....	5	2	9	1
Octave complete except seventh and third..............	1	....	....	....	1	....	2	....
Octave complete except seventh and second............	11	3	1	5	9	4	21	4
Octave complete except sixth..........	15	4	2	10	12	5	29	5
Octave complete except sixth and fifth.	....	....	1	5	....	....	1	....
Octave complete except sixth and fourth.............	1	....	....	....	2	1	3	....
Octave complete except sixth and second..............	1	....	....	....	4	2	5	1

[1] These songs are minor in tonality, the mediant being a minor third above the tonic and the submediant a minor sixth above the tonic. (See p. 14, footnote.)

MELODIC ANALYSIS—continued

TABLE 6A.—TONE MATERIAL—continued

	Chippewa songs.		Sioux songs recorded by Chippewa.		Sioux songs.		Total.	
	Number.	Per cent.	Number.	Per cent.	Number.	Per cent.	Number.	Per cent.
Octave complete except sixth, fifth, and second.........	....	....	1	5	1	....	2	....
Octave complete except sixth and third..............	....	....	....	....	1	....	1	....
Octave complete except fifth and second...............	....	....	....	....	1	....	1	....
Octave complete except fourth........	5	2	....	....	10	4	15	2
Octave complete except fourth and third..............	1	....	....	....	....	....	1	....
Octave complete except fourth and second...............	1	....	....	....	3	1	4	1
Octave complete except third..........	1	....	....	....	....	....	1	....
Octave complete except third and second...............	....	....	....	....	1	....	1	....
Octave complete except second.......	10	3	....	....	11	5	21	4
Minor third and fourth..............	3	1	....	....	1	....	4	1
First, second, and fifth tones.........	1	....	....	....	....	....	1	....
First, fourth, and fifth tones..............	....	....	....	....	1	....	1	....
First, second, fourth, and fifth tones.....	1	....	....	....	....	....	1	....
First, second, fifth, and sixth tones....	6	2	....	....	....	....	6	1
Other combinations of tones...........	9	3	1	5	2	1	12	2
Total.........	340	....	20	....	240	....	600	....

TABLE 7A.—ACCIDENTALS

	Chippewa songs.		Sioux songs recorded by Chippewa.		Sioux songs.		Total.	
	Number.	Per cent.	Number.	Per cent.	Number.	Per cent.	Number.	Per cent.
Songs containing—								
No accidentals...	288	85	18	90	196	82	502	85
Seventh raised a semitone.......	4	1	1	5	10	4	15	2

MELODIC ANALYSIS—continued

TABLE 7A.—ACCIDENTALS—continued

	Chippewa songs.		Sioux songs recorded by Chippewa.		Sioux songs.		Total.	
	Number.	Per cent.	Number.	Per cent.	Number.	Per cent.	Number.	Per cent.
Songs, containing— continued								
Sixth raised a semitone.......	9	3	1	5	3	1	13	2
Sixth and third raised a semitone..........	....	....	....	....	1	....	1	....
Fourth raised a semitone.......	2	1	....	....	6	2	8	1
Third raised a semitone.......	1	....	....	....	....	....	1	....
Second raised a semitone.......	3	1	....	....	3	1	6	1
Fourth and seventh raised a semitone.......	1	....	....	....	1	....	2	....
Fourth raised a semitone and second lowered a semitone.....	1	....	....	....	....	....	1	....
Second raised a semitone and sixth lowered a semitone.......	1	....	....	....	....	....	1	....
Seventh lowered a semitone.....	1	....	....	....	3	1	4	....
Seventh and fourth lowered a semitone.....	....	....	....	....	1	....	1	....
Sixth lowered a semitone.......	16	5	....	....	5	2	21	4
Fifth lowered a semitone.......	1	....	....	....	....	....	1	....
Fourth lowered a semitone.......	2	....	....	....	3	1	5	....
Third lowered a semitone.......	3	1	....	....	3	1	6	1
Second lowered a semitone.......	6	2	....	....	2	1	8	1
Third and second lowered, and fourth raised a semitone.......	0	....	....	....	1	....	1	....
Second, third, and sixth lowered a semitone.	1	....	....	....	....	....	1	....
Irregular............	....	....	....	....	2	1	2	....
Total..........	340	....	20	....	240	....	600	....

MELODIC ANALYSIS—continued

TABLE 8A.—STRUCTURE

	Chippewa songs.		Sioux songs recorded by Chippewa.		Sioux songs.		Total.	
	Number.	Per cent.	Number.	Per cent.	Number.	Per cent.	Number.	Per cent.
Melodic [1]	222	65	17	85	158	66	397	66
Melodic with harmonic framework [2]	35	10	3	15	47	20	85	14
Harmonic [3]	83	24	....	....	33	14	116	19
Irregular	....	....	....	....	2	1	2	....
Total	340	....	20	....	240	....	600	....

[1] Songs are thus classified if contiguous accented tones do not bear a simple chord-relation to each other.
[2] Songs are thus classified if only a portion of the contiguous accented tones bear a chord-relation to each other.
[3] Songs are thus classified if contiguous accented tones bear a simple chord-relation to each other.

TABLE 9A.—FIRST PROGRESSION—DOWNWARD AND UPWARD

	Chippewa songs.		Sioux songs recorded by Chippewa.		Sioux songs.		Total.	
	Number.	Per cent.	Number.	Per cent.	Number.	Per cent.	Number.	Per cent.
Downward	238	70	12	60	165	69	415	69
Upward	102	30	8	40	75	31	185	31
Total	340	....	20	....	240	....	600	....

TABLE 10A.—TOTAL NUMBER OF PROGRESSIONS—DOWNWARD AND UPWARD

	Chippewa songs.		Sioux songs recorded by Chippewa.		Sioux songs.		Total.	
	Number.	Per cent.	Number.	Per cent.	Number.	Per cent.	Number.	Per cent.
Downward	5,422	65	346	64	4,651	63	10,419	64
Upward	2,864	35	198	36	2,674	37	5,736	36
Total	8,286	....	544	....	7,325	....	16,155	....

TABLE 11A.—INTERVALS IN DOWNWARD PROGRESSION

	Chippewa songs.		Sioux songs recorded by Chippewa.		Sioux songs.		Total.	
	Number.	Per cent.	Number.	Per cent.	Number.	Per cent.	Number.	Per cent.
Interval of a—								
Twelfth	1	....	....	....	....	....	1	....
Ninth	1	....	....	....	....	....	1	....
Octave	2	....	....	....	....	....	2	....
Seventh	2	....	....	....	....	....	2	....

MELODIC ANALYSIS—continued

TABLE 11A.—INTERVALS IN DOWNWARD PROGRESSION—continued

	Chippewa songs.		Sioux songs recorded by Chippewa.		Sioux songs.		Total.	
	Number.	Per cent.	Number.	Per cent.	Number.	Per cent.	Number.	Per cent.
Interval of a—contd.								
Major sixth	12				1		13	
Minor sixth					6		6	
Fifth	59	1	3		26	1	88	1
Fourth	421	8	22	6	525	11	968	9
Major third	628	11	4	1	343	7	975	9
Minor third	1,824	34	114	33	1,396	30	3,334	32
Augmented second			1		5		6	
Major second	2,472	42	198	57	2,085	45	4,755	46
Minor second			4	1	264	6	268	3
Total	5,422		346		4,651		10,419	

TABLE 12A.—INTERVALS IN UPWARD PROGRESSION

	Chippewa songs.		Sioux songs recorded by Chippewa.		Sioux songs.		Total.	
	Number.	Per cent.	Number.	Per cent.	Number.	Per cent.	Number.	Per cent.
Interval of a—								
Fourteenth	1						1	
Twelfth	17						17	
Eleventh	3				1		4	
Tenth	4		1		6		11	
Ninth	2		2	1	6		10	2
Octave	43	1	2	1	63	2	108	2
Seventh	9				13		22	
Major sixth	47	2	1		16		64	1
Minor sixth			3	1	30	1	33	1
Fifth	196	7	11	6	151	6	358	6
Fourth	388	14	31	16	422	16	841	15
Major third	345	12	9	4	271	10	625	11
Minor third	800	29	51	26	710	27	1,561	27
Major second	1,009	35	85	43	818	31	1,912	33
Minor second			2	1	167	6	169	3
Total	2,864		198		2,674		5,736	

MELODIC ANALYSIS—continued

TABLE 13A.—AVERAGE NUMBER OF SEMITONES IN AN INTERVAL

	Number of songs.	Number of intervals.	Number of semitones.	Average number of semitones in an interval.
Chippewa songs...	340	8,286	25,791	3.1
Sioux songs of Drum-presentation ceremony, recorded by Chippewa......................................	20	544	1,592	2.93
Old Sioux songs..	147	4,445	12,864	2.89
Comparatively modern Sioux songs...................	93	2,880	8,558	2.97
Total..	600	16,155	48,805	3.02

TABLE 14A.—KEY

	Chippewa songs.		Sioux songs recorded by Chippewa.		Sioux songs.		Total.	
	Number.	Per cent.	Number.	Per cent.	Number.	Per cent.	Number.	Per cent.
Key of [1]—								
A major..........	19	6	....	....	12	5	31	5
A minor.........	18	5	3	15	15	6	36	6
B flat major......	17	5	....	....	13	5	30	5
B flat minor.....	6	2	....	....	11	5	17	3
B major..........	7	2	....	....	11	5	18	3
B minor.........	17	5	1	5	16	7	34	6
C major..........	13	3	2	10	6	2	21	4
C major..........	13	3	1	5	14	6	28	5
D flat major.....	17	5	2	10	5	2	24	4
C sharp minor...	14	4	....	....	5	2	19	3
D major.........	7	3	1	5	11	5	19	3
D minor.........	12	3	1	5	15	6	28	5
E flat major......	9	3	....	....	8	3	17	3
E flat minor.....	17	5	2	10	8	3	27	5
E major..........	6	2	1	5	7	3	14	2
E minor.........	5	2	....	....	8	3	13	2
F major..........	29	9	1	5	8	3	38	6
F minor.........	10	3	....	....	14	6	24	4
G flat major......	23	7	1	5	3	1	27	5
F sharp major...	....	....	....	....	1	....	1	....
F sharp minor...	6	2	1	5	10	4	17	3
G major..........	36	11	3	15	10	4	49	8
G minor.........	11	3	....	....	17	7	28	5
A flat major......	17	5	....	....	4	2	21	4
G sharp minor...	8	3	....	....	6	2	14	2
Beginning major, ending minor..........	2	....	....	....	....	....	2	....
Beginning minor, ending major.......	1	....	....	....	....	....	1	....
Irregular............	....	....	....	....	2	1	2	....
Total..........	340	....	20	....	240	....	600	....

[1] The term "key" is here used in its broad sense, as applicable to nonharmonic music, inclusive of modes.

RHYTHMIC ANALYSIS

TABLE 15A.—PART OF MEASURE ON WHICH SONG BEGINS

	Chippewa songs.		Sioux songs recorded by Chippewa.		Sioux songs.		Total.	
	Number.	Per cent.	Number.	Per cent.	Number.	Per cent.	Number.	Per cent.
Beginning on unaccented part of measure............	109	37	12	60	96	40	217	39
Beginning on accented part of measure............	189	63	8	40	144	60	341	61
Transcribed in outline[1]................	42	....	....	....	....	....	42	....
Total..........	340	....	20	....	240	....	600	....

TABLE 16A.—RHYTHM OF FIRST MEASURE

	Chippewa songs.		Sioux songs recorded by Chippewa.		Sioux songs.		Total.	
	Number.	Per cent.	Number.	Per cent.	Number.	Per cent.	Number.	Per cent.
First measure in—								
2–4 time.........	149	50	9	45	142	59	300	54
2–2 time.........	2	....	....	....	....	....	2	....
3–8 time.........	4	2	....	....	....	....	4	1
3–4 time.........	120	40	6	30	94	39	220	39
4–8 time.........	....	....	....	....	3	1	3	1
4–4 time.........	9	3	....	....	....	....	9	2
5–8 time.........	2	....	1	5	1	1	4	1
5–4 time.........	9	3	4	20	....	....	13	2
6–4 time.........	1	....	....	....	....	....	1	....
7–4 time.........	2	....	....	....	....	....	2	....
Transcribed in outline[1]................	42	....	....	....	....	....	42	....
Total..........	340	....	20	....	240	....	600	....

[1] Excluded in computing percentage.

RHYTHMIC ANALYSIS—continued

TABLE 17A.—CHANGE OF TIME (MEASURE-LENGTHS)

	Chippewa songs.		Sioux songs recorded by Chippewa.		Sioux songs.		Total.	
	Number.	Per cent.	Number.	Per cent.	Number.	Per cent.	Number.	Per cent.
Songs containing no change of time.....	69	23	1	5	18	8	88	16
Songs containing a change of time.....	229	77	19	95	222	92	470	84
Transcribed in outline [1]...............	42	....	....	....	....	....	42	....
Total..........	340	....	20	....	240	....	600	....

TABLE 18A.—RHYTHM OF DRUM [2]

	Chippewa songs.		Sioux songs recorded by Chippewa.		Sioux songs.		Total.	
	Number.	Per cent.	Number.	Per cent.	Number.	Per cent.	Number.	Per cent.
Sixteenth notes unaccented..............	....	....	....	....	1	1	1	....
Eighth notes unaccented..............	89	40	12	60	42	34	143	40
Quarter notes unaccented..............	12	5	....	....	44	36	56	15
Half notes unaccented..............	1	....	2	10	2	2	5	1
Eighth notes accented in groups of two...	10	4	....	....	11	9	21	6
Each beat preceded by an unaccented beat corresponding to third count of triplet..............	96	43	6	30	22	18	124	34
Each beat followed by an unaccented beat corresponding to second count of triplet.................	2	1	....	....	....	....	2	1
Each beat preceded by an unaccented beat corresponding to fourth count of group of four sixteenth notes [3]......	14	6	....	....	....	....	14	3
Drum not recorded [1]..	116	....	....	....	118	....	234	....
Total..........	340	....	20	....	240	....	600	....

[1] Excluded in computing percentage.
[2] Examples of these rhythms are cited on p. 19, in footnote.
[3] See Bulletin 53, p. 240.

RHYTHMIC ANALYSIS—continued

TABLE 19A.—RHYTHMIC UNIT [1] OF SONG

	Chippewa songs.		Sioux songs recorded by Chippewa.		Sioux songs.		Total.	
	Number.	Per cent.	Number.	Per cent.	Number.	Per cent.	Number.	Per cent.
Songs containing—								
No rhythmic unit..	107	36	7	35	71	29	185	33
One rhythmic unit.	186	62	10	50	139	57	335	60
Two rhythmic units	4	1	3	15	25	10	32	6
Three rhythmic units............	1	....	....	....	3	1	4	1
Four rhythmic units.............	....	....	....	....	1	....	1	....
Five rhythmic units............	....	....	....	....	1	....	1	....
Songs transcribed in outline [2]	42	....	....	....	....	....	42	....
Total..........	340	....	20	....	240	....	600	....

[1] For the purpose of this analysis a rhythmic unit is defined as a group of tones of various lengths, usually comprising more than one count of a measure, occurring more than twice in a song, and having an evident influence on the rhythm of the entire song.

[2] Excluded in computing percentage.

TABLE 20A.—METRIC UNIT OF VOICE (TEMPO)

	Chippewa songs.		Sioux songs recorded by Chippewa.		Sioux songs.		Total.	
	Number.	Per cent.	Number.	Per cent.	Number.	Per cent.	Number.	Per cent.
Metronome—								
44...............	1	....	....	....	....	....	1	....
48...............	....	....	....	....	1	....	1	....
50...............	1	....	....	....	....	....	1	....
52...............	2	....	....	....	3	1	5	....
54...............	2	....	....	....	3	1	5	....
56...............	1	....	....	....	3	1	4	....
58...............	....	....	....	....	5	2	5	....
60...............	9	3	....	....	9	4	18	3
63...............	4	1	....	....	12	5	16	3
66...............	5	2	....	....	16	6	21	4
69...............	8	3	....	....	10	4	18	3
72...............	16	5	....	....	15	6	31	6
76...............	11	4	1	5	20	8	32	6
80...............	11	4	3	15	21	8	35	6
84...............	14	5	3	15	15	6	32	6
88...............	15	5	5	25	12	5	32	6
92...............	16	6	3	15	19	8	38	7
96...............	22	7	....	....	15	6	37	7
100..............	18	6	....	....	11	2	29	5
104..............	20	7	1	5	7	3	28	5
108..............	18	6	1	5	5	2	24	4
112..............	18	6	....	....	5	2	23	4

RHYTHMIC ANALYSIS—continued

TABLE 20A.—METRIC UNIT OF VOICE (TEMPO)—continued

	Chippewa songs.		Sioux songs recorded by Chippewa.		Sioux songs.		Total.	
	Number.	Per cent.	Number.	Per cent.	Number.	Per cent.	Number.	Per cent.
Metronome—contd.								
116.................	10	3	....	....	5	2	15	3
120.................	14	5	1	5	1	....	16	3
126.................	7	2	....	....	4	1	11	2
132.................	3	1	....	....	4	1	7	2
138.................	2	....	....	....	2	....	4	....
144.................	7	2	....	....	5	2	12	2
152.................	5	2	....	....	....	....	5	1
160.................	9	3	....	....	3	1	12	3
168.................	13	4	....	....	3	1	16	3
176.................	3	1	1	5	5	2	8	1
184.................	3	1	1	5	....	....	5	....
192.................	5	2	....	....	1	....	6	....
200.................	6	2	....	....	....	....	6	1
208.................	2	....	....	....	....	....	2	....
Rubato[1].........	2	....	....	....	....	....	2	....
Transcribed in outline[1].............	37	....	....	....	....	....	37	....
Total..........	340	....	20	....	240	....	600	....

[1] Excluded in computing percentage.

TABLE 21A.—METRIC UNIT OF DRUM (TEMPO)

	Chippewa songs.		Sioux songs recorded by Chippewa.		Sioux songs.		Total.	
	Number.	Per cent.	Number.	Per cent.	Number.	Per cent.	Number.	Per cent.
Metronome—								
56..................	....	....	....	....	2	2	2	....
60..................	....	....	....	....	4	3	4	1
63..................	....	....	....	....	4	3	4	1
66..................	....	....	....	....	5	4	5	1
69..................	....	....	....	....	1	....	1	....
72.................	1	....	....	....	5	4	6	1
76.................	2	....	1	5	7	6	10	3
80.................	9	4	2	10	11	9	22	6
84.................	4	2	1	5	5	4	10	3
88.................	8	2	4	20	10	8	22	6
92.................	15	7	4	20	9	8	28	8
96.................	15	7	5	25	11	9	31	8
100.................	15	7	....	....	5	4	20	5
104.................	26	11	2	10	7	6	35	9
108.................	25	11	....	....	5	4	30	8
112.................	25	11	....	....	2	2	27	7
116.................	21	9	1	5	5	4	27	7
120.................	22	10	....	....	2	2	24	6
126.................	13	6	....	....	1	....	14	4

RHYTHMIC ANALYSIS—continued

TABLE 21A.—METRIC UNIT OF DRUM (TEMPO)—continued

	Chippewa songs.		Sioux songs recorded by Chippewa.		Sioux songs.		Total.	
	Number.	Per cent.	Number.	Per cent.	Number.	Per cent.	Number.	Per cent.
Metronome—contd.								
132...............	13	6	....	....	4	3	17	5
138...............	4	2	....	....	4	3	8	2
144...............	2	....	....	....	3	2	5	1
152...............	2	....	....	....	2	2	4	1
160...............	1	....	....	....	3	2	4	1
168...............	....	....	....	....	5	4	5	1
176...............	1	....	....	....	....	....	1	....
Drum not recorded[1]..	116	....	....	....	118	....	234	....
Total..........	340	....	20	....	240	....	600	....

TABLE 22A.—COMPARISON OF METRIC UNIT OF VOICE AND DRUM (TEMPO)

	Chippewa songs.		Sioux songs recorded by Chippewa.		Sioux songs.		Total.	
	Number.	Per cent.	Number.	Per cent.	Number.	Per cent.	Number.	Per cent.
Drum and voice having the same metric unit...............	80	36	7	35	76	62	163	44
Drum faster than voice...............	103	46	11	55	24	20	138	38
Drum slower than voice...............	41	18	2	10	22	18	65	18
Drum not recorded[1]..	116	....	....	....	118	....	234	....
Total..........	340	....	20	....	240	....	600	....

[1] Excluded in computing percentage.

ANALYSIS OF SIOUX AND CHIPPEWA SONGS

The purpose of this chapter is to present in descriptive and diagrammatic form [1] the more important data contained in the tabulated analyses immediately preceding.

Table 1A.—In this table the songs are grouped according to tonality, which is defined as "the quality or peculiarity of a tonal system." (See p. 12, footnote.)   The first step in analyzing a song is the determination of the keynote or tonic by observing the tones which occur in the song and their general progressions.   The next step in the analysis is the determination of the tonality.   In ascertaining this, if the song contains several tones, we observe especially the pitch of the third and sixth above the keynote, as these tones are a semitone lower in minor than in major tonality.   The sixth is absent from 138 of the songs under analysis, while the third is absent from only 17 songs; the third is therefore the principal factor in judging the tonality of a

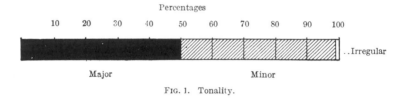

Fig. 1.   Tonality.

song.   If the third is four semitones (a major third) above the keynote, the song is said to be major in tonality, and if three semitones (a minor third) above the keynote, minor in tonality.   Classifying the songs according to this basis, we find 50 per cent major in tonality and 49 per cent minor, 1 per cent being irregular in form.   (Fig. 1.)

We usually associate a minor key with the idea of sadness, but this association of ideas does not appear to be present to the same degree in the mind of the Indians.   It seems more probable that a preference for the major tonality shown in many groups of songs may be due to the fact that the major third is one of the more prominent overtones of a fundamental tone (see p. 41).   Helmholtz states that the "minor triad is very decidedly less harmonious than the major triad, in consequence of the combinational tones, which must consequently be . . taken into consideration"; [2] also that "minor chords do not represent

---

[1] The writer gratefully acknowledges her indebtedness to Dr. Aleš Hrdlička, curator of physical anthropology, United States National Museum, for suggestions concerning the graphic methods used in the accompanying diagrams.

[2] Helmholtz, The Sensations of Tone (translated by A. J. Ellis), pt. 2, p. 214, London, 1885.

the compound tone of their root as well as the major chords; their third, indeed, does not form any part of this compound tone."[1] In this connection it is observed that the tonality of a song does not determine its general character as much in Indian music as in that of the white race. The melodic feeling in many Chippewa and Sioux songs seems to be for the interval between successive tones, while the melodies of the white race are based upon "keys," which are groups of tones having a systematic and definite relation to a key-note. Subsequent analyses will show that the prevailing interval of progression in a song may be minor, though the interval between the keynote and its third is major, thus giving a predominance of minor intervals in a song of major tonality.[2]

Table 2A.—Before considering this phase of analysis let us recall certain fundamental principles of the musical system developed by the white race. In that system the tonic chord, or triad on the key-note, may be said to be the framework of the group of tones called a key. This chord is based on the laws of acoustics and comprises, if the chord be major, the first four overtones of the keynote or fundamental tone. It is understood, of course, that the tone produced by a stretched string or other body capable of strong sympathetic vibration is a compound, not a simple sound. In addition to the tone produced by the vibrations of the entire body there are higher tones which are less distinct, but which can be perceived. These are called overtones, or upper partial tones.

Helmholtz says:

We must . . . not hold it to be an illusion of the ear, or to be mere imagination, when in the musical tone of a single note emanating from a musical instrument, we distinguish many partial tones. . . If we admitted this, we should have also to look upon the colours of the spectrum which are separated from white light, as a mere illusion of the eye. The real outward existence of partial tones in nature can be established at any moment by a sympathetically vibrating membrane which casts up the sand strewn upon it.[3]

The series of these upper partial tones is precisely the same for all compound musical tones which correspond to a uniformly periodical motion of the air. It is as follows:

The first upper partial tone . . . is the upper Octave of the prime tone, and makes double the number of vibrations in the same time.

The second upper partial tone . . . is the Fifth of this Octave . . . making three times as many vibrations in the same time as the prime.

The third partial . . . is the second higher Octave . . . making four times as many vibrations as the prime in the same time.

The fourth upper partial tone is the major Third of this second higher Octave . . . with five times as many vibrations as the prime in the same time.

. . . And thus they go on, becoming continually fainter, to tones making 7, 8, 9, &c., times as many vibrations in the same time, as the prime tone.[4]

---

[1] Helmholtz, The Sensations of Tone (translated by A. J. Ellis), pt. 3, p. 300, London, 1885.
[2] See analyses of songs Nos. 175, 177, 187.
[3] Helmholtz, op. cit., pt. 1, p. 48.
[4] Ibid., p. 22.

In musical notation, with C, second space bass clef, as a fundamental, this part of the series is as follows (fig. 2).

It is noted that the first overtone is an octave above the fundamental and the second is 12 tones (fifth in the first higher octave) above the fundamental, while the fourth overtone (third in the second higher octave) supplies the major third, completing the tones of the triad or common chord of C, the fundamental tone.

Fundamental   1st   2d   3d   4th overtones
     C   c   g   c'   e'

FIG. 2.   Fundamental and first four overtones.

We will now turn to the Indian songs under analysis. Figure 3 indicates the intervals on which the songs begin, omitting groups of less than 1 per cent, shown in Table 2A. Twenty-one per cent begin on the octave (first or third overtone), and 23 per cent, having a compass of 12 tones above the keynote, on the twelfth (second overtone). Thus, if the keynote were C, as in figure 2, the octave is c, and the twelfth g. But before proceeding further let us note the range of the human voice, also the fact that the ear seems to accept tones an

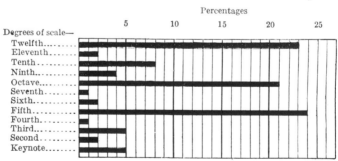

FIG. 3.   First note of song—its relation to keynote.

octave apart as being the same tone.[1]   Not all voices have a range of 12 tones, and a large majority of the songs under analysis have a compass smaller than that number of tones. With the songs beginning on the twelfth should be included, therefore, those on the fifth, which (supposing the keynote to be C) would be G, an octave lower than the tone designated as g. Twenty-four per cent begin on the fifth above the keynote, making a total of 47 per cent beginning on this interval of the scale. Few voices have a range of two octaves, but two of these songs (Nos. 195, 202) begin on the second

---

[1] "It is very easy to make a mistake of an octave."—HELMHOLTZ, op. cit., p. 62.

octave above the keynote (third overtone). We find that, next to the percentages already cited, the largest proportion is that of songs beginning on the third and tenth above the keynote. With C as a keynote these tones are E and e, readily seen to be the fourth overtone, sung in the two lower octaves, which are within the compass of the voice. Thirteen per cent of the songs begin on these tones and 5 per cent begin on the keynote, these melodies lying partly above and partly below the keynote. Thus 86 per cent of the songs under analysis begin on the keynote and its first four overtones. These, as already indicated, comprise the tones of a common chord.

Table 3A.—The results of this analysis serve to emphasize the preceding paragraph. It is here shown that all except two of the songs

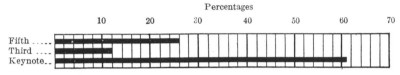

Percentages

| 10 | 20 | 30 | 40 | 50 | 60 | 70 |

Fifth .....
Third ....
Keynote..

FIG. 4. Last note of song—its relation to keynote.

under analysis end on the keynote, its third or fifth. Twenty-six per cent end on the fifth (corresponding to the second overtone), 12 per cent on the third (corresponding to the fourth overtone), and 61 per cent on the keynote. (See fig. 4.) Two songs are so irregular in form that no tone is designated as a keynote.

Table 4A.—This table shows that the structure of 90 per cent of the songs is above the final tone. The preceding table indicated the final tone to be the keynote in 61 per cent of the songs. These tables

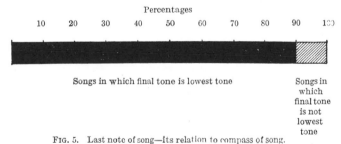

Percentages

| 10 | 20 | 30 | 40 | 50 | 60 | 70 | 80 | 90 | 100 |

Songs in which final tone is lowest tone   Songs in
                                                        which
                                                        final tone
                                                        is not
                                                        lowest
                                                        tone

FIG. 5. Last note of song—its relation to compass of song.

supplement Table 2A in showing the melodic structure of these songs. This structure appears to rest on a fundamental tone, usually the keynote. The trend is downward and this frequently is not heard until the closing measures. A typical outline is as follows, the intervals being repeated several times and bytones introduced: g–e–c–A–G–E–C.

In 10 per cent of the songs the final tone is not the lowest tone. In these instances the final tone is usually the keynote, preceded by an ascent of a small interval, as though at the close of the above outline there were a descending interval, with a return to C as the final tone. (See fig. 5.)

Table 5A.—The compass of the songs is shown in this table. The present analysis differs from that of Table 2A in that it concerns the entire range of the song, while Table 2A indicated the interval between the keynote and the first note. There is accordingly a difference in percentages. For instance, 25 per cent of the songs have a compass of 12 tones, but only 23 per cent begin on the twelfth above the keynote. In this, as in Table 2A, the largest percentages are on eight and twelve. It is noted in Table 5A, though not shown on the diagram, that three songs have a

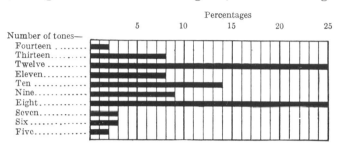

FIG. 6.   Number of tones comprising compass of song.

compass of 17 tones, or two octaves and two tones. The singers of these songs were men with falsetto voices. (See fig. 6.)

Table 6A.—The percentages shown in this table are not the same as those shown in figure 7, though both are concerned with the tone material of the songs. The table indicates the *character* of the tone material by referring it to a keynote, while the diagram indicates the *amount* of the tone material, or the number of scale degrees in the song. Attention is directed to four groups in the table: The second five-toned scale (minor pentatonic), comprising 12 per cent; the

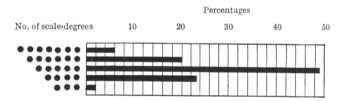

FIG. 7.   Number of degrees of scale used in song.

fourth five-toned scale (major pentatonic), comprising 23 per cent; the group containing only the tones of the major or minor triad, comprising slightly more than 1 per cent; and the group comprising all the tones of the diatonic octave, 6 per cent. In compiling the data shown in figure 7 a degree of the scale occurring in two octaves is, of course, counted only once. It is thus seen that 49 per cent of these songs contain only 5 scale-degrees, 23 per cent contain 4 scale-degrees, and 20 per cent, 6 scale-degrees, while 6 and 2 per cent contain, respectively, 7 and 3 degrees of the scale.

Table 7A.—The purpose of this analysis is to ascertain whether these songs adhere to the intervals of the diatonic scale or whether, while having a keynote and a feeling for the tonic chord of the key, they still use tones which are a semitone higher or lower than the tones of that key. The analysis shows that 85 per cent of the songs contain only the tones of the diatonic scale. In the remaining 15 per cent the tones most frequently raised or lowered are the seventh, sixth, fourth, and second. (See fig. 8.) In only 10 songs is the pitch of the third altered, and the fifth is changed in only one song. This keeping of the diatonic pitch on the tones of the tonic chord is a

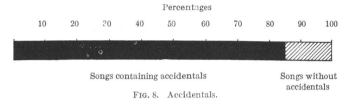

Percentages

| 10 | 20 | 30 | 40 | 50 | 60 | 70 | 80 | 90 | 100 |

Songs containing accidentals   Songs without
                                                accidentals

FIG. 8. Accidentals.

peculiarity which emphasizes the points mentioned in connection with Table 2A.

Table 8A.—Thus far we have considered the tones in a song chiefly with reference to the keynote of the song. The purpose of the present table is to determine the structure of the songs by observing the interval relation of accented tones. Thus if contiguous accented tones bear a simple chord-relation to each other the song is classified as harmonic in structure; if such chord-relation does not exist it is classified as melodic in structure, while an intermediate type is classified as melodic with harmonic framework. An example of

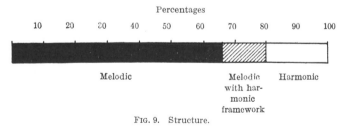

Percentages

| 10 | 20 | 30 | 40 | 50 | 60 | 70 | 80 | 90 | 100 |

Melodic   Melodic   Harmonic
                                 with har-
                                 monic
                                 framework

FIG. 9. Structure.

the latter is a song containing the tones C–E–G–A–C, with the accent placed consecutively on G, A, and G. The framework of the melody is harmonic and comprises the chord C–E–G, but the consecutive accents on G, A, G do not imply a simple chord of the key of C. The song, therefore, is not purely melodic nor strictly harmonic according to the basis adopted for classification. Nineteen per cent of the songs are harmonic in structure, every accented tone having a simple chord-relation to a contiguous accented tone, these chord-relations being within the key implied by the keynote. A much larger proportion are melodic in structure. (See fig. 9.)

Tables 9A, 10A.—Continuing observation of the tones with reference to contiguous tones, we note in Table 9A that 69 per cent of the songs begin with a downward progression. Table 10A shows the entire number of progressions in the song, 64 per cent of which are downward and 36 per cent upward. This is in accordance with Table 2A, which shows that many of the songs begin on high intervals, and with Table 4A, which shows that the last tone is the lowest tone in

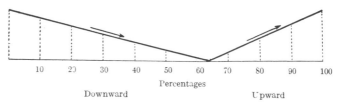

Fig. 10. Downward and upward progressions.

a majority of the songs. This is a further indication that the general trend of these melodies is downward. (See fig. 10.)

Tables 11A, 12A.—An interesting point shown in Tables 11A and 12A is that the descending intervals are smaller than the ascending intervals. Thus it is seen that only 19 per cent of the downward progressions in contrast with 36 per cent of the upward progressions, are larger than a minor third. This is due in part to a peculiarity of these songs in beginning on a high tone and descending, then returning to the original

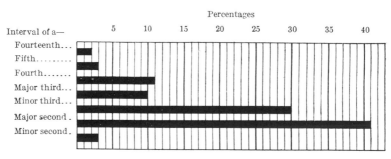

Fig. 11. Size of downward and upward progressions.

pitch or to one almost as high, and again descending by small intervals. Figure 11 shows all the intervals which occur in these songs and are represented in Tables 11A and 12A. Only 5 per cent of the intervals are larger than a fourth. The minor third constitutes 30 per cent of the number, the major second (interval of a whole tone), 41 per cent, and the minor second (interval of a semitone), 3 per cent. This small proportion of semitone intervals does not tend to encourage the theory that Indians habitually use intervals smaller than a semitone.

It is admitted that they frequently produce vocal sounds which differ one from another by a number of vibrations less than that comprised in a semitone, but the writer finds no evidence, on phonographic records of about a thousand songs, that such sounds are part of a system, consciously used by the Indians. Animals express emotion by means of sounds which glide from one pitch to another. Such expression is primal, but into song there enters an intellectual element which tends to produce definiteness of tonal intervals.

Table 13A.—This table shows the largest, smallest, and average interval, expressed in semitones. Figure 12 presents the same data in graphic form, the horizontal lines representing semitones. It should especially be noted that this diagram shows the sizes of the intervals and does not indicate the number of times they occur. The largest interval in these songs is a fourteenth, comprising 23 semitones, and the smallest is a minor third, comprising one semitone. The number of occurrences of these and other intervals is shown in Tables 11A and 12A, in connection with which it has already been noted that the larger intervals are of less frequent occurrence than the smaller. In making the computations for Table 13A the number of occurrences of each interval was multiplied

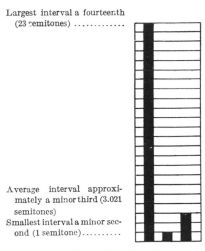

Largest interval a fourteenth (23 semitones) ....

Average interval approximately a minor third (3.021 semitones)
Smallest interval a minor second (1 semitone)..........

FIG. 12.   Largest, smallest, and average intervals (horizontal lines represent semitones).

by the number of semitones which it contains. Having obtained the total number of intervals and of semitones, the average number of semitones in an interval was secured. The average of the entire series is found to be 3.021 semitones, slightly more than a minor third.

Table 14A.—In this table it should be observed that 30 per cent of the songs have as their keynote G, G sharp (or A flat), and A. This is a larger proportion than on any other three consecutive semitones, and suggests the natural range of voice among these Indians. In this connection it should be stated that the speed of the phonograph is the same when the songs are played for transcription as when they are recorded, and that the pitch of the tones is decided by comparing the tones of the phonograph with those of a piano tuned to standard pitch (a′ 435 vd).

Table 15A.—We now enter on the consideration of the rhythm of these songs and of the drum with which many of them were accompanied. Table 15A concerns only the rhythm of the voice, and its purpose is to determine directness of "attack" in beginning a song. The analysis shows that 61 per cent of the songs begin on the accented part of the measure. Table 2A shows that a majority of the songs begin on the tones of the tonic chord. Taken together, these tables suggest a clearness of musical concept on the part of the Indian. (See fig. 13.)

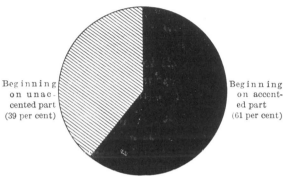

Beginning on unaccented part (39 per cent)

Beginning on accented part (61 per cent)

FIG. 13.   Part of measure on which song begins.

Table 16A.—Like the preceding table, this concerns the rhythm of the voice. In the phonograph records of these songs the accented tones usually are unmistakable and clear. As already stated, a measure in the transcription represents the period of time between two accented tones. The division of this time period into two parts is the simplest possible division. In 54 per cent of the songs the first measure is in double time (2–4 or 2–2) and in 40 per cent in triple time (3–4 or 3–8), 6 per cent of the songs beginning in combinations of these rhythms. (See fig. 14.)

Table 17A.—A change of time (measure-lengths) is found in 84 per cent of these songs (see fig. 15). Such a change in the music of civilized peo-

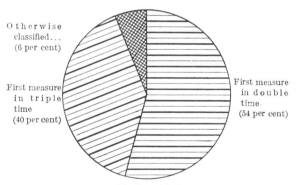

Otherwise classified... (6 per cent)

First measure in triple time (40 per cent)

First measure in double time (54 per cent)

FIG. 14.   Rhythm of first measure.

ples usually affects an entire section of a melody or composition. Changes in time in the songs under analysis, on the other hand, commonly affect single measures or only a few measures. These alternations of measure lengths usually find what may be termed their rhythmic explanation, in the rhythmic unit of the song or in the rhythm of the song as a whole. (See fig. 15.)

Table 18A.—This analysis concerns only the rhythm of the drum. There were recorded without the accompaniment of the drum 234 songs; these were excluded in computing the percentages. In 56 per cent of the songs recorded with drum it is found that the beats of the drum are not divided into groups by accented strokes, but are an unaccented pulsation. The metric unit of the drumbeats is indicated as an eighth, quarter, or half note, according to the note value which constitutes the metric unit of the song. In 6 per cent of the songs the drumbeats are accented in groups of two, and in more than 34 per cent the drum is in a triple division, two parts of which are

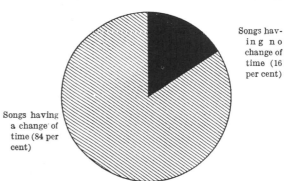

FIG. 15.   Change of time (measure-lengths).

marked by drumbeats and one by a rest. With a few exceptions the unaccented drumbeat immediately precedes the accented beat. In 3 per cent of the songs the drum is in quadruple division, the accented stroke being preceded by a short unaccented stroke. (See fig. 16.)

Table 19A.—On examining these songs it was found that many contain a group of tones which form a distinct phrase, this phrase being repeated either consecutively or at intervals throughout the song. In order to use this peculiarity as a basis of classification it became necessary to formulate a definition. This phrase (or *motif*) was accordingly called a "rhythmic unit," and defined as "a group of tones of various lengths, usually comprising more than one count of a measure, occurring at least twice in a song and having an evident influence on the rhythm of the entire song." Having recognized the rhythmic unit as an important part of the structure of these songs, it was noted that many songs contained two or more of these

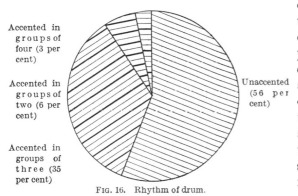

FIG. 16.   Rhythm of drum.

units, each clear, and given with exactness in every rendition of the song. It was further noted that, when two or more such units occur, there is a resemblance among them. In many instances the note-values of the first unit are reversed in the second, while in others the second unit is what might be termed a "complementary" or "answering" phrase. Thirty-three per cent of the songs do not show a rhythmic unit, but in many of these the song itself is a rhythmic whole. Instead of being composed of rhythmic units it is itself a long phrase, with a rhythmic completeness which is satisfactory to the ear. Sixty per cent of the songs contain one rhythmic unit, and 7 per cent contain two, three, four, or five such units. The rhythmic structure of these songs gives evidence of a primitive musical culture. (See fig. 17.)

Tables 20A, 21A.—In these tables are shown the metric units of voice and drum. The metric unit is determined by comparing the phono-

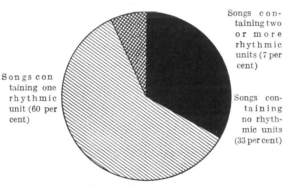

Songs containing two or more rhythmic units (7 per cent)

Songs containing one rhythmic unit (60 per cent)

Songs containing no rhythmic units (33 per cent)

FIG. 17.   Rhythmic unit.

graph record with the speed of a Maelzel metronome (which has been tested for accuracy). The numbers at the left of the analysis tables indicate the number of "ticks" of the metronome per minute. In the rhythmic analysis this corresponds to the comparison of the

phonograph record with the piano in the melodic analysis. On comparing Tables 20A and 21A it is seen that the speed of the drum is slightly faster than that of the voice. Thus in the voice table, 37 per cent have a speed of 100 or more, while in the drum table, 57 per cent have a speed of 100 or more. In each instance the note value indicated in connection with the metronome speed is the same for voice and drum.

Table 22A.—The data in Tables 20A and 21A suggest a discrepancy between the tempo of voice and drum which is further shown in this table. Only 44 per cent of the songs have the same metric unit of voice and drum. This does not signify that in every instance there is one drumbeat to each quarter note of the melody, if the metric unit be indicated as a quarter note. The metric unit of the melody may be a quarter note, the speed being 90 ($\quarternote$ =90), and the drum may be in rapid beats, two of which are equivalent in time to 90. Thus the metric unit would be the same, the drum being indicated as in eighth notes. In 56 per cent of these songs, however, the metric units of voice and drum are different. In a very few instances these are in the ratio of 2 to 3, but the difference is usually too slight to suggest any proportion. Furthermore, the pulses of voice and drum do not coincide at frequent intervals, as they probably would if there were a relation between them in the mind of the performer. The inference in such instances is' rather that the voice and the drum are the expressions of separate impulses, these expressions being simultaneous, but having no relation to each other. (See fig. 18.)

Summary of pages 40–51.—Thus it appears that the songs under analysis resemble the music of civilization in the use of the keynote, third, fifth, and oc-tave and in a unit of rhythm and differ from it in the irreg-ularity of time and in the discrepancy between the tempo of voice and accom-panying drum. It appears also that these songs are char-acterized by a de-scending trend; that the melody tones are chiefly diatonic; and that the most prominent interval is the minor third.

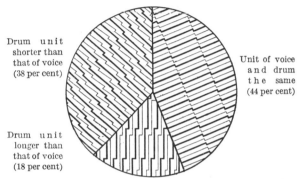

Drum unit shorter than that of voice (38 per cent)

Unit of voice and drum the same (44 per cent)

Drum unit longer than that of voice (18 per cent)

FIG. 18.   Comparison of metric unit of voice and drum.

GRAPHIC REPRESENTATIONS OR "PLOTS"

A form of graphic representation, or "plotting," of melodies has been devised by the writer and is here introduced for the purpose of making the trend of Sioux melodies more apparent to the eye than in musical transcription. The general method employed is similar to that used in showing graphically the course of a moving object. The loci of the object at given periods of time are determined and recorded, the several positions being connected by straight lines. In any use of this method the interest centers in the several points at which the object is located, it being understood that the lines con-necting these points are used merely as an aid to observation. In the present adaptation of this method the pitch of the accented tones in a melody is indicated by dots placed at the intersections of coordinate lines, the horizontal coordinates representing scale degrees and the ver-tical coordinates representing measure-lengths. These dots are con-nected by straight lines, though the course of the melody between the accented tones would, in many instances, vary widely from these lines if it were accurately plotted. The use of accented tones exclusively in analyzing these songs has already been employed, the structure of the melodies being determined by the pitch of contiguous accented tones (see Table 8, footnote). One consideration which seems to justify this usage is the fact that, when differences appear in the several renditions of an Indian song, these differences almost without exception are in unimportant progressions between unaccented tones. Since the sole purpose of these plots is to show the trend of the melodies, it seems permissible to omit from the representation, not only the unaccented tones occurring in the melody, but also a distinction between whole tones and semitones in progressions, and a distinction between double and triple time in measure-lengths. It is obviously desirable that the graphic representation be as simple as possible, the more detailed observation of the melodies being contained in mathematical and descriptive analyses.

A plot of each Sioux melody having been made, these plots were compared, and as a result it was found that there are five types which may be considered the primary outlines, a majority of the others being combinations or modifications of these. The simplest of these types are designated as A and B (see fig. 19), the former being a descending trend with no ascending intervals, and the latter showing what might be termed a horizontal progression, followed by a descent to the final tone. These types appear throughout the series and seem to have no relation to the content of the song. On comparing the plots representing types C, D, and E with the titles of respective songs, it was found that the plots of songs having similar titles or uses resemble each other. This suggests a relation between the content and the form of the song, a somewhat tentative conclusion, which, in another form, was presented in the study of Chippewa songs (see Bulletin 53, pages 50–58).

The song selected as an example of Type A' is No. 195, a song of the grass dance. Comparison with the musical transcription will show the progressions, the song having a compass of two octaves. It will be noted that in this song there are no ascending intervals in the series of accented tones. In addition to this song, the following songs contain a similar outline: Nos. 31, 56, 120, 151, 152, 210, 215. Reference to the list of songs will show that these are divided among almost all classes of songs, a fact which indicates that the type is persistent. This is confirmed by general observation of the structure of Indian songs. Plots of other songs of this type are shown on pages 204, 245, 283, 419. Many other songs resemble this type in outline, but contain one or more ascending intervals in the accented tones.

The example selected to represent Type B is No. 68, a song of the sacred stones. It will be noted that the melody progresses at first horizontally, afterwards descending to the lowest tone.   Other songs resembling this in outline are Nos. 50, 51, 52, 64, 67, 68, 74, 75, 76, 96, 109, 113, 117, 118, 136, 139.   Plots of some of these songs are shown on pages 245, 419.   All these are found among songs a majority of which are believed to be more than 50 years old; they are distributed among the various classes of these songs, but no song of the outline of No. 68 appears among the comparatively modern songs.

The characteristic of Type C is a repetition of the lowest tone, usually the keynote, the melody descending to the keynote, returning

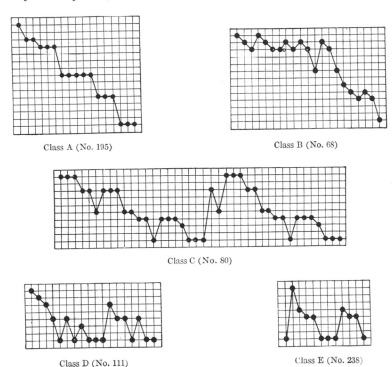

Class A (No. 195)   Class B (No. 68)

Class C (No. 80)

Class D (No. 111)   Class E (No. 238)

FIG. 19.   Plots, Group 1.

to a higher tone and again descending to the lowest tone, with a repetition of that tone.   The example of this type is No. 80, a song used in the treatment of the sick.   It will be recalled that the element of affirmation was very strong in the treatment of the sick, the medicine-man endeavoring to instill in his patient a confidence in the former's ability to effect a cure.   Reference to the analyses of songs used in treating the sick will show a large proportion of these songs ending on the keynote.   Many songs emphasizing the lowest tone or keynote appear in this series, the type being subject to even more variation than Types A and B.   The following list was compiled as the result of an examination of the plots of the songs. Comparison with the list of song titles will show that in a majority of instances the song contains the idea of strength, victory, or self-confidence. The list is as follows: 5, 7, 11, 12, 13, 15, 40, 42, 45, 70, 72, 81, 82, 83, 84, 92, 93, 119, 123, 124, 125, 130, 131, 134, 142, 145, 147, 148, 150, 153, 154, 156, 160, 161, 164, 165, 168, 170, 171, 175, 176, 177, 184, 185, 186, 187, 188, 190, 191, 196, 214, 222, 223, 224, 229, 230. Plots of several of these are shown on pages 283, 419.

Type D was first noted in the songs of Dream societies, named for animals which appeared in dreams, many of these songs being said to have been received from the animals. This type is characterized by a short ascent and descent frequently repeated in the melody. On grouping a number of songs having this characteristic and comparing the song numbers with their respective titles, it was found that practically all are songs concerning men or animals in motion. No. 111 is an example of this class. The plots of Nos. 55 and 58, songs of Dream societies, are shown on page 204. Plots of Nos. 99, 100, 111, 127, 145, 146, 161, and 174, which are songs concerning men or animals and usually suggesting motion, are shown on page 419. Other instances of similar outline are Nos. 66 and 179, which are not plotted.

Type E is noted in songs expressive of grief, or of dissatisfaction. (See p. 519.) There are other songs in which the first progression is an ascending progression. It will be noted that this plot shows only the relation of accented tones, or tones which (in musical terminology) appear at the beginning of measures.

COMPARISON BETWEEN ANALYSES OF CHIPPEWA AND SIOUX SONGS

We will next consider a comparison between the characteristics of Chippewa and Sioux songs, as shown by the percentages in the Tables of Analysis on pages 26–39. The Sioux songs of the Drum-presentation ceremony, sung by Chippewa, are not included in this comparison.

In Table 1 we note that 42 per cent of the Chippewa songs are minor in tonality, while 60 per cent of the Sioux songs are minor. The proportion beginning on the twelfth or fifth is 52 per cent in the Chippewa and 41 per cent in the Sioux, but the proportion beginning on the octave, tenth, and third is larger in the Sioux. The Chippewa show a larger percentage ending on the keynote, but about the same percentage in which the final tone is the lowest in the song. The Chippewa have a much larger proportion of songs with a range of 12 tones, but the Sioux have the larger proportion with a range of 10 tones and of an octave. In songs on the five-toned scales the Chippewa have a larger proportion, but in songs with the octave complete or nearly complete, the percentage is almost identical. A slightly larger percentage of the Chippewa songs contain no accidentals, and the number of purely melodic songs differs by only 1 per cent in the two groups. The difference in songs beginning with a downward progression is also only 1 per cent, and the proportion of ascending and descending progressions differs by 2 per cent. Differences of 1 to 6 per cent mark the frequency of occurrence of various intervals of progression. The average interval in the Sioux songs is slightly smaller than in the Chippewa.

In key the Chippewa songs show a preference for F, F sharp, and G. A slightly larger proportion of the Chippewa songs begin on the accented part of the measure, and a smaller percentage begin in 2–4 time. The percentage of Sioux songs having a change of measure-lengths is considerably larger than that of the Chippewa. In the rhythm of the drum there is a difference, the Chippewa having a much larger percentage with the accented drumbeat preceded by a short, unaccented beat. The proportion of songs containing rhythmic units is 64 per cent in the Chippewa and 68 per cent in the Sioux. The metric unit of the voice shows greater variety among the Chippewa but the drum shows the greater variety among the Sioux. The metric unit of voice and drum shows much greater divergence among the Chippewa, only 36 per cent having the same metric unit, while among the Sioux the corresponding proportion is 62.

Referring to the table of rhythmic units (19A), we note that the percentage of Sioux songs which contain a rhythmic unit is larger than that of the Chippewa.

Of the Sioux songs 169 contain one or more rhythmic units, these units, or phrases, being transcribed on pages 528 et seq. in groups similar to those which appear in the text of the work. Examining these units, we find no duplications except the following phrase, ♩♪.♪♩., which occurs in 11 songs (Nos. 35, 36, 58, 115, 164, 194, 195, 225, 226, 229, 230). We note also that an accented sixteenth note followed by a dotted eighth note, which characterizes this phrase, is the first count-division in the rhythmic units of 26 songs (Nos. 7, 26, 33, 41, 113, 116, 119, 131, 134, 155, 156, 160, 166, 167, 170, 171, 186, 188, 199, 202, 220, 221, 222, 231, 235, 238). Thus it is seen that this count-division characterizes the rhythmic units of more than 16 per cent of the Sioux songs under analysis. Turning to the rhythmic units of the Chippewa songs (Bull. 53, pp. 309–333), it is found that this count-division is present at the opening of slightly less than 3 per cent of the entire number (Nos. 110, Bull. 45, and Nos. 64, 90, 92, 116, 131, 153, 163, 174, Bull. 53). In the summary of analyses in Bulletin 53 (p. 11) it is stated that—

There is . . . a division of a count ♪♫ which occurs in Chippewa songs recorded on a reservation showing Sioux influence, and which is found also in Sioux songs. This

division of the count occurs in 15 per cent of the songs recorded at Waba′cĭñg. . . .
The same phrase is found in 10 per cent of the Sioux songs of the Drum-presentation
Ceremony . . . and also in about 10 per cent of the Sun-dance songs of the Teton
Sioux recorded by the writer at Standing Rock, North Dakota.

From these data it appears that an accented sixteenth note, followed either by an eighth or a dotted eighth note, may be regarded as
a rhythmic characteristic of the Sioux songs under analysis.

No rhythmic peculiarity of equal importance was noted among
the songs of the Chippewa. It therefore appears that the rhythmic
sense is more strongly developed among the Sioux than among the
Chippewa.

Briefly summarizing the comparison between the Chippewa and
Sioux songs as sung by the people of each tribe, it may be said that
the tabulated analyses show differences between the music of the two
tribes, but not such as can safely be traced to definite causes. The
resemblances may be due to the fact that the two tribes have been
in contact for many generations and the music of the one undoubtedly has been influenced to some extent by that of the other. It
is possible that the resemblances and differences between the two
may be seen to have more significance as the study of Indian music is
extended to include a comparison between the songs of other and more
widely separated tribes.

Test of Pitch Discrimination Among Chippewa and Sioux

In order to obtain data on the pitch discrimination of Indians
certain tests were made by the writer during the summer of 1915. [1]
These were made among the Mandan, Hidatsa, Chippewa, and Sioux
Indians, but only the results obtained among the latter two tribes will
be presented. In each of these tribes 10 persons were submitted
to the test, including men and women who are known as being
good singers, and also a few "old timers" who are not musicians.
The limited number of persons tested, as well as the very unfavorable
conditions under which the tests were made, renders the results far
from conclusive, but they have a bearing on the subject of Indian
music, and also suggest interesting points for further investigation.

The tests were made by means of a set of tuning forks comprising
a fork giving the tone a′ (435 vibrations, international pitch), this
being the fundamental tone of the series, and 10 other forks pro-
ducing tones respectively $\frac{1}{2}$, 1, 2, 3, 5, 8, 12, 17, 23, and 30 vibrations
above the fundamental.

---

[1] The writer gratefully acknowledges her indebtedness to Prof. C. E. Seashore, dean of the Graduate
College, University of Iowa, for his courtesy in lending the tuning forks with which the tests were made,
also for valuable suggestions regarding the formulation of the results. The method used in the tests was
essentially that described by Prof. Seashore in his monograph, "The Measurement of Pitch Discrimination; A Preliminary Report," in *Psychological Monographs*, vol. 13, No. 1, Review Publishing Co., Lancaster, Pa., and Baltimore, Md., 1910.

As a preliminary to the recorded test the person was asked to listen to various intervals, interspersed with unisons, two forks being sounded in rapid succession and the person stating whether they sounded alike or different. Many could recognize the unison whenever it occurred (the same fork being sounded twice), while others could hear no difference between tones which were three or even five vibrations apart. After the subject had thus become somewhat accustomed to the sound of the forks, the regular test was given and repeated 20 times, each reply being noted, together with the interval used in the test. As in the preliminary tests, two forks were sounded in rapid succession, and in this the subject was asked which tone was the higher, the first or the second. The fundamental fork was not always used in this test, the forks being sounded in irregular order, making the test the more difficult. The intervals used in the test and the correctness of the replies formed a basis for judging the pitch discrimination of the individual. Thus a man who failed on a majority of tests comprising intervals of fewer than three vibrations and answered correctly on a majority of tests comprising intervals of three or more vibrations may be considered as having three vibrations as the limit of his pitch discrimination. The direct result of these tests can be shown quantitatively, but in addition to this result there are observations of equal importance which depend to a large extent on personal knowledge of the individuals being tested. For instance, men whom the writer knows from an acquaintance of several years to be men of great firmness and independence of character showed special power of concentration and recognized small intervals (1, 2, or 3 vibrations) in the early part of the test, while men of less strong individuality did not make their best record until the test was almost completed. A particularly clear example of this occurred among the Chippewa.

A man and two of his sons were tested, all being prominent singers on the White Earth Reservation. The father and one of the sons (known respectively as Big Bear and George Big Bear) recorded songs for the writer during her musical study among the Chippewa. The older man retains much of the native character, while his sons are somewhat divided in their sympathies, having much in common with the older Indians but having progressed so far in the white man's way that when these tests were made they were employed as carpenters by the Government. A record of the tests of these three men indicates the pitch discrimination of the older man as about three vibrations, and that of his two sons as about five vibrations.

The pitch discrimination of the older Chippewa and Sioux Indians was, generally speaking, about 3 vibrations. As the interval between a′ and b′ is 54 vibrations, the interval of 5 vibrations is approximately one-eleventh of a tone, and the interval of 3 vibrations is approximately one-eighteenth of a tone.

The following tables give the record of the tests made on 10 persons in each tribe:

CHIPPEWA

Number of vibrations in interval.	Number of times this interval was used in test.	Correct answers.	Per cent.	Incorrect answers.	Per cent.
½ to 4	62	32	51	30	49
5 to 10	96	67	70	29	30
11 to 30	42	34	81	8	19
Total	200	133	66. 5	67	33. 5

SIOUX

½ to 4	57	34	60	23	40
5 to 10	79	67	85	12	15
11 to 30	64	52	81	12	19
Total	200	153	76. 5	47	23. 5

It may be seen that there is no significant difference in the average ability of these two groups as shown in the small number of records here given. After comparing these records with those of American whites under various conditions, Professor Seashore is of the opinion that the abilities here shown are about as good as one would find among the average American whites under similar circumstances.

Music as a Cultivated Art Among Chippewa and Sioux [1]

From the structural data given in the foregoing tables and from the descriptions of the singers and their manner of singing contained in the following pages, it seems permissible to make some observations concerning music as a cultivated art among the Chippewa and the Sioux. In this, as in the melodic and rhythmic analyses, we may bear in mind certain fundamental principles of music as an art among white races. The musical standards of civilized peoples have been gradually developed and are concerned with composition and manner of rendition. The music of Chippewa and Sioux will be considered with reference to both these standards.

In the phonographic recording of about 1,000 Indian songs and in contact with a large number of Indian singers the writer has found

[1] This chapter was read by a delegation of Sioux who were in Washington on tribal business. The delegation was composed of five men, one each from the Standing Rock, Pine Ridge, Rosebud, Crow Creek, and Lower Brule Agencies. They pronounced the standards of Indian musical criticism to be correctly set forth, adding only that in order to be a good musician among the Indians a man must be able to learn a melody quickly, and that a good musician could sing a melody correctly after hearing it two or three times.

unmistakable evidence of musical criticism. Certain men are generally acknowledged to be "good singers" and certain songs are said to be "good songs." This implies that the songs and the singers satisfy some standard of evaluation. The Indian may not be able to formulate this standard, but its existence is evidence of an esthetic impulse.

We may note at this time a few observations on this subject, opening it for further investigation. First, in the matter of composition it is observed that the oldest songs, which are considered the best songs, were "composed in dreams." This means that they came in a supposedly supernatural manner to the mind of a man who was hoping for such experiences and who had established the mental and physical conditions under which they were believed to occur. In this we have the native concept of what we call "inspiration." The Indian isolated himself by going away from the camp, while the white musician or poet locks his door, but both realize the necessity of freedom from distraction. A majority of the songs said to have been thus received by the Indians have a rhythmic and melodic unity which is not always present in songs said to have been "made up." Thus the writer once heard a song which was said to have been recently composed, and on inquiry learned that several men had "composed it together." This was evidenced by a lack of unity in the melody, which contained too many peculiarities. The form of the melody suggested the possibility that each man had incorporated in it a favorite interval, or some other musical fancy of his own. The result was a composite rather than a unit.

The comparative analyses in Bulletin 53 (pp. 51–58) suggest a relation between mental concept and the form of its musical expression. The significant prominence of the ascending and descending interval of a fourth in songs concerning motion was noted in Bulletin 53 (pp. 99–101) and is found also in songs of the present series. A comparison of the structure of the old songs with that of songs said to be somewhat modern shows that the more recent songs contain a smaller compass, larger number of progressions and a more regular rhythm. The latter tendency was shown by the following incident: In recording a Chippewa song from an old Indian the writer found the rhythm peculiar, with frequent changes of measure lengths; later the same song was recorded by a young man, said to be an excellent singer. On comparing the phonographic records it was found that the younger singer had slightly changed the rhythm so as to avoid the irregularity in the measure lengths. The song had lost its native character and also its musical interest.

The various occasions of music which exist among civilized races are found also among the Indians. It is a custom that songs connected with ceremonial acts shall be sung only by those who have received them in dreams, or who have inherited or purchased the right to sing them. Such songs form one class of Indian music. To another class belong songs of games and dances, songs of war and of the hunt, as well as songs which celebrate the deeds of a chief or successful warrior. The words of all these songs, while often showing high degree of poetic feeling, appear to be less subjective in character than the words of similar English songs. It is difficult to state what Indian songs correspond to the folk songs of the white race, but in such a group should probably be included the songs connected with folk tales. These are many in number and usually are represented as being sung by animals. An example of this is the story and song of the crawfish (Bulletin 53, p. 305). Songs of this class are found to vary more than any others in their rendition by different people; perhaps because they were more generally known and sung than others, with less criticism as to correctness of rendition.

Among musicians of civilized races the standards of excellence in a singer include (1) intonation, (2) quality of tone, (3) range of voice, (4) memory, and (5) interpretation (intellectual and emotional).

(1) *Intonation.*—Observing Indian singers according to these standards, the writer has noticed that "good singers" keep the pitch of their tones approximately that of the tones of the diatonic scale, and that in songs recorded by such men and women the pitch of "accidentals" is practically the same in every rendition of the song. This is not the case in songs phonographically recorded by men whose musical standing among their own people is not so high. An instance of this is as follows: On the transcription of a song recorded by an old man it was found that the melody showed no feeling for a keynote. Inquiry among the Indians disclosed the fact that the man was not considered by them to be a good singer. The same song was accordingly obtained from a man of acknowledged musical proficiency, and on comparing the renditions it was found that by slight alterations in pitch the song had become diatonic in character, the intervals closely resembling those of the scale and ending on a keynote. Experience in listening to the melodies of Chippewa and Sioux makes it possible to distinguish between a melody which has unusual native peculiarities and one which is distorted by a poor singer.

The accuracy of an Indian in repeating a song should also be considered. For this purpose several consecutive repetitions of each song were recorded. As an evidence of accuracy in repeating ceremonial songs the following incident may be cited: In 1912 the writer recorded four songs of the Creek Women's society of the Mandan, from Mrs. Holding Eagle, one of its members. In 1915 Mrs. Holding Eagle recorded the songs a second time, and on comparison it was found that the pitch and metronome speed of all the songs was the same in the second as in the first records. In two of the songs there was no difference in the slightest respect; in one what appeared as a glissando progression in the first recording was sung in definite intervals in the second; and in the fourth song there was a slight difference in the opening measures but none in the part containing the words. Several consecutive renditions of the songs were recorded on both occasions. Another and similar instance occurred among the Chippewa. Ŏdjib'we (See Bulletin 53) recorded certain songs in August, 1909, and March, 1910, the two recordings showing the same pitch of the song as a whole, and also a slight deviation from diatonic pitch on the same tones, this deviation being perceptible but not enough to be indicated by an accidental.

See also analysis of song No. 209 of this volume.

(2) *Quality of tone.*—The manner of tone production by the Indian is different from that of the white man. The former cultivates and greatly admires a pronounced vibrato; a falsetto tone is also considered a mark of musical proficiency. An instance of this is mentioned in Bulletin 53 (p. 252): A singer at Red Lake, Minn., "sang in falsetto voice with a peculiar throaty *vibrato*. He said that he discovered his ability to do this when he was a boy and had cultivated it ever since." This vibrato is not invariably found in a good singer, but, as in the white race, it is frequently present. A peculiar nasal tone is always used in the Love songs, so that one accustomed to the music of these tribes can recognize these songs by the tone quality, as well as by a melodic freedom greater than that in other songs. Another quality of tone is that used in the songs of hopeless illness, or in the "wailing songs" after a death. To these may be added the crooning tone of the lullabies. Other tone qualities are undoubtedly and perhaps intentionally used, these being, however, the most easily recognized.

(3) *Compass of voice.*—An expanded compass is admired among the Chippewa and Sioux as well as among musicians of the white race. Songs Nos. 55, 195, 202, have each a compass of 17 tones; two of these were recorded by Kills-at-Night, who has a wide reputation as a singer. Other songs have a compass of 13 or 14 tones each.

(4) *Memory.*—The memory test ("repertoire") obtains among these Indians as well as among civilized musicians. The writer has never attempted to exhaust the number of songs which could be recorded by a good singer. The largest number of songs recorded by one individual are those of Ŏdjib'we in Bulletin 53. As he was recording songs known to no other person he was asked to record more than 80. These were songs which were practically all of the same class; he doubtless remembered many others of different kinds. The recording of 50 or 60 songs by one individual is not unusual in the present work, selections being made from this number after tran-

scription, and many records being used for comparison with records of the same song by other singers.

(5) *Interpretation (intellectual and emotional).*—Among these Indians, as among white musicians, there must be a convincing quality in a singer's rendition of a song. It has frequently been said to the writer, "So-and-so knows the old songs, but he is not a good singer; he can give you the melody, but it will not be well sung." Into this "convincing quality" there enters another element—the personality of the singer. It is required that a good singer among Indians, as well as among white men, shall carry with him full confidence in himself, and do his work with authority.

From the foregoing data it appears that in general character the musical standards of the Chippewa and Sioux Indians bear a resemblance to those of the white race.

CEREMONIES

The White Buffalo Calf Pipe (Ptehin'ćala Ćanoŋ'pa)

It is fitting that a narrative of the gift of the White Buffalo Calf pipe to the Sioux should introduce the present account of the ceremonies and customs of the tribe. Throughout this memoir reference will be made to ceremonial acts performed in accordance with the instructions of the White Buffalo Maiden, a supernatural being through whose agency the ceremonial pipe was given to the Sioux.[1]

The narrative in its present form was given by Iśna'la-wića' (Lone Man; see pl. 23), and is recorded in the words of the interpreter, Mr. Robert P. Higheagle. Preceding this recital by Lone Man, the subject had been studied with other informants for more than two years. A summary of this study was read to Lone Man and discussed with him, after which he was requested to give the narrative in connected form, incorporating therewith material which he wished to add.[2]

The ancient and sacred tradition of the Sioux was given by Lone Man as follows:

In the olden times it was a general custom for the Sioux tribe (especially the Teton band of Sioux) to assemble in a body once at least during the year. This gathering took place usually about that time of midsummer when everything looked beautiful and everybody rejoiced to live to see nature at its best—that was the season when the Sun-dance ceremony took place and vows were made and fulfilled. Sometimes the tribal gathering took place in the fall when wild game was in the best condition, when wild fruits of all kinds were ripe, and when the leaves on the trees and plants were the brightest.

One reason why the people gathered as they did was that the tribe as a whole might celebrate the victories, successes on the warpath, and other good fortunes which had occurred during the year while the bands were scattered and each band was acting somewhat independently. Another reason was that certain rules or laws were made by the head chiefs and other leaders of the tribe, by which each band of the tribe was governed. For instance, if a certain band got into trouble with some other tribe, as the Crows, the Sioux tribe as a whole should be notified. Or if an enemy or enemies came on their hunting grounds the tribe should be notified at once. In this way the Teton band of Sioux was protected as to its territory and its hunting grounds.

After these gatherings there was a scattering of the various bands. On one such occasion the Sans Arc band started toward the west. They were moving from place to place, expecting to find buffalo and other game which they would lay up for their winter supply, but they failed to find anything. A council was called and two young men were selected to go in quest of buffalo and other game. They started on foot. When they were out of sight they each went in a different direction, but met again at a place which they had agreed upon. While they were planning and planning

---

[1] In connection with this chapter see Fletcher, Alice C., The White Buffalo Festival of the Uncpapas, *Peabody Museum Reports*, III, Nos. 3 and 4, pp. 260–75, Cambridge, 1884.

[2] Other material obtained from Lone Man is found in the chapter on the Sun dance (p. 92), the *heyo'ka* (pp. 159–170), and the sacred stones (pp. 214–217).

what to do, there appeared from the west a solitary object advancing toward them. It did not look like a buffalo; it looked more like a human being than anything else. They could not make out what it was, but it was coming rapidly. Both considered themselves brave, so they concluded that they would face whatever it might be. They stood still and gazed at it very eagerly. At last they saw that it was a beautiful young maiden. She wore a beautiful fringed buckskin dress, leggings, and moccasins. Her hair was hanging loose except at the left side, where was tied a tuft of shedded buffalo hair. [See pp. 126, 458.] In her right hand she carried a fan made of flat sage. Her face was painted with red vertical stripes. Not knowing what to do or say, they hesitated, saying nothing to her.

She spoke first, thus: "I am sent by the Buffalo tribe to visit the people you represent. You have been chosen to perform a difficult task. It is right that you should try to carry out the wishes of your people, and you must try to accomplish your purpose. Go home and tell the chief and headmen to put up a special lodge in the middle of the camp circle, with the door of the lodge and the entrance into the camp toward the direction where the sun rolls off the earth. Let them spread sage at the place of honor, and back of the fireplace let a small square place [1] be prepared. Back of this and the sage let a certain frame, or rack, be made. Right in front of the rack a buffalo skull should be placed. I have something of importance to present to the tribe, which will have a great deal to do with their future welfare. I shall be in the camp about sunrise."

While she was thus speaking to the young men one of them had impure thoughts. A cloud came down and enveloped this young man. When the cloud left the earth the young man was left there—only a skeleton. The Maiden commanded the other young man to turn his back toward her and face in the direction of the camp, then to start for home. He was ordered not to look back.

When the young man came in sight of the camp he ran in a zigzag course, this being a signal required of such parties on returning home from a searching or scouting expedition. The people in the camp were on the alert for the signal, and preparations were begun at once to escort the party home. Just outside the council lodge, in front of the door, an old man qualified to perform the ceremony was waiting anxiously for the party. He knelt in the direction of the coming of the party to receive the report of the expedition. [See p. 441.] A row of old men were kneeling behind him. The young man arrived at the lodge. Great curiosity was shown by the people on account of the missing member of the party. The report was made, and the people received it with enthusiasm.

The special lodge was made, and the other requirements were carried out. The crier announced in the whole camp what was to take place on the following morning. Great preparations were made for the occasion. Early the next morning, at daybreak, men, women, and children assembled around the special lodge. Young men who were known to bear unblemished characters were chosen to escort the Maiden into the camp. [See pp. 72; 103, 111.] Promptly at sunrise she was in sight. Everybody was anxious. All eyes were fixed on the Maiden. Slowly she walked into the camp. She was dressed as when she first appeared to the two young men except that instead of the sage fan she carried a pipe—the stem was carried with her right hand and the bowl with the left.

The chief, who was qualified and authorized to receive the guest in behalf of the Sioux tribe, sat outside, right in front of the door of the lodge, facing the direction of the coming of the Maiden. When she was at the door the chief stepped aside and made room for her to enter. She entered the lodge, went to the left of the door, and was seated at the place of honor.

---

[1] The square space of mellowed earth, the spread sage, the buffalo skull, and pipe rack are frequently mentioned in this work. Among other instances the following are cited: pp. 71, 122, 229, 232, 235, 328. The earth space in the spirit-keeping lodge was round instead of square (p. 82).

The chief made a speech welcoming the Maiden, as follows:

"My dear relatives: This day Wakaŋ'taŋka has again looked down and smiled upon us by sending us this young Maiden, whom we shall recognize and consider as a sister. She has come to our rescue just as we are in great need. Wakaŋ'taŋka wishes us to live. This day we lift up our eyes to the sun, the giver of light, that opens our eyes and gives us this beautiful day to see our visiting sister. Sister, we are glad that you have come to us, and trust that whatever message you have brought we may be able to abide by it. We are poor, but we have a great respect to visitors, especially relatives. It is our custom to serve our guests with some special food. We are at present needy and all we have to offer you is water, that falls from the clouds. Take it, drink it, and remember that we are very poor."

Then braided sweet grass was dipped into a buffalo horn containing rain water and was offered to the Maiden. The chief said, "Sister, we are now ready to hear the good message you have brought." The pipe, which was in the hands of the Maiden, was lowered and placed on the rack. Then the Maiden sipped the water from the sweet grass.

Then, taking up the pipe again, she arose and said:

"My relatives, brothers and sisters: Wakaŋ'taŋka has looked down, and smiles upon us this day because we have met as belonging to one family. The best thing in a family is good feeling toward every member of the family. I am proud to become a member of your family—a sister to you all. The sun is your grandfather, and he is the same to me. Your tribe has the distinction of being always very faithful to promises, and of possessing great respect and reverence toward sacred things. It is known also that nothing but good feeling prevails in the tribe, and that whenever any member has been found guilty of committing any wrong, that member has been cast out and not allowed to mingle with the other members of the tribe. For all these good qualities in the tribe you have been chosen as worthy and deserving of all good gifts. I represent the Buffalo tribe, who have sent you this pipe. You are to receive this pipe in the name of all the common people [Indians]. Take it, and use it according to my directions. The bowl of the pipe is red stone—a stone not very common and found only at a certain place. This pipe shall be used as a peacemaker.[1] The time will come when you shall cease hostilities against other nations. Whenever peace is agreed upon between two tribes or parties this pipe shall be a binding instrument. By this pipe the medicine-men shall be called to administer help to the sick."

Turning to the women, she said:

"My dear sisters, the women: You have a hard life to live in this world, yet without you this life would not be what it is. Wakaŋ'taŋka intends that you shall bear much sorrow—comfort others in time of sorrow. By your hands the family moves. You have been given the knowledge of making clothing and of feeding the family. Wakaŋ'taŋka is with you in your sorrows and joins you in your griefs. He has given you the great gift of kindness toward every living creature on earth. You he has chosen to have a feeling for the dead who are gone. He knows that you remember the dead longer than do the men. He knows that you love your children dearly."

Then turning to the children:

"My little brothers and sisters: Your parents were once little children like you, but in the course of time they became men and women. All living creatures were once small, but if no one took care of them they would never grow up. Your parents love you and have made many sacrifices for your sake in order that Wakaŋ'taŋka may listen to them, and that nothing but good may come to you as you grow up. I have brought this pipe for them, and you shall reap some benefit from it. Learn to

---

[1] Cf. Bulletin 53, pp. 143, 144, in which a woman is said to have been the supernatural means of bringing permanent peace between the Chippewa and Sioux.

respect and reverence this pipe, and above all, lead pure lives. Wakaŋ'taŋka is your great grandfather."

Turning to the men:

"Now my dear brothers: In giving you this pipe you are expected to use it for nothing but good purposes. The tribe as a whole shall depend upon it for their necessary needs. You realize that all your necessities of life come from the earth below, the sky above, and the four winds. Whenever you do anything wrong against these ele-ments they will always take some revenge upon you. You should reverence them. Offer sacrifices through this pipe. When you are in need of buffalo meat, smoke this pipe and ask for what you need and it shall be granted you. On you it depends to be a strong help to the women in the raising of children. Share the women's sorrow. Wakaŋ'taŋka smiles on the man who has a kind feeling for a woman, because the woman is weak. Take this pipe, and offer it to Wakaŋ'taŋka daily. Be good and kind to the little children."

Turning to the chief:

"My older brother: You have been chosen by these people to receive this pipe in the name of the whole Sioux tribe. Wakaŋ'taŋka is pleased and glad this day because you have done what it is required and expected that every good leader should do. By this pipe the tribe shall live. It is your duty to see that this pipe is respected and reverenced. I am proud to be called a sister. May Wakaŋ'taŋka look down on us and take pity on us and provide us with what we need. Now we shall smoke the pipe."

Then she took the buffalo chip which lay on the ground, lighted the pipe, and pointing to the sky with the stem of the pipe, she said, "I offer this to Wakaŋ'taŋka for all the good that comes from above." (Pointing to the earth:) "I offer this to the earth, whence come all good gifts." (Pointing to the cardinal points:) "I offer this to the four winds, whence come all good things." Then she took a puff of the pipe, passed it to the chief, and said, "Now my dear brothers and sisters, I have done the work for which I was sent here and now I will go, but I do not wish any escort. I only ask that the way be cleared before me."

Then, rising, she started, leaving the pipe with the chief, who ordered that the people be quiet until their sister was out of sight. She came out of the tent on the left side, walking very slowly; as soon as she was outside the entrance she turned into a white buffalo calf.[1]

It is said that the chief who received the pipe from the White Buffalo Maiden was Buffalo Stands Upward (Tataŋ'ka-woslal'-naźiŋ). The pipe has been handed down from one generation to another, and is said to be now in the possession of Elk Head (Heĺia'ka-pa), who lives at Thunder Butte, on the Cheyenne River Reservation. He is said to be of "about the third generation" which has kept the pipe, and is 98 years of age.[2] Each preceding keeper of the pipe lived to be more than a hundred years old.

The Indians named the pipe the White Buffalo Calf pipe. Dupli-cates of it were made, and soon every male member of the tribe carried a similar pipe. The stem was made to resemble the wind-pipe of a calf. Whenever this pipe is used in a smoking circle, or even when two men are smoking together, the rule is that the pipe

---

[1] It is interesting to observe that the identity of a dream object often is unrecognized until it turns to depart. See Bulletin 53, p. 207; also p. 185 of this volume.

[2] Elk Head died in January, 1916, after the above paragraph was written.

be passed to the left, because that was the direction taken by the White Buffalo Maiden when she went away. The one who lights this pipe is required to make an offering.

It is said that the following song was sung by the White Buffalo Maiden as she entered the camp. This song is sung in the Spirit-keeping ceremony when the man who is keeping the spirit of his child can afford to have a white buffalo robe used in the ceremony. (See pp. 82, 446.) The words "scarlet relic" refer to the scarlet-wrapped packet in the lodge of those who are "keeping a spirit."

No. 1. Song of the White Buffalo Maiden (Catalogue No. 569)[1]

Sung by CHARGING THUNDER

VOICE ♩= 58
DRUM not recorded

Ni - ya taŋ-iŋ-yaŋ ma-wa-ni   ye   ni - ya taŋ-iŋ-yaŋ ma-wa-ni

ye   e   e   o - ya - te le   i - ma - wa - ni   na *ho* *ho*

ho - taŋ - iŋ-yaŋ ma - wa-ni   ye   *ye* *ye*   *ye* *a* *ye* *a*

ye   ni - ya   taŋ - iŋ-yaŋ ma - wa - ni   ye   e   e   wa -

lu - ta le   i - ma - wa - ni   na *ho* *ho*

ho - taŋ - iŋ-yaŋ ma-wa-ni   ye   *ye* *ye*   *ye* *a* *ye* *a* *ye*

---

[1] The catalogue numbers used throughout this memoir correspond respectively with the numbers designating the phonograph record of the songs, which are preserved in the Bureau of American Ethnology.

niya′ taŋiŋ′yaŋ .... with visible breath [1]
mawa′ni ye .... I am walking
oya′te [2] le .... this nation (the Buffalo nation)
ima′wani .... I walk toward
na .... and
ho′taŋiŋyaŋ .... my voice is heard
mawa′ni ye .... I am walking
niya′ taŋiŋ′yaŋ .... with visible breath
mawa′ni ye .... I am walking
walu′ta le .... this scarlet relic
ima′wani ye .... (for it) I am walking

Analysis.[3]—This song is minor in tonality and melodic in structure. Thirty-four progressions are found in the melody, 22 (65 per cent) of which are minor thirds. This is an unusually large proportion of any one interval in a song. Ten of the remaining intervals (29 per cent) are major seconds, the others being an ascending fifth and a descending fourth. The tempo of the song is slow, and the short tones at the end of the first and similar measures were given in correct time. As in all the songs, vocables are here italicized. In this song they were sung with marked emphasis.

The final measure of this song is transcribed as a complete measure, though the song begins on an unaccented tone. This precedent will be followed throughout the present work, instances in which the repetition of a song begins without a break in the time being indicated by the usual mark for repeat.

The Alo′waŋpi Ceremony

This ceremony has been used by the Pawnee, Omaha, Osage, Ponca, Iowa, Oto, and Dakota tribes. The ceremony among the Omaha and Pawnee has been studied by Miss Alice C. Fletcher, whose research includes the ceremonial songs of these tribes.[4] As the ceremony has been in disuse among the Dakota for many years it was impossible to study it exhaustively, but sufficient information was available for a general comparison with the customs of the above-mentioned tribes. From this comparison it is evident that the

---

[1] In cold weather the breath of a herd of buffalo, rising in the frosty air, could be plainly seen.

[2] The word *oya′te* is of frequent occurrence in these songs. When reference is made to the Indians the word is translated "tribe", but it is often used in connection with animals (see p. 162, footnote).

[3] The descriptive analyses of these songs should not be regarded as exhaustive. It is their purpose merely to point out peculiarities of melody or rhythm which may aid the reader in a further investigation of the subject. Moreover, the phraseology of these analyses should be understood as general in character. Thus, the term "accurate intonation" should not be considered to mean that in every instance the Indian sang the exact interval, but that, so far as concerns the present work, the interval was practically correct. These descriptive analyses are based on tabulated analyses of individual songs, which are not herewith presented, but are incorporated in the tables of analysis found at the close of the groups of songs, and also in the tables on pp. 12-21.

[4] Cf. Fletcher, Alice C., The "Wawaⁿ", or Pipe Dance of the Omahas, in *Peabody Mus. Rep.*, III, Nos. 3, 4, pp. 308-333, Cambridge, Mass., 1884; also The Hako; a Pawnee Ceremony, by the same author, in *Twenty-second Rep. Bur. Amer. Ethn.*, pt. 2, 1904.

ceremony in transmission to another tribe and locality has undergone modifications and changes in detail.

Among the Teton Sioux the ceremony is known as Alo'waŋpi, meaning "to sing for someone," and also as the Huŋka, this being the name applied to the child who fills an important role in the ceremony.

Among the Sioux this ceremony was closely associated with the White Buffalo Maiden and her mysterious visit to the tribe. The following account concerns the usage of the Teton Sioux. The subject was studied by the writer during two visits to the reservation, and Mr. Higheagle continued the work for several months, consulting the older Indians as he had opportunity. The material embodies the original narrative by Weasel Bear and also many points contributed by Chased-by-Bears, Eagle Shield, White-paw Bear, Jaw, and others

FIG. 20.   Drawing from picture-calendar—the year of the first Alo'waŋpi ceremony.

who were qualified to express opinions on the subject. The account in its final form was translated to, and pronounced correct by, Weasel Bear and others equally well informed.

In a picture-calendar of the Teton Sioux there occurs a native drawing of this ceremony (fig. 20), the year represented by the drawing being called "Awi'ća alo'waŋpi wani'yetu," meaning literally "truthfully singing winter;" understood as "ceremonial singing winter." This is the first year recorded on this calendar, and the writer's informant said it represented the first year in which the Alo'waŋpi ceremony was held by the Standing Rock Sioux. The date corresponds to the year 1801. The calendar, which is owned by Black Thunder, of Eagle River, closes with a representation of the Black Hills council which took place in 1912. The dates of other historical events are correctly indicated.

In describing the purport of the ceremony Looking Elk (Heḣa'ka-wa'kita), a Teton Sioux, said:

The great result of this ceremony is that the man who performed it was regarded as a father by the child for whom he performed it. He made a solemn vow taking that child under his protection until one or the other died. He became like a brother to the man whose children he sang over and painted with the huŋka stripes. In all the great ceremonies of the Sioux there is not one that binds two men together so strongly as this.

The keynote, or central idea, of this ceremony (as held by the Teton Sioux) is the affection of a father for his child, and his desire that only good should come to it. The following statement is given in the words of Mr. Higheagle:

It is strictly believed and understood by the Sioux that a child is the greatest gift from Wakaŋ'taŋka, in response to many devout prayers, sacrifices, and promises. Therefore the child is considered "sent by Wakaŋ'taŋka," through some element—namely, the element of human being. That the child may grow up in health with all the virtues expected, and especially that no serious misfortune may befall the child, the father makes promises or vows to Wakaŋ'taŋka as manifested by the different elements of the earth and sky. During the period of youthful blessedness the father spared no pains to let the people know of his great love for his child or children. This was measured by his fellow men according to the sacrifices or gifts given, or the number of ceremonies performed. In order to have a standard by which this love could be shown, the first thing taken into consideration and adopted was the White Buffalo Maiden, sent to the Sioux tribe by the Buffalo tribe. The impression left upon the people by the Maiden and her extraordinary good qualities were things that were much admired by every parent as a model for his children. This Maiden was pure white, without a blemish—that was the principal desire of the father for the character of his child. The Maiden addressed men, women, and children.

It had been told by the Maiden that good things would come to the people by means of the pipe, so it seemed necessary that there be a ceremony, having connection with the Maiden and with the pipe. For this reason the essential article in the Alo'waŋpi ceremony is the "Huŋka Ćanoŋ'pa," a decorated wand, which represents the pipe given to the Indians by the Maiden, the original pipe not being available when needed for this ceremony.[1] This wand, or pipestem, was carried and employed by the *itaŋ'ćaŋ*, "leader"[2] during the ceremony, and when that was finished it was given to the child for whom the ceremony had been performed. In many families such a pipestem was handed down for many generations. The manner of decorating the pipestem has also been handed down, and neither the shape nor the decoration can be changed. A new pipestem might be made by some one who had undergone the ceremony, but an old one was generally used. The wand, or pipestem, was usually about 20 inches long. On it were fastened tufts of the feathers of the kaŋke'ća, pileated woodpecker, and above each tuft of feathers was the head of

[1 In stating that the wand represented the pipe, the tradition related by the informant seems to have confused the symbolic meaning of the two. See article *Calumet*, by J. N. B. Hewitt, in Handbook of American Indians, pt. 1.]

[2 The exact significance of this word may be understood from the connection in which it is used (cf. pp. 162, 180, footnotes), or other words may be added to make the meaning more definite. Thus certain officers in the spirit lodge, and the leader of dancers in the Sun dance were called merely *itaŋ'ćaŋ* (see pp. 81, 98). Other officers in the spirit lodge were designated, respectively, *waśpaŋ'ka iḣpe'ya itaŋ'ćaŋ*, 'leader in charge of food'; *wo'waśi itaŋ'ćaŋ*, literally 'labor leader', and *itaŋ'ćaŋ iya'taŋ ki'yapi*, 'leader who lights the pipe' while the master of the entire spirit-keeping ceremony was known as *a'taya itaŋ'ćaŋ* (see pp. 80, 81). An intensified form of the word, *in'itaŋ'ćaŋ*, 'supreme leader', appears on p. 216.]

a woodpecker (*Phleoeotomus pileatus*). [¹] The tail feathers of an eagle, in the form of a fan, and also strands of horsehair, were hung from the wand. [See pl. 3.] ²

In explaining the use of the woodpecker in decorating the Huŋka Ċanoŋ'pa it was said that this is "a simple, humble bird, which stays near its nest and is seldom seen." ³ This bird seems to have been considered especially appropriate, because children who underwent this ceremony were more closely guarded and protected than others. They usually belonged to well-to-do families, in which the girls were seldom seen in public until they were grown up. The ceremony could be held for several children at a time, and often took place in fulfillment of a vow.⁴

The wish of the parents that this ceremony be performed for their child or children was first declared. An invitation was then sent to the man whom the father desired to perform the ceremony, and who thereafter would be bound to the father by a tie even stronger than that of natural brotherhood, because he had assumed a responsibility not placed on him by nature. An invitation was usually conveyed by means of a pipe, but for this ceremony a different form of invitation was used. The father of the child made a case from the dried bladder of a buffalo, into which he put many little packages of tobacco, one or two pipefuls being wrapped in membrane, similar to the packets fastened to sticks as offerings at the Sun dance (p. 102). The case, after being tied or sealed, was wrapped in a cloth. This was taken to the man selected to perform the ceremony. If he accepted the invitation, he opened the case; otherwise he returned it unopened.

On acceptance of the invitation great preparations were begun. Two large lodges were erected in the middle of the camp circle and united so as to make one lodge of double the usual size, opening toward the west. This and the other details of the ceremony were in accordance with the instructions given by the White Buffalo Maiden on her first appearance to the Indians. The lodge was like the one which they built to receive her. There was no fire within, but opposite the door and slightly back of the middle of the lodge a square of exposed and "mellowed" earth was prepared. (See p. 64, footnote.) In the two corners of this square farthest from the door

[¹ The decorations of the calumet more frequently consisted of the feathers or heads of the duck, owl, eagle, or other birds. See J. N. B. Hewitt, art. *Calumet* in Handbook of American Indians, pt. 1.]

² The pileated woodpecker is commonly called woodcock, and, through misunderstanding, the bird heads shown in pl. 3 are those of the common woodcock.

³ Cf. the following instances in which the characteristics of a bird or an animal were desired by the Indians who, in some cases, wore a part of the bird or animal on their persons; the deer (in a decoration), because this animal can endure thirst a long time (p. 125); the hawk as "the surest bird of prey" (p. 139); the elk, in gallantry (p. 176); the frog, in watchfulness (p. 160); the owl, in "night-wisdom and gentle ways" (p. 181); the bear, which "though fierce, has given many medicinal herbs for the good of man" (p. 195); the kit-fox, which is "active and wily" (p. 314); the crow, which is especially direct as well as swift in flight (p. 319), and the wolf, in hardihood (p. 388).

⁴ Cf. the piercing of a child's ears at the Sun dance in fulfillment of a similar vow (p. 137).

were placed two buffalo chips, which were used in lighting the ceremonial pipes. Sweet grass also was made ready for lighting the pipes.
Fresh sage was spread on the ground in the rear of the square, and on
this was laid a buffalo skull painted with red lines and having the openings filled with sage. (See pp. 64, 185.) The nose of the skull was near,
but did not touch the side of the square. Strips of red flannel were
tied on the horns. Back of the buffalo skull stood a pipe rack formed
of two upright sticks, each having a crotch at the top, between which
was laid a cross-bar; the whole was painted blue. This pipe rack
was similar to that used in the Sun dance, but the position of the
pipe (or wand) was reversed, the bowl of the Sun-dance pipe resting
against the forehead of the buffalo skull, as shown in plate 20, while
the Huŋka pipe was placed with the stem toward the skull. If more
than one child was to be "sung over," there was a pipe for each, beneath
which was laid the white eagle-plume to be tied on the head of the
child during the ceremony. The rattle to be used by the itaŋ'ćaŋ
leaned against one of the posts of the pipe rack. Against the pipe
rack was placed also an ear of corn on a stick, decorated in blue as
shown in plate 3. It was essential that this be particularly regular
in form, with an even number of kernels arranged in straight lines.[1]
Thus the ceremonial articles comprised the ear of corn, the decorated pipe (or wand), the pipe rack and the tuft of white down, and
also a bunch of shed buffalo hair which was used in the ceremony.
These were provided by the man who performed the ceremony, who
kept them wrapped in a red cloth. The preparation of the lodge was
completed by the erection around it of a barricade of hides, so placed
as to keep spectators at a proper distance.

The Teton Sioux were not originally an agricultural people, and
the use of corn in this ceremony formed the subject of considerable
inquiry. In response to this inquiry the writer was told the following legend of the coming of the corn, which, in its final form, is given
in the words of the interpreter, Mr. Higheagle:

There was an old couple living on the bank of a river. They had been married a
long time, but did not have any children, though they had often asked Wakaŋ'taŋka
to send them a child. This special request was always made when they were in the
sweat-bath booth. On one of these occasions, while they were praying, they heard
some one outside saying that their prayer had been heard and would be granted on
the following morning. They were very much pleased and felt overanxious.

On the next morning the old man went out, and there, right in front of the door,
peeped out of the ground a greenish opening of some seed—out of the ground. The
old man was very much excited, and, not knowing what to do, they both went into
the sweat-bath booth and asked what they should do. As before, they heard a voice

_____

[1] Articles for ceremonial use were required to be as perfect as possible. Cf. choice of the buffalo skull,
and the tree for the sacred pole, in the Sun dance (pp. 102, 111), also the ax used in cutting the tree (p. 112).
The sacred stones were regular in outline and untouched by a tool (p. 205). Purity of life was required of
leaders in all ceremonies. See also the statement on p. 173, footnote, that what is genuine should be preferred to what is artificial.

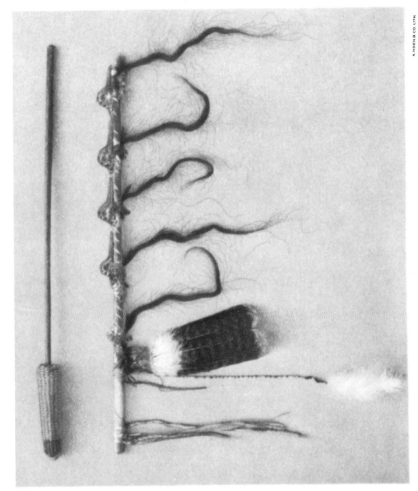

WAND AND EAR OF CORN USED IN HUNKA CEREMONY

saying: "Fear not. This plant which you behold is going to grow into the most beautiful child you ever saw. Watch for its development. Take good care of it. Give it
plenty of air, sunshine, and water. Let no other plant or shrub grow near it." So
they, realizing this was the child they had been desiring, went out and did as they
were told. The plant grew up, had green clothing, and beautiful whitish hair. It
grew to be tall. Finally beautiful corn, nicely enveloped in green covering, grew out.
As soon as the coverings had turned to another color the corn was taken out. So from
this they concluded that Wakaŋ'taŋka had sent them something to keep and to raise.

In the old times this ceremony extended through several days, and
many ceremonial songs were sung. In its later observance by the
Teton Sioux it is said that the entire ceremony was concluded in one
day. Only two of the songs were recorded by the writer.

It was said that at the opening of the ceremony the itaŋ'ćaŋ came
from the double lodge and started to get the children for whom the
ceremony was to be performed. They pretended that they did not
know where the children lived and went through the camp singing
the following song:

No. 2. Song of Pretended Search   (Catalogue No. 649)

Sung by WEASEL BEAR

VOICE ♩ = 112
DRUM not recorded

E - ća tu-kte ti - pi so

WORDS (FREE TRANSLATION)

eća'	I wonder
tukte'	where
ti'pi so	they live

Analysis.—It is interesting to observe here the rhythmic unit in
connection with the use of the song. As already stated, this is a song
of search, the singer going around the camp pretending to seek a
certain tent. He hastened to a tent, paused, and then passed on,
repeating this procedure until he came to the tent which was his
destination. Thus in the rhythmic unit we find a hurried triplet of
eighth notes, followed in the next measure by a tone prolonged to
the length of four quarter notes. The song is simple in form and has
a compass of eight tones, descending from the octave to the tonic.
The tones are those of the second five-toned scale, and the tonic
chord is prominent in the melody. One-third of the intervals are

minor thirds.   Five renditions were recorded with no break in the time; these are uniform in every respect.

When the man (or men) arrived at the door of the children's home they did not enter at once, but began to tell of their deeds in the past as an evidence of their right to perform the Alo'waŋpi ceremony. Without this narration they would not be allowed to enter and get the children, as none but those who had in the past, and who still had, the necessary qualifications could perform this sacred rite over children.

If the children were small they were carried to the double lodge in blankets on the backs of the itaŋ'ċaŋ.   On their way to the lodge the men stopped four times (see pp. 78, 83, 113, 116, 167, 328) giving the "wolf howl", which was used to signalize approach.   When they reached the double lodge the itaŋ'ċaŋ sat in the place of honor, back of the pipe rack.   There might be one man for each child who was to be "sung over," and each of these men had his own pipe, or wand, which was placed against the pipe rack.

Describing the enacting of the ceremony for his two daughters, Weasel Bear said:

Everyone could see the old man as he painted the faces of the girls.   He painted a blue line from the hair-parting down to the end of the nose, then across the upper part of the forehead and down to the cheek, ending at a point opposite the end of the nose. Red stripes could be added after the blue paint had been put on the face.   The red stripes were narrow, extending downward from the line across the forehead and being the same length as the vertical blue lines.   Additional red stripes could be added at any time by a person qualified to do it, a horse being given for the right to wear two or three more stripes.

On many important occasions this decoration of the face was used by those who had the right to use it.   A white eagle plume was fastened in the hair of a girl whose face was to be painted.   In plate 8 is shown a spirit post decorated with the plume which was worn by the daughter of Weasel Bear in the Alo'waŋpi ceremony, described by him; the tip of the quill was covered with duck feathers similar to those used on a Sun-dance pipe.   With the eagle plume was fastened a strand of horse hair colored red, the whole being suspended by a narrow strip of hide, so that it hung lightly.

Continuing his narrative, Weasel Bear said:

After the faces of the girls were painted the itaŋ'ċaŋ stood with his rattle in his right hand and the decorated wand in his left, and waved the wand over them as he sang the following song.   Each girl held in her hand a decorated ear of corn as the song was sung.   [This scene is shown in a native drawing on cloth made by Jaw (pl. 4).]

PART OF HUŊKA CEREMONY (NATIVE DRAWING)

No. 3. Ceremonial Song   (Catalogue No. 648)

Sung by WEASEL BEAR

VOICE ♩ = 52
DRUM not recorded

Le huŋ - ka   ye   e   le   huŋ - ka   a   ya   ya   le   huŋ-

ka   ya   ya   ya   le   huŋ - ka   ya   ya   ya   e - ca

waŋ - ka - tu kiŋ   le   huŋ - ka   ya   ya   ya   le   huŋ - ka

WORDS

(*First rendition*)

le huŋ′ka.................... this honored one
eća′........................... behold
waŋkaŋ′tu kiŋ................. you who are above

(*Second rendition*)

le huŋ′ka.................... this honored one
eća′........................... behold
maka′ kiŋ..................... you who are in the earth

(*Third rendition*)

le huŋ′ka.................... this honored one
eća′........................... behold
wiyo′ḣpeyata................. you who dwells where the sun falls (west)

(*Fourth rendition*)

le huŋ′ka.................... this honored one
eća′........................... behold
wazi′yata..................... you who dwell in the home of the giant (north)

(*Fifth rendition*)

le huŋ′ka.................... this honored one
eća′........................... behold
wiyo′hiyaŋpata................ you who dwell where the sun continually
                              returns (east)

(*Sixth rendition*)

le huŋ′ka.................... this honored one
eća′........................... behold
ito′kaǧata.................... you who dwell in the direction we face with
                              outstretched arms (south)

Analysis.—This song contains only the tones of the minor triad and fourth.   Similar tone material is found in so many of these songs that it deserves special observation.   Reference to Table 6 shows that it constitutes the tone material of 12 per cent of the songs, this being the largest proportion except that of the second five-toned scale (13 per cent) and the fourth five-toned scale (18 per cent).   There are two ways in which this tone material may be regarded—as a minor triad with the fourth as a passing tone and as a combination of tones leading toward the second five-tone scale.   If the first be the correct standpoint, we may expect a large proportion of songs containing either the minor triad alone or with some other tone used as a passing tone, but such is not found.   We note only 1 per cent containing the minor triad alone, and less than 1 per cent with another tone as a passing tone.   Regarding the matter from the second standpoint, we note that the percentage of songs on the second five-toned scale is less than that of those on the fourth five-toned scale. It is observed, however, that the proportion of songs containing the major triad and sixth is 12 per cent.   This bears the same relation to the complete fourth five-toned scale that the minor triad and fourth bears to the complete second five-toned scale.   In this connection, see Bulletin 53, pages 4–5.   Tests and comparisons similar to the foregoing are presented merely as suggestions for the practical use of the present method of analyzing Indian music.

Like the preceding song, this has a compass of 12 tones, beginning on the octave and ending on the tonic.   It is, however, harmonic in structure, while the preceding is melodic.   The proportion of minor thirds is larger than in the preceding song, constituting about 39 per cent of the intervals.   As in the preceding song, the vocables were slightly emphasized, and the words of the many renditions were distinctly sung.   Neither this nor the preceding song contains a change of time.   Only 23 per cent of the 340 Chippewa songs are without change of time, and this continuity appears in only 16 per cent of this series.

After the ceremony (which, as already stated, was not studied in detail by the writer) the decorated pipe (or wand) and the corn became the property of the child for whom the ceremony had been performed. In departing with the children the Itaŋ'ćaŋ, pausing four times, gave the long "wolf call" which had signalized their approach to the ceremonial lodge.   Liberal rewards were given those who performed this ceremony, Weasel Bear stating that he bestowed three horses and a pipe on the old man who painted and "sang over" his daughters.

The celebration of this ceremony placed a child in a highly respected position in the tribe.   Such a child was regarded as possessing that which would "make it nothing but good in every way," and was "recognized by all as ranking above an ordinary child."

DECORATED ROBE

A young girl for whom the Alo'waŋpi ceremony had been performed might wear a calfskin robe similar to that shown in plate 5. The decoration on this robe indicates that the wearer had taken part in the Huŋka ceremony, and also that her relatives had been successful in war. Red, blue, and yellow are the colors used in the decorations. It was said that "red represents blood, blue is a 'blue cloud,' indicating success, and yellow is the color of the sky at morning."[1] The stripes on the head of the calfskin are red and represent the Huŋka stripes painted on the face of the child for whom the ceremony was performed. The two lines bordering the entire decoration are blue, and the space between them is yellow. Near the left margin are red lines, said to represent a spider's web. The crescents along the right margin represent the phases of the moon, blue being used to represent a quarter moon and red a full moon. These are the phases in which the child's relative engaged in the war expeditions noted in the decoration of the robe. Next to this border are parallel lines, the dots on which represent the number of camps made during a certain expedition. The panel in the center of the robe represents the "warrior's path." A war party with eight camps is here shown, each round dot representing a camp. Such a robe could be made only by a woman whose relative had been successful in war. The robe illustrated was made by the wife of Dog Eagle. (See p. 349.)

THE CEREMONY OF SPIRIT-KEEPING[2] (WAKI'ĆAĠAPI)

In the old days a Sioux, filled with grief at the death of a near relative, might prolong his period of mourning by "keeping the spirit" for several months or a year, and then "letting it go" by means of a certain ceremony. This was a custom which exacted a great deal and which, having been begun, must be carried out consistently, either by the man who undertook it, or in the event of his death by his nearest relative. A man considered this before he announced his intention of "keeping the spirit" of a relative. He considered the fact that for many months he could not hunt, nor go to war, nor share in the social activities of the tribe, and he also counted the cost of gifts which he must distribute at the feast for releasing the spirit. If he felt that he could meet these requirements he made known his decision, and those who wished to join him were at liberty to do so, each providing a "spirit bundle" (wana'ġi wapa'ḱta)

---

[1] Other symbolisms mentioned in this work are as follows: The white buffalo robe used in Huŋka ceremony (p. 80); colors—red, blue, yellow, white, and black (p. 124); ascending smoke of sweet grass (p.127, footnote); a hoop (pp. 139,295); water, fire, and steam (p. 167); outline and structure of the sacred stones, by Chased-by-Bears (p.205); by Brave Buffalo (p. 208); a hand (p. 330). The symbolism of the "earth space" is given on page 122, footnote.

[2] See in this connection Fletcher, Alice C., The Shadow or Ghost Lodge: A Ceremony of the Ogallala Sioux, *Peabody Mus. Reps.*, III, Nos. 3, 4, pp. 296–307; also Dorsey, James Owen, A Study of Siouan Cults, in *Eleventh Rep. Bur. Ethn.*, pp. 487–89, 1894.

to represent the spirit of a relative, and also his share of food and gifts for the final feast.

The Ceremony of Spirit-keeping, like the Alo'waŋpi, had its inspiration in the Coming of the White Buffalo Maiden, and everything was done in accordance with her instructions. The manner of studying this subject was similar to that used in connection with the two preceding chapters. The spirit of a child was "kept" more frequently than that of a grown person, and the writer's first work on this ceremony consisted in taking down a narrative by Weasel Bear (interpreted by Mrs. McLaughlin), in which he told of keeping the spirit of a little daughter. A year later this narrative was discussed by Bear Face[1] and other old men (Mr. Higheagle interpreting), and many points were added. In its final form the first part is based on a narrative by Bear Face, while in the latter part the information given by Weasel Bear has been incorporated, together with details supplied by other reliable informants.

Concerning this ceremony Bear Face (Mato'-ite') said:

It is one of the great undertakings of the tribe, not simply in the honor which surrounds it, but because of the work and obligation it involves, so that a man who can carry this through successfully is recognized by the tribe as a man who is qualified to fulfill large responsibilities.

Bear Face said that his first spirit keeping was for a son who died at the age of 15. The body of the boy was placed on a scaffold, and his best horse was killed beneath it. Before this was done the father decided to keep the boy's spirit and so announced to the tribe. He requested a man whose record was without blemish to cut a lock of the boy's hair to be put in the spirit bundle. The man came at his request, and before going near the body of the boy he purified his hands and also his knife with the smoke of sweet grass. When about to cut the hair he made three motions as if to do so and then cut it with the fourth motion. (See references on p. 74.) The lock cut was over one eye. When the hair had been cut it was wrapped in red cloth. (The remainder of the narrative is a compilation from several informants.) If desired, some article which had been worn next the body of the child could be used instead of a lock of hair. Thus Weasel Bear said that when keeping the spirit of his little girl, he used the ornaments which she had worn on her hair as the central article in the spirit bundle.

After wrapping this selected article in red cloth the proposed spirit-keeper took the little packet in his arms as if it were the body of a child and rode around the camp circle, lamenting the child's death. This was his announcement to the tribe that he had taken upon himself the responsibilities of a spirit-keeper (wana'ǧi yuha'pi) and wished to be considered as such. Afterwards a decorated case was

---

[1] Bear Face died in December, 1914.

OUTER WRAPPING FOR SPIRIT BUNDLE AND BRAIDED SWEET GRASS

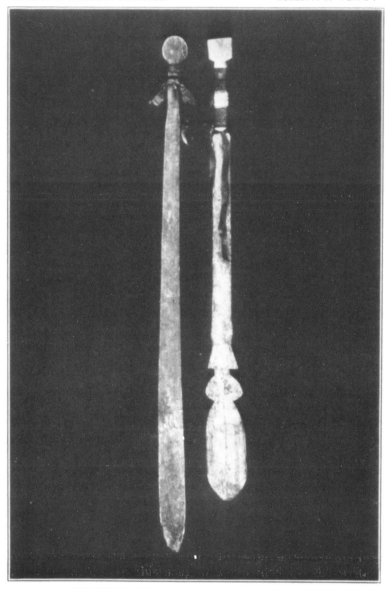

IMPLEMENTS USED IN HANDLING COALS IN SPIRIT LODGE

brought, and in this was placed the packet containing the hair, also sweet grass and the shed hair of the buffalo. This case was wrapped in red cloth. The spirit-keeper or his friends then selected the straightest pole they could find, pine being preferred for the purpose. This pole was erected outside his door, and the spirit bundle was tied on it. The bundle was supposed to stay there four days and nights before being taken down. During these four days a special wrapping (*wi'ćaśke*) of soft-tanned hide was made for it, and feasts were given to those who had kept spirits. At the end of four days the bundle was taken down by men who had kept spirits and was placed in its wrapping, which was elaborately decorated but had no sewing about it. With it were placed articles intended as gifts to those who took part in the ceremony. Small articles were placed in a decorated case and large articles, as pieces of red cloth, were folded smoothly.

Plate 6 shows a "spirit wrap" and a braid of sweet grass which was placed in the spirit bundle. Mrs. James McLaughlin said she "purchased it 30 years ago from Black Moon's mother, who said it was then about 80 years old and had been used in keeping the spirits of her grandfather, her mother, and other relatives." The porcupine quills on it were dyed with native dyes, and the wrap is so fragile that it had been used in recent years as an inner instead of an outer wrapping. A braid of sweet grass was usually placed in a spirit bundle, and an old one had been preserved with this wrapping. According to Mrs. McLaughlin, beads were seldom used on any of the wrappings of a spirit bundle, as beads were unknown among the Sioux when the White Buffalo Maiden came to them.

After the spirit bundle was complete they prepared three stakes, painted red and decorated with quill work, also decorated thongs with which to fasten the bundle in place. Two of the stakes were tied together near the top, and the bundle was tied across them, the third stake being used as a support for the other two, which faced the door of the spirit-keeper's tipi. The tripod was about 6 steps from this tipi, which was known as *wana'ǵi ti'pi*, or "spirit lodge."

When the tripod had been put in place they made a decorated case (*paŋ*) of soft-tanned hide. In it were put gifts for the itaŋ'ćaŋ who would have charge of the final ceremony. These gifts, which were gradually collected, comprised needles, awls, knives, tobacco, and sometimes as many as 50 pipes. In the tipi, between the fire and the place of honor, a certain area of the earth floor was "mellowed." This was round, not square as in the Huŋka and the Sun dance. In the center of this space was placed a buffalo chip, and beside it two implements (pl. 7) made of wood, about 3 feet in length, one broad at the end and the other pointed. When sweet grass was to be burned it was the custom to use the pointed stick in pushing a coal on the other implement, with which it was lifted and laid on the buffalo chip. The spirit-keeper and his wife wore no ornaments during this period, and their faces were painted all the time. Their manner was always quiet and reverent, as though the body of the relative whom they mourned was in the lodge. It was expected that those who kept a spirit would hold charitable thoughts toward everyone in the tribe, and all unkind or harsh words were forbidden in the spirit lodge.

The tripod and spirit bundle were brought into the lodge at night and also in bad weather. The bundle was laid in the place of honor and treated with great respect, no one passing between it and the fire. Weasel Bear said: "At evening I burned sweet grass and my wife passed her hands over the smoke, rubbing the fragrance on her face, hair, hands, and neck. Then she took the tripod in her arms and carried it into the tipi, turning toward the left as she entered. In the morning she again made herself fragrant and took the tripod and its burden outside the lodge."

The thing most desired was that a man might have the robe of a white buffalo to spread in the place of honor. On this the tripod and spirit bundle would rest when they were in the lodge. Such a robe signified that the spirit being kept was pure, and that all the articles connected with it had been purified. No one was allowed to touch the robe with bare hands nor pass between it and the fire. The only person permitted to touch it was a medicine-man who was known to be qualified for the act. Bear Face said that he had such a robe when he kept the spirit of his son, and that the only person allowed to touch or move it was a man, whom he engaged, who was noted for this ceremony. If he needed help he was obliged to call on some one as fully qualified as himself and to give him half of the compensation for such services. The only exception is in favor of children who have been through the Huŋka ceremony. These children may lift the white buffalo robe and carry it out of the lodge when the ceremony is finished.

Weasel Bear said further that during the period of keeping a spirit the contents of his lodge were supposed to belong to the tribe. Thus if a man came to his lodge saying, "I have come for some of my tobacco and red willow," he gave him what he required. Weasel Bear continued his narrative as follows:

I selected a virtuous old man as one of the officers of the spirit lodge. He was called *waśpaŋ'ka iḣpe'ya itaŋ'ćaŋ*, meaning "leader in charge of food." He came to the tipi for a short time every day, and if he wished to sleep there at night he was at liberty to do so. Every morning I put beef in a dish; he took a small piece of the meat, offered a prayer, and put it in a small dish provided for that purpose. This duty was never omitted. When the dish was full he emptied it into the fire, saying, "Grandchild, this is our food, but we give it to you to eat before us." This was continued from early winter, when my child died, until the next autumn, when we

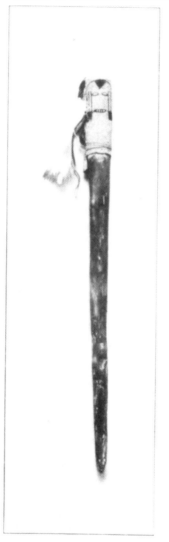

PARTIALLY DECORATED

DECORATED WITH CLOTHING

SPIRIT POST

released her spirit. During that time we collected many gifts for the final feast. Our relatives helped us in this, the women making many articles with their own hands. As I was withheld from the ordinary duties of life I had a man called *wo' waśi itaŋ'ćaŋ* (literally "laborer leader"), who carried messages for me, kept us supplied with wood and water, swept the lodge, and kept clean the space around the spirit bundle. He also cut red willow [*ćaŋsa'sa*] and dried it, so that I would have plenty to give away at the final feast.

The man who kept a spirit was frequently invited to feasts of the various societies and was expected to attend them. It was understood that if valuable presents were being given away he would be first to receive one. In return for these favors he invited the societies to attend the feasts, which were held outside the lodge, when the time came for releasing the spirit. The time for keeping a spirit varied from several months to a year or even longer. At the expiration of this time the final ceremony and feast were held. This was called *waki' ćaġa*, meaning the act of completing the undertaking. All the band gathered for the event and the various societies had their special tents. The societies took a prominent part in such features of the spirit releasing as took place outside the lodge, but their members did not enter the lodge unless they were men who themselves had kept spirits.

If several spirits were to be released, the man who first announced his intention of keeping a spirit was considered the leader of the spirit-keepers. Early in the morning, on the day of the spirit releasing, he sent a filled pipe to an old man who was to be master of the whole ceremony and who was designated *a'taya itaŋ'ćaŋ*.

Weasel Bear said: "On that day I was to lay aside all signs of mourning, so I painted myself gaily and put on all my finest attire. I was only 28 years old, but I had won a war-honor feather and I wore it that day. My wife arrayed herself like a young girl." (See reference to the bright adornments in the Ceremony of Restoring the Mourners, in Bulletin 53, p. 153.)

One man was selected for each spirit; he was known merely as itaŋ'caŋ,[1] and was a man who had kept the spirit of a relative. It was his duty to prepare the "spirit post" (*wana'ġi gele'pi*) and to perform other parts of the ceremony pertaining to the individual spirit in whose service he had been employed. The spirit post was made in the spirit lodge. According to Weasel Bear cottonwood was generally used for this purpose (cf. pp. 111, 118), and the man who made it always sat with his face toward the east and whittled upward, moving the knife away from him. Before doing this he purified his hands and knife with the smoke of sweet grass. A post for a child's spirit was smaller than for that of an adult. The post shown in plate 8 is 35 inches long; this was made by Weasel Bear to

---

[1] See p. 70, footnote.

represent the one used when the spirit of his little girl was released. The features of the face are worked with beads on buckskin, and the lines of the paint are those which would be used for a girl who had been through the Alo'waŋpi ceremony. The feather is that worn by Weasel Bear's daughter when she was "sung over" in that ceremony. Both the lines and feather belonged to a daughter somewhat older than the one whose spirit he kept. When the features had been delineated on the posts each itaŋ'ćaŋ opened the case (*paŋ*) containing the articles of clothing to be placed on the posts. These, which had been previously exhibited outside the lodge, were garments worn by the person whose spirit was to be released. After the ceremony these garments were given to the man who painted the post.

After the dressing of the posts the woman in charge of the cooking brought food, a plate of which she put in front of each spirit post, after purifying the food in the smoke of sweet grass. Taking a round piece of pounded meat, each itaŋ'ćaŋ held it to the painted mouth on a spirit post. At this time any orphan in need of help might appear and ask in the name of the spirit to be released, that it be fed and cared for. Such a request was never refused. Any others in need of help might make an appeal at this time, four opportunities being given during the "feeding of the spirits."

When this was finished within the spirit lodge there was a distribution of gifts to the people in the camp. These gifts had been accumulated by the family of the spirit-keeper and already had been exhibited to the people. Weasel Bear said that his wife put up frames for this purpose, laying poles across forked stakes and hanging belts, moccasins, leggings, and other articles on the poles. At this time the spirit-keeper sent gifts to the societies, who preserved order in the camp. A gift to a society was said to be something about equal in value to the gifts which the spirit-keeper had received from that society, and to be something which could be divided among the members. Thus Weasel Bear said that he gave a war bonnet to the Tokala society, and that the feathers were distributed among the men. There was much feasting in the camp and this was an occasion on which prominent families announced publicly the names which they had given their children, or had the ears of their children pierced in the same manner as at the Sun dance. (See p. 137.)

The ceremony within the lodge was not studied in detail. Only former spirit-keepers were allowed to enter, and the man selected as *a'taya itaŋ'ćaŋ* was "prepared with proper songs and prayers and was also qualified to give lamentations for the dead."

If a white buffalo robe were used, song No. 1 was sung. Mention has been made of a filled pipe placed beside the round space of mellowed earth in the spirit lodge. A man was appointed to light this pipe, and was known as *itaŋ'ćaŋ iya'taŋ ki'yapi*, or "leader who lights the pipe." This man put lighted sweet grass on the buffalo chip which lay on the mellowed earth. He did not do this with directness, but, lowering the grass a short distance, he paused for a moment; then lowering it farther, he paused again, making four downward motions, after which he moved it four times in a circle, "with the sun," and placed it on the buffalo chip. The a'taya itaŋ'ćaŋ held the pipe in the ascending smoke and repeated the words which the White Buffalo Maiden said to the Sioux when she appeared to them. This ceremonial speech was not recorded, as none of the writer's informants on this subject were able to repeat it.) The a'taya itaŋ'ćaŋ then turned the pipe and held it as if he would smoke it. Having done this three times, he put it to his lips, ready for lighting. More grass was put on the buffalo chip, and the man who was to light the pipe rubbed the fragrant smoke on his hands and face, after which he lit the pipe and the a'taya itaŋ'ćaŋ smoked it freely. Weasel Bear said:

After he had smoked for awhile I sat down close to him and he pointed the stem of the pipe toward me, saying, "Young man, you are going to smoke this pipe. It was brought to us by a woman, and drawing it will lead you to be as straight and truthful as the stem of the pipe." I smoked it without touching the bowl, and the old man in taking it from me passed his hand downward over my face. The pipe was then passed around the lodge, going toward the left. When it was smoked out itaŋ'ćaŋ iya'taŋ ki'yapi took it and three times pretended to empty the ashes on the buffalo chip, emptying them with the fourth motion.

During the day of the ceremony the spirit bundles lay beside their respective spirit posts. The actual release of the spirits came when these bundles were opened. This was done by the a'taya itaŋ'ćaŋ. Weasel Bear said:

He did not take all the wrapping from a spirit bundle at once. He removed a portion and then made a brief discourse, doing this in such a manner that there were four acts of unwrapping, the last one occurring about an hour before sunset. Then he unfolded the last wrapping and let the spirit of my child depart.

The lock of hair, or other object which formed the nucleus of the spirit bundle, was kept by the family, and the itaŋ'ćaŋ kept such articles from the bundle as he desired, the remainder being distributed among the people in the lodge. The spirit-keeper and his wife then gave away practically all they possessed except the clothing they wore.

If the principal spirit-keeper made use of a white buffalo robe in the spirit lodge there was much interest at the close of the ceremony in seeing who would have the honor of carrying it out of the lodge. A man having the necessary qualifications might do this, and children who had been through the Alo'waŋpi ceremony might take hold of it and help him carry it. The qualifications included uprightness of life and the former possession of a white buffalo robe. Outside the lodge a crude effigy of a buffalo had been erected of small trees.   After being carried from the lodge the white buffalo robe was laid over this framework, and on it were placed valuable garments, as an elk-tooth dress or an eagle war bonnet.   The white buffalo robe, together with the articles placed upon it, were given to the society which had given most assistance to the spirit-keeper.   In every society there is one man who is qualified to take charge of such a robe if the society decides to keep it intact, and such a man may make drawings on it.   The society is at liberty, however, to cut it in pieces and divide it among the members, or to sell it if so desired.

Weasel Bear said:

When it was time for the people to depart, the itaŋ´ćaŋ went first, carrying his share of the bundle in which for so long I had detained the spirit of my little daughter.   My wife stood at the door of the tipi and said to the people, "if you have no leather you may cut up this tipi."   The women came like a rush of wind and cut up the tipi very quickly.   My wife even let them have a little tipi in which we kept our cooking utensils and other things not connected with the spirit-keeping.   They even took away the tipi poles.   Nothing was left except the grass on which we stood and the little spirit post.   My wife and I had parted with everything.   We walked side by side, and I thought with some regret of all I had given away.   We went and sat down under a tree in a deep study.

That evening one of our relatives came and put up a tipi, led us to it and said. "This is your home."   Others brought kettles, blankets, provisions, and clothing for us.   Our relatives did all this for us, in order that we might begin our lives again.

After a time the camp moved to another place and we left the spirit post standing there.   No matter where we were, if a woman came and said, "I cleared the ground around your daughter's post," my wife would give her food.   Sometimes, if there is a spirit post in the camp, a person who is hungry will go and clear the ground around the post.   The relatives of the dead person will see this and cook food and carry the kettles to the place, that the hungry may eat and be satisfied.   But if a spirit-keeper so desires, he may, after a certain time, take up the spirit post and bury it."

After finishing his narrative, Weasel Bear added: "All this came to us through the white buffalo and is one of the reasons why everything connected with the buffalo is so highly regarded by us."

THE SUN DANCE

In the myths of the Indians, as in the mythology of ancient peoples, the sun was a prominent figure.   Doctor Swanton [1] states that "the Natchez believed the universe to be filled with spirits in human forms, and that there were differences in power among these, the most powerful of all being a sky deity resident in or connected with the Sun."   Many other tribes held a similar belief, and the worship of such a deity was widespread among the Indians of North America.   This worship assumed various forms, presenting contrasts in many important characteristics.   The Sun dance was a

[1] Indian Tribes of the Lower Mississippi Valley and Adjacent Coast of the Gulf of Mexico, *Bull. 43, Bur. Amer. Ethn.*, p. 174, 1911.

ceremony whose observance was limited to certain Plains tribes.[1]   In
the Sun dance the Indian considered that he offered to Wakaŋ'taŋka[2]

---

[1] See bibliography, pp. 86, 87, footnote, of this work, also article *Sun Dance*, by G. A. Dorsey, in Handbook of American Indians, pt. 2, p. 649.

[2] Throughout this work the term Wakaŋ'taŋka will be used in preference to the term Great Spirit, which is commonly accepted as its English equivalent. The word Wakaŋ'taŋka is composed of *wa'kaŋ* (mysterious) and *taŋ'ka* (great). There is nothing in the term to suggest "spirit," the Sioux having other words to express that idea. The statement has been made that the term Wakaŋ'taŋka, as well as the idea which it is used to express, is a result of the teachings of missionaries, the native religion being a worship of Ta'kuwakan, a *numen* or a mysterious thing (hence a spirit or divinity). Rev. J. Owen Dorsey, who went among the Siouan tribes first as a missionary and afterwards as a philologist, wrote: "The missionaries, not the laymen, are the ones who make the positive statements about the absence of a belief in one Great Spirit. (See *Eleventh Rep. Bur. Ethn.*, p. 432.) During several seasons' work among the Teton Sioux the writer has made diligent inquiry concerning this matter, and the unvarying opinion of the old men is that the Sioux have always believed in Wakaŋ'taŋka. The exact significance of the term in the mind of the Sioux is as difficult to formulate as the exact meaning of the word God in the mind of Christians. (See p. 96.) In old times the term Wakaŋ'taŋka was not used in ordinary conversation, because it was held too sacred to be spoken except with due reverence and at a proper time. In this connection it will be recalled that many tribes of Indians avoid mentioning a man's name, especially in his presence. That which remains unspoken must be considered in the study of any deep phase of Indian thought. A full and complete expression is not in accordance with Indian custom. The unspoken element may be a matter of mutual understanding, no indication of which appears in words, or it may be something which is indicated in such a manner as to be intelligible only to those for whom it is intended. Thus there is a "sacred language" used by medicine-men in which familiar words take on an occult meaning. (See p. 120, footnote.) In attempting to express the meaning of the word *wakaŋ* the following statement was made to the writer by several old Indians, after consultation: "An ordinary man has natural ways of doing things. Occasionally there is a man who has a gift for doing extraordinary things, and he is called *wakaŋ*. Although this is a supernatural gift, he can use it only by effort and study. A man may be able to do things in a mysterious way, but none has ever been found who could command the sun and moon or change the seasons. The most wonderful things which man can do are different from the works of nature. When the seasons changed we regarded it as a gift from the sun, which is the strongest of all mysterious *wakaŋ* powers." (See p. 96.) In another consideration of the subject it was said: "We use the words *taku wakaŋ* for anything which we can see for ourselves has mysterious power. Thus a pipe is *taku* (something) *wakaŋ*, for with it supplications may be made and good obtained. We can not see the thunder, and we say it is *wakaŋ*, but we see the lightning and we know that the thunder and lighting are a sign of rain, which does good to the earth. Anything which has similar power is *wakaŋ*, but above all is the sun, which has most power of all." Other conversations, similar to the preceding, expressed the conviction in the minds of the Sioux that their people had always believed in a mysterious power whose greatest manifestation is the sun, and that Wakaŋ'taŋka was the designation of that power. The belief in lesser "deities" will not be considered at this time.

The following citations indicate the manner in which Wakaŋ'taŋka is regarded by the Sioux: Should be reverenced (p. 88); "I conquered by the help of Wakaŋ'taŋka" (p. 96); "Wakaŋ'taŋka, pity me" (p. 135); is to be petitioned reverently (p. 184); provides food (p. 185); is maker of all (p. 208); Wakaŋ'taŋka represented by sacred stones (p. 214); medicinal herbs are a gift from Wakaŋ'taŋka (p. 268); is all powerful (p. 87); is a help in sickness (p. 275); gives success (p. 341). See also prayers to Wakaŋ'taŋka, p. 95, footnote.

The following authorities on this subject may be consulted, some holding opinions differing from the above statement: Rev. G. H. Pond, writing in 1866, said: "Evidence is also wanting to show that the Dakotas embraced in their religious tenets the idea of one Supreme Existence, whose existence is expressed by the term 'Great Spirit.'" (*Colls. Minn. Hist. Soc.*, vol. 2, pt. 3, p. 33, 1867.) Rev. S. R. Riggs mentions nine "Dakota gods," saying, "this enumeration of the *Dakota gods* is not intended to be exhaustive." (See Riggs, Stephen Return, Tah-koo Wah-kan', pp. 61-75, Boston [1869]; also, by the same author, The Theogony of The Sioux, in *Amer. Antiq.* for April-June, II, No. 4, pp. 265-70, 1880, in which the elements of earth, air, and water have each a special deity.

Among certain Siouan tribes the term *wakaŋ'da* was used. Concerning this word Dr. W J McGee says "The idea expressed by the term . . . can not justly be rendered into 'spirit,' much less into 'Great Spirit' . . . . It appears that, in so far as they grasped the theistic concept, the Sioux Indians were polytheist; that their mysteries or deities varied in rank and power; . . . and that their dispositions and motives resembled those found among mankind." (McGee, W J, The Siouan Indians, in *Fifteenth Rep. Bur. Ethn.*, pp. 182-83.) Miss Fletcher states that among the Omaha and Ponca tribes the word *wakaŋ'da* was used to designate a "mysterious power or permeating life," and that "this word is now used to designate the Deity." (Fletcher, Alice C., The Emblematic Use of the Tree in the Dakotan Group, in *Proc. Amer. Assoc. Adv. Sci.*, 1896, p. 193, Salem, 1897.) See also Fletcher and La Flesche, The Omaha Tribe, in *Twenty-seventh Rep. Bur. Amer. Ethn.* pp. 597-599, Washington, 1911; Fletcher, Wakondagi, in *Amer. Anthr.*, XIV., pp. 106-108, Lancaster, 1912.

what was strongest in his nature and training—namely, the ability to endure physical pain.   He did this in fulfillment of a vow made in time of anxiety, usually when on the warpath.   Strange as it may seem, the element of pain, which ennobled the ceremony in the mind of the Indian, was a cause of its misunderstanding by the white man.   The voluntary suffering impressed the beholder, while its deep significance was not evident.   It is probable that no Indian ceremony has been misinterpreted so widely and so persistently as the Sun dance.

V. T. McGillicuddy, agent at Pine Ridge, S. Dak., wrote in his report for 1882: "The heathenish annual ceremony termed 'the Sun dance,' will, I trust, . . . be soon a thing of the past."[1] James G. Wright, agent on the Rosebud Reservation, in the same State, characterized the Sun dance as an "aboriginal and barbarous festival."[2]   The stand point of the Sioux concerning the Sun dance is indicated by the following statement of Red Bird, a thoughtful member of the tribe.   In describing the Sun dance to the writer he said:

There is a great deal in what a man *believes*, and if a man's religion is changed for the better or for the worse he will know it.   The Sun dance was our first and our only religion.   We believed that there is a mysterious power greater than all others, which is represented by nature, one form of representation being the sun.   Thus we made sacrifices to the sun, and our petitions were granted.   The Indians lived longer in the old days than now.   I would not say this change is due to throwing away the old religion; there may be other reasons, but in the old times the Sun dance was held annually and was looked forward to with eagerness.   I believe we had true faith at that time.   But there came a year when "the sun died."   There was a period of darkness,[3] and from that day a new religion came to the Indians.   It is the white man's religion.   We are timid about it, as we are about the other ways of the white man.   In the old days our faith was strong and our lives were cared for; now our *faith* is weaker, and we die.

The ceremony of the Sun dance varied among different tribes.[4]

[1] *Ind. Aff. Rep.* for 1882, p. 39, 1882.

[2] Ibid. for 1886, p. 82, 1886.

[3] [The Indians stated that this referred to an eclipse of the sun in 1868, but the reference is probably to the total eclipse which took place August 7, 1869.]

[4] Concerning the Sun-dance customs of various tribes the following authorities, among others, may be consulted:

Among the Sioux:

Fletcher, Alice C., The Sun dance of the Ogalalla Sioux, in *Proc. Amer. Assoc. Adv. Sci.*, 1882, pp. 580–84, Salem, Mass., 1883.

Description by Bushotter, in Dorsey, George A., A Study of Siouan Cults, in *Eleventh Rep. Bur. Ethn.*, pp. 450–64.   Also description by Capt. John G. Bourke, U. S. A., ibid., pp. 464–66.

Clarke, W. P., Indian Sign Language, p. 361, Philadelphia, Pa., 1885.

Catlin, George, The Manners, Customs, and Condition of the North American Indians, I, pp. 232, 233, London, 1841.

Lynd, James W., Religion of the Dakotas, in *Colls. Hist. Soc. Minn.*, vol. 2, pt. 2, pp. 78, 79, St. Paul, Minn., 1865.

Pond, G. H. (quoting from Rev. S. R. Riggs), Dakota Superstitions, ibid., pt. 3, pp. 46–49, 1867.

Beckwith, Paul, Notes on Customs of the Dakotahs, in *Smithson. Rep.* for 1886, pt. 1, p. 250, 1889.

Among the Crows:

Lowie, Robert H., The Sun Dance of the Crow Indians, in *Amer. Mus. Nat. Hist., Anthr. Papers*, XVI, pt. 1, New York, 1915.

The form of the ceremony herewith presented is that of the Sioux on the Standing Rock Reservation, in Dakota, a majority of whom belong to the Teton division. In old times the tribe was so large and so widely scattered that Sun dances were held at more than one locality, the Teton and Yanktonai usually uniting in a ceremony, which was held on the western portion of the Dakota prairie. Thus their traditions of the ceremony have much in common, while the Sun-dance customs of the Santee, Sisseton, and other divisions of the tribe living toward the east, present many radical differences.

THE SUN DANCE OF THE TETON SIOUX

The writer's study of the Sun dance was made in 1911 among the Teton and Yanktonai Sioux on the Standing Rock Reservation, in North and South Dakota. The principal part of the work was done in a series of conferences covering a period of several weeks, these being held at the Standing Rock Agency. Fifteen men took part, and about 40 others were interviewed. These informants, who were carefully selected, lived within a radius of about 80 miles. Below will be found a brief sketch of each of the men who took part in the conferences. Ten are of pure Teton blood. Several of these men have been prominent in the history of the tribe and its negotiations with the Government. With one exception—a noted warrior who took part in the battle known as the Custer massacre—they were friendly to the white men during the troublous days on the frontier. Six of the men have steadily refused to be influenced by the missionaries and still retain the native religious beliefs.

Among the Cheyenne:

Dorsey, George A., The Cheyenne, pt. 2, in *Pubs. Field Col. Mus., Anthr. ser.*, IX, No. 2, Chicago, 1905.

Hayden, F. V., Contributions to the Ethnography and Philology of the Indian Tribes of the Missouri Valley, p. 280, Philadelphia, 1862.

Mooney, James, The Cheyenne Indians, in *Mems. Amer. Anthr. Assoc.*, vol. 1, pp. 369, 417, Lancaster, Pa., 1905–1907.

Among the Arapaho:

Dorsey, George A., The Arapaho Sun Dance; The Ceremony of the Offerings Lodge, op. cit., IV, 1903.

Among the Ponca:

Dorsey, James Owen, A Study of Siouan Cults, in *Eleventh Rep. Bur. Ethn.*, p. 378, 1894

Among the Kiowa:

Scott, Hugh Lenox, Notes on the Kado, or Sun dance of the Kiowa, in *Amer. Anthr.*, XIII, No. 3, pp. 345–79, Lancaster, Pa., 1911.

Among the Mandan:

Catlin describes and illustrates a ceremony similar in some respects to the Sun dance, under the title "Annual Religious Ceremony;" see Catlin, op. cit., pp. 155–77.

This ceremony is also described as the "Okippe" of the Mandan by Maximilian, Prince of Wied, in Travels in the Interior of North America (translated from the German by H. Evans Lloyd), pp. 372–78, London, 1893.

Among the Blackfoot:

Wilson, R. N., The Sacrificial Rite of the Blackfoot, in *Proc. and Trans. Roy. Soc. Canada*, 1909, 3d ser., vol. 3, sec. II, pp. 3–21, Ottawa, 1910.

Among the Minitari (a division of the Hidatsa):

Matthews, Washington, Ethnography and Philology of the Hidatsa Indians, *U. S. Geol. and Geogr. Surv., Misc. Pub.* No. 7, pp. 45, 46, 1877.

James, Edwin, Account of an Expedition from Pittsburgh to the Rocky Mountains, performed in the years 1819 and '20, under the command of Maj. Stephen H. Long, pp. 276, 277, Philadelphia, 1823.

See also articles *Sun dance* and *Ceremony* by George A. Dorsey in Handbook of American Indians.

(1) Ituŋ'kasaŋ-lu'ta (Red Weasel), a member of the Teton division of the tribe.   Concerning the Sun dance Red Weasel is considered the highest authority among the Teton Sioux.   He acted as Intercessor four times, the last occasion being the Sun dance of 1881, the final ceremony held by the Teton in Dakota.   He also took part in the dance four times, once by being suspended from the pole and three times by receiving cuts on his arms.   In earlier years he was trained for the office of Intercessor (*Kuwa' Kiya'pi*) [1] by Wi-ihaŋ'bla (Dreamer-of-the-Sun), who died about the middle of the last century. Before giving his information concerning the Sun dance Red Weasel said:

> I am not boasting; I am telling you what I myself know and I must speak for myself as there is no man living who can vouch for me.   What I tell you is what I learned from Dreamer-of-the-Sun, who taught me as he was taught.   Beyond that I can not tell you the history of the Sun dance.   Dreamer-of-the-Sun was my uncle.   He had many relatives, but he selected me as one who was peculiarly fitted to succeed him if I lived to grow up.   He thus decided to instruct me and began my training at an early age.   One of the first and most important things I was taught was that I must have the greatest reverence for Wakaŋ'taŋka.   Dreamer-of-the-Sun told me that if I would obey his instructions I would be a help to the Sioux nation, and that, if properly prepared for the duties of the highest office in the Sun dance, I need have no anxiety when filling the office as the proper thing to do would come to my mind at the time.   In regard to the songs, Dreamer-of-the-Sun told me that I may pray with my mouth and the prayer will be heard, but if I *sing* the prayer it will be heard *sooner* by Wakaŋ'taŋka.   All the prayers which I offered in the Sun dance and which are still in my mind are prayers which were taught me by Dreamer-of-the-Sun.

When Red Weasel gave his information concerning the Sun dance he was about 80 years old and bowed with the weight of his years.   He traveled 43 miles by wagon in order to confer with the writer.   The sun shone in a cloudless sky while he was at the agency, and his presence was so highly esteemed by the old people that many said, "We have fine weather because Red Weasel is with us."

(2) Mato'-kuwa'pi (Chased-by-Bears), a Santee-Yanktonai (pl. 13) took part in the Sun dance twice as Leader of the Dancers and was present at the final Sun dance of the Teton.   His first participation in the dance was in 1867, when at the age of 24 years he had "spoken the vow" of a war party.   (See p. 97.)   On that occasion as well as at other Sun dances he cut the arms of the men, suspended them to the pole or fastened the buffalo skulls to their flesh, according to the nature of their vows.   He said that he once saw a vision.   He was dancing in the Sun dance, and as he looked steadily at the sun he saw

---

[1] One of the most important of the Intercessor's duties was considered to be the offering of prayers as representative of the people, and for this reason the term "Intercessor" was adopted by Mr. Higheagle to designate this office.   A majority of English words expressing religious ideas are associated with the teachings of Christianity.   In many instances, therefore, the native idea must be gained largely from the connection in which a word is used.

a man beneath the sun, the man's face being painted red and white.[1] Chased-by-Bears died in February, 1915.

(3) ZINTKA′LA-LU′TA[2] (RED BIRD), plate 22, a Teton Sioux, took part in the Sun dance at the age of 24 years, receiving 100 cuts on his arms in fulfillment of a Sun-dance vow.[3] His uncle was an Intercessor in the Sun dance and Red Bird was receiving instructions from him with a view to filling that office when the Sun dance was discontinued. His uncle's name was Taća′gula (His Lungs) who died in the year 1868.

(4) PEŹI′ (GRASS), plate 73, bears also the name Mato′-wata′-kpe (Charging Bear); he is best known, however, as John Grass. His father also was known as John Grass, and in addition to this he bore the name Waha′ćaŋka-ya′pi (Used-as-a-Shield); he was noted as a warrior against other tribes, but was always friendly to the white men. John Grass is a Teton and was a successful leader of war parties against the Mandan, Arikaree, and Crow Indians. When the Black Hills treaty and other treaties were made with the Government he was the principal speaker for the Sioux tribe. Since that time he has constantly influenced his people to adopt the customs of civilization. He has been to Washington as a tribal delegate and for 30 years has been the leading judge of the Court of Indian Offenses on the Standing Rock Reservation. As a young man he was selected to choose the Sun-dance pole, but never made a Sun-dance vow.

(5) ITUŊ′KASAŊ-MATO′ (WEASEL BEAR) is a Teton Sioux. He was once selected to choose the Sun-dance pole but never fulfilled a vow at a Sun dance. He once made a similar vow, which, however, was fulfilled privately. When on the warpath against the Crows he vowed that if he were successful he would give part of his flesh to Wakaŋ′taŋka, but did not say that he would do so at the Sun dance. The war party was successful, and on the way home his arms were cut with 100 gashes in fulfillment of the vow, the cutting being done by a man who had taken part in the Sun dance. Weasel Bear is hereditary chief of a large band and belongs to one of its wealthiest families. As a young man he was successful in war, a prominent member of the White Horse Riders, and a leader in the grass dance. When negotiations with the Government were begun he was one of

---

[1] For other descriptions of dreams see: Dream of the rising sun (p. 139); a dream of "a man in the sun," by Red Bird (p. 149); of the thunderbirds, by Lone Man (pp. 159–161); of the thunderbirds, and of wolves, by Charging Thunder (pp. 170–181); of the buffalo, elk, wolf, and sacred stones, by Brave Buffalo (pp. 173–179, 207–208); of the crow and owl, by Śiya′ka (pp. 184–188); of the wolf, by Two Shields and by Weasel Bear (pp. 188–190); of a rainbow (p. 214); a strange vision in the sky, in which a sacred stone appeared, by Goose (p. 251); a dream of a badger by Eagle Shield (p. 266.)

[2] This is the generic term for small birds but is commonly translated simply "bird."

[3] Red Bird died a few weeks after the study of the Sun dance was completed. On returning to the reservation the writer asked whether the death of Red Bird was attributed to the information given concerning the Sun dance and was assured it was not. Indeed Red Bird said during his last illness that he was greatly comforted by the thought that he had helped to preserve the songs and beliefs of his people.

the tribal delegates to Washington. In his later years he is known as one of the most prosperous native farmers on the reservation.

(6) WAKIŊ'YAŊ-WATA'KPE (CHARGING THUNDER), plate 24, a Teton Sioux, is an hereditary chief of a band and a highly respected member of the tribe. He took part in the Sun dance four times, at the ages of 21,23, 24, and 25. On each occasion he had vowed that 100 cuts should be made on his arms, but the last time there was not room for all the cuts on his arms, so about 20 were made on his chest. He is a man of genial countenance and powerful physique. In speaking of himself he said, "My prayer has been heard and I have lived long."

(7) MAĠA' (GOOSE), plate 31, was a member of the Teton division, and at the time of giving his information was 76 years of age. He still continued the practice of native medicine and was considered the best Indian doctor on the reservation. He took part in the Sun dance at the age of 27, being suspended from the Sun-dance pole. Goose served for a time in the United States Army. The records of the War Department show that he enlisted September 11, 1876, in Buffalo County, Dakota Territory, as a scout, U. S. A., and served almost continuously in that capacity until July 10, 1882. He again enlisted June 11, 1891, at Fort Yates, North Dakota, and was honorably discharged April 30, 1893, a private of Company I, 22d United States Infantry. He was a corporal from October 16, 1891, to October 18, 1892. Goose died in September, 1915.

(8) ŚIYA'KA (TEAL DUCK), plate 1, who bore also the name Waŋbli'wana'peya (EAGLE-WHO-FRIGHTENS), was a Yanktonai-Teton. Instead of being known by the English equivalent of his Sioux name he was known as Śiya'ka, the name used in the present work. He was not an hereditary chief, but was elected chief of a band. He took part in the Sun dance twice as a young man and was also one of the four young men selected to choose the Sun-dance pole. The first time he took part in the Sun dance was at the age of 21 in fulfilment of a vow made on the warpath. He went with a party of 26 warriors on an expedition against the Mandan and Arikaree. About 20 of the warriors, including himself, vowed to take part in the next Sun dance by dancing, and the other members of the party vowed to participate in other ways., One battle was fought, and all the party returned home alive. His second participation in the Sun dance was at the age of 25, and he bore three long scars on each arm as an evidence of the ordeal. He was once a tribal delegate to Washington. Śiya'ka died in March, 1913.

(9) TOKA'LA-LU'TA (RED FOX), plate 56, is a member of the Teton band. He was prominent in the Sun dance, taking part three times, at the ages of 19, about 30, and 40 years. The last time he had sev-

BUFFALO BOY

NO HEART

WHITE-BUFFALO-WALKING

eral buffalo skulls fastened to his back.   As evidence of his other Sundance vows he bears nine long scars on each arm, three near the wrist, four near the elbow, and two on the upper arm.

(10) Hogaṇ'-lu'ta (Red Fish), plate 74, a Santee-Yanktonai, is a chief and is a prominent man in the councils of the tribe.   He took part in the Sun dance twice, first when he was 26 years old, and the second time at the age of 40.   (See song No. 192.)

(11) Iśna'la-wiĆa' (Lone Man), plate 23, a Teton, took part in the Sun dance when 20 and when 31 years of age, and has 100 scars on each arm.   He was chosen on one occasion to help select the Sundance pole and on another occasion to sing at the drum.   He was prominent in tribal wars and took part in the Custer massacre.

(12) Ma'zakaṇ'-wiĆa'ki (Seizes-the-Gun-away-from-Them), a Teton, took part in the Sun dance, being suspended from the pole. He stated that when he was on the warpath all the warriors made a Sun-dance vow, so he joined them, asking that he might conquer the enemy and capture horses, also that he might find his friends alive when he reached home.   In fulfilling this vow he remained suspended for more than an hour, after which he was "jerked down," but the flesh still refused to tear and only the sticks were broken.   The flesh was then cut and the splinters of wood remaining underneath were removed, after which a tiny portion of flesh was offered as in the case of that cut from the arms.

(13) Tataṇ'ka-hokśi'la (Buffalo Boy), plate 9, is a Santee-Yanktonai.   At the age of 30 he carried six buffalo skulls when fulfilling a Sun-dance vow.   Ten years later he took part in the dance again.   He received his name from a dream in which he saw the buffalo.

(14) Caṇte'-wani'Ća (No Heart) (plate 10), a Yanktonai, is a well known medicine-man of the tribe and is able to depict events by means of drawings.   (See pl. 16.)   He took part in the Sun dance when 20 years of age and has 100 scars on each arm.

(15) Ptesaṇ'-ma'ni (White-Buffalo-Walking), plate 11, is a Teton and took part in the final Sun dance in 1882.

The above-mentioned men were the principal informants concerning the Sun dance, the work being done in a series of conferences. As already stated, about 40 additional men were interviewed.   All were members of the Teton, Santee, and Yanktonai divisions of the tribe.   The purpose of the interviews was to ascertain the facts concerning the ceremony which were remembered by those who attended as spectators, and also to ascertain the manner in which the men who took part in the conferences were regarded by members of the tribe.   Thus the importance given the opinions expressed by these men was influenced somewhat by the authority accorded them by these scattered members of the tribe. The facts brought out during these interviews did not conflict with statements made in the conferences, but served to corroborate them and to add minor details.

Not all the men in the foregoing list were present at every conference. Thus on the first occasion it was possible for only 9 to attend. It was considered desirable that at least 12 persons be present, and as no other elderly man was acceptable to the council, an invitation was extended to Thomas Frosted, a full-blood Santee-Yanktonai, who witnessed several Sun dances when too young to make a Sundance vow, and who has given much consideration to its history and beliefs. Robert P. Higheagle, the interpreter, also witnessed a Sun dance when a child. These men, with the writer, completed the desired number and no other persons were allowed in the room. Two days were occupied by the discussions, and several men remained longer to record songs.

Concerning these conferences Iśŋa'la-wića' (Lone Man) said to the writer:

> When we heard that you had come for the facts concerning the Sun dance we consulted together in our homes. Some hesitated. We have discarded the old ways, yet to talk of them is "sacred talk" to us. If we were to talk of the Sun dance there should be at least 12 persons present, so that no disrespect would be shown, and no young people should be allowed to come from curiosity. When we decided to come to the council we reviewed all the facts of the Sun dance and asked Wakaŋ'taŋka that we might give a true account. We prayed that no bad weather would prevent the presence of anyone chosen to attend, and see, during all this week the sound of the thunder has not been heard, the sky has been fair by day and the moon has shone brightly by night, so we know that Wakaŋ'taŋka heard our prayer.

Seated in a circle, according to the old custom, the Indians listened to the statements concerning the Sun dance as they had already been given to the writer. According to an agreeement there were no interruptions as the manuscript was translated. The man at the southern end of the row held a pipe, which he occasionally lit and handed to the man at his left. Silently the pipe was passed from one to another, each man puffing it for a moment. The closest attention was given throughout the reading. A member of the white race can never know what reminiscences it brought to the silent Indians—what scenes of departed glory, what dignity and pride of race. After this the men conferred together concerning the work.

That night until a late hour the subject was discussed in the camp of Indians. The next morning the principal session of the council took place. At this time the expression of opinion was general and after each discussion a man was designated to state the decision through the interpreter. Sometimes one man and sometimes another made the final statement, but nothing was written down which did not represent a consensus of opinion.   Throughout the councils care was taken that the form of a question did not suggest a possible answer by the Indians.

On the afternoon of that day the entire party drove across the prairie to the place, about a mile and a half from the Standing Rock Agency, where the last Sun dance of these bands was held in 1882.

A majority of the Indians who went to the site of the Sun dance with the writer were men who took part in the Sun dance of 1882 and had not visited the place since that time.   When nearing the place they scanned the horizon, measuring the distance to the Missouri River and the buttes.   At last they gave a signal for the wagons to stop, and, springing to the ground, began to search the prairie. In a short time they found the exact spot where the ceremony was held.   The scars were still on the prairie as they were on their own bodies.   A depression about 2 inches in depth still square in outline and not fully overgrown with grass showed where the earth had been exposed for the *owaŋ'ka wakaŋ'* ("sacred place"); see page 122.   Only 3 or 4 feet away lay a broken buffalo skull.   Eagerly the Indians lifted it and saw traces of red paint upon it—could it be other than the skull used in that ceremony?   They looked if perchance they might find a trace of the location of the pole.   It should be about 15 feet east of the "sacred place."   There it was—a spot of hard, bare ground 18 inches in diameter.

One said, "Here you can see where the shade-house stood."   This shade-house, or shelter of boughs, was built entirely around the Sun-dance circle except for a wide entrance at the east.   It was possible to trace part of it, the outline being particularly clear on the west of the circle; to the east the position of the posts at the entrance was also recognized.   The two sunken places (where the posts had stood) were about 15 feet apart, and the center of the space between them was directly in line with the site of the pole and the center of the "sacred place" at the west of it.[1]   More than 29 years had passed since the ceremony.   It is strange that the wind had not sown seeds on those spots of earth.

The little party assembled again around the buffalo skull.   Mr. Higheagle gathered fresh sage, which he put beside the "sacred place;" he then laid the broken buffalo skull upon it and rested a Sun-dance pipe against the skull, with stem uplifted.   He, too, had his memories.   As a boy of 6 years he was present at that final Sun dance, wearing the Indian garb and living the tribal life. Between that day and the present lay the years of education in the white man's way.   Some of the Indians put on their war bonnets

---

[1] These measurements were verified by the writer at a subsequent time.

and their jackets of deerskin with the long fringes. (Pl. 12.) How bright were the porcupine quills on the tobacco bags! "Yes, it is good that we came here today." Pass the pipe from hand to hand in the old way. Jest a little. Yonder man tells too fine a story of his part in the Sun dance—let him show his scars! Yet the memories, how they return! One old man said with trembling lips: "I was young then. My wife and my children were with me. They went away many years ago. I wish I could have gone with them."

The sky was blue above the little gathering, and all around the vast silent prairie seemed waiting, listening. The Indians were its children—would the white man understand them aright?

A few weeks later the material was again discussed point by point with men who came 10 miles for the purpose. Chief among these was Red Bird, who was under instruction for the office of Intercessor when the Sun dance was discontinued. He was present at the first council, but some facts had come to his mind in the meantime, and he wished to have them included in the narrative. These men met four times for the discussion of the subject, the phonograph records being played for them and approved, and some ceremonial songs being added to the series. A few days later a conference was held with five other men, most of whom were present at the council of August 28 and 29. The session lasted an entire day, the narrative which had been prepared being translated into Sioux and the phonograph records played for them, as for the previous group of men. With one exception all the men present were chiefs.

Throughout this series of conferences the principal points of the account remained unchanged. Each session added information, placed events in the proper order, furnished detail of description, and gave reasons for various ceremonial acts. The councils were not marked by controversy, a spirit of cordiality prevailing, but the open discussion assisted in recalling facts and nothing was recorded which was not pronounced correct by the council as a whole.

A message was then sent to Ituŋ'kasaŋ-lu'ta (Red Weasel), an aged man who acted as Intercessor at the last Sun dance, asking him to come and give his opinion on the material. He came and with three others went over the subject in another all-day council. His training and experience enabled him to recall details concerning the special duties of the Intercessor, and he also sang four songs which he received from Wi-ihaŋ'bla (Dreamer-of-the-Sun) together with the instructions concerning the duties of his office. These songs are Nos. 14, 15, 16, and 18 in the present memoir. Before

PARTICIPANTS IN SUN DANCE

CHASED-BY-BEARS

singing the first song the aged man bowed his head and made the following prayer,[1] which was recorded by the phonograph:

Ho Wakaŋ'taŋka nama'ħon wo.　Aŋpe'tu le el ni'oiĕ waŋźi' obla'kiŋ ktelo'.　Tka ta'ku wo'waħtani wanil' ya obla'kiŋ ktelo'.　Oya'te wića'ni ktelo'.　Huku'ćiyela waoŋ' taŋyaŋ' ama'bleza yo.　Mi'waŋkapataŋhaŋ waŋyaŋg' nama'jiŋ yo.　Wića'yaka eće kiŋ on taŋyaŋ' ho ana'maġoptaŋ ye.　Le mita'kuye yaŋka'pi kiŋ ob taŋyaŋ' to'ka e'waćiŋ śniyaŋ waoŋ' ktelo'.　Hećéća kiŋ toka'ta oi'najiŋ waŋ oŋyeglepi kiŋ ekta' hountaŋiŋ pi kta nuŋwe'.

(Translation)

Wakaŋ'taŋka, hear me.　This day I am to tell your word.　But without sin I shall speak.　The tribe shall live.　Behold me for I am humble.　From above watch me. You are always the truth, listen to me.　My friends and relatives, sitting here, and I shall be at peace.　May our voices be heard at the future goal you have prepared for us.

The foregoing prayer was uttered in so low a voice that the phonogram was read with difficulty.　It is uncertain whether the aged man intended that it should be recorded, but as he had seated himself before the phonograph preparatory to singing, it was possible to put the machine in motion without attracting his attention.　He began the prayer with head bowed and right hand extended, later raising his face and using the same gestures which he would have used when filling his ceremonial office.

The final work on this material was done with Chased-by-Bears, (pl. 13), a man who had twice acted as Leader of the Dancers, had "spoken the Sun-dance vow" of a war party (see p. 97), and had frequently inflicted the tortures at the ceremony.　He was a particularly thoughtful man, remaining steadfast in the ancient beliefs of his people.　Few details were added to the description of the ceremony at this time, but its teachings received special attention.　Chased-by-Bears' recital of his understanding of the Sun dance was not given consecutively, though it is herewith presented in connected form. This material represents several conferences with the writer, and also talks between Mr. Higheagle and Chased-by-Bears which took place during long drives across the prairie.　In order to give opportunity for these conversations the interpreter brought Chased-by-Bears to the agency every day in his own conveyance.　Thus the information was gradually secured.　When it had been put in its present form, it was translated into Sioux for Chased-by-Bears, who said that it was correct in every particular.

The statement of Chased-by-Bears concerning the Sun dance was as follows:

The Sun dance is so sacred to us that we do not talk of it often.　Before talking of holy things we prepare ourselves by offerings.　If only two are to talk together, one

---

[1] Other prayers, either incorporated in narratives or made before songs and recorded by phonograph, are as follows: By Chased-by-Bears (p. 97); by Lone Man (pp. 160, 163, 216); by Eagle Shield (p. 266); by White-paw Bear (p. 268); by Jaw (p. 389).

will fill his pipe and hand it to the other, who will light it and offer it to the sky and the earth. Then they will smoke together, and after smoking they will be ready to talk of holy things.

The cutting of the bodies in fulfillment of a Sun dance vow is different from the cutting of the flesh when people are in sorrow. A man's body is his own, and when he gives his body or his flesh he is giving the only thing which really belongs to him. We know that all the creatures on the earth were placed here by Wakaŋ′taŋka. Thus, if a man says he will give a horse to Wakaŋ′taŋka, he is only giving to Wakaŋ′taŋka that which already belongs to him. I might give tobacco or other articles in the Sun dance, but if I gave these and kept back the best no one would believe that I was in earnest. I must give something that I really value to show that my whole being goes with the lesser gifts; therefore I promise to give my body.

A child believes that only the action of some one who is unfriendly can cause pain, but in the Sun dance we acknowledge first the goodness of Wakaŋ′taŋka, and then we suffer pain because of what he has done for us. To this day I have never joined a Christian Church. The old belief which I have always held is still with me.

When a *man* does a piece of work which is admired by all we say that it is wonderful; but when we see the changes of day and night, the sun, moon, and stars in the sky, and the changing seasons upon the earth, with their ripening fruits, anyone must realize that it is the work of some one more powerful than man. Greatest of all is the sun, without which we could not live. The birds and the beasts, the trees and the rocks, are the work of some great power. Sometimes men say that they can understand the meaning of the songs of birds. I can believe this is true. They say that they can understand the call and cry of the animals, and I can believe this also is true, for these creatures and man are alike the work of a great power. We often wish for things to come, as the rain or the snow. They do not always come when we wish, but they are sure to come in time, for they are under the control of a power that is greater than man.

It is right that men should repent when they make or fulfill a vow to Wakaŋ′taŋka. No matter how good a man may appear to others, there are always things he has done for which he ought to be sorry, and he will feel better if he repents of them. Men often weep in the Sun dance and cry aloud. They are asking something of Wakaŋ′-taŋka, and are like children who wish to show their sorrow, and who also know that a request is more readily granted to a child who cries.[1] (See p. 185.)

We talk to Wakaŋ′taŋka and are sure that he hears us, and yet it is hard to explain what we believe about this. It is the general belief of the Indians that after a man dies his spirit is somewhere on the earth or in the sky, we do not know exactly where, but we are sure that his spirit still lives. Sometimes people have agreed together that if it were found possible for spirits to speak to men, they would make themselves known to their friends after they died, but they never came to speak to us again, unless, perhaps, in our sleeping dreams. So it is with Wakaŋ′taŋka. We believe that he is everywhere, yet he is to us as the spirits of our friends, whose voices we can not hear. (See p. 85.)

My first Sun-dance vow was made when I was 24 years of age. I was alone and far from the camp when I saw an Arikaree approaching on horseback, leading a horse. I knew that my life was in danger, so I said, ''Wakaŋ′taŋka, if you will let me kill this man and capture his horse with this lariat, I will give you my flesh at the next Sun dance.''

I was successful, and when I reached home I told my friends that I had conquered by the help of Wakaŋ′taŋka and had made a Sun-dance vow. It happened that I was the first who had done this after the Sun dance of that summer, so my friends said that I should be the Leader of the Dancers at the next ceremony. (See p. 102.) In

---

[1] See Dorsey, James Owen, A Study of Siouan Cults, in *Eleventh Rep. Bur. Ethn.*, p. 435, 1894.

fulfilling this vow I carried the lariat I had used in capturing the horse (fig. 21) fastened to the flesh of my right shoulder and the figure of a horse cut from rawhide fastened to my left shoulder. [Fig. 21 shows the lariat and whistle carried by Chased-by-Bears.]

Later in the same year I went with a party of about 20 warriors. As we approached the enemy some of the men came to me saying that they desired to make Sun-dance vows and asking if I would "speak the vow" for the party. (See p. 101.) Each man came to me alone and made some gift with the request. He also stated what gifts he would make at the Sun dance, but did not always say what part he intended to take in the dance. One man said, "I will give my whole body to Wakaŋ'taŋka." I did not understand what he meant, nor was it necessary that I should do so, but at the time of the Sun dance he asked that his body be suspended entirely above the ground.

Just before sunrise I told the warriors to stand side by side facing the East. I stood behind them and told them to raise their right hands. I raised my right hand with them and said: "Wakaŋ'taŋka, these men have requested me to make this vow for them. I pray you take pity on us and on our families at home. We are now between life and death. For the sake of our families and relatives we desire that you will help us conquer the enemy and capture his horses to take home with us. Because they are thankful for your goodness and will be thankful if you grant this request these men promise that they will take part in the next Sun dance. Each man has some offering to give at the proper time."

We were successful and returned home victorious. Knowing that these men had vowed to take part in the Sun dance, I saw that their vows were fulfilled at the next ceremony and personally did the cutting of their arms and the suspension of their bodies. I did this in addition to acting as Leader of the Dancers and fulfilling my own vow.

The second time I fulfilled a Sun-dance vow I also acted as Leader of the Dancers. At that time I carried four buffalo skulls. They were so heavy that I could not stand erect, but bowed myself upon a stick which I was permitted to use and danced in that position (p. 133).

When the work with Chased-by-Bears was finished he went with the writer and the interpreter to the spot where the final Sun dance was held, a place which had been visited by the council of Indians a few weeks before. The purpose of this visit was that Chased-by-Bears might arrange the ceremonial articles on the "sacred place" as would be done in a ceremony.

The outline of the "sacred place" was made clear and intersecting white lines were traced on the exposed earth. (See page 122.)

A buffalo skull had been secured and brought to the place. Chased-by-Bears spread fresh sage beside the "sacred place" and laid the buffalo skull upon it. He then made a frame to support a pipe and placed in ceremonial position a pipe which had been decorated by the woman who decorated the Sun-dance pipe for the last tribal ceremony. The group of articles was then photographed. (See pl. 20.) Suddenly Chased-by-Bears threw himself, face downward, on the ground, with his head pressed against the top of the buffalo skull. This was the position permitted a Leader of the Dancers when resting during the Sun dance. (See p. 130.) After a few silent moments, he rose to his feet. The white cross was then obliterated, and fresh sage was carefully strewn over the bare, brown earth, so that no chance passer-by would pause to wonder.

The study of the Sun dance was finished.

FIG. 21. Lariat and whistle carried in Sun dance.

DESCRIPTION OF A TETON SIOUX SUN DANCE

The Sun dance was called by the Sioux Wi waŋ′yaŋg waći′pi, which is literally translated "Sun-watching dance." It was their only tribal gathering of a religious character and was held every year at the full moon of midsummer, "when all nature and even men were rejoicing." The trees were in full leaf and the june berries were ripe. Further, the wild sage was fully grown—a thing especially desired, as the sage was used in the ceremony.

The place where the Sun dance was held changed from year to year, but was known to all the tribe. Across the prairie came the little companies of Sioux, some traveling a long distance to attend the ceremony. One band after another arrived and erected its tipis in the accustomed part of the tribal circle. Each band constructed a vapor lodge ("sweat bath") near its' camp for the use of those who took part in the dance, also a larger lodge in which the dancers assembled before and after the ceremony.

The Sun dance was held in the center of the great circle of tents. The opening of this tribal circle was toward the East, and the tent of the itaŋ′ćaŋ [1] (Leader of the Dancers) was opposite. A short distance in front of his tent was the council tent, larger than the others and without decoration. There the chiefs and leading men met to

---

[1] The meaning of this word is "leader," and its exact significance is understood from the connection in which it is used.   (See p. 70, footnote.)

transact the business of the tribe, and thence the various orders pertaining to the ceremony were carried to the people by the Crier. Members of the tribe did not approach, and children and dogs were kept away from the vicinity because the buffalo skull to be used in the ceremony of the Sun dance lay at the west of this tent. During the four days preceding the ceremony the skull lay on a bed of fresh sage outside the council tent, in a position corresponding to the place of honor inside the tent. The ceremonial lines of red paint had not yet been placed on the skull, but the openings in it were filled with sage. The use of sage around the buffalo skull was in accordance with the instructions given by the White Buffalo Maiden. (See p. 64.) It was said, too, that "the sage was used because the buffalo sought for it on the prairie and rolled their great bodies on its fragrant leaves." The sage used in this connection was identified as *Artemisia gnaphalodes* Nutt.

A month before the Sun dance the *wakaŋ'haŋ* (medicine-men; see p. 245) prayed for fair weather, singing, burning sweet grass, and offering their pipes to the sky, the earth, and the cardinal points. Before burning the sweet grass, a medicine-man prepared a spot of bare ground, placing a few coals in the middle of it. Then, taking a bunch of sweet grass, he offered it to the sky, the earth, and the cardinal points, after which he singed it over the coals. While it was smoking, he offered it again to the sky, the earth, and the cardinal points. It is said that the efforts of the medicine-men were always successful, and that the oldest men can not remember the falling of rain during a Sun dance.

The following song was especially favored for securing fair weather; it is one of the songs which have descended from Dreamer-of-the-Sun, who died about the year 1845. (See p. 88.)

No. 4. Song for Securing Fair Weather   (Catalogue No. 497)

Sung by RED BIRD

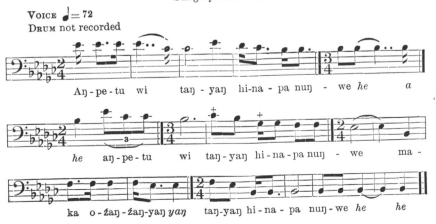

VOICE ♩ = 72
DRUM not recorded

Aŋ - pe - tu wi   taŋ - yaŋ hi - na - pa nuŋ - we *he*   *a*

he   aŋ - pe - tu   wi   taŋ - yaŋ hi - na - pa nuŋ - we   ma -

ka o - źaŋ - źaŋ - yaŋ *yaŋ*   taŋ - yaŋ hi - na - pa nuŋ - we *he*   *he*

WORDS

(*First rendition*)

aŋpe′tu wi taŋyaŋ′ hina′pa nuŋwe′... may the sun rise well
maka′ oźaŋ′źaŋyaŋ taŋyaŋ′....... may the earth appear
hina′pa nuŋwe′.................... brightly shone upon

(*Second rendition*)

haŋhe′pi wi taŋyaŋ′ hina′pa nuŋwe′. may the moon rise well
maka′ oźaŋ′źaŋyaŋ taŋyaŋ′...... may the earth appear
hina′pa nuŋwe′.................... brightly shone upon

Analysis.—Like all the ceremonial songs of the Sun dance, this song was sung with much flexibility of both time and intonation, and therefore can not be fully represented by notation. In the opinion of the writer it is not necessary, however, that variations of less than a semitone be represented to the eye, since in this instance they differ in the several renditions, while the larger features of the song do not show a corresponding difference. The same words are always accented, and the general ratios of the rhythm are steadily preserved. Thus a comparison of several renditions shows that the rhythm used in singing the word *hinapa* can be indicated with reasonable accuracy by a sixteenth note followed by a dotted eighth. E flat above the staff and E flat on the staff were sung with an intonation which was almost correct, showing a feeling for the interval of the octave. B flat, the fifth of the key, was sometimes sung quite accurately and at other times was very faulty, the same being true of F, the second of the key. It was noted among the Chippewa songs that the octave and fifth were sung with more accuracy of intonation than other intervals. (Bulletin 45, p. 5.) C flat in the seventh measure of the present song was always sung too high, and might have been considered an accidental except that the intonation is faulty in the entire measure in which it occurs, some of the progressions in this measure being glissando. Thus the character of the song and in many instances that of the singer as well must be taken into consideration in judging the importance of points which appear in the song.

About three-fourths of the intervals are downward progressions, and the song is melodic in structure. It has a range of eleven tones and comprises all the tones of the octave except the fourth.

The danger from enemies was not forgotten in the season of rejoicing. The horses were herded near the camp, and young men guarded them during the day, bringing them nearer the tents and picketing them at night.

There were many greetings among the people. Events of the year were reviewed, and tales of war were told again and again. War was an absorbing interest, and the Sun dance would see the fulfillment of many a warrior's vow.

When in danger, it was customary for an entire war party to vow that its members would take part in the next Sun dance. The vow was usually made at sunrise and spoken by a warrior who had fulfilled a similar vow. (See p. 97.) If there were time to secure a proper offering, each man held this in his left hand, raising his right hand as the vow was spoken. It was a rite, which could be varied by the individual. Thus it was said that some made the vow more impressive by bowing the head or lowering the right hand slowly toward the earth. A man's spoken vow was only that he would take part in the dance, but deep in his heart was hidden a private vow concerning the part which he would take.[1] Some had left little children at home, or sick relatives or friends whom they longed to see again. They vowed that at the next Sun dance they would dance, or would be suspended by their flesh, or that many gashes would be cut in their arms; they felt that no extreme of heroic endurance would be too great an expression of thankfulness if they were reunited with their friends, yet they knew that their vow must be fulfilled even if they returned defeated or to an empty lodge.

During the months which intervened between their return and the Sun dance they prepared for the fulfillment of their vows. Well they knew that if they failed to do this of their own accord it would be exacted of them by the forces of nature. More than one man who disregarded his vow to the sun had perished in a lightning flash; or if he escaped punishment himself, it was known that disaster had befallen his family or his horses. The old men knew of every vow and watched for its fulfillment.

The leading men of the tribe belonged to various military societies, as the Strong Heart, the Crow-owners, the Wolf, Badger and Fox societies, or the White Horse Riders. (See pp. 314–332.) During the four days next preceding the Sun dance these societies met together for the purpose of electing the *Kuwa' Kiya'pi* (Intercessor), the *Itaŋ'ćaŋ* (Leader of the Dancers), the four young men who were to select the tree for the sacred pole, and the four young women who were to cut it down. The chiefs were also in the council tent whenever business was transacted. It was generally known in advance who would be chosen Intercessor and Leader of the Dancers. The former office required long and special preparation and was repeatedly filled by the same man. His duties included the offering of prayers on behalf of the people, the singing of songs as he performed certain ceremonial acts, the painting of the *caŋ wakaŋ'* (sacred pole) and the preparation of· the *owaŋ'ka wakaŋ'* (sacred place). The ceremonial songs must either be composed by the man who sang them, or purchased from some one who had previously

---

[1] Among other instances see Red Fox (p. 376) and Jaw (p. 390).

held the office and instructed him in its duties. A large amount was paid for the instructions and songs. The tribe knew when a young man aspired to this office, and if his preparation were complete he was elected as soon as occasion offered.

Red Bird made the statement: "The tribe would never appoint an unworthy man to the office of Intercessor. In his prayers and offerings he represented the people, and if he were not a good man Wakaŋ'taŋka might not answer his petitions and grant fair weather; he even might send disaster upon the tribe." Chased-by-Bears said that no man who had committed a great wrong could act as Intercessor, no matter how fully he had repented. The record of an Intercessor must be absolutely without blemish.

The Leader of the Dancers was usually the warrior who first returned successful from the warpath, stating that he had made a Sundance vow and that he wished to act as Leader of the Dancers at the next ceremony. As with the office of Intercessor, the qualifications were so well known that a man who lacked them would not presume to seek the position. He must have a reputation above reproach and be able to fill the office with credit to himself and the tribe; he must furnish the various offerings placed upon the sacred pole, and the buffalo fat in which the pole was embedded; he was also expected to offer a Sun-dance pipe and provide the buffalo skull upon which it rested during the ceremony, a skull without defect selected by him from the many that strewed the prairie.

The Sun-dance pipe (pl. 14), furnished by the Leader of the Dancers, was decorated at his request by one of the most skillful women of the tribe. It was considered a great honor to decorate this pipe, which was prepared some time before the ceremony. There was no prescribed pattern, but the decoration consisted of porcupine-quill work and did not cover the entire stem. The men who fulfilled their vows also made certain offerings, which they prepared before the ceremony; these varied in value according to the wealth of the man. Thus a man of large means might give a pipe, a quantity of tobacco, a buffalo robe, and other goods, while a man of small means gave only tobacco. Like the offerings made during the ceremony by the Intercessor, these were regarded as gifts to Wakaŋ'taŋka. A difference between the two classes of offerings was shown by the fact that the goods offered by the Intercessor were left undisturbed on the prairie, while those offered by the dancers were free to anyone who wished to appropriate them. The reason given by Red Bird was that "the Intercessor represented the whole tribe and his offerings were to Wakaŋ'taŋka, while the dancers were all alike and their offerings were among themselves."

The tobacco offered by the dancers was tied in little packets, each holding about a pipeful, and each being fastened to a stick (pl. 15).

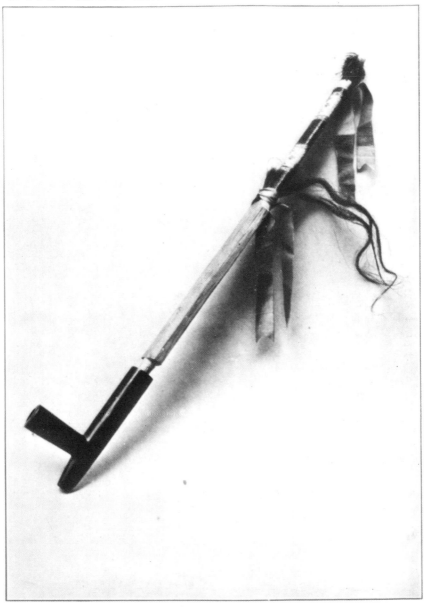

SUN-DANCE PIPE

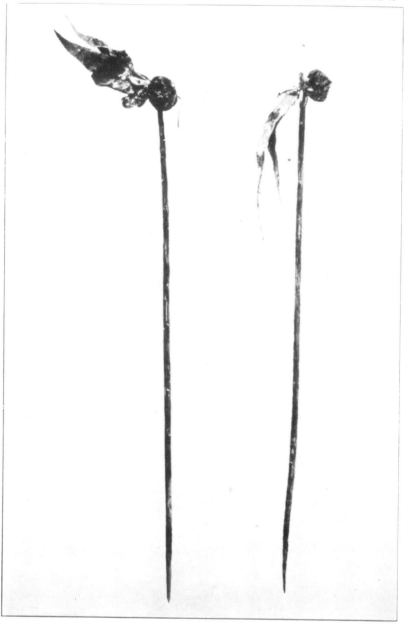

GIFTS OF TOBACCO

In the specimens illustrated the tobacco is wrapped in the dried bladder of a steer, buffalo bladder being formerly used. The number of these packets varied; 10 was the usual number, though a dancer sometimes gave 100. The sticks bearing the packets were placed upright in the ground or left in any available place, and, like the other gifts of the dancers, were taken by the poor of the tribe.

If a man's vow involved the cutting of his flesh he was permitted to offer a pipe similar to that of the Intercessor, filled with tobacco, sealed with buffalo fat, and placed beside the Intercessor's pipe during the ceremony. Iśna'la-wića' (Lone Man) stated that his Sun-dance vow included the offering of a pipe; he therefore offered a pipe when fulfilling his vow and had kept the pipe with greatest care. This was smoked when the members of the Sun-dance council revisited the site of the final Sun dance, August 29, 1911, and was again placed on the square of exposed earth, which was still discernible on the prairie. (See p. 93.)

Preparation for the Sun dance included the choice of others who were to take part in the ceremony. It was required that the four young men who were to select the tree for the sacred pole should be unmarried, members of prominent families and men of unquestioned integrity. The four women were selected from among the virgins of the tribe. Great care was exercised in these selections, and each choice could be challenged by the tribe. There was, however, no open rivalry at the time of the election, it being known who would probably be chosen.

Twenty or more men were selected who should carry the sacred pole to the camp and erect it in the Sun-dance circle; these men also sang at the drum, together with special singers, both men and women.

During the days before a Sun dance several begging dances were held. The begging dance, which was performed at every Sioux gathering, resembled a serenade rather than a dance. A party of men and women carrying a drum went from tent to tent, pausing before each and singing and dancing until food was given them. A man went in advance of the party and placed a stick upright in the ground before each tent where the serenaders expected to sing. This was a signal to the occupants of the tent, the stick being removed by the singers after they had been supplied with food.[1]

To those who were to take part in the Sun dance the days preceding the ceremony were a season of preparation, including visits to the vapor lodges of their respective bands. During this time the dancers usually made the arrangements for the painting of their bodies. The painting was done by men of known ability, who were paid by the individual dancers. Often there was some formality

---

[1] See Bull. 53, pp. 228–33; also pp. 320, 327, 481 of the present work.

connected with the making of this request, which was enacted for the writer by Zintka'la-lu'ta (Red Bird), who represented the dancer, and Iśna'la-wiĉa' (Lone Man), who represented the man who was asked to apply the paint. Red Bird made the request, but his friend pretended to hesitate, finally extending both hands tightly closed. Lone Man then tried to open his friend's hands. After succeeding in this with seeming difficulty, he placed a pipe in them, which his friend accepted and smoked. After a few moments Red Bird asked for the return of the pipe, but was met with the same reluctance as before. Finally he was obliged to pry his friend's hands from the pipe as he had forced them open when the pipe was offered. This was said to constitute an agreement that one man would paint the body of the other, and in it the "artistic temperament" was typified in an unmistakable manner.

For four nights just before the Sun dance there were rehearsals of those who were to drum, sing, or dance, each person being carefully instructed in his part of the ceremony.

Announcements were made by the Crier, who was a picturesque and important figure in every tribal gathering. An old man was preferred, as it was said that "the old men were more careful than the young men in making the announcements." [1] Mounted on horseback, handsomely dressed, wearing a single eagle feather erect in his hair and carrying an eagle-wing fan, the Crier went the round of the camp circle, close to the tent doors, announcing the decisions of the council, the commands of the Intercessor, or the events of the day. He was also ready to answer any inquiries regarding the ceremony, as the Intercessor and the Leader of the Dancers were supposed to talk only when it was necessary for them to do so.

During the days immediately preceding the Sun dance it was customary for each military society to hold one or more dances called braves' dances, which were followed by feasts. The term "braves' dances" is a general one, referring to the dances of the various military societies. It was said that a dance of the Strong Heart society might be announced by the Crier in the following words:

Ĉaŋte' Tiŋ'za waŋ! I'mnahaŋ waya'tiŋ ktelo'. Hiyu' po! (Strong Hearts! You are going to eat to your hearts' content. Come on!)

In response to this summons the members of the Strong Heart society would come in finest array. This society was composed of warriors, and the leaders of the tribe were usually among its members. (See p. 329.) They paraded around the camp circle before the dance, singing the songs which they used on the warpath.

---

[1] The writer heard a Sioux Crier who was said to be 103 years old, but whose voice in announcing an evening council was as the sound of a trumpet, full, clear, and of wonderful carrying quality.

The following song was commonly used at the dances preceding a Sun dance. It is a "Chief song" and is analyzed with similar songs on page 462.

No. 5. "We Are Coming"   (Catalogue No. 456)

Sung by ŚIYA′KA

WORDS

kola′pila	friends
blihe′ićiya po	take courage
he lel	right here
oŋku′pi kiŋ	we are coming
waŋoŋ′yaŋka pelo′	they see us

Analysis—This melody is particularly forceful and direct. It is a song which would inspire confidence, and is also rhythmic for dancing. The tonic triad is emphasized, the song consisting only of the tonic triad and fourth. In one instance the fourth was accented and has no apparent chord relation to contiguous accented tones. The song is therefore classified as "melodic with harmonic framework," instead of "harmonic" in structure. Descending progressions are used effectively in this melody, the first rhythmic unit containing such progressions in double and the second in triple time. It is interesting to note throughout these songs the effect produced by slight changes in rhythm. For instance, in the first occurrence of the second rhythmic unit the second measure was sung in every rendition with two eighth notes on the second count. It will be seen that in other occurrences of this unit the first note of this measure is a dotted eighth. In all renditions of this song the time was increased with the introduction of the words, and the song closed in the original tempo. The return to this tempo was usually gradual, being made sooner in some renditions than in others. The time of the drum did not change with the increased tempo of the voice, the drum-rhythm being continuous, as indicated. Similar instances were noted among the Chippewa; these are considered in Bulletin 53, page 206. In the present work the following instances of change of time are found:

Songs in which the voice changes tempo, the song being recorded with drum, which is continuous and does not change in tempo—Nos. 5, 83, 114, 133, 188.

Songs in which the voice changes tempo, the song being recorded without drum—Nos. 55, 58, 88, 137, 140, 145, 153, 156, 166, 170, 171, 174. In this song occurs one instance of the omission of a syllable, the third syllable of bliheiċiya being omitted by the singer. Among other songs containing this peculiarity are Nos. 17, 38. The omission and addition of syllables was frequently noted in the Chippewa songs. Throughout the present work all interpolated syllables are indicated by italics. These cnanges in the words of songs represent an Indian custom and do not in any wise affect the meaning.

The following song was also used in the braves' dance; it is estimated to be about 180 years old, as the singer, who was a man past middle life, stated that his father said that his grandfather sang it. The age of a song can usually be determined in this manner with a fair degree of accuracy.

No. 6. Song of the Braves' Dance   (Catalogue No. 498)

Sung by RED BIRD

VOICE ♩= 80
DRUM ♩= 80
See drum-rhythm below

Drum-rhythm

Analysis.—This song is minor in tonality and contains all the tones of the octave except the sixth and second. In three instances the seventh is raised a semitone. Twelve tones are comprised in the compass of the song, which has a steadily descending trend. The song contains two rhythmic units, each occurring twice. As is usual in such instances, the rhythmic units resemble each other, the second seeming to be an "answering phrase."

The tree to be used for the sacred pole was selected and cut, and the sacred pole was decorated and raised on the morning of the day preceding the Sun dance. All the tribe were present when the four young men set out from the camp to select the tree. For some time before their departure the drummers and singers sang the songs of war, for the tree was regarded as something to be conquered. The following song might be sung as the people assembled. This song was composed by the singer, a man who is known in the tribe as a composer of war songs.

No. 7. "With Dauntless Courage"   (Catalogue No. 488)

Sung by Lone Man

VOICE ♩ = 96
DRUM not recorded

E - ća   o - zu - ye kiŋ - haŋ   tu - we - ni wa -

la - ke   śni   ća   bli - he - ći - ya   wa-oŋ   we - lo

WORDS

eća′ ozu′ye kiŋhaŋ′.......... on the warpath
tuwe′ni walake′ śni ća...... I give place to none
blihe′ićiya waöŋ′ welo′....... with dauntless courage I live

Analysis.—The descending interval of a fourth comprises more than a third of the entire number of intervals in this song. Three rhythmic units appear, and a comparison of them is of interest. The count-divisions of the first unit are reversed in the second. The third unit begins with two eighth notes, like the first, but these are followed by a reversal of the count-division found in the first unit. The ascent of a twelfth, which occurs with the introduction of the words, was given quite accurately, but the intonation on the measure containing the words *waöŋ′ welo′* was faulty, approaching a glissando in the descent from one tone to another.

The following song was frequently used in this connection, and was used also before the departure of a party going on the warpath or in search of buffalo:

No. 8. " The Many Lands You Fear "   (Catalogue No. 450)

Sung by Śiya′ka

VOICE ♩ = 104
DRUM ♩ = 96

Drum in accented eighth notes*

(1)

Ko - la   o - te ma-ko - ćе waŋ ko - ya-ki - pa - pi   he - na ko-

(2)

ki - pe   śni o - ma - wa - ni   e   u   i te - sa - bye ća o-wa-

le

*Drum-rhythm

WORDS

kola′..	friends
o′te mako′će............................	the many lands
koya′kipapi waŋ......................	you fear
hena′ koki′pe śni oma′wani..........	in them without fear I have walked
ite′sabye ća............................	the black face-paint (see p. 359.)
owa′le....................................	I seek

Analysis.—The principal interest of this song is in the number of minor thirds which it contains. The song contains 23 intervals 15 (about 54 per cent) of which are minor thirds. The minor third E–G is the framework of the opening measures, followed by the minor triad A–C–E; after a single measure of the tonic triad there is a return to the minor thirds A–C and E–G, the latter forming the closing interval of the song. The tones of the melody are those of the fourth five-toned scale, but the tonic triad appears only in the seventh measure. The song contains two rhythmic units, the count divisions of both being the same, but the accent being changed in the second unit. The first part of the song is based on the rhythmic unit, and the latter part on the second unit.

The relative time-duration of quarter notes in voice and drum, as given in the preceding song, are shown, by means of linear measurements, drawn to scale in the accompanying illustration.[1]

A Melody as transcribed above.
B Time of melody expressed in quarter notes.
C Time of drum expressed in quarter notes.
D Drumbeats as given by performer.

Comparison of the phonograph record with the metronome shows the speed of the voice to be equivalent to 104 quarter notes per minute ($\d=104$), while that of the drum is equivalent to only 96 quarter notes per minute ($\d=96$). If there were no deviation from regularity, there would be a coincidence of voice and drum at the fourteenth pulsation (quarter note) of the voice; this, however, is entirely theoretical, as a slight variation in either part would change the ratio between the two. In this and many similar instances it would appear that voice and drum represent separate impulses, expressed simultaneously, but having no time-relation to each other.

The following song of departure was reserved for use at the Sun dance; this was usually sung as the four young men left the camp for the woods to select the tree which should form the sacred pole . . .

No. 9. Song of the Departure of the Young Men (Catalogue No. 480)

Sung by LONE MAN

Voice = 96
Drum = 104
Drum-rhythm similar to No. 5

[1] The writer gratefully acknowledges her indebtedness to Mr. C. K. Wead, examiner, United States Patent Office, for suggestions concerning the above graphic representation.

Analysis.—This melody contains only the tones A flat–C–E flat–G flat. These are not the tones comprised in the key of A flat, as the term is used by musicians, but the sequence of the tones is such as to suggest A flat as a satisfactory tonic. A test by the ear seems permissible in such an instance as this, and the song is accordingly transcribed with A flat as its tonic and G flat as an accidental. The tonic triad constitutes the first seven measures of the melody, the descending fourth from the tonic to the dominant forming the outline of the remainder of the song, with the flatted seventh as an accidental. A rhythmic unit occurs, forming part of both double and triple measures. It is varied slightly in repetition, the second count being in some instances a quarter note and in others two eighth notes. The triplet on the first count, however, is distinctive and is steadily repeated. Two-thirds of the progressions are downward.

Any who wished to accompany the young men were permitted to do so, but they had no part in choosing the tree. On arriving at the woods the young men searched for a straight, slender tree. It was stated that cottonwood was preferred for the sacred pole and for all the articles of wood used in the Sun dance, because the white down of the cottonwood seed resembles the downy eagle feathers used in the ceremony.[1] If a cottonwood could not be obtained, elm was selected, because the elm is the first tree to blossom in the spring. The tree for the Sun-dance pole must be a standing tree and particularly fine with respect to straightness, branching, and fullness of leaf. It was required that the first tree selected should be cut, no change of choice being allowed. It is interesting to note that all articles devoted to a ceremonial use must be the best obtainable. A high standard of excellence prevailed among the Sioux, and this is especially shown in their ceremonies which expressed their highest ideals.

When the young men had decided on a tree they returned to make their report to the Intercessor. Their return had been anxiously awaited, and in response to their signal a number of friends went on horseback to meet them, riding around them in wide circles and escorting them to the camp. There they found their friends dancing around the drum and singing the following song, which was used also to welcome a returning war party or men who had gone in search of buffalo. After the singing and dancing a feast was provided by the friends of the young men. There was abundance of food, and all were invited to partake.

---

[1] Cottonwood was used also for the post in the spirit lodge. (See p. 81, also in offering placed on Sun-dance pole, p. 118.

No. 10. Song of the Return of the Young Men   (Catalogue No. 481)

Sung by LONE MAN

VOICE ♩= 112
DRUM ♩= 104
Drum-rhythm similar to No. 5

Analysis—An unusual feature of this song is that seven of the 12 intervals which it contains are fourths, four being ascending, and 3 descending, progressions. The tonic occurs only in the upper octave, the song closing on the dominant. The seventh and second tones of the octave are not found in the song, which is major in tonality and harmonic in structure.

The announcement of a choice was followed by preparation for cutting the tree and bringing it to the camp. The cutting of the tree for the Sun-dance pole was an important part of the ceremony, and many went to witness it. Some went from curiosity, and others wished to make offerings when the tree was cut. Even the children went to see the cutting of the pole. The young people, riding their fleet ponies, circled around the party. The leading members of the company were the Intercessor (or, in his absence, one of the old medicine-men), the four young men who selected the tree, the four young women who were to cut the tree, and the pole-bearers, who were to carry it. to the camp. It was the duty of the Leader of the Dancers to provide the ax with which the tree was felled, but he did not accompany the party who went to cut it. In the old days a primitive implement was used; in later times this was replaced by an ax purchased from the trader, but it was required that the ax be a new one, never used before.

Great interest centered in the selection of the tree, and when it was indicated by the young men the Intercessor raised his pipe, holding the stem toward the top of the tree and lowering it slowly to the earth, repeating a prayer in a low tone. When he held the pipe toward the top of the tree, he spoke of the kingbird; lowering it about one-third of the distance to the ground, he spoke of the eagle; lowering it half the remaining distance, he spoke of the yellow-hammer, and holding it toward the ground he spoke of the spider. The tree was regarded as an enemy, and in explanation of the reference to these animals it was said that "the kingbird, though small, is feared by all its enemies; the eagle is the boldest of birds; the yellowhammer can not overcome its enemies in open fight but is expert in dodging them, darting from one side of the tree-trunk to another; while the spider defeats its enemies by craftiness and cunning."

One of the four virgins was selected to cut the tree, but she did not fell it at once. It was considered that she had been given the honor of conquering an enemy, and before she wielded the ax a kinsman was permitted to relate one of his valiant deeds on the warpath. The maiden then lifted the ax and made a feint of striking the tree. Each of the four virgins did likewise, the action of each being preceded by the telling of a victory tale by one of her kinsmen. The ax was then returned to the first virgin, who swung it with effect, cutting the tree in such a manner that it fell toward the south (see p. 78). While the tree was being felled, no one was allowed near it except those who wielded the ax, the Intercessor, those who wished to make offerings, and those who were to carry the pole. At this time the following song was sung:

No. 11. Song of Cutting the Sacred Pole (Catalogue No. 451)

Sung by ŚIYA′KA

WORDS

(*First rendition*)

ite′sabye	the black face-paint (see p. 359.)
owa′le	I seek
ća he′ćamoŋ	therefore I have done this

(Second rendition)

suŋka′ke	horses
owa′le	I seek
ća he′ćamoŋ	therefore I have done this

Analysis.—This melody comprises the tones of the fourth five-toned scale. In two instances the sixth is lowered a semitone. A dotted eighth note either preceded or followed by a sixteenth note is a count division which characterizes the song, though it contains no rhythmic unit. This song begins on the third above the tonic and ends on the third in the lower octave. A beginning and ending on the dominant is of more frequent occurrence than on the third of the scale. A majority of both Sioux and Chippewa songs end on the tonic, which is also the lowest tone in the song. (See Table 3A, p. 27.)

Throughout this part of the ceremony the tree was regarded as an enemy, and a shout of victory arose as it swayed and fell. Care was taken that it should not touch the ground. The medicine men, some of whom usually accompanied the party, burned sweet grass, and offerings were presented. The branches of the tree were cut off close to the trunk except one branch about one-fourth of the distance from the top, which was left a few inches long in order that the crossbar of the pole might be fastened to it. In some cases a small branch with leaves on it was also left at the top of the pole. From this time the pole was regarded as sacred and no one was allowed to step over it, or over any of the branches which had been cut from it. Jealousy frequently arose among the women in regard to the privilege of cutting the tree, and it is said that on one occasion a woman was so angry because she was not chosen for the purpose that she stepped over the pole. Half an hour later she was thrown from her horse, dragged some distance, and killed. The horse was known to be a gentle animal, and the event was considered a punishment justly visited on the woman.

Between 20 and 40 men were required to carry the sacred pole to the camp. These walked two abreast, each pair carrying between them a stick about 2 feet long on which the pole rested as on a litter. The pole was carried with the top in advance, and the Intercessor or his representative walked behind the bearers. No one was allowed to walk before the sacred pole.

The songs of carrying home the pole were songs of victory. The following song could be used at any time after the pole had been cut and was frequently sung as it was carried to the camp:

No. 12. Song of Victory over the Sacred Pole (Catalogue No. 486)

Sung by LONE MAN

VOICE ♩= 144

DRUM 𝅗𝅥 = 72

See drum-rhythm below

Miś - na - la wi - ma - ća   ye - lo e - he - ćoŋ wi

ća - ya - ke śni ye na - ke će - ya i - la - le

Drum-rhythm

WORDS (ADDRESSED TO THE SACRED POLE)

miśna'la wima'ća yelo'....... "I only am a man"
ehe'ćoŋ wića'yake śni ye... you falsely implied
nake' će'ya ila'le............. now you cry

Analysis.—The rhythmic unit of this song is less interesting than the rhythm of the song as a whole, which has a decided "swing." The melody begins on the fifth above the tonic and ends on the third in the lower octave. Many songs have a greater range than this, but few have a compass of a tenth in three measures, as occurs in this song with the introduction of the words. This part of the song was sung quite accurately, but in the measures containing the last two words and in the corresponding measures of the first section of the song the intonation was so unsteady as to make transcription difficult. It has been frequently noted among the Sioux, as among the Chippewa, that large intervals are sung with more accuracy than small ones. The drumbeat was in half notes, representing a very slow tempo. In the double measures the drumbeat coincided quite regularly with the corresponding tone of the song.

Around the pole-bearers circled the young men and women of the tribe on their ponies. It was the custom of the young people to decorate their ponies with trailing vines and to wreathe the vines around their own bodies. They made hoops of slender branches, with crossbars like the framework of a shield, and on this they draped vines and leaves, thus forming a striking contrast to the dignified procession of pole-bearers.

Four times on the way to the camp the pole-bearers were allowed to rest. (See p. 74.) The signal for each halt—a throbbing call beginning on a high tone and descending like a wail—was given by the Intercessor. At this signal, the pole was lowered for a few moments upon crotched sticks provided for the purpose.

The sacred pole was brought into the Sun-dance circle as it had been carried, with the top in advance. As the pole-bearers walked across the circle the medicine-men cried, "Now is the time to make a wish or bring an offering." The people crowded forward, shouting and offering gifts of various kinds. So great excitement prevailed that no one knew who brought a gift, and a man could scarcely hear his own voice.

The Intercessor then prepared the sacred pole, first removing the rough outer bark, fragments of which were eagerly seized and carried away by the people. After the pole had been made sufficiently smooth, it was painted by the Intercessor; native red paint or vermilion [1] was used. The pole was painted in perpendicular stripes, beginning at the branch where the cross bar would be fastened and extending to the base.

As the Intercessor painted the sacred pole, he sang the following song, which, like the other songs pertaining to his ceremonial office, was sung alone and without the drum, the people listening attentively:

---

[1] On the Standing Rock Reservation is found a yellow ocherous substance which, after being reduced to a fine powder, is used by the Indians in making yellow paint. This substance, when treated by means of heat, yields the vermilion used on all ceremonial articles as well as in painting the bodies of the Indians. The baking of this ocherous substance—a process which requires skill—is done by the women. First, the substance mixed with water is formed into a ball. A hole is dug in the ground in which a fire of oak bark is made. When the ground is baked, the coals are removed, the ball is placed in the hole, and a fire is built above it. This fire is maintained at a gentle, even heat for about an hour, which is sufficient for the amount of the substance usually prepared at a time. The action of the heat changes the color of the substance to red. When the ball is cold, it is pounded to powder. In the old days this red powder was mixed with buffalo fat in making the paint, but at the present time it is mixed with water. White, black, and blue paints were obtained by mixing colored earthy substances with buffalo fat. The blue was found in southern Minnesota (this required no treatment by heat), and the white and black in Dakota. (See p. 173.) It is said that white paint was preferred for the painting of horses (see p. 353) because it was a "genuine color," and also because other colors could be applied to advantage above it. Brown earth is mentioned in song No. 62. The symbolisms of various colors used in paint are noted on pp. 77 and 124.

No. 13. Song of Painting the Sacred Pole   (Catalogue No. 452)

Sung by ŚIYA'KA

VOICE ♩ = 160

DRUM ♩ = 80

Drum-rhythm similar to No. 12

A - te le - na   ta - wa ma - ki - ye   a - te le -

na   ta - wa ma-ki - ye   ćaŋ ma-ko - ba - za na - źiŋ hi -

ye - ya ćiŋ a - te le - na   ta-wa ma - ki - ye

a - te le - na   ta - wa ma-ki - ye   ćaŋ ma-ko-ba - za na -

źiŋ hi - ye - ye ćiŋ a - te le - na   ta - wa ma - ki - ye

WORDS

ate′	father
lena′ ta′wa maki′ye	all these he has made me own
ćaŋ mako′baza	the trees and the forests
na′źiŋ	standing
hiye′ye ćiŋ	in their places

Analysis.—This melody contains only the tones of the minor triad and fourth. The rhythmic unit is long, its repetitions comprising the entire song except two periods of six measures each, which consist principally of quarter notes. The sustained tones were always given the indicated time. The words are continuous throughout the song. Among the Chippewa, as well as among the Sioux, this occurs more often in "medicine songs" than in other classes of songs. The final tone, though very low in pitch, was sung with distinctness.

The Sun-dance pole was usually about 35 feet in length and 6 to 8 inches in diameter. A crossbar "the length of a man" was tied on the pole, being securely fastened to the short branch left for the purpose. At the intersection of the pole and the crossbar there was tied with rawhide thongs a bag, which constituted one of the offerings made by the Leader of the Dancers. This bag was about 2 feet square, made of rawhide decorated with beads, tassels, and fringe, and was wrapped in cherry branches 4 or 5 feet long which completely concealed it. Inside the bag was a smaller bag of tanned buffalo hide containing the offering, which consisted of a large piece of buffalo hump, on a sharpened stick painted red. The stick was cottonwood and, according to Mato'-kuwa' (Chased-by-Bears), symbolized the arrow with which the buffalo had been killed and also the picket stake to which a horse stolen from an enemy was fastened when it was being brought to the camp. The additional offerings fastened to the crossbar were two effigies (see pl. 21) cut from rawhide, one in the form of an Indian and the other in the form of a buffalo, indicating that the enemy and also the buffalo had been conquered by supernatural help. To the crossbar were fastened also the thongs, or cords, by which the men would be suspended. One cord was made ready for each man, the middle of it being fastened to the crossbar and the two ends hanging, to be fastened to the sticks passed through the flesh of the man's chest. At the top of the pole was hung a tanned robe of buffalo calfskin. In the later ceremonies a banner of red list cloth was used instead of the buffalo robe.

After painting the sacred pole, the Intercessor examined the hole which had been prepared for its erection, in which he placed an abundance of buffalo fat. It was said that, while doing this, he "prayed and talked in a low voice."

The command to raise the pole was followed by absolute silence on the part of the assembled people. Thus they watched the pole as it was raised slowly and carefully by the men who had brought it to the camp. The moment it was in place all gave way to cheers and rejoicing, and the three following songs were sung. These three songs were recorded by a man said to be the only Teton Sioux living (1911) who had filled the office of Intercessor. These songs comprised part of the instructions he received from the man who preceded him in that office. The singer was about 80 years of age when the songs were recorded. (See p. 88.)

No. 14. Song Sung after Raising the Sacred Pole (a)   (Catalogue No. 628)

Sung by RED WEASEL

VOICE ♩ = 63

Recorded without drum

WORDS (NOT TRANSCRIBED)

(*The pole speaks*)

wakaŋ′yaŋ.................................. sacred
nawa′źiŋ ye................................ I stand
waŋma′yaŋka yo........................... behold me
ema′kiye ćoŋ.............................. was said to me

Analysis.—The conciseness of this melody is interesting, especially
in view of the fact that it was sung by an aged man, who said he
learned it in his youth. The rhythmic units are clear-cut, and their
repetitions comprise the entire song except two short parts somewhat similar to each other. Both intonation and time were remarkably good, considering the age of the singer. His voice was as strong
as that of a young man. This has been noted by the writer to be the
case among old men who, in their younger days, were accustomed to
address large numbers of people on the open prairie. Red Weasel,
who had held responsible positions in tribal ceremonies, had developed this quality of voice. In this connection the pitch of his songs
should be noted.

This melody contains all the tones of the octave except the
seventh. In structure it is classified as melodic with harmonic
framework. About two-thirds of the intervals are downward
progressions, the principal accented tones being those of the descending series A, F sharp, D, B, F sharp. Only two ascending progressions appear between accented tones.

No. 15. Song after Raising the Sacred Pole (b)   (Catalogue No. 629)

Sung by RED WEASEL

VOICE ♩ = 66
DRUM not recorded

WORDS (NOT TRANSCRIBED)

(*The pole speaks*)

maka′ ćokaŋ′yaŋ.............. at the center of the earth [1]
wa′kil na′źiŋ po.............. stand looking around you
oya′te iye′kiya................ recognizing the tribe
wa′kil na′źiŋ po.............. stand looking around you

---

[1] This is an instance of the "sacred language" mentioned on p. 85. A language of this kind was said to be necessary in order that persons intimate with supernatural things could communicate without being understood by the common people. The term "center of the earth" occurs in a narrative on p. 214 and also in song No. 137, translated as follows: "At the center of the earth I stand . . . at the wind center (where the winds blow toward me from every side) I stand." Songs Nos. 16 and 75 mention the places whence the winds blow, the former containing the words "at the places of the four winds may you be reverenced," and the latter, "At the four places . . . the places from which the winds blow . . . to stand I was required:" also "the homes of the four winds," p. 127. The following instances may also be cited: An expression similar to this occurs in song No. 93—*ćaŋte′ mato′kćaćeća*, also translated "with a heart that is different," but carrying the idea of the fierceness of a bear. The term *yatin′kte*, literally translated "you will eat," is a phrase used only by medicine-men when addressing the sick (song No. 57). The words "a scarlet relic" in song No. 1 refer to the custom of spirit keeping and would not be understood by those who were unfamiliar with that ceremony. The term "grandfather" is found in No. 21, which is the opening prayer of the Sun dance. The word *tunkaŋ′*, 'sacred stones,' is said to be derived from *tuŋka′sila*, 'grandfather.' (See p. 205.) In songs Nos. 41, 93, and 105 there is shown something approaching the personification of a wind and a rainbow, the idea being that these possess or wear the man who has dreamed of them and has not

Analysis.—This song contains two rhythmic units, but the rhythmic structure of the song differs from that of most songs under analysis in that these two units appear to have no influence on each other. The first is in triple, the second in double, time, and none of the count-divisions are alike. The song is melodic in structure and contains the tones of the fourth five-toned scale. The descending fourth from the tonic to the dominant occurs with frequency.

No. 16. Song Sung after Raising the Sacred Pole (c)   (Catalogue No. 630)

Sung by Red Weasel

VOICE ♩ = 76
DRUM not recorded

WORDS (NOT TRANSCRIBED)

tuŋka′ŝila	grandfather
to′pakiya	at the places of the four winds (see p. 120, footnote).
wakaŋ′ nila′pi nuŋwe′	may you be reverenced
ta′ku koyag′ mayaye′	you made me wear something sacred
oya′te waŋ wakaŋ′yaŋ yaŋka′pi	the tribe sitting in reverence
niwa′ćiŋpi	they wish to live

yet enacted his dream, even as a medicine-man wears an object, or the symbol of an object, which is subject to his commands. Thus No. 41 contains the words, "a wind wears me"; No. 93, "a wind comes to get me;" and No. 105, "a hoop (rainbow) wears me." The term *wahu′noŋ′pa*, or its abbreviation *hu noŋ′pa*, literally "two-legged object," is used by those who treat the sick as referring to a human being (Nos. 76, 90) and the term *ćaŋte′to′kĕća*, 'a heart that is different,' is used by them to indicate anger. (Songs Nos. 58, 93.) The phrases "in a sacred manner," or "I have made it sacred," are not unusual and can not be regarded as an adequate translation of the Sioux. In the mind of the Sioux the meaning of the word *wakaŋ* contains more of mystery and a greater element of the supernatural than we are accustomed to associate with the words "sacred" or "holy," though these are used as its English equivalent. (See footnote, p. 88.)

Analysis.—Two intervals of a fourth form the framework of this melody, the first being C–F and the second G–C. The tonic is especially prominent, as it occurs in both these intervals and is frequently repeated. The song is minor in tonality and contains only the tones of the minor triad and fourth. A monotony in the melody is shown by the fact that it contains 27 measures and only 12 progressions. It has been noted that the average number of progressions in this class of songs is 31.3. The rhythmic unit occurs six times and its count-divisions were clearly given by the singer.

The sacred pole was placed in such a manner that the crossbar extended north and south, and the earth was packed solidly around the base.

The dance enclosure was about 50 feet in diameter, with a wide entrance at the east. (See p. 93.) The sacred pole stood in the center of this circle, and about 15 feet west of the pole a square of earth was exposed, all vegetation being carefully removed and the ground finely pulverized. This square of earth was called *owaŋ'ka wakaŋ'*, "sacred place," and no one was allowed to pass between it and the pole.[1] Two intersecting lines were traced within the square of earth, forming a cross, these lines being parallel to the sides of the square but not touching them.[2] After tracing these lines in the soil, the Intercessor filled the incisions with tobacco which had been offered to the sky, the earth, and the cardinal points. He then covered the tobacco with vermilion paint-powder, over which he spread shining white "mica dust."[3] At the intersection and ends of the lines he placed bunches of downy white eagle feathers. Very beautiful was the contrast of green turf, soft brown earth, shining white lines, and downy eagle feathers. West of this was placed a bed of fresh sage, on which the buffalo skull would be laid during the ceremony. (Pls. 16, 17.)

The Intercessor sang the following song as he prepared the square of earth. When this and similar songs were sung by the Intercessor, there was absolute silence in the great gathering of people.

---

[1] Miss Fletcher states (in *Peabody Mus. Reps.*, III, p. 284, note, Cambridge, 1887): "The mellowed earth space . . . has never been absent from any religious exercise I have yet seen or learned of from the Indians. It represents the unappropriated life or power of the earth, hence man may obtain it."

[2] Concerning this outline, which is widely used by the Indians, Mr. W. H. Holmes writes (in Handbook Amer. Inds., pt. 1, p. 366): "Primitive man adjusts himself to his environment, real and imaginary, by keeping in mind the cardinal points as he understands them. When the Indian considers the world about him, he thinks of it as divided into four quarters, and when he communicates with the mysterious beings and powers with which his imagination peoples it—the rulers of the winds and rains—he turns his face to the four directions in stipulated order and addresses them to make his appeals and his offerings. Thus his worship, his ceremonies, his games, and even his more ordinary occupations in many cases are arranged to conform to the cardinal points, and the various symbolic representations associated with them assume the form of the cross."

[3] A specimen of the "mica" was secured, and was identified as "Gypsum, variety Selenite," by Dr. G. S. Merrill, curator of the department of geology of the U. S. National Museum.

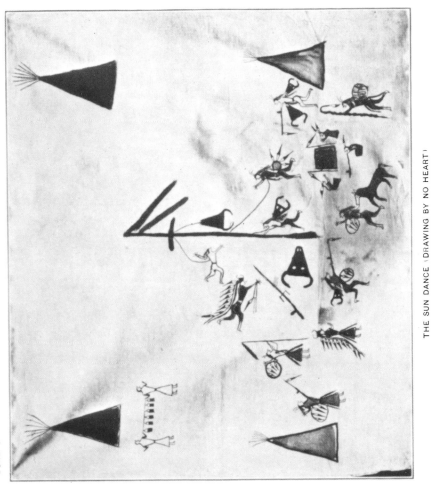

THE SUN DANCE (DRAWING BY NO HEART)

THE SUN DANCE (NATIVE DRAWINGS)
A. BY EAGLE SHIELD
B. BY JAW

No. 17. Song of Preparing the Sacred Place   (Catalogue No. 500)

Sung by RED BIRD

VOICE ♩ = 60
DRUM not recorded

To-pa- ki - ya ma-ka- ta   ćе-wa - ki ye - lo   e   to-pa- ki - ya ma-ka-

ta će-wa - ki ye - lo   e   o-waŋ-ka ka - ġiŋ kta   ća   o - ya -

te waŋ-la-ka pe-lo   e   to-pa-ki- ya ma-ka-ta će-wa-ki ye-lo   e

WORDS

to'pakiya maka'ta će'waki yelo'..	four times to the earth I prayed
owaŋ'ka	a place
waka'ġiŋ kta ća.................	I will prepare
oya'te...........................	O tribe
waŋla'ka pelo'...................	behold

Analysis—All the tones of the octave except the fourth occur in this melody, which is minor in tonality and melodic in structure. A feeling for the tonic triad is evident throughout the song, but there is more freedom of progression than in many of the songs under analysis. The second of the key is unusually prominent, and the progressions in the sixth and seventh measures are interesting, as they include the tonic and the tone immediately above and below it. About two-thirds of the intervals are downward progressions.

After the sacred pole was erected and the "sacred place" prepared, a shelter, or "shade-house," was built entirely around the Sundance circle, any who wished to share in this work being permitted to do so. Posts about 6 feet high were erected, and upon these were placed a light framework of poles. This framework was covered with buffalo hides and decorated with freshly cut boughs. Beneath this shade sat the old people, the relatives of the dancers, and any who attended the ceremony merely as spectators.

On the morning of the Sun dance those who were to take part in the ceremony were allowed to eat a full meal, after which they entered the vapor lodge while the following song was sung:

No. 18. Song of Final Visit to the Vapor Lodge (Catalogue No. 631)

Sung by Red Weasel

Drum ♩= 63
Drum not recorded

WORDS (NOT TRANSCRIBED)

ho	a voice
u wa′yin kte	I will send
nama′hon ye	hear me
maka′	the land
sito′mniyaŋ	all over
ho	a voice
ye waye′lo	I am sending
nama′hon ye	hear me
wani′ ktelo′	I will live

Analysis.—This song contains 20 measures and only 15 progressions. In its lack of progression it resembles Nos. 14, 15, and 16, rendered by the same singer. (See analysis of No. 16.) Two-thirds of the progressions are downward, the song beginning on the dominant above the tonic and ending on the dominant below the tonic. The melody contains the tones of the second five-toned scale and is melodic in structure.

After their vapor bath, the dancers were painted by the men whom they had selected for that purpose. A few of the writer's informants stated that the bodies of the dancers were painted white on the first day of the ceremony, the colors being added on the morning of the second day, but others, including Ituŋ′kasaŋ-lu′ta (Red Weasel) stated positively that the painting in colors was done before the opening of the dance. Red Bird stated that each man who was accustomed to paint the dancers had a special color, which was "associated with his dream," and that he used this color first in the painting. The colors employed were red (the "tribal color"), blue, yellow, white, and black, each color being a symbolism connected with the sky. Thus, it was said that red corresponds to the red clouds of sunset, which indicate fair weather; blue represents the cloudless sky; yellow, the forked lightning; white corresponds to the

SUN-DANCE WHISTLE

light; and black was used for everything associated with night, even the moon being painted black because it belonged to the hours of darkness. (See p. 77, footnote.)

Śiya'ka (Teal Duck) stated that when he took part in the Sun dance his face and body were painted yellow, with dark-blue lines extending down the arms and branching at the wrist to lines which terminated at the base of the thumb and the little finger. Similar lines extended down the legs, branching at the ankles. There was also a dark-blue line across his forehead and down each cheek. A black deer's head was painted over his mouth, the man who painted him saying that this decoration he used because the deer could endure thirst for a long time without losing its strength. On his chest was painted a red disk representing the sun, and outlining this disk he wore a hoop of wood wound with otter fur and decorated with four white eagle feathers tipped with black. (See p. 139.) On his back was painted a dark crescent representing the moon. Bands of rabbit fur were worn around the wrists and ankles.

Those who took part in the Sun dance wore their hair loose on the shoulders after the manner of men who had recently killed an enemy. A lock of hair was tied at the back of the head and to this was fastened upright a white downy eagle feather. Small sticks about 8 inches long were also fastened in the hair, four being the usual number. These sticks were decorated with porcupine quills, beads, and tassels. (Fig. 22.) A dancer was not allowed to touch his body during the ceremony, the decorated sticks being taken from his hair and used for that purpose.

No moccasins were worn by the dancers. Each man wore a white deerskin apron (nite'iyapehe), which was fastened at the waist and extended below the knees both front and back; he had also a robe of buffalo skin in which he was wrapped while going to the Sun-dance circle and returning to his lodge. A whistle was hung around his neck by a cord. This whistle was made of the wingbone of an eagle, wound with braiding of porcupine quills and tipped with a downy white eagle feather fastened above the opening so that the breath of the dancer moved the snowy filaments. The mouthpiece was surrounded with fresh sage. The man blew this whistle as he danced. The instrument (illustrated in pl. 18) was decorated by the woman who decorated the Sun-dance pipe.[1]

After being painted and arrayed, the men who were to take part in the ceremony assembled in the dancers' lodges of their respective bands and awaited the summons of the Crier.

---

[1] The bone of this whistle was identified at the U. S. National Museum as the ulna of the golden eagle (Aquila chrysaetus). The specimen is thus described by Mr. E. H. Hawley, curator of musical instruments: "Length, 8 inches; average diameter, $\frac{7}{16}$ inch. It has a triangular sound hole, its apex toward the lower or open end, which is $4\frac{1}{8}$ inches distant. To the lower end of the whistle is sewed with sinew a fluffy eagle feather $13\frac{3}{4}$ inches long. This feather grows under the tail-feathers of an eagle." (Cf. p. 98.)

The Leader of the Dancers was with the Intercessor in the council tent. His costume was not necessarily different from that of the dancers. Chased-by-Bears stated that when acting as Leader of the Dancers he was painted white with black streaks across his forehead and down his cheeks. The deerskin *nite'iyapehe* which he wore was elaborately wrought with porcupine quills by the women among his relatives, who wished to do the work although such decoration was not required.

The costume worn by an Intercessor was somewhat similar to that of the dancers, but on his wrists and ankles he frequently wore bands of buffalo skin on which the hair was loosening, and his robe was the skin of a buffalo killed at the time when it was shedding its hair. Bits of hair shed by the buffalo were tied to his own hair (see pp. 64, 458), and he wore buffalo horns on his head, or he might wear a strip of buffalo skin fastened to his hair and hanging down his back. (See pl. 19.) In contrast to the dancers his hair was braided, but like them he wore one white downy eagle feather. His face and hands were painted red. The

FIG. 22. Decorated stick worn in Sun dance.

costume of an Intercessor varied slightly with the individual, Red Weasel stating that he wore otter skin around his wrists and ankles, that the braids of his hair were wound with otter skin, and that he wore a shirt of buffalo hide trimmed with human hair, which was supposed to represent the hair of an enemy.

On the morning of the day appointed for the Sun dance the Crier went around the camp circle, announcing the opening of the ceremony in the following words: "Wana' u po. Wana' yuśtanpe. Inali'ni po!" ("Now all come. Now it is finished. Hasten!")

In the procession which approached the Sun-dance circle the Intercessor was the most prominent figure, the others acting as his escort. The Intercessor held before him with uplifted stem his

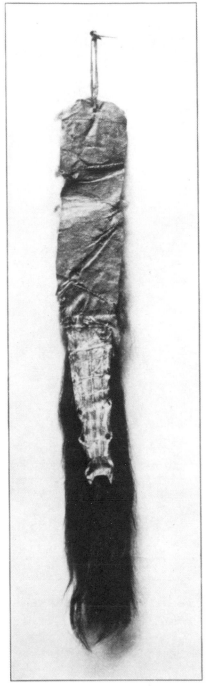

HAIR ORNAMENT OF BUFFALO HIDE WORN IN SUN DANCE

CEREMONIAL GROUPING OF ARTICLES IN SUN DANCE

Sun-dance pipe, which would be smoked during the ceremony.　The Leader of the Dancers walked beside him, carrying the ceremonial buffalo skull, which had been painted with stripes of red extending from the nostrils to the horns.　Near him walked some close relative or friend, who carried the Leader's sealed pipe, which would be placed with the buffalo skull beside the square of exposed earth. Those who were to fulfill their vows walked on either side of the Intercessor and the Leader of the Dancers, and around them were the war societies and other organizations of the tribe.　On reaching the entrance of the Sun-dance circle the procession paused.　The Intercessor directed the attention of the people to the east, and it was understood that each man offered a silent prayer; this action was repeated toward the south, the west, and the north, after which they entered the inclosure.　Amid impressive silence the procession passed along the southern "side" of the circle to the western "side," where the Leader of the Dancers, pausing, laid the buffalo skull on the bed of sage, with its face toward the east.　He then placed his sealed pipe in its ceremonial position, the bowl resting on the buffalo skull and the stem supported by a slight frame of sticks painted blue (see pp. 64, 72), the mouthpiece of the pipe being extended toward the Sun-dance pole (pl. 20).　When the Intercessor rose to sing or pray, he held this pipe in his hand, afterward replacing it in its ceremonial position; it was also extended toward the sky, the earth, and the cardinal points, but the seal on it was not broken until after the ceremony.

The pipe which was smoked at the ceremony was that of the Intercessor.　He first burned sweet grass, the ascending smoke of which was said to symbolize prayer.[1]　Then he lit the· pipe, and extended the stem toward the sky, the earth, and the cardinal points.　The following explanation of this action was given by Wakiŋ'yaŋ-wata'-kpe (Charging Thunder): "When we hold the pipe toward the sky, we are offering it to Wakaŋ'taŋka.　We offer it to the earth because that is our home and we are thankful to be here; we offer it to the east, south, west, and north because those are the homes of the four winds; a storm may come from any direction, therefore we wish to make peace with the winds that bring the storms."　After this action, the Intercessor, having first smoked the pipe himself, offered it to the Leader and all the dancers.　This procedure was repeated at infrequent intervals during the period of dancing.

Beside the Sun-dance pole the men who were to fulfill their vows stood facing the sun, with hands upraised.　The Intercessor cried, "Repent, repent!",[2] whereupon a cry of lamentation rose from the entire assembly.

---

[1] See article *Incense*, by James Mooney, in Handbook Amer. Inds., pt. 1, p. 604.

[2] Certain features of the ceremony seem to show the influence of Christian teaching.　See footnoe p. 88.

The opening song of the ceremony was sung three times with a tremolo drumbeat, after which the drum changed to a definite, even stroke, and the men began to dance with faces still turned toward the sun and with hands upraised.

No. 19. Opening Song of the Sun Dance (a)   (Catalogue No. 453)

Sung by ŚIYA'KA

* Drum-rhythm

Analysis.—This transcription shows the song and also the manner in which it was changed by the singer in repetition. Thus the song itself ends with the third measure preceding the change of time, and only that part of the transcription is considered in the analysis. In songs expressive of desire it is not unusual for the tempo to be increased with repetitions of the song (see p. 481). Thus the second tempo in this instance is faster than the first. Comparing the two portions of the transcription, we note a persistence of important and slight changes in unimportant phrases, a peculiarity which has been frequently noted in the musical performances of both Chippewa and Sioux. Contrasted with these instances are those in which many renditions of the song are identical in every respect.

This song is transcribed and analyzed in the key of D minor, though the second and fifth of that key are not present. The melody is broadly outlined by the descending intervals F–C, C–F, F–D, with a return to F at the close. One accidental occurs—the fourth lowered a semitone. The number of downward and upward intervals is about equal, there being 25 of the former and 22 of the latter in the song.

The following song also could be used at this time:

No. 20. Opening Song of the Sun Dance (b)   (Catalogue No. 479)

Sung by LONE MAN

VOICE ♩= 80
DRUM ♩= 84
Drum-rhythm similar to No. 19

Analysis.—The rhythmic unit occurs twice at the opening of this song, the latter part of the song showing an accented sixteenth note in several measures but having little rhythmic interest. The purpose of the latter part seems to be merely the carrying of the melody down to the final tone. The range of the melody is 13 tones. Only 11 per cent of the Chippewa songs have a compass of more than 12 tones, and a similar range is found in only 10 per cent of the present series. (See Table 5A, p. 28.) This song is minor in tonality, lacking only the sixth tone of the complete octave.

During the excitement of the opening dance many gifts were given to the poor or exchanged among the people, and many "paid their respects" to the parents of young men who were taking part in the dance for the first time.

The drum used in the Sun dance was placed south of the pole. It was a large dance drum of the usual type and elaborately decorated, the sides being hung with bead work and fur, and the supports wound with beads and fur. In addition to the drum a stiff rawhide was beaten. This gave to the accompaniment of the songs a peculiar quality of tone, which marked a difference between that of the ordinary dances and that of a religious ceremony. The men who had carried the sacred pole were seated at the drum and the rawhide, together with special singers, both men and women, the latter sitting behind the men and forming an outer circle. The voices of the women singers were an octave higher than the voices of the men.

The Intercessor was seated west of the "sacred place" during the entire ceremony. The Leader of the Dancers was with the others who were fulfilling their vows, but during the brief periods of rest which were allowed the dancers he lay on the ground at the west of the "sacred place," face downward, with his head pressed against the top of the buffalo skull. (See p. 97.)

The man who had spoken the vow for a war party assumed some responsibility in the proper fulfillment of their vows, and the dancers were attended by the men who had painted them. All who took part in the dance were required to abstain from food and water during the entire period of dancing.

At the conclusion of the opening dance the following prayer was sung by the Intercessor, all the people listening with reverence:

No. 21. Opening Prayer of the Sun Dance   (Catalogue No. 501)

Sung by RED BIRD

VOICE ♩ = 168
DRUM not recorded

Tuŋ-ka-śi-la   ho u-wa-yiŋ kte   tuŋ-ka-śi-la

ho   u-wa-yiŋ kte na-ma-ḣoŋ ye   ma-ka si-to-mni-

yaŋ   ho   u-wa-yiŋ   kte   na-ma-ḣoŋ   ye

tuŋ-ka-śi-la   wa-ni kte-lo   e-pe-lo

WORDS

tuŋka′śila	grandfather. (See p. 120, footnote)
ho uwa′yiŋ kte	a voice I am going send
nama′hon ye	hear me
maka′ sito′mniyaŋ	all over the universe
ho uwa′yiŋ kte	a voice I am going to send
nama′hon ye	hear me
tuŋka′śila	grandfather
wani′ ktelo′	I will live
epelo′	I have said it

Analysis.—Peculiar strength is given this melody by the fact that a quarter note is the shortest note occurring in the rhythmic unit. The time of the sustained tones was accurate in all the renditions. Two-thirds of the progressions are downward, the melody beginning on the fifth above the tonic and ending on the third in the lower octave. All the tones of the octave are found in the song, which is minor in tonality and melodic in structure. The words are continuous. As already stated, continuous words are found most frequently in songs connected with "medicine."

A man might take part in the Sun dance in one of six ways, according to the nature of his vow. The requirement of fasting was the same in every vow. The first way of taking part in the Sun dance consisted merely in dancing, the second added a laceration of the flesh, and the other four required that a stick be thrust through the flesh and strain placed upon it until the flesh tore or was cut. The Indians stated that the stick, or skewer, was "put through the skin," and probably it pierced also the subcutaneous fascia.[1] The two most common forms of this treatment consisted in the piercing of the flesh over the chest with skewers attached by cords to the crossbar of the sacred pole, and the fastening of buffalo skulls to the flesh of the back and arms. The two more severe and less employed forms were the suspending of the entire body by the flesh of the back, and the fastening of the flesh of both back and chest to four poles at some distance from the body, the poles being placed at the corners of a square.[2]

If a horse had carried a man on the warpath when his vow was made, the man might fasten the horse to the thong by which he was suspended from the pole, thus hastening his release, or he might fasten in a similar manner the bridle and whip which he carried on

---

[1] As the word "skin" is commonly applied to the cuticle, the word "flesh" is used in this chapter as indicating more clearly the severity of the ordeal.

[2] In this connection it should be borne in mind that the present memoir concerns only the customs of the Teton Sioux, as described by members of that tribe who took part in the dance.

the warpath, or he might hold the bridle and whip in his hand as he danced.   Chased-by-Bears stated that in fulfilling his first Sun-dance vow he caused a skewer to be put through the flesh of his arm and from it suspended the rawhide lariat which he carried when on the warpath, and with which he later captured a horse.   (See p. 97.)

Women sometimes took part in the Sun dance by fasting and standing beside some relative who was dancing, or by assuming part of the obligation of a vow made by some relative and permitting their arms to be cut.   (See p. 135.)   The gifts distributed by relatives of the dancers and the feasts given in their honor were also the work of the women.

Even the simplest form of the Sun-dance was a severe test of a man's endurance.   He was required to abstain from food and water, to dance with face upraised to the sun from morning until night, and to continue dancing during the night and on the following day until he fell exhausted.[1]

If he had vowed to have his arms cut, he left the line of dancers and seated himself beside the pole for the operation, after which he resumed his dancing.   The number of cuts varied from 10 to 100 or even 200, according to the man's vow, though if the vow required the larger numbers named part of the number was usually assumed by his relatives.   The cutting was done by a man of experience, to whom the dancer gave one or more horses.   The man had an assist-ant, who lifted a small portion of flesh on the point of an awl, where-upon the man then severed it with a quick stroke of a knife, lifting the first portion which he cut toward the sky, saying, ''This man promised to give you his flesh; he now fulfills his vow.''   (See p. 96.) The cuts were usually placed close together.   The writer has seen ·the scars of a man whose arms were cut 100 times—small dots on the upper arm, about half an inch apart, in regular order.

Another manner of cutting the arm was by gashes, which left broad white scars.   As already stated, the relatives of a man might assume part of the obligation of his vow by allowing their arms to be cut.   Thus Lone Man said that he vowed 200 gashes, but his relatives divided half the number among themselves.

If a man vowed that he would be suspended from the pole the operation of fastening the thongs to his chest was as follows: The dancer lay on the ground, and the man who performed the operation, bending over him, lifted the flesh of the chest between his thumb and finger; then thrusting an awl through the flesh, he followed this with the insertion of the pointed stick.   This stick was painted blue, and the man moistened it with his lips before inserting it in the flesh. He then lifted the man to his feet and tied the thongs hanging from the crossbar of the pole to the sticks in the man's flesh.   Medicine was applied if the bleeding was excessive.   In old days the awl used in this operation was of bone.   Chased-by-Bears, who performed this

---

[1] Intervals permitted for rest are noted on p. 134.

BULLETIN 61 PLATE 21

EFFIGIES

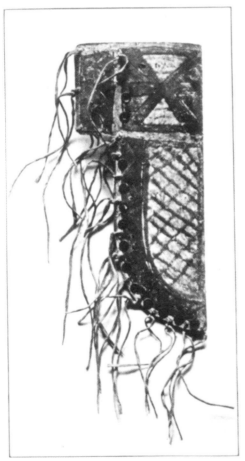

KNIFE CASE

KNIFE

ARTICLES USED IN SUN DANCE

office many times in the Sun dance, stated that he used a knife, the blade being ground to a point, and the handle and part of the blade being wrapped with rawhide (pl. 21).

The thongs by which a man was suspended were usually of a length permitting only his toes to touch the ground, though the height of the suspension depended somewhat upon the man's physical strength. When first suspended each man was given a stick by means of which he might raise his body slightly to ease the strain upon the flesh of his chest. After discarding this support any effort at rest or any cessation of the motion of dancing only increased the suffering.

The men were suspended soon after 9 o'clock in the morning on the north side of the pole in such a position that their upraised faces were in the full glare of the sun. It was expected that they would make an effort to free themselves as soon as possible. Sometimes this was accomplished in half an hour, and according to John Grass and other informants a man seldom remained in that position more than an hour. If he was unable to tear the flesh in that time by means of the motion of dancing, he might give horses for his release, or his relatives might give them in his behalf. In that event the man who had done the cutting was allowed to cut through the flesh either partially or entirely. If a considerable time elapsed and the man could not free himself, and neither he nor his relatives could give the requisite horses, he was jerked downward until the flesh gave way. While suspended, each man held his eagle-bone whistle in his mouth, blowing it from time to time.

If a man vowed to take part in the Sun dance by carrying buffalo skulls, the number varied from two to eight. If two were used they were fastened to the flesh of the upper part of the back, near the spine. The flesh having been lifted on an awl, a small stick was inserted. A thong of buffalo hide was fastened to this stick, the other end of the thong being passed through the nostril-openings of of the buffalo skull, suspending it at some distance from the ground. The man then danced until the tearing of the flesh released the skull. If four skulls were used, the additional pair was fastened to the back, halfway between the spine and the point of the shoulder. With six skulls, the third pair was fastened to the upper arm. If more than six were used, the additional skulls were fastened anywhere on the upper part of the back, it being permitted also to fasten more than one skull to a thong. When several skulls were employed, their weight made it impossible for a man to stand erect, hence the man had to lean forward upon a stick, dancing in a bowed position. The scales indicated 25 pounds weight for a buffalo skull which was obtained by the writer. The skull was shown to Chased-by-Bears who after lifting it, said that although the specimen was a large one it was not unusual for men to carry such in the Sun dance.

Buffalo Boy stated that he carried six buffalo skulls for four or five hours, at the expiration of which he was set free by the cutting of the flesh from which they were suspended, the proper number of horses being given for his release.

A more severe form of torture was the hanging of the body clear of the ground by means of thongs passed through the flesh on each side of the lower part of the back. Seizes-the-Gun-away-from-Them told of an instance in which a man rode to the sacred pole, and was suspended by his back, after which the horse was led away. The most severe form of torture was the suspension of the body between four poles, by means of thongs passing through the flesh of both chest and back, the body hanging so that only the toes touched the ground. Under these conditions the flesh tore less readily. John Grass stated that a man had been known to remain in that position from one morning until the evening of the next day, when gifts were given for his release.

While the men were dancing, they "prayed for all in the tribe, especially the sick and the old." Red Bird said:

The warriors went on the warpath for the protection of the tribe and its hunting grounds. All the people shared in this benefit, so when the warrior fulfilled his vow he wanted all the tribe to share in its benefits. He believed that Wakaŋ'taŋka is more ready to grant the requests of those who make vows and fulfill them than of those who are careless of all their obligations; also that an act performed publicly is more effective than the same thing done privately. So when a man was fulfilling his vow, he prayed for all the members of the tribe and for all the branches of the tribe, wherever they might be.

As soon as a man enduring torture was set free by the breaking of the flesh, it was customary to apply to the wound a medicine in the form of a powder. It was said that the wounds healed readily, blood poisoning and even swelling being unknown. The writer saw a large number of Sun-dance scars, which appeared slight considering the severity of the ordeal.

After the medicine was applied, the man returned to his place with the dancers, continuing his fast and dancing until exhausted. During the period of dancing the men who painted the dancer occasionally offered a pipe, holding the bowl as the man puffed; also putting the dancer's whistle into his mouth, as participants were not allowed to touch any objects while dancing.

Each man remained in one place as he danced, merely turning so that he continually faced the sun, toward which he raised his face. In dancing he raised himself on the ball of his foot with rhythmic regularity. At intervals of a few hours the men at the drum were allowed to rest, and the dancers might stand in their places or even sit down and smoke for a short time, but if they showed any hesitation in resuming the dance they were forced to their feet by the men who did the cutting of the arms and superintended the fulfillment of the vows.

Women whose relatives were fulfilling vows frequently danced beside them during part of the time. Taśi'na-skawiŋ (White Robe), singer of the following song, stated that she composed it while taking part in a Sun-dance in which her brother was fulfilling a vow. As the result of a successful raid against the Crows, he brought home many horses, which were divided among his relatives, she receiving part of the number. He had vowed that if he were successful he would be suspended from the pole and would also have 200 cuts made on his arms. She and her sister assumed one-half of this number, each having her arms cut 50 times. She and his other female relatives danced while he was dancing, and without preparation she sang this song, which was readily learned and sung by all the women:

No. 22. "Wakaŋ'taŋka, Pity Me"   (Catalogue No. 688)

Sung by TAŚI'NA-SKAWIŊ (WHITE ROBE)

VOICE ♩= 63
DRUM not recorded

WORDS (NOT TRANSCRIBED)

Waŋbli'-iya'li'	Climbing Eagle (man's name)
heye' le	said this
Wakaŋ'taŋka	"Wakaŋ'taŋka
oŋ'śimala ye yo	pity me
letaŋ'haŋ	from henceforth
te'haŋ wani' ktelo'	for a long time I will live"
eyiŋ' na'haŋ	he is saying this, and
teħi'ya na'żiŋ ye	stands there, enduring

Analysis.—The third and second tones of the octave are lacking in this melody, which, as already stated, was said to have been composed by a woman. The absence of the third in songs composed by women is considered in Bulletin 53 (p. 140). Only four other instances of the absence of the third occur in the present series. These are Nos. 5, 42, 99, 131, 169, and the present song is the only one of the group which was composed or sung by a woman. One accidental occurs—the fourth raised a semitone. The manner of using this accidental introduces two intervals, one of which seems particularly difficult for an Indian to sing, namely, the minor second. The other interval is the augmented fourth, in the descent from D sharp to A. All these intervals, as well as the ascent of the octave, were sung with good intonation. The song is minor in tonality and freely melodic in structure.

The aged members of the tribe were seated comfortably in the "shade house" on the outer edge of the dancing circle. There they listened attentively to all that took place; indeed, the utmost reverence and respect for the ceremony were shown by all who attended. The spectators realized that when prayer was offered by the Intercessor "it was their duty to join in his prayer with their hearts."

Meantime many incidents were taking place in the great tribal gathering. Those who rejoiced were asking others to rejoice with them, while still others joined their friends in lamenting chiefs who had died during the year, or warriors who had been slain by the enemy. The relatives of those who took part in the Sun dance provided feasts, and little groups were seen feasting here and there in the camp while at the same time songs of lamentation could be heard. The following song was used at a Sun dance in commemoration of Kaŋġi'-iyo'take (Sitting Crow), a Sioux warrior who was killed in a fight with the Crows. The words of this song are a warrior's best memorial.

No. 23. Song of Lamentation   (Catalogue No. 437)

Sung by LONE MAN

Kaŋ - ġi - i - yo - ta - ke   he - ćel yuŋ - kiŋ kte ħćiŋ e - ćel   yuŋ - ka he

WORDS

Kaŋǵi′-iyo′take................ Sitting Crow (man's name)
he′ćel yuŋkiŋ′ kte hćiŋ...... that is the way he wished to lie
ećel yuŋka′ he................ he is lying as he desired

Analysis.—Five renditions of this song were recorded; these are entirely uniform. The upward progressions in the measure containing the first word are interesting, also the upward progression necessary in beginning a repetition of the song. These intervals were sung with good intonation. From the writer's observation an Indian may vary the pitch of unimportant intervals, but very rarely loses the pitch of what might be called the "outline" of a melody. In structure this song is freely melodic, yet the tonic triad is felt throughout the song. The minor third is of frequent occurrence and constitutes 37 per cent of the entire number of intervals. The melody tones are those of the second five-toned scale.

Even the children had a part in the Sun dance, which consisted in the piercing of their ears. Frequently this was done in fulfillment of a vow made by their parents; for instance, in the event of a child's illness the parents might vow that if the child should live until the next Sun dance its ears would be pierced. This was considered an honor, and the gifts which were required made it impossible for poorer members of the tribe. The piercing of the ears was done publicly by any experienced person, in some instances by the Intercessor, assisted by those who cut the arms of persons fulfilling vows at the ceremony. The parents of the child gave gifts to those who pierced its ears, the gifts varying according to their means. Some gave 1 horse, some 10 horses, and wealthy persons added large and valuable presents of goods to show their affection for the child. A wealthy family provided also rich furs on which the child was laid during the operation—soft robes of otter, beaver, or buffalo, elaborately wrought on the inner side with beads or porcupine quills, and brought a pillow filled with the soft hair scraped from the deer's hide, or the down of the cat-tail reeds that grow in the marshes. All these articles were left in their places after being used and were appropriated by the poor of the tribe.

The piercing of the ear was originally done with a bone awl, this instrument being replaced later by one of metal. After the puncture, a piece of copper was inserted so that the wound would heal rapidly. One or both ears might be pierced, and if desired more than one hole was made in each ear.

The children whose ears were thus pierced were considered somewhat related in status to the men whose flesh was lacerated in the Sun dance, and feasts were given by their relatives in honor of the event.

About noon of either the first or second day of the dancing the Intercessor sang the following song, the drum being silent and the entire assembly listening as he sang:

No. 24. Noon Song   (Catalogue No. 506)

Sung by RED BIRD

VOICE ♩ = 58
DRUM not recorded

WORDS (NOT TRANSCRIBED)

(*First rendition*)

to'kiya	where
wakaŋ'	holy
waŋla'ke	you behold
wi ohi'nape ta	in the place where the sun rises
wakaŋ	holy
waŋla'ka nuŋwe'	may you behold

(*Second rendition*)

to'kiya	where
wakaŋ'	holy
wáŋla'ke	you behold
wi ohi'ya ye ta	in the place where the sun passes us on his course
wakaŋ'	holy
waŋla'ke	you behold

(*Third rendition*)

to'kiya	where
waśte'	goodness
waŋla'ke	you behold
wi oë'kawiŋġe te	at the turning back of the sun
waśte'	goodness
waŋla'ka nuŋwe'	may you behold

Analysis.—The principal characteristic of this melody is that 9 of the 16 progressions are intervals of the minor third. The tones are those of the fourth five-toned scale, and the melody is freely melodic in structure. Several renditions were recorded, each repetition beginning at the point indicated by the marks for repeat. Thus the first part of the song may be regarded as an introduction.

The following song was sung by the Intercessor during one of the periods when the drummers rested; the people listened attentively.   In explanation of this song Red Bird said:

This is a song concerning a dream of an Intercessor.   In his dream he saw the rising sun with rays streaming out around it.   He made an ornament which represented this.   At first he alone wore it, but afterward others wore the same ornament.   [See p. 89.]   It is a hoop with feathers fastened lightly to it.   The hoop represents the sun, and the feathers fastened to it are feathers of the eagle, which is the bird of day, the crane, which is the bird of night, and the hawk, which is the surest bird of prey.

No. 25. Song concerning the Sun and Moon   (Catalogue No. 504)

Sung by RED BIRD

VOICE ♩ = 58
DRUM not recorded

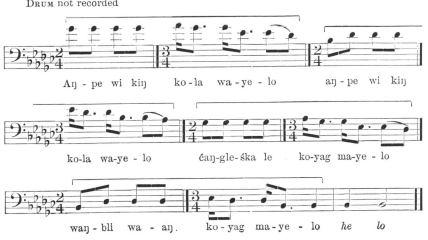

WORDS

(*First rendition*)

aŋpe′ wi kiŋ	the sun
kola′ waye′lo	is my friend
ćaŋgle′śka le	a hoop
koyag′ maye′lo	it has made me wear
waŋbli′ waŋ	an eagle
koyag′ maye′lo	it has made me wear

(*Second rendition*)

haŋye′ wi kiŋ	the moon
kola′ waye′lo	is my friend
pehaŋ′ waŋ	a crane
koyag′ maye′lo	it has made me wear
ćetaŋ′ waŋ	a hawk
koyag′ maye′lo	it has made me wear

Analysis.—In many songs the rhythmic unit is merely a short phrase which lacks completeness in itself, but which appears frequently throughout the melody and influences the rhythmic divisions of the entire melody. The song now under analysis, however, contains a rhythmic unit which is complete in itself, and which was sung with a distinct "phrase perception." Repetitions of this unit constitute the entire song except the closing measure. The melody tones are those of the fourth five-toned scale. The only intervals here found are the major second and minor third. Descending intervals comprise about two-thirds of the entire number.

The songs of the hours of dancing are peculiarly rhythmic, the following being examples. These songs were not used exclusively in the Sun dance, some of them being songs of the various War societies.

No. 26. "Wakaŋ'taŋka Hears Me"   (Catalogue No. 483)

Sung by LONE MAN

VOICE ♩ = 88
DRUM ♩ = 88
Drum-rhythm similar to No. 6

Wa-kaŋ - taŋ - ka   ća wa - ki - ya   ćaŋ -na na-ma - ḣoŋ e

ta-ku waś-te ma-ḳu we-lo

WORDS

Wakaŋ'taŋka	Wakaŋ'taŋka
ća wa'kiya ćaŋ'na	when I pray to him
nama'ḣoŋ e	heard me
ta'ku waśte'	whatever is good
maḳu' welo'	he grants me

Analysis.—The distinct minor character of this song is of interest. The fourth and seventh tones of the octave are lacking in the melody. It will be noted that these are the tones omitted from the fourth five-toned scale, which is major in tonality, while this song is minor in tonality, the third and sixth being minor intervals. This tone-material is found in four Chippewa songs (see Table 6A); it is considered in Bulletin 53 (p. 188). Similar songs of the present series are Nos. 73, 89, 115, 126, 194. The interval of the fourth is prominent, comprising about one-fourth of the entire number of intervals. Two rhythmic units occur, but have no resemblance to each other. It has been noted that when several rhythmic units appear in a song they usually have some characteristics in common.

No. 27. "Black Face-paint He Grants Me" (Catalogue No. 503)

Sung by Red Bird

Voice ♩ = 76
Drum ♩ = 76
Drum-rhythm similar to No. 6

Wa-kaŋ - taŋ-ka ća wa - ki - ya ćaŋ- na i - te - sa - bye

ma-ķu we-lo

WORDS

Wakaŋ'taŋka .... Wakaŋ'taŋka
će wa'kiya ćaŋ'na............ when I pray to him
ite'sabye..................... black face-paint (see p. 359)
maķu' welo'.................. he grants me

Analysis.—This song is major in tonality, yet the minor third constitutes more than half the entire number of intervals. This peculiarity is of frequent occurrence in the present series and was noted among the Chippewa songs. (See Bulletin 53, p. 263.) All the tones of the octave except the seventh are present

in the melody.   An ascent of 10 tones is accomplished in the space
of three measures, about midway through the song.   It will be
noted that a measure division similar to that in the second measure
of the rhythmic unit is of frequent occurrence, though the rhythmic unit occurs only three times.

The following song commemorates a victory over the enemy:

No. 28. "I Have Conquered Them"   (Catalogue No. 484)

Sung by LONE MAN

VOICE ♩= 92
DRUM ♩= 92
Drum-rhythm similar to No. 19

E - ća   o - zu - ye   waŋ   he

u - kte se - će - lo   wa - na   hi - ye - lo   wa - ka - so - ta   he

WORDS

eća′ ozu′ye waŋ he............ well, a war party
ukte′ se′ćelo.................... which was supposed to come
wana′ hiyelo′.................. now is here
waka′sota he.................. I have obliterated every trace of them

Analysis.—An interesting peculiarity of this song is the progression E–D–E, showing a whole tone between the seventh and eighth of a minor key. This occurs immediately before the words and also at the close of the song. The ascent of an octave in two progressions (with the introduction of the words) is also interesting, as these intervals were sung with more correctness than many smaller intervals in the song. All the tones of the octave except the sixth are present in the song, which is freely melodic in structure.

No. 29. Dancing Song (a)   (Catalogue No. 499)

Sung by RED BIRD

VOICE ♩ = 80
DRUM ♩ = 60
Drum-rhythm similar to No. 6

Analysis.—A notable feature of this song is the difference in tempo between voice and drum. Occasionally the two coincided on the first count of a measure, but this appears to have been accidental, the two parts being entirely distinct. (See analysis of No. 8.) The time of the voice is not rigidly maintained, though the variations are neither sufficient nor regular enough to be indicated except on the E which was shortened in every rendition, and is so marked in the transcription. The structure of the melody is more regular than that of the majority of the songs under analysis. It comprises three periods of four measures each, with one additional measure after the second period. The melody tones are those of the fourth five-toned scale, and two-thirds of the progressions are downward.

No. 30. Dancing Song (b)   (Catalogue No. 505)

Sung by RED BIRD

Analysis.—The count-division which characterizes this song consists of two sixteenth notes followed by an eighth note. This is combined with other divisions of a quarter note to form five distinct phrases of one measure each. The repetition of these short phrases, or rhythmic units, comprises the entire song except the closing measure. The first rhythmic unit occurs twice, the second three times, the third three times, the fourth six times, and the fifth twice. The irregular order of these phrases prevents their grouping into periods, but the rhythm of the song as a whole is complete and interesting. In structure the song is harmonic, the principal tones being those of the tonic triad. All the tones of the octave except the fourth are found in the melody. An ascent of 11 tones in two measures is noted in the seventh and eighth measures before the close. The small count-divisions were clearly given by the peculiar action of the throat which characterizes Indian singing. (See Bulletin 53, p. 13.) Half the intervals (19) are major seconds, all but two of which are in descending progression.

No. 31. Dancing Song (c)   (Catalogue No. 482)

Sung by LONE MAN

VOICE ♩ = 84
DRUM ♩ = 84
Drum-rhythm similar to No. 6

Analysis.—The intonation was wavering in both renditions of this song. Drum and voice have the same metric unit, but the drum invariably precedes the voice. The rhythmic unit, which is short, appears three times. No change of time (measure-lengths) occurs in the melody. This is somewhat unusual, a majority of both Sioux and Chippewa songs containing a change of time. (See Table 17A.)

No. 32. Dancing Song (d)   (Catalogue No. 485)

Sung by LONE MAN

VOICE ♩ = 176
DRUM ♩ = 176
Drum-rhythm similar to No. 19

Analysis.—Wide intervals characterize this melody, one-fourth of these being larger than a major third. The compass of 13 tones is somewhat unusual. The song is major in tonality and is especially lively and inspiring. All the tones of the octave are used except the seventh. In structure the song is classified as melodic with harmonic framework. The drumbeat is tremolo in the opening measures and then changes to the indicated rhythm, which was steadily maintained in all the repetitions of the song.

No. 33. Dancing Song (e)   (Catalogue No. 457)

Sung by ŚIYA′KA

VOICE ♩ = 176
DRUM ♩ = 176

Drum-rhythm similar to No. 6

Analysis.—This melody is transcribed in the key of D minor, but in the opening phrases and also near the close of the song there is a feeling of "interval formation" which is stronger than the feeling for a keynote or its related chords. These parts of the song are based on the descending interval of a fourth. (See p. 418 of this work, also Bulletin 53, p. 99.) Two rhythmic units occur in the song, the second reversing the count-divisions of the first. The drumbeat in this, as in the preceding song, is a rapid tremolo during the opening measures, changing to the rhythm indicated in the transcription. About 45 per cent of the intervals are major seconds.

No. 34. Dancing Song (f)　　　　(Catalogue No. 458)

Sung by ŚIYA'KA

Analysis.—This melody is minor in tonality and contains all the tones of the octave. It has a compass of 13 tones. In structure it is melodic with harmonic framework, special prominence being given the tones B and F. The principal interest of the song is in its rhythm, which is vigorous and well defined. Two rhythmic units occur, the second being a complement or "answering phrase" to the first. There is no change of tempo in the melody. After singing the song as transcribed, the part indicated as a repeat was sung three times with no break in the time.

No. 35. Dancing Song (g)   (Catalogue No. 459)

Sung by Síya′ka

VOICE ♩ = 84
DRUM ♩ = 84
Drum-rhythm similar to No. 19

Analysis.—This melody contains a large number of progressions (69) and has a compass of 13 tones. The trend of the melody is steadily downward, and the song is peculiar in the wide range which is repeatedly employed within two or three measures; thus the sixth and seventh measures comprise a compass of 10 tones. In the parts of the song having a simple rhythm the drum and voice coincided, but in other parts the drumbeat was hastened slightly and bore no relation to the voice.

All night the men danced, with the intervals of rest already described. As the sun rose on the second day, the Intercessor greeted it with the following song:

No. 36. Song at Sunrise   (Catalogue No. 502)

Sung by RED BIRD

VOICE ♩ = 88
DRUM not recorded

RED BIRD

WORDS (NOT TRANSCRIBED)

(*First rendition*)

le miye′ yelo′................ here am I
waŋma′yaŋkiye′ yo........... behold me
aŋpe′ wi ḳoŋ miye′ yelo′..... I am the sun
waŋma′yaŋka yo.............. behold me

(*Second rendition*)

le miye′ yelo′................ here am I
waŋma′yaŋka yo.............. behold me
heya′ u welo′................. it said as it rose
haŋye′ wi ḳoŋ he miye′ yelo′ I am the moon
waŋma′yaŋka yo.............. behold me

Analysis.—Beyond a varied use of the sixteenth and dotted eighth note count-division this melody presents little of special interest. The trend is persistently downward without the return to a high note, which usually occurs. The melody tones are those of the fourth five-toned scale.

On the second day the men were allowed a brief intermission; they might even return to their lodges, but were not allowed to take food or water. During this day the men, one after another, fell from exhaustion. Red Bird (pl. 22) said that he had a vision in the Sun dance. On the second day, as he was dancing, he noticed that the Intercessor held a small mirror in his hand, and that he threw the light reflected from this mirror into the face of one dancer after another, each man falling to the ground when it flashed into his eyes. At last Red Bird felt the flash of light in his own face and fell unconscious. Then he saw something in the sun; it was a man's face, painted, and as he looked at it he saw that the man in the sun was the Intercessor. It was said that this vision was sufficient to entitle Red Bird to act as Intercessor, after he had received the proper instructions concerning the duties of that office.

As soon as a man fell from exhaustion he was carried into the shade, where he gradually regained consciousness.

Those who had taken part in the Sun dance returned to their respective lodges at the close of the dancing. Before partaking of food or water they spent some time in the vapor lodge. Their first sip of water was taken in the following manner: A large bowl was filled with water, and beside it was placed a bunch of sweet grass. Having dipped this into the water, the dancer placed it to his lips. He was then given a small piece of cooked buffalo meat, and later sat down to a meal which was spread in his own lodge.

When the entire ceremony was finished the Intercessor took from its ceremonial position the pipe given by the Leader of the Dancers, and carried it to his own lodge. There he broke the seal of buffalo fat, and having lighted the pipe, offered it to such of his friends as felt themselves worthy to smoke it. No one who knew himself to be unworthy ever dared to touch the Sun-dance pipe.

FIG. 23. Reed whistle used in boys' Sun dance.

Among the Indians here dealt with camp had to be broken before the evening of the second day. The sacred pole and its offerings, the red-painted buffalo skull, and the ·bits of white eagle down remained on the prairie. As the last man left the camping ground, he looked back and saw them in their places. Then he left them with Wakaŋ'taŋka and the silent prairie.

After the people reached their homes the boys of the tribe began a childish enactment of the Sun dance, which continued at intervals during the entire summer. Boys whose fathers or grandfathers had taken part in the ceremony were given preference in the assigning of parts. Mr. Robert P. Higheagle, the interpreter, stated that he well remembered the gravity with which the grandson of an Intercessor imitated the actions of that official. A fine was exacted from any boy who failed to do his part in the proper manner, or who showed disrespect toward the performance. Whistles in imitation of Sun-dance whistles were made of reeds (see fig. 23), the plumy blossom representing the eagle down, and long red and green grasses being wound around the reed in imitation of the porcupine-quill decoration.

Through the summer woods the boys sought for wild grapes and berries with which to color their bodies and their decorations.

Removing the outer bark from trees, they took long, thin layers of the inner bark for streamers, coloring these with the juice of the grapes and berries. The tree for their sacred pole was carefully selected, and was brought home with much pomp and ceremony. Boys with good voices were assigned the part of singers and seated themselves around an old pan. A hoop was sometimes covered with a bright handkerchief or cloth; this more nearly resembled the Sun-dance drum in appearance, but the pan was considered more satisfying. The torture was imitated by thrusting a stiff cactus-spine through a boy's skin; this was fastened to the pole by means of a very frail thread. When his movements in dancing broke this thread the boy was considered released.

Thus the boys of the tribe were trained in their play to become the men of the future.

The desire of children to imitate the actions of older people is further illustrated by the children's Games of War contained in Bulletin 53, pages 137–139. These games included a sham fight on the part of the boys, while the little girls sang of relatives who had been wounded while on the warpath.

OLD SONGS [1]

1. CEREMONIAL SONGS

This group comprises such songs of the Alo'waŋpi, Spirit-keeping, and Sun-dance ceremonies as are sung only by persons specially qualified to sing them. The song of the Spirit-keeping ceremony (No. 1) is given in connection with the account of the Gift of the White Buffalo Calf Pipe, and its ceremonial use is described on page 82. The Huŋka songs are Nos. 2 and 3, and the Sun-dance songs Nos. 4, 11, 12, 13, 14, 15, 16, 17, 19, 20, 21, 36; the latter group being sung only by the Intercessor, and forming part of the instructions which he received in qualifying himself for that office.

MELODIC ANALYSIS

TONALITY

	Number of songs	Serial Nos. of songs
Major tonality...............................	4	11, 14, 15, 36
Minor tonality...............................	11	1, 2, 3, 4, 12, 13, 16, 17, 19, 20, 21
Total	15	

FIRST NOTE OF SONG—ITS RELATION TO KEYNOTE

Beginning on the—		
Twelfth...............................	2	13, 17
Eleventh...............................	1	19
Tenth...............................	1	20
Octave...............................	3	2, 3, 15
Fifth...............................	6	1, 12, 14, 16, 21, 36
Third...............................	1	11
Tonic...............................	1	4
Total...............................	15	

LAST NOTE OF SONG—ITS RELATION TO KEYNOTE

Ending on the—		
Fifth...............................	3	1, 14, 20
Third...............................	6	4, 11, 12, 19, 21, 36
Tonic...............................	6	2, 3, 13, 15, 16, 17
Total...............................	15	

[1] This group comprises songs a majority of which are believed to be 50 to 150 years old.

152

Old Songs—(1) Ceremonial Songs—Continued

Melodic Analysis—Continued

LAST NOTE OF SONG—ITS RELATION TO COMPASS OF SONG

	Number of songs	Serial Nos. of songs
Songs in which final tone is lowest tone in song........	13	1, 2, 3, 4, 11, 12, 13, 14, 15, 17, 20, 21, 36
Songs containing a minor fourth below the final tone..	1	16
Songs containing a minor third below the final tone....	1	
Total...	15	

NUMBER OF TONES COMPRISING COMPASS OF SONG

Compass of—		
Thirteen tones...................................	1	20
Twelve tones.....................................	1	13
Eleven tones.....................................	2	4, 19
Ten tones..	3	12, 21, 36
Nine tones.......................................	2	13, 14
Eight tones......................................	6	1, 2, 3, 11, 15, 16
Total..	15	

TONE MATERIAL

Second five-toned scale.............................	1	2
Fourth five-toned scale.............................	3	11, 15, 36
Minor triad and fourth.............................	2	3, 16
Octave complete...................................	1	21
Octave complete except seventh....................	1	14
Octave complete except seventh and second..........	1	12
Octave complete except sixth......................	1	20
Octave complete except sixth and fourth.............	1	1
Octave complete except sixth and second............	1	13
Octave complete except fifth and second.............	1	19
Octave complete except fourth.....................	2	4, 17
Total..	15	

ACCIDENTALS

Songs containing—		
No accidentals...................................	13	1, 2, 3, 4, 12, 13, 14, 15, 16, 17, 20, 21, 36
Sixth lowered a semitone..........................	1	11
Fourth lowered a semitone.........................	1	19
Total..	15	

STRUCTURE

Melodic..	11	1, 2, 4, 11, 13, 15, 16, 17, 19, 20, 21
Melodic with harmonic framework....................	3	12, 14, 36
Harmonic...	1	1
Total..	15	

Old Songs—(1) *Ceremonial Songs*—Continued

MELODIC ANALYSIS—Continued

FIRST PROGRESSION—DOWNWARD AND UPWARD

	Number of songs	Serial Nos. of songs
Downward	14	1, 2, 3, 4, 11, 12, 13, 15, 16, 17, 19, 20, 21, 36
Upward	1	14
.Total	15	

TOTAL NUMBER OF PROGRESSIONS—DOWNWARD AND UPWARD

Downward	239
Upward	135
Total	374

INTERVALS IN DOWNWARD PROGRESSION

Interval of a—	
Fifth	4
Fourth	26
Major third	23
Minor third	66
Major second	94
Minor second	26
Total	239

INTERVALS IN UPWARD PROGRESSION

Interval of—	
Octave	1
Major sixth	1
Minor sixth	1
Fifth	8
Fourth	16
Major third	15
Minor third	42
Major second	37
Minor second	14
Total	135

AVERAGE NUMBER OF SEMITONES IN AN INTERVAL

Total number of intervals, ascending and descending	374
Total number of semitones	1,101
Average number of semitones in each interval	3.5

Old Songs—(1) Ceremonial Songs—Continued

MELODIC ANALYSIS—Continued

KEY

	Number of songs	Serial Nos. of songs
Key of—		
A major	1	36
A minor	1	17
B flat minor	1	21
B minor	1	12
C minor	2	2, 3
D flat major	1	15
C sharp minor	1	16
D major	1	14
D minor	2	19, 20
E flat major	1	11
E flat minor	1	4
F sharp minor	1	10
G minor	1	1
Total	15	

RHYTHMIC ANALYSIS

PART OF MEASURE ON WHICH SONG BEGINS

	Number of songs	Serial Nos. of songs
Beginning on unaccented part of measure	8	1, 2, 4, 13, 16, 17, 19, 36
Beginning on accented part of measure	7	3, 11, 12, 14, 15, 20, 21
Total	15	

RHYTHM OF FIRST MEASURE

	Number of songs	Serial Nos. of songs
First measure in—		
2–4 time	10	1, 2, 4, 11, 13, 14, 17, 19, 20, 36
3–4 time	5	3, 12, 15, 18, 21
Total	15	

CHANGE OF TIME (MEASURE-LENGTHS)

Songs containing no change of time	5	2, 3, 14, 17, 21
Songs containing a change of time	10	1, 4, 11, 12. 13, 15, 16, 19, 20, 36
Total	15	

RHYTHM OF DRUM

Eighth notes unaccented	2	19, 20
Quarter notes unaccented	1	11
Half notes unaccented	2	12, 13
Drum not recorded	10	1, 2, 3, 4, 14, 15, 16, 17, 21, 36
Total	15	

Old Songs—(*1*) *Ceremonial Songs*—Continued

RHYTHMIC ANALYSIS—Continued

RHYTHMIC UNIT OF SONG

	Number of songs	Serial Nos. of songs
Songs containing—		
No rhythmic unit	3	4, 11
1 rhythmic unit	11	1, 2, 12, 13, 14, 16, 17, 19, 20, 21, 36
2 rhythmic units	1	15
Total	15	

METRIC UNIT OF VOICE (TEMPO)

	Number of songs	Serial Nos. of songs
Metronome—		
52	1	3
58	1	1
60	1	17
63	1	14
66	1	15
72	1	4
76	1	16
80	2	11, 20
88	1	36
112	1	2
144	2	12, 19
160	1	13
168	1	21
Total	15	

METRIC UNIT OF DRUM (TEMPO)

	Number of songs	Serial Nos. of songs
Metronome—		
72	1	12
80	2	11, 13
84	1	20
144	1	19
Drum not recorded	10	1, 2, 3, 4, 14, 15, 16, 17, 21, 36
Total	15	

COMPARISON OF METRIC UNIT OF VOICE AND DRUM (TEMPO)

	Number of songs	Serial Nos. of songs
Drum and voice having the same metric unit	2	11, 19
Drum faster than voice	1	20
Drum slower than voice	2	12, 13
Recorded without drum	10	1, 2, 3, 4, 14, 15, 16, 17, 21, 36
Total	15	

DREAMS AND THEIR OBLIGATIONS

The obligation of a dream was as binding as the necessity of fulfilling a vow, and disregard of either was said to be punished by the forces of nature, usually by a stroke of lightning. Dreams were sought by the Sioux, but it was recognized that the dream would correspond to the character of the man. Thus it was said that "a young man would not be great in mind so his dream would not be like that of a chief; it would be ordinary in kind, yet he would have to do whatever the dream directed him to do." The first obligation of a dream was usually its announcement to the tribe. This was by means of a performance which indicated the nature of the dream and allied the man to others who had similar dreams. If the dream were connected with the sacred stones, or with herbs or animals concerned in the treatment of the sick, it was considered obligatory that the man avail himself of the supernatural aid vouchsafed to him in the dream, and arrange his life in accordance with it.

Below will be found three groups of dream songs which, as noted among Chippewa as well as Sioux, are songs believed to be supernaturally received in dreams. The first of these groups comprises the songs of the Heyo'ka (dreamers of the thunderbird) and songs of those who dreamed of birds or animals. The numbers of these songs are 37–58, inclusive; with few exceptions they were recorded by the men who received them in their dreams. Two other groups follow; these comprise songs of the sacred stones and songs connected with the treatment of the sick.

HEYO'KA KA'GA (FOOL IMPERSONATION)

A dream of the thunderbirds [1] was considered the greatest honor which could come to a man from a supernatural source, and for this reason the obligation of the dream was heavier than that of any other.

The manner in which the thunderbirds are regarded was indicated by Shooter, who said:

Dreamers have told us of these great birds in the sky, enwrapped in the clouds. If the bear and other vicious beasts are regarded as dangerous, how much more should we fear the thunderbirds that cause destruction on the face of the earth. It is said that the thunderbirds once came to the earth in the form of giants. These giants did

---

[1] The thunderbirds (wakiŋ'yaŋ) are defined by Riggs as "the cause of thunder and lightning, supposed by the Dakota to be a great bird." (See Contr. N. Amer. Ethn., VII, p. 514, 1890). Cf. article Thunderbird by Dr. J. R. Swanton, in Handbook Amer. Inds., pt. 2, 1910.

wonderful things, such as digging the ditches where the rivers run. At last they died of old age, and their spirits went again to the clouds and resumed their form as thunderbirds. While they were on earth, the rain fell without sound of thunder or flash of lightning, but after their return to the sky the lightning came—it is the flash of their eyes, and the thunder is the sound of their terrible song. When they are angry, the lightning strikes a rock or tree as a warning to men. The bodies of these giants became stone, and parts of them are found in many places, indeed the whole body of more than one of these giants has been found in the land of the Dakotas.

The Heyo'ka Ka'ga was a ceremony of public humiliation in which the man who had been selected by the thunderbirds to receive a manifestation of their presence in a dream voluntarily exposed himself to the ridicule of the lowest element in the tribe.[1] His self-abasement was exaggerated to the greatest possible degree. The superficial and unthinking heaped their scorn and derision upon him, but the wise of the tribe understood that, to the end of his life, that man could command the powers of the sky to help him in his undertakings. In the opinion of the writer's informants the enacting of the part of a fool in connection with a thunderbird dream was an example of the antithesis by which Indians sometimes disguise their meaning. In this it might be said to resemble the "sacred language" (see p. 120, footnote), which is unintelligible to those who are not initiated into its mysteries.

Several of the writer's informants, after consultation, gave the following meanings (or uses) for the word *heyo'ka:* A man who has dreamed of the thunderbirds; a person who does things contrary to the natural way of doing them; and, in some instances, a joker. In connection with the ceremony in fulfillment of a thunderbird dream the word is translated "fool," because only a foolish or half-witted person would behave, under such circumstances, in the manner assumed by the dreamer, while the merriment provoked by the action gives rise to the term "clown." The writer's informants stated that in their youth they had never heard of heyo'ka being regarded as gods by the Teton Sioux. In their opinion the heyo'ka resembled characters in the field of folk tales, rather than in that of religion. Holding the opposite view, both Riggs and Pond enumerate heyo'ka among the Dakota gods.[2] The reason for not regarding heyo'ka as gods, on the part of the writer's informants, seemed to be that they are not accredited with supernatural power. Writing on this subject J. Owen Dorsey says:[3] "Dr. Brinton has confounded the Heyoka with the Wakinyan.[4] The two are distinct classes of powers, though there is some connection between them, as may be inferred from the

---

[1] Cf. Wissler, Clark, Societies and Ceremonial Associations in the Oglala Division of the Teton-Dakota, n *Anthr. Papers, Amer. Mus. Nat. Hist.*, XI, pt. 1, pp. 82–85, New York, 1912; also Lowie, Robert H., Dance Associations of the Eastern Dakota, ibid., pt. 2, pp. 113–117, 1913.

[2] Riggs, in Tah-koo Wahkan, p. 66 Boston [1869]. Pond, G. H., in *Colls. Minn. Hist. Soc.* for 1867, p. 44. St. Paul, 1867.

[3] See A Study of Siouan Cults, *Eleventh Rep. Bur. Ethn.* p. 469, 1894.

[4] It is said that the thunderbirds are related also to the sacred stones. (See p. 208.)

LONE MAN

following stories in the Bushotter collection." Dorsey then relates the story of a heyo'ka man who predicted the time of his death and was killed by lightning as he rode on his horse pointing the stem of his pipe toward the clouds; also the story of a heyo'ka woman who was killed by lightning. Further, he quotes Bushotter as saying—

Women used to dream about the Thunder-beings, just as the men did, and in those dreams the heyoka man or woman made promises to the Thunder-beings. If the dreamers kept their promises, it was thought that the Thunder-beings helped them to obtain whatever things they desired; but if they broke their promises, they were sure to be killed by the Thunder-beings during some storm.

Riggs states further that—

The nature of the *Ha yo'-ka* is the very opposite of nature. He expresses joy by sighs and groans . . . and sorrow and pain by the opposite sounds and looks. Heat causes his flesh to shiver . . . while cold makes him perspire. In the coldest weather, when the mercury congeals, these gods seek some prominence on the prairie, where they put up bushes to shield themselves as they swelter with heat. . . . They feel perfect confidence when beset with dangers, and quake with fear when safe.

In his Dakota Dictionary, Riggs (under *Heyo'ka*) says: "Heyoka is represented as a little old man with a cocked hat on his head, a bow and arrows in his hands, and a quiver on his back. In winter he goes naked, and in summer he wraps his buffalo-robe about him." "The little hills on the prairie are . . . the houses of Heyoka." Mythical "little men" enter into the beliefs of many tribes of Indians. Thus among the White River Ute, on the Uinta Reservation, in Utah, the writer was informed of "little green men," who lived in the mountains and often appeared to the Indians, telling them of "medicines" and teaching them songs.[1]

Two dreams of the thunderbirds were related to the writer, one by Lone Man (pl. 23), followed by an account of the Heyo'ka ceremony in fulfillment of his dream, the other by Charging Thunder (see p. 170), this dream being the source of his name, which is literally translated "Charger-of-the-Thunderbird." In describing his dream Lone Man said:

One day when I was on the warpath I sat down to rest and was at some distance from the other members of the party. I looked up at the sky and the rolling clouds. I fell asleep, and while I slept I had a dream. My face was toward the west, and I heard thunder in that direction. There was a sound of hoofs, and I saw nine riders coming toward me in a cloud, each man on a horse of a different color. Then I heard a sound in the north and saw nine riders coming toward me from that direction, each on a white horse. They joined the riders from the west and came toward me. One of them spoke to me, and said they had appointed me to make the first attack upon the enemy. He said the man to be attacked was painted red and was standing in the water, and he said that if I could conquer that man I would gain something which would be useful to me all the rest of my life. Then a voice from among the company of riders said that, having been appointed to make this attack, I would be considered

---

[1] Two dreams of the thunderbirds, with the songs which they taught the dreamers, were recorded (Bull. 53, pp. 158, 198) among the Chippewa of Wisconsin, and two similar songs, without the story of the dreams, among the Chippewa of northern Minnesota. (See Bull. 53, pp. 264, 274.)

part of their company and could always call on them for help in time of need. [See p. 170.]

In my dream I found the enemy as they had described. I ran at him, thrust him through with my spear, and was bearing him away when he was transformed into a reed standing in the water. The same voices spoke again, hailing me as one of their number and saying that ever after I would be able to do things which no ordinary man could do, because I had obeyed them. They also told me that the frog must not be harmed, as he watches everything in the water and has been given this peculiar power. They told me a great deal about the creatures that live in the water, saying they are taken care of, and water is sent them from the sky when they need it; therefore they should never be treated cruelly.

The horsemen in the cloud then told me to look down at the earth and observe everything on the land and in the water, and to consider them all as mine. The voice also said, "The sacred stones will look upon you as a man whom they are to guard and protect." Concerning this they taught me a song.

Before recording this song Lone Man made the following prayer, speaking reverently and in a low tone. His position before the phonograph made it possible to secure a record of this prayer, which was afterwards translated.

Ho tuŋka′śila ake′ nita′olo′waŋ waŋźi′ awa′hiyayiŋ kta ća taŋyaŋ′ an′am ag′optaŋ yo. Lena′ aŋpe′tu iyo′hi waŋźig′źi kiksu′ye mayaśi′ ḳoŋ lehaŋl′ aŋpe′tu kiŋ waŋźi′ wek′suyiŋ ktelo′.

(Translation)

Great grandfather, again one of your songs I shall sing, listen to me. These you required me to sing each day, and now, this day, I shall recall one.

No. 37. "The Horsemen in the Cloud" (Catalogue No. 492)

Sung by Lone Man

maka′ta.................................. the earth
e′toŋwaŋ yo............................. behold
lena′.................................... all these
nita′wa................................. yours
ktelo′.................................. will be
maka′ta................................. the earth
e′toŋwaŋ yo............................. behold
lena′..·................................ all these
nita′wa yelo′.......................... (are) yours

Analysis.—The opening of this melody is unusual, consisting in a descent from the fifth to the second of a minor key. In the third measure the third of the key appears, the tonic enters in the sixth measure, followed by five measures in which the tonic and third are emphasized. Two descending fourths (A–E and E–B) carry the melody down toward the tonic in the lower octave, which is given as the closing tone. The melody comprises all the tones of the octave except the seventh. It will be noted that the opening tones of the song contain the beginning of the rhythmic unit, which appears in complete form in the succeeding measures and occurs three times in the song.

Continuing his narrative, Lone Man said:

Before the riders in the cloud went away they gave me a charm (*wo′tahe*), which I always carried. If I were in great danger and escaped alive I attributed it to the charm and sang a song in its honor. The song relates to the swallow whose flying precedes a thunderstorm. When I sang the song of my charm I fastened the skin of a swallow on my head. This bird is so closely related to the thunderbird that the thunderbird is honored by its use. The action of a swallow is very agile. The greatest aid to a warrior is a good horse, and what a warrior desires most for his horse is that it may be as swift as the swallow in dodging the enemy or in direct flight.[1] For this reason my song is in honor of the swallow as well as of my charm.

---

1 See footnote 3, p. 71.

No. 38. "Before the Gathering of the Clouds" (Catalogue No. 493)

Sung by Lone Man

Voice ♩ = 100
Drum not recorded

Ka -ċa- mna - ya - ya- aŋ kiŋ-yaŋ ye wa-ye ki - ċa - mna -

ya - ya- aŋ kiŋ-yaŋ ye wa-ye - lo u - pi - ża-ta o - ya - te

waŋ ki - ċa - mna wa-ye - lo he yo ma-ħpi-ya o - gli-na -

żiŋ ta i - to - ka- bya ya yo ki - ċa-mna wa - ye - lo mi -

ta -śuŋ-ke u - pi - ża - ta ċa kiŋ-yaŋ-yaŋ iŋ - a-yaŋ-ke - lo he

WORDS

kiċa′mnayaŋ	in erratic
kiŋyaŋ′	flight
ye wa′yelo	I have sent
upi′żata oya′te [1] waŋ	a Swallow nation
kiċa′mna	the erratic (flight)
wa′yelo	I have caused
maħpi′ya ogli′nażiŋ ta ito′kabya	before the gathering of the clouds
kiċa′mna	the erratic (flight)
wa′yelo	I have caused
mita′śuŋke	my horse
upi′żata	(as) a swallow
ċa	it was
kiŋyaŋ′yaŋ	flying
iŋ′ayaŋ′kelo	running

Analysis.—This song as a whole is decidedly rhythmic, yet it does not contain a rhythmic unit. The melody tones are those of the

---

[1] The word *oya′te*, when referring to the Sioux, is translated "tribe"; when used with reference to birds or animals, it is translated "nation." The following uses of this term are cited: Thunderbird nation, No. 43; Wolf nation, Nos. 52, 67; Swallow nation, Blackbird nation, No. 54; Deer nation, Eagle nation, No. 55; Sacred-stone nation, Nos. 59, 68; Horse nation, Nos. 61, 111, 112.

fourth five-toned scale, and about two-thirds of the intervals are downward progressions. The occasional ómission of syllables by the singer does not affect the meaning of the words.

Lone Man said:

When I found myself in danger, I remembered my dream of the riders in the clouds and their promise to give me help. Therefore I painted my horse with streaks of lightning and sang the following song.

Before singing Lone Man made this prayer, which was recorded by the phonograph:

Ake' tuŋka' śila nita' olo'waŋ waŋźi' wek'suya ća awa'hiya yiŋ ktelo'.

(*Translation*)

Again, great grandfather, one of your songs I have remembered and I shall now sing it.

No. 39. Song in Time of Danger (Catalogue No. 496)

Sung by Lone Man

Voice ♩ = 72
Drum ♩ = 152
Drum-rhythm similar to No. 19

Ko - la mi- ta - śuŋ- ke   waŋ-yaŋ - ki -ye   yo   *he*   ko -

la mi ta - śuŋ- ke   iŋ - yaŋ - kiŋ kte waŋ-yaŋ- ki -ye   *o* e - ma - ki

ye - lo ko - la mi - ta - śuŋ - ke kiŋ-yaŋ-yaŋ iŋ -yaŋ - ke ye - lo

WORDS

kola'............................ friends
mita'śuŋke.................... my horse
waŋyaŋ' kiye yo.............. behold it
kola'............................ friends
mita' śuŋke................... my horse
iŋ'yaŋkiŋ kte .... will run
waŋyaŋ'kiye .... behold it
ema'ki yelo'.................. was said to me
kola'............................ friends
mita'śuŋke.................... my horse
kiŋyaŋ'yaŋ.................... flying (as it were)
iŋyaŋ'ke yelo'................ is running

Analysis.—The rhythm of this song shows remarkable clearness of concept. There are two rhythmic units, the entire song being composed of their repetitions. The order of their occurrence is irregular, but this feature seems to give an interesting unity to the rhythm of the song as a whole. The melody tones are those of the fourth five-toned scale. The tempo of the drum indicates four drumbeats to one melody note, and this proportion was maintained during most of the melody, drum and voice coinciding on the first part of each count. As in many other melodies of the present series, the downward progressions comprise about two-thirds of the whole number.

Resuming the story of his dream, Lone Man said:

After my return to the camp I wanted to do something to show that I realized my unworthiness of the honor given me by the thunderbirds. No one told me that I ought to do this, and yet all who dream of the thunderbirds in any of their manifestations have a deep sense of their own unworthiness. I knew that I was only an ordinary mortal and had often done wrong, yet the riders in the air had disregarded this. By appearing to me they had given me a chance to redeem myself. I wanted to make a public humiliation to show how deeply I realized my unworthiness. I wanted to do as others had done who saw the thunderbirds in their dreams, so I made the following song.

No. 40. Song Concerning a Dream of the Thunderbirds (Catalogue No. 491)

Sung by Lone Man

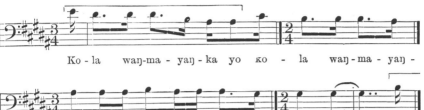

Ko - la   waŋ-ma - yaŋ - ka yo ĸo - la   waŋ - ma - yaŋ -

ka yo wa - kaŋ ma - ka - ġa   *ġa*   pe - lo   ko -

la waŋ-ma-yaŋ-ka yo wa - kaŋ-yaŋ ma-ka-ġa pe - lo *he*   ko -

la waŋ-ma-yaŋ-ka yo wa - kaŋ-yaŋ ma-ka-ġa pe - lo *he*   ma-ħpi-

ya   o - gli - na - źiŋ   ta wa - kaŋ   ma-ka - ġa pe - lo

ma-ħpi - ya o - gli - na - źiŋ ta wa - kaŋ ma-ka-ġa pe - lo

he   ko-la waŋ-ma-yaŋ-ka yo wa - kaŋ ma-ka-ġa pe - lo *he* *yo*

WORDS

kola′.............................. friends
waŋma′yaŋka yo .... behold
wakaŋ′.......................... sacred
maka′ġa pelo′ .... I have been made
kola′.............................. friends
waŋma′yaŋka yo .... behold
wakaŋ′yaŋ .... in a sacred manner
maka′ġa pelo′ .... I have been influenced
maħpi′ya ogli′naźiŋ ta .... at the gathering of the clouds (before a thun-
                                              derstorm)

4840°—Bull. 61—18——13

wakaŋ'......................... sacred
maka'ġa pelo' .... I have been made
kola'........................... friends
wanma'yaŋka yo .... behold
wakaŋ'......................... sacred
maka'ġa pelo' .... I have been made

Analysis.—This song contains several points of unusual interest. First among these may be mentioned its compass of 14 tones, beginning on the fourteenth above the tonic and ending on the tonic. (See Table 5.) We note also the upward progression of a tenth, which is found midway through the song and again at the beginning of the repeated part. The low tone at the close of the song (G flat) in some instances was given accurately, while in others the singer found difficulty in reaching it and sang it a trifle sharp. It is strange that a song characterized by a range of almost two octaves and by one particularly large interval should contain also an unusual number of minor seconds—the smallest interval recognized in these analyses. Many songs do not contain even one minor second, but in this melody 18 (44 per cent) of the entire number of intervals are minor seconds. The song contains all the tones of the octave and is melodic in structure.

As already stated, the ceremony called Heyo'ka Ka'ġa is a ceremony of public humiliation and is enacted chiefly by those who have dreamed of the thunderbirds. A man is required to be leader in only one such ceremony, but when other thunderbird dreamers are enacting the ceremony for themselves he is expected to join them. If a man who has seen the thunderbird in a dream should become arrogant or fail to express his unworthiness, it is said that Wakaŋ'taŋka would punish him through the agency of some of the great forces of nature. Thus every man who has been favored with this wonderful dream tries to demonstrate that in his own estimation he is below the least in the tribe. A man signifies his intention of performing this ceremony by placing a decorated robe, tobacco, or some other offering to the thunderbirds high on the poles of his tent. All who see such offerings know that the man intends to fulfill the obligations of his dream at the earliest opportunity, after which he will feel free to mingle with his relatives and friends.

The ceremony may be held at any time after the thunderstorms begin in the spring. In fulfilling the obligation of his dream Lone Man erected within the tribal circle a tent such as only the poorest member of the tribe would use, in this, as in other respects, following the custom of the ceremony. The tent was often ragged, and its furnishings were always of the most inferior quality. On the day of the ceremony he clad himself in the poorest garments.

Lone Man said:

A man enacting this ceremony often tied a bunch of grass or sage to the lock of hair over his forehead, wearing this as a warrior would wear his medicine. Some were so humble that they covered their faces. It was the custom that a man go with bare head, and he often had his face painted in black and white, or blue and white, his arms and legs being painted with streaks of lightning. If a man wished to express the greatest possible humiliation and did not feel that he could even go through the ceremony, he cut off part of his hair and put it with the entire body of a dog which had been killed for the purpose, both being placed on a pole beside his lodge.

The man who was to show his humiliation engaged the services of a medicine-man to have charge of the ceremony. For this he selected a man who had had many dreams of the wolf, horse, and other animals, and compensated him liberally, probably giving him a horse.

On the appointed day the Crier announced to the tribe that a certain man (giving his name) had had a dream of the thunderbird and wished to fufill the dream, and that he requested all who had had similar dreams to join him in the ceremony of humiliation. Sometimes women also had these dreams, and they were under the same obligations as the men.

The medicine-man led the dreamer in tattered garments out of his tent. If the man were rich a horse was ready for him to ride, one was provided for the medicine-man, and his relatives accompanied him on horseback as he went around the tribal circle, followed by a jeering crowd, who treated the matter as a jest. On their return they dismounted, sang, and told their dreams. A fire was burning in front of the specially erected tent, and a pot of boiling water was hung over the fire. For this pot the man provided as valuable an offering of meat as he could afford; this might be a buffalo tongue and sometimes a dog was given. He did not put this into the pot himself, but gave it to the medicine-man, who held it toward the west, then toward the north, east, and south as he sang of his own dreams and also told the dreams of the man who was making his humiliation. He then turned toward the pot and pretended that he would throw the meat into it. He did this three times, and the fourth time he released the meat [see p. 74], which sped through the air, falling into the pot without splashing the water. All who joined him in the ceremony put some meat in the pot. These constituted an offering to the thunderbird and were symbolic.

Lone Man gave the following explanation of this symbolism:

The water comes from the clouds, the fire is the sun which warms the earth, the meat is from the animals, which are placed here for the use of the Indians, and over the pot are the clouds of steam like the clouds in the sky. These are to teach the people to meditate how Wakaŋ'taŋka by these means is taking care of them.

After the meat was cooked there was a command to take it out of the water. This was an important part of the ceremony, as the men had to plunge their bare arms into the boiling water to take out the meat, and it was in this action that medicines to prevent scalding were tested.[1] These medicines consisted of herbs prepared with water,

[1] The ability to walk upon hot stones or through fire, or to plunge the hand into boiling liquid, without injury, has been noted among many Indian tribes. The following descriptions are cited:

Among the Chippewa: Hoffman, W. J., in The Midewiwin or "Grand Medicine Society" of the Ojibwa, in *Seventh Rep. Bur. Ethn.*, p. 157, 1891; also Chippewa Music, *Bull. 45, Bur. Amer. Ethn.*, 1910.

Among the Menominee: Hoffman, W. J., The Menomini Indians, in *Fourteenth Rep. Bur. Ethn.*, p. 151, 1896.

Among the Mandan: Lowie, R.H., Societies of the Crow, Hidatsa, and Mandan Indians, in *Anthr. Papers Amer. Mus. Nat. Hist.*, XI, pt. 3, p. 308, New York, 1913.

See also Lynd, account of Heyoka Feast, in *Minn. Hist. Soc. Colls.* for 1864, vol. 2, pt. 2, pp. 70, 71, St. Paul, 1865.

which were rubbed on the hands and arms. A specimen of the herb most often used for this purpose was secured by the writer and was identified as *Malvastrum coccineum* A. Gray.

The man for whom the ceremony was given was the first to put his hand into the boiling water, and it was expected that he would try to take out the piece of meat he had put into the pot. He did not eat it himself but gave it to some one in the assembly. The other dreamers followed him, and the meat was distributed. No other food was eaten at the time, and the occasion was not regarded as a feast. It was a ceremony enacted to teach a great lesson. Ignorant persons or children laughed at the tattered garments and the actions of the dreamers, who in every movement attempted to imitate persons not only poor but lacking in judgment. All intelligent members of the tribe, however, regarded the ceremony with greatest reverence.

This and the following song were sung by Lone Man when enacting his part in this ceremony. The words of the song require explanation. From the time of a dream until the time when the dreamer has fulfilled its requirements he regards himself as belonging to the elements and under an obligation of obedience to them. A medicineman may wear the head of a bird as a sign of his power, indicating that bird to be subject to his commands. So in this song, the elements are said to be "wearing" the singer, who has not yet fulfilled his obligations to them. In the second rendition of the song the word meaning 'wind' was replaced by *wasu'ća*, 'hail'; in the third by *wakaŋ'glića*, 'lightning'; and in the fourth by *maḣpi'ya*, 'clouds.'

No. 41. "A Wind"   (Catalogue No. 494)

Sung by Lone Man

Voice ♩ = 104 (or ♪ = 208)
Drum ♩ = 144

Drum-rhythm similar to No. 6

He a-ki-ći-ta   ća wa-mi-ćoŋ - ze-lo   he a-ki-ći-ta

ća wa-mi-ćoŋ - ze-lo ta-te   wan ko-ma-ya-

ke-lo wan-yan-ki   ye o wa-kan ye-lo   *he*

WORDS

he...............................	it was
aki′ćita ća.....................	a guard
wami′ćoŋzelo...................	predicted for me
tate′ waŋ......................	a wind
koma′yakelo...................	wears me [1] (as a medicine-man wears that which is subject to his commands)
waŋyaŋ′ki ye...................	behold it
wakaŋ	sacred
yelo′...........................	it is

Analysis.—The changes of measure-lengths as well as the relative tempo of voice and drum are interesting features of this song. Two renditions were recorded, each with a repeated part, as indicated; between the renditions was a pause, during which the drum continued its steady beat. The rhythm of the voice was uniform in the two renditions. The measures containing six eighth notes are not indicated as being in 6–8 time, as they are in groups of two, and not in triplets. Melodic in structure, the song contains all the tones of the octave except the second. The rhythmic unit appears twice, but its count-divisions do not seem to influence the rhythm of the remainder of the song.

No. 42. "In a Sacred Manner I Return" (Catalogue No. 495)

Sung by LONE MAN

VOICE ♩ = 92

DRUM not recorded

Ko - la waŋ-ma-yaŋ - ka yo ko - la waŋ-ma-yaŋ-ka yo

wa - kaŋ-yaŋ wa-ku we-lo o - ya - te waŋ - ma-yaŋ-ka yo

wa-kaŋ-yaŋ wa-ku we-lo *he* o - ya - te wa-kaŋ yaŋ-ke kiŋ

ko - la waŋ-ma- yaŋ - ka yo wa-kaŋ-yaŋ wa - ku we - lo

o - ya - te waŋ-ma-yaŋ-ka yo wa-kaŋ-yaŋ wa-ku we-lo *he yo*

---

[1] Cf. words of songs Nos. 93 and 105. See also p. 120, footnote.

WORDS

kola'............................ friends
waŋma'yaŋka yo............... behold me
wakaŋ'yaŋ..................... in a sacred manner
waku' welo'.................... I return
oya'te......................... you, tribe
waŋma'yaŋka yo............... behold me
wakaŋ'yaŋ..................... in a sacred manner
waku' welo'.................... I return
oya'te wakaŋ' yaŋke' kiŋ..... the nation sitting holy
kola'............................ friends
waŋma'yaŋka yo............... behold me
wakaŋ'yaŋ..................... in a sacred manner
waku' welo'.................... I return
oya'te......................... you, tribe
waŋma'yaŋka yo............... behold me
wakaŋ'yaŋ..................... in a sacred manner
waku' welo'.................... I return

Analysis.—This song contains only the tones B flat, C, and F and is transcribed in the key of B flat, as the sequence of tones, especially at the close of the song, suggests B flat as a keynote satisfactory to the ear. Sixteen progressions occur in the song, seven of which are fourths and eight of which are major seconds. This melody is an excellent example of the influence of a rhythmic unit on those parts of the song in which it is not found, the count divisions of the second measure of the unit appearing frequently throughout the melody.

Charging Thunder (pl. 24) related his dream of the thunderbirds, in which, as in Lone Man's dream, they assumed the form of men riding on horses. From this dream he received his name Wakiŋ'yaŋ wata'kpe. This is literally translated "Charger-of-the-Thunderbird," but he is commonly called Charging Thunder. His earlier dreams of the wolf and buffalo are described on pages 181–184.

In narrating his dream of the thunderbird, Charging Thunder said:

Soon after the Standing Rock Agency was established I asked the agent (an Army officer) if I might go hunting. I said that before I settled down and adopted the ways of the white man I would like to go hunting for an indefinite length of time. Permission was granted, and I went out alone. As I was going north, near Timber Lake, I saw a deer coming toward me from the north. I wanted to shoot the animal, but thought I would wait until it came nearer. The deer must have come very slowly, for while I was waiting I fell asleep and dreamed. In this dream I saw the deer still coming toward me, and behind it were several men riding on painted horses with grass tied on their forelocks. The riders seemed to be pursuing some object. I became one of these riders, and they told me to lead the party. Then they told me to make a charge on the object which they were pursuing. At first I was not sure what this was, but I soon saw it was a wolf standing toward the west with its face toward the north. I was chosen to do this. because some day I would need the protection of these riders, who were thunderbirds who had assumed human form. They told me that because I had

CHARGING THUNDER

been chosen to make that charge and had become one of their number I would ever thereafter be called Wakiŋ'yaŋ wata'kpe [Charger-of-the-Thunderbird]. After I had attacked and defeated the wolf I saw beyond it a camp with many horses and a man lying dead on the ground. This signified that some day I would conquer an enemy and capture his horses. Ever since that time my greatest enemy has always seemed to me like a wolf, and whenever there is a thunderstorm I am reminded of my dream.

The following is the song of Charging Thunder's dream:

No. 43.　　"**The Thunderbird Nation**"　　(Catalogue No. 571)

Sung by Charging Thunder

Voice ♩ = 76
Drum not recorded

Le - na-ke　　wa - ku - wa-pi kte　　le - na - ke　　wa - ku -

wa-pi kte - lo　*he*　　*o*　wa - kiŋ - yaŋ o - ya - te　pi ća　*yo*

yo　si - to - mni　　wa - ku - wa-pi kte　　si - to - mni - yaŋ

wan - la - ka - pi kte　　si - to-mni - yaŋ　　wa-ku - wa-pi kte-lo　*he*

WORDS

lena'ke	all these
waku'wapi kte	shall pursue
lena'ke	all these
waku'wapi ktelo'	shall pursue
wakiŋ'yaŋ oya'te pi ća	the Thunderbird nation (see p. 162, footnote)
sito'mni	everyone
waku'wapi kte	shall pursue
sito'mniyaŋ'	everyone
waŋla'kapi kte	you shall behold
sito'mniyaŋ	everyone
waku'wapi ktelo'	shall pursue

Analysis.—The tones of this melody are those of the fourth five-toned scale. It has a range of 14 tones, ending on a particularly low tone. This tone on the phonograph cylinder is not ⌣oud, but is distinct, corresponding to the indicated tone on the piano. The adjustment of the phonograph is believed to be the same as when the song was recorded, hence the transcription indicates the tone actually sung by the singer. The song is melodic in structure and contains 20 progressions, three-fourths of which are descending intervals.

DREAMS CONCERNING ANIMALS

A dream concerning an animal was greatly desired by the Sioux. Brave Buffalo (see pp. 207 et seq., 248 et seq.) said:

> I have noticed in my life that all men have a liking for some special animal, tree, plant, or spot of earth. If men would pay more attention to these preferences and seek what is best to do in order to make themselves worthy of that toward which they are so attracted, they might have dreams which would purify their lives. Let a man decide upon his favorite animal and make a study of it, learning its innocent ways. Let him learn to understand its sounds and motions. The animals want to communicate with man, but Wakaŋ'taŋka does not intend they shall do so directly—man must do the greater part in securing an understanding.

This suggests that a fancy for a certain animal preceded a dream concerning it.

Shooter, a thoughtful man and well versed in the old customs, made the following statement, given in the words of Mr. Higheagle, the interpreter:

> All living creatures and all plants derive their life from the sun. If it were not for the sun, there would be darkness and nothing could grow—the earth would be without life. Yet the sun must have the help of the earth. If the sun alone were to act upon animals and plants, the heat would be so great that they would die, but there are clouds that bring rain, and the action of the sun and earth together supply the moisture that is needed for life. The roots of a plant go down, and the deeper they go the more moisture they find. This is according to the laws of nature and is one of the evidences of the wisdom of Wakaŋ'taŋka. Plants are sent by Wakaŋ'taŋka and come from the ground at his command, the part to be affected by the sun and rain appearing above the ground and the roots pressing downward to find the moisture which is supplied for them. Animals and plants are taught by Wakaŋ'taŋka what they are to do. Wakaŋ'taŋka teaches the birds to make nests, yet the nests of all birds are not alike. Wakaŋ'taŋka gives them merely the outline. Some make better nests than others. In the same way some animals are satisfied with very rough dwellings, while others make attractive places in which to live. Some animals also take better care of their young than others. The forest is the home of many birds and other animals, and the water is the home of fish and reptiles, All birds, even those of the same species, are not alike, and it is the same with animals and with human beings. The reason Wakaŋ'taŋka does not make two birds, or animals, or human beings exactly alike is because each is placed here by Wakaŋ'taŋka to be an independent individuality and to rely on itself. Some animals are made to live in the ground. The stones and the minerals are placed in the ground by Wakaŋ'taŋka, some stones being more exposed than others. When a medicine-man says that he talks with the sacred stones, it is because of all the substance in the ground these are the ones which most often appear in dreams and are able to communicate with men.
>
> All animals have not the same disposition. The horse, dog, bear, and buffalo all have their own characteristics. This is also true of the fowls of the air, the living creatures in the water, and even the insects, they all have their own ways. Thus a man may enjoy the singing of all the birds and yet have a preference for the melodies

BUREAU OF AMERICAN ETHNOLOGY

BRAVE BUFFALO

of certain *kinds* of birds.   Or he may like all animals and yet have a favorite among them.

From my boyhood I have observed leaves, trees, and grass, and I have never found two alike.   They may have a general likeness, but on examination I have found that they differ slightly.   Plants are of different families, each being adapted to growth in a certain locality.   It is the same with animals; they are widely scattered, and yet each will be found in the environment to which it is best adapted.   It is the same with human beings, there is some place which is best adapted to each.   The seeds of the plants are blown about by the wind until they reach the place where they will grow best—where the action of the sun and the presence of moisture are most favorable to them, and there they take root and grow.   All living creatures and all plants are a benefit to something.   Certain animals fulfill their purpose by definite acts.   The crows, buzzards, and flies are somewhat similar in their use, and even the snakes have a purpose in being.   In the early days the animals probably roamed over a very wide country until they found their proper place.   An animal depends a great deal on the natural conditions around it.   If the buffalo were here to-day, I think they would be different from the buffalo of the old days because all the natural conditions have changed.   They would not find the same food nor the same surroundings.   We see the change in our ponies.   In the old days they could stand great hardship and travel long distances without water.   They lived on certain kinds of food and drank pure water.   Now our horses require a mixture of food; they have less endurance and must have constant care.   It is the same with the Indians; they have less freedom and they fall an easy prey to disease.   In the old days they were rugged and healthy, drinking pure water and eating the meat of the buffalo, which had a wide range, not being shut up like cattle of the present day.   The water of the Missouri River is not pure, as it used to be, and many of the creeks are no longer good for us to drink.

A man ought to desire that which is genuine instead of that which is artificial.   [See pp. 205, 330.]   Long ago there was no such thing as a mixture of earths to make paint.   There were only three colors of native earth paint—red, white, and black.[1]   These could be obtained only in certain places.   When other colors were desired, the Indians mixed the juices of plants, but it was found that these mixed colors faded and it could always be told when the red was genuine—the red made of burned clay.

Four men told their personal dreams of animals and sang the songs which, they said, were received by them in these dreams. Brave Buffalo related his dreams of the buffalo, elk, and wolves; Charging Thunder, his dream of the wolves; and Śiya'ka, his dream of the crow and the owl.   (Dreams of the thunderbirds by Lone Man and Charging Thunder are contained in the preceding section on the Heyo'ka.   The following group comprises, in addition to narratives by the dreamers, certain accounts of dreams and their songs which were given by men who had heard them related by others, and also a few dream songs whose history is unknown.

DREAMS CONCERNING THE BUFFALO

Brave Buffalo (pl. 25) gave the following narrative concerning his first dream, from which he received his name:

When I was 10 years old, I dreamed a dream, and in my dream a buffalo appeared to me.   I dreamed that I was in the mountains and fell asleep in the shade of a tree.

[1 See p. 116, footnote, which includes blue, obtained from blue clay found in Minnesota.   The above list evidently includes only those colors found in the country of the Teton Sioux.]

Something shook my blanket. It was a buffalo, who said, "Rise and follow me." I obeyed. He took a path, and I followed. The path was above the ground. We did not touch the earth. The path led upward and was smooth like smooth black rock. It was a narrow path, just wide enough for us to travel. We went upward a long distance and came to a tent made of buffalo hide, the door of which faced us. Two buffalo came out of the tent and escorted me in. I found the tent filled with buffalo and was placed in the midst of them.

The chief buffalo told me that I had been selected to represent them in life. He said the buffalo play a larger part in life than men realize, and in order that I might understand the buffalo better day by day they gave me a plain stick (or cane) and told me that when I looked at it I should remember that I had been appointed to represent them. The cane was similar to the one which I now carry and have carried for many years. I would not part with this cane for a fortune. [See pl. 25, in which Brave Buffalo is represented leaning on his staff.]

Brave Buffalo said that the following song was given him in the lodge filled with buffalo, and that by it he received power to engage in the practice of medicine:

No. 44. "A Buffalo Said to Me"   (Catalogue No. 606)

Sung by BRAVE BUFFALO

VOICE ♩ = 69

DRUM ♩ = 69

Drum-rhythm similar to No. 19.

Wa - hi - na - wa - piŋ kte waŋ - ma - yaŋ - ka yo   he   yo   wa -

hi - na - wa - piŋ kte waŋ - ma - yaŋ - ka yo   he   yo   wa -

hi - na - wa - piŋ kte waŋ - ma - yaŋ - ka yo   he   yo   ta - taŋ - ka waŋ

he - ma - ki - ya   he   yo wa - hi - na - wa - piŋ kte waŋ - ma - yaŋ - ka yo   he   yo

WORDS

wahi′nawa′piŋ kte .... I will appear
waŋma′yaŋka yo............. behold me
tataŋ′ka waŋ................... a buffalo
hema′kiya...................... said to me

Analysis.—This song comprises five periods, four of which contain the rhythmic unit while one has a different rhythm. Observing the melodic form, we note that the first period consists, of three measures and is based on the minor triad, B flat, D flat, F, the tones occurring in descending order. In the fourth measure the accidental B double flat leads downward to A flat, and for several measures the melody is based on the descending minor third A flat–F. This is followed by a return to the minor triad in the upper octave and a descent to A, and a recurrence of the accidental, the song closing with the descending minor third A flat–F. Five tones are found in the melody, which is distinctly major in tonality. The sequence of tones is such as to suggest D flat as a keynote, and the song is accordingly transcribed and analyzed in the key of D flat with one accidental—the sixth lowered a semitone. It is interesting, however, to note the intervals in this song. With the number of their occurrences these are as follows: Minor sixth, 1; major third, 3; minor third, 9; major second, 7; and minor second, 9—a total of 29. It will be noted that about 65 per cent of the intervals are minor. A predominance of minor intervals in songs of major tonality has been frequently observed. (See Bulletin 53, p. 263.) It will be recalled that the minor second is a somewhat infrequent interval in Sioux songs. (Cf. analysis of No. 40.) The pitch of the tones transcribed as B double flat and A flat was not always given with absolute exactness, but in every rendition the tones were clearly differentiated. Three renditions were recorded, all being marked by the carefulness which characterizes the following song by the same singer. Drum and voice did not coincide, though the metric unit of the two is the same.

Continuing his narrative, Brave Buffalo said:

The buffalo in my dream told me that I would live to be 102 years old. Then they said: "If you are to show people the great value of the buffalo one proof which you must give them is a demonstration of your endurance. After properly qualifying yourself you will be able to show that weapons can not harm you, and you may challenge anyone to shoot you with arrows or with a gun.

Brave Buffalo said that on waking from his dream, he went home and thought the matter over seriously. After qualifying himself for the ordeal, he requested his relatives to erect a very large tent of buffalo hide in which he would give his demonstration and challenge anyone to shoot him with arrows. He clothed himself in an entire buffalo hide with the head and the horns. The whole tribe came to see whether anyone could wound him. Many tried with arrows, but could not do so. The arrows did not penetrate his skin. Several years later the test was repeated with guns, and Brave Buffalo stated that they were not able to injure him.

Brave Buffalo said that he sang the following song before being made a target for arrows and bullets. No words were sung, Brave Buffalo saying that "the words were in his heart."

No. 45. Weapon Song

(Catalogue No. 608)

Sung by BRAVE BUFFALO

Analysis.—The tones comprised in this melody are those of the minor triad and fourth. The song was sung as transcribed, the repetition being without a break in the time. The singer then gave the calls or cries which are frequently interspersed with renditions of a song, following them with another double repetition of the melody. All repetitions were accurately given, and there was an evidence of carefulness in the manner of singing. Both time and intonation were good. The song is distinctly minor in tonality and is melodic in structure.

DREAMS CONCERNING THE ELK

A dream of the elk has a peculiar significance. The elk is a favorite animal among the young men. Shooter explained this as follows:

The best part of a man's life is between the ages of 18 and 33. Then he is at his best. He has the strength and ability to accomplish his aims. He is brave to defend himself and others and is free to do much good. He is kind to all, especially to the poor and needy. The tribe looks to him as a defender, and he is expected to shield the women. His physical strength is at its best. He is light on his feet and can reduce long distances to short ones. He is taught true politeness and is very gallant. What animal has these traits more than any other? It is the elk, which is the emblem of beauty, gallantry, and protection. The elk lives in the forest and is in harmony with all his beautiful surroundings. He goes easily through the thickets, notwithstanding his broad branching horns. In observing the carcass of an elk it is found that two teeth remain after everything else has crumbled to dust. These teeth will last longer than the life of a man, and for that reason the elk tooth has become the emblem of long life. We desire long life for ourselves and our friends. When a child is born its parents desire long life for it, and for this reason an elk tooth is given to a child if its parents can afford the gift.

Brave Buffalo gave the following narrative concerning his dream of the elk:

When I was about 25 years of age I was able to think for myself. I was not afraid to go into the woods, on a mountain, or in any dangerous place. At that time I was at my best in health and in worthiness, for I had conducted myself rightly in my youth, complying with all that is required of a boy and young man and living in a manner worthy of my parents and grandparents. I had a clean record when I dreamed of the elk.

The dream came to me when I was asleep in a tent. Some one came to the door of the tent. He said he had come for me, and I arose and followed him. It was a long and difficult journey, but at last he led me to a beautiful lodge. All the surroundings were beautiful. The lodge was painted yellow outside, and the door faced the southeast. On entering the lodge I saw drawings on the walls. At the right of the entrance was a drawing of a crane holding a pipe with the stem upward, and at the left was a drawing of a crow holding a pipe with the stem downward. I could see that the occupants of the lodge were living happily and luxuriously. I was escorted to the seat of honor opposite the entrance and reached it with difficulty, as the lodge was filled with brush, and I was not accustomed to making my way through thickets. [At this point the occupants of the lodge seem to have been recognized as elks.[1]] The elks in the lodge watched me with interest and encouraged me to go on, saying they had something they wished to tell me. At last I managed to reach the seat assigned me, and when I was seated the elks rose and said they had heard that I was a great friend of the buffalo, and that they wanted me to be their friend also. They said they had tested me by requiring me to reach this difficult place, and as I had succeeded in doing so they were glad to receive me. They then said that they were going to sing a song and wished me to learn it. They sang the following song, which has no words.

No. 46. Song of the Elks   (Catalogue No. 609)

Sung by BRAVE BUFFALO

VOICE ♩ = 60
DRUM ♩ = 120
Drum-rhythm similar to No. 8

Analysis.—The descending fourths E flat–B flat, and B flat–F are prominent in the framework of this melody, though the interval is usually broken, the progressions being a major second followed by a minor third. The interval of a fourth in songs concerning animals has been frequently noted. (See Bulletin 53, p. 101.) One interval of a minor second occurs in the song, but was sung too large. It has been observed that the minor second is found less frequently than

[1 The identity of a dream object is frequently unrecognized until it turns to depart. Cf. Bulletin 53, p. 207; also p. 66 of the present work.]

the major second, and seemingly is sung with difficulty.   The melody contains all the tones of the octave except the sixth and seventh.

After teaching Brave Buffalo this song the elks gave him numerous instructions.   He noticed that every elk had a downy white eagle feather tied on its right horn to indicate that it could run as fast as the eagle flies.   He was told to wear a similar feather on his head, and at the time of giving this narrative he had a downy eagle plume fastened on the right side of his felt hat.   (See p. 248.)   The elks told him to paint his tipi in a manner similar to theirs, yellow outside with drawings of the crane and the crow on its inner walls, saying that these birds would protect him.   This style of painting the tipi he has always carried out.   The elks told him further that before he would be fully entitled to make a request for help from them he must go through a performance which he himself should devise, by which he would show the people that he was acting under their patronage.

On reaching home Brave Buffalo made a mask of elk hide, using for this purpose the skin of the head with the horns.   He then painted himself yellow and held in each hand a hoop wound with elk hide and decorated with an herb which is much liked by the elks.[1]   A specimen of this herb was secured and identified as *Monarda mollis L.*, commonly known as wild bergamot.   This was used by the young men chiefly on account of its fragrance.   Another variety of the "elk herb" was used by Eagle Shield in his practice of medicine.   (See p. 270.) Brave Buffalo made also a hoop (pl. 26, which he said was similiar to the one he carried when enacting his dream.   As the flowers of the "elk herb" were not then in season, he used flowers resembling them as nearly as possible, and also such fur as was available.

Brave Buffalo said that after arraying himself as described he went around the camp, passing close to the tents.   Two virgins preceded him, carrying his pipe.   As he was making this circuit and imitating the actions of the elk, a thought occurred to him: "Now I have done everything as I was directed to do it, and I wish I might show these people that I have the power of the elk.   There is a spot of damp ground before me.   I wish that when I step on this damp ground I may leave the footprints of an elk."

A crowd of people followed him, and after he had passed over this spot they saw the footprints of an elk instead of those of a man.

He was not required to repeat this demonstration, but if another elk dreamer were giving a similar performance and asked him to join he would do so, wearing the same mask as on the first occasion.   (See p. 166.)   During a demonstration of an elk dream no woman is

---

[1] This hoop is mentioned in Song 105 and its symbolism described in connection therewith.

HOOP CARRIED BY ELK DREAMER

HAIR ORNAMENT WORN BY ELK DREAMER

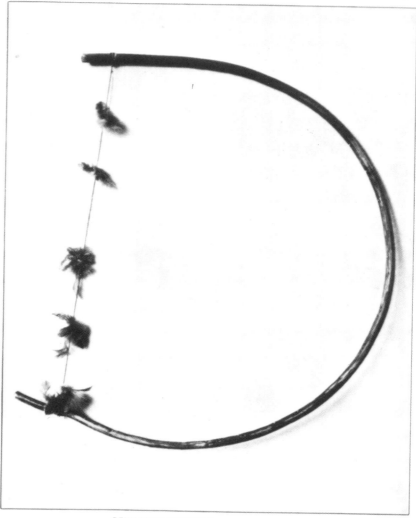

BENT STICK CARRIED BY WOLF DREAMER

allowed on the windward side of the person giving the demonstration and no one is allowed to come near him.

Brave Buffalo stated that after this demonstration the elks gave him power to find medicinal herbs. At the present time if he is in doubt what herb to use in treating a sick person, he appeals to the elks and they tell him what to use and where to find it.

The emblem of the elk is a circle, exemplified by the hoop which an elk dreamer carries in his hand when "acting out his dream." The young men wear a hair ornament consisting of a small hoop wound with porcupine quills and having a downy white eagle feather suspended in the center. Such an ornament is shown in plate 27; the eagle feather is suspended by a tiny loop of hide at the end of the quill. This ornament is fastened by a narrow strip of hide to a lock of hair on top and at the left side of a man's head. The fastening is from the center of the hoop so that the ornament hangs lightly above the ear.

DREAMS CONCERNING THE WOLF

Brave Buffalo stated that about two years after his dream of the elk he had a dream of a wolf. This dream came to him as he was hunting alone. He had been wandering for several days in search of game when he met a pack of wolves. They formed a circle around him, and as they stood looking at him he noticed that their nostrils and paws were painted red. They came toward him, whereupon he grew dizzy. When they reached him, he was unconscious. They stood around him until he regained his senses; then they moved on, telling him to follow them. They led the way to a wolf den on top of a high hill. While he was there, more wolves came out of the hole, painted like the others. The wolves have always been wanderers, not knowing where they would find food. They knew he had been hunting and had had much difficulty in finding game, and they wanted to help him. They said there was a certain herb which, if dried, would enable him to catch all kinds of snakes. He was told to dry this herb, and put it on the ground where the snakes are wont to come. He did so and caught a live rattlesnake. The wolves told him to carry this live snake when giving the demonstration of his wolf dream. Instead of the mask of elk hide which he wore in his former demonstration, he used a similar mask of wolf skin, wearing practically the entire hide[1] and carrying in his hand a bent stick somewhat resembling a bow, which was painted red. A duplicate of this stick made by Brave Buffalo for the writer is shown in plate 28. Brave Buffalo stated that he carried this and the snake in the same hand, the snake coiling itself around the bow. He held the snake close to its head during the demonstration and let it go after the demonstration was closed. The

---

[1] Cf. the wearing of a wolf hide by warriors, p. 388.

wolves told him that when he was making this demonstration a live owl would alight on his back.   Brave Buffalo said that this actually happened.   After this dream and its demonstration he "prayed to the wolves" when he wanted to locate game, and they always told him where to secure it.

The following song, which was taught Brave Buffalo in this dream, is one which he afterwards used in treating the sick.   He said that it was his custom to sing this song every night.

No. 47. "Owls Hooting"   (Catalogue No. 607)

Sung by BRAVE BUFFALO

VOICE ♩ = 92
DRUM ♩ = 92
Drum-rhythm similar to No. 8

Hiŋ-haŋ ho-tuŋ pe - lo hiŋ - haŋ ho - tuŋ pe   hiŋ -

haŋ ho - tuŋ pe - lo hiŋ-haŋ ho - tuŋ pe   hiŋ - haŋ ho - tuŋ

pe - lo hiŋ-haŋ ho - tuŋ pe   haŋ-he-pi hi - ya - ye - ćin hiŋ -

haŋ ·ho - tuŋ pe   hiŋ - haŋ ho - tuŋ pe - lo hiŋ-haŋ ho - tuŋ

pe   hiŋ - haŋ ho - tuŋ pe - lo hiŋ-haŋ ho - tuŋ pe

WORDS

hiŋhaŋ' .... owls
ho'tuŋ [1] pelo'.................. (were) hooting
haŋhe'pi hiya'yećiŋ........... in the passing of the night
hiŋhaŋ'.......................... owls
ho'tuŋ pelo' [2].................. (were) hooting

---

[1] Riggs gives the following definition of the word *ho*: "*the voice* either of a man or of any animal or thing; *sound* in general." Its exact meaning is understood from its use (cf. *itaŋ'ćaŋ*, p. 70).   When *ho* is used concerning an animal, it is understood to refer to the peculiar call or cry of that animal.   Thus in this memoir, in addition to the present song, it appears as follows: With reference to wolves in song No. 48, to buffalo in song No. 54, to owls and wolves in No. 160, to owls and crows in No. 50, to the bear in No. 84, and to the horse in Nos. 109, 111.

[2] The final syllable of this word was often omitted by the singer.

Analysis.—This melody as a whole is of unusual interest. Three renditions were recorded on one cylinder; these show no variations. Three renditions recorded at a later time were found to be identical. The intonation is not so good as in other songs by the same singer, an uncertainty, or wavering of the tone, occurring at the same point in all the renditions. The customary "calls" or "cries" were given between the repetitions of the song. About one-fourth of the intervals are minor seconds which, as already noted, are found less frequently than major seconds in both Chippewa and Sioux songs.

Some medicine-men consider the owl especially sacred among birds. Two reasons were given for this by an Indian, who said:

> The owl moves at night when men are asleep. The medicine-man gets his power through dreams at night and believes that his dream is clear, like the owl's sight. So he promises that he will never harm an owl. If he did so, his power would leave him. For this reason some medicine-men wear owl feathers. The medicine-man also regards the owl as having very soft, gentle ways, and when he begins to treat sick persons he is supposed to treat them very gently. So in night wisdom and in the manner of carrying itself the owl is greatly respected by the medicine-men of the tribe.

Charging Thunder had three dreams of animals. The first was the dream of the thunderbirds, from which he received his name (see pp. 170, 171); the second was a dream of wolves, which is here described; and the third was a dream of buffalo. This last dream occurred about a year after his dream of the wolves. He did not relate the dream of buffalo, but said that because of it he was often sent to look for buffalo, the leaders sending him alone instead of a searching party as described in the account of the hunt on page 439. Charging Thunder said that he had faithfully fulfilled all the obligations of his dreams, and believed that he had received great benefit thereby, but that none of his dreams required him to engage in the practice of medicine. They required other acts, which he had duly performed.

In describing his dream of the wolves, Charging Thunder said:

> When I was about 22 years of age I dreamed that I came to a wolf den and found the little wolves unprotected by either father or mother. They seemed to say, "We are left here helpless, but our parents will soon return." [1] I learned their song, which was as follows:

[1 A dream similar to this is recorded by J. Owen Dorsey in *Eleventh Rep. Bur. Ethn.*, pp. 478–479.]

No. 48. Song of the Young Wolves   (Catalogue No. 570)

Sung by CHARGING THUNDER

VOICE ♩ = 56
DRUM not recorded

A - te to - ki-ya ho ku-we - lo   i - na to - ki-ya ho ku-we - lo   ćiŋ-

ća   zi wa - ku   na   i - na to - ki-ya ho   ku - we - lo   wa-

na - a - ka ku - ʾu-we he   lo   he   e   e   e   he   e   e   ha

e   a   e   ha   e   ya he   wa - kaŋ - yaŋ ho a ku - we - lo

WORDS

ate′	father
to′kiya	somewhere
ho [1] ku′welo	comes home-howling
ina′	mother
to′kiya	somewhere
ho ku′welo	comes home howling
ćinća′ zi waŋ [2]	a young calf
aku′	(father) is bringing
na	and
ina′	mother
to′kiya	somewhere
ho ku′welo	comes home howling
wana′ka	now
ku′we	she is returning
wakaŋ′yaŋ	in a sacred manner
ho ku′welo	she is coming home

Analysis.—The final tone of this song is indistinct on the phonograph cylinder, as it evidently was below the natural range of the singer's voice. It is interesting to note the uncertainty of intonation on G. This tone is first approached by a descent of a minor third, which is an interval frequently sung too small, and in its next occurrence it alternates with F, constituting a repeated major second. A repetition of small intervals appears to be difficult for Sioux or Chippewa. (See analysis of song No. 100, Bulletin 53.) The time

---

[1] See p. 180, footnote.   [2] This word is elided with the following and sung as *waku*.

in this, as in many similar songs, was not rigidly maintained.   Three renditions were recorded, the repetitions being without a break in the time.

Resuming the narrative of his dream, Charging Thunder said:

Soon I saw the old wolf returning and behind him came a buffalo calf.   This old wolf told me how to make a pipe, telling me to smoke it when I was on the warpath and saying that the smell of the pipe would be so strong that the enemy would not detect my approach and thus I would be able to steal their horses.   The old wolf said that by the aid of this pipe I would be able to outwit the wisest and craftiest of my enemies.   I made the pipe as he directed and carried it on the warpath and had good success.   It did not look any different from an ordinary pipe, but it had been "made sacred" by a medicine-man.[1]   The following song was taught me by the old wolf:

No. 49. Song of the Old Wolf   (Catalogue No. 568)

Sung by CHARGING THUNDER

WORDS

wakaŋ′yaŋ............................	in a sacred manner
mića′kelo...........................	he made for me
ćanoŋ′pa waŋ to′keća..........	a pipe that is different
wakaŋ′yaŋ.........................	in a sacred manner
mića′kelo..........................	he made for me
naġi ksa′pa waŋ.................	a wise spirit
maka′hewaye.....................	I met
wakaŋ′yaŋ........................	in a sacred manner
mića′kelo.........................	he made (it) for me
kola′..............................	friend
waŋma′yaŋka yo...............	behold me

[1 The ability to make objects "sacred," thus giving them mysterious power, was said to belong only to men who had the ability to talk with such objects and to understand what they said.   (Cf. section on Sacred Stones, pp. 218, 230, 231, 234, 236, 238, in which men talk with the stones and receive their messages.)   When making a pipe "sacred" the medicine-man filled it, incensed it with burning sweet grass, and offered it to the sky and the cardinal points.]

Analysis.—Three renditions of this song were recorded, with an interruption of the time between the repetitions. In this, as in many similar songs, the time was not strictly maintained. From the beginning of the song to the fifth measure before its close the melody is framed on the chord F sharp–A–C sharp–E, a minor triad with minor seventh added. Other tones occur, and the descending fourth C sharp–G sharp is noted, but this chord is felt as a framework. The song closes with a repetition of the descending minor third E–C sharp. The song is melodic in structure, and about two-thirds of the intervals are descending progressions.

See plot of this melody on page 204.

DREAM OF THE CROW AND OWL

Śiya'ka in his youth dreamed of a crow and an owl. His narrative as here given reveals the manner in which a dream was sought and also the importance attached to it:

All classes of people know that when human power fails they must look to a higher power for the fulfillment of their desires. There are many ways in which the request for help from this higher power can be made. This depends on the person. Some like to be quiet, and others want to do everything in public. Some like to go alone, away from the crowd, to meditate upon many things. In order to secure a fulfillment of his desire a man must qualify himself to make his request. Lack of preparation would mean failure to secure a response to his petition. Therefore when a man makes up his mind to ask a favor of Wakaŋ'taŋka he makes due preparation. It is not fitting that a man should suddenly go out and make a request of Wakaŋ'taŋka. When a man shuts his eyes, he sees a great deal. He then enters his own mind, and things become clear to him, but objects passing before his eyes would distract him. For that reason a dreamer makes known his request through what he sees when his eyes are closed. It has long been his intention to make his request of Wakaŋ'taŋka, and he resolves to seek seclusion on the top of a butte or other high place. When at last he goes there he closes his eyes, and his mind is upon Wakaŋ'taŋka and his work. The man who does this usually has in mind some animal which he would like for protection and help. No man can succeed in life alone, and he can not get the help he wants from men; therefore he seeks help through some bird or animal which Wakaŋ'-taŋka sends for his assistance. Many animals have ways from which a man can learn a great deal, even from the fact that horses are restless before a storm.

When I was a young man I wanted a dream through which I could know what to depend upon for help. Having this desire, I went to a medicine-man [1] and told him about it. He instructed me what to do, and I followed his instructions in everything. He told me to get four well-tanned robes, with one for my own use, also a decorated pipe and offerings of tobacco, and to appear before him on a certain day prepared to seek my vision. I prepared the articles as he directed and went to him on that day. He painted my face white, and before leaving him we went together into the sweat lodge, and while we were there he told me of his own dream and gave me an idea of what a dream was like. I had already selected a hill on which to await my dream, and after leaving him I went to this hilltop to follow his instructions.[2]

[1] In a similar manner Lone Man consulted a medicine-man in his youth. (See p. 211.)
[2] Cf. Old Buffalo's fasting vigil on a hilltop, pp. 274–275.]

I was not required to fast before seeking the vision but of course took no food with me when I went to the hilltop. In the middle of this hilltop I dug a hollow about 2 feet deep and large enough so that I could crouch against its side when weary with standing. At each of the four points of the compass I placed one of the robes and some of the tobacco. These offerings were to show that I desired messages from the directions of the four winds and was waiting anxiously to hear the voice of some bird or animal speaking to me in a dream.

Having placed these offerings in position, and according to the advice of the medicine-man, I stood facing the west and watched the sun disappear. As soon as the sun was out of sight I closed my eyes and turned my face toward the east, standing thus for awhile, then facing the north and the south. So I stood, wrapped in a buffalo robe. I was not exactly singing, but more nearly lamenting, like a child asking for something. [Cf. p. 96.] In the crying or lamenting of a young man seeking a vision two things are especially desired: First, that he may have long life, and second, that he may succeed in taking horses from the enemy.

Beside me, at the north, was placed a buffalo skull, the face of which was painted with blue stripes.[1] The openings of the skull were filled with fresh sage, and it was laid on a bed of sage. The skull was placed with its face toward the south. The reason for this was that when the buffalo come from the north, traveling toward the south, they bring news that Wakaŋ'taŋka has provided food for the Indians and there will not be a famine. During part of the time I rested my pipe against the buffalo skull, with the stem pointing toward the north. Part of the time I held the pipe in my hands, with the stem away from me. The pipe was filled, but not to be lighted until I returned to the medicine-man after my dream. [Cf. sealed pipe in Sun dance, pp. 149, 150.]

As I still faced the west, after the sun had set and when it was almost dark, I heard a sound like the flying of a bird around my head, and I heard a voice saying, "Young man, you are recognized by Wakaŋ'taŋka." This was all the voice said.

All night I stood with my eyes closed. Just before daybreak I saw a bright light coming toward me from the east. It was a man. His head was tied up, and he held a tomahawk in his hand. He said, "Follow me," and in an instant he changed into a crow. In my dream I followed the crow to a village. He entered the largest tent. When he entered the tent he changed to a man again. Opposite the entrance sat a young man, painted red, who welcomed me. When I was thus received I felt highly honored, for as this was the largest tent I knew it must be the tent of the chief. The young man said he was pleased to see me there. He said, further, that all the animals and birds were his friends, and that he wished me to follow the way he had used to secure their friendship. He told me to lift my head. I did this and saw dragon flies, butterflies, and all kinds of small insects, while above them flew all kinds of birds. As soon as I cast down my eyes again and looked at the young man and at the man who had brought me thither, I saw that the young man had become transformed into an owl, and that my escort had changed again into a crow. The following is the song of this part of my dream.

[1 It will be recalled that the stripes on the buffalo skull used in the Alo'waŋpi ceremony and in the Sun dance were red, and that in the Huŋka ceremony the skull was laid facing the west and in the Sun dance facing the east. In both these instances the skull was laid on a bed of fresh sage. In a narrative concerning the "calling of the buffalo" by a medicine-man it is stated that a buffalo skull was painted with both red and blue stripes. (See pp. 72, 127, 444.)]

No. 50. Song of the Crow and Owl   (Catalogue No. 473)

Sung by ŚIYA′KA

VOICE ♩ = 69
DRUM not recorded

Haŋ-ye-tu ma-wa - ni haŋ-ye-tu ma-wa-ni nuŋ-

we e o haŋ-ye - tu ma - wa-ni ta-to he - ya

ma - wa - ni nuŋ - we haŋ-ye-tu ma-wa - *wa*-ni hiŋ -

haŋ *wa* ho - toŋ-haŋ ma-wa - ni nuŋ - we *he* o

WORDS

(First rendition)

haŋye′tu	at night
mawa′ni nuŋwe′	may I roam
tato′ heya′	against the winds
mawa′ni nuŋwe′	may I roam
haŋye′tu	at night
mawa′ni	(may) I roam
hiŋhaŋ′	(when) the owl
ho′toŋhaŋ	(is) hooting (see p. 180, footnote)
mawa′ni nuŋwe′	may I roam

(Second rendition)

aŋ′paö	at dawn
mawa′ni nuŋwe′	may I roam
tato′ heya′	against the winds
mawa′ni nuŋwe′	may I roam
aŋ′paö	at dawn
mawa′ni	(may) I roam
kaŋġi′	(when) the crow
ho′toŋhaŋ	(is) calling
mawa′ni nuŋwe′	may I roam

Analysis.—This melody contains only three intervals larger than a minor third, about half the intervals being major seconds. It is minor in tonality and lacks the sixth and second tones of the complete octave. In structure it is melodic, and the trend is steadily downward from the eleventh to the tonic. The subdominant is more prominent in this than in many of the songs under analysis.

Śiya′ka continued:

The owl said, "Always look toward the west when you make a petition, and you will have a long life." After this the owl commanded me to look at him. As soon as I did this he was changed to an elk, and at his feet were the elk medicine and a hoop. [See pp. 178, 295.] As soon as I saw him changing, I began to wonder what marvel would be next. Then I heard a song. I tried to learn the song, and before I realized what I was doing I was singing the song.

The following is the song taught me by the elk in my dream.

No. 51. "Where the Wind is Blowing" (Catalogue No. 474)

Sung by Śiya′ka

WORDS

to′ki............................	where
tate′............................	the wind
uye′ ćiŋ........................	is blowing
tate′............................	the wind
ića′limuŋyaŋ....................	is roaring
nawa′żiŋ ye....................	I stand
wiyo′lipeyata...................	westward
tate′............................	the wind
uye′ ćiŋ........................	is blowing
tate′............................	the wind
ića′limuŋyaŋ....................	is roaring
nawa′żiŋ ye....................	I stand

Analysis.—Two renditions of this song were recorded, the principal difference between them being that in the second rendition the half note at the end of the third measure was sung a quarter note and the last note of the following measure a half note, thus comprising five counts in the two measures, but distributing them differently. The intonation was wavering throughout the renditions, making the song especially difficult of transcription. This was undoubtedly due in part to the presence of the accidental. It was clearly the intention of the singer to differentiate the tones transcribed respectively as D sharp and D natural, but the interval between the two was not always an exact minor second. As already stated, the minor second is not of frequent occurrence. It is frequently sung too small, but not with sufficient uniformity to justify the belief that a definite interval smaller than a semitone is in the mind of the singer. The measure transcribed in 3–8 time was uniformly sung in all the renditions. The melody tones are those of the second five-toned scale with the fourth raised a semitone as an accidental. The song is melodic in structure and has a compass of 12 tones.

Śiya′ka said further:

The hilltop where I had my dream was quite a distance from the camp. My friends knew I had gone there, and in the early morning they sent a man with my horse. I came home, and the first thing I did was to take a sweat bath. In the lodge with the medicine-man I told him my dream.

I was a young man at that time and eager to go on the warpath and make a name for myself. After this dream, my stronghold was in the east, but the west was also a source from which I could get help. All the birds and insects which I had seen in my dream were things on which I knew I should keep my mind and learn their ways. When the season returns, the birds and insects return with the same colorings as the previous year. They are not all on the earth, but are *above* it. My mind must be the same. The elk is brave, always helping the women, and in that way the elk has saved a large proportion of his tribe. In this I should follow the elk, remembering that the elk, the birds, and the insects are my helpers. I never killed an elk nor ate its flesh. The birds that continually fly in the air I would not kill. I may kill water birds and grass birds if suitable for food, but only these.

Śiya′ka was deeply affected by the telling of this dream and the singing of the songs. Shaking hands with the writer, he said that he had given her his most cherished possession.[1]

Two Shields related the following dream, which is a tradition in the tribe, and sang the song which is said to have been received in the dream:

Many years ago a war party were in their camp when they heard what they believed to be the song of a young man approaching them. They could hear the words of the song and supposed the singer was one of their party, but as he came nearer they saw that he was an old wolf, so old that he had no teeth, and there was no brush on his tail.

[1] Śiya′ka's narrative was given in November, 1912; he died in March, 1913.

He could scarcely move, and he lay down beside their fire. They cut up their best buffalo meat and fed him. Afterward they learned his song, which was the beginning of all the wolf songs (war songs). After this, too, the warriors began the custom of carrying a wolf-skin medicine bag.

The writer was told by Looking Elk and others that the wolf-skin medicine bag carried by warriors had been known to "come to life" and walk about the camp, and it had been heard to sing this, the first wolf song of the Sioux:

No. 52. "I Made It Walk"   (Catalogue No. 533)

Sung by TWO SHIELDS

VOICE ♩ = 168
DRUM ♩ = 138
Drum-rhythm similar to No. 19

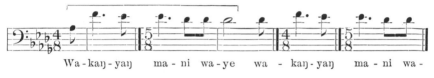

Wa - kaŋ - yaŋ   ma - ni wa - ye   wa - kaŋ - yaŋ   ma - ni wa -

ye   śuŋ - ka o - ya - te waŋ wa - kaŋ - yaŋ   ma - ni wa -

ye   wa - kaŋ - yaŋ   ma - ni wa - ye   wa - kaŋ - yaŋ

ma - ni wa - ye   wa - kaŋ - yaŋ   ma - ni wa - ye

WORDS

wakaŋ′yaŋ	by my supernatural power
ma′ni waye′	I made it walk
śuŋ′ka oya′te waŋ	a wolf nation (see p. 162, footnote)
wakaŋ′yaŋ	by my supernatural power
ma′ni waye′	I made it walk

Analysis.—The same peculiarities of rhythm occur in all renditions of this song. The time is exactly maintained throughout. The melody tones are those of the major triad and second—an unusual tone material. The ascent of a sixth at the opening of the song is also unusual. The song has a compass of 13 tones. Two-thirds of the progressions are major seconds, and a majority of the other intervals are fourths.

Weasel Bear related the following incident, which he said took place when his father was a young man. His father, whose name was

Metal Knee (Hu′pahu-ma′za), was with a number of men on the war-path. On stopping beside a hill, they heard what they believed to be a man singing. They counted their party, but all were there. One of them climbed the hill and, looking over, saw a wolf sitting with his back to the hill. The wolf was looking away off and singing. The words of the four renditions suggest the change from enthusiasm to caution, and are interesting as being sung by an old wolf to the young warriors. The warriors listened and learned the song, which was as follows:

No. 53. Song of a Wolf   (Catalogue No. 650)

Sung by WEASEL BEAR

VOICE ♩ = 100
DRUM ♩ = 88

Drum-rhythm similar to No. 19

Aŋ - pa - o ćaŋ - na o - ma - wa - ni ye ka - to - na -

oŋk o - ma - wa - ni ye

WORDS

(First rendition)

aŋ′paö ćaŋ′na	at daybreak
oma′wani ye	I roam
kato′naöŋk	galloping
oma′wani ye	I roam

(Second rendition)

aŋ′paö ćaŋ′na	at daybreak
oma′wani ye	I roam
kaćaŋ′ćaŋ	trotting
oma′wani ye	I roam

(Third rendition)

aŋ′paö ćaŋ′na	at daybreak
oma′wani ye	I roam
napa′pa	in a timid manner
oma′wani ye	I roam

(Fourth rendition)

aŋ′paö ćaŋ′na	at daybreak
oma′wani ye	I roam
wakta′kta	watching cautiously
oma′wani ye	I roam

Analysis.—An interesting peculiarity of this song is the difference in tempo of voice and drum, the latter being slightly the slower. The song showed no differences in the several renditions. The melody tones are those of the fourth five-toned scale. Of the intervals 52 per cent are major seconds and 35 per cent minor thirds; the remaining three intervals are upward progressions of a major third, a fourth, and a fifth. The character of the song is lively and entirely unlike the earlier songs of this group.

The following song concerning a dream of a buffalo was sung by Old Buffalo. In this and the four succeeding numbers the song remains, but the story of the dream is lost.

No. 54. "Toward Them I Walk"　　　(Catalogue No. 639)

Sung by OLD BUFFALO

Voice ♩ = 176

Drum not recorded

WORDS

(*First rendition*)

tataŋ′ka....................... a buffalo
ċa........................... it was
ho′ye....................... a voice (see p. 180, footnote)
wa′yelo....................... I sent forth
nuŋwe′....................... be it so
wa′ħpetaŋka oya′te.......... a Blackbird nation (see p. 162, footnote)
ċa........................... it was
itoye′ya.................... toward them
mawa′ni ye.................... I walk

(*Second rendition*)

tataŋ'ka	a buffalo
ća	it was
ho'ye	a voice
wa'yelo	I sent forth
nuŋwe'	be it so
upi'źata oya'te	a Swallow nation
ća	it was
itoye'ya	toward them
mawa'niye	I walk

Analysis.—The tones comprised in this song are those of the second five-toned scale, A being the keynote. The chord of A minor forms the framework of all the melody except the closing measures, which consists of the minor third E–G. Throughout the melody the minor third is prominent, comprising 41 per cent of the entire number of intervals. Two rhythmic units are found in the song. The time of the sustained tones was uniform in all the renditions. In this, as in a majority of such instances, the long-sustained tones contain an uneven number of counts.

In explanation of the words of the following song Śiya'ka said:

The reference to the deer and the scarlet object is because venison is red and is the bait used to catch the eagle. The reference to blue is because when trying to catch an eagle we look at the sky so steadily that everything appears blue.

No. 55. "An Eagle Nation is Coming"   (Catalogue No. 472)

Sung by Śiya′ka

VOICE ♩= 132
DRUM not recorded

Ta - ĥća   o - ya - te   waŋ   a - u we-lo   wa - lu -

ta   waŋ   e   *ya*   a - u we   wa - yaŋ - ka   yo

WORDS

(*First rendition*)

ta′ĥća [1] oya′te waŋ............ a Deer nation (see p. 162, footnote)
aü′ welo′...................... is coming
walu′ta waŋ.................. a scarlet object
·aü′ we...................... is coming
wayaŋ′ka yo.................. behold it

---

[1] According to Riggs *ta′ĥća* is a contraction of *t′ĥiŋća*, meaning "the common deer, *Cervus capreolus.*"

(Second rendition)

wanbli′ oya′te wan............ an Eagle nation
aü′ we........................ is coming
maka′to wan.................... a blue object
aü′ we........................ is coming
wayan′ka yo................... behold it

Analysis.—The compass of this song is 17 tones. Among the
Chippewa no songs were recorded which had a compass of more
than 14 tones, but three songs in the present series have a compass
of 17; the others are Nos. 196 and 202. The final tone is faint, but
discernible on the phonograph record. The rapid tempo and wide
intervals cause more uncertainty of intonation than is usual in these
songs. However, in this, as in No. 58, the exactness of the smaller
intervals is of less importance than the fact that 27 of the intervals
(37 per cent) are larger than a major third. An equal number of
intervals are major seconds, and the remaining 15 intervals are
minor thirds. Changes of time occur as indicated. (See song No. 5.)

No narrative was given with this song. Four dream songs concerning deer were recorded among the Chippewa—Nos. 95–98 in
Bulletin 53.

See plot of this melody on page 204.

No. 56. "A Blacktail Deer"   (Catalogue No. 564)

Sung by CHARGING THUNDER

VOICE ♩ = 84
DRUM not recorded

Wa-kan mi-ća-ġe   wa-kan mi-ća-ġe   sin-te sa-

pe-la wan wa-kan mi-ća   ġe   wa-kan mi-ća-ġe

he-na-ki-ya wan-la-ka-pi kon   *hi*   *yo*

WORDS

wakaŋ'.	. . . .	sacred
mi'ćaġe.	. . . .	he made for me
wakaŋ'.	. . . .	sacred
mi'ćaġe.	. . . .	he made for me
siŋte' sa'pela waŋ	. . . .	a blacktail deer [1]
wakaŋ'.	. . . .	sacred
mi'ćaġe.	. . . .	he made for me
hena'kiya.	. . . .	those
waŋla'kapi ḳoŋ	. . . .	you had seen

Analysis.—The interval of the minor third characterizes this melody and constitutes 41 per cent of the entire number of intervals. The trend of the melody is steadily downward, about two-thirds of the intervals being downward progressions. The compass of the melody is 14 tones, lacking only 1 tone of 2 octaves. Three renditions were recorded; these show no points of variation.

See plot of this melody on page 204.

SONGS CONCERNING THE BEAR

Two Shields said:

The bear is the only animal which is dreamed of as offering to give herbs for the healing of man. The bear is not afraid of either animals or men and it is considered ill-tempered, and yet it is the only animal which has shown us this kindness; therefore the medicines received from the bear are supposed to be especially effective.

In somewhat similar strain Śiya'ka said:

The bear is quick-tempered and is fierce in many ways, and yet he pays attention to herbs which no other animal notices at all. The bear digs these for his own use. The bear is the only animal which eats roots from the earth and is also especially fond of acorns, june berries, and cherries. These three are frequently compounded with other herbs in making medicine, and if a person is fond of cherries we say he is like a bear. We consider the bear as chief of all animals in regard to herb medicine, and therefore it is understood that if a man dreams of a bear he will be expert in the use of herbs for curing illness. The bear is regarded as an animal well acquainted with herbs because no other animal has such good claws for digging roots.

---

[1] This animal was mentioned by Lewis and Clark in the account of their journey on the upper Missouri. In September, 1804, Clark wrote, "I walked on Shore Saw Goats, Elk, Buffalow, Black tail Deer & the Common Deer." (Original Journals of the Lewis and Clark Expedition, vol. 1, p. 155.) A footnote on this passage in the Coues edition is as follows: "*Cariacus macrotis,* also called mule deer. The tail is mostly white, but tipped with black." (History of the Expedition under the Command of Lewis and Clark, edited by Elliott Coues, vol. 1, p. 122, footnote, 1893.) The common deer is mentioned in Śiya'ka's song, No. 55.

No. 57. "A Bear Said This"[1]   (Catalogue No. 581)

Sung by SHOOTER

WORDS

peźi'huta wan .... a medicine (root of herb)
yatin' kte .... you will eat (to live) [2]
kahan'tu .... at that place
na'źiŋye .... it stands
mato' .... a bear
hema'kiye .... said this to me

Analysis.—The complex rhythmic form of this song, together with its clearness in repetition, suggests that it is an old song and was correctly sung. Four rhythmic phrases are found in the song. It will be noted that the opening of the first and second are alike, and that the opening of the third and fourth also have a resemblance to each

---

[1] Other dream songs of the bear (Nos. 87–89) are used by Eagle Shield in his practice of medicine. (See also No. 58.)

[2] This is an expression used by medicine-men. When giving medicine to a sick person they said, "You will eat this in order to live, or to recover." (Cf. words of Song No. 83.)

other, the remainder of each phrase being individual. The melody tones are those of the second five-toned scale. There are 52 progressions in the song, 37 (71 per cent) of which are major seconds. Many of the accented tones were given with a peculiar attack, much used by this singer, which consisted in sounding first a tone slightly above the principal tone and immediately sliding downward to that tone.

No narrative was given with this song.

No. 58. "He Comes to Attack" (Catalogue No. 562)

Sung by Charging Thunder

Voice ♩ = 84

Drum not recorded

WORDS

wazi′yatan	from the north
natan′ hina′pe lo	he comes to attack
ekta′	in that direction
e′tonwin ye	behold him
maka′	dust
we′ćon	I threw upon myself
na	and
ćante′	(with) a heart
to′keća	that is different [1]
wa′u we	I came
he yelo′	he said

[1] In the usage of the medicine-men this phrase indicates anger. (See footnote, p. 120.)

Analysis.—Two renditions of this song were.recorded, in both of which the intonation, especially in. the first part, was wavering. This was probably due in part to the difficulty of the progressions and in part to the fact that it was the first song recorded by Charging Thunder. The transcription of such a song should be regarded as approximate, so far as many of the smaller intervals are concerned. This, however, does not affect the broad lines of the melody. Thus in the present instance we note that 17 (45 per cent) of the intervals are larger than a major third. The fourth is especially prominent in this melody, though 15 (39 per cent) of the intervals are minor thirds. The change of tempo occurs in both renditions of the song. (See song No. 5.)

See plot of this melody on page 204.

The analyses of two other groups of dream songs are on pp. 239, 278.

Old Songs[1]—(2) Songs Concerning Personal Dreams

MELODIC ANALYSIS

TONALITY

	Number of songs.	Serial Nos. of songs.
Major tonality	9	38, 39, 42, 43, 44, 48, 52, 53, 55
Minor tonality	13	37, 40, 41, 45, 46, 47, 49, 50, 51, 54, 56, 57, 58
Total	22	

FIRST NOTE OF SONG—ITS RELATION TO KEYNOTE

	Number of songs.	Serial Nos. of songs.
Beginning on the—		
Fourteenth	1	40
Twelfth	3	37, 51, 56
Eleventh	2	46, 50
Tenth	4	38, 39, 43, 48
Octave	4	41, 45, 55, 58
Sixth	1	54
Fifth	5	42, 44, 49, 52, 53
Fourth	2	47, 57
Total	22	

LAST NOTE OF SONG—ITS RELATION TO KEYNOTE

	Number of songs.	Serial Nos. of songs.
Ending on the—		
Fifth	10	39, 41, 42, 43, 44, 48, 49, 52, 53, 54
Third	2	38, 57
Key note	10	37, 40, 45, 46, 47, 50, 51, 55, 56, 58
Total	22	

[1] A majority of these songs are believed to be 50 to 150 years old.

Old Songs—(2) Songs Concerning Personal Dreams—Continued

MELODIC ANALYSIS—Continued

LAST NOTE OF SONG—ITS RELATION TO COMPASS OF SONG

	Number of songs.	Serial Nos. of songs.
Songs in which final tone is lowest tone in song........	20	37, 38, 39, 40, 41, 42, 43, 44, 45, 46, 48, 49, 50, 51, 52, 53, 54, 55, 56, 58
Songs containing a major third below the final tone.....	1	47
Songs containing a minor third below the final tone...	1	57
Total..	22	

NUMBER OF TONES COMPRISING COMPASS OF SONG

	Number of songs.	Serial Nos. of songs.
Compass of—		
Seventeen tones	1	55
Fourteen tones..................................	3	40, 43, 56
Thirteen tones..................................	3	39, 48, 52
Twelve tones....................................	2	37, 51
Eleven tones....................................	2	46, 50
Ten tones......................................	2	41, 49
Nine tones.....................................	3	53, 54, 57
Eight tones....................................	6	38, 42, 44, 45, 47, 58
Total...	22	

TONE MATERIAL

	Number of songs.	Serial Nos. of songs.
Second five-toned scale.............................	2	51, 54
Fourth five-toned scale.............................	6	38, 39, 43, 44, 53, 57
Major triad and second..............................	2	52, 55
Minor triad and fourth..............................	1	45
Octave complete....................................	1	40
Octave complete except seventh......................	2	37, 47
Octave complete except seventh and sixth............	1	46
Octave complete except seventh and second..........	1	58
Octave complete except sixth........................	2	43, 56
Octave complete except sixth and second............	1	50
Octave complete except fourth.......................	1	48
Octave complete except second.......................	1	41
First, fourth, and fifth tones........................	1	42
Total...	22	

Old Songs—*(2) Songs Concerning Personal Dreams*—Continued

MELODIC ANALYSIS—Continued

ACCIDENTALS

	Number of songs.	Serial Nos. of songs.
Songs containing—		
No accidentals	19	37, 38, 39, 40, 41, 42, 43, 45, 46, 48, 49, 50, 52, 53, 54, 55, 56, 57, 58
Fourth raised a semitone	1	51
Sixth lowered a semitone	1	44
Fourth lowered a semitone	1	47
Total	22	

STRUCTURE

	Number of songs.	Serial Nos. of songs.
Melodic	19	37, 38, 40, 41, 42, 43, 44, 45, 46, 47, 48, 49, 50, 51, 52, 53, 55, 56, 57
Melodic with harmonic framework	2	39, 54
Harmonic	1	58
Total	22	

FIRST PROGRESSION—DOWNWARD AND UPWARD

	Number of songs.	Serial Nos. of songs.
Downward	16	37, 38, 39, 40, 42, 43, 44. 45, 46, 47, 48, 50, 51, 54, 57, 58
Upward	6	41, 49, 52, 53, 55, 56
Total	22	

TOTAL NUMBER OF PROGRESSIONS—DOWNWARD AND UPWARD

Downward	420
Upward	215
Total	635

INTERVALS IN DOWNWARD PROGRESSION

Interval of a—	
Minor sixth	5
Fifth	4
Fourth	46
Major third	31
Minor third	109
Major second	190
Minor second	35
Total	420

Old Songs—(2) *Songs Concerning Personal Dreams*—Continued

MELODIC ANALYSIS—Continued

INTERVALS IN UPWARD PROGRESSION

	Number of songs.	Serial Nos. of songs.
Interval of a—		
Tenth	1	
Ninth	2	
Octave	4	
Major sixth	2	
Minor sixth	6	
Fifth	16	
Fourth	36	
Major third	13	
Minor third	46	
Major second	73	
Minor second	16	
Total	215	

AVERAGE NUMBER OF SEMITONES IN EACH INTERVAL

Total number of intervals	635	
Total number of semitones	1,966	
Average number of semitones in each interval	309	

KEY

	Number of songs.	Serial Nos. of songs.
Key of—		
A major	3	37, 51, 54
B flat major	1	48
B flat minor	1	46
B major	1	38
B minor	1	50
C minor	1	58
D flat major	2	39, 42
D major	2	44, 52
D minor	1	57
E major	1	53
F major	1	55
F minor	1	41
F sharp minor	2	45, 49
G major	1	43
G minor	1	56
G sharp minor	2	40, 47
Total	22	

Old Songs—(2) Songs Concerning Personal Dreams—Continued

RHYTHMIC ANALYSIS

PART OF MEASURE ON WHICH SONG BEGINS

	Number of songs.	Serial Nos. of songs.
Beginning on unaccented part of measure............	14	37, 39, 40, 43, 44, 46, 47, 48, 49, 50, 52 53, 54, 55
Beginning on accented part of measure...............	8	38, 41, 42, 45, 51, 56, 57, 58
Total...	22	

RHYTHM OF FIRST MEASURE

	Number of songs.	Serial Nos. of songs.
First measure in—		
2-4 time...	12	37, 38, 39, 42, 44, 47, 48, 49, 50, 53, 56, 58
3-4 time...	9	40, 41, 43, 45, 46, 51, 54, 55, 57
4-8 time...	1	52
Total...	22	

CHANGE OF TIME (MEASURE-LENGTHS)

	Number of songs.	Serial Nos. of songs.
Songs containing no change of time..................	2	39, 47
Songs containing a change of time...................	20	37, 38, 40, 41, 42, 43, 44, 45, 46, 48, 49, 50 51, 52, 53, 54, 55, 56, 57, 58
Total...	22	

RHYTHM OF DRUM

	Number of songs.	Serial Nos. of songs.
Eighth notes accented in groups of two..............	1	46
Eighth notes unaccented...........................	5	39, 44, 47, 52, 53
Quarter notes unaccented..........................	1	41
Drum not recorded	15	37, 38, 40, 42, 43, 45, 48, 49, 50, 51, 54, 55 56, 57, 58
Total...	22	

RHYTHMIC UNIT OF SONG

	Number of songs.	Serial Nos. of songs.
Songs containing—		
No rhythmic unit................................	7	38, 45, 46, 48, 49, 53, 55
One rhythmic unit...............................	13	37, 40, 41, 42. 43, 44, 47, 50, 51, 52, 54, 56, 58
Two rhythmic units.............................	1	39
Four rhythmic units.............................	1	57
Total...	22	

Old Songs—(2) Songs Concerning Personal Dreams—Continued

RHYTHMIC ANALYSIS—Continued

METRIC UNIT OF VOICE (TEMPO)

	Number of songs.	Serial Nos. of songs.
Metronome—		
54	1	51
56	1	48
60	2	45, 46
63	1	37
69	2	44, 50
72	2	39, 49
76	2	40, 43
84	2	56, 58
88	1	57
92	2	42, 47
100	2	38, 53
132	1	55
168	1	52
176	1	54
208	1	41
Total	22	

METRIC UNIT OF DRUM (TEMPO)

	Number of songs.	Serial Nos. of songs.
Metronome—		
69	1	44
88	1	53
92	1	47
120	1	46
138	1	52
144	1	41
152	1	39
Drum not recorded	15	37, 38, 40, 42, 43, 45, 48, 49, 50, 51, 54, 55, 56, 57, 58
Total	22	

COMPARISON OF METRIC UNIT OF VOICE AND DRUM (TEMPO)

	Number of songs.	Serial Nos. of songs.
Drum and voice having the same metric unit	2	44, 47
Drum faster than voice	2	39, 46
Drum slower than voice	3	41, 52, 53
Drum not recorded	15	37, 38, 40, 42, 43, 45, 48, 49, 50, 51, 54, 55, 56, 57, 58
Total	22	

PLOTS OF SONGS (DREAMS ABOUT ANIMALS)

From among the plots of the preceding group of songs four are herewith presented. No 56 is an example of Class A (see fig. 19) and contains no ascending intervals. No. 49 resembles it but contains short intervals which frequently occur in songs concerning animals or suggesting motion, as shown in Class D. We note that the title of this song is "Song of the old wolf," but that no suggestion of motion is found in the words. No. 55 has the wide compass and "rambling" outline which characterize songs of Class D. The title

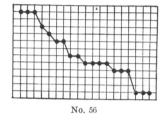

No. 56

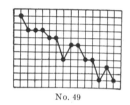

No. 49

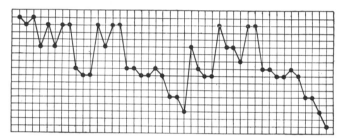

No. 55

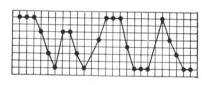

No. 58

Fig. 24. Plots, Group 2.

of this song is "An Eagle nation is coming." No. 58, while said to have been received in a dream of an animal, is a song used in the treatment of the sick, and in it may be observed the emphasis on the keynote, which characterizes Class C, as well as the divergence, which characterizes Class D.

THE SACRED STONES (TUŊKAŊ')

Songs relating to the sacred stones constitute the second group of songs received in dreams. To dream of a small stone was regarded by the Teton Sioux as a sign of great import, indicating that the dreamer, by fulfilling the requirements of his dream, would become possessed of supernatural power, in the exercise of which he would use the sacred stones. This power would be shown in an ability to cure sickness, to predict future events, and to tell the location of objects beyond the range of his natural vision. The stones were the native brown sandstone, usually spherical in shape, though oval stones and stones slightly flattened were also used, the principal requirements being that they should be regular in outline and untouched by a tool. The symbolism of the stones was given by Chased-by-Bears[1] as follows:

The outline of the stone is round, having no end and no beginning; like the power of the stone it is endless. The stone is perfect of its kind and is the work of nature, no artificial means being used in shaping it. Outwardly it is not beautiful, but its structure is solid, like a solid house in which one may safely dwell. It is not composed of many substances, but is of one substance, which is genuine and not an imitation of anything else. [2]

The term used by the Sioux in speaking of these stones is *tuŋkaŋ'*, said to be an abbreviation of *tuŋka'śila*, 'grandfather.' The word *tuŋkaŋ'* is an example of the "sacred language" mentioned on p. 120. Riggs (in the Dakota Dictionary) gives the meaning of this word as, "In the sacred language, *a stone*, and *the moon*." Thus is it seen that the term "sacred stones," used in the present work, is not a translation of *tuŋkaŋ'*, but is a term expressing more nearly the idea in the mind of the Sioux. (Cf. footnote, p. 88.)

It is said that a medicine-man, in demonstrating his power to acquire information by means of the sacred stones, sends them long distances. After a time the stones return and give him the desired information. He is the only person who can understand what they say, and therefore he repeats their message to the man who requested him to make the inquiry. During a demonstration for the curing of the sick it is said that the stones, flying through the air in the darkened tent, sometimes strike those who have refused to believe in them. This power of the sacred stones to move through the air is connected in the mind of the Sioux with *Ta'kuśkaŋśkaŋ'*, this term being composed of *ta'ku*, 'something', and *śkaŋśkaŋ'* (defined by Riggs as "*v. red.* of śkaŋ; *to stir, move about, change place*"). Several of the writer's most reliable informants, after consultation, expressed the opinion that Ta'kuśkaŋśkaŋ' could correctly be said to be one of the native Dakota gods. Pond regards this as one of the native gods, and writes: "The significance of the term 'Takuśkaŋśkaŋ' is *that which stirs*. This god is too subtle in essence to be perceived

---

[1] See Chased-by-Bears' account of the meaning of the Sun dance, p. 95. Other symbolisms are noted on p. 77, footnote.

[2] An emphasis on genuineness is found also on pp. 173, 330.

by the human senses. . . . His symbol is the bowlder. . . . He lives, also in what is termed 'the four winds.' " [1] Dorsey writes:

Takuśkaŋśkaŋ, the moving deity . . . is the most powerful of their [the Dakota] gods; the one most to be feared and propitiated, since, more than all others, he influences human weal and woe. He is supposed to live in the four winds, and the four black spirits of night do his bidding.[2]

Miss Alice C. Fletcher uses the term "Something that moves," and a connection between this mysterious power and the small stones appears in her article on "The religious ceremony of the Four Winds." [3] Miss Fletcher says:

An intelligent Santee Indian said to me: . . . "The Four Winds are sent by 'the Something that moves'. There is a 'Something that moves' at each of the 'Four Directions or Quarters'. . . . Among the Santee (Sioux) Indians the Four Winds are symbolized by the raven and a small black stone, less than a hen's egg in size.

The desire for a dream of this small black stone and the manner of its treatment, as described by this author, are similar to those connected with the sacred stones which form the subject of the present discussion.

Distinct from these small stones, which were carried on the person, were the large stones or rocks in the field which were "objects of worship." Riggs says, "Large bowlders were selected and adorned with red and green paint, whither the devout Dakota might go to pray and offer his sacrifice." [4] An interesting account of such a stone, known as Eyay Shah, "Red Rock," is given by Hovey. This stone was situated near the site of St. Paul, Minn., and was last visited by the Sioux shortly before their outbreak in 1862.[5] Many stones on the Dakota prairie are said to have been similarly regarded by the Sioux.

To talk of these stones is "sacred talk" to the Sioux, and the material comprised in this chapter was treated with the same reverence as that relating to the dream of the thunderbird or the ceremony of the Sun dance.

Songs and information concerning the sacred stones were secured from men who, in their relation to these objects, may be said to represent five different standpoints, as follows:

(1) Men who have dreamed of the sacred stones, possess one or more of them, and have used them successfully in treating the sick or in locating lost articles. Those of this class who furnished information were Brave Buffalo (Tataŋ'ka-ohi'tika) and Goose (Maǧa').

(2) Men who possess sacred stones, and believe they have been helped in various ways by their presence. Chased-by-Bears (Mato'-

[1] Pond, G. H., Dakota Superstitions, *Colls. Minn. Hist. Soc.* for 1867, vol. 2, pt. 3, pp. 43–44, St. Paul, 1867.

[2] Dorsey, James Owen, A Study of Siouan Cults, in *Eleventh Rep. Bur. Ethn.*, p. 445.

[3] In *Peabody Mus. Rep.*, III, pp. 289–90, Cambridge, Mass., 1887.

[4] Riggs, Stephen R., Theogony of the Sioux, *Amer. Antiq.*, II, No. IV, p. 268, Chicago, 1880.

[5] Hovey, H. C., D. D., Eyay Shah: A Sacrificial Stone near St. Paul, ibid., IX, No. I, pp. 35–36, 1887.

kuwa) had in his possession more than 40 years a sacred stone, which he acquired by purchase. He appealed to it when in danger and anxiety, but never attempted to secure through its use benefits for others than his immediate family. Lone Man (Iśna'la-wića') possesses one stone, and believes he has been greatly helped by wearing it on his person.

(3) A man who possesses a stone but does not use it. Charging Thunder (Wakiŋ'yaŋ-wata'kpe) has had a sacred stone for many years, but has not been able to command it as the medicine-men do. He attributes this lack of efficiency to the fact that he "does not place his faith wholly upon it, but believes in the help of many other agencies." The stone was given him at a time when he was sick, in the belief that it would restore him to health and also act as a charm. His father was skilled in the use of the stones, and Charging Thunder recorded songs which he said were composed by his father.

(4) A man who has not used the sacred stones, but who was one of the singers when White Shield (Waha'ćaŋka-ska) gave his wonderful demonstrations with them. It was customary for six or eight singers to sit at the drum and sing with the man who was giving the demonstration. Two Shields (Waha'ćuŋka-noŋ'pa) recorded two songs of White Shields's which had been used on such occasions. Two Shields is a close adherent of the the old beliefs, the missionaries having made no impression on him (pl. 47).

(5) Men who have witnessed demonstrations with the sacred stones in the camp, on the hunt, and on the warpath and were familiar with songs used at such times. Songs were recorded by Gray Whirlwind (Wamni'yomni-ho'ta), Shooter (Oku'te), Teal Duck (Śiya'ka), and Bear Eagle (Mato'waŋbli). Additional information, as well as corroboration and personal reminiscence, was furnished by Buffalo Head (Tataŋ'ka-pa) and Standing Soldier (Aki'ćita-na'źiŋ[1]).

Among the above-mentioned informants the man whose use of the sacred stones is most open at the present time is Brave Buffalo, a prominent medicine-man of the Standing Rock Reservation. He was born near the present site of Pollock, N. Dak., and at the time of giving his information was about 73 years of age. His father (see p. 250) was a leading medicine-man of the tribe. In describing his dream of the sacred stone Brave Buffalo said:

When I was 10 years of age I looked at the land and the rivers, the sky above, and the animals around me and could not fail to realize that they were made by some great power. I was so anxious to understand this power that I questioned the trees and the bushes. It seemed as though the flowers were staring at me, and I wanted to ask them "Who made you?" I looked at the moss-covered stones; some of them seemed to have the features of a man, but they could not answer me. Then I had a

---

[1] Died March, 1915.

dream, and in my dream one of these small round stones appeared to me and told me that the maker of all was Wakaŋ'taŋka, and that in order to honor him I must honor his works in nature. The stone said that by my search I had shown myself worthy of supernatural help. It said that if I were curing a sick person I might ask its assistance, and that all the forces of nature would help me work a cure.

Soon after this dream Brave Buffalo found on the top of a high butte his first sacred stone, which is still in his possession. About a month later he found several others, one of which is in the possession of the writer (pl. 29). This is almost a perfect sphere. On one side is a number of dots, the grouping of which suggests a tiny face, a characteristic pointed out by Brave Buffalo. The stone is dyed red with native dye. The color, which is a favorite color of Brave Buffalo, has no significance. The stone, surrounded by eagle down, is kept in a wrapping of red cotton cloth. It was said that "there is something between the eagle down and the stone, because when surrounded by eagle down, it can not get away." The stone can be sent on errands of observation by its owner, and when not in use is imprisoned by the downy eagle feathers.

Brave Buffalo said that he had cured many illnesses by means of this stone, which he said is "a brother of the first stone" he found. He said further that he "had no authority to secure its sisters, but that it was good to have several brothers of the original stone to cooperate with it." He "can feel if he is near a relative of the original stone" and always secures it. These relatives he may give away if he so desires, but the original stone has been seen by very few except the sick persons in whose treatment it has been used. (See p. 211.)

Concerning the nature of the sacred stones, Brave Buffalo said:

It is significant that these stones are not found buried in the earth, but are on the top of high buttes. They are round, like the sun and moon, and we know that all things which are round are related to each other. Things which are alike in their nature grow to look like each other, and these stones have lain there a long time, looking at the sun. Many pebbles and stones have been shaped in the current of a stream, but these stones were found far from the water and have been exposed only to the sun and the wind. The earth contains many thousand such stones hidden beneath its surface. The thunderbird is said to be related to these stones [see p. 158] and when a man or an animal is to be punished, the thunderbird strikes the person, and if it were possible to follow the course of the lightning, one of these stones would be found embedded in the earth. Some believe that these stones descend with the lightning, but I believe they are on the ground and are projected downward by the bolt. In all my life I have been faithful to the sacred stones. I have lived according to their requirements, and they have helped me in all my troubles. I have tried to qualify myself as well as possible to handle these sacred stones, yet I know that I am not worthy to speak to Wakaŋ'taŋka. I make my request of the stones and they are my intercessors. (See p. 88, footnote.)

UNWRAPPED   WRAPPED

PARTIALLY WRAPPED

SACRED STONE OWNED BY BRAVE BUFFALO

No. 59. "May You Behold a Sacred Stone Nation" (Catalogue No. 602)

Sung by BRAVE BUFFALO

VOICE ♩ = 80
DRUM ♩ = 168
Drum-rhythm similar to No. 19

Ko - la - pi - la   le - haŋl ko - la waŋ - la -

ka nuŋ-we o tuŋ-kaŋ le o - ya - te waŋ ko - la waŋ-la -

ka nuŋ - we le - na si - to - mni-yaŋ le - haŋl ko -

la waŋ-la - ka nuŋ-we o tuŋ-kaŋ le o - ya -

te waŋ ko - la waŋ - la - ka nuŋ-we o - *he* *e*

WORDS

kola′pila	friends
lehaŋl′	now
kola′	friend
waŋla′ka nuŋwe′	may you behold
tuŋkaŋ′ le oya′te waŋ	a Sacred-stone nation (see p. 162, footnote).
kola′	friend
waŋla′ka nuŋwe′	may you behold
lena′	these
sito′mniyaŋ	all (the stones)
lehaŋl′	now
kola′	friend
waŋla′ka nuŋwe′	may you behold
tuŋkaŋ′ le′oya′te waŋ	a Sacred Stone nation
waŋla′ka nuŋwe′	may you behold

Analysis.—This melody is minor in tonality and contains all the tones of the octave except the seventh and second. In structure it is classified as melodic with harmonic framework, the E flat in the third and the eleventh measures being the only accented tones other than those of the tonic triad. The major second and major third constitute 80 per cent of the intervals, though the tonality of the song is distinctly minor. The drum-beat is so rapid as to be practically a tremolo. The form of the melody is regular, consisting of four periods. One rhythmic unit occurs in the first and third phrases and a second rhythmic unit in the second and fourth phrases. These units show a similar division in the opening measure, followed by slightly different divisions. It is as though the second were an "answering phrase," the two combining to form a satisfactory whole.

See plot of this melody on page 245.

Goose, a prominent medicine-man, also dreamed of the sacred stones. (See p. 251.) He said that he had two of these stones in his possession some time before he tested his power over them. One day a fur trader ridiculed the medicine-men in his hearing. This white man said that all the medicine-men did was by sleight of hand, and that he would have to see an instance of their power before he would believe it. Goose entered into conversation with the trader on the subject, who offered him 10 articles, including cloth and blankets, if he would call a buffalo to the spot where they were standing. Goose sent both the sacred stones to summon a buffalo. The trader brought his field glasses and looked across the prairie, saying in derision, "Where is the buffalo you were to summon?" Suddenly the trader saw a moving object, far away. It came nearer until they could see it without the aid of the glasses. It was a buffalo, and it came so near that they shot it from the spot where they stood.

At a subsequent time Goose found a rifle which had fallen into the water. This occurred near the present site of Pierre, S. Dak. Some horses were being taken across the river on a ferry and others were compelled to swim. In the confusion a white man dropped his rifle into the river. The man regretted his loss, but made no effort to recover the rifle. After the man had gone, Goose decided to try to find it by the aid of the sacred stones. Accordingly he took the stones with him, and rowed on the river until the stones told him to dive. Doing so, he found the rifle on the bed of the river, a strange circumstance being that when he was in the water it appeared clear instead of cloudy as usual. Goose afterwards had an opportunity to restore the rifle to its owner, who rewarded him liberally.

(2) In addition to the stone purchased from Brave Buffalo another stone was transferred to the writer by Chased-by-Bears in July, 1912. This (pl. 30) is slightly larger than that of Brave Buffalo; the surface

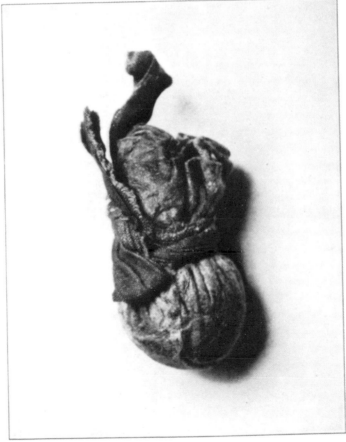

SACRED STONE OWNED BY CHASED-BY-BEARS

is smooth and not dyed. The stone was wrapped in a piece of deerskin and surrounded by the finely powdered root of an herb. Chased-by-Bears said that he used this herb as a "charm" and also took it internally. When parting with the stone he refused to give the writer any of this herb, but it was secured and identified later.

This stone had been in the possession of Chased-by-Bears 40 years, and during that time he had faithfully fulfilled its requirements of character and action. Throughout this period, moreover, he had not lost one of his children, illness was almost unknown in his family, and he had suffered no great misfortune from any cause. In time of anxiety, either through fear of sickness or disaster, he had carried the stone in his medicine bag. Chased-by-Bears was 64 years old when he gave this information and seemed to be in perfect health. He said that the stone formerly belonged to a very powerful medicine-man named White Shield, who then lived at Standing Rock but had since moved to Poplar Creek, Mont. He warned the writer that the stone was still subject to a summons from White Shield and that at some time it might disappear from its wrappings, but that if such were the case she need feel no anxiety, as it would return. He said that White Shield had many such stones, one of which was for his personal use; this was always worn in a buckskin bag around his neck. The others were the "helpers" of this stone, and he could sell them, though he retained the right to recall them if he so desired. White Shield had dreamed of the sacred stones, had qualified himself to use them in treating the sick and in other ways, and had composed many songs concerning them.

White Shield's stone came into the possession of Chased-by-Bears in the following manner: About 40 years previous to giving this information a daughter of Chased-by-Bears was ill, and he sent for White Shield to treat her. White Shield showed him the sacred stone, then it disappeared and the tent was darkened. After a time the light was restored, whereupon the stone was found on the person of the girl, who at once began to recover. Chased-by-Bears then asked for the stone which White Shield had used in performing the cure, and White Shield transferred it to him together with the song which he sang at the time and which he said should always be sung when any request was made of the stone. In exchange for these Chased-by-Bears gave a horse. The song, which follows, is believed to have been composed by White Shield.

No. 60. "The Sacred Stones Come to See You" (Catalogue No. 675)

Sung by CHASED-BY-BEARS

VOICE ♩ = 60
DRUM ♩ = 168
Drum-rhythm similar to No. 19

He waŋ-ni - yaŋk   a - u   we

tuŋ-kaŋ

kiŋ   si - to - mni - yaŋ waŋ - ni - yaŋk a - u   we

WORDS

he waŋni′yaŋk..................	to see you
aü′ we.........................	they come
tuŋkaŋ′ kiŋ sito′mniyaŋ.....	all the sacred stones
waŋni′yaŋk....................	to see you
aü′ we........................	they come

Analysis.—This melody consists of 32 measures, which group themselves in 4 periods of 8 measures each. The first and third of these periods are based on the triad of F minor, and the second and fourth periods on the minor third C–E flat. The song is transcribed and analyzed in the key of C minor, though the fifth of that key does not occur. The rhythm of the first and second halves of the song is alike except for slight changes in the part containing the words. The rhythmic unit is short and occurs frequently. Two renditions, on separate cylinders, show no material points of difference.

In parting with the sacred stone and in singing its song, Chased-by-Bears seemed actuated by a sincere desire that his grandchildren should understand the native religious ideas which had governed his life, and that the white man might better know the mind of the Sioux. But misfortune followed his action. After a few weeks the writer on returning to the reservation was informed that Chased-by-Bears had suffered a stroke of paralysis,[1] which was attributed to his sale of the sacred stone and its song. Mr. Higheagle was requested to visit Chased-by-Bears and ascertain whether the report were correct. It was found that Chased-by-Bears seemed to be in danger of death. Mr. Higheagle was then instructed to tell him that the stone would be returned to him as soon as it had been measured, weighed, and photographed. Every effort was made to allay the nervous tension under which the aged man was suffering. After a time Chased-by-Bears was well enough to come and camp near the agency. He walked heavily, leaning on his cane. Food was sent to his camp, and when he was able to come to the writer's office she played for him the phonograph records of sacred-stone songs which others had sung, endeavoring to impress him with the idea that he had not transgressed more than they. At length the subject of the herb used with the stone was broached, and it was suggested that if the stone were to be returned perhaps he would be willing to loan a portion of the herb for identification, which, together with the stone, would subsequently be given him by Mr. Higheagle. After several conferences Chased-by-Bears brought the plant, which was identified at Washington as *Aster* sp. With this he had in his medicine bag a root which, he said, he powdered and mixed with the root of the first plant. It was a pithy root, but as none of the upper part of the plant was available it could not be identified. Chased-by-Bears was encouraged to be present when other Indians were recording songs, and it was observed that his health steadily improved. When the writer left the reservation a few weeks later he had almost regained his strength, and a year afterwards he appeared to be in his usual health.[2] Both the stone and the herbs were returned at the earliest opportunity, but it is interesting to note that the man's physical recovery began before these were actually restored to his possession. Chased-by-Bears' misfortune did not seem to arouse any antagonism toward the writer or her work. In conversation with those who were considered authorities on the subject it was said that he "should have known better than to sell a stone when he had only *one*." A medicine-man could sell the "helpers" of his special stone, but even a medicine-man would not part with the stone which was the center of his power.

---

[1] It is the belief of the Chippewa that those who offend the "manido" are punished by paralysis. Thus the writer saw at a remote Chippewa village on the northern shore of Lake Superior a man who had suffered paralysis of one side of his face and body, and whose personal record was not good. It is said by the Chippewa that many offending members of the Mĭdĕ′wĭwĭn become paralyzed.

[2] Chased-by-Bears died in February, 1915, more than two years after the paralytic stroke.

As an introduction to his narrative concerning the sacred stones, Lone Man said:

Ever since I have known the old Indians and their customs, I have seen that in any great undertaking it is not enough for a man to depend simply upon himself. Most people place their dependence on the medicine-men, who understand this life and all its surroundings and are able to predict what will come to pass. They have the right to make these predictions. If as we sit here we should hear a voice speaking from above, it would be because we had the right to hear what others could not hear, or we might see what others had not the right to see because they were not properly qualified. Such are some of the rights and privileges of the medicine-men, and those who desire to know mysterious things must seek their aid. If a man desires success in war or the hunt, or if he wishes to make the greatest of all requests, which is the request for long life, he should make it through a medicine-man, who will give him a charm, probably a root of herb wrapped in buckskin, and he will wear this charm. [See p. 161.] It is not enough for a man to make known his request. There is a way which it has been found best to follow, and that is to make an offering with the request.

When I was a young man I went to a medicine-man for advice concerning my future. The medicine-man said: "I have not much to tell you except to help you understand this earth on which you live. If a man is to succeed on the hunt or the warpath, he must not be governed by his inclination, but by an understanding of the ways of animals and of his natural surroundings, gained through close observation.[1] The earth is large, and on it live many animals. This earth is under the protection of something which at times becomes visible to the eye. One would think this would be at the center of the earth [see p. 120], but its representations appear everywhere, in large and small forms—they are the sacred stones. The presence of a sacred stone will protect you from misfortune."[2] He then gave me a sacred stone which he himself had worn. I kept it with me wherever I went and was helped by it. He also told me where I might find one for myself. Wakaŋ'taŋka tells the sacred stones many things which may happen to people. The medicine-man told me to observe my natural surroundings, and after my talk with him I observed them closely. I watched the changes of the weather, the habits of animals, and all the things by which I might be guided in the future, and I stored this knowledge in my mind.

The medicine-man also told me that the sacred stone may appear in the form of a person who talks and sings many wonderful songs. Among these was the following song, in which the sacred stone says that all living creatures look to him for protection. This and the song next following were composed and used by Ite'-oksaŋ-lu'ta [Red-Streaked-around-the-Face], a man who dreamed of the rainbow and therefore painted his face with an arch of color. He used red for this arch, as red was his favorite among the colors of the rainbow.

[1] In this connection it is interesting to note the following statement by Father De Smet, a native of Belgium, who came to America in 1821 and for many years labored as a Jesuit missionary among the Sioux, writing extensively of their conditions and needs. He says: "Some writers have supposed that the Indians are guided by instinct, and have even ventured to assert that their children would find their way through the forests as well as those further advanced in age. I have consulted some of the most intelligent Indians on this subject, and they uniformly told me that they acquire this practical knowledge by long and close attention to the growth of plants and trees, and to the sun and stars. . . . Parents teach their children to remark such things, and these in their turn sometimes add new discoveries to those of their fathers." (Life, Letters, and Travels of Father Pierre-Jean De Smet, S. J., edited by Hiram Martin Chittenden and Alfred Talbot Richardson, III, p. 1016, New York, 1905.)]

[2] The carrying of a sacred stone in order to secure a benefit from its presence is, in the mind of the Sioux, on an entirely different plane from the wearing of a "charm" (wo'tahe). This is one of many instances in which the English language lacks a brief equivalent for the shades of meaning in an Indian language.]

No. 61. "I Sing for the Animals"   (Catalogue No. 489)

Sung by LONE MAN

VOICE ♩ = 84
DRUM ♩ = 96
Drum-rhythm similar to No. 6

Ma - ka taŋ-haŋ wa - ki - lo - waŋ   ye - lo *he*   *yo* ma -

ka taŋ-haŋ wa - ki - lo-waŋ   ye - lo *he* śuŋ - ka-wa-kaŋ o - ya -

te wa - ki - lo - waŋ lo *he*   ma - ka taŋ-haŋ wa - ki - lo-waŋ

ye - lo *he*   *yo*   ma - kaś - kaŋ   wa - ki - lo - waŋ

ye - lo *he* śuŋ - ka - wa - kaŋ o - ya - te wa - ki - lo -

waŋ lo *he*   kaś - kaŋ wa - ki - lo - waŋ   ye - lo *he*

WORDS

maka′ taŋhaŋ′.................. out of the earth
waki′lowaŋ yelo′............... I sing for them
śuŋka′wakaŋ oya′te........... a Horse nation (see p. 162, footnote)
waki′lowaŋ yelo′ [1]............. I sing for them
maka′ taŋhaŋ′.................. out of the earth
waki′lowaŋ yelo′............. I sing for them
wama′kaśkaŋ [2].................. the animals
waki′lowaŋ yelo............... I sing for them

Analysis.—This melody comprises the tones of the fourth five-toned scale, beginning on the dominant above the tonic and ending on the third in the lower octave, a somewhat unusual melodic out-

---

[1] The first syllable of this word was omitted by the singer.
[2] One or two syllables of this word were omitted by the singer.

line.   The rhythmic unit occurs three times, and there are two other phrases in the melody which closely resemble it.   One of these appears at the close of the song.   Three renditions were recorded. Throughout these the time was less steadily maintained than in a majority of the songs under analysis.

After singing this song Lone Man bowed his head and reverently made the following prayer.   It was not his expectation that this and the prayers which preceded two other songs (Nos. 53, 55) would be recorded, but as he was seated at the phonograph it was possible to secure the records without attracting his attention, and the records were afterwards translated.   His prayer was as follows:

Maka'taŋhaŋ wića'śa waŋ wićo'ħaŋ waŋ awa'hiyaya tka hena' oŋ oŋ'śimala yo, tuwa' waŋka'taŋhaŋ in'itaŋćaŋ he'ćina.

(Translation)

A man from the earth I am, I have sung concerning an event, for which have compassion on me, whoever from above, you [who are] the supreme ruler.

Continuing his narrative, Lone Man said:

Another instruction given me by the medicine-man was that all herbs and roots are made for the benefit of animals or man.   Some herbs and roots vary in color according to the season of the year, and others do not.   All are carefully tested, and if one is found to be a cure for a certain disease, it should be regarded as a gift from Wakaŋ'-taŋka, and intended especially as a remedy for that disease.   It should be reverenced, and this reverence should be closely observed, as without it the herb will have no effect.   Because of the reverence due to these medicinal herbs certain songs are used expressing this feeling.   This, like the preceding song, was used by the man who dreamed of a rainbow.   It may have been used when painting a horse on the warpath.   [See pp. 350, 353.]

No. 62. "My Horse"   (Catalogue No. 490)

Sung by LONE MAN

VOICE $\quad \downarrow = 104$

DRUM $\quad \downarrow = 104$

Drum-rhythm similar to No. 6

Mi - ta - śuŋ - ke   kiŋ - yaŋ   ye   wa - ye - lo   *he*   pe -

źu - ta waŋ ko - yag   wa - ki   ye - lo   kiŋ - yaŋ   ye   wa - ye

he   mi-ta - śuŋ - ke   kiŋ - yaŋ   ye   wa - ye - lo   *he*

WORDS

mita′šuŋke	my horse
kiŋyaŋ′	flying
ye	along
wa′yelo	I have caused
peźu′ta waŋ	a medicine
koyag′	to wear
waki′ yelo′	I caused my own
kiŋyaŋ′	flying
ye	along
wa′ye	I have caused
mita′šuŋke	my horse
kiŋyaŋ′	flying
ye	along
wa′yelo	I have caused

Analysis.—Four renditions of this song were recorded. In the first and fourth renditions the word *peźu′ta* was sung, as indicated in the transcription. This is an abbreviation of *peźi′huta,* "a root of herb," but commonly used in the sense of "medicine," the herb having either a curative or (as in this case) a mysterious power to benefit by its presence. In the second rendition this word was replaced by *maka′ġi,* "brown earth," and in the third by *maka′to,* "blue earth." Both these earths were used in the making of paint, which was used on horses as well as the bodies of men and on their possessions. (See p. 116.) This song begins with an upward progression of a fifth, which is somewhat unusual, yet only about one-fourth of the progressions in the song are upward. The song is minor in tonality and melodic in structure. The seventh and second tones of the octave are not found in the melody. A rhythmic quality is somewhat lacking in the song, which contains no rhythmic unit.

In closing, Lone Man said:

After the medicine-man had given me this advice and instruction and had taught me the songs, he told me how to act in various emergencies, after which I realized that I must depend on myself, and that if I failed I must seek help from other sources, as he did not expect that I would return to him.

(3) Four songs concerning the sacred stones were recorded by Charging Thunder, who does not use the stones himself, but who learned the songs from his father, Bear Necklace (Mato′napin), a prominent medicine-man. The first of these songs was received in a dream of the sacred stones.

Charging Thunder said that his father, while on a buffalo hunt, was thrown from his horse, falling on a pile of stones and injuring his head. He lay unconscious almost all day and was found in the evening. His wound was dressed, and when he regained consciousness he said that all the rocks and stones "were people turned to stone."

After this he found some stones (similar to those in pls. 29 and 30). He could talk to them and depended on them for help. Once a war party had been gone two months; no news of them had been received, and it was feared that all were killed. In their anxiety the people appealed to Bear Necklace, asking him to ascertain, by means of the sacred stones, what had become of the war party. Bear Necklace requested them to tie his arms behind him, then to tie his fingers and toes, interlacing them with twisted sinew. He was then wrapped in a buffalo robe and tied with ropes. His medicine drum, medicine bag, and a bell were hung high on the tent poles, and he was laid on the ground beneath them. The tent was darkened, he sang the following song and told his dreams. Then the tent began to tremble, the articles hanging from the pole dropped to the ground, his cords loosened, and he stood entirely free. As soon as the medicine articles fell to the ground there appeared a row of four or five small round stones ready to tell him what he wanted to know. Sitting Bull was present and made an offering of a buffalo robe to the sacred stones and asked that he might become famous.[1] Bear Necklace wrapped one of the stones in buckskin and gave it to him. Sitting Bull wore it in a bag around his neck to the time of his death, and it was buried with him.

Bear Necklace then gave correct information concerning the absent war party. At that time he proved his power to give information by the help of the sacred stones, and afterwards the stones always told him the names of those who were killed in war, the names of the survivors, and the day on which they would return. This information was always correct.

The following song was composed by Bear Necklace at the time he was hurt, and was sung by him when demonstrating his power. The words refer to the passing of the stones through the air in the darkened tent while an exhibition of his power was in progress. It is said that a person who did not believe in the power of the stones was frequently struck by them, or by other objects hurtling through the air in the spirit-filled darkness.

---

[1] See account of Sitting Bull, p. 458; also songs Nos. 91, 92.

No. 63. "Worthy of Reverence"   (Catalogue No. 563)

Sung by CHARGING THUNDER

WORDS [1]

(First rendition)

niyo'ḣpeyata	in the direction of the sunset
tate'[2]	the wind
uye'ćiŋ	is blowing
na	and
tuŋkaŋ' le	these stones
mime'	one round
me'ya	another round
kiŋyaŋ[1]	flying
kiyu'ze	continuing to fly
waŋyaŋ'kiye	behold them

(Second rendition)

wazi'yata	in the direction of the home of the giant
tate'	the wind
uye'ćiŋ	is blowing
ta'ku	something
wakaŋ'	worthy of reverence
kiŋyaŋ'	(the stones) flying
aü' we	toward us
waŋyaŋ'kiye	behold them

(Third rendition)

wiyo'hiŋyaŋpa'ta	in the direction of the sunrise
tate'	the wind
uye'ćiŋ	is blowing
tuŋkaŋ'	stones
mime'	one round
me'ya	another round
kiŋyaŋ'	flying
aü' we	toward us
waŋyaŋ'kiye	behold them

---

[1] Cf. song No. 24.

[2] The singer elided the final *e*, substituting therefor the first letter of the following word, singing *tatu*.

(Fourth rendition)

ito′kaǵata	in the direction before us
ta′ku	something
wakaŋ′	worthy of reverence
o′ta	many (of the stones)
kiŋyaŋ′	flying
kiyu′ze	continuing to fly
waŋyaŋ′kiye	behold them

Analysis.—This melody comprises the tones of the fourth five-toned scale with the sharped second as an accidental. The descending interval of an augmented second was clearly given. This interval occurs also in songs Nos. 106 and 225. Four renditions of this song were recorded, the repetitions beginning without a break in the time. About 75 per cent of the intervals are downward progressions.

The three songs following were also composed and used by Bear Necklace.

No. 64. "A Sacred Stone Nation Is Speaking"   (Catalogue No. 566)

Sung by CHARGING THUNDER

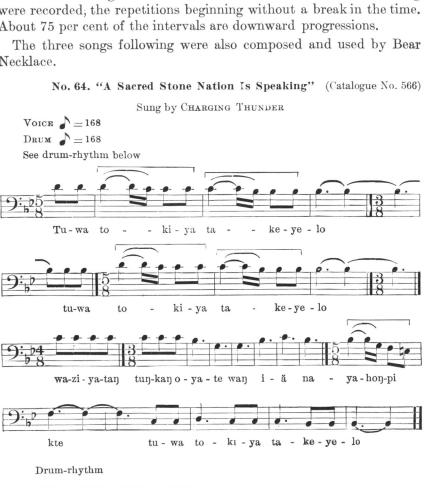

Drum-rhythm

WORDS

tu′wa	some one
to′kiya	somewhere
take′yelo	is speaking
wazi′yataŋ	from the north
tuŋkaŋ′ oya′te waŋ	a Sacred-stone nation
iä′	is speaking
naya′hoŋpi kte	you will hear
tu′wa	some one
to′kiya	somewhere
take′yelo	is speaking

Analysis.—This melody is major in tonality, and contains all the tones of the octave except the seventh. One accidental occurs—the fourth raised a semitone. The 5–8 time is clearly given in all the renditions. This is the only song in the entire work which begins in 5–8 time, but this measure–division is found also in Nos. 41, 68, 125, 169, and 223. Only 19 progressions are found in the song—an unusually small number in a song of this length. About two-thirds of the intervals are downward progressions.

No. 65. "They Move With a Purpose"   (Catalogue No. 567)

Sung by CHARGING THUNDER

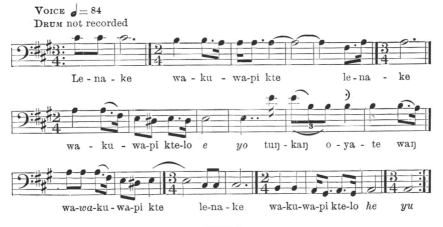

WORDS

lena′ke	all these
waku′wapi kte	move with a purpose
lena′ke	all these
waku′wapi ktelo′	move with a purpose
tuŋkaŋ′ oya′te waŋ	a Sacred-stone nation
waku′wapi kte	moves with a purpose
lena′ke	all these
waku′wapi ktelo′	move with a purpose

Analysis.—This song, like the preceding, is major in tonality and contains all the tones of the octave except the seventh. The repetitions begin without a break in the time. In this, as in numerous other instances, the tone marked ·) was similarly shortened in all the renditions. The song is melodic in structure, yet we note that the first six measures are based on the minor triad of F sharp; the melody then ascends to E, and the tonic chord appears in the downward progression. A prominence of the submediant triad (minor) at the opening of a song in a major key was observed in the Chippewa songs and is of frequent occurrence in the present series.

No. 66. "From Everywhere They Come" (Catalogue No. 565)

Sung by CHARGING THUNDER

WORDS

to′kiyataŋ ḳeya′	....	from everywhere
aü′ we	....	they come
kiŋyaŋ′	....	flying
wazi′yataŋ	....	(from) the north
tatu′ye	....	the wind is blowing
maka′ta	....	to earth

ićas'na...................... rattling
kiŋyaŋ'...................... flying
aü' we....................... they come
aü' we....................... they come
to'kiyataŋ ḳeya'............. from everywhere
aü' we....................... they come

Analysis.—Almost two-thirds of the intervals in this song are minor thirds. In the first part the descending minor third E flat–C forms the basis of the melody. In the eighth measure the descending minor third D flat–B flat is introduced and continues for several measures, followed by the minor third A flat–F, the song ending with D flat–B flat, making a satisfactory close on the tonic. All the tones of the octave are present in this song and the feeling of a keynote is well established, yet it is noted that the tones are not grouped along the lines of triad chords, but of single intervals. This "interval formation" was given extended consideration in Bulletin 53, pages 7–8.

(4) In giving a complete demonstration of the sacred stones, it was customary for the man who was proving his power to tell his dreams and sing the songs of the dreams, these being in the nature of credentials. The two following songs were used in this manner by White Shield and recorded by Two Shields. The words are obscure, as in the majority of dream songs.

In songs Nos. 70, 71, and 72 the sacred stones address their owner as "father," or "grandfather."

No. 67. "A Wolf Nation Called Me 'Father'" (Catalogue No. 541)

Sung by Two Shields

VOICE ♩ = 92
DRUM ♩ = 138
Drum-rhythm similar to No. 19

Tu-wa he - ma - ki ye - lo   tu-wa he - ma - ki ye-

lo śuŋ-ka o - ya - te waŋ   a - te e - ma - ki ye-

lo   tu-wa he - ma - ki ye - lo śuŋ-ka o - ya - te waŋ

a - te e - ma - ki ye - lo   tu-wa he - ma - ki ye-

lo śuŋ-ka o - ya - te waŋ   a - te e - ma - ki ye - lo

WORDS

tu′wa......................... some one
hema′ki yelo′................. told me
śuŋ′ka oya′te waŋ............. (that) a Wolf nation (see p. 162, footnote)
ate′ ema′ki yelo′............. called me "father"

Analysis.—It is not unusual to note a song in a major key beginning with the submediant chord, which is minor. In this instance,
however, a song in a minor key begins with the submediant triad,
which is major. The eighth measure introduces the descending
minor third A–F sharp, which forms the framework of the melody to
the sixteenth measure. This is followed by a return to the submediant triad, the song closing with the descending minor third A–F
sharp. If these tones (F sharp–A–C sharp–E) were used consecutively, it might be said that the melody is based on the minor triad
with minor seventh added, but this chord relation is not suggested by
the framework of the melody. This song is melodic in structure and
lacks the sixth and second tones of the complete octave. The

rhythmic unit is well defined, and its repetitions comprise the entire song except the closing measures of each section.

Two Shields stated that he had frequently sung at the drum when White Shield used this song, the singers at the drum carrying the song with him. In the second rendition the words "Wolf nation" were used instead of those for "Stone nation." It was said that on more than one occasion when the words "Wolf nation" were used a wolfskin medicine bag became alive and walked around.

No. 68. "I Have Caused Them to Roam"   (Catalogue No. 539)

Sung by Two Shields

VOICE ♪ = 160
DRUM ♪ = 138
Drum-rhythm similar to No. 19

Wa-kaŋ-yaŋ ma - ni wa-ye wa - kaŋ-yaŋ ma - ni wa - ye

tuŋ-kaŋ o - ya - te waŋ wa - kaŋ - yaŋ ma - ni wa -

ye wa - kaŋ - yaŋ ma - ni wa-ye wa - kaŋ - yaŋ

ma - ni wa-ye wa - kaŋ-yaŋ ma - ni wa-ye

WORDS

wakaŋ'yaŋ........................ in a sacred manner
ma'ni waye' tuŋkaŋ' oya'te waŋ. I have caused a Sacred-stone nation to roam
                                 (see p. 162, footnote)
wakaŋ'yaŋ........................ in a sacred manner
ma'ni waye'...................... I have caused them to roam

Analysis.—This is one of the comparatively few songs containing 5–8 measures. (See song No. 64.) The frequent occurrence of the descending fourth recalls the observation among Chippewa songs that the interval of the fourth seems to characterize songs concerning animals, especially men and animals in motion. (See Bulletin 53, pp.

99–101.)   This progression is especially noted in the descent C–G–D, in the seventh and eighth measures from the end.   Two-thirds of the intervals in the song are major seconds.   The metric unit of the drum is slightly slower than that of the voice and is steadily maintained.

See plot of this melody on page 245.

(5) Gray Whirlwind also sang a song, which was used by White Shield in his demonstrations.

No. 69. "These Are My Spies"   (Catalogue No. 667)

Sung by GRAY WHIRLWIND

VOICE ♩ = 92
DRUM ♩ = 132

Drum-rhythm similar to No. 19

He-na mi-ta toŋ-we - ya *i ya i yo* kiŋ-yaŋ   a-ku we he -

na   mi - ta   toŋ- we - ya   *ya*   *ya* kiŋ-yaŋ   a-ku we tuŋ -

kaŋ o - ya - te kiŋ a-ku he - na mi-ta toŋ- we - ya   kiŋ - yaŋ

WORDS

he′na............................ these (are)
mita′............................ my
toŋwe′ya........................ spies
kiŋyaŋ′.......................... flying
a′ku we .... returning
tuŋkaŋ′ oya′te kiŋ.............. the Sacred-stone nation (see p. 162, footnote)
á′ku............................. returning
he′na............................ these (are)
mita′............................ my
toŋwe′ya........................ spies
kiŋyaŋ′.......................... flying

Analysis.—This song contains only three tones—those of the tonic triad—and therefore is necessarily harmonic in structure.   Only four Chippewa songs (1 per cent) in a series of 340 contained this tone material, and it is found in only about 1 per cent of the present series.   Only two upward progressions are found in the song.   Three renditions were recorded.   Between the renditions the singer gave prolonged cries or calls. In one of these instances the drum was continued, and in the other it was silent. The usual custom is for the drumbeat to be continued during these cries or calls.

In the following song the stone addresses its owner as "grandfather":

No. 70. "I Am Required to Roam"   (Catalogue No. 668)

Sung by GRAY WHIRLWIND

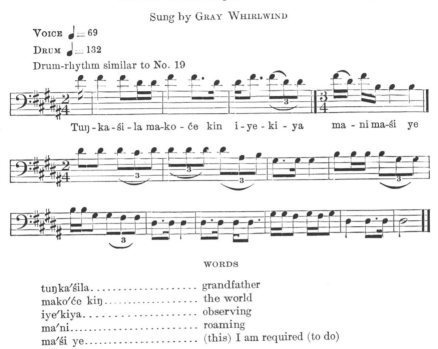

WORDS

tuŋka′śila................... grandfather
mako′ćo kiŋ................ the world
iye′kiya................... observing
ma′ni..................... roaming
ma′śi ye................... (this) I am required (to do)

Analysis.—This is one of the songs in which a single change in the time seems to give a certain "swing" to the entire rhythm of the song. This rhythmic peculiarity was frequently observed among the Chippewa' songs. Thus, in two of three renditions of this song the fourth measure was sung as transcribed, while in the other rendition an additional measure was inserted, the first two counts of the fourth measure forming a measure in double time, followed by B flat (final count of the fourth measure) prolonged into a triple measure. An additional measure does not seem to trouble an Indian singer, as the form of a song as a whole seems to be less definite among Indians than among musicians of the white race.

This melody is major in tonality and harmonic in structure. The tonic triad forms the framework of the first four measures, after which the descending minor third B–G sharp appears, the song closing with a descent to the third of the key. This melodic outline is unusual and interesting. The opening of the song has force and definiteness, and the prominence of the fourth in the latter portion reminds us that this interval frequently characterizes songs concerning motion. The upward and downward intervals are more nearly equal than is commonly the case. See plot of this melody on page 245.

In this and the following song the sacred stones are addressing their owner. These songs were recorded by Shooter (Oku'te), a man who is familiar with the ancient customs of his people. (See pp. 157–158, 172, 173.)

No. 71. "Father, Behold Me"   (Catalogue No. 574)

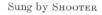

Sung by SHOOTER

Voice ♩ = 69
Drum ♩ = 160
Drum-rhythm similar to No. 19

A - te ma-ka kiŋ o-wa-ki-yiŋ kte   a - - te waŋ-ma-yaŋ -

ka yo   a - te   ma - ka kiŋ   o - wa - ki - yiŋ kte   a -

te   waŋ - ma - yaŋ - ka   yo   yo   e   yo

WORDS

ate'............................ father
maka' kiŋ.................... the earth
o'wakiyiŋ kte................ I intend to help
ate'............................ father
waŋma'yaŋka yo............. behold me

Analysis.—This melody begins on the octave of the tonic and ends on the dominant below the tonic—a somewhat unusual outline. The first progression is upward, but the trend of the melody as a whole is downward, the tonic being more strongly emphasized than in most of the songs under analysis. The division of the first count in the first measure characterizes the entire song, but there is no recurrent phrase which can be considered a rhythmic unit.

See plot of this melody on page 245.

No. 72. "I Was Ordered to Return" (Catalogue No. 582)

Sung by SHOOTER

VOICE ♩ = 72
DRUM ♩ = 152
Drum-rhythm similar to No. 19

Tuŋ - ka - ṡi-la e - ya ku ma-yaŋ pe-

lo

WORDS

tuŋka′ṡila .... grandfather
e′ya ku .... to return
mayaŋ′ pelo′ .... I was ordered

Analysis.—All the accented tones in this song are those of the tonic chord, showing the song to be strongly harmonic in structure. The melody tones are those of the fourth five-toned scale. The interval of a fourth is prominent in both ascending and descending progression, as has frequently been noted in songs concerning motion. About two-thirds of the intervals in this song are downward progressions.

Ṡiya′ka (see pl. 1 and pp. 184 et seq., 439 et seq.) sang three songs of the sacred stones and related instances in which he had heard of their use in locating buffalo and finding the enemy. He first described a performance by Crooked Foot (Siha′ĺimin), who died in 1877. Crooked Foot was asked to ascertain by means of the sacred stones where buffalo could be found. The stone which he used was egg-shaped, and he was said to have found it on top of the highest butte near his home. When giving this performance Crooked Foot had the stone encased in a bag. He said: "The stone has now gone to look for the buffalo, but when it comes back you will see it." The people then prepared a place on which it was expected that the stone would appear. This was done by pulverizing the earth for a space about a foot square and covering this place with buffalo hide or with part of a red blanket. All watched this place, and after a time the stone appeared upon it. Crooked Foot questioned the stone concerning the location of the buffalo, and the tribe, acting on his advice, found the herd as he had indicated. If he had been employed by an individual to locate horses or other property which was lost, the man employing him would have lighted a pipe and offered it to the stone as soon as it appeared. Before passing the pipe to the assembly this man would have questioned the stone. The replies would have been given by the owner of the stone, as he was supposed to be the only person present who understood what the stone said. He repeated what the stone said to him, and the man who employed him received it as the message of the stone. In the words of Crooked Foot's song the stone is represented as speaking to its owner, calling him "father" and asking that he will not require of it anything unreasonable.

No. 73. "Father, Sing to Me" (Catalogue No. 462)

Sung by Śíya′ka

VOICE ♩ = 126
DRUM not recorded

A - te ma - ki - lo - waŋ yo wa - na hi - bu we a -
te ma - ki - lo - waŋ yo wa - na hi - bu we he ta - ku a - i -
ye - ćiŋ a - te ma - ki - lo - waŋ yo wa - na hi - bu we a -
te ma - ki - lo - waŋ yo wa - na hi - bu we
he ta - ku a - i - ye - ćiŋ a - te ma - ki - lo - waŋ yo wa - na
hi - bu we a - te ma - ki - lo - waŋ yo wa - na hi - bu we

WORDS

ate′.............................	father
maki′lowaŋ yo...................	sing to me
wana′...........................	now
hibu′ we........................	I come
he.............................	in this
ta′ku...........................	thing
aïye′ćiŋ........................	be reasonable

Analysis.—This song is minor in tonality and lacks the seventh and fourth tones of the complete octave. (See song No. 26,) The rhythmic unit is lengthy and continuously repeated, giving little opportunity for taking breath. Between the renditions of the song were given the high calls which frequently interrupt Indian singing, but in these calls, or cries, the tempo of the song was maintained, so there was no break in the time during the entire performance. This song begins on the twelfth and progresses steadily downward to the tonic at the close.

When Śiya′ka was on the warpath the sacred stones were invoked by Heḣa′ka-na′źiŋ (Standing Elk), who sent them on their customary search, and then said to the warriors:

In the early morning you will meet one man and kill him. You will meet a wolf coming from the north before you see this enemy. Let each man pray to the wolf, calling him "grandfather" and asking that he may get a count.[1] You will also meet a large crow flying toward you from the north. Let each man make the same prayer to the crow. After seeing the crow you will see one enemy coming also from the north.

Everything came to pass as the stone had predicted. They met the wolf and the crow; then they saw one man and killed him. The man was a scout, but the Sioux did not know this. The war party of the enemy, following the scout, made a charge on the Sioux. There were 19 in the enemy's party and 4 brave Sioux stood against them and drove them back. The enemies were Arikaree and Mandan. After peace was established the Sioux talked with them about this battle and learned that the name of the scout was One Feather. Śiya′ka was one of the four men who drove them back and won a count at that time. He said that the following song was used by Standing Elk in making his request of the stones. No drum was used with this song.

---

[1] The right to wear a war-honor feather in the hair.

No. 74. "A Spirit Has Come"   (Catalogue No. 461)

Sung by ŚIYA′KA

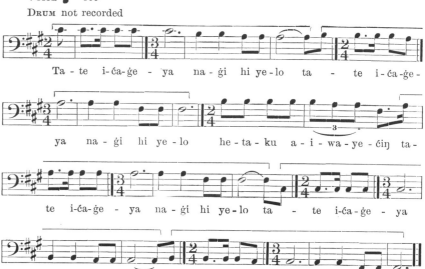

WORDS

tate′ iċa′ġeya	with the wind
naġi′	a spirit
hi yelo′	has come
heta′ku	something
aï′waye′ċiŋ	I foretold

Analysis.—Three renditions of this song were recorded; these were not continuous, but were separated by cries and short spoken sentences. Repetitions of the rhythmic unit comprise the entire song except two measures, in the second of which the time was retarded to permit a clear enunciation of the words. It will be noted that the rhythmic unit occurs five times, and divides the song into five periods. This irregularity in the number of periods is of frequent occurrence in Sioux and Chippewa songs. This melody begins on the twelfth and ends on the tonic, two-thirds of the progressions being downward.

See plot of this melody on page 245.

At another time Śiya′ka was with a war party, the leader of which was Waŋbli′-wiċa′śa (Eagle Man), who was also a medicine-man. Eagle Man had an assistant named He-lu′ta (Red Horn). They started out and had gone some distance when Eagle Man said he would ask the sacred stones for news of the enemy. He told his followers to prepare a spot of ground and to bring him a small pebble. Having painted the pebble red, he laid it on the red blanket which had been spread over the prepared earth. He then sang the following song:

No. 75. "From Whence the Winds Blow" (Catalogue No. 463)

Sung by ŚIYA′KA

VOICE ♩ = 100

DRUM not recorded

WORDS

to′pakiya	at the four places
ina′źiŋ	to stand
maye′	I was required
tate′ oü′ye	the places from which the winds blow (see p. 120, footnote)
to′pakiya	at the four places
he′na waŋyaŋk′ ya	behold
to′pakiya	at the four places
ina′źiŋ	to stand
maye′	I was required
tate′ oü′ye	the places from which the winds blow
to′pakiya	at the four places
he′na waŋyaŋk′ ya	behold
to′pakiya	at the four places
ina′źiŋ	to stand
maye′	I was required

Analysis.—This song is unusual in that it contains only two upward progressions. The melody descends from the dominant above the tonic to the dominant below the tonic, which is the final tone. In every instance the entire rhythmic unit is sung on one tone.

Red Horn then offered the pipe to the little red stone and asked it to go before them as a scout. Eagle Man sang his song again, and the stone disappeared. The war party went on and made a camp for the night. Toward morning Eagle Man said that the stone had returned, and that, on being questioned concerning the enemy, the stone had stated that they would meet the enemy the next day, but did not name the hour, adding that there would not be more than 10 men in the enemy's party. The stone was left on the red blanket where it appeared after its quest.

That morning the war party went on again, and Śiya'ka and another man were chosen to act as scouts. They found six men drinking at a water hole, whereupon they immediately returned and reported this to the war party. They tried to surround the men but failed, and the six escaped. However, they met one man—an Omaha—coming to join this party and killed him. Red Horn shot him, thus securing the first "count", and Śiya'ka secured the fourth count.

Eagle Man sang the following song during this demonstration by the sacred stones:

No. 76. "Something I Foretold"   (Catalogue No. 464)

Sung by ŚIYA'KA

VOICE ♩ = 100
DRUM not recorded

He tu - wa wa-koŋ - za   ti - ya - ta   hi - na· źiŋ wa - ye

he tu-wa wa-koŋ - za   ti - ya - ta   hi - na - źiŋ wa - ye

hu noŋ-pa wa-koŋ - za   ti - ya - ta   hi - na - źiŋ wa - ye

he tu - wa wa - koŋ- za   ti - ya - ta   hi - na - źiŋ wa - ye

WORDS

he tu′wa	one whom
wakoŋ′za	I pretend to be
tiya′ta hina′źiŋ waye′	stands at the place where I have caused him (to stand)
hu noŋ′pa [1]	a man
wakoŋ′za	I pretend to be
tiya′ta hina′źiŋ waye′	(he who) stands at the place where I have caused him (to stand)
he tu′wa	one whom
wakoŋ′za	I pretend to be
tiya′ta hina′źiŋ waye′	stands at the place where I have caused him (to stand)

Analysis.—The rhythmic unit of this song consists of five measures, and, as in the preceding song, its repetitions comprise the entire melody. The first note in the second measure of the unit was invariably shortened, as indicated. Four renditions were recorded, separated by calls or short spoken sentences. In tonality the song is minor, the melody tones being those of the minor triad and fourth.

See plot of this melody on page 245.

A remarkable demonstration of the sacred stones by White Shield was related by Śiya′ka. Three of White Shield's sacred-stone songs have already been given. (See Nos. 67, 68, 69.) Śiya′ka said that on one occasion he had lost two horses and asked White Shield to locate them. Before being bound with sinews (see p. 218) White Shield asked, "What sign shall the stone bring to show whether your horses are by a creek or on the prairie?" Śiya′ka replied: "If they are by a creek, let the stone bring a little turtle and a piece of clamshell, and if they are on the prairie let the stone bring a meadow lark."

White Shield then sent the stone on its quest. While the stone was absent the people prepared a square of finely pulverized earth as already described. It was evening when the stone returned. The tepee was dark, as the fire had been smothered, but there was dry grass ready to put on it when White Shield ordered light. At last the stone appeared on the place prepared for it, and beside it was a little turtle with a small piece of clamshell in one of its claws. Thereupon White Shield said to Śiya′ka: "Your horses are 15 miles west of the Porcupine Hills at a fork of the Porcupine Creek. If you do not want to go for them there is a traveler coming that way who will get them and bring them in for you." This proved true. A neighbor of Śiya′ka's had been out looking for wild fruit and on his way home he saw the horses at the fork of the Porcupine Creek; recognizing them as Śiya′ka's, he brought them back.

---

[1] The full form of this expression is *wahu′ noŋ′pa*, "two-legged object", used by the medicine-men to designate a man. (See p. 120, footnote.) The full form occurs in song No. 78.

Mato'-waŋbli' (Bear Eagle) said that he was once leader of a war party against the Crows. One member of the party was Paŋke'-ska-napin' (Shell Necklace), who could inquire of the sacred stones. One night in the camp Eagle Man asked Shell Necklace to secure news of the enemy. A place on the ground was prepared and covered with a red blanket. When the stone returned Shell Necklace covered himself with a buffalo robe, head and all, and asked what news it brought. When the usual pipe was offered to the sacred stone a wolf was heard howling in the distance. Shell Necklace said the stone reported that the next day they would meet two men on horseback and see a large camp of the enemy. The stone told the men to be ready, and they would kill the enemy, who would fall on "prepared" or soft ground. Then the stones said that they wanted a buffalo as a reward in the morning, that the men would kill the buffalo with an arrow, and that it would fall with its head toward the south. The next morning the men killed a buffalo as the stone had predicted and put fresh sage in the wound. Beside the prepared ground where the stone had lain was a painted gift-stick with tobacco tied at the top. (See pl. 15.) They laid this stick at the head of the buffalo they had killed, leaving it on the prairie as an offering. That day they met two enemies and killed them both.

The two following songs were said to have been sung by Shell Necklace while giving this demonstration. The first concerns himself, setting forth his qualifications to ask favors of the sacred stones. The second concerns his power as a medicine-man, which enables him to control persons at a distance.

No. 77. "In a Sacred Manner I Live"   (Catalogue No. 632)

Sung by BEAR EAGLE

VOICE ♩ = 100
DRUM not recorded

Wa - kaŋ - kaŋ   yaŋ wa - oŋ *we* wa - kaŋ - kaŋ   yaŋ wa -

oŋ *we* ma-ḣpi - ya   ta wa - ki - ta   ye   wa - kaŋ -

kaŋ yaŋ wa-oŋ *we* mi - ta - śuŋ-ke o - ta   ye - lo *he*

WORDS

wakaŋ′kaŋ yaŋ	in a sacred manner
waöŋ′	I live
maḣpi′ya ta	to the heavens
wa′kita ye	I gazed
wakaŋ′kaŋ yaŋ	in a sacred manner
waöŋ′	I live
mita′śuŋke	my horses
o′ta yelo′	are many

Analysis.—The structure of this song is interesting. With one exception all the accented tones are those of the minor triad B flat–D flat–F, and the song is accordingly analyzed as being in the key of B flat minor, yet the progressions in the last four measures are such as to suggest the relative major chord. Sixteen intervals occur in the song, only five of which are upward progressions.

No. 78. "A Voice I Sent"   (Catalogue No. 633)

Sung by BEAR EAGLE

WORDS

aŋpe′tu kiŋ	to-day
mita′waye	is mine (I claimed)
wahu′ noŋ′pa waŋ	(to) a man
ho′ye	a voice
waki′ye	I sent
ćoŋ maya′ḳu welo′	you grant me
aŋpe′tu le	this day
mita′waye	is mine (I claimed)

wahu′ noŋ′pa waŋ................ (to) a man
ho′ye............................ a voice
waki′ye ćiŋ...................... I sent
wana′........................... now
hi.............................. here
yelo′........................... (he) is

Analysis.—This song begins on the dominant above the tonic and ends on the dominant below the tonic, two-thirds of the progressions being downward. All the tones of the octave except the seventh are present in the melody. One accidental appears—the fourth raised a semitone.

The following account of a performance by White Shield differs from preceding narratives in that it took place in a house, and the stone was held in White Shield's hand instead of being laid on the ground. The narrative was given by Bull Head, who witnessed the performance. He said it occurred when the Government first issued harness and wagons to the Indians. At that time the old people "kept close track" of everything which was issued to them by the Government and prized it very highly. One old man lost part of a harness. Knowing that White Shield often recovered lost articles by the aid of the sacred stones, he appealed to him, asking him to find the missing part of his harness and also a handsome tobacco bag and pipe. White Shield came, and in giving the performance held the stone in the palm of his hand, saying, "This will disappear." Bull Head said that though he watched it very closely, it suddenly vanished from before his eyes. The length of time that a stone is absent depends on the distance it must travel in finding the lost object. In this instance the stone was gone a long time. At last a rattle was heard at the door. White Shield stopped the singing, and said, "The stone has returned; be ready to receive it." He then opened the door, and the stone was found on the doorstep. White Shield brought it in and heard the message. The stone said that the missing articles had been taken by a certain man who, for fear of detection, had thrown them into the river. The stone said further that the articles would be brought back that night and left where they had been last seen. The next morning all the missing articles were found in the place where they had been last seen. Their appearance indicated that they had been under the water for several days.

The following is the second analysis group of dream songs, comprising those concerning the sacred stones (Nos. 59–78, inclusive). The aid of the sacred stones was invoked to locate the camp of an enemy (p. 348); also in finding a missing man (p. 496). Other analyses of dream songs are on pages 198 and 278.

Old Songs—(3) Songs Concerning the Sacred Stones

MELODIC ANALYSIS

TONALITY

	Number of songs.	Serial Nos. of songs.
Major tonality	8	61, 63, 64, 65, 68, 70, 71, 78
Minor tonality	12	59, 60, 62, 66, 67, 69, 72, 73, 74, 75, 76, 77
Total	20	

FIRST NOTE OF SONG—ITS RELATION TO KEYNOTE

	Number of songs.	Serial Nos. of songs.
Beginning on the—		
Twelfth	6	63, 67, 69, 73, 74, 76
Eleventh	1	66
Tenth	2	64, 65
Octave	3	60, 62, 71
Sixth	1	59
Fifth	7	61, 68, 70, 72, 75, 77, 78
Total	20	

LAST NOTE OF SONG—ITS RELATION TO KEYNOTE

	Number of songs.	Serial Nos. of songs.
Ending on the—		
Fifth	5	68, 71, 75, 77, 78
Third	2	61, 70
Keynote	13	59, 60, 62, 63, 64, 65, 66, 67, 69, 72, 73, 74, 76
Total	20	

LAST NOTE OF SONG—ITS RELATION TO COMPASS OF SONG

	Number of songs.	Serial Nos. of songs.
Songs in which final tone is—		
Lowest tone in song	18	59, 60, 61, 62, 63, 64, 66, 67, 68, 69, 70, 71, 72, 73, 74, 75, 76, 77
Immediately preceded by semitone below	1	65
Song containing a minor third below the final tone	1	78
Total	20	

Old Songs—(3) Songs Concerning the Sacred Stones—Continued

MELODIC ANALYSIS—Continued

NUMBER OF TONES COMPRISING COMPASS OF SONG

	Number of songs.	Serial Nos. of songs.
Compass of—		
Fourteen tones	1	67
Thirteen tones	3	59, 65, 68
Twelve tones	8	62, 63, 66, 69, 71, 73, 74, 76
Ten tones	5	60, 61, 64, 70, 72
Eight tones	3	75, 77, 78
Total	20	

TONE MATERIAL

	Number of songs.	Serial Nos. of songs.
Fourth five-toned scale	3	61, 63, 72
Minor triad	1	69
Minor triad and seventh	1	77
Minor triad and fourth	3	74, 75, 76
Octave complete	1	66
Octave complete except seventh	3	64, 65, 78
Octave complete except seventh, sixth, and fourth	1	68
Octave complete except seventh and fourth	1	73
Octave complete except seventh and second	2	59, 62
Octave complete except sixth and second	1	67
Octave complete except fifth and second	1	60
Octave complete except fourth	2	70, 71
Total	20	

ACCIDENTALS

	Number of songs.	Serial Nos. of songs.
Songs containing—		
No accidentals	16	59, 60, 61, 62, 66, 67, 68, 69, 70, 71, 72, 73, 74, 75, 76, 77
Fourth raised a semitone	3	64, 65, 78
Second raised a semitone	1	63
Total	20	

STRUCTURE

	Number of songs.	Serial Nos. of songs.
Melodic	13	61, 62, 64, 65, 66, 67, 68, 71, 73, 74, 75, 76, 78
Melodic with harmonic framework	4	59, 60, 63, 77
Harmonic	3	69, 70, 72
Total	20	

Old Songs—(3) Songs Concerning the Sacred Stones—Continued

Melodic Analysis—Continued

FIRST PROGRESSION—DOWNWARD AND UPWARD

	Number of songs.	Serial Nos. of songs.
Downward	14	59, 60, 61, 63, 64, 65, 66, 69, 70, 73, 74, 75, 76, 78
Upward	6	62, 67, 68, 71, 72, 77
Total	20	

TOTAL NUMBER OF PROGRESSIONS—DOWNWARD AND UPWARD

Downward	324
Upward	162
Total	486

INTERVALS IN DOWNWARD PROGRESSION

Intervals of a—	
Fifth	2
Fourth	23
Major third	30
Minor third	106
Augmented second	1
Major second	144
Minor second	18
Total	324

INTERVALS IN UPWARD PROGRESSION

Intervals of a—	
Tenth	1
Octave	2
Major sixth	1
Minor sixth	1
Fifth	7
Fourth	24
Major third	19
Minor third	55
Major second	40
Minor second	12
Total	162

AVERAGE NUMBER OF SEMITONES IN AN INTERVAL

Total number of intervals	486
Total number of semitones	1,435
Average number of semitones in an interval	2.9

Old Songs—(3) Songs Concerning the Sacred Stones—Continued

MELODIC ANALYSIS—Continued

KEY

	Number of songs.	Serial Nos. of songs.
Key of—		
A major	1	65
B flat major	1	78
B flat minor	3	69, 73, 77
B major	1	70
B minor	2	59, 66
C major	1	68
C minor	1	60
D flat major	1	72
E flat major	1	64
F major	1	63
F minor	3	67, 75, 76
G flat major	1	61
F sharp minor	1	74
G major	1	71
G minor	1	62
Total	20	

RHYTHMIC ANALYSIS

PART OF MEASURE ON WHICH SONG BEGINS

	Number of songs.	Serial Nos. of songs.
Beginning on unaccented part of measure	16	59, 61, 63, 64, 65, 66, 67, 68, 69, 70, 71, 72, 73, 74, 75, 78
Beginning on accented part of measure	4	60, 62, 76, 77
Total	20	

RHYTHM OF FIRST MEASURE

	Number of songs.	Serial Nos. of songs.
First measure in—		
2–4 time	12	59, 60, 63, 66, 69, 70, 71, 73, 74, 75, 76, 77
3–4 time	6	61, 62, 65, 67, 72, 78
4–8 time	1	68
5–8 time	1	64
Total	20	

Old Songs—(3) Songs Concerning the Sacred Stones—Continued

RHYTHMIC ANALYSIS—Continued

CHANGE OF TIME (MEASURE LENGTHS)

	Number of songs.	Serial Nos. of songs.
Songs containing no change of time....................	None.	
Songs containing a change of time.....................	20	59, 60, 61, 62, 63, 64, 65, 66, 67, 68, 69, 70, 71, 72, 73, 74, 75, 76, 77, 78
Total..	20	

RHYTHM OF DRUM

	Number of songs.	Serial Nos. of songs.
Sixteenth notes unaccented...........................	1	64
Eighth notes unaccented.............................	8	59, 60, 67, 68, 69, 70, 71, 72
Quarter notes unaccented............................	2	61, 62
Each beat preceded by an unaccented beat corresponding to third count of a triplet.	1	66
Drum not recorded	8	63, 65, 73, 74, 75, 76, 77, 78
Total..	20	

RHYTHMIC UNIT OF SONG

	Number of songs.	Serial Nos. of songs.
Songs containing—		
No rhythmic unit...............................	9	60, 62, 63, 65, 66, 69, 71, 72, 78
One rhythmic unit...............................	11	59, 61, 64, 67, 68, 70, 73, 74, 75, 76, 77
Total..	20	

METRIC UNIT OF VOICE (TEMPO)

	Number of songs.	Serial Nos. of songs.
Metronome—		
60...	1	60
69...	3	63, 70, 71
72...	1	72
76...	1	66
80...	1	59
84...	2	61, 65
92...	2	67, 78
96...	1	69
100..	4	74, 75, 76, 77
104..	1	62
126..	1	73
160..	1	68
168..	1	64
Total..	20	

Old Songs—(3) *Songs Concerning the Sacred Stones*—Continued

RHYTHMIC ANALYSIS—Continued

METRIC UNIT OF DRUM (TEMPO)

	Number of songs.	Serial Nos. of songs.
Metronome—		
76	1	66
96	1	61
104	1	62
132	2	69, 70
138	2	67, 68
152	1	72
160	2	59, 71
168	2	60, 64
Drum not recorded	8	63, 65, 73, 74, 75, 76, 77, 78
Total	20	

COMPARISON OF METRIC UNIT (TEMPO) OF VOICE AND DRUM

	Number of songs.	Serial Nos. of songs.
Drum and voice having the same metric unit	3	62, 64, 66
Drum faster than voice	8	59, 60, 61, 67, 69, 70, 71, 72
Drum slower than voice	1	68
Drum not recorded	8	63, 65, 73, 74, 75, 76, 77, 78
Total	20	

PLOTS OF SONGS (THE SACRED STONES)

The songs concerning the sacred stones contain no examples of a song without ascending progressions. (Class A, fig. 19.) Song No. 59 is the nearest to this type and contains one ascending interval. No. 71 has a strongly descending trend but contains three ascending intervals. No 68 is an example of Class B, and Nos. 76 and 74 have the same general outline. No. 70 suggests Class D, though having the descending trend which characterizes Class A. The title of this song is "I am required to roam." It will be recalled that songs of Class D concern animals or contain the idea of motion.

TREATMENT OF THE SICK

This is the third of the groups of songs received in dreams. All treatment of the sick was in accordance with dreams. No one attempted to treat the sick unless he had received a dream telling him to do so, and no one ever disregarded the obligations of such a dream. Each man treated only the diseases for which his dream had given him the remedies. Thus Shooter said:

In the old days the Indians had few diseases, and so there was not a demand for a large variety of medicines. A medicine-man usually treated one special disease and treated it successfully. He did this in accordance with his dream. A medicine-man would not try to dream of *all* herbs and treat *all* diseases, for then he could not expect to succeed in all nor to fulfill properly the dream of any one herb or animal. He would depend on too many and fail in all. That is one reason why our medicine-men lost their power when so many diseases came among us with the advent of the white man.

Three methods of treating the sick were used by the Sioux—by means of the sacred stones, "conjuring," and the giving of herbs. The first kind of treatment might be given by a *wakaŋ'haŋ*. This term was applied to the highest type of medicine-men—those qualified to command the sacred stones, to bring fair weather, or to fill

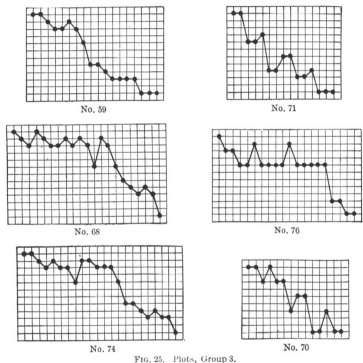

No. 59   No. 71

No. 68   No. 76

No. 74   No. 70

Fig. 25. Plots, Group 3.

such important ceremonial positions as that of Intercessor in the Sun dance. A man who "conjured" the sick was called *wapi'ya*, "one who repairs," and a man who treated the sick by means of herbs was called *peźu'ta wića'ku*, "one who places his confidence in roots of herbs." It was not unusual for the same man to use more than one of these methods, but he was best known by the one which he employed the most.

Treatment of the sick by means of the sacred stones and by conjuring has been forbidden by the Government in recent years, but certain of the old men are allowed to continue treating the sick by administering herbs. Four such men described the method they were using at the time of giving the .information; one (Used-as-a-Shield) gave an account of "conjuring" from the standpoint of the patient; another (Old Buffalo) narrated his fasting prayer for a sick relative; and additional information was received from other informants.

When a man skillful in the use of the sacred stones was called to attend a sick person he was expected to give a demonstration of his supernatural power. Many were invited to witness this exhibition, and it is said that harm would come to those who did not "believe in the sacred stones." The sick person filled a pipe, which he gave to the medicine-man. After smoking it the man was tightly bound with thongs, even his fingers and toes being interlaced with sinews like those of which bowstrings are made, after which he was firmly tied in a hide. The tent was dark, and the medicine-man sang songs addressed to the sacred stones; he sang also his own dream songs. Strange sounds were heard in the darkness, and objects were felt to be flying through the air. Voices of animals were speaking. One said, "My grandchild, you are very sick, but I will cure you." Frequently a buffalo came, and those who did not believe in the sacred stones were kicked by the buffalo or struck by a flying stone or bundle of clothing. At last the medicine-man called, "Hasten, make a light!" Dry grass, which was ready, was placed on the fire. In its light the man was seen wedged between the poles near the top of the tipi, with all the restraining cords cast from him.[1]

Brave Buffalo said that in treating a person by means of the sacred stones he rolled a stone on the person's body "to locate the ailment," and that if the sick person wished to hold the stone in his mouth he was allowed to do so, as this produced an internal effect.

In many instances of treating the sick by "conjuring" no medicines were given, the conjuror claiming that he removed the disease from the person's body by sucking it out. A performance of this kind was described to the writer by Mrs. James McLaughlin, who witnessed it on the Devils Lake Reservation, in North Dakota. Mrs. McLaughlin said, concerning this Santee demonstration:

I saw a conjuror named Śip'to (Beads) give a performance in an attempt to cure a boy who was suffering from hemorrhages of the lungs. Śip'to was an old man. He wore nothing but his breechcloth, his whole body was painted red, his face also was painted red, and his hair was short and loose. The boy lay in a tipi. If a conjuring performance were held in a log house it was necessary to take up a portion of the floor, as the conjuring must be done on bare ground. I have seen a house in which a large portion of the floor had been cut away for this purpose.

When I entered the tipi the conjuror was in the place of honor, opposite the door. This place was clean of turf, and the bare ground had been made very smooth. The boy lay with his head near the conjuror. In the middle of the lodge was a fire with many red coals. A young girl brought water and placed it beside the conjuror. When

---

[1] Similar demonstrations were made by the medicine-men of other tribes. A description of the custom among the Chippewa is given in Bulletin 45, pp. 123-25. (Cf. also p. 218 of this work.)

this had been done, the conjuror rinsed his mouth, put a piece of root in his mouth, and chewed it. Removing a coal from the fire with a stick, he took it up in his hands and put it in his mouth. He then dropped on all fours and began to tear up the ground with his fingers and toes, as though they were claws. He made a cry like an animal and approached the boy as though he were a wild beast. With the coal still in his mouth he stooped over the boy's chest and sucked so violently that the blood came to the surface. Then he gave a whistling, puffing sound [see p. 254] and spit into a dish which was partly filled with water. When this performance was completed he sat down in a dripping perspiration and immediately the boy had a hemorrhage from the lungs.

The same performance was enacted four times and after each time the boy had a hemorrhage. Then the boy complained that the treatment was making him worse, and the boy's father asked the conjuror not to work over the boy any longer. The boy's father gave the conjuror a horse, as it is the belief of the Santee that sickness will return if the "doctor" is not paid.

The following is an account of a somewhat similar treatment, which included the administering of medicine. This account was given by Used-as-a-Shield, a reliable informant, who sang a number of songs in the present work and took part in several discussions of serious topics by the old men. He described his own experience in receiving treatment by a conjurer, saying:

The first thing done in summoning a medicine-man to treat a sick person was to put black paint on the stem of a pipe. Charcoal was ordinarily used in making this paint, which was smeared on the stem of the pipe, an eagle feather being tied next the mouth-piece. A messenger took this painted pipe to the medicine-man's lodge, carrying it with the bowl next him. If the medicine-man were at home, the messenger entered the lodge, turning toward the left. Without speaking he handed the pipe to the medicine-man, who smoked it in token of his assent. A request to visit a sick person was never refused unless the medicine-man were physically unable to go. If the man were not at home the messenger left the pipe in the place of honor, with the bowl toward the door.[1] The relatives of the medicine-man then made an effort to find him soon as possible.

It was in this manner that many years ago, I sent for a medicine-man to treat me. When he entered my lodge he seated himself back of the fire. After a time he came and sat by my head, looking me over. He then took up a lock of hair on my forehead and tied a wisp of grass around it, letting the rest of my hair hang loose. Then he had me placed so that I lay facing the east and he began his preparations for the treatment. Opening a bundle, he took from it a whistle [*ši'yotaŋka*], a small drum [*čaŋ'čeǧa*], and a rattle [*wagmu'ha*] which he used in beating the drum. He also took out a black cloth, which he tied over his eyes. Then he dropped on one knee, facing me, holding the drum in his right hand and the rattle in his left hand. Beating the drum rapidly with the rattle, he said: "Young man, try to remember what I tell you. You shall see the power from which I have the right to cure sicknesses, and this power shall be used on you this day." Then he told the dream by which he received his power as a medicine-man. When he rose to his feet I noticed that a horse's tail hung at his side, being fastened to his belt. Standing, he offered his drum to the cardinal points, then beat it as hard as he could, sometimes louder, sometimes softer. A wooden bowl which he carried was placed next my head. Then he came toward me, still beating his drum. As he came near me his breath was so forcible it seemed as if it would blow me before it. Just before he reached me, and while blowing his breath so strongly, he struck his body on the right side and on the left side. He was still telling his dream

---

[1] [Cf. position of the pipe, pp. 72, 127, 185.]

and singing, but when he paused for an instant I could hear the sound of a red hawk; some who were there even said they could see the head of a red hawk coming out of his mouth. He bent over me and I expected that he would suck the poison from my body with his mouth, but instead I felt the beak of a bird over the place where the pain was. It penetrated so far that I could feel the feathers of the bird. The medicine-man kept perfectly still for a time; then he got up with a jerk to signify that he had gotten out the trouble. Still it was the beak of a bird which I felt. A boy stood near, holding a filled pipe. It was soon apparent that the medicine-man had swallowed the poison. He took four whiffs of the pipe. Then he must get rid of the poison. This part of the performance was marked by great activity and pounding of the drum. At times he kicked the bare ground in his effort to get rid of the poison; he paced back and forth, stamped his feet, and used both rattle and drum. Finally he ejected the poison into the wooden bowl. Then he told the people that he had sucked out all the poison, that none remained in my body, and that I would recover.

Opening his medicine bag, he took out some herbs and placed them in a cup of cold water. He stirred it up and told me to drink it and to repeat the dose next morning, and that in less than ten days I would be well. I did as he told me, and in about 10 days I was entirely well.

Brave Buffalo is considered one of the most powerful medicine-men on the Standing Rock Reservation, and was actively engaged in the practice of native medicine when he held his conferences with the writer. In describing his treatment of the sick he said:

Fig. 26.   Drawing on mirror used in treatment of the sick.

Some people have an idea that we medicine-men, who get our power from different sources, are the worst of human beings; they even say that we get our power from the evil one, but no one could disregard such dreams as I have had, and no one could fail to admire the sacred stones. Wakaŋ′taŋka is all-powerful, and if we reverence his work he will surely let us prove to all men that these things are indeed his doing. It is a very strict requirement that a medicine-man shall act out his dream [see p. 157], and that he maintain absolute integrity of character. If he fails to do this he will be punished and will not live long. I am not required to fast, only to smoke, showing that I am at peace with all men. Dreams come to me now in a natural way. Often during the day when I am alone on a journey, and my mind is on many things, I stop to rest awhile. I observe what is around me, and then I become drowsy and dream. Often I see the sacred stones in my dreams.

Brave Buffalo's conference with the writer was interrupted by a call to visit a sick person many miles away. On his return, several days later, he said that he left his patient recovering. He had with him a bag containing articles which he had used in treating this sick person, and on his hat he wore a bone about 5 inches long instead of a feather which had been fastened to his hatband on his previous visit. In describing his treatment he said that he "sucked out the disease" through the bone, and ejected it from his mouth into a bowl of water. Opening his bag, he took from it a small mirror inclosed in a flat frame of unpainted wood, the whole being about 4 by 6 inches. On the mirror was a drawing of a new moon and a star. This design was copied by Brave Buffalo and is shown in figure 26. He said: "I hold this mirror in front of the sick person and see his disease reflected in it; then I can cure the disease."

Concerning the drawing on the glass Brave Buffalo said: "The new moon is my sign. I am strongest when the moon is full; I grow weaker as the moon wanes, and when the moon dies my strength is all gone until the moon comes back again."

One of the songs used by Brave Buffalo in treating the sick was recorded. Before singing this he said: "Some diseases are affected by the day and others by the night. I use this song in the cases which are worse at night. I composed it myself and always sing it at night, whether I am treating a sick person or not. I offer smoke to the four winds and sing this song." This song was received by Brave Buffalo in his dream of a wolf. (See Song No. 47.)

The following song also was used by Brave Buffalo, but the occasion of its use was not designated.

No. 79. "The Sunrise"   (Catalogue No. 603)

Sung by BRAVE BUFFALO

VOICE ♩= 84

DRUM ♩= 72

Drum-rhythm similar to No. 19

Wi hi-na - pe waŋ-la - ka nuŋ - we wi hi - na - pe waŋ-la - ka

nuŋ - we • lo wi hi - na - pe waŋ-la - ka nuŋ - we

lo wi hi - na - pe wan-la - ka nuŋ - we a he

WORDS

wi hina′pe...................... sunrise
waŋla′ka nuŋwe′ lo.......... may you behold

Analysis.—This is one of the few songs in which a rest occurs. Other songs of the present series containing rests are Nos. 117, 123, 144, 159, 188, 203, 208, 206, 207, 230. The lack of a rest, or seeming breathing place, is noted in Chippewa as well as Sioux songs, this feature occurring in only 13 of the 340 recorded from the Chippewa. In the song under analysis the rest is short, but clearly defined. Two renditions were recorded; these are uniform except that the intonation is more wavering in the second than in the first rendition. In both, the repeated part begins with the third measure, the opening bars not containing the rhythmic unit. Observation of recorded songs shows that the rhythmic unit is usually found at the beginning of the song. See plot of this melody on page 283.

Brave Buffalo sang also one of his father's medicine songs. Crow Bear (Kaŋġi'-mato), the father of Brave Buffalo, was a famous singer and medicine-man, who lived to the age of 80 years. In one of his dreams he saw a bear, and a majority of the songs he composed concerned or were addressed to the bear. The song recorded by Brave Buffalo was not of this number, but was a song which his father sang every morning, as required by one of his dreams. In a dream it was required also that anyone who passed him, even though he were smoking or eating, must pass in front of him. If anyone accidentally passed behind him the physical effect was immediate. His teeth chattered and he became unconscious, much effort being necessary to restore him.

No. 80. "Behold the Dawn"   (Catalogue No. 610)
Sung by BRAVE BUFFALO

VOICE ♩ = 138
DRUM ♩ = 138
Drum-rhythm similar to No. 6

WORDS

aŋ'paŏ waŋ	....	a dawn
hina'pelo	....	appears
waŋyaŋ'ka yo	....	behold it

GOOSE

Analysis.—Three renditions of this song were recorded, and show no points of difference. Between the renditions the singer gave glissando "calls" or "cries," but the repetition began on the the same tone as the original rendition. No change of time occurs in the song—an unusual feature—and the rhythmic unit is more continuously repeated than in a majority of the songs. The first tone of the rhythmic unit was strongly accented. The only tones are those of the minor triad and fourth, and the structure of the song is melodic with harmonic framework, the accented G precluding its classification as harmonic in structure. Two-thirds of the progressions are downward, the melody descending steadily from the tenth to the tonic.

See plot of this melody on page 283.

Goose (pl. 31), a widely-known medicine-man, is what might be termed a specialist in the treatment of consumption and is said to have had no small degree of success in his work. Information concerning the Sun dance and the sacred stones was also given by him. (See pp. 90, 210.) Goose narrated the dream by which he felt himself authorized to undertake the treatment of the sick. It was impossible to record the songs when the story of the dream was given, and unfortunately another opportunity did not occur. In describing the dream Goose said:

When I was a young man I was an excellent marksman with bow and arrows. After coming in contact with the Army I was given a rifle and cartridges and never missed my aim. One morning I arose before daybreak to go on a hunting trip. As I went around a butte I saw an antelope, which came toward me and stood still a short distance away from me. The antelope looked at me and then began to graze. I took my rifle and fired several shots with no effect. I fired 16 cartridges and wondered what could be the matter. I put in four more cartridges and fired again, but with no effect whatever. Then the animal stopped grazing and began to move slowly away. Then I heard a voice speaking three times, then a fourth time, and the voice said it was going to sing something, and I must listen. The voice was above me and commanded me to look at the sun. I looked and saw that the rising sun had the face of a man and was commanding all the animals and trees and everything in nature to look up. In the air, in front of the sun, was a booth made of boughs. In front of the booth was a very bright object and between this and the booth was a man, painted and wearing an eagle-down feather, while around him flew all kinds of birds. The bright object was a sacred stone, and it was heated red hot. After seeing this I heard another voice telling me to look and receive what would be given me. Something in the form of a bird came down, and where it touched the ground an herb sprang up. This occurred three times. The voice above me said that I was to use these three herbs in the cure of the sick. The fourth time the descending object started in the form of a bird, but a human skeleton came to the ground. Then the voice above me told me to observe the structure of the human body. I then saw blood run into the skeleton, and a buffalo horn appeared on the back, between the shoulders, and drew the blood out of the skeleton. The voice above me said this was a sign that I would have power more than any other to cure diseases of the blood. The voice came from the sacred stone and said I must use the buffalo horn in curing diseases of the blood, a practice which I have followed ever since. I do not consider that I dreamed this as one dreams in sleep; it appeared to me when I was early on the chase.

One of the greatest things it taught me is that the first thing a sick person should do is to take a sweat bath, to take out all the impurities, so that the body will respond to remedies.   The booth showed how the sweat lodge must be constructed, and the hot stone showed the use of heated stones in the lodge.   The hot stone is taken into the lodge, and water is sprinkled upon it.   The oftener this bath is taken, the healthier a person will be.   In case of illness, the sick person must take this bath the first thing, and as often afterward as the medicine-man directs.   I always prescribe the sweat bath the first thing.   I also claim that a sick person can not recover unless the diet is changed.   Certain kinds of food and of wild fruit are bad in certain illnesses, and certain kinds of game or venison are injurious to a sick person.   The food must be lighter than usual, and the person must avoid unnecessary exertion.   My requirements are the sweat bath, light diet, and rest.   I have treated consumption, and if the disease is not too far advanced the person usually recovers.   The treatment depends on the seriousness of the case.   All three herbs which I saw in my dream were prepared in a certain way and were intended for use in consumption, which is caused by improper circulation of the blood.   I do not want the patient to make any undue exertion, but I try especially to keep up his circulation.   The sweat bath makes the circulation better.   In the old days a person did not take cold after a sweat bath.   The sick person did not jump immediately into cold water, as is sometimes stated, but was covered with furs and allowed to cool off gradually.

Many years ago there lived among the Sioux a medicine-man named Ćeha'kiŋ (Carry-the-Kettle), who was said to have wakaŋ' power in a remarkable degree.   A gourd rattle [1] (pl. 32) used by him in treating the sick became the possession of the writer.

Such a rattle is called by the Sioux wagmu'ha.[2]   This is, however, not the only type of rattle used among the Sioux in treating the sick, the form of rattle depending on the choice of the medicine-man.

Every medicine-man had a bag or case in which he kept his supply of herbs and the articles used by him in treating the sick.   In some instances the outer case was of decorated rawhide.   A man's medicine bag was hung on a pole outside the lodge and usually brought in at night; it was often "incensed" with burning sweet grass.   It was believed that the presence of "the wrong kind of person" in the lodge would affect the efficacy of the medicine, and that if it were exposed to such influence for any considerable time its power would be entirely destroyed.   The writer secured three of these medicine bags.   One (pl. 33) belonged to a medicine-man named Waŋbli'iyo'take (Sitting Eagle), who lived many years ago.   The bag is made of four antelope ears.   When Sitting Eagle died the medicine bag and its contents passed into the possession of his niece, who emptied most of the small bags contained in the pouch, but kept the pouch and two of the

[1] This specimen is described as follows by Mr. E. H. Hawley, curator of musical instruments, U. S. National Museum: "Total length, 10 inches; body length, 6 inches; diameter, 5¾ to 6 inches. An irregular gourd shell with a short neck.   A wooden handle enters the neck and comes out at the blossom end.   Three-sixteenth-inch holes are made in the neck and a strip of leather sewed to the neck through these holes; this leather is brought down over the handle and bound to it by a strip of bright cloth.   This gives a firm attachment between the gourd and handle.   Near the outer end of the handle a groove is cut; in it is tied a strip of twisted cloth so it can be worn on the arm or hung up.   The gourd incloses pebbles."

[2] A rattle similar to this is pictured by Skinner as part of a charm used by the Menomini to call the buffalo. (Skinner, Alanson, Social Life and Ceremonial Bundles of the Menomini Indians, Amer. Mus. Nat. Hist., Anthr Papers, XIII, pt 1, p. 157, New York, 1913.)

GOURD RATTLE

MEDICINE BAG WITH ARTICLES USED BY OWNER IN TREATING THE SICK

MEDICINE BAG OF BADGER PAWS

MEDICINE BAG OF MINK HIDE

remedies.   The niece's name was Maka'-peźu'tawiŋ (Earth-medicine Woman).   One of her songs (No. 146) is contained in this work.   In the pouch were seven empty medicine bags, the entire foot of an eagle, and a small piece of bone of an elk.   On the inner edge of each medicine bag was a small mark by which the contents could be identified. Earth-medicine Woman said that her uncle used the eagle claw in treating scrofulous sores, especially on the neck.   For this purpose he scraped the surface of the claw, mixed a small quantity of the scrapings with hot water, and applied the mixture to the skin.   The elk bone was said to be an effective remedy for broken bones.   It was prepared in the same way as the eagle claw, but the mixture was taken internally.

A medicine pouch made of badger's paws is shown in plate 34; this was secured among the Teton Sioux, but its history is unknown.

Eagle Shield said that he received his knowledge of herbs from the bear and the badger, the former giving him instructions concerning most of the remedies which he used for adults, and the latter telling him of remedies for children.   As already noted, those who dreamed of the bear were supposed to have particularly effective remedies.   (See p. 195.)   Like others who gave valuable information, Eagle Shield at first hesitated, but afterwards became interested, expressing a desire to make his part of the work as complete as possible.[1] For this reason he sold his medicine-bag and four small bags containing herbs which he always took with him when visiting the sick.   He also secured fresh specimens of many medicinal herbs which he used in his practice.   These were sent to Washington for identification, with a view to ascertaining whether any of them are used in the medical practice of the white race.   Further, Eagle Shield permitted the photographing of a bear claw which he said had been in his possession 48 years and was constantly used by him in treating the sick. (Fig. 27.)

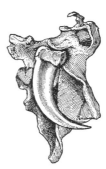

FIG. 27.   Bear claw used in treatment of the sick.

Eagle Shield's medicine-bag (pl. 35) was made of the entire skin of an animal called by the Sioux i'kusana, 'white chin.'[2]   He said that he killed this animal 44 years ago, on the present site of Fort Keogh, Mont.   He was hunting large game in the autumn, after the leaves had fallen, and had two antelope on his horse when he killed this little creature near the water.   Ever since that time he had used the hide as a medicine pouch.   The matted fur around the neck shows the manner in which it was carried.   In this pouch were placed

[1] The material furnished by Eagle Shield and White-paw Bear in this section was interpreted by Mrs. James McLaughlin.
[2] On examination of this specimen at the U. S. National Museum the animal was identified as a mink, subspecies *Mustela vison lacustris.*

small buckskin packets of herbs, the large supply being in a bundle which was placed outside his lodge during the day and brought inside every night, being treated with great respect. The number of small packets in a medicine-pouch varied according to the man who used them. Thus the medicine-pouch belonging to Sitting Eagle contained seven small packets, which were said to be only part of the remedies used by him. Eagle Shield had four principal remedies, the most important of which was contained in a beaded case. This herb is described in connection with song No. 81. His four medicine-packets, together with a small spoon of white bone used in giving medicine to children, are shown in plate 36.

As already stated, an Indian doctor in the old days did not pretend to have a remedy for every disease. Thus Eagle Shield said that if an Indian were suffering from a malady he would go to a doctor and say, "Have you a remedy for such and such an ailment?" The doctor had no hesitation in saying he lacked the remedy if such were the case, as he was not expected to have any remedies except such as various animals had revealed to him, unless he may have acquired a few from other medicine-men.

The herb kept by Eagle Shield in the decorated bag (pl. 36) was called *taö'pi pežu'ta*, 'herb for the wounded.' Many remarkable cures are said to have been wrought by Eagle Shield through the use of this remedy. A fresh specimen of the herb was secured and identified as *Achillea lanulosa* Nutt. (yarrow). It was said to "grow on hills and in the Bad Lands." The entire plant was dried, and instead of being prepared as a tea the patient was required to chew it. Eagle Shield said that he had treated men shot through the body and they had recovered. One man thus treated was personally known to the writer. The man had attempted suicide by shooting himself in the left side, the bullet passing through the body and breaking the edge of the shoulder blade. As a result of the wound his arm was paralyzed, and two doctors of the white race said that it must be amputated. Eagle Shield undertook the treatment of the case and did his work so effectually that the man appears to have as free use of one arm as of the other. For this treatment Eagle Shield received a fee of $100, a new white tent, a revolver, and a steer.

Eagle Shield said that he sang the following song when treating wounded persons with this herb. Between the renditions of all these songs he gave deep groans, like those of a man in extreme distress, frequently interspersing these with a hissing exhalation of the breath. (See Bulletin 53, p. 264; also p. 247 of this work.)

SMALL BAGS OF MEDICINE AND SPOON

No. 81. "Behold All These Things" (Catalogue No. 511)

Sung by EAGLE·SHIELD

VOICE ♩= 66
DRUM not recorded

I - ho le - na waŋ-yaŋ-ka yo i - ho le - na waŋ-yaŋ-ka yo

ta - ku waŋ   he - ha - ka - se   waŋ - la - ke ćiŋ

on ya - ni pi kte - lo

WORDS

(First rendition)

iho′ lena′ waŋyaŋ′ka yo....... behold all these things
ta′ku waŋ..................... something
haha′kase.................... elklike
waŋla′ke ćin................. you behold
yani′ pi ktelo′.............. you will live

(Second rendition)

iho′ lena′ waŋyaŋ′ka yo...... behold all these things
ta′ku waŋ.................... something
tataŋ′kase.................. buffalolike
waŋlake ćiŋ................ you behold
yani′ pi ktelo′ .... you will live

Analysis.—More than 60 per cent of the intervals in this song are larger than a minor third. This is an unusual proportion of large intervals. Fifteen of these intervals are fourths, nine are fifths, and one is an octave. Two renditions were recorded; these show no points of difference. The melody is minor in tonality and contains all the tones of the octave except the sixth and seventh.

See plot of this melody on page 283.

The following song was used with the same herb as the preceding and was sung when the patient began to improve.

No. 82. "I Am Sitting"   (Catalogue No. 515)

Sung by EAGLE SHIELD

VOICE ♩ = 184

DRUM not recorded

Wa - kaŋ-yaŋ ma - ke   lo   wa - kaŋ - yaŋ ma - ke   lo

ma - to   ti - pi   ća   wa - kaŋ - yaŋ ma - ke   lo

haŋ - ya - ke   o - ma - ni - yaŋ   he - ma - ki - ye   yo

WORDS

wakaŋ'yaŋ.................... in a sacred manner
make' lo...................... I am sitting
mato' ti'pi ća................ at bear lodge [1]
wakaŋ'yaŋ.................... in a sacred manner
make' lo..................... I am sitting
haŋya'ke..................... at night
oma'niyaŋ................... roaming about
hema'kiye yo................ is said to me

Analysis.—This song contains only one interval larger than a minor third and is an interesting contrast to the song next preceding, in which more than half the intervals were larger than a minor third.

---

[1] This probably refers to Bear Butte in the Black Hills. The Teton speak of two buttes by this name, one in South Dakota, and one in Montana which is higher and is probably the one mentioned by Red Fox in connection with his war expedition. (See p. 376.) Concerning the one which seems to be referred to in this song, Rev. J. Owen Dorsey says (*Eleventh Rep. Bur. Ethn.*, p. 448): "Eight miles from Fort Meade, S. Dakota, is Mato tipi, Grizzly Bear Lodge, known to the white people as Bear Butte. It can be seen from a distance of a hundred miles. Of this landmark Bushotter writes thus: 'The Teton used to camp at a flat-topped mountain, and pray to it. This mountain had many large rocks on it, and a pine forest at the summit. The children prayed to the rocks as if to their guardian spirits.'"

The first half of this song is based on the triad C–E flat–G. This part includes the repetitions of the rhythmic unit. The latter part contains only the tones of the minor third G–B flat, and the song is considered to be in the key of G minor though the fifth of that key does not appear. The rhythmic unit of this song is longer than that of many of the songs and is interesting. The rhythm of the latter part of the song is somewhat similar but does not duplicate any of the count-divisions of the unit. The song begins and ends on the same tone, a peculiarity occurring in only 11 Chippewa songs (see Bull. 53, p. 222). The following other songs in the present series have this structure: Nos. 97, 99, 207, 212, 220, 221, 234, 238. Five renditions of this song were recorded. There was no break between the first and second rendition, but a short pause was made between the others.

A remedy used by Eagle Shield for those suffering from loss of appetite was called *loće'pi śni peźi'huta*. The plant was said to grow "near creeks and in gravel." The root only was used. This herb was identified as *Astragalus carolinianus* L. (loco weed). The following song was sung in connection with its use. In a short speech before singing the song Eagle Shield said that it was the song of a bear.

No. 83. "We Will Eat"   (Catalogue No. 512)

Sung by EAGLE SHIELD

VOICE ♩= 63

DRUM not recorded

He tu-wa hi-yu-ye e-ma'-ki-ya će   he tu-wa hi-yu-

ye e - ma - ki - ya *he ya* će pe - źi - hu - ta

uŋ - yu - tiŋ kta *ya* *ye* he tu - wa hi - yu -

ye *ya* e - ya će - yo he tu - wa hi - yu - ye e - ma -

ki - ya *he ya* će ho - śu - pa waŋ uŋ - yu -tiŋ - tka *o wa*

ye he tu - wa hi - yu - ye *a* e - ya će - yo

WORDS

he tu′wa	some one
hiyu′ye	"come here" (a command)
ema′kiya će	said to me
peźi′huta	medicine (herbs)
uŋyu′tiŋ kta	we will eat (together)
he tu′wa	some one
hiyu′ye	"come here"
eya′ ćeyo′	has said
he tu′wa	some one
hiyu′ye	"come here"
ema′kiya će	said to me
hośu′pa waŋ	fish intestines
uŋyu′tiŋ tka	we will eat
he tu′wa	some one
hiyu′ye	"come here"
eya′ ćeyo′	has said

Analysis.—This song is characterized by the interval of the fourth, which constitutes 18 per cent of the entire number of intervals. It appears in the first part of the song as the descending progression E–B, and later as A–E; the ascent of an octave gives a return of the interval E–B, followed again by A–E, descending to the tonic. The melody tones are only those of the minor triad and fourth, and the song is harmonic in structure. The rhythmic unit is short and is a phrase which is not unusual in these songs.

For those suffering from headache Eagle Shield had a special remedy—an herb called *nasu'la yazaŋ'pi ipi'ya*, 'no appetite medicine,' which grew on the prairie. The root, dried and powdered, was sprinkled on hot coals, the patient inhaling the fumes. This plan was identified as *Artemisia frigida* Willd. (Colorado sage).

Before recording the song Eagle Shield spoke the following sentences:

Peźu'ta ćiću' ktelo' tka waśte' ća yani' ktelo' lena'ke waśte' ke'yape.

(*Translation*) Herbs I shall give you, but (they are) good, so you shall recover, all these (are) good, they say.[1]

The following song was sung during the treatment.

No. 84. "These Are Good"   (Catalogue No. 513)
Sung by EAGLE SHIELD

Le-na-ke waś - te ke-ya - pe - lɔ ho-ye-

ya   na-źiŋ

WORDS

lena'ke	. . . .	all these
waśte'	. . . .	(are) good
ke'yapelo	. . . .	they say
ho'yeya [2]	. . . .	with a noise
na'źiŋ	. . . .	(they) stand erect

[1] Chippewa doctors also use strong affirmations when treating the sick (Bulletin 45, p. 92).

[2] This refers to the sounds made by a bear standing erect, preparatory to making an attack. (See p. 180, footnote.)

Analysis.—Few songs of the present series have the upward and downward intervals so nearly equal as this song, in which 27 progressions are upward and 32 are downward. The major second occurs 11 times in upward and 11 times in downward progression, and the minor second is found 10 times in upward and 10 times in downward progression, yet the melody is not monotonous, and the intonation on these small intervals was better than in a majority of such instances. The song begins on the octave and ends on the tonic. All the tones of the octave are present except the sixth. It is interesting to observe that the interval between the seventh and eighth is in some instances a semitone and in others a whole tone. The transcription is from the first rendition, which gives the entire song, the second and third renditions omitting the first four measures. This is in accordance with a custom which has been noted among both Chippewa and Sioux, that the first phrase of a song seems in many instances to serve as an introduction to the performance.

An herb called *cante' yazaŋ'pi iću'wa* was prepared as a tea and used for those suffering from "heart trouble or pain in the stomach." This plant was identified as *Astragalus* sp. (loco weed).

Before singing Eagle Shield said:

Te'han mawa'ni kte śni ećan'ni ķe'yaśi to'kśa eća'na maya'ni ketlo'.

(*Translation*) A long time before I can walk you may think, but (in) only a short time you shall be able to walk.[1]

The following song was sung as the herb was administered.

No. 85. "You Will Walk"   (Catalogue No. 514)
Sung by Eagle Shield

Voice ♩=72

Drum not recorded

Ta - ku wa - kaŋ   ya - tiŋ kte - lo   ka - haŋ - tu - ke

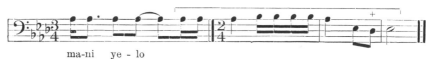

ma-ni   ye - lo

WORDS

ta'ku wakaŋ'	something sacred
ya'tin ktelo'	you will eat
kahaŋ'tuke	now
ma'ni yelo	you will walk

---

[1] Compare words of song No. 47, Bulletin 45: "You will recover, you will walk again. It is I who say it. My power is great. Through our white shell I will enable you to walk again."

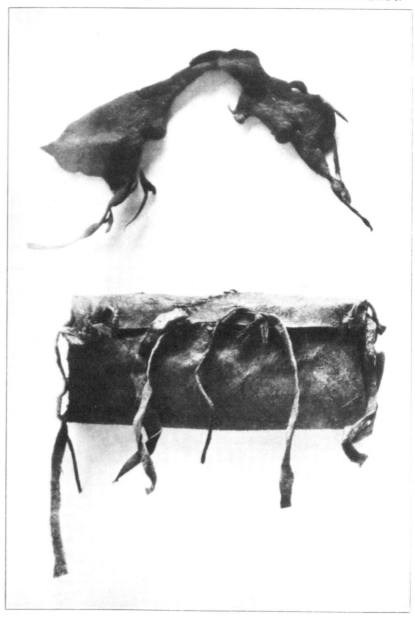

SPLINT AND MATTED DEER HAIR USED IN TREATING FRACTURES

Analysis.—The interval of a fourth is prominent in the first part of
this melody. It appears, in the opening measures, as the descending
interval E flat–B flat; the tone A also occurs, and the descent from
B flat to A flat introduces the tonic chord. The fourth then appears
as the descending interval A flat–E flat. The subdominant of the key
occurs twice and in both instances was sung a trifle sharp, as indicated in the transcription. The song is major in tonality and contains all the tones of the octave except the sixth and seventh. Four
renditions were recorded, which are uniform in every respect.

Eagle Shield might be called a specialist in the treatment of broken
bones. In this treatment he used an herb identified as *Allionia
nyctaginea* Michx., and called by the Sioux *hu'huweñankan peźu'ta,*[1]
which was said to grow in the woods. The dried leaves and root of
this plant were mixed with soft grease. When treating a fracture
Eagle Shield covered his hands with this mixture and after holding
them over the coals until they were warm, he rubbed the flesh above
the broken bone. He said the patient often was so relieved by this
treatment that he fell asleep. The treatment was repeated three
times a day and continued "until the fracture was healed." He
said that when an arm or leg was first broken he "pulled it until the
bone slipped into place," then covered it with a parfleche case,
laced together with thongs. This case was removed for the treatment described above, but he emphasized the need of keeping the
case firmly laced, and of tightening it whenever the thongs seemed to
be loosening. He said the purpose of the rubbing was to keep the
muscles from becoming stiff. He added that he had treated four
cases in which the large bone of the leg was broken, and that in each
instance the patient was able to walk in a month. One was a fracture near the hip. It had been put in iron braces by a white doctor,
but the patient, not being able to stand the treatment, came to him.

Eagle Shield made a small "splint" of parfleche, 8 inches in
length, saying this was the size he would use for a broken wrist. In it,
with Indian accuracy, he put a piece of old, soft flannel, saying that
was what he "would put next the person's arm." He sold to the
writer a matted portion of soft hair, which he said was the shed hair
of the deer; this was thick with grease. Eagle Shield said he had
used this in treating fractures for more than forty years, holding it in
his hand as he rubbed the flesh. (See pl. 37.)

The song used by Eagle Shield in treating fractures was sung four
times "while getting ready to apply the medicine."

---

[1] A specimen of the same herb was given by Bear-with-White-Paw, who said it was "good to reduce
swelling." (See p. 270.)

No. 86. Song Preceding Treatment of Fractures (Catalogue No. 516)

Sung by EAGLE SHIELD

VOICE ♩= 88

DRUM not recorded

Ko - la wa - na hi - yu - ye ma - to o - ma ki - ya - ke

ko - la hi - yu - ye   le - na wa-yaŋk hi - yu - ye

wa-yaŋk hi-yu - ye   ma - to o-ma - ki - ya - ke

WORDS

kola'............................ friend
wana'............................ now
hiyu'ye............................ come
mato'............................ bear (who)
oma'kiyake............................ told me this[1] (said)
kola'............................ friend
hiyu'ye............................ come
lena' wayaŋk'............................ behold all these
hiyu'ye............................ come
mato'............................ bear
oma'kiyake............................ told me this

Analysis.—Three renditions of this song were recorded, which are uniform in every respect. The melody progressions are somewhat peculiar, but their exact repetition shows that they were clear in the mind of the singer. There was a slight lowering of pitch in the sustained tone which occurs in the sixth and seventh measures. The song is melodic in structure and contains all the tones of the octave except the sixth. One accidental occurs—the seventh lowered a semitone.

See plot of this melody on page 283.

Another remedy imparted to Eagle Shield by the bear was a remedy for diseases of the kidneys. This plant, which grew on the prairie, was called by the Sioux *azuŋ'tka yazaŋ'pi oŋ'piyapi*, and was identified as *Lactuca pulchella* DC. (wild lettuce). It was dried and prepared in the form of a decoction. Eagle Shield said that not more than three doses should be prepared at a time, as it must not be allowed

---

[1] Referring to the manner in which the patient was being treated.

to stand overnight. This decoction was to be taken three times a day, and the effect was said to be better if it were taken with food. Eagle Shield said: "No matter how much a person is suffering, as soon as this medicine reaches the spot it relieves the pain. This is usually done by the time six doses have been taken."

A song was sung four times during treatment with this remedy. In the words of the song the bear is addressed as "father."

No. 87. An Appeal to the Bear   (Catalogue No. 517)

Sung by EAGLE SHIELD

VOICE ♩ = 84
DRUM not recorded

A- te ho-ye - ya   a -te ho-ye - ya   i -yo -ti - ye wa -ki -

ye   a - te ho-ye -̇ ya   i -yo - ti - ye wa -ki - ye   yo

WORDS

ate′	father
ho′yeya	send a voice
ate′	father
ho′yeya	send a voice
iyo′tiye	a hard task
wa′kiye	I am having
ate′	father
ho′yeya	send a voice
iyo′tiye	a hard task
wa′kiye yo	I am having

Analysis.—This is a pleasing melody, with no striking characteristics. Three-fourths of the intervals are major seconds, the remainder comprising a fifth, a fourth, and a minor third; the song is minor in tonality and melodic in structure, containing all the tones of the octave except the seventh and second. Three renditions were recorded, interspersed with the groans as given with songs for the sick. The renditions were uniform in all respects.

The following song is that of the bear, which digs roots with its claws. The herb used in connection with this song was identified as *Glycyrrhiza lepidota* Nutt. (wild licorice). The song and herb were used in the treatment of the sick. Eagle Shield said that when administering the herb the song was sung only three times.

No. 88. Song of the Bear   (Catalogue No. 518)

Sung by EAGLE SHIELD

VOICE ♩ = 80

DRUM not recorded

Mi - na - pe kiŋ wa - kaŋ ye - lo pe - źi - hu - ta o - ta ye - lo ye - lo mi - na - pe kiŋ pe - źi - hu - ta o - ta ye - lo

WORDS

(*First rendition*)

mina′pe kiŋ wakaŋ′ yelo′...... my paw is sacred
peźi′huta o′ta yelo′........... herbs are plentiful

(*Second rendition*)

mina′pe kiŋ wakaŋ′ yelo′...... my paw is sacred
ta′ku iyu′ha o′ta yelo′......... all things are sacred

Analysis.—The fourth constitutes 31 per cent of the intervals in this song. The only interval larger than this is the ascending eleventh, which appears with the introduction of the words. This interval occurs in no other song of this series and is found only three times in 340 Chippewa songs. The interval was correctly sung in the three renditions of the song. The change of time was the same in all renditions. (See song No. 5.) This melody contains two rhythmic units, both of which are found in the first part of the song. The rhythm of the latter part, containing the words, has no resemblance to the rhythm of the unit.

A remedy to check hemorrhages, arising either from wounds or from some internal cause, was supplied by an herb called by the Sioux *wiŋa'wazi hutkaŋ,* 'root of the bur,' and identified as *Ratibida colum-naris* (Sims) Don. (cone flower).   This was found in damp places, along creeks.   For pain in the side a tea was made of the stalk and leaves of this plant, and for earache a decoction was made of the root and a drop put into the ear.   The following song accompanied the use of this herb.

No. 89. "Bear Told Me"   (Catalogue No. 519)

Sung by EAGLE SHIELD

VOICE ♩ = 80

(or ♪ = 160)

DRUM not recorded

WORDS

kan'tuhuwa lu'ta waŋ........	a scarlet buckbrush
mato'............................	bear
oma'kiyaka....................	told me about
ta'ku sito'mniyaŋ............	all things
kola'.............................	friend
oma'kiyaka....................	told me about
kan'tuhuwa lu'ta waŋ........	a scarlet buckbrush
mato'............................	bear
oma'kiyaka....................	told me about

Analysis.—Three renditions of this song were recorded, and in them all the changes of measure-lengths occur as in the transcription, the time being unusually well maintained.   It is impossible to indicate an eighth note as the metric unit of the first and similar measures, as 6–8 time implies a group of two triplets, while the three counts in these measures are clearly defined.   The rhythmic unit is interesting, and parts of it are found in parts of the song which do not contain the complete unit.   The song is minor in tonality and lacks the seventh and fourth tones of the complete octave.   (See song No. 26.)

The fourth constitutes 37 per cent of the entire number of intervals in this song, a proportion even larger than that in the preceding song. In the descending fourth D–G the lowest tone was invariably sung a trifle sharp in this song, offering a contrast to the preceding song, in which the fourth was sung with good intonation.

Eagle Shield gave the following narrative concerning his dream of the badger, from which he secured his remedies for children.   The remedies for adults, as already stated, were received from the bear.

Eagle Shield said:

A man appeared to me in a dream, showed me a plant, and said, "My friend, remember this plant well. Be sure to get the right one, as this is good." It was a badger, who appeared to me in the form of a man and said this. It was the first time that the badger came to me, but afterward he brought me other herbs. There were no songs with any of the herbs which the badger brought me. In return for the kindness of the badger I took tobacco, cut it up fine, and dug a hole in the ground. I buried the tobacco and said, "Badger, I give you this in return for what you have told me." When the badger is alive he eats this herb. Whatever herb the badger introduces is especially good. Some consider his medicine stronger than that of the bear, as he digs deeper and farther into the ground.

Eagle Shield said that he buried a little tobacco as an offering to the badger whenever he dug any of these roots.   He said also that before giving these remedies to a child he always made a supplication similar to the following: "Wakaŋ'taŋka, you have made these herbs.   We are going to give them to this child.   We hope you will make the child well, and we hope nothing will come to prevent the usefulness of these herbs."

The first remedy imparted to Eagle Shield by the badger was a plant identified as *Leptilon canadense* (L.) Britton (horseweed).   This was used as a remedy for pain in the bowels and for diarrhea.   As it is a mild remedy and the size of the plant varies, it was difficult to describe the amount to be used as a dose.   Eagle Shield said that if a plant were small it would be necessary to use all the root and a few inches of the stalk, but that if the plant were large it would be sufficient to use half the root for a dose.   A decoction was made, and he said it was "well to smell the tea to judge its strength, as it should smell of the root to be right."   He said it "should be taken before meals, the morning

BEAR-WITH-WHITE-PAW

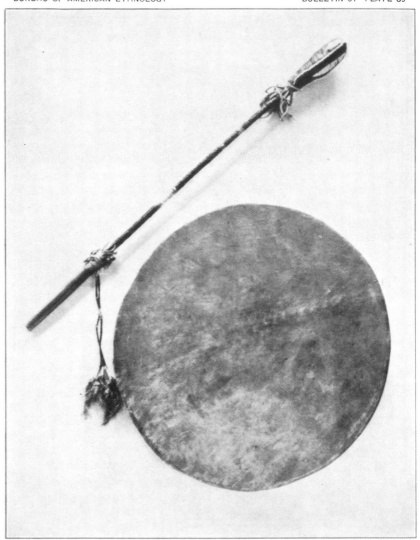

DRUM AND DECORATED DRUMSTICK

EAGLE SHIELD

NECKLACE WORN WHEN TREATING THE SICK

dose being the largest. If a person should take this after a meal it would cause distress, but when taken before a meal it prepares the stomach to receive and digest the food." A small spoon made of white bone was used in giving medicine to children. (See pl. 36.)

The second of Eagle Shield's remedies for children was identified as *Chenopodium album* L. (lamb's-quarters). A decoction of the entire plant was used in cases of bloody dysentery. It could be given from the time a child was old enough to drink water, the dose being increased according to the age of the child.

The third remedy was for diarrhea, and was seemingly stronger than the others, as the dose was about a teaspoonful and only two or three doses were usually given. The herb was not boiled, but hot water was poured over it to make a tea. This was identified as *Aquilegia canadensis* L. (wild columbine).

The fourth remedy was for fever and headache. In this instance the herb was to be steeped. Some was given internally, and the child's entire body was rubbed with it. This herb was identified as *Rumex* sp. (dock).

———————

Mato'-nape'-ska (Bear-with-White-Paw) (pl. 38) was a man who showed much seriousness in describing his practice of medicine. He said that when treating the sick he wore one side of his hair unbraided, as shown in the illustration. (See p. 64.) The drum which he holds is that which he used when singing his medicine songs. The term *čaŋ'čeġa* is applied by the Sioux to all drums, the large dance drums as well as the hand drum. The specimen here shown (pl. 39) has a single head of rawhide and is held by means of two iron wires at the back, which are passed through a short section of iron tubing, thus forming a handle. Thongs or strips of stout cloth are also used for holds on these drums, which are common to many tribes of Indians. (See Bulletin 53, p. 62.) Drums of this type appear in the hands of members of the Kaŋġi'yuha in a native drawing by Eagle Shield (pl. 40). The drumstick used by Bear-with-White-Paw is elaborately decorated with porcupine quills and could be used with a large dance drum as well as with a hand drum. Such a stick might be carried to a gathering by a man who expected to sing at the drum.

A "necklace" which Bear-with-White-Paw said that he had worn for many years when attending the sick is shown in plate 41. He said that when summoned to visit a sick person it was his custom to put on this "necklace," consisting of a strip of hide to which are attached two small bags of "medicine" and a bear's claw. He said further that he pressed this claw into the flesh of the patient in order that the medicine might enter more easily and be more effectual. Eagle Shield also used a bear's claw in treating the sick (p. 253).

Like Eagle Shield, Bear-with-White-Paw received his knowledge of healing herbs from the bear. He said, "The bear is very truthful. He has a soul like ours, and his soul talks to mine in my sleep and tells me what to do."

Six herbs were described to the writer by Bear-with-White-Paw, and fresh specimens were furnished for identification.

Before beginning his account of the herbs and their uses he made the following supplication to the bear, a supplication which he said he would use when treating the sick:

Ho mita′kola oŋ maśi′ke taŋyaŋ′ ana′maġoptaŋ yo. Aŋpe′tu kiŋ lehaŋl′ ta′ku waŋźi′ awa′ćaŋ mi he oći′ćiyakiŋ ktelo′. Peźu′ta lena′ke slolye′ mayaki′yiŋ na ta′ku ećoŋ′ maya′śi na wo′yazaŋ waŋ′źigźi api′ye ma′yaśi na hena′ iyo′kihe kta ke′he ḳoŋ wana′ lehaŋl′ iya′ḣpe wa′yiŋ kta tka he′će iyu′ha owa′kihi kta. Wo′yazaŋ hena′ ḣeyab′ iya′yiŋ kte.

Translated as follows by Mr. Higheagle:

My friend, I am poor and needy. Listen well to me. This day I have something in my mind, and I wish to tell you. All these medicines you have made known to me, and you have commanded me to perform certain things in order to attend to certain sicknesses, and you have told me that these medicines have certain powers in them. Now I wish to use them with effect. These sicknesses, I want them to go away.

Bear-with-White-Paw said that he had only one song, which he sang in connection with the use of all these herbs. This song is as follows:

No. 90. Song of Healing   (Catalogue No. 674)
Sung by BEAR-WITH-WHITE-PAW

ate′	father
hiyu′ye yo	come forth
hu noŋ′pa	a two-legged object (see footnote, p. 120)
maka′ta yuŋka′ ća	lying in the earth
piya′wakaǵe′	I have renewed
ate′	father
hiyu′ye yo	come forth
ina′	mother
hiyu′ye yo	come forth
hu noŋ′pa	a two-legged object
maka′ta yuŋka′ ća	lying in the earth
piya′wakaǵe′	I have renewed
ina′	mother
hiyu′ye yo	come forth

Analysis.—This is the only song recorded by this singer. It is an interesting melody and was sung twice. There is no difference between the renditions, and the singer's performance was characterized by a marked degree of carefulness, like that of Brave Buffalo when singing similar songs. The tonic chord (D minor) is in evidence throughout this song which, however, is classified as melodic with harmonic framework because of the accented G, which appears four times. The last tone of the rhythmic unit was slightly shortened in every instance, as indicated in the transcription. The song contains 32 intervals, only two of which are larger than a minor third.

The herbs furnished by Bear-with-White-Paw, with the directions for their use, are as follows:

(1) Identified as *Cheirinia aspera* (DC.) Britton (western wallflower). This was said to be a very rare plant among the Sioux, though it can occasionally be found on level ground or along a river. It was used as a remedy for cramps in the stomach or bowels. The plant has long slender seed pods, somewhat resembling pine needles. In preparing the medicine these seed pods are opened and the seeds removed and crushed. Warm (not hot) water is poured over them, whereupon the water becomes yellow. This mixture is taken internally and also applied externally. It is a very strong medicine, and if the person has been sick only one day a single dose of the remedy is usually sufficient.

(2) Identified as *Heuchera hispida* Pursh (alum root). This plant was said to grow on high ground. The root only was used; this is so strong that a fragment of a small root about half an inch long was a sufficient dose for a child. It is a powerful astringent and was used as a remedy for chronic diarrhea. Only two or three doses were usually given.

(3) Identified as *Lithospermum linearifolium* Goldie (puccoon). This was used as a remedy for hemorrhages from the lungs. The

plant grows on the hills and has fragrant white flowers. Bear-with-White-Paw said, "The odor of these flowers goes to every plant that brings cure to men. It makes them sweeter and strengthens them as they grow in the field." He said also that the medicine-men keep this or some other fragrant herb in the bundle with their roots during the winter. (Compare p. 79.)

(4) Identified as *Echinacea angustifolia* DC. ("nigger head"). A specimen of this herb was also brought by Jaw (pl. 59), who, like Bear-with-White-Paw, said that he used it as a remedy for toothache. Bear-with-White-Paw gave other uses for it, saying that he used it also for pain in the bowels; that it would cure tonsilitis, and was frequently employed in combination with other herbs. Only the root of this plant was used.

(5)′ Identified as *Monarda fistulosa* L. (horsemint). This was said to be an "elk herb" but is not the same variety of plant as that called the "elk herb" in the description of Brave Buffalo's dream, which was identified as *Monarda scabra* Beck. (See p. 178.) This remedy was used to reduce fever, and was also said to be "good for a hard cold." The blossoms only were used, and Bear-with-White-Paw said they were so strong that "only a little" should be used in making the tea.

(6) This herb, identified as *Allionia nyctaginea* Michx. (umbrellawort), is the same as that a specimen of which was furnished by Eagle Shield and used externally by him in the treatment of broken bones. Bear-with-White-Paw gave the following directions for its use: "Grate the root, moisten it, and rub it on the skin wherever there is a swelling." He said it grew close to the water and was adapted only for external use.

The narrative concerning these medicines was given at intervals through a period of several weeks, as considerable time was required for finding suitable specimens of the herbs. Bear-with-White-Paw understood the purpose of the analysis, and the plants he brought were especially large and typical. When the work was completed he assured the writer of the sincerity with which he had done his part, saying again, "These are the medicines which I use for the purposes I have told you, and the song which I sing when I use them."

In addition to the herbs secured from Eagle Shield and Bear-with-White-Paw, two plants were procured from Jaw, one mentioned above and another which was said to be an unfailing cure for rheumatism; this was identified as *Parmelia* sp. (a lichen). No songs were recorded by Jaw in connection with the use of these herbs.

In order to ascertain whether the herbs used by Eagle Shield, Bear-with-White-Paw, and Jaw have a known medicinal value the specimens of plants were submitted to the United States Department of

Agriculture, from which the following report was received.[1] The species marked (*), or, in some cases, other species of the same genus, were reported by the late Mrs. Stevenson as being used medicinally among the Zuñi.[2] Those marked (†) have been noted among the Tewa.[3]

†Achillea lanulosa Nutt .... Not known as possessing medicinal value (p. 254).

*Astragalus carolinianus L ..... None (p. 257).

†Artemisia frigida Willd .... Known as Colorado sage; has considerable reputation as a medicinal herb among miners and others in the Rocky Mountain region in the treatment of their mountain fevers (p. 259).

*Astragalus sp................. Species of *Astragalus* in this country are best known for their poisonous action upon animals (p. 260).

Lactuca pulchella DC........... None (p. 262).

†Allionia nyctaginea Michx .... None (pp. 261, 270).

Glycyrrhiza lepidota Nutt...... Has the taste of the true licorice root, but is not used medicinally (p. 263).

*Ratibida columnaris (Sims) Don None (p. 265).

*Leptilon canadense (L.) Britton Herb used for hemorrhages of various kinds; also employed in diarrhea and dropsy. Volatile oil, known as oil of erigeron, obtained by distillation of the fresh flowering herb (p. 266).

*Chenopodium album L........ Leaves said to have sedative and diuretic properties (p. 267).

Aquilegia canadensis L.......... Plant said to have diuretic, emmenagogue, sudorific, and tonic properties (p. 267).

*Rumex sp..................... The roots of *Rumex crispus* and *R. obtusifolius* are employed medicinally for their astringent and tonic properties. *Rumex hymenosepalus* of the Southwestern States is used for tanning purposes (p. 267).

Cheirinia aspera (DC) Britton.. None (pp. 269, 389).

Heuchera hispida Pursh........ Root said to be employed by hunters and prospectors of the Northwest as an astringent to check diarrhea (p. 269).

*Lithospermum   linearifolium None (p. 269).
   Goldie.

Echinacea angustifolia DC ..... Root used for its alterative properties (pp. 270, 389).

†Monarda fistulosa L .... Leaves and tops sometimes used as a substitute for *M. punctata*, and employed as a stimulant, carminative, sudorific, diuretic, and anti-emetic. Furnishes a sharp and pungent oil (p. 270).

*Erigeron pumilus Nutt .... None (p. 389).

†Lacinaria   punctata   (Hook.) None (p. 389).
   Kuntze.

Parmelia sp................... None (p. 270).

[1] The writer gratefully acknowledges the assistance of Mr. Paul C. Standley, assistant curator, Division of Plants, U. S. National Museum, who identified these specimens; also that of Miss Alice Henkel, assistant in economic and systematic botany, Bureau of Plant Industry, U. S. Department of Agriculture, who reported on their medicinal properties, as here given.

[2] Ethnobotany of the Zuñi Indians, in *Thirtieth Rep. Bur. Amer. Ethn.*, pp. 101–102.

[3] Robbins, Harrington, and Freire-Marreco, Ethnobotany of the Tewa Indians, *Bull. 55, Bur. Amer. Ethn.*, pp. 121–123.

The two following songs are said to have been used by Sitting Bull in treating the sick and were sung by his nephew Tataŋ′kawaŋźi′la (One Buffalo), literally One Buffalo Bull. (Pl. 57.) A brief account of the life of Sitting Bull followed by two of his songs is given on page 458 and an incident in his early life is related in connection with a demonstration of the sacred stones on page 218.

No. 91. Sitting Bull's Medicine Song (a)   (Catalogue No. 654)

Sung by ONE BUFFALO

VOICE ♩= 63

DRUM not recorded

WORDS (NOT TRANSCRIBED)

Wakaŋ′taŋka.....................	Wakaŋ′taŋka
ta′ku wa′yelo....................	to him I am related
Wakaŋ′taŋka waśte′............	Wakaŋ′taŋka (is) good
ta′ku wa′yelo....................	to him I am related
waŋkaŋ′taŋhaŋ..................	from above
oya′te waŋ......................	a tribe
kola′ wa′yelo...................	is my friend
waŋkaŋ′taŋhaŋ..................	from above
heha′ka waŋ.....................	an elk
kola′ wa′yelo...................	is my friend
waŋkaŋ′taŋhaŋ..................	from above
wića′śa waŋ....................	a man
kola′ wa′yelo...................	is my friend

Analysis.—This melody is simple in form and without striking characteristics. It contains all the tones of the octave except the seventh, and is major in tonality and melodic in structure. The first interval is an ascending progression of a major sixth, which is the only interval in the song larger than a minor third.

See plot of this melody on page 283.

No. 92. Sitting Bull's Medicine Song (b)　(Catalogue No. 655)

Sung by ONE BUFFALO

VOICE ♩= 96

DRUM not recorded

To - pa ki - ya　ko - la　ni - wa - kaŋ nuŋ - we　to - pa - ki -

ya　ko - la　ni - wa - kaŋ nuŋ - we　to - pa - ki -

ya　ko - la ni - wa - kaŋ nuŋ - we　tu - we - ni wa - kaŋ śni

ye - lo e - he - ćuŋ to - pa ki - ya　ko - la ni - wa - kaŋ nuŋ -

we　to - pa - ki - ya　ko - la　ni - wa - kaŋ nuŋ - we

WORDS

to′pa ki′ya.....................	in four places
kola′.............................	friend
ni′wakaŋ nuŋwe′..............	may you be sacred
tuwe′ni wakaŋ′ śni yelo′.......	no one is sacred
ehe′ćuŋ	you said
to′pa ki′ya.....................	in four places
kola′.............................	friend
ni′wakaŋ nuŋwe′..............	may you be sacred

Analysis.—This melody contains 23 measures, but only 11 progressions, 6 of which are downward and 5 upward. It has a compass of only 6 tones. Among 340 Chippewa songs 7 per cent have a compass of 6 or fewer tones, and in the present series 5 per cent have this range. The rhythmic unit is long and interesting, having a completeness which is frequently lacking in these units. The melody tones are those of the fourth five-toned scale. The tonic chord is clearly felt throughout the melody, which would be classified as harmonic in structure except for the accented C, occurring once in the song.

NARRATIVE OF A VIGIL AND PRAYER FOR THE SICK

By Tataŋk'-ehaŋ'ni (Old Buffalo)

It was with no little hesitation that Old Buffalo told this story and depicted the event in a drawing (pl. 42) It is an account of a prayer vigil which he kept for a niece who was very ill and who, he believed, recovered because of this action on his part. Such a vigil is called by the Sioux *haŋble'ćapi*, 'prayers offered standing.'[1]

This narrative is given in the present tense, as it was related, and the words of the interpreter (Mrs. James McLaughlin) are followed as closely as possible. Old Buffalo said:

I have a sister older than myself. We are children of one father and one mother. As my sister's child is growing up to be a young girl, she is taken sick, and is so thin that there is no flesh on her bones. She can not rise from her bed. I sit beside her. She asks me to bring her a drink of water. My heart is very sad. As I see her my thought is, "I will call on Wakaŋ'taŋka for help." I had heard that when men came to helplessness in sickness they did this. I could not bear the thought of going many miles barefoot, but I wanted the girl to recover.

I go on a high hill and make a vow, saying, "Wakaŋ'taŋka, I call upon you. Have pity on me. My niece is on her deathbed. Have pity on her, so she can live on earth and see you. Give me strength to do what is right and honest. I will give you four sacrifices. I will smoke a fine pipe. It is a Chief pipe, so you can bless it. I will do this in your honor if you will spare her life."

The girl gets better. She drinks water and eats a little food.

Now I am going to fulfill my vow to Wakaŋ'taŋka. It is July, and the weather is very hot. They make a lodge for me at some distance from the village. It is a lodge of branches. Several men take the big-leaf sage and spread it on the ground in the lodge, then they bring hot stones and pour water on them. As I sit in the lodge it is filled with steam. When I am wet with perspiration the men rub me with sage. They take a buffalo robe, put it around me with the fur outside, and tie it across my chest. The discomfort of wearing this heavy robe is part of my sacrifice, as well as the disgrace of being dressed like a woman. No moccasins are on my feet. So I start for the distant hill where I am to offer my prayer. I carry a pipe decorated with ribbons and mallard-duck feathers, holding the stem upward in front of me as I walk. The sun has not long risen as I leave the village, and I reach the hill before noon. There I find a buffalo skull, which a man has brought from the village. It is a large skull with horns on it. My friends have also prepared a soft place on the ground for me and covered it with sage leaves, that I may rest when I am too weary from standing. That afternoon I hold the pipe and follow the sun with it. At night I lie face down on the sage.

Now the sun has risen. I stand up again, facing the east and holding the pipe. All day I follow the sun with the stem of the pipe. The second night I stand up all night, until the daylight appears. Then I put my pipe against the buffalo skull and lie down with my head near it. When the sun is fully risen I stand up again and cry, saying "Give me strength for long life, and strength to be right and honest in all I do." On the third day I put a piece of red cloth [*waóŋ'yapi*] at each of the four directions.

Just as the sun is getting low on this day they come for me. I leave the buffalo skull, the pipe, and the four offerings of red cloth on the hill. Now I am going back

---

[1] Cf. vigil by Śiya'ka (pp. 184–188)

FASTING VIGIL (DRAWING BY OLD BUFFALO)

OLD BUFFALO

with my friends, still walking with bare feet. They have made a new sweat lodge near the old one, and I am the first to enter it. Again they bring hot stones and pour water on them, and again they rub me with the sage leaves. After this I put on moccasins and leggings, and go away.

This is the means by which we prolonged our lives in the old days. My niece recovered.

The writer then asked some question about the care given the girl by the medicine-man (or doctor) and Old Buffalo replied indignantly: "It was Wakaŋ'taŋka who saved her life; not the doctor. She lived in answer to my prayer."

This song is commonly used by medicine-men of the tribe:

No. 93. "A Wind from the North"　　(Catalogue No. 536)

Sung by Two Shields

WORDS

ćaŋte′	my heart
mato′kećaća	is different (see footnote, p. 120)
waŋma′yaŋka yo	behold me
ćaŋte′	my heart
mato′kećaća	is different
heiya′ye waye′	I have shown it
wazi′yata	from the north
tate′	a wind
hiyo′ ma aü′ we	comes to get me (cf. words of Nos. 41, 105; also footnote, p. 120).

Analysis.—This song contains the tones of the fourth five-toned scale. In structure it is melodic with harmonic framework, the tonic chord being strongly in evidence throughout the melody. Concerning the change of tempo see song No. 5. In this instance the phrase indicated as the rhythmic unit of the song is long and not accurately repeated. Three reasons seem to justify this: (1) the phrase forms the rhythmic divisions of the entire song; (2) the phrase in every instance opens with the same measure-divisions; (3) the note values of the phrase are in some instances necessarily changed to conform to the words. Two-thirds of the progressions are downward, and the song contains only three intervals larger than a minor third. See plot of this melody on page 283.

In this song we meet a strange phase of the life of a medicine-man. Two Shields, who recorded the song, said that "White Shield used to sing this song when he was worried or disappointed." Strangely human is this little melody. Two Shields said also that when singing the song he would mention the direction on which the wind was blowing that day, as "every man who performs ceremonies respects the various winds."

No. 94. "May This be the Day"   (Catalogue No. 540)

Sung by Two SHIELDS

VOICE ♩ = 176
DRUM ♩ = 132
Drum-rhythm similar to No. 19

Aŋ-pe-tu mi-ta-wa ḳoŋ le - tu nuŋ-we aŋ-pe-tu

mi-ta-wa ḳoŋ le - tu nuŋ-we wa-zi-ya-ta

ta-te u-ye ćiŋ aŋ-pe-tu mi-ta-wa ḳoŋ le -

tu nuŋ-we aŋ-pe-tu mi-ta-wa ḳoŋ le -

tu nuŋ-we aŋ-pe-tu mi-ta-wa ḳoŋ le - tu nuŋ-

we aŋ-pe-tu mi-ta-wa ḳoŋ le - tu nuŋ-we

WORDS

aŋpe′tu mita′wa ḳoŋ le′tu nuŋwe′	may this be the day which I considered mine
wazi′yata......................	from the north
tate′ uye′ ćiŋ....................	the wind is blowing
aŋpe′tu mita′wa ḳoŋ le′tu nuŋwe′	may this be the day which I considered mine

Analysis.—In this song voice and drum are entirely independent in tempo, the drum beating unaccented eighths in a tempo ♩ = 132, while the tempo of the voice is ♩ = 176. Both are steadily maintained. The song is distinguished by the number of major seconds it contains, this interval forming 16 per cent of the progressions. The melody has a compass of 10 tones and is on the fourth five-toned scale. The rhythmic unit is interesting and is continuously repeated. Three

4840°—Bull. 61—18——20

renditions were recorded, the repetitions being separated by shrill cries during which the drumbeat was steadily continued.

This is the third analysis group of dream songs and comprises those used in treating the sick. In this, as in the songs analyzed on pages 198 and 239, a large majority of the songs were recorded by those who themselves received them in dreams. The numbers of these songs are 79 to 94, inclusive.

Old Songs—(4) Songs Used in Treatment of the Sick
MELODIC ANALYSIS
TONALITY

	Number of songs.	Serial Nos. of songs.
Major tonality	6	85, 86, 91, 92, 93, 94
Minor tonality	10	79, 80, 81, 82, 83, 84, 87, 88, 89, 90
Total	16	

FIRST NOTE OF SONG—ITS RELATION TO KEYNOTE

	Number of songs.	Serial Nos. of songs.
Beginning on the—		
Tenth	4	79, 80, 86, 94
Ninth	1	81
Octave	4	83, 84, 87, 90
Fifth	4	85, 89, 91, 93
Third	1	92
Keynote	2	82, 88
Total	16	

LAST NOTE OF SONG—ITS RELATION TO KEYNOTE

	Number of songs.	Serial Nos. of songs.
Ending on the—		
Fifth	3	85, 88, 89
Third	2	91, 93
Keynote	11	79, 80, 81, 82, 83, 84, 86, 87, 90, 92, 94
Total	16	

LAST NOTE OF SONG—ITS RELATION TO COMPASS OF SONG

	Number of songs.	Serial Nos. of songs.
Songs in which final tone is—		
Lowest tone in song	14	79, 80, 81, 82, 83, 84, 86, 87, 88, 89, 90, 91, 93, 94
Immediately preceded by whole tone below	1	85
Songs containing a fourth below the final tone	1	92
Total	16	

Old Songs—(4) Songs Used in Treatment of the Sick—Continued

Melodic Analysis—Continued

NUMBER OF TONES COMPRISING COMPASS OF SONG

	Number of songs.	Serial Nos. of songs.
Compass of—		
Twelve tones....................................	1	88
Ten tones..	6	79, 80, 84, 86, 93, 94
Nine tones.......................................	2	81, 85
Eight tones......................................	5	83, 87, 89, 90, 91
Six tones..	2	82, 92
Total..	16	

TONE MATERIAL

	Number of songs.	Serial Nos. of songs.
Fourth five-toned scale ......,......................	3	92, 93, 94
Minor triad and fourth..............................	3	80, 83, 90
Octave complete except seventh......................	1	91
Octave complete except seventh and sixth............	2	81, 85
Octave complete except seventh, fifth, and second....	1	82
Octave complete except seventh and fourth...........	1	89
Octave complete except seventh and second...........	1	87
Octave complete except sixth........................	4	79, 84, 86, 88
Total..	16	

ACCIDENTALS

	Number of songs.	Serial Nos. of songs.
Songs containing—		
No accidentals...................................	13	79, 80, 81, 82, 83, 85, 87, 89, 90, 91, 92, 93, 94
Seventh raised a semitone........................	1	88
Fourth and seventh raised a semitone.............	1	84
Seventh lowered a semitone.......................	1	86
Total..	16	

STRUCTURE

	Number of songs.	Serial Nos. of songs.
Melodic..	5	79, 86, 87, 91, 94
Melodic with harmonic framework.....................	8	80, 81, 82, 85, 88, 90, 92, 93
Harmonic..	3	83, 84, 89
Total..	16	

Old Songs—(4) Songs Used in Treatment of the Sick—Continued

MELODIC ANALYSIS—Continued

FIRST PROGRESSION—DOWNWARD AND UPWARD

	Number of songs.	Serial Nos. of songs.
Downward..	12	79, 80, 81, 83, 85, 86, 87, 89, 90, 92, 93, 94
Upward..	4	82, 84, 88, 91
Total..	16	

TOTAL NUMBER OF PROGRESSIONS—DOWNWARD AND UPWARD

Downward..	292
Upward..	186
Total..	478

INTERVALS IN DOWNWARD PROGRESSION

Interval of a—	
Fifth..	3
Fourth.......................................	53
Major third..................................	13
Minor third..................................	68
Major second.................................	135
Minor second.................................	20
Total..	292

INTERVALS IN UPWARD PROGRESSION

Interval of a—	
Eleventh.....................................	1
Tenth..	1
Octave.......................................	5
Major sixth..................................	2
Minor sixth..................................	1
Fifth..	8
Fourth.......................................	33
Major third..................................	9
Minor third..................................	45
Major second.................................	66
Minor second.................................	15
Total..	186

AVERAGE NUMBER OF SEMITONES IN AN INTERVAL

Total number of intervals...........................	478
Total number of semitones	1,461
Average number of semitones in an interval...........	3.05

Old Songs—(4) Songs Used in Treatment of the Sick—Continued

MELODIC ANALYSIS—Continued

KEY

	Number of songs.	Serial Nos. of songs.
Key of—		
A major	1	93
B flat major	2	91, 92
B major	2	86, 94
D minor	4	79, 80, 84, 90
E flat minor	2	87, 88
E minor	2	81, 83
G minor	2	82, 89
A flat major	1	85
Total	16	

RHYTHMIC ANALYSIS

PART OF MEASURE ON WHICH SONG BEGINS

	Number of songs.	Serial Nos. of songs.
Beginning on unaccented part of measure	8	79, 81, 82, 83, 84, 88, 91, 92
Beginning on accented part of measure	8	80, 85, 86, 87, 89, 90, 93, 94
Total	16	

RHYTHM OF FIRST MEASURE

	Number of songs.	Serial Nos. of songs.
First measure in—		
2–4 time	10	79, 80, 81, 83, 84, 85, 87, 88, 90, 91
3–4 time	5	86, 89, 92, 93, 94
4–8 time	1	82
Total	16	

CHANGE OF TIME (MEASURE-LENGTHS)

	Number of songs.	Serial Nos. of songs.
Songs containing no change of time	1	80
Songs containing a change of time	15	79, 91, 82, 83, 84, 85, 86, 87, 88, 89, 90, 91, 92, 93, 94
Total	16	

Old Songs—(4) Songs Used in Treatment of the Sick—Continued

RHYTHMIC ANALYSIS—Continued

RHYTHM OF DRUM

	Number of songs.	Serial Nos. of songs.
Eighth notes unaccented	3	79, 93, 94
Quarter notes unaccented	1	80
Drum not recorded	12	81, 82, 83, 84, 85, 86, 87, 88, 89, 90, 91, 92
Total	16	

RHYTHMIC UNIT OF SONG

	Number of songs.	Serial Nos. of songs.
Songs containing—		
No rhythmic unit	1	86
One rhythmic unit	13	79, 80, 81, 82, 83, 84, 85, 87, 89, 90, 92, 93, 9
Two rhythmic units	2	88, 91
Total	16	

METRIC UNIT OF VOICE (TEMPO)

	Number of songs.	Serial Nos. of songs.
Metronome—		
63	2	83, 91
66	2	81, 90
72	1	85
80	2	84, 88
84	2	79, 87
88	2	86, 89
96	1	92
132	1	93
138	1	80
176	1	94
184	1	82
Total	16	

METRIC UNIT OF DRUM (TEMPO)

	Number of songs.	Serial Nos. of songs.
Metronome—		
72	1	79
132	1	94
138	1	80
160	1	93
Drum not recorded	12	81, 82, 83, 84, 85, 86, 87, 88, 89, 90, 91, 92
Total	16	

Old Songs—(4) Songs Used in Treatment of the Sick—Continued

RHYTHMIC ANALYSIS—Continued

COMPARISON OF METRIC UNIT OF VOICE AND DRUM (TEMPO)

	Number of songs.	Serial Nos. of songs.
Drum and voice having the same metric unit.........	1	80
Drum faster than voice.............................	1	93
Drum slower than voice.............................	2	79, 94
Drum not recorded.................................	12	81, 82, 83, 84, 85, 86, 87, 88, 89, 90, 91, 92
Total...	16	

PLOTS OF SONGS USED IN TREATMENT OF THE SICK

Among the plots selected from those of the preceding group may be noted three which resemble Class A (see fig. 19) but contain scending progressions; these are Nos. 79, 86, and 91. Examples

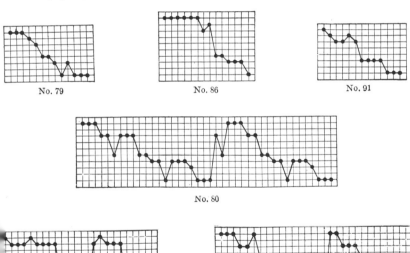

No. 79   No. 86   No. 91

No. 80

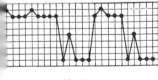

No. 81

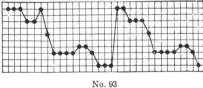

No. 93

FIG. 28. Plots, Group 4.

Class C are shown in Nos. 80 and 81, the recurrence and dwelling n the keynote suggesting the confidence which the medicine-man elt in his own power and which he wished to impress on the mind f his patient. The outline of song No. 93 suggests Class C in its repeated tones but bears also a resemblance to Class D. The title f this song is "A wind from the north."

SOCIETIES (OKO'LAKÍĆIYE)

Two classes of societies existed among the Sioux—dream societies and military societies. Both classes are mentioned by Hayden, one of the earliest writers on the Indians of the upper plains. Hayden enumerates the Sioux societies as the "Bull Head, Elk, and Bear" (the first being properly translated "buffalo" and all being dream societies); also the "Scalp, Strong Heart, Fox, Big Owl, and Soldier." [1] In every instance the Sioux equivalent is given, identifying the societies with organizations of comparatively recent times.

Societies based on dreams (known as "dream societies") were composed of men who, in their fasting visions, had seen the same animal. The common experience of the vision bound the men together and societies were thus formed. These societies had their meetings, to which were admitted only those who had dreamed of the animal for which the society was named. Concerning these societies Miss Fletcher writes:

Among the Siouan family of Indians there are societies, religious in character, which are distinguished by the name of some animal. . . . Membership in these societies is not confined to any particular gens, or grouping of gens, but depends upon supernatural indications over which the individual has no control. The animal which appears to a man in a vision during his religious fasting determines to which society he must belong.[2]

Among the Teton Sioux there are some societies which belong unmistakably to one of these groups and others which, according to the writer's informants, probably had their origin in a dream of the name-animal, but are now open to men who have distinguished themselves in war. Thus the Elk and the Buffalo are distinctly dream societies, and the Strong Heart, Miwa'tani, and White Horse Riders are distinctly military in character, while the great military society of the Kaŋǵi'yuha is said to have originated in a dream of an owl. The writer secured an account of a dream of a wolf, but the terms "Wolf society" and "Fox society" seem to some extent interchangeable at the present time. Mention was made of a Horse society, but no dream of a horse was recorded; it was, however, a dream society, and is included by Wissler in his list of "dream cults"

---

[1] Hayden, F. V., Ethnography and Philology of the Indian Tribes of the Missouri Valley, p. 281, Philadelphia, 1862.

[2] Fletcher, Alice C., The Elk Mystery or Festival. Ogallala Sioux, in *Reps. Peabody Museum*, III, pp. 276, 277, Cambridge, 1887. Cf. also Wissler, Clark, Societies and Ceremonial Associations of the Teton-Dakota, *Anthr. Papers, Amer. Mus. Nat. Hist.*, XI, pt. 1, pp. 81-98, New York, 1912.

BUFFALO-DANCE SHIELD

among the Oglala.[1] Mention of "horse songs" is made also by Dorsey.[2]

It is probable that these societies held no regular meetings, and that no new members of the military organizations had been elected during a period of about 30 years prior to the collecting of this material. It is impossible, therefore, to secure much reliable information on the history of these societies among the Teton Sioux.

DREAM SOCIETIES

BUFFALO SOCIETY

Concerning the Buffalo society Dr. Lowie writes:

Among the Santee the men performing the Buffalo dance [Tataⁿ'k watcĭpi] had had visions of the buffalo, though apparently the sons of such men were also entitled to join. One man might dream that he   . . .   had been shot by an arrow so that he could barely get home. . . . Such a man painted himself vermilion to represent the trickling down of the blood. Another man dreamed of being shot with a gun. Such a one would act out his dream during a Buffalo dance.[3]

Catlin mentions the Buffalo dance in one of his letters,[4] stating that he witnessed it at Fort Snelling, Minn. The writer saw a Buffalo dance at Bull Head, S. Dak., on the Fourth of July, 1913.   In this dance it is customary for the dancers to wear headdresses adorned with buffalo horns, and to imitate the actions of buffalo. A shield carried in the buffalo dance is shown in plate 43.

The following songs were said to have been sung in the Buffalo society. Some of these songs were said to have been received, or composed, in a dream of buffalo, but the story of the dream had been forgotten, only the songs remaining as a tradition in the tribe.

---

[1] Ibid., p. 95.

[2] In *Eleventh Rep. Bur. Ethn.*, p. 479.

[3] Lowie, Robert H., Dance Associations of the Eastern Dakota, *Anthr. Papers, Amer. Mus. Nat. Hist.*, XI, pt. 2, p. 119, New York, 1913.

[4] Catlin, George, The Manners, Customs, and Conditions of the North American Indian, vol. 2, p. 35, London, 1841.

No. 95. "Northward They Are Walking"   (Catalogue No 663)

Sung by WAKAŊ'-ĆIKA'NA (LITTLE CONJUROR)

VOICE ♩ = 96
DRUM ♩ = 96
Drum-rhythm similar to No. 6

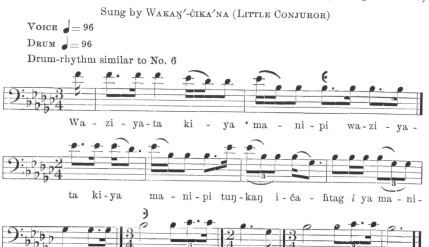

Wa - zi - ya - ta   ki - ya ' ma - ni - pi   wa - zi - ya -

ta ki - ya   ma - ni - pi tuŋ - kaŋ i - ća - ħtag i ya ma - ni -

. pi

WORDS

wazi'yata ki'ya................. northward
ma'nipi.......................... they are walking
tuŋkaŋ'.......................... a sacred stone
ića'ħtag ya...................... they touch
ma'nipi.......................... they are walking

Analysis.—This song and the two following songs were recorded at Sisseton among Sioux who belong to the Santee division of the tribe. (See p. 512.)   These three songs are characterized by the ascending interval of a major third in the closing measures.   In two instances this is an ascent to the final tone, which is usually the lowest tone in the song.   Two of these songs are minor and one is major, but this interval occurs in all.   The song under analysis is characterized by the interval of the fourth, which forms about 28 per cent of the whole number of intervals.   Six renditions were recorded, which show no differences.   Between the repetitions of the song the drumbeat changed to a tremolo, instead of being steadily maintained, as usual, in the rhythm which accompanied the song.

No. 96. "My Goal"   (Catalogue No. 664)

Sung by LITTLE CONJUROR

VOICE ♩= 72
DRUM ♩= 88
Drum-rhythm similar to No. 19

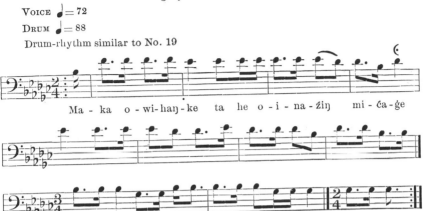

Ma - ka   o - wi- haŋ - ke   ta   he   o - i - na - źiŋ   mi - ća - ge

WORDS

maka′ owi′haŋke ta.............. toward the end of the earth
he oï′naźiŋ..................... my goal
mi′ćaġe........................ he has made

Analysis.—Six renditions of this song were recorded, and in each the time of the second and third measures before the close was a little slower than in the rest of the song, the original tempo being resumed with the last measure, and the repetition following without a pause. The song has a compass of only seven tones, and yet two-thirds of the progressions are downward. The first part of the song is based upon the minor triad B flat–D flat–F but the progressions in the latter part suggest G flat as a keynote, and the song is accordingly transcribed and analyzed in that key.

No. 97. "In the North"   (Catalogue No. 660)

Sung by MAḢPI′YA-TO (BLUE CLOUD)

VOICE ♩ = 132
DRUM ♩ = 92
Drum-rhythm similar to No. 6

Wa - zi-ya-ta ta - te u-ya
ma - ni - pi wa - su i - bo - a - bdu - ya ma - ni - pi

WORDS

wazi′yata ki′ya..............	in the north
tate′..........................	the wind
uya′...........................	blows
ma′nipi.......................	they are walking
wasu′.........................	the hail
ibo′bduya....................	beats
ma′nipi.......................	they are walking

Analysis.—The words of this song are in the Santee dialect, as this song, like the two next preceding, was recorded at Sisseton. This melody begins and ends on the same tone. (See song No. 82.) Although this song is minor in tonality, it contains only two minor thirds, nine of the intervals (31 per cent) being major thirds. Three renditions were recorded, the transcription being from the second rendition. The last two measures containing words were sung slightly slower, but without enough change of time to be indicated by a metronome mark. The repetitions of this song were less accurate than in a large majority of instances, seemingly because of the personality of the singer. The rhythm was more exactly repeated than the melody, though the changes in the latter were unimportant. For instance, in the first measure containing words the progression B flat–F was sometimes substituted for F–B flat, and in the last measure of the words the tone B flat was sometimes sung instead of D. It will be readily observed that these changes did not affect the harmonic framework of the measures, but seemed inserted by way of variety. Some indifference as to the form of ending is shown by the fact that in the first rendition the entire section from the tenth to the fourth measure from the end was omitted, while in the third rendition the last three measures were not sung. As stated, the transcription was from the second rendition, which was the clearest in form. The rhythmic unit, which is interesting, occurs three times.

No. 98. "Their Voices Could Be Heard"   (Catalogue No. 555)

Sung by GRAY HAWK (Ćetaŋ'hota)[1]

VOICE 𝅘𝅥 = 116
DRUM 𝅘𝅥 = 116
Drum-rhythm similar to No. 6

O - ya-te waŋ   ho   taŋ-iŋ-yaŋ ma - ni - pi

o - ya-te waŋ   ho taŋ-iŋ-yaŋ ma - ni - pi   e - yaŋ-pa-ha

ho   taŋ-iŋ-yaŋ ma - ni - pi

WORDS

oya'te waŋ...................... a tribe
ho............................. their voices
taŋiŋ'yaŋ...................... could be heard
ma'nipi....................... (as) they walk
e'yaŋpaha.................... the heralds (leaders of the herd)
ho............................. their voices
taŋiŋ'yaŋ...................... could be heard
ma'nipi....................... (as) they walk

Analysis.—This song contains only the tones of the minor triad and fourth, beginning on the dominant above the tonic and ending on the dominant below the tonic. Three renditions were recorded;

---
[1] See pl. 71.

these show no points of difference. The rhythmic unit is long, but its divisions were clearly given. In the second occurrence of the unit an accent was placed on the final tone, this accent being unmistakable though the corresponding tone in the first occurrence of the unit is unaccented. The interval of the fourth is prominent, constituting 38 per cent of the entire number of intervals. As in many other songs used in dancing, the intonation was wavering. In the first part of the song the drum precedes the voice, but in the closing measures the drum and voice coincide.

No. 99. "Against the Wind"   (Catalogue No. 556)

Sung by GRAY HAWK

VOICE ♩ = 100
DRUM ♩ = 100
Drum-rhythm similar to No. 6

I - te   a   i - te ta - te   i - ya - pa   wa - ye

wa - hu - ke - za   o - waŋ - ċa wa - ye

WORDS

ite′ tate′ iya′pe waye′........ I caused the face to strike against the wind
wahu′keza owaŋ′ċa waye′..... a lance I sent forth to cover all

Analysis.—A free translation of the words of this song would be, "I drove the tribe against the wind, which struck their faces like a lance." Four renditions were recorded, the time being interrupted between the repetitions. In each rendition the drum was with the voice in the last measure, though it had slightly preceded the voice in the earlier part of the song. Concerning the beginning and ending of a song on the same tone, see song No. 82. The tonic chord is felt throughout the melody, which, nevertheless, is melodic, not harmonic, in structure. The melody tones are those of the first five-toned scale, which lacks the third and seventh of the complete octave. (See p. 7.) See plot of this melody on page 419.

The following song is undoubtedly that of a man who dreamed of a buffalo, but the origin of the song was not given:

No. 100. "I Come"   (Catalogue No. 546)

Sung by GRAY HAWK

VOICE ♩ = 92
DRUM ♩ = 96
Drum-rhythm similar to No. 19

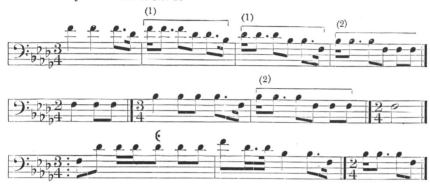

Ta- taŋ - ka - o - ḣi - ti - ka   mi-ye   wa-hi - ye

WORDS

Tataŋ′ka-oḣi′tika.............. Brave Buffalo (a man's name)[1]
miye′.......................... I am
wahi′ye........................ I come

Analysis.—Three renditions of this song were recorded, the time being interrupted between the renditions. The song is unusual in that it contains no interval smaller than a minor third. It is characterized by the interval of a fourth, 58 per cent of the intervals being fourths. The melody contains only the tones of the minor triad, a tone material found in only three other songs of this series. Eight tones comprise the compass of the song, which is harmonic in structure. In every instance the two rhythmic units were sung as transcribed, the last count of the second unit being different from that of the first. The tempo of the drum was slightly faster than that of the voice. See plot of this melody on page 419.

---

[1] This does not refer to the medicine-man mentioned in previous chapters of this work.

No. 101. Buffalo Society Song (a)   (Catalogue No. 549)

Sung by GRAY HAWK

VOICE ♩ = 92
DRUM ♩ = 92
Drum-rhythm similar to No. 6

Analysis.—Three renditions of this song were recorded, the time being interrupted between the repetitions. This is a pleasing and simple minor melody containing all the tones of the octave except the second. It is harmonic in structure, following first the triad of C minor and then the triad of G minor. Two-thirds of the progressions are downward and comprise only the minor third and major second. In the first part of the song the drum precedes and seems to hurry the voice, but at the close the drum and voice coincide. The same peculiarity has been noted in some other songs by this singer. See plot of this melody on page 419.

No. 102. Buffalo Society Song (b)   (Catalogue No. 550)

Sung by GRAY HAWK

VOICE ♩ = 126
DRUM ♩ = 120
Drum-rhythm similar to No. 19

Analysis.—This song is characterized by an unusual prominence of the interval of a fifth, about 16 per cent of the entire number of intervals being ascending fifths; yet the song has a compass of only seven tones. More than half the intervals are major seconds, and on these the intonation was wavering. The rapid tempo and small count-divisions would make a correct intonation difficult. The drum was persistently slower than the voice. This song contains a rhythmic unit which, though short, is interesting. Two renditions were recorded.

No. 103. Buffalo Society Song (c)   (Catalogue No. 577)

Sung by SHOOTER

VOICE ♩ = 112

DRUM ♩ = 112

Drum-rhythm similar to No. 6

Analysis.—This song is on the second five-toned scale and is melodic in structure. Its compass is small, being only six tones. Two-thirds of the progressions are downward, and two intervals occur which are larger than a minor third. Several renditions were recorded, all being uniform. The rhythmic form of the song is interesting. There are two occurrences of the rhythmic unit, then a pause of one count, after which the unit again appears twice, the remainder of the song resembling the unit but not repeating it. Such definiteness of form suggests that the song is clear in the mind of the singer and is being correctly sung. The interval between B and A sharp was not always an exact semitone, but the A natural in the third from the last measure was in every instance given as a much larger interval, showing it was the intention of the singer to sing another tone than that which had been given in the preceding measures

ELK SOCIETY

The men who had dreamed of the elk (see p. 176 et seq.) banded themselves together and called themselves the Elk society. Two Shields was one of the singers and drummers in this society, the last meeting of which was held about 30 years ago. He sang the following song, which was used in this society, and which he said had been handed down for many generations. He stated that the song is still sung at dances and must always be paid for by the man who asks that it be sung. Such a man is usually an elk dreamer.

No. 104. Song of the Elk Society   (Catalogue No. 538)

Sung by Two Shields

Voice ♩ = 80
Drum ♩ = 88
Drum-rhythm similar to No. 19

Tu-wa

waś - te - i - ći - la   waŋ - ma - yaŋ - ka ćaŋ - na

ćaŋ-te wa-ni-će

WORDS

tuwa′.............................. whoever
waśte′ićila...................... consider themselves beautiful (in character
                                              and appearance)
waŋma′yaŋka caŋ′na............ after seeing me
ćaŋte′ wani′će.................. has no heart

Analysis.—Three renditions of this song were recorded, and in every instance the tones transcribed, respectively, as D flat and D natural were distinguished clearly, though the intonation on them was not exact. The intonation of these tones was best in the opening measures. The renditions were uniform, but the song was especially difficult of transcription, as the tone was vibrato and the time not absolutely regular. On analyzing the melody, we find that 55 per cent of the intervals are seconds, either major or minor. The tones comprised in the melody are those of the fourth five-toned scale, with the sixth flatted as an accidental. Though the tonality is major, we note that almost 18 per cent of the intervals are minor thirds. The final count of the rhythmic unit differs somewhat in its repetitions. Throughout the song the metric unit of the drum was slightly slower than that of the voice.

The hoop carried by an elk dreamer is mentioned in the following song as "a rainbow." The following was given as an explanation of the use of this term: "Part of the rainbow is visible in the clouds, and part disappears in the ground. What we see is in the shape of a hoop. This word is employed by medicine-men and especially by dreamers of the elements of the air and the earth." (For songs of a man who dreamed of a rainbow, see Nos. 61 and 62.) The hoop of an elk dreamer was considered sacred, and the dreamer took great pride in it. When carrying it he sometimes put it around his neck or thrust one arm through it and carried it on his shoulder. Such a hoop is shown in plate 26 and is described in connection with Brave Buffalo's dream of the elk.

No. 105. "Something Sacred I Wear" (Catalogue No. 471)

Sung by ŚIYA'KA

WORDS

(*Part 1*)

ta′ku	something
wakaŋ′	sacred
komaŋ′ya kelo′	wears me (cf. words of Nos. 41, 93)
sito′mniyaŋ	all
waŋma′yaŋk	behold me
aü′ we	coming

(*Part 2*)

ćaŋgle′śka waŋ	a hoop (rainbow)
komaŋ′ya kelo′	wears me
sito′mniyaŋ	all
waŋma′yaŋk	behold me
aü′ we	coming

Analysis.—This song contains 40 intervals, all but 3 of which are minor thirds and major seconds. The intonation was particularly good considering the smallness of the intervals. The rhythmic unit, which is interesting, appears four times, one of the tones invariably being shortened. Parts of the rhythmic unit occur, as well as its complete repetitions. Two renditions were recorded, separated by shrill cries while the drum was beaten tremolo. Drum and voice have the same metric unit, but coincidences are met with only in the closing measures. (See song No. 101.) The song contains only the tones of the minor triad and fourth and is melodic in structure.

No. 106. "My Life Is Such"   (Catalogue No. 575)

Sung by Shooter

VOICE ♩ = 69
DRUM not recorded

Mi - o - oŋ - ća - ġe   le - će - ća - ye   mi - o - oŋ - ća - ġe waŋ - yaŋ -

ka yo e - ye - lo   mi - oŋ - ća - ġe   le - će - ća-ye waŋ-yaŋ-ka yo yo

WORDS

miöŋ′ćaġe	my life
le′ćećaye	is such
miöŋ′ćaġe	my life
waŋyaŋ′ka yo	behold me
eye′lo	it is said
miöŋ′ćaġe	my life
le′ćećaye	is such
waŋyaŋ′ka yo	behold me

Analysis.—The first four measures of this song are based on the tonic chord.   Among both Chippewa and Sioux it is unusual for the tonic chord to be given out at the opening of a song.   In the present instance these measures serve as an introduction to the performance of the song, being sung only once while the repeated part was sung six times without a break in the tempo.   The high tones in this song, especially the accented tones, were given with a sharp attack, which began slightly above the tone and immediately descended to it. This was a mannerism of the singer impossible to indicate in notation. An augmented second is found in the song and this, as well as the minor second, was given with particularly good intonation.   An augmented second occurs also in songs Nos. 63 and 225.   This song contains the tones of the fourth five-toned scale and is melodic in structure.   Only two intervals larger than a minor third appear in the song

No. 107. "An Elk Am I"   (Catalogue No. 622)

Sung by WI′YAKA-WAŊŹI′LA (ONE FEATHER)

WORDS

heȟa′ka waŋ...................	an elk
miye′ yelo′...................	am I
nake′noŋla...................	(a) short life
waöŋ′ welo′...................	I am living

Analysis.—The fourth constitutes 55 per cent of the intervals in this song, a peculiarity frequently noted in songs concerning animals. Many other intervals in this song are seconds, which form part of the descent of a fourth. An ascent of an eleventh is accomplished in two intervals, with the introduction of the words. This represents the entire compass of the song, which contains the tones of the fourth five-toned scale and is melodic in structure. Two rhythmic units occur, entirely different from each other. It is frequently noted that two rhythmic units in a song have one or more measure divisions alike.

HORSE SOCIETY

No dream of a horse was related to the writer, but there is among the Teton Sioux an organization called the Horse society. It was said that some of the songs in the following group were used in this society, and were used also on the warpath to make a horse swift and sure. The estimation in which the horse is held by the Sioux is shown by a speech by Brave Buffalo. This speech was made before the singing of his first song, and was recorded by the phonograph. Freely translated it is as follows:

Of all the animals the horse is the best friend of the Indian, for without it he could not go on long journeys. A horse is the Indian's most valuable piece of property. If an Indian wishes to gain something, he promises his horse that if the horse will help him he will paint it with native dye, that all may see that help has come to him through the aid of his horse.

Śiya'ka said that on one occasion when he was hard pressed on the warpath, he dismounted, and standing in front of his horse, spoke to him, saying—

We are in danger. Obey me promptly that we may conquer. If you have to run for your life and mine, do your best, and if we reach home I will give you the best eagle feather I can get and the finest *sina' lu'ta*, and you shall be painted with the best paint.[1]

---

[1] The eagle feather was tied to the horse's tail, and the *sina' lu'ta* was a strip of red cloth fastened around the horse's neck. (See p. 388.)

No. 108. "My Horse Flies like a Bird"   (Catalogue No. 573)

Sung by BRAVE BUFFALO

Voice ♩ = 84

DRUM not recorded

Ko - la mi - ta - śuŋ - ke kiŋ-yaŋ   yaŋ   iŋ - yaŋ - ke

lo

WORDS

kola'............................. friend
mita'śuŋke...................... my horse
kiŋyaŋ' yaŋ.................... flies like a bird
iŋ'yaŋke lo.................... as it runs

Analysis.—This is one of the instances in which the signature indicates the pitch of the tones as sung by the singer but does not imply a "key" in the musical sense of the term.   The song is classified as "irregular." (See table on p. 305.)   It will be noted that the progressions of the first 12 measures are based on the major triad B–D sharp–F sharp, yet the presence of E sharp makes it impossible to consider that part of the song in the key of B.   The remainder of the song suggests the key of B minor.   In the first part of the song Brave Buffalo sang E sharp and D sharp, and in the latter part he sang E natural and D natural, these tones being given clearly and unmistakably. A comparison of the tone C, registered at the beginning of the cylinder, with C on the piano, shows that the phonograph was properly adjusted when the record was made, so that the change of pitch is not due to any slackening of speed in the recording machine, which might have been the case if the machine had been partially run down. Two renditions were recorded, with a pause and some conversation between them, and the peculiarities of the first rendition were repeated exactly in the second.   The personality of the singer should be taken into account in considering a song of marked peculiarity, and Brave Buffalo, who made this record, was not a man given to seeking effects, as some of the young men occasionally do. He recorded nine songs, and his manner of singing was marked by more than usual carefulness. This was the first song he recorded and he did it quite reluctantly. The transcription has been compared with the phonograph record many times, at long intervals, in order that the test of the ear might be renewed. It is, therefore, the opinion of the writer that the transcription indicates as nearly as possible the song as it was sung by Brave Buffalo. It is a peculiar melody, but the purpose of the present work is to ascertain what the singer sang, not to adapt his song to a white musician's standard, either of time or of key.

Of the intervals in the song 60 per cent are major seconds, and the song contains only two intervals larger than a minor third. It has been noted frequently that an Indian has great difficulty in keeping the adjustment of a melody in which a majority of the progressions are small intervals.

No. 109. "When a Horse Neighs"   (Catalogue No. 604)

Sung by Brave Buffalo

VOICE ♩ = 76
DRUM ♩ = 126
Drum-rhythm similar to No. 19

Aŋ-pa - o

hi - na - pe ćiŋ - haŋ   o   śuŋ-ka - kaŋ waŋ ho-toŋ - we

WORDS

aŋ′paŏ	daybreak
hina′pe	appears
ćiŋhaŋ′	when
śuŋka′kaŋ [1] waŋ	a horse
hotoŋ′we	neighs (see p. 180, footnote)

[1] This is a shortened form of the word śuŋka′wakaŋ.

Analysis.—It is interesting to compare this with other songs concerning the horse, not only in this group, but in the songs of war (Nos. 138, 139, 140, 145). The tempo is slower, and the rhythm is not the galloping rhythm of some of the other songs. There is in it a little of the dignity and solemnity which seems always present in the mind of the Sioux when he sings of the dawn. The drum is a rapid tremolo. Two renditions were recorded, which are identical in all respects. The song contains only the tones of the minor triad and fourth. Of the intervals 65 per cent are major seconds, and the trend of the melody is downward from the twelfth to the tonic.

No. 110. "Horses Are Coming"   (Catalogue No. 605)

Sung by BRAVE BUFFALO

VOICE ♩ = 72
DRUM ♩ = 132
Drum-rhythm similar to No. 19

Ta -te   o - u - ye   to - pa   kiŋ   śuŋ-ka - wa-kaŋ waŋ-źig - źi

a - u   we - lo   e   a - u   a   we - lo

WORDS

tate′ oü′ye to′pa kiŋ............ the four winds are blowing
śuŋka′wakaŋ waŋźig′źi......... some horses
aü′ welo′...................... are coming

Analysis.—Two renditions of this song were recorded; these are alike except that the second is slightly lower in pitch. It has been noted that some singers will pause after the first rendition of a song, and then begin a second rendition on exactly the same pitch as the first, while others will begin slightly higher or lower. This song contains no rhythmic unit, but the song as a whole has a rhythmic completeness, which is interesting. The first and last phrases resemble each other in some of the count-divisions, notably in the first triple measure.

No. 111. "Prancing They Come"   (Catalogue No. 537)

Sung by Two Shields

Voice ♩ = 104
Drum ♩ = 104
Drum-rhythm similar to No. 6

WORDS

he′na	....	see them
waći′	....	prancing
aü′ we	....	they come
hoton′	....	neighing (see p. 180, footnote)
aü′ welo′	....	they come
śun′kawakan oya′te wan	....	a Horse nation (see p. 162, footnote)
he′na	....	see them
waći′	....	prancing
aü′ we	....	they come
hoton′	....	neighing
aü′ welo′	....	they come

Analysis.—This is a peculiarly rhythmic melody, which was sung four times. Drum and voice have the same metric unit, but the drum-beat follows the voice. The song is strongly harmonic in feeling, but the accented E classifies the structure of the song as melodic with harmonic framework. The compass of the song is an octave, and the trend of the melody is steadily downward. The melody is very bright and lively, yet more than half the intervals are minor thirds. See plot of this melody on page 419.

No. 112. "Chasing, They Walked"   (Catalogue No. 470)

Sung by ŚIYA'KA

VOICE ♩ = 116
DRUM ♩ = 116
Drum-rhythm similar to No. 6

Wa - ku - wa ma - ni - pi   wa - ku - wa ma - ni - pi   le

śuŋ - ka - wa - kaŋ   o - ya - te   le   wa - ku - wa

ma - ni - pi   wa - ku - wa   ma - ni - pi   yo   hi   yo

WORDS

waku'wa...................... chasing
ma'nipi...................... they walked
le........................... this
śuŋ'kawakaŋ oya'te........... Horse nation (see p. 162, footnote)
waku'wa...................... chasing
ma'nipi...................... they walked

Analysis.—The words of this song refer to the free, almost playful, action of a herd of horses. This melody is especially rhythmic. Three double renditions were recorded, which show no differences except a slight lowering of pitch. All but three of the intervals are major seconds. Difficulty in keeping the adjustment of a melody containing small intervals has been frequently noted. The song has a range of 10 tones and is based on the fourth five-toned scale. Before beginning to sing, Two Shields beat the drum in a rapid tremolo, the indicated time of the drum not being fully established until the first few measures of the song had been sung, after which it was steadily maintained.

No. 113. "A Root of Herb"   (Catalogue No. 467)

Sung by ŚIYA'KA

VOICE ♩= 138

DRUM not recorded

Pe- źu - ta wa-kaŋ   ća wa - wa - ku-wa ye   pe- źu -

ta wa-kaŋ   ća wa - wa-ku-wa ye   hu noŋ - pa o - ya-

te yuŋ-kaŋ hel i - to - he - - ya wa-wa - ku-wa ye

pe- źu - ta wa-kaŋ   ća *wi*   wa - wa-ku-wa ye   hu-noŋ -

pa o - ya - te yuŋ-kaŋ hel i - to - he - - ya wa-wa -

ku-wa ye   hel i - to - he - ya   ća wa - wa-ku-wa ye

WORDS

peźu'ta (contraction of peźi'huta).   a root of herb
wakaŋ'......................... sacred
ća............................ it is
wawa'kuwa ye................. (that which) I have used
hu noŋ'pa oya'te............. the tribe of men
yuŋkaŋ'...................... therefore
hel ito'heya.................. toward them
ća............................ it is
wawa'kuwa ye................ I have used it

Analysis.—This song contains two rhythmic units, the opening measures of the two being alike, but the first having four complete measures and the second six measures.   The repetitions of these units comprise every note in the song.   In tonality the melody is distinctly minor, but only one interval of a minor third is found in it; a descent from E flat to C occurs several times, but always with D as a passing tone.   The song contains only the tones of the minor triad and second—a somewhat unusual tone material.   The interval of a second is especially prominent in the melody.   Two renditions were recorded; these are alike in every respect.

This group comprises the songs of such societies as are composed of men having similar dreams, the name of the society indicating the animal which appeared in the dream (songs Nos. 95–113).   Undoubtedly many of the songs in this group are songs which were "received in dreams," but the names of the original owners are forgotten and the songs are now the common songs of the societies.

Old Songs—(5) Songs of Dream Societies

MELODIC ANALYSIS

TONALITY

	Number of songs.	Serial Nos. of songs.
Major tonality	7	96, 99, 102, 104, 106, 107, 112
Minor tonality	11	95, 97, 98, 100, 101, 103, 105, 109, 110, 111, 113
Irregular	1	108
Total	19	

FIRST NOTE OF SONG—ITS RELATION TO KEYNOTE

	Number of songs.	Serial Nos. of songs.
Beginning on the—		
Twelfth	1	109
Eleventh	1	105
Tenth	1	113
Ninth	2	104, 110
Octave	1	101
Seventh	1	102
Fifth	7	98, 99, 100, 103, 106, 107, 111
Third	2	96, 112
Second	1	95
Keynote	1	97
Irregular	1	108
Total	19	

Old Songs—(5) *Songs of Dream Societies*—Continued

MELODIC ANALYSIS—Continued

LAST NOTE OF SONG—ITS RELATION TO KEYNOTE

	Number of songs.	Serial Nos. of songs.
Ending on the—		
Fifth	8	95, 98, 99, 100, 104, 107, 110, 111
Third	1	106
Keynote	9	96, 97, 101, 102, 103, 105, 109, 112, 113
Irregular	1	108
Total	19	

LAST NOTE OF SONG—ITS RELATION TO COMPASS OF SONG

	Number of songs.	Serial Nos. of songs.
Songs in which final tone is—		
Lowest tone in song	5	96, 98, 99, 100, 101, 102, 104, 105, 106, 107, 109, 110, 111, 112, 113
Immediately preceded by semitone below	1	103
Songs containing a major third below the final tone	2	95, 97
Irregular	1	108
Total	19	

NUMBER OF TONES COMPRISING COMPASS OF SONG

	Number of songs.	Serial Nos. of songs.
Compass of—		
Twelve tones	4	104, 105, 108, 109
Ten tones	4	106, 110, 112, 113
Nine tones	1	95
Eight tones	6	97, 98, 99, 100, 101, 111
Seven tones	3	96, 102, 111
Six tones	1	103
Total	19	

Old Songs—(5) Songs of Dream Societies—Continued

MELODIC ANALYSIS—Continued

TONE MATERIAL

	Number of songs.	Serial Nos. of songs.
Second five-toned scale	2	103, 111
Fourth five-toned scale	4	104, 106, 107, 112
Minor triad	1	100
Minor triad and fourth	3	98, 105, 109
Octave complete	1	113
Octave complete except seventh	1	97
Octave complete except seventh and sixth	1	110
Octave complete except seventh and third	1	99
Octave complete except fourth	1	95
Octave complete except fourth and second	2	96, 102
Octave complete except second	1	101
Other combinations of tones	1	108
Total	19	

ACCIDENTALS

	Number of songs.	Serial Nos. of songs.
Songs containing—		
No accidentals	15	95, 96, 97, 98, 99, 100, 101, 102, 105, 107, 109, 110, 111, 112, 113
Seventh raised a semitone	1	103
Second raised a semitone	1	106
Sixth lowered a semitone	1	104
Irregular	1	108
Total	19	

STRUCTURE

	Number of songs.	Serial Nos. of songs.
Melodic	15	95, 96, 97, 98, 99, 102, 103, 104, 105, 106, 107, 109, 110, 112, 113
Melodic with harmonic framework	1	111
Harmonic	2	100, 101
Irregular	1	108
Total	19	

Old Songs—*(5) Songs of Dream Societies*—Continued

MELODIC ANALYSIS—Continued

FIRST PROGRESSION—DOWNWARD AND UPWARD

	Number of songs.	Serial Nos. of songs.
Downward..	13	95, 98, 100, 101, 102, 103, 104, 106, 108, 109, 111, 112, 113
Upward...	6	96, 97, 99, 105, 107, 110
Total..	19	

TOTAL NUMBER OF PROGRESSIONS—DOWNWARD AND UPWARD

Downward...	295
Upward..	169
Total...	464

INTERVALS IN DOWNWARD PROGRESSION

Interval of a—	
Fifth...	2
Fourth..	34
Major third.......................................	39
Minor third.......................................	73
Augmented second.................................	1
Major second......................................	132
Minor second......................................	14
Total...	295

INTERVALS IN UPWARD PROGRESSION

Interval of a—	
Tenth..	1
Octave...	3
Seventh..	1
Minor sixth......................................	2
Fifth..	16
Fourth...	31
Major third......................................	15
Minor third......................................	22
Major second.....................................	70
Minor second.....................................	8
Total...	169

AVERAGE NUMBER OF SEMITONES IN AN INTERVAL

Total number of intervals............................	464
Total number of semitones............................	1,436
Average number of semitones in an interval...........	3.09

Old Songs—(5) Songs of Dream Societies—Continued

MELODIC ANALYSIS—Continued

KEY

	Number of songs.	Serial Nos. of songs.
Key of—		
A minor	1	109
B flat major	1	100
B flat minor	2	97, 98
B major	1	99
B minor	3	103, 105, 111
C major	1	106
C minor	1	113
E flat major	1	112
E flat minor	1	95
E minor	1	110
F major	2	104, 107
G flat major	1	96
G major	1	102
G minor	1	101
Irregular	1	108
Total	19	

RHYTHMIC ANALYSIS

PART OF MEASURE ON WHICH SONG BEGINS

	Number of songs.	Serial Nos. of songs.
Beginning on unaccented part of measure	4	95, 96, 107, 113
Beginning on accented part of measure	15	97, 98, 99, 100, 101, 102, 103, 104, 105, 106, 108, 109, 110, 111, 112
Total	19	

RHYTHM OF FIRST MEASURE

	Number of songs.	Serial Nos. of songs.
First measure in—		
2–4 time	12	96, 97, 99, 101, 102, 103, 105, 106, 108, 110, 112, 113
3–4 time	7	95, 98, 100, 104, 107, 109, 111
Total	19	

CHANGE OF TIME, MEASURE (LENGTHS)

	Number of songs.	Serial Nos. of songs.
Songs containing no change of time	None.	
Songs containing a change of time	19	95, 96, 97, 98, 99, 100, 101, 102, 103, 104, 105, 106, 107, 108, 109, 110, 111, 112, 113
Total	19	

Old Songs—*(5)* *Songs of Dream Societies*—Continued

RHYTHMIC ANALYSIS—Continued

RHYTHM OF DRUM

	Number of songs.	Serial Nos. of songs.
Eighth notes unaccented.............................	3	100, 102, 104
Quarter notes unaccented............................	9	95, 96, 97, 98, 99, 101, 103, 111, 112
Eighth notes accented in groups of two...............	3	105, 109, 110
Total...	15	

RHYTHMIC UNIT OF SONG

	Number of songs.	Serial Nos. of songs.
Songs containing—		
No rhythmic unit.................................	6	95, 96, 99, 108, 109, 110
One rhythmic unit................................	10	97, 98, 101, 102, 103, 104, 105, 106, 112, 113
Two rhythmic units...............................	3	100, 107, 111
Total...	19	

METRIC UNIT OF VOICE (TEMPO)

	Number of songs.	Serial Nos. of songs.
Metronome—		
69...	1	106
72...	2	96, 110
76...	2	105, 109
80...	1	104
84...	1	108
92...	1	100
96...	1	95
100..	2	99, 101
104..	1	111
112..	1	103
116..	2	98, 112
126..	2	102, 107
132..	1	97
138..	1	113
Total...	19	

Old Songs—(5) Songs of Dream Societies—Continued

RHYTHMIC ANALYSIS—Continued

METRIC UNIT OF DRUM (TEMPO)

	Number of songs.	Serial Nos. of songs.
Metronome—		
80	1	105
88	2	96, 104
92	1	97
96	2	95, 100
110	2	99, 101
104	1	111
112	1	103
116	2	98, 112
120	1	102
126	1	100
132	1	110
Drum not recorded	4	106, 107, 108, 113
Total	19	

COMPARISON OF METRIC UNIT OF VOICE AND DRUM (TEMPO)

	Number of songs.	Serial Nos. of songs.
Drum and voice having same metric unit	5	95, 98, 99, 101, 105
Drum faster than voice	7	96, 100, 104, 109, 110, 111, 112
Drum slower than voice	3	97, 102, 103
Drum not recorded	4	106, 107, 108, 113
Total	19	

MILITARY SOCIETIES

Organizations of warriors existed among all the Plains tribes. The term "wolf" was applied to the warriors of several tribes, while among others the term "dog soldiers" was used. A condensed account of the military organizations of the Plains Indians is given by Clark,[1] who places the number of societies in the Siouan peoples at 11. Writers concerning individual tribes have described the customs of such tribes, the following being representative citations.

Among the Kiowa:

The Kiowa have an elaborate military organization, now fast becoming obsolete, known as *Yä'pähe*, "Warriors." A similar organization is found among most of the prairie tribes, and is commonly known to the whites as the Dog-soldier society, from an imperfect rendering of the name of one of the principal bands. The Kiowa organization consists of six orders, each having its own dance, songs, insignia, and duties.[2]

[1] Clark W. P., The Indian Sign Language, p. 355, Philadelphia, 1885.
[2] Mooney, James, Calendar History of the Kiowa, *Seventeenth Rep. Bur. Ethn.*, pt. 1, p. 229, Washington, 1898.

Among the Arapaho:

Among the Arapaho the organization was called *Bĕni'nĕna*, "Warriors," and consisted of eight degrees or orders, including nearly all the men of the tribe above the age of about 17. [1]

Among the Cheyenne:

These warriors he [the Great Prophet] grouped into five societies, who, with the chief, were responsible for the conduct of the tribe. The societies were called the Red-Shield, Hoof-Rattle, Coyote, Dog-Men's, and Inverted or Bow-String. [2]

Among the Omaha:

There were two classes of societies among the Omaha—social and secret. Membership in the social class was open to those able to perform the acts required for eligibility. To this class belong the warrior societies, as well as those for social purposes only. [This is followed by an extended consideration of the war societies.] [3]

Among the Blackfeet:

[The] association of the All Comrades consisted of a dozen or more secret societies, graded according to age, the whole constituting an association which was in part benevolent and helpful and in part military, but whose main function was to punish offenses against society at large. [4]

This association appears to resemble that of the Aki'ćita among several other tribes. (See pp. 313, 314.)

Lewis and Clark made what is probably the first recorded mention of societies among the men of the Sioux tribe. Under date of August 30, 1804, their Journal contains the following section written by Clark: [5]

I will here remark a SOCIETY which I had never before this day heard was in any nation of Indians, four of which is at this time present and all who remain of this Band. Those who become Members of this Society must be brave active young men who take a *Vow* never to give back let the danger be what it may, in War Parties they always go forward without screening themselves behind trees or anything else to this Vow they Strictly adhier dureing their Lives. an instance which happened not long sence, on a party in Crossing the R Missourie on the ice, a whole was in the ice imediately in their Course which might easily have been avoided by going around, the foremost man went on and was lost the others wer draged around by the party. in a battle with the Crow (Kite) Indians who inhabit the *Cout Noir* or Black Mountain out of 22 of this Society 18 was killed, the remaining four was draged off by their Party. Those men are likely fellows the[y] Set together Camp & Dance together. This Society is an imitation of the Societies of the de Curbo or Crow (*De Corbeau, Kite*) Indians, whom they imitate.

This evidently refers to one of the military societies of the tribe, and the action described is that of the Aki'ćita. An old man on the Standing Rock Reservation said to the writer, "Many military soci-

[1] Mooney, James, The Ghost Dance Religion, *Fourteenth Rep. Bur. Ethn.*, pt. 2, p. 986, Washington, 1896.
[2] Dorsey, George A., The Cheyenne, *Field Columb. Mus. Pub. 99*, Anthr. Ser., IX, No. 1, p. 15, Chicago, 1905.
[3] Fletcher, Alice C., and La Flesche, Francis, The Omaha Tribe, *Twenty-seventh Rep. Bur. Ethn.*, pp. 459–486, Washington, 1911.
[4] Grinnell, George Bird, Blackfoot Lodge Tales, p. 220, New York, 1892.
[5] Original Journals of the Lewis and Clark Expedition, 1804–1806, edited by Reuben Gold Thwaites, I, p. 130, New York, 1904.

eties had their origin in a dream, but the organization of these societies and their meetings were more public than those of the regular 'dream societies.' "

In his study among the Oglala Sioux Dr. Wissler has divided the societies for men into Aki′ćita societies, Headmen's societies, and War societies.[1]   Six Aki′ćita societies are enumerated by him as existing at the time of his observation, among the Oglala on the Pine Ridge and Rosebud Reservations, in South Dakota, these being the Toka′la (Kit Fox), Kaṅġi′yuha (Crow Owners), Ćaṅte′-tiṇza (Strong Heart), Iḣo′ka (Badgers), Sotka′yuha (Bare-lance Owners), and Wi′ćiska (White-marked).   Only the first four of these societies were found by the writer among the Teton Sioux on the Standing Rock Reservation.

Another society mentioned by the writer's informants was said to be known by two names, the Silent Eaters (A′inila wo′ta) and Strong Heart at Night (Ahe′pi ćaṅte′tiṇza).   This was a secret society, entirely distinct from the Strong Heart society, described in this section.   No songs and no further information concerning this society were obtained.

Before proceeding to a consideration of these societies and their songs it may be well to consider briefly the meaning of the term *aki′ćita*.

The word *aki′ćita* is commonly translated "soldier," but its meaning is akin to "guard" or "police," the proper word for "warrior" being *iki′ćize*.   Thus the Aki′ćita societies were those whose members could be required to act as guards or marshals when the tribe was moving, or as "police" in the village.   The aki′ćita were primarily associated with the buffalo hunt, in which they saw that no one disregarded the laws of the chase (see p. 442); they also preserved order in the camp and punished all offenders.   They were primarily civil officers, though aki′ćita might also be appointed to act in connection with a large war party.   Hennepin notes an instance of punishment by aki′ćita among the Santee, or eastern Sioux.   In 1680 Hennepin and his party were descending the Mississippi River and were "in the Islands of the River," not far below the Falls of St. Anthony (probably near the site of St. Paul, Minn.).   The Indians set food before them, but while they were eating, there came other Indians, who took the food from them and plundered the tipi.   Hennepin says:

We knew not what these Savages were at first; but it appear'd they were some of those that we had left above at the Fall of St. *Anthony*. One of them, who call'd himself my Uncle, told me, that those who had given us Victuals, had done basely to go and forestall the others in the Chase; and that according to the Laws and Customs of their Country, 'twas lawful for them to plunder them, since they had been

1 Wissler, Clark, Societies and Ceremonial Associations in the Oglala Division of the Teton-Dakota, *Anthr. Papers, Amer. Mus. Nat. Hist.*, XI, pt. 1, p. 5, New York, 1912.

the cause that the Bulls were all run away, before the Nation could get together, which was a great Injury to the Publick.[1]

Lewis and Clark refer to these men as follows:

Those people have Some brave men which they make use of as Soldiers those men attend to the police of the Village Correct all errors I saw one of them today whip 2 Squars, who appeared to have fallen out, when he approach[d]. all about appeared to flee with great turrow [terror]. at night they keep two 3, 4, 5 men at different Distances walking around Camp Singing the accurrunces of the night [2]

The aki'ćita are mentioned also by many writers on the tribes of the Plains. Rev. J. Owen Dorsey states that "The Akitcita, soldiers or guards (policemen), form an important body among the Asiniboin as they do among other Siouan tribes."[3]

Wissler states that the manner of selecting aki'ćita was as follows: The chiefs chose the four "head aki'ćita" from one society, who in turn chose their assistants from the society to which they themselves belonged. Thus the choice of the four head aki'ćita was practically the choice of a certain society for this duty. The selection was usually made at the beginning of the summer hunt, and service continued to the close of the season. It seems to have been customary, but not obligatory, for the chiefs to choose from the societies in rotation.[4]

Concerning the organizations of these societies, Wissler states:[5]

We find a surprising degree of uniformity in details. All were liable to be called into aki'ćita service, while other societies never rendered such service. . . . The scheme of officers is practically the same. All have from four to six lance bearers, who are the most conspicuous, if not the most important personages in the society. They are usually grouped in pairs, as in fact are nearly all the other officers; . . . Next in rank to the two leaders stands another pair, among the cante tinza and the wiciska they are known as bonnet bearers, and among the others as pipe bearers, but their functions are much the same. These two ranking pairs are sometimes spoken of as the four chiefs in charge of the organization. There are two whip bearers in all [the societies] except the kaŋgi'yuha. . . . As to food passers, drummers, and singers, there is general uniformity throughout. It is thus clear that whatever may have been the origin of these societies, they were all brought to an approximation of the one type.

FOX SOCIETY

In his account of the Toka'la, or Kit-fox society, Wissler says:[6]

The society is so named because its members are supposed to be as active and wily on the warpath as this little animal is known to be in his native state. . . . The members wear a kit-fox skin around the neck, the head before, the tail behind. To

[1] Hennepin, Father Louis, A New Discovery of a Vast Country in America (reprinted from the second London issue of 1698), Reuben Gold Thwaites ed., I, p. 280, Chicago, 1903.
[2] Original Journals of the Lewis and Clark Expedition, op. cit., I, p. 168.
[3] Dorsey, James Owen, Siouan Sociology, Fifteenth Rep. Bur. Ethn., p. 224, Washington, 1894.
[4] Wissler, Clark, Societies and Ceremonial Associations in the Oglala Division of the Teton-Dakota, op. cit., XI, pt. 1, p. 10.
[5] Ibid., p. 63.
[6] Ibid., pp. 14–23.

the nose part some small bags of medicine are attached. [See p. 389.] The edges, feet, and ears may be worked in porcupine quills and hung with bells according to the tastes of the individual owners. They take the jawbones of the toka′la, paint them red or blue (the old native colors), fasten them on a strip of otterskin or some similar material, and wear the bones on the forehead. On the back of the head is fastened a bunch of crow tail feathers sidewise, and sticking up are two eagle feathers. . . . When participating in a dance, the officers paint their bodies yellow.

The teachings. of the society inculcated "bravery, generosity, chivalry, morality, and fraternity for fellow members." Men who joined the society were required to promise obedience to these teachings, and the whip bearers had whips of a peculiar kind with which they scourged those who disregarded their vows. One of the officers of the society was the custodian of the drum.

The "kit-fox dance" as held by the Santee Sioux is described by Dr. Lowie,[1] his account differing but slightly from that already quoted. Maximilian notes a society of "the foxes" among the Arikara about the year 1833.[2] The "Kit-fox society" is included by Dr. Lowie in his list of the Hidatsa[3] and also of the Mandan societies.[4] The same authority states that, among the Crows, "the Foxes and Lumpwoods had become the most important military societies in the decades immediately preceding the breakdown of the old tribal life."[5] Some of the songs of this society are still sung at Fort Berthold, N. Dak., and have been recorded by the writer.

Miss Fletcher mentions the Toka′lo (Toka′la) among the Omaha as one of two "social societies that were borrowed or introduced from the Dakota. . . . There are no words to the songs—a fact which makes it probable that the music was adopted from another tribe, the foreign words being dropped."[6]

In the writer's study among the Teton on the Standing Rock Reservation it was said that "fox songs and coyote songs are the same." It was also decided that certain songs called wolf songs or "Wolf society songs" should be included in this section. In this connection it is interesting to note that Dr. Lowie found the kit-fox dance called the coyote dance by the Santee at Fort Totten, N. Dak.,[7] and that among the Crows of Montana he was told that "all the societies were originated by the mythical Old Man Coyote."[8] A similar correspondence in the terms "fox" and "coyote" is found in the names of the societies of the Cheyenne, Mooney giving one

[1] Lowie, Robert H., Dance Associations of the Eastern Dakota, Anthr. Papers, Amer. Mus. Nat. Hist., XI, pt. 2, p. 105, New York, 1913.
[2] Maximilian, Prince of Wied, Travels in the Interior of North America (translated from the German by H. Evans Lloyd), p. 407, London, 1843.
[3] Lowie, Robert H., Societies of the Crow, Hidatsa and Mandan Indians, op. cit., pt. 3, p. 253.
[4] Ibid., p. 296.
[5] Ibid., p. 155.
[6] Fletcher, Alice C., and La Flesche, Francis, The Omaha Tribe, op. cit., p. 486.
[7] Lowie, Robert H., Dance Associations of the Eastern Dakota, op cit., p. 106.
[8] Lowie, Robert H., Societies of the Crow, Hidatsa and Mandan Indians, op. cit., p. 156, footnote.

of the Cheyenne societies as the "foxmen (specifically, the kit, or swift, fox);"[1] while George A. Dorsey mentions the Coyote as one of the original Cheyenne societies.[2]

Two songs of the Fox society are given herewith, and a third (No. 178) appears in the personal war narrative of Old Buffalo, who was a member of the society. Song No. 147 was composed in honor of a member of the society who was killed on the warpath.

The following song of the Fox society was sung by Bear Soldier (Mato'-aki'ćita) a nephew of Rain-in-the-Face:

No. 114. Song of the Fox Society (a)   (Catalogue No. 677)

Sung by BEAR SOLDIER

[1] Mooney, James, The Cheyenne Indians, *Mem. Amer. Anthr. Assoc.*, I, pt. 6, p. 412, Lancaster, Pa., 1907.

[2] Dorsey, George A., The Cheyenne, *Field Columbian Mus. Pub. 99*, Anthr. ser., IX, No. 1, pp. 15, 19, Chicago, 1905.

Toka′la kiŋ	the Fox (society)
ta′ku yaka′pi ćaŋ′na	whenever you propose to do anything
iyo′taŋ[1] mići′la	I consider myself foremost
ķoŋ	but (now)
iyo′tiye	a hard time
waki′ yelo′	I am having

Analysis.—This is the only song recorded by this singer, but its rhythmic form shows that it was clear in his mind. Two renditions were recorded; these show no points of difference. Three accidentals occur—the second and third lowered a semitone, and the fourth raised a semitone. In the first part of the song C sharp and D sharp were sung slightly below pitch, but these appear in a series of the small intervals which seem difficult for an Indian to sing correctly. All the tones of the octave are present in the song, and almost 56 per cent of the intervals are major seconds. A change of tempo occurs in the song. (See song No. 5.)

No. 115. Song of the Fox Society (b)   (Catalogue No. 580)

Sung by SHOOTER

VOICE ♩ = 84
DRUM ♩ = 84
Drum-rhythm similar to No. 5

Ko-la   *a*   ta-ku ya-ka-pi kiŋ

ta-moŋ-ka śni ye-lo

kola′	friends
ta′ku yaka′pi kiŋ	whatever you council about
tamoŋ′ka śni yelo′	I consider a difficult undertaking

Analysis.—This melody is minor in tonality and lacks the seventh and fourth tones of the complete octave. (See analysis of song No. 26.) The minor third is not found in the song; instead we find that the major third constitutes about one fourth of the intervals.

---

[1] In one instance the final syllable of this word was omitted by the singer.

The song has a compass of an octave, beginning on the dominant above and ending on the dominant below the tonic.   Three renditions were recorded, which show no points of difference.

KAŊĠI'YUHA (CROW-OWNERS)[1]

This society, like other military and social organizations, was widespread among the tribes of the Plains.   Miss Fletcher states that, among the Omaha, "the wolf and the crow were not only connected with carnage but they had a mythical relation to the office of 'soldiers,' the designation given to certain men on the annual tribal hunt who acted as marshals."[2]   A full description of "the crow" worn by the Omaha, with an account of its symbolism, is given by Miss Fletcher.[3]   Among the northern tribes the crow and the raven appear to be connected exclusively with success in war, the skin of the bird being worn around the neck or attached to the spear which was carried in war.   A "Crow or Raven society" was noted among the Mandan and was mentioned by Maximilian.[4]

The Crow-owners society of the Teton Sioux and the Raven-bearers society of the Mandan, as studied by the present writer, appear to be similar in essential features.   Lowie, however, uses the term Crow society in his list of Mandan organizations.[5]   A Crow-owners society is noted by the same authority, among the Crow Indians.[6]   The Raven-owners society is mentioned by Lowie in his observations among the eastern Dakota,[7] and the Raven-bearers by Wissler, among the Blackfoot Indians.[8]

The full organization of the Crow-owners society is given as follows by Wissler:[9]

The Kaŋġi' yuha (they that have the crow) was an organization similar to the Toka'la, the scheme being as follows:

2 leaders	4 lance bearers
2 rattle bearers	x lay members
2 pipe keepers	4 drum bearers and singers, two of whom
2 short-lance bearers	carry rattles and sit about the drum
2 crow-skin bearers	1 herald

---

[1] The writer's informant concerning the Kaŋġi'yuha was Eagle Shield (Waŋbli'-waha'ćuŋka), who was a member of the society. In pl. 43 he is shown wearing the "crow-skin necklace," (kaŋġi'wanà'pi), which was the insignia of the society.

[2] Fletcher and La Flesche, op. cit., p. 442.

[3] Ibid., p. 441.

[4] Reise in das Innere Nord-America in den Jahren 1832 bis 1834, von Maximilian Prinz zu Wied, II, p. 140, Coblenz, 1841. "Die zweite Classe oder Bande sind die * * * Krähen- oder Rabenbande (La bande du corbeau), junge Leute, von 20 bis 25 Jahren."

[5] Lowie, Robert H., Societies of the Crow, Hidatsa and Mandan Indians, op. cit., p. 309.

[6] Ibid., p. 199.

[7] Lowie, Robert H., Dance Associations of the Eastern Dakota, op. cit., p. 109.

[8] Wissler, Clark, Societies and Dance Associations of the Blackfoot Indians, Anthr. Papers, Amer. Mus. Nat. Hist., XI, pt 4, p. 392, New York, 1913.

[9] Wissler, Clark, Societies and Ceremonial Associations in the Oglala Division of the Teton-Dakota, op. cit., p. 23.

CROW-SKIN NECKLACE AND CASE

When asked why the crow was honored by the society, Eagle Shield said:

We want our arrows to fly as swift and straight as the crow. The crow is always the first to arrive at the gathering of the animals in the Black Hills. The reason why the Black Hills were so long unknown to the white man was that Wakaŋ'taŋka created them as a meeting place for the animals. The Indians had always known this and regarded the law of Wakaŋ'taŋka concerning it. By this law they were forbidden to kill any of the animals during their great gatherings. In the Black Hills there is a ridge of land around which is a smooth, grassy place called the "race course."[1] This is where the animals have the races, during their gatherings. Even small animals like the turtle are there. The crow is always first to arrive, and the other birds come before the animals, while insects and creatures like the frog travel slowly and arrive last. Sometimes it takes 10 years for all the animals to arrive, as they come from long distances and camp wherever winter overtakes them.

Eagle Shield said further that among the Teton of Standing Rock the Crow-owners society had originally but 10 members, but that later it became a large organization to which only successful warriors could belong. Such men of distinction could be admitted by making the request of the leader and giving a feast to the members of the society.

A special tent in the village was used by this society as its meeting place. Eagle Shield said, "the village was full of noise, with children shouting at their games and women singing and dancing, and the members of the Kaŋġi'yuha liked to spend the evenings in their lodge, singing and enjoying themselves." Over the door of this lodge was hung the "Crow lance" in its wrappings. According to Eagle Shield, this lance was decorated with a crow skin next to the lance head. Before a fight the lance was unwrapped and passed over the smoke of burning sweet grass. When stuck in the ground during a fight it marked a place from which the members of the society could not retreat unless they took the lance with them.[2]

When going to war each man carried his crow-skin "necklace" in a rawhide case (pl. 44), and before putting it around his neck he passed it over the smoke of burning sweet grass. Feathers for head

[1] This is undoubtedly the mound referred to by Clark in the Original Journals of the Lewis and Clark Expedition, vol. 1, pp. 121-123. Clark writes, under date of August 25, 1804, as follows: "Capt. Lewis and Myself concluded to go and See the Mound . . . which the Indians Call Mountain of *little people or Spirits*. . . . The Surrounding Plains is open Void of Timber and leavel to a great extent, hence the wind from whatever quarter it may blow, drives with unusial force over the naked Plains and against this hill; the insects of various kinds are thus involuntaryly driven to the Mound by the force of the wind, or fly to its Leeward Side for Shelter; the Small Birds whoes food they are, Consequently resort in great numbers to this place in Surch of them; Perticularly the Small brown Martin of which we saw a vast number hovering on the Leeward Side of the hill, when we approached it in the act of catching those insects; they were so gentle that they did not quit the place untill we had arriv⁴ within a fiew feet of them.

One evidence which the Indˢ give for believeing this place to be the residence of Some unusial Sperits is that they frequently discover a large assemblage of Birds about this Mound [this] is in my opinion a Sufficient proof to produce in the Savage Mind a Confident belief of all the properties which they ascribe [to] it.

[2] Cf. Wissler (op. cit., p. 24): "When attacking the enemy they were required to thrust the lances into the ground and not leave the spot unless released by some of their party pulling up the lances. . . . The lances are short and covered with otterskin; at the top there is an eagle feather and at the other end, a spear. Near the spear is (*sic*) fastened the neck and head of a crow."

decoration were also carried in this case.   Eagle Shield said that before
a fight the warriors always put on their finest regalia, so that, if
they were killed, they would die in a manner worthy of their position.
The sleeves of the war shirts were not sewed, but were tied together
under the length of the arm.   Before a fight the warrior untied
these fastenings and threw back the sleeves to permit free use of his
arms.

Concerning the "aki'ćita duties" of members of this society,
Eagle Shield said: "These men were among those who protected
the people and watched for buffalo when the camp was moving, and
who assisted in the selection of suitable places for the winter camps."

A "praise song," *iwa'kićipi olo'waŋ* (No. 158) of this society was
sung by One Feather, this song being in honor of Sitting Crow, a
member of the society.   One of the dancing songs (No. 164) was sung
by Eagle Shield; this is given in connection with a narrative of his
personal experience on the warpath.

ĆAŊTE' TIŊŹA (STRONG HEART)

This term is translated "Stout-hearted ones" by Bushotter,[1] and
"the dauntless" and "the braves" by Wissler.[2]   In the present work
it will be translated "Strong Heart," according to the explanation
given by the writer's interpreters on the Standing Rock Reservation.
Lowie does not include this society in his list of eastern Dakota
societies.[3]   A full account of its organization is, however, given by
Wissler.[4]

A Sioux once said to the writer, "Indian patience and philosophy
are matters of long training."   This was a training which began
in childhood.   Thus Red Fox said that when he ran away with a
war party the men frightened him "to make his heart strong."
(See p. 375.)

It was said that the Strong Heart society among the Teton Sioux,
as it existed within the memory of the writer's informants, was
organized by Sitting Bull, Gall, and Crow King, prominent chiefs,
who were practically in command of all the warriors.   It was their
desire to have a body of fearless warriors to meet any emergency, and
for that purpose this society was organized.   If a man were known to
be fully qualified for the honor of membership, it was not necessary
for him to undergo any tests.   All he had to do when initiated was
to promise to be brave in the defense of the tribe, to take care of
the poor and needy, and to maintain a good moral character.   The

[1] See Dorsey, James Owen, A Study of Siouan Cults, *Eleventh Rep. Bur. Ethn.*, p. 463.
[2] Wissler, Clark, Societies and Ceremonial Associations in the Oglala Division of the Teton Dakota, op. cit., p. 25.
[3] Lowie, Robert H., Dance Associations of the Eastern Dakota, op. cit., p. 104.
[4] Wissler, op. cit., pp. 25-31.

distinctive headdress of the society was a war bonnet made of the
tail feathers of the eagle and having a pair of horns attached in
front.   Each member had one of these headdresses, which he wore
only when going on the warpath or in actual battle.   If a man had
been uniformly successful and had never shown any sign of cowardice,
he might be buried with this bonnet on his head; but if he showed
cowardice on the warpath, he was punished on his return by being

FIG. 29. Woman with banner of the Strong Heart society.

severely reprimanded in the presence of all the members, his headdress was taken away, and he was expelled from the society.

Members of this society were allowed to carry a banner made by
fastening feathers to a long strip of flannel, which was attached to
a pole.   This was called *wapa'ha   kamini'mini*, 'waving banner.'
Women whose relatives were members of this society and had been
killed in war were allowed to carry this banner.   Pahi'wiŋ (Yellow
Hair) said that six of her uncles had been members of this society,
and that she was entitled to carry the Strong Heart society banner

(fig. 29). A similar custom was noted at White Earth, Minn., among the Chippewa. In plate 16, Bulletin 53, is shown a Chippewa woman, the daughter of a chief, carrying such a banner, which belonged to her father.

The distinctive rattle of the Strong Heart society is shown in plate 45. This consists of a rawhide receptacle on which are traced the lines of a turtle. It contains a few small stones or shot. This rattle was used by the dancers.

One of the customs of this society seems to have been designed to increase the self-control of its members. An informant said:

In the old days there were four lodges of the Strong Hearts in the center of the village. Every morning the Strong Heart men met in one of these lodges and sang their songs. Then two young men with rattles and two with bows and arrows went around the village and killed dogs which were to be eaten in their lodge. Some Indians are short tempered, and the Strong Hearts did not kill their dogs. They killed the dogs of prominent families and when the dog was shot they shouted and shook their rattles. It strengthened a man's heart to have his dog killed and not show anger. The women singed the dogs, cooked them, and took them to one of the Strong Heart lodges. There they all sang and danced, and the dogs were part of the feast.

No. 116. Song of the Strong Heart Society (a)   (Catalogue No. 509)

Sung by EAGLE SHIELD

Ko-la tu-wa na-pe-ći-ra-haŋ   o-pa kte śni

ye

WORDS

kola'............................. friends
tu'wa......................... whoever
nape' ćinahaŋ .... runs away
o'pa kte śni ye .... shall not be admitted

STRONG HEART SOCIETY RATTLE

Analysis.—This melody has a compass of 12 tones. This range is not so unusual as is the frequency with which large intervals are spanned. Thus an ascent of 12 tones is accomplished in two progressions at the introduction of the words, and in two instances a descent of a seventh is made in two progressions. Of the intervals 22 per cent are fourths. The song contains all the tones of the octave except the fourth and in structure is classified as melodic with harmonic framework.

No. 117. Song of the Strong Heart Society (b)   (Catalogue No. 544)

Sung by GRAY HAWK

VOICE ♩ = 88
DRUM ♩ = 88
Drum-rhythm similar to No. 19

Analysis.—This song is minor in tonality and progresses largely by intervals of a major second, this constituting about 64 per cent of the entire number of intervals. Four renditions were recorded, uniform in all respects. The final tone was sung slightly flat, but the repeated part and the repetitions of the melody always began on F sharp. The song contains one rest. (See analysis of song No. 79.) The triplet divisions of the count were given clearly. In structure the song is melodic, containing all the tones of the octave.

This and the four songs next following were recorded by Gray Hawk (Ćetaŋ'-hota) (see pl. 71), a well-known member of the tribe, who also contributed interesting material concerning the buffalo hunt (p. 436).

No. 118. Song of the Strong Heart Society [1] (c)   (Catalogue No. 548)

Sung by GRAY HAWK

VOICE ♩ = 104
DRUM ♩ = 104
Drum-rhythm similar to No. 8

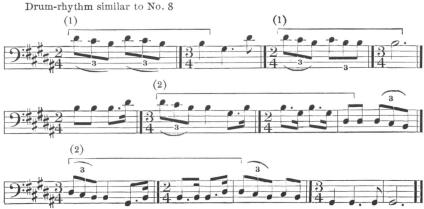

Analysis.—The rhythmic form of this melody is clear and interesting. Two rhythmic units are present, the first count in each having a triplet division. The melody tones are those of the minor triad and fourth. About 31 per cent of the intervals are minor thirds, and one-half are major seconds. The song is harmonic in structure and has a compass of 12 tones.

No. 119. Song of the Strong Heart Society (d)   (Catalogue No. 557)

Sung by GRAY HAWK

VOICE ♩ = 88
DRUM ♩ = 96
Drum-rhythm similar to No. 5

Analysis.—This is a simple melody and three uniform renditions show that it was clear in the mind of the singer. The tone A in the first triple measure was sometimes sung below pitch, but the intona-

---

[1] An additional song of this society is No. 231.

tion of the remainder of the song was excellent.   The melody tones
are those of the minor triad and fourth, yet about one-third of the
progressions are major thirds.   The drum was slightly faster than
the voice and was beaten steadily while the shrill cries were given
between the renditions of the song.

BADGER SOCIETY

The fourth Aki'ćita society, according to Wissler, was the Badger
society.   This is noted by him among the Oglala Sioux,[1] also by Lowie
among the eastern Dakota[2] and the Mandan.[3]   It is said to have
become extinct about 20 years ago.   Two songs of this society were
recorded at Standing Rock.

No. 120. Song of the Badger Society (a)   (Catalogue No. 553)

Sung by GRAY HAWK

VOICE ♩ = 80
DRUM ♩ = 80
Drum-rhythm similar to No. 6

Analysis.—This song is minor in tonality and contains the tones
of the second five-toned scale.   The tones transcribed as C natural
and C sharp are clearly distinguished in the three renditions, the
semitone at the beginning of the second measure being sung with
particularly good intonation.   The minor third is of frequent occurrence, constituting 40 per cent of the intervals.   The rhythmic
form of the song is good and the rhythmic unit, though short, is
interesting.   The drum was slightly behind the voice in all the renditions.

See plot of this melody on page 419.

1 Wissler, Clark, Societies of the Teton-Dakota, op. cit., p. 31.
2 Lowie, Robert H., Dance Associations of the Eastern Dakota, op. cit., p. 109.
3 Lowie, Robert H., Societies of the Crow, Hidatsa, and Mandan, op. cit., p. 322.

No. 121. Song of the Badger Society (b)   (Catalogue No. 554)

Sung by GRAY HAWK

VOICE ♩ = 104
DRUM ♩ = 104
Drum-rhythm similar to No. 19

Analysis.—This song is distinctly major in tonality, yet one-third of the intervals are minor thirds. Five renditions were recorded, the song being sung three times without a break in the time, then a short pause being made, after which it was sung twice. These repetitions are uniform throughout. The tonic triad forms the basis of the melody, but the accented A makes it necessary to classify the song as melodic with harmonic framework. The triplets of eighth notes were clearly enunciated. This count-division is frequently found in dancing songs. About two-thirds of the progressions are downward. The drum slightly preceded the voice, though the metric unit of the two is the same.

MIWA′TANI

The Miwa′tani was an important military society among the Teton Sioux, the members of which were exempt from aki′ćita duty. Charging Thunder said that he belonged to this society, that it was originated long ago by a man who dreamed of an owl, and that the society was sometimes erroneously called the Owl society. The word *miwa′tani* is not fully explainable, as it is not found in the common speech of the Sioux. Two informants said it is not a Sioux word, and that they thought it meant "owl feathers." Wissler says:[1]

According to one informant, this society, which by the way, is regarded as a very ancient one, was so named because an owl-being in conferring the ritual said, "My name is Miwa′tani." . . . Our informants are all agreed that the term is associated with no concept other than that of a particular society. It is also their name for Mandan, the tradition being that the latter were named because of some resemblance to the Miwa′tani society.

The Omaha word for Mandan is Mawa′dani,[2] and a "Mandan dancing society" among the Omaha is mentioned and one of its feasts described by Rev. J. Owen Dorsey.[3]

[1] Societies and Ceremonial Associations in the Oglala Division of the Teton-Dakota, op. cit., p. 42.

[2] Fletcher and La Flesche, The Omaha Tribe, op. cit., p. 102.

[3] Omaha Sociology, *Third Rep. Bur. Ethn.*, p. 273. See also Dorsey, *Eleventh Rep. Bur. Ethn.*, p. 463.

Wissler[1] states that the organization of the Miwa'tani consisted of:

2 leaders	x lay members
2 sash bearers, or bonnet men	1 drum bearer
2 whip bearers	8 singers
1 food passer	1 herald

Charging Thunder said the Miwa'tani society, besides being one of the most difficult to enter, was one of the most exacting in its requirements. Each member pledged himself to sacrifice his own life in defense of a wounded member, if such sacrifice became necessary on the warpath. When anything was needed by the society the principal officer appointed some one to collect what was required, and the demand was never refused. The collecting was usually done at a public meeting of the society and formed one of the tests by which the leaders of the tribe determined which men were qualified to be useful to the tribe.

If an officer of this society saw in the camp a supply of provisions which should have been donated to the society, he could take it, either for the use of the medicine-men who conducted the ceremonies or for the use of the organization as a whole. He had the right to do this, and it was even expected that he would do so if donations were wilfully withheld.

According to Charging Thunder the purpose of this society was to promote friendliness and helpfulness among its members. The more important of its meetings were for the initiation of new members. Any member of the tribe could apply for membership, and if his application was accepted he was notified by the crier.

Before a meeting for initiation the candidates as well as members of the society were required to fast partially for four days. They assembled in their lodge, and once each day the leader brought in a pail of water, and after dipping into this a bunch of sweet grass, handed the latter to each member, with a very small piece of buffalo meat. This was all the nourishment they were allowed, hence the end of the four days found them greatly weakened.

Two old men, after consultation, described the initiation to the writer. On the day of the ceremony the officers of the society, wearing headdresses of owl feathers (*hiŋhaŋ' šuŋ wapa'ha*), took their position in the place of honor, opposite the entrance of the lodge. In their hands they held the owl-feather headdresses which the new members were to receive. All the members of the tribe were gathered to witness the installation of the new members. It was required that the newly elected men should show that they were qualified for the honor which had been conferred on them. Back of the fire was a

---

[1] Societies and Ceremonial Associations in the Oglala Division of the Teton-Dakota, op. cit., p. 42.

"mellowed-earth space" (see p. 122, footnote), and the men were.required to carry live coals in their hands and put them on the earth. Each man, rising from his seat, took coals in the palm of his hand, and turning to the left, walked slowly around the lodge. After the first round of the lodge, pausing at the mellowed-earth space, he pretended that he would place the coals upon it.   This was done three times, and after the fourth round of the lodge, slowly lowering his hand, he gently rolled the coals to the softened earth. (See p. 74.) If he could do this without being burned he was considered qualified to be a member of the society.

As already stated, a headdress of owl feathers had been prepared for each of the new members. These headdresses were long, like war bonnets, but were made of owl feathers instead of eagle feathers. Quite a heap of coals lay on the mellowed earth after all the men had made the circuit of the lodge. Sweet grass was placed on this heap, and the headdresses were held in the fragrant smoke, after which they were placed on the heads of the newly installed members.

The following ceremonial song was sung as the headdresses were placed upon the heads of the men, who were understood then to be fully received into the society.

No. 122. Ceremonial Song of the Miwa'tani   (Catalogue No. 572)

Sung by CHARGING THUNDER

VOICE ♩ = 66

DRUM not recorded

Tu - wa   wa - kaŋ ḳoŋ   le mi - ća - ġe

WORDS

tu'wa wakaŋ' ḳoŋ............ the one who is holy
le mi'ćaġe................... has made this for me

Analysis.—This melody contains the tones of the second five-toned scale, with G sharp as a keynote. The accidental (F double sharp) was clearly given in all the renditions. The song is harmonic in structure and has a compass of 12 tones. Three-fourths of the progressions are downward, the trend of the melody being steadily downward from the twelfth to the tonic. The time in the first two measures is peculiar and was maintained less steadily than in the latter part of the song.

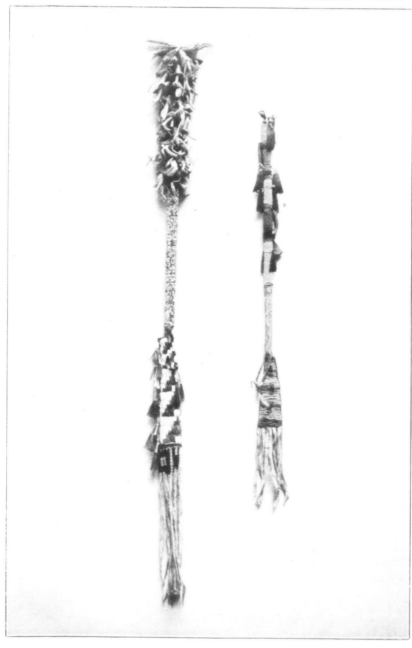

DANCE RATTLE   MIWA'TANI SOCIETY RATTLE

RATTLES

After a man was admitted to this society he donated his best horse to the society, no matter what its value might be. He also hired a man to make his paraphernalia, usually giving a horse as compensation for this service. One of the articles with which he provided himself was a whistle made of the wing bone of an eagle; this whistle was closely decorated with beads (fig. 30), and hung around his neck. Each member had also a rattle fastened to a wand (pl. 46) which he carried during the dances of the society. This rattle was made by boiling the hoof of the deer and cutting the hard, outer part into pieces of the desired shape and size. All the feathers used in adornment by members of this society were owl feathers, tipped with red down. The feathers of the owl were used also on their arrows.

Two of the dancing songs of this society (Nos. 156, 165) occur in connection with the personal war narratives of Eagle Shield and One Feather.

A rattle of dew claws (pl. 46) was used in many Sioux dances.

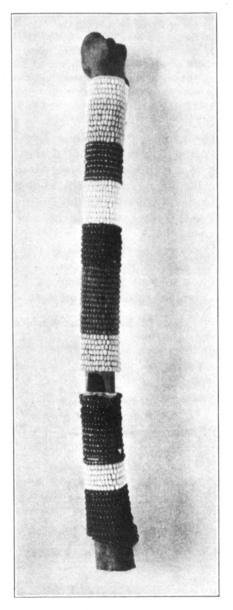

FIG. 30. Miwa'tani society whistle.

WHITE HORSE RIDERS (Śuŋk'ska-akaŋ'yaŋka)

The White Horse Riders were not considered a tribal society, like those already described, but were an old organization which, in the opinion of some informants, was local in character. The term "white horse riders" is not an exact translation of the Sioux designation, the first word of which means "white horse," while the second is a compound word indicating age and experience. One informant said:

The White Horse Riders were principally the old warriors. Those older people had a special liking for painting their horses on parades or on the warpath, as by that means they could show that the horse's owner had done some brave deed. They rode white horses for two reasons. They liked the white color, because it was regarded as a *genuine* color [see pp. 173, 205], and also because a white horse was the only one on which the paint would show well. The usual decoration was a horse's hoofprint and a hand, the hand being understood to represent the hand of the enemy. To people with an understanding the arrangement of these designs told the story of the man's brave deeds. (See p. 77, footnote.)

The parade of the White Horse Riders was greatly admired in the camp. It is said that if the White Horse Riders came to the tent of a man who had been wounded in war, they fired their guns into the air, whereupon the women of the family cooked a quantity of food and placed it in the middle of the camp circle. The custom was that "those who had no one to cook for them went and ate this food."

The songs of the White Horse Riders were favorites among the Sioux, and the words of these songs were often changed. Thus No. 225 is a song of this society in which the name Ptesaŋ'-noŋ'pawiŋ has been substituted for another name.

No. 123. Song of the White Horse Riders (a)   (Catalogue No. 534)

Sung by Two Shields

VOICE ♩ = 66
DRUM ♩ = 66
Drum-rhythm similar to No. 6

Analysis.—This song contains an unusual number of progressions. There are 52 intervals in the song. It has been stated that the average number of progressions in comparatively modern songs is 31.3. Thirty (58 per cent) of these intervals are thirds, 18 being major and 12 being minor thirds. It is interesting to note the large number of minor thirds in a song which is distinctly major in tonality; these intervals, however, are usually part of the tonic triad, which forms the framework of the melody. Two rests are found in the song. (See No. 79.) The two renditions show no points of difference, the small count-divisions being clearly given. Drum and voice have the same metric unit and were coincident.

No. 124. Song of the White Horse Riders (b)   (Catalogue No. 535)

Sung by Two Shields

Analysis.—Two renditions of this song were recorded, in both of which renditions G in the upper octave was sung G flat, and in the lower octave G natural. This was probably because the higher tone was above the compass of the singer's voice. Two rhythmic units are present, their repetitions comprising most of the song. The melody tones are those of the major triad and second, a tone material found in only 3 of 340 Chippewa songs, and in 8 songs of the present series. About 38 per cent of the intervals are fourths. The average interval is not large, but a compass of 13 tones is accomplished in three measures, about midway through the song. The tempo of the drum is slightly slower than that of the voice.

WAR SONGS (OZU'YE OLO'WAŊ)

CONSECUTIVE SONGS OF A TYPICAL WAR EXPEDITION

War expeditions were of two kinds—tribal and individual. In the former the tribe acted as a unit, as they did on the buffalo hunt. Thus, if the tribe as a whole needed horses, the only way to secure them was by stealing them from the enemy. The matter was discussed either in the tribal council or in the council of the chiefs. Scouts were selected by the council, or each military society could choose some of its members to act in that capacity, the procedure of selecting and sending the searching party being similar to that which preceded the search for the pole to be used in the Sun dance or a buffalo hunt. (See pp. 109, 439.) The scouts started at night, having been given instructions where to go, and also what to do if they saw the enemy. When the scouts had returned and made their report, the tribe took up its journey. The organization was similar to that of the buffalo hunt, the men being restrained by the aki'ćita from any individual action until the time came for the tribe to act as a unit.

An individual war party could be organized at any time when the tribe was not on a general expedition. A man desiring to organize an individual war party called on his relatives and friends at night, explained his purpose, and asked them to join him. If they were willing to do so they smoked a pipe in token of their acceptance. Such an invitation could scarcely be refused, and the man who gave it became leader of the party. Everything concerning the expedition was carefully discussed before starting. The country through which they would pass and the enemies they would meet were somewhat familiar to the warriors, so that the leader could explain verbally the route which he proposed they should take. It was not uncommon, however, for a map to be sketched on the bare ground, and quite customary for a war party to leave behind a "map" on buckskin, showing the hills and streams they expected to pass, so that other parties could find them if desirable.

(Used by permission.)

TWO SHIELDS

It was not considered a great honor to be asked to join a war·party, and no demonstration was made when they left the village. As an old warrior said, "the honor was in coming home victorious, and the demonstration was reserved to see whether it would be needed when we returned."

The following section presents in consecutive order certain songs which might be sung on a war expedition. Many details of description are omitted, as they are comprised in the personal narratives which follow this section.

The next 10 songs are common war songs, or "wolf songs," which were sung in the societies or other gatherings before the departure of a war party. Many of them mention the wolf, as the life of a warrior was supposed to be like that of the wolf. Two Shields (pl. 47), who recorded several of these songs, is a leading singer at every tribal gathering.

No. 125. "Those Are Not My Interest" (Catalogue No. 528)

Sung by Two Shields

WORDS

kola′pila	friends
epe′ćoŋ [1]	I have said
ti i′kćeya	in common life
wićo′haŋ kiŋ	the customs
o′ta yelo′	are many
kola′	friend
he′na	those
e śni	are not (do not interest me)
yelo′ epe′lo	I have said

Analysis.—This song was recorded by the same singer on two occasions. The duplication was accidental, and a comparison of the result is, therefore, the more interesting. Both renditions were transcribed and are herewith presented. It will readily be seen that the points of difference are slight and unimportant. This is usually the case when a song is repeated by the same singer or sung by two equally good singers. The rhythm, which is peculiar, was exactly repeated. It has been frequently noted that the rhythm of a song is more accurately repeated than the melody progressions. The foregoing transcription was from the second "recording," in which the song was sung three times, while in the first recording it was sung only once, with a repetition of the first part. The transcription which follows this analysis is from the first recording of the song, in which the pitch was slightly lower, and the tempo slower, than in the second. Probably it was because of this low pitch that the singer closed both parts of the song on the third instead of on the tonic. The drumbeat was alike in both recordings, but was specially clear in the second, as is shown in the foregoing transcription. It is not customary to vary the rhythm of the drum as in this instance, but Two Shields is a particularly efficient singer at the drum when large gatherings are held, and such "leading drummers" frequently elaborate their part, especially in songs of this kind. It is probably unnecessary to state that the writing of the drum part on a staff does not imply pitch. Drum and voice coincided throughout the performance. Between the three renditions recorded at this time the drumbeat was continuous. The pause in the voice was about equal to two measures, but was not exact; in one instance it was interrupted by shrill cries. The time in the five–eight and three–eight measures was absolutely exact, and the triplet and couplet groups are indicated according to the rhythm in which the passage was sung. The melody contains the tones of the second five-toned scale. About one-fourth of the intervals are minor thirds, but the melody progresses principally by whole tones, the major second forming 49 per cent of the entire number of intervals.

---

[1] Contraction of *epe′ći ḳoŋ.*

The words of the following are identical with those of No. 125:

Duplication of No. 125

Sung by Two SHIELDS

Ko - la - pi - la e - pe - ći ḳoŋ *he*

a hi ye ti i - kće - ya wi - ćo - haŋ kiŋ ˙ o - ta ye - lo

ko - la he - na e śni ye - lo e - pe - lo *he* *yo*

An Indian warrior wanders like a wolf, and his life is expressed in the following song.

No. 126. "Like a Wolf I Roam" (Catalogue No. 656)

Sung by ONE BUFFALO (TATAŊ′KA-WAŊŹI′LA)

Śuŋ - ka i - śna - la mi - ye - lo ća ma - ka o - ka wiŋ - łiya o - ma - wa -

ni ḳoŋ he - ći - ya ta - moŋ - ka śni ye - lo

WORDS

śuŋ'ka iśna'la	lone wolf
miye'lo ća	I am
maka' o'ka wiŋ'ħya	in different places
oma'wani	I roam
ķoŋ	but
heći'ya	there
tamoŋ'ka sni yelo'	I am tired out

Analysis.—Considering F sharp as the keynote of this song, we find the melody tones to be those of the second five-toned scale. The basis of the melody is the minor triad with minor seventh added. (See analysis of song No. 49.) Nearly half of the intervals are minor thirds. The song is melodic in structure and has a compass of 10 tones.

No. 127. "Watch Your Horses"   (Catalogue No. 532)

Sung by Two Shields

Voice ♩=92
Drum ♩=92
Drum-rhythm similar to No. 5

Kaŋ-ġi wi - ća - śa kiŋ śuŋk a - waŋ-gla - ka po

e ya suŋ - ka wa - ma - noŋ sa mi - ye ye - lo

WORDS

Kaŋġi'[1] wića'śa	Crow Indian
kiŋ suŋk awaŋ'glaka po	you must watch your horses
suŋ'ka wama'noŋ	a horse thief
sa	often
miye' yelo'	am I

---

[1] Kaŋġi' is the Sioux equivalent for Crow. Concerning the name of this tribe the Handbook of American Indians (pt. 1, p. 367) states: "trans., through French *gens des corbeaux*, of their own name *Absaroke*, crow, sparrowhawk, or bird people." The following forms occur in the words of these songs: Kaŋġi' wića'sa (Crow people), Nos. 127, 149, 179; Kaŋġi' to'ka (Crow enemies), Nos. 169, 174; Psa'loka (corruption of Absaroka, Teton dialect), Nos. 167, 168; Psa'doka (Santee dialect), No. 192.

Analysis.—About half of the intervals in this song are minor thirds, though the interval of a fourth is also prominent. All the tones of the octave except the seventh and second appear in the song, which is melodic in structure and has a compass of an octave. Several renditions were recorded; these show no points of difference.

See plot of this melody on page 419.

No. 128. "Friends, Go-On"   (Catalogue No. 527)

Sung by Two Shields

Voice ♩ = 92
Drum ♩ = 92
Drum-rhythm similar to No. 5

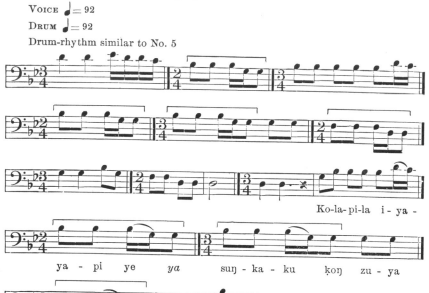

Ko-la-pi-la i-ya-ya-pi ye *ya* suŋ-ka-ku ḳoŋ zu-ya u ye-lo

WORDS

kola′pila........................ friends
iya′yapi ye..................... you go on
suŋka′ku ḳoŋ.................. even that younger brother
zuya′ u yelo′.................. is coming on the warpath

Analysis.—The framework of this melody is one which is familiar in these songs. The submediant chord forms the basis of the opening measures, followed by a descent from the dominant to the mediant, a descent of a minor third; after this the melody returns to the submediant chord, and the song closes on the mediant. Comparison with the preceding song will show the same outline in that melody. About half of the intervals in this song are minor thirds. The intonation is good, and the melody contains all the tones of the octave except the seventh. The rhythm of the drum is one found frequently in the Chippewa songs, but is much less common among the Sioux.

No. 129. "A Wolf I Considered Myself"　(Catalogue No. 547)

Sung by GRAY HAWK

VOICE ♩ = 104
DRUM ♩ = 104
Drum-rhythm similar to No. 8

Śuŋ-ka mi-çi - la yuŋ-kaŋ　　ta-ku wa-te śni yuŋ-kaŋ

na-źiŋ wa-ka - piŋ ye-lo

WORDS

(*First rendition*)

śuŋ'ka	a wolf
miçi'la	I considered myself
yuŋ'kaŋ	but
ta'ku wa'te śni	I have eaten nothing
yuŋ'kaŋ	therefore
na'źiŋ	from standing
wakapiŋ' yelo'	I am tired out

(*Second rendition*)

śuŋ'ka	a wolf
miçi'la	I considered myself
yuŋ'kaŋ	but
hiŋhaŋ'	the owls
hotoŋ'pi	are hooting (see p. 180, footnote)
yuŋ'kaŋ	and
haŋko'waki pelo'	the night I fear

Analysis.—The interval of a fourth is prominent in this melody, constituting about 25 per cent of the intervals, while the major second constitutes 53 per cent of the number. In many instances the major second is a passing tone in a descent of a fourth. This song has a compass of 13 tones and is melodic in structure. The rhythm is of special interest, as the song contains three rhythmic units, every tone in the melody being comprised in these units.

No. 130. "Adventures I Seek"   (Catalogue No. 523)

Sung by Two SHIELDS

si - to-mni-yaŋ wi - ĉo-haŋ o-wa-le he *e a e e*   *e* i-

yo - ti - ye - ki - ya   o - ma-wa - ni *hi*   *a*

WORDS

maka′ sito′mniyaŋ.............. in all lands
wiĉo′haŋ........................ adventures
owa′le.......................... I seek
he............................. hence
iyo′tiyekiya oma′wani......... amid hardships I have walked

Analysis.—This is a particularly interesting example of a song which is harmonic in structure and based on the fourth five-toned scale. At the opening of the song the tonic chord appears in the upper octave and there is a descent through the submediant to the tonic chord in the lower octave. An ascent of 12 tones is accomplished in two progressions, and the melody, with the introduction of the words, returns to the tonic chord in the upper octave, descending, as before, through G to the tonic chord in the lower octave, ending on the tonic. Though the song is so regular in melodic form and so distinctly major in tonality, 40 per cent of the intervals are minor thirds. The song contains 60 progressions, 37 of which are downward and 23 upward. It will be recalled that the average number of progressions in comparatively modern songs is 31.3.

No. 131. "His Horses He Granted Me" (Catalogue No. 543)

Sung by Two Shields

WORDS

Wakaŋ′taŋka	Wakaŋ′taŋka
ćewa′kiya	I pray to
awa′ku we	bringing home
taśuŋ′ke	his horses
ko	also
ma′ku welo′	(he) granted me

Analysis.—In determining the keynote of a song the test by the ear seems permissible, and by this test the song under analysis is transcribed as being in the key of A, although the seventh and third tones of that key do not appear in the melody. The omission of these tones places the song in the first five-toned scale, according to the system of pentatonic scales given by Helmholtz. (See p. 7.) One instance of a song on the first five-toned scale is found in the analyzed Chippewa songs. (See song No. 116, Bulletin 53.) A descending fourth characterizes this melody. It appears as E–B in the first two measures, followed by D–A and A–E, these progressions being repeated in the latter part of the song, which contains the words. The tonality of the song is major, though more than half the intervals are minor thirds.

No. 132. "Those Hills I Trod Upon" (Catalogue No. 670)

Sung by MANY WOUNDS

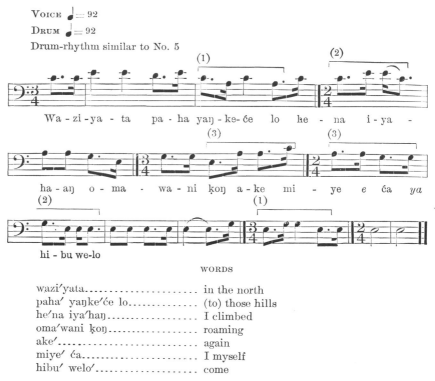

VOICE ♩= 92
DRUM ♩= 92
Drum-rhythm similar to No. 5

Wa - zi - ya - ta   pa - ha yaŋ - ke- ćе   lo   he - na   i - ya -

ha - aŋ   o - ma - wa - ni ķoŋ a - ke   mi - ye   e   ća   ya

hi - bu we-lo

WORDS

wazi′yata...................... in the north
paha′ yaŋke′će lo.............. (to) those hills
he′na iya′haŋ.................. I climbed
oma′wani ķoŋ.................. roaming
ake′........................... again
miye′ ća...................... I myself
hibu′ welo′................... come

Analysis.—This is a favorite song of the Sioux, a fact which explains why it was recorded by three singers on widely separated parts of the reservation. The words of the first two singers are practically the same, while the third singer mentions the streams, instead of the hills of the north country; the differences in the melody are slight. The rendition by Many Wounds is the one used in the tabulated analyses. The song is based on the fourth five-toned scale and contains a large percentage of minor thirds. It is melodic in structure and has a compass of an octave.

Duplication of No. 132

Sung by ONE FEATHER

VOICE ♩= 96
DRUM ♩= 96
Drum-rhythm similar to No. 5

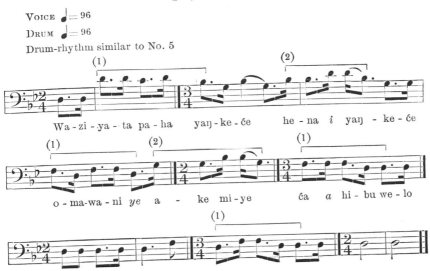

Wa - zi - ya - ta pa - ha   yaŋ - ke - će   he - na i yaŋ - ke - će

o - ma-wa - ni ye a - ke mi - ye   ća a hi - bu we - lo

As already stated, this is a duplication, the song being sung on
different occasions by three singers. This transcription is given for
purposes of comparison. The words of this are the same as No. 132
except that the word *iya'han* (I climbed) is omitted. Other duplications transcribed are Nos. 125 and 133.

This and the following duplication of No. 132 begin and end on the
same tone. Other songs of this series showing the same peculiarity
are Nos. 99, 127, 203, 205, 212, 220, 221, 228, 234, 238. (See Bull.
53, page 222.)

Duplication of No. 132

Sung by Two Shields

VOICE ♩ = 96
DRUM ♩ = 96
Drum-rhythm similar to No. 5

Wa - zi -

ya - ta wa-kpa   yuŋ - ke-ćin   he   he - na   o - yuŋk -

ya ya o - ma - wa   ni ye   a - ke   mi - ye   ća   ya   hi - bu

we - lo

WORDS

wazi′yata	in the north
wakpa′	(by) streams
yuŋke′ćin	that are
hena′	there
oyuŋk′ya	my bed is
oma′wani ye	I have roamed
ake′	again
miye′ ca	I myself
hibu′ welo	come

In this instance the words are slightly different from those sung by One Feather with the same melody.

No. 133. Wolf Song   (Catalogue No. 524)

Sung by Two Shields

VOICE ♩ = 96
DRUM ♩ = 96
Drum-rhythm similar to No. 19

E - ća   šuŋ-ka mi - ći - la yuŋ-kaŋ

ta - ku wa-te   šni yuŋ-kaŋ na-ziŋ wa-ka - piŋ ye

WORDS

e′ća............................ well
šuŋ′ka.......................... a wolf
mići′la......................... I considered myself
yuŋ′kaŋ......................... and yet
ta′ku wa′te šni................. I have eaten nothing
yuŋ′kaŋ......................... and
na′žiŋ waka′piŋ ye.............. I can scarcely stand

Analysis.—The words of this song are the same as those of the
first rendition of No. 129, embodying an idea which was commonly
expressed in connection with the warpath—that the life of a warrior
was like that of a wolf. On examining the phonograph records
it was found that the same melody had been recorded by Śiya′ka,
different words being used. It is probable that the words used by
Śiya′ka are also very old. Both transcriptions are given for the purpose of comparison. It will be readily seen that the differences are
about the same as in other duplications; the actual comparison, however, can be made only by means of structural analyses. On comparing these, it is found that both renditions contain only the tones
of the second five-toned scale, have a range of 12 tones, and are
harmonic in structure. The rhythmic unit is the same in each, also

the rhythm of the drum. The tempo is slightly different and the key is higher, which suggests a difference in the adjustment of the phonograph. It is found that the rendition by Two Shields contains 53 progressions and that by Śiya'ka 59; the former contains 18 and the latter 20 minor thirds; the former 25 and the latter 29 major seconds; the former 5 and the latter 6 ascending major thirds. The differences are therefore shown to be slight and unimportant. A change of tempo occurs in the rendition by Two Shields.

Duplication of No. 133

Sung by ŚIYA'KA

VOICE ♩ = 108

DRUM ♩ = 108

Drum-rhythm similar to No. 19

E - ća   wi   o - blu - spa yuŋ - kaŋ   śuŋ-ka - wa-kaŋ

ni   ni - ća   e - ma - ki - ya   ca   ma - ka si - to - mni

o - ma - wa-ni   ye

WORDS

e'ća............................ well
wi oblu'spa yuŋ'kaŋ.......... when I was courting
śuŋka'wakaŋ ni nića'.......... "horses you have none"
ema'kiya...................... to me was said
ća........................... therefore
maka' sito'mni............... over all the land
oma'wani ye.................. I roam

This is not entirely similar to the preceding songs, as it is a personal rather than a society song, but is placed here as it may be supposed to have been sung prior to the departure of a war party. In some respects the words of this song resemble those of Red Fox's war song (No. 155), yet the idea is exactly the opposite, for in this song a reluctant boy is being urged to bravery by his older brothers.

No. 134. "It Is Difficult"   (Catalogue No. 611)

Sung by USED-AS-A-SHIELD

<pre>
VOICE ♩ = 80
DRUM not recorded
</pre>

Zu-ya   wa-u   kta yuŋ - kaŋ   ći - ye   he-ya - pe - lo

ta - ku   waŋ-la - ke   ćiŋ   a - pe - wa - ćiŋ   yo

ći - ye   he - ya - pi   tka   ta - moŋ - ka   śni ye - lo

WORDS

zuya′	on the warpath
waü′ kta	I was coming
yuŋ′kaŋ	when
ćiye′	brothers
heya′ pelo	said
ta′ku	anything (see p. 349, footnote 2)
waŋla′ke ćiŋ	you see
ape′waćiŋ yo	try to strike it (see p. 359)
ćiye′	brothers
heya′pi	said this
tka	hence
tamoŋ′ka śni yelo′	I realize difficulties

Analysis.—In structure as well as in idea this song closely resembles No. 155; indeed it was said by some Indians to be the same song. On comparison of the two transcriptions it is noted that 53 instead of 75 per cent of the intervals are thirds, the major and minor thirds being equal in number. The rhythmic unit is shorter but has the same division of the first count. The compass is the same, but No. 134 contains all the tones of the octave except the seventh and second, while song No. 155 contains only the major triad.

The warriors carried extra moccasins, and each man took his own cup or cooking utensil, these features of the preparation being indicated in the personal war narratives which follow. The war party took also a supply of medicines for the treatment of the wounded.

The leader usually carried the skin of a wolf with the head pointing in the direction they were going. When the party camped he laid the wolfskin on the ground with its head toward the enemy's country, and when they resumed their journey the head still pointed the way. No drum or rattle was used, the men walking silently. If there chanced to be a man in the party who had dreamed of a wolf, he was asked to perform certain ceremonies. For instance, as the warriors approached the camp of the enemy they desired bad weather, especially a drizzling rain, to cover their attack. Then the medicine-man would sprinkle water on the wolf hide, sing his personal song, and offer a prayer, saying that the warriors wished for a storm in which to attack their enemies. It is said that a storm usually followed this procedure on the part of a medicine-man. If they had difficulty in locating the enemy because the latter's camp had been moved, they again called on a medicine-man to search for the enemy by means of his power. If he were able to command the sacred stones, he would use them for that purpose.

From an old warrior the writer secured a decorated shield which, he said, he had carried in wars against the Crows (pls. 48, 49). The shield is made of rawhide stretched over a hoop and laced with a strip of hide. The greatest diameter is 16 inches. The decoration on the shield was said to refer to a dream of a bear. The eight segments were painted alternately red and yellow, the painting on the yellow segments, in black, representing bears' paws, while the space below the paws was white. The warrior said that the decoration commemorated a fight with the Crows, and that certain features of the painting showed that the fight, though in the Black Hills, took place in a level, open place. He said that he was "in the middle of the shield and the enemies were all around him, but the claws of the bear were on every side to protect him," hence he was not hurt in the battle.

A typical Sioux war bonnet is shown in plate 50. These head-dresses were made of the tail feathers of the eagle, and many of them were tipped with horsehair or white down.

WAR SHIELD (OBVERSE)

WAR SHIELD (REVERSE)

SIOUX WAR BONNET

Men on the warpath sought the highest points from which to spy the enemy and estimate distances; they often piled up stones to shield them from the sight of the enemy. Many of these heaps of stones are still seen in the Sioux country. Some of them are said to have been erected as landmarks to guide the members of a war party back to their rendezvous. This statement, however, is erroneous. The place and time of meeting were understood before an attack was made on the enemy, but the men were obliged to find their way to it as best they could.

Śuŋ′ka-waŋbli′[1] (Dog Eagle) said that when he went on the warpath this song was sung at night in the camp to "strengthen their hearts." They sang very low, and sometimes imitated an owl.

No. 135. Song of the Camp   (Catalogue No. 657)

Sung by Dog Eagle

VOICE ♩ = 80
DRUM ♩ = 80
Drum-rhythm similar to No. 5

Ta-ku   le - će - ča he
to-ki i-huŋ - ni a ka   e - ha - haŋ pe - lo śuŋ-ka - wa-kaŋ he hi-yo
wa - u   we - lo

WORDS

ta′ku[2].......................... something (referring to a person)
le′ćeća he...................... like this
to′ki ihuŋ′ni ka............... is not likely to reach anywhere
eha′haŋ pelo′..... .... you are saying
śuŋ′kawakaŋ.................. horses
hiyo′ waü′ welo′.............. I am coming after

---

[1] The word *suŋ′ka* may be translated either "wolf" or "dog," but in proper names the latter meaning is commonly used.

[2] The word *taku* when used in this manner is an expression of contempt. A free translation of the words is as follows: "You are saying that such a person as I will never arrive at anything, but I am coming after horses." Cf. *taku* in songs Nos. 134, 156.

Analysis.—This song contains only the tones of the minor triad and fourth. The melody progresses largely by whole tones, as 56 per cent of the intervals are major seconds. The interval of the fourth also is prominent, comprising 20 per cent of the progressions. Several renditions were recorded; these are uniform in every respect. The rhythm of the song is such as to suggest the presence of a rhythmic unit, but it will be noted that no rhythmic phrase is repeated in the melody.

When the warriors were acting as scouts or wished for any reason to be unobserved, each wore a white cloth arranged like a blanket and frequently having eagle feathers fastened at the shoulders. Sometimes a separate cloth covered the head, as shown in the drawing by Jaw (pl. 59), but the hands were always covered. It was said that on seeing an enemy in the distance the warrior strung his bow, making ready to shoot. As he came nearer the enemy he took an arrow from his quiver, and putting the quiver close under his armpit, held the bow below it with the arrow in position, so that in a moment he could throw open his blanket and send the arrow on its way. Plate 51 shows two Sioux in this costume, enacting the part of scouts. This was a feature of a celebration of the Fourth of July, 1913, at Bull Head, S. Dak.

If an open fight was expected the warriors put on their gayest regalia. Feather ornaments had been carried in a rawhide case and these, with the decorated war shirts, were donned by the warriors. Sometimes the men wore little clothing and rubbed "war medicine" on their bodies. It was said that they mixed earth which a mole had "worked up," with a powdered herb, rubbing it on their own bodies and on those of their horses. A specimen of this herb was secured, which was identified as *Gutierrezia sarothrae* (Pursh) B. & R. This specimen grew close to one of the old buffalo wallows on the prairie.

Some warriors preferred to be painted by the medicine-men.

Little Buffalo (Tataŋ'ka-ćika'la) was a man who "made medicine" for the warriors. Using blue clay mixed with "medicine," he painted a band across the man's forehead with a branching end on each cheek bone, the painting being done only in war. In addition to this the "medicine" was rubbed on the body and limbs of the warrior.

Bear Eagle (Mato'-waŋbli'), who had been painted in this manner by Little Buffalo, recorded the two following songs. He said that the first one was sung by Little Buffalo alone as he painted them, and the second by the warriors after the painting was finished. He said further that they did not sing in a loud voice, but that, having mounted their horses, they sang this song of the man who had painted them.

MEN IN COSTUME OF SCOUTS

No. 136. "Clear the Way, I Come"   (Catalogue No. 634)

Sung by BEAR EAGLE

VOICE ♩ = 112
DRUM not recorded

Haŋ - ta yo   wa-kaŋ-yaŋ hi - bu we - lo   e   o   haŋ - ta

a   yo wa - kaŋ-yaŋ hi - bu we - lo   e   ma - ka

kiŋ mi - ta - wa   ća wa - kaŋ-yaŋ hi - bu we - lo   e   haŋ - ta

a   yo   o   wa - kaŋ-yaŋ hi - bu we - lo   e   yo

WORDS

haŋ'ta yo	clear the way
wakaŋ'yaŋ	in a sacred manner
hibu' welo'	I come
maka' kiŋ	the earth
mita' wa	(is) mine
ća	hence
wakaŋ'yaŋ	in a sacred manner
hibu' welo'	I come
haŋ'ta yo	clear the way
wakaŋ'yaŋ	in a sacred manner
hibu' welo'	I come

Analysis.—This melody is based on the minor triad A–C–E, though D and G frequently appear as accented tones. The song has a compass of 12 tones, beginning on the twelfth and descending steadily to the tonic along the tones of the second five-toned scale. It is minor in tonality, and about one-third of the intervals are minor thirds. The intonation was particularly good in this and the following song by the same singer. Three renditions were recorded, which are uniform throughout.

See plot of this melody on p. 419.

No. 137. "At the Wind Center I Stand"   (Catalogue No. 635)

Sung by BEAR EAGLE

VOICE ♩= 80
DRUM not recorded

Ma - ka kiŋ ćo-ka-ya na-wa-źiŋ-ye   waŋ-ma-yaŋ-ka   yo

ta - te-yo ćo - ka-ya na-wa-źiŋ-ye   waŋ-ma-yaŋ-ka   yo   e pe -

źi - hu-ta ća na - wa-źiŋ-ye   ta - te-yo na - wa-źiŋ-ye

WORDS

maka' kiŋ ćoka'ya........... at the center of the earth
nawa'źiŋye.................. I stand
waŋma'yaŋka yo............. behold me
tate'yo ćoka'ya............. at the wind center (where the winds blow to-
                             ward me from every side (see p. 120, footnote)
nawa'źiŋye.................. I stand
waŋma'yaŋka yo............. behold me
peźi' huta.................. a root of herb (medicine)
ća......................... therefore
nawa'źiŋye.................. I stand
tate'yo.................... at the wind center
nawa'źiŋye.................. I stand

Analysis.—Two renditions of this song were recorded, both containing the change of tempo indicated in the transcription. This change is sudden and definite, but the second tempo is not sustained to the end of the song, the first rendition closing in almost the original tempo. (See song No. 5.) Throughout the renditions there are variations in time too slight to be indicated, but the rhythmic unit is clearly given, showing that the song had a rhythmic clearness in the mind of the singer. The intonation was good. The song is analyzed in the key of C major; the minor triad A–C–E, however, is prominent in the melody, and about 52 per cent of the intervals are minor thirds.

A somewhat similar description of war painting was given by Śiya′ka, who said that he and four others were in a war party and that their horses were painted by a man named Holy Horse (Taśuŋ′ka-wakaŋ′). He painted the horses with white clay, drawing zigzag lines from the mouth down the front legs, branching at the hoofs, and the same on the hind legs; there was also a band across the forehead and spots on the chest. All the horses were painted alike.

The four men had their faces painted brown with a white line across the forehead extending down the cheeks and forked at the end. Their hair was tied in a bunch on the forehead and in it was tied some of the same "medicine" which had been put on their bodies.

When the men were ready to start they mounted their horses with their faces toward the east and walked single file in a great circle, Holy Horse following close behind them. The three following songs were said to have been sung by Holy Horse and the men whom he had thus painted. It seems probable that, as in the preceding narrative, the first song was sung by Holy Horse alone, as he painted the men and their horses, and the others by the warriors after the painting was finished.

No. 138. Song Concerning War Paint (Catalogue No. 465)

Sung by Śiya′ka

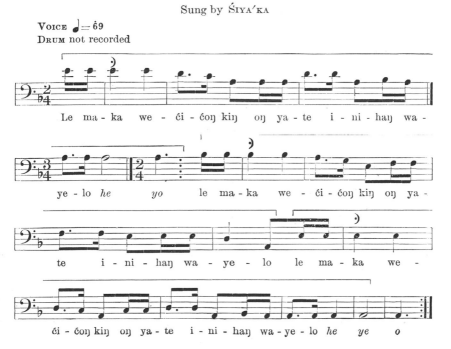

le............................	this
maka'.........................	earth
we'ćićoŋ kiŋ..................	I had used as paint
oŋ............................	causes
oya'te [1].....................	the tribe (of the enemy)
ini'haŋ waye'lo................	much excitement

Analysis.—The repetitions of the rhythmic unit constitute the whole of this song, these repetitions differing only in the lengths of the last two tones. One-third of the intervals are minor seconds, this being an unusual proportion of this interval. The major seconds are almost as many in number, and the remaining intervals comprise four minor thirds, four fourths, and an ascending fifth. The song is minor in tonality, melodic in structure, and contains all the tones of the octave.

The two following songs were sung after a horse had been painted for the warpath:

No. 139. "Tremble, O Tribe of the Enemy" (Catalogue No. 466)

Sung by ŚIYA'KA

VOICE ♩ = 144
DRUM not recorded

Wa-na-ka ho hi-yu-wa-ye si - to-mni-yaŋ ni-hiŋ-ći-ya yo o

ye   o   wa-na-ka ho hi - yu-wa-ye si - to-mni-yaŋ

ni - hiŋ - ći - ya yo *he*   o - ya - te wa-kaŋ -

yaŋ yaŋ-ke-ćiŋ si - to - mni-yaŋ ni-hiŋ - ći - ya yo *yo*   *he*   *yo*

---

[1] The first syllable of this word was omitted by the singer.

WORDS

wana′ka......................	now at this time
ho...........................	a voice
hiyu′waye....................	I sent forth
sito′mniyaŋ..................	all
nihiŋ′ćiya yo................	tremble
oya′te.......................	O tribe (of the enemy)
wakaŋ′yaŋ...................	in a sacred manner
yaŋke′ćiŋ....................	sitting
sito′mniyaŋ..................	all
nihiŋ′ćiya yo................	tremble

Analysis.—This song is divided into three rhythmic periods, the third of which differs slightly from the others in the division of the opening measure. The tempo was slightly slower on the word *sito′mniyaŋ*, but not sufficiently so to be indicated. Three renditions were recorded, which are alike in every respect. The melody tones are those of the minor triad and fourth, and the song has a compass of 12 tones. Only five intervals occur which are larger than a minor third, yet the melody is interesting and not lacking in vigor.

No. 140. "Behold My Horse"   (Catalogue No. 468)

Sung by ŚIYA′KA

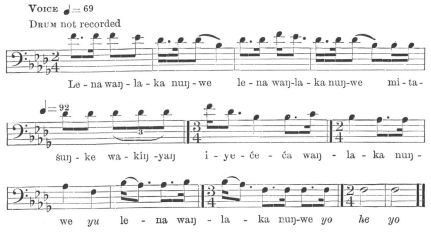

WORDS

le′na........................	these (the painted horse and the herbs)
waŋla′ ka nuŋwe′............	may you behold
mita′ śuŋke.................	my horse
wakiŋ′yaŋ iye′ćeća.........	like the thunderbird
waŋla′ka nuŋwe′............	may you behold

Analysis.—In every rendition of this song the tempo was hastened in the latter part. (See song No. 5.) The song is minor in tonality and contains all the tones of the octave except the sixth. In structure it is harmonic, the accented tones descending along the intervals of the chord of B flat minor. One-third of the progressions are minor thirds.

Before entering the camp of the enemy a warrior might strike another member of the party as a sign that he was willing to die in that man's place if such a sacrifice became necessary.

No. 141. "See My Desire" (Catalogue No. 616)

Sung by USED-AS-A-SHIELD

VOICE ♩ = 48
DRUM not recorded

Ta - ku wo-wi-taŋ o - ya-le pi - *i* - ća ko - la- pi-la miś-e-ya waŋ-

yaŋ - ke wa-ćaŋ - mi wa-na ti-ya -ta *wa* ća - že   ma -ya-ta pe-lo

WORDS

ta′ku wowi′taŋ.................. some honor
oya′le pića′....................... you seek
kola′pila....................... friends
miś′eya........................ I, myself
waŋyaŋ′ke...................... see
waćaŋ′mi .... my desire
wana′........................ now
tiya′ta........................ at home
ćaźe′ maya′ta pelo′............ (it) is mentioned

Analysis.—This song contains only two intervals larger than a minor third, these being an ascending fourth and a descending major third. Half of the intervals are minor thirds, with the result that the melody has a wailing effect. Four renditions were recorded, the first and second being without a break in the time, as indicated in the transcription. The song contains all the tones of the octave except the second, and in structure is melodic with harmonic framework.

The following song was sung during or after a fight:

No. 142. "The Earth Only Endures"   (Catalogue No. 617)

SUNG BY USED-AS-A-SHIELD

VOICE ♩ = 63
DRUM ♩ = 63
Drum-rhythm similar to No. 6

Wi-ća-hća-la kiŋ he-ya

pe   lo ma-ka kiŋ le-će-la te-haŋ yuŋ-ke-lo e-ha

pe - lo   e-haŋ-ke-ćoŋ wi - ća - ya-ka pe-lo

WORDS

wića′hćala kiŋ.................. the old men
heya′ pelo′..................... say
maka′ kiŋ..................... the earth
leće′la........................ only
tehaŋ′ yuŋke′lo................ endures
eha′ pelo′..................... you spoke
ehaŋ′kećoŋ.................... truly
wića′ yaka pelo′................ you are right

Analysis.—This song contains the tones of the minor triad and fourth, and the effect of minor tonality is very strong, yet the major and minor thirds are almost equal in number, there being 16 major and 15 minor thirds in the melody. The song is harmonic in structure, the accented tones following the intervals of the tonic chord.

Not all who went on the warpath were impelled by love of war. It is said that a young man once went because some one told him that the girl he expected to marry was untrue to him. The report was false, but he went with the warriors. Before a fight he asked his comrades to tell the girl, when they returned, that he hoped he would be killed. This was his song.

No. 143. "Tell Her"   (Catalogue No. 621)

Sung by USED-AS-A-SHIELD

VOICE ♩ = 76

DRUM ♩ = 76

Drum-rhythm similar to No. 6

WORDS

iŋćiŋ' yaki' ki'nahaŋ...........	when you reach home
he oki'ćiyaka yo...............	tell her
ehaŋ'naĥći....................	long before then
ena' waki' yelo'...............	I will have finished

Analysis.—This song contains two sections, the latter parts of which are alike. Words are found in the second but not in the first. There are in the song 65 progressions, almost 62 per cent of which are minor thirds and major seconds. Two renditions were recorded, which are alike in every respect. The song has a compass of 12 tones, and contains all the tones of the octave except the second. A phrase consisting of two eighth notes followed by a quarter note appears frequently, but is not marked as a rhythmic unit because it characterizes the song less than the dotted eighth and sixteenth count-division, which occurs in various combinations

The latter, however, is so short a phrase, and is used so diversely, that it can not be said to constitute a unit of rhythm. A triple measure followed by a double measure is an interesting peculiarity of this song.

The purpose of a man in going to war was to gain honor and to capture horses. The honor could come to him either from loyalty to his comrades or from conquering the enemy. If a man carried either a wounded friend or a captive on his back, on his return he could place a certain decoration on his tobacco bag or on his blanket. (Fig. 31.) By this sign everyone knew of his act. If two relatives were together on a war party, and one was wounded and deserted by his kinsman, a stranger who saved him was accorded special honor. Thenceforth he was called *Wawo'kiyapi*, 'Helper of the helpless.' To desert a wounded friend on the warpath was considered the greatest perfidy. (See song No. 167.)

The custom of wearing feathers and painting the face, as well as that of "counting coup," probably differs among various tribes or bands. The following was given by the writer's informants as the custom of the Teton Sioux on that reservation. It was said that if a party of warriors attacked the enemy and killed several men, the first warrior who killed an enemy had the right to wear the "black face paint"; thus many of the war songs contain the words "the black face paint I seek." (See songs Nos. 8, 11, 27, 171.) This paint was worn by

FIG. 31. Decoration denoting bravery.

the man in the dances which followed his return from war. Usually it covered only the face, although a man might paint his entire body if he so desired. The second warrior to kill an enemy might "strike the enemy," for doing which he might, on his return, let his hair hang loose, but not paint his face. The time for continuing this practice varied according to the individual, but was usually about a month. If a war party defeated the enemy without loss to themselves, it was permitted to the first four who killed enemies, and also to their women relatives, to use the black face paint. In such an event special songs would be sung, and at any large gathering these four men would appear, the tribe considering them all to be equally entitled to the honor of using the black paint.

If a man had killed an enemy without injury to himself he was entitled to wear a feather erect at the back of his head. If he killed two or more he could wear a corresponding number of feathers, but the enemies must all have been killed in the same battle. If he succeeded in striking an enemy he could wear a feather horizontally at the back of his head. Four men could "count coup" by striking the same enemy. (See an instance of striking an enemy, p. 376.)

At the final camp a returning war party prepared the scalps which they had taken for use in the victory dance.   Eagle Shield said:

They selected a man who had dreamed of a carnivorous animal which attacks human beings, if such a man were in the party.   This man scraped the flesh from the inside of the scalp, and having mixed the fat from it with gunpowder, rubbed it on his face and hands.   He did this because of his dream of an animal that devours human beings.   Then, making a little hoop, he sewed the scalp inside it and fastened it at the end of a pole.[1]

Plate 52 shows a scalp captured by a Sioux warrior.   This seems not to have been placed in a hoop, but dried by stretching with two short sticks, the mark of one being clearly discernible.   The texture of the skin made it possible for this specimen to be fully identified at the United States National Museum as a human scalp. A dance ornament made of human hair (pl. 52) was obtained among the Sioux, but does not represent a custom of that tribe. This ornament is said to have been worn by the Crows in dancing. It was later used by the Mandan and Hidatsa, with whom the Sioux were frequently at war and from whom this article was undoubtedly taken.   When among the Mandan at Fort Berthold the writer was told that ornaments of this sort were frequently seen in the old days, and that they were made, not from scalps of an enemy, but from hair which had been cut or had fallen out and been kept for the making of the ornament.   The strands of hair were secured at intervals with spruce or other gum, and the ornament was fastened to the wearer's head, the hair hanging down his back.

A victorious war party approached the village on its return, bearing the scalps aloft on poles.   Dog Eagle said that he sang this song when he came in sight of the camp on his return from war.   It was used also in the dances which followed.

---

[1] Concerning the usage of the Chippewa in preparing a scarp see Bull. 53, p. 118; of the Menomini, see Skinner, Alanson, War Customs of the Menomini Indians, *Amer. Anthr.*, XIII, No. 2, p. 309, Lancaster, Pa., 1911; and of the Osage, see *Eleventh Rep. Bur. Ethn.*, p. 526.

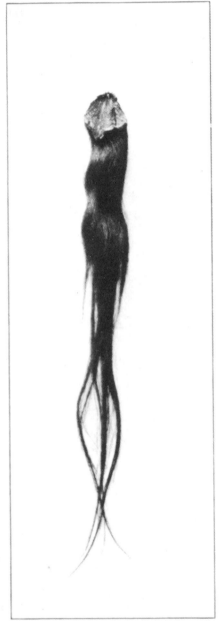

SCALP

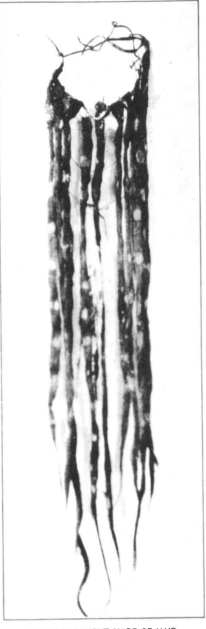

DANCE ORNAMENT MADE OF HAIR

No. 144. "She Stands There Smiling"   (Catalogue No. 658)

Sung by Dog Eagle

Voice ♩ = 69

Drum not recorded

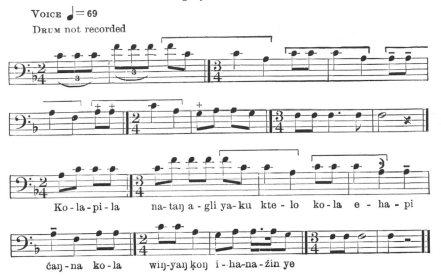

Ko-la-pi-la   na-taŋ a-gli ya-ku kte-lo   ko-la   e-ha-pi

ćaŋ-na   ko-la   wiŋ-yaŋ ḳoŋ   i--ha-na-źin ye

WORDS

kola′pila........................ friends
nataŋ′ [1] agli′ ya′ku ktelo′..... the attacking party will return
kola′............................ friend
eha′pi′ ćaŋ′na.................. whenever you said this
kola′............................ friend
wiŋyaŋ′ ḳoŋ................... that woman
iha′naźiŋ ye................. stands there smiling

Analysis.—This song is rhythmic and lively, yet very simple. The only tones are those of the major triad and second, the tonic triad forming the framework of the melody. The song has a compass of an octave, and the intonation was wavering in all the renditions. Nearly two-thirds of the progressions are downward.

As the warriors approached the village the women came to meet them. War was for the defense of the home and of the helpless, and a man usually gave to the women of his immediate family the scalps which he had taken. (Cf. Bulletin 53, pp. 118–126.) The return of the war party was followed by preparations for the victory dances. Songs in honor of victorious warriors were sung in these dances, and the scalps on the poles were carried by the women. When the celebration was finished it was the custom to take the scalps to the top of the highest butte, where the poles were set upright in the ground and food was placed beside them. Neither the food nor the scalps was ever molested.

---

[1] This word, translated "attacking," refers to the manner in which a returning war party approached the village, coming with a rush as though attacking an enemy.

At subsequent gatherings of the tribe a woman was allowed to carry evidences of her husband's success in war. Such a privilege as this was greatly prized by the women. Plate 53 shows a gathering at Bull Head, S. Dak. In the foreground appears a woman seated, holding a pole on which are the trophies of her husband's success in war, the wisp of horsehair representing a scalp. (See also fig. 29.)

If a young man had been successful on his first war party, it was expected that at the first large gathering after his return he would give away many horses and receive his manhood name, suggestive of his deed of valor. After that he discarded his childhood or boyhood names. If he went on the warpath again and excelled his first achievement, on his return he could be given still another name to correspond with his second victory.

A man who captured horses usually gave some of them to the women of his family. This custom is expressed in the following song:

No. 145. "Horses I Am Bringing"   (Catalogue No. 529)

Sung by Two Shields

Taŋ-ke hi - na - pa   yo   taŋ - ke   hi - na -
pa   yo   śuŋ - ka - wa - kaŋ   a - wa - ku - we
taŋ-ke hi - na-piŋ na waŋ-źi o-yus-pa yo

WORDS

taŋke′............................	older sister
hina′pa yo.....................	come outside
śuŋka′wakaŋ..................	horses
awa′kuwe......................	I am bringing back

WOMAN WITH WAR INSIGNIA OF A RELATIVE

taŋke´........................... older sister
hina´piŋ [1]..................... come outside
na............................. and
waŋźi´ oyus´payo.............. you may catch one of them

Analysis.—This is a particularly lively melody, and is unique in that all the downward progressions are minor thirds and major seconds. These descending intervals comprise more than 76 per cent of the intervals. Concerning the change of tempo, see song No. 5. The song is melodic in structure and contains all the tones of the octave except the second. See plot of this melody on page 419.

The songs of the victory, or scalp, dance were many. These were known as *iwa´kiĉi´pi* 'scalp dance,' the equivalent for "songs" being unexpressed, according to Sioux custom. This term, however, is applied to a large number of songs the words of which do not concern the killing of an enemy, and in this connection the term is translated "praise song." The words of many of the praise songs deal with a man's generosity, and the adaptation of the term *iwa´kiĉi´pi* is evident, the man being praised in the scalp dance for his valor, and the song being used later as a means of securing gifts from him; after he had proven his liberality as well as his valor, another set of words expressing that fact could be composed. In this manner the term *iwa´kiĉi´pi* became applied to a wide range of songs.

The following song, in both words and melody, is a typical *iwa´kiĉi´pi* in the original meaning of the word.

Maka´-peźu´tawiŋ (Earth-medicine Woman) sang this concerning her cousin, Peźu´ta-wakaŋ´ (Holy Medicine).[2] She said that when she was 13 years of age he went in the middle of the winter to "look for Crow horses." Thirty Crows met them, of whom he killed one, bringing home the scalp.[3]

---

[1] This is less imperative than *yo*, which appears in other parts of the song.

[2] As already stated (p. 217) the full form of "Pezu´ta" is Pezi´huta, meaning literally "a root or herb" but commonly translated medicine, it being understood to refer only to preparations of roots and herbs.

[3] Concerning the manner of removing a scalp, see Bull. 53, p. 86.

No. 146. "He Is Returning"   (Catalogue No. 689)

Sung by EARTH-MEDICINE WOMAN

VOICE ♩ = 56

DRUM not recorded

i - yo - ki - pi wa - ćiŋ na   *he*   e Pe - źu - ta - wa -

kaŋ o - wa - ki - ya - ka yuŋ-kaŋ   ke wa - na waŋ-źi - kte   na ku-we

he   *i* Pe - źu - wa-kaŋ *hi ye*   *he*   *a he*

WORDS

oï'yokipi...................... pleasant times
waćiŋ'......................... I wish
na............................. and
Peźu'ta-wakaŋ................. Holy Medicine
owa'kiyaka.................... I told
yuŋ'kaŋ he.................... hence
wana'......................... now
waŋźi'kte..................... he has killed one
na............................. and
kuwe'......................... is returning
Peźu'wakaŋ   (contraction   of
  above name)

Analysis.—This song progresses largely by whole tones, about half the intervals being major seconds. Six minor seconds also occur, forming more than 13 per cent of the intervals. The general character of the melody is similar to that sung by Silent Woman (song No. 149). Like that song, it is minor in tonality, but the latter song has a compass of 13 tones, while this has a range of only 9 tones. See plot of this melody on page 419.

The grief of those whose relatives were killed on the warpath was intense. Many of the women cut gashes in the flesh of the entire body and limbs, and cropped the hair close to their heads. Many

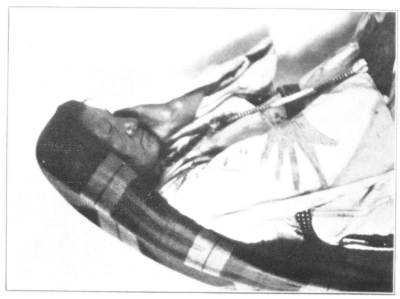

SILENT WOMAN

MRS. HATTIE LAWRENCE

of the men thrust skewers through the flesh on the outside of their legs. It was the custom for them to go around the village circle displaying these signs of mourning, and as they went they sang a song in which they inserted the name of their dead relative, or they might compose an entirely new song in his honor.

The following song was sung by Mrs. Hattie Lawrence (pl. 54), whose Sioux name is Čaŋku'lawiŋ (Road). Mrs. Lawrence has been a student at Carlisle, but retains an unusually clear knowledge of old war customs. She assisted the writer at McLaughlin, S. Dak., by acting as interpreter for part of the material furnished by Jaw, Old Buffalo, and Swift Dog. Mrs. Lawrence said that when she was 10 years of age her cousin, named Kimi'mila-ska (White Butterfly), was killed by the Crows, and that she remembered hearing her aunt sing this song when the war party returned with the news of his death.

No. 147. Song Concerning White Butterfly   (Catalogue No. 686)

Sung by Mrs. Lawrence

WORDS

Toka'la toka'he ḳoŋ.............	that Fox leader
wana'.........................	now
ku śni ye......................	did not return
eha'pi yuŋ'kaŋ.................	you said
Kimi'mila-ska.................	White Butterfly
ḳoŋ he yaka'pi.................	is whom you mean
ićiŋ'keyaś.....................	but then
he'ća ole'yaća he'ćuŋ we......	he went looking for this and it has come to pass

Analysis.—This is a strange melody. The tonality of the song as a whole is minor, the tone most satisfactory to the ear as a keynote, being C sharp, yet the major third occurs six times and the minor third only twice. A wailing effect is given by the prominence of the minor second, which appears 18 times, comprising 46 per cent of the intervals. It will be recalled that this interval is entirely absent from a large majority of these songs. All the tones of the octave except the fourth are found in the melody, the seventh being sharped as an accidental. Two renditions were recorded. In both the accidental was clearly given, but the intonation as a whole was somewhat wavering, owing doubtless in part to the large proportion of semitone progressions.

Mrs. Lawrence said that her aunt lost another son in addition to White Butterfly, and that she sang this song as she went around the village, mourning his death:

No. 148. "He Lies Over There"   (Catalogue No. 687)

Sung by Mrs. Lawrence

WORDS

Huŋ′kpapaya hokśi′la . . . . boys of the Hunkpapa band
ta′ku kuwa′pi caŋ′na . . . . whenever you pursue anything
Tataŋ′ka-haŋ′ska . . . . Long Buffalo

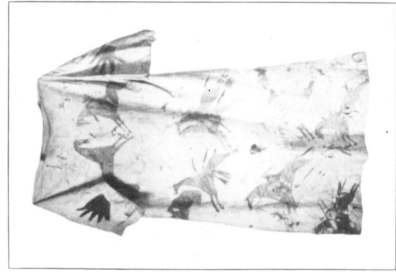

FRONT

BACK

WOMAN'S DRESS DECORATED WITH DRAWINGS

he iyo'taŋ...................... is foremost
waćiŋ' eha'pi yelo'............ you said
eći'yana yuŋ'ka ke'yapi........ he lies over there

Analysis.—In many respects this song is like No. 149. It is in the same key and has the same compass and tone-material. Like song No. 149, it begins with an ascending fifth and contains no rhythmic unit. This song, however, contains fewer progressions, and the singer gave the lowest tone with less distinctness. The minor second occurs with about the same frequency as in the latter, but the proportion of minor thirds is larger in this melody. Both are characteristic of the songs which are sung by women.

The following song was sung by Ini'laoŋ'wiŋ (Silent Woman) concerning her younger brother, who was killed by the Crows. This singer is shown in plate 54 in a pose often assumed by the women singers when they wish to "throw" the voice. Placing the hand beside the mouth, they are able to make the sound carry a long distance. In this picture she is shown wearing the decorated dress (pl. 55), the use of which was permitted only to those whose relatives had been killed in battle. This dress is a type of costume worn in the old days, but the history of the exploits pictured on the garment is lost. It was in a collection of Sioux articles owned by Mrs. James McLaughlin and was photographed with her permission.

No. 149. "Learn the Songs of Victory"   (Catalogue No. 685)

Sung by SILENT WOMAN

VOICE ♩ = 116

DRUM not recorded

Ma - to - oŋ - źiŋ - ća   he   he - yiŋ

na   ha   i - ya - ye   he   he   e   Kaŋ -

ġi   wi - ća - śa   ya   o - wa - le   kte - lo   o

he - yiŋ   na   ha   i - ya - ye   -ye   a   he   he   taŋ -

ke   lo - waŋ - pi   kiŋ   oŋ - spe   i - ći - ći - ya - yo

WORDS

Mato'-onźin'ća................	Bobtail Bear (man's name)
he heyin'....................	said this
na..........................	and
iya'ye......................	went away, never to return—
Kaŋġi' wića'śa...............	"[the] Crow Indians

owa'le ktelo'.................... I will seek"
heyiŋ'......................... he said
na............................ and
iya'ye he..................... went away, never to return—
taŋke'........................ "older sister
lowaŋ'pi kiŋ.................. the songs [in honor of warriors who return
　　　　　　　　　　　　　　　victorious]
oŋspe' iċi'ċiya yo............. you must learn"

Analysis.—This song has a compass of 13 tones, both the highest and lowest tones being clearly given. Like song No. 147, this melody abounds in semitone progressions, which give a peculiar, wailing effect. About 13 per cent of the progressions are semitones, an interval which is entirely absent from a large majority of these songs. The minor third constitutes about 24 per cent of the intervals. An ascent of 13 tones is accomplished in three measures with the introduction of the words. The intonation was good throughout the song.

The following song was sung in honor of one of the prominent warriors of the tribe:

No. 150. Song in Honor of Oni'haŋ　　(Catalogue No. 460)

Sung by ŚIYA'KA

VOICE ♩ = 76
DRUM not recorded

ni - *hi* - haŋ　*he e*　i - ki - ċi - ze　ḳoŋ　wa - na　he -

na - he - ċa　ye

WORDS

Oni'haŋ........................ Oni'haŋ (man's name, meaning "excited")
iki'ċize ḳoŋ.................... that warrior
wana'......................... now
hena'heċa ye.................. is no more

Analysis.—This is a rather simple melody on the second five-toned scale with the minor third as one-third of the intervals. The rhythmic unit is brief but forms the basis of the rhythm of the entire song. The compass of 11 tones is accomplished in two progressions with the introduction of the words of the song.

The four following songs might be called "love songs connected with war." [1] It was said that in the old days all the love songs were associated with a man's qualification to wed, this being determined by his success in war or in the buffalo hunt. (See duplication of song No. 133.) No narratives concerning these songs were secured.

Two renditions of the following song were recorded, one by Two Shields and the other by Śiya′ka. This duplication, which was unintentional, gives an opportunity for comparison, as Two Shields and Śiya′ka were equally good singers, and neither knew that the other sang the song. (See song No. 133.) The words are slightly different but express the same idea. It is not unusual for the words of a song to differ in this manner when the song is sung by another singer. Both records are transcribed, and it will be seen that the melody progressions are the same in both.

No. 151. "You May Go on the Warpath" (Catalogue No. 531)

Sung by Two Shields

VOICE ♩ = 92
DRUM ♩ = 92
Drum-rhythm similar to No. 5

Ho - we   zu - ya   ya - ye   ho - we   zu - ya   ya - ye

ho - we   zu - ya   ya - ye   to - kśa   ća - źe   na - ći -

hoŋ kiŋ-haŋ hiŋ-gna   ći-yiŋ kte a

WORDS

ho′ we.......................... you may
zuya′ ya′ye...................... go on the warpath
to′kśa........................... when

---

[1] For comparatively modern love songs, see Nos. 232–234.

čaže′	your name
nači′hoŋ	I hear [announced among the victors]
kiŋhaŋ′	then
hiŋgna′ čiyiŋ′ kte	I will marry you

Analysis.— This melody contains the tones of the fourth five-toned scale and has a compass of an octave, extending from the dominant above the tonic to the dominant below the tonic. Of the progressions 61 per cent are major seconds, and about one-fourth are major thirds. The wider intervals comprise two intervals of a fourth and one ascending fifth. In structure the song is melodic. It is a lively melody and particularly rhythmic, though the rhythmic unit is found only twice.

Duplication of No. 151. "When You Return"

Sung by ŚIYA′KA

VOICE ♩ = 100
DRUM ♩ = 100
Drum-rhythm similar to No. 5

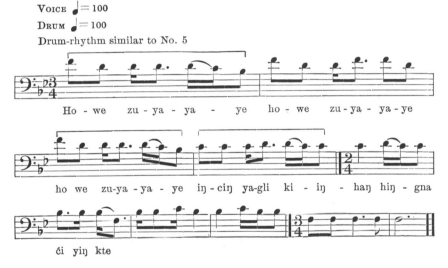

WORDS

ho we	you may
zuya′ yaye	go on the warpath
iŋciŋ′	when
yagli′ kiŋhaŋ′	you return
hiŋgna′ čiyiŋ′ kte	I will marry you

Analysis.—A comparison of the rhythm of this and the rendition of the same song by Two Shields (No. 151) is of special interest. It will be seen that the same rhythmic unit occurs in both renditions, though not always on the same phrase of the song.

The words of the following song tell its story. Doubtless it is a song which was often heard in the old days, when many who went forth with the war parties did not return.

No. 152. "I Look for Him in Vain"   (Catalogue No. 530

Sung by Two Shields

Voice ♩ = 92

Drum not recorded

Ko - ŝka - la - ka kiŋ   a - hi - ya-ya ćaŋ - na

a - wa - ton-waŋ   he - lo   to - haŋ - ni

a - ke i - ya-ya huŋ-ŝe   ta-ku ćan-ze-ma - ye

WORDS

koŝka′ laka kiŋ ahi′yaya ćaŋ′na. as the young men go by
awa′tonwaŋ helo′. . . . . I was looking for him
to′haŋ ni ake′. . . . . it surprises me anew
iya′ya huŋŝe′. . . . . that he has gone
ta′ku. . . . . (it is) something
ćaŋ ze′maye. . . . . to which I can not be reconciled

Analysis.—The intonation throughout the renditions of this song was wavering, yet the rapid tones in the sixth measure were clear and different from a *vibrato*. The song is melodic in form and begins with an ascending fifth; this is somewhat unusual. The tones are those of the second five-toned scale, and about two-thirds of the progressions are downward. No rhythmic unit appears, but the song as a whole is especially rhythmic in character.

Like the preceding song, this seems to require no explanation other than that contained in the words of the song. It represents the life of the camp, the everyday life of Indian women.

No. 153. "He Is Again Gone on the Warpath" (Catalogue No. 591)

Sung by SWIFT DOG

WORDS

he	the one
hiŋgna′ wayiŋ′ kte ćuŋ	I was going to marry
he	is
ake′	again
iya′yelo′	gone (on the warpath)
he miye′ makiŋ′na he′yahe lo	it was I whom she meant by saying this

Analysis.—This song is based on the fourth five-toned scale, has a range of nine tones, and is melodic in structure. Twenty-eight progressions are downward and 21 are upward, these numbers being more nearly equal than in most of the songs under analysis. The tones transcribed as A natural and A sharp were clearly distinguished, the tone transcribed as A sharp being even sung a trifle above the proper pitch. The song contains a change of tempo. (See song No. 5.)

No. 154. "You Should Give Up the Warpath"   (Catalogue No. 576)

Sung by SHOOTER

VOICE ♩ = 116
DRUM ♩ = 116
Drum-rhythm similar to No. 5

Zu - ya - pi kiŋ he a-yuś-

taŋ na o - waŋ - źi - la hi yaŋ-ke wa - ćiŋ na

a -.taŋ-se - la he - ćel yaŋ-ka na

WORDS

zuya′pi kiŋ he	going on the warpath
ayuś′taŋ	you should give up
na	and
owaŋ′źila	(to) settle
yaŋ′ke	down
waćiŋ′	you should desire
na	and
ataŋ′sela	stop
hećel′ yaŋ′ka na	for good

Analysis.—This song is minor in tonality, 35 per cent of the intervals being minor thirds. The compass is 13 tones, and all the tones of the octave except the seventh are found in the melody. The rhythm is interesting, but contains no repeated phrase. The song was recorded on two occasions, several renditions being recorded each time. The differences are only in the number of repetitions of the final tone, or occasionally in the length of unimportant tones.

RED FOX

PERSONAL NARRATIVE BY RED FOX

Red Fox (Tokala-lu'ta), plate 56, gave the following narrative, telling how he entered on the career of a warrior:

My mother was a good and beautiful woman. She wore her hair in long braids, and I remember how she looked as she said, "If my son ever goes on the warpath I shall take a lariat and hang myself." I was a very little boy, and it made a great impression on me, as my mother intended it should do. Of course, she did not really mean it, but she did not want me to run away and go with a war party. Yet that is exactly what I did.

One day when I was about 12 years old I took my bow and arrows and went to shoot birds. The arrows were the blunt arrows that children used. I noticed there were a number of men going away from the village, gaily dressed, and followed by little boys carrying packs. I said to another little boy, "Where are they going?" He replied, "They are going north on the warpath." This was the first time I ever saw a war party. The other little boy said, "They are our friends who are carrying those packs; let us go, too." So we followed the war party. We did not go home nor take any extra moccasins; we had only the little calfskin robes we wore and the blunt arrows with which we were going to kill birds, but we overtook the war party and went with them. Of course the boys who had started with the warriors were well supplied with clothing and provisions.

In every war expedition there is an advance party, which precedes the main body of men. My father was one of the warriors in this company, and I afterward learned that my cousin Hairy Chin was in the advance party. We had gone a long distance before any of the older members of the party saw me. Then one of them called to my father and said, "here is your boy." My father told me to sit down beside him and questioned me, saying, "Did you have permission from your mother?" I said, "No; we were hunting birds and we just came along to join you." He said, "You had better camp with the advance party when we overtake them; you will have better food and bed than if you stay with us." I learned that the advance party always has a good camp, while the others sleep as best they can. The day we left home the rear party killed a buffalo, and they shared the meat with the advance party who were waiting for them on a butte.

When my cousin saw me he came over and said, "Why did you come, brother-in-law?"[1] I replied, "We were hunting birds." He said, "Come with me." So he took me to his camp. When we entered all the men said, "What a little boy to go on the warpath!" I leaned over my dish and began to cut and eat my meat. While I was eating I heard the men say, "There is some one coming on horseback, singing." The man came nearer and we could hear him saying, "The news is flung about the camp that a little boy ran away with the war party, and that his mother took a lariat and hung herself." Then I began to cry, and I said, "That must be my mother; she said that she would do that if I ever ran away with a war party."

One man said: "They are doing that to make your heart strong. They are only fooling you. You will be fooled many times while you are on the warpath." But that did not make any difference. I thought of my mother, and I kept on crying.

After 10 days' journey we came on a previous war party of six Sioux, all of whom had been killed by the Crows. I remember the names of only four; they were Mato'-ina'pa (Bear Appears), Kaŋġi'-śuŋka' (Crow Dog), Ma'za-ska (White Metal), and E'gna-iŋ'yaŋke (Runs Amidst). When I saw the dead bodies lying there with the heads scalped, I asked, "What are these?" The reply was, "These are our friends who went on the warpath." I said, "By whom were they killed?" The reply was,

---

[1 A term used in familiar speech without necessarily implying relationship.]

"By our enemies." I asked, "What will you do with these bodies?" The men replied, "We will wrap them up and take them home with us." Then I exclaimed, "When I grow up I will have my revenge, and I will slay the Indians who killed my people." So I became a warrior.

Our expedition was absent from the village 20 days. My mother did not say a word when I came back. She did not reprove me nor tell me how anxious she had been. While the men were away on the warpath the women made moccasins. While I was gone my mother went on making moccasins. When I returned she gave me the moccasins, and I wore them, but I could scarcely move, I was so closely watched. For a long time, whenever I left the lodge she asked me where I was going.

Continuing his narrative, Red Fox said:

I went on 45 war parties. I even followed the west branch of the Missouri River to the place where the snow never melts on the mountains. I will tell you of the war party on which I first killed an enemy. On this expedition I rode a beautiful white horse with brown ears. Just before we started there was a Sun dance in the village, and the leaders said, "If anyone wants to be successful in war let him come and join the Sun dance." There were a hundred men standing abreast in the circle. We were asked "What offer will you make to the great sun shining over your head? Will you give him tobacco? Will you give him your flesh and blood?" When the Intercessor came to me and asked these questions, I said in reply, "I will give my flesh and blood that I may conquer my enemies." I fulfilled this vow at a Sun dance when I returned victorious from war. My arms were cut 7 times below the elbow and 2 times above the elbow, making 18 wounds in all. [Compare description on p. 91.]

After making my Sun-dance vow, I started on the warpath. We had traveled five days and had reached the end of the Missouri River, when the scouts said, "The Crow Indians are having a great buffalo hunt." We went where they directed and saw three Crows: one had a gun, one had a bow and arrows, and the third had a revolver. The first two pointed their weapons at us, and the third flourished his revolver, but we were able to go up to them and strike each of them with a coup stick while they were alive. We killed those three and also two more. Then we went farther and saw another Crow party, but they did not see us. They went into the timber, made a fire, and cooked some meat. After a time one of them came out and pointed his gun all around. I rode up and hit him with a club. My Sun-dance vow made me fearless. This was the fourth coup I counted on that expedition. We watched for the man and afterward killed him. From there we went on until we came to a village of the Blackfeet. The borders of the river were heavily timbered, and the Blackfeet were camped there. This was beyond the country of the Crows. When in sight of the Blackfoot village I put on my war bonnet, mounted my white horse, and ran toward the village. I charged them and got about 50 horses from the center of their herd. They shot and shot at me, but did not hit me.

On the second night of our homeward journey we camped at a place called Bear Butte.[1] Some of our horses were tired out and when the rest of the war party went on their way, I stayed behind, having two young men with me. We traveled more slowly than the rest, and as we were going along the side of a foothill, I saw four Crow warriors coming toward us. I said to the young men: "Come near and stand by me. Four warriors are coming." The young men said, "Let us run and hide." I said: "Wakaŋ'taŋka has but one path. No matter how or where you die you must go by that path. Let us stand together and fight."

[1 There were said to be two or more places called Bear Butte. One of these, situated in Montana, and probably referred to in this song, was said to be higher than the one in South Dakota, probably referred to in song No. 82, p. 256.]

I had a gun and two revolvers, one of the young mèn had a quiver of arrows, and the other had a double-barreled gun.   I sang my death song[1] for I felt sure that I was soon to die.   I sang as I pointed my gun.   I said to my companions, "I will see which of the four has a gun, and I will fire at him, then our numbers will be even."   They all said, *ho*.   There was an immense rock in front of us, and in a crack of the rock grew a cherry tree.   It was through this crack that I watched the warriors.   One had his hair combed high and carried a gun; the others had bows and arrows, and as they came nearer I saw that one of them was only a boy.   I said to my companions: "Now work and be brave. We have only three to fight, as one of them is a boy."   When they came opposite the crack in the rock I fired, but my gun snapped and did not go off.   A branch of the cherry tree interfered with it.   The man with the gun saw me and aimed at me, but I grabbed his arm so he could not fire.   My companions chased the others, and I fought hand to hand with the man for an hour.   Then I called my companions; they succeeded in taking the gun from the man, and I had the satisfaction of killing him.

The boy ran away, but my companions brought back the two Crows, whom they had taken captive.   One of them said: "We are Crow Indians.   We want to live. We give you our bodies, and we give you the right to wear the feathers, only let us go."   So we gave them back their lives.   Because of that act I was appointed a chief, for it was considered a brave deed to spare the lives of two enemies.

Red Fox then recorded the song which he said that he sang when he fired at the Crow. The words are those of a boy who wishes to go on the warpath, but is opposed by older brothers. He is divided between obedience and ambition, and, while he shows no sign of yielding, he finds his difficulties increased by this opposition. This recalls the story of Red Fox's first war expedition, when he was a boy.

[1 A song sung under these circumstances indicated that the man realized the probability of death and was ready to meet it.   Red Fox's song is given as No. 155.]

No. 155. Song of the Warpath   (Catalogue No. 676)

Sung by RED FOX

Zu-ya   wa-u kte ćoŋ he-haŋ

ći - ye   he ye - lo   a - wi - ća - u - pi kte ka-wiŋḣ-wa-ćiŋ yo

ći - ye   he - ya   tka   o   ta-moŋ - ka śni - ye - lo *he*

WORDS

zuya′............................. on the warpath
waü′ kte ćoŋ.................... I was coming
hehaŋ′........................... then
ćiye′............................. older brothers
he yelo′......................... said
awi′ćaüpi kte.................. if they chase you
kawiŋḣ′waćiŋ yo.............. try to turn back
ćiye′............................. older brothers
heya′............................. said
tka.............................. hence
tamoŋ′ka śni yelo′............. I realize difficulties

Analysis.—This song contains only the tones of the major triad, a tone material which is found in only 5 Chippewa songs in a series of 340. This is its only occurrence in this series. Three-fourths of the intervals are thirds, one-half being minor thirds, and a fourth major thirds. The song has a compass of an octave, extending from the dominant above to the dominant below the tonic. In the latter part of the song the division of the final count in the rhythmic unit is changed to conform to the words. The song contains no change of time. Compare analysis of Song No. 134.

Personal Narrative by Eagle Shield

An individual war expedition was described by Eagle Shield, Mrs. Jas. McLaughlin acting as interpreter. Eagle Shield said:

Many years ago, in the middle of the winter, I wanted to get up a war party, so I cooked food and invited some men to a feast. While they were eating I said, "I want to go somewhere; that is why I invited you here." They asked where I wished to go, and I replied, "On the warpath." "Why do you go on the warpath?" they asked; and I answered: "It is winter. The Crows do not tie their horses so near the tipis as in summer, so we can get them more easily. We will ask the women to make moccasins for us all day tomorrow, and we will start in the evening."

The next day, toward evening, 3 men came to my lodge, then more came until there were 16 men, though I had asked only 10. We sat in a circle and smoked in my lodge until the village was asleep. Then we started away. The snow was deep, and walking was slow and difficult. At our first camp we cut low plum trees and made a bed of branches in the snow. As we journeyed we sometimes saw a herd of buffalo. Then we killed one for food, cooking the meat on pointed sticks. We used the hide for a bed, but left it when we went on our way.

After camping the tenth night I said, "Two of us will go ahead and see if we can see the enemy's village." A third man asked to go with us, and early the next morning we started. We had traveled some distance when my companion said, "Let us climb that butte and look over." We climbed the butte, and looking over the top, we saw a very large Crow settlement, and beyond the tipis was a herd of horses like a cloud. My companion said, "Let us take two horses and go back." But I replied: "No. The Crows will follow us, and as we will be the only ones on horseback the others will be killed."

We at once turned back toward our camp, traveling a little way at a dogtrot, then stopping to rest, and then taking up the dogtrot again. It was just daybreak when we approached the camp. I gave the wolf howl by which a war party announces its return, and I heard our friends cry: "The scouts are coming back. The scouts are coming back. Come and meet them."

The people stood in a line to receive us. In front of them a stick was placed upright in the ground, and I knocked down this stick as a guaranty that I would tell the truth. [See p. 441.] My companions joined me in the long-drawn wolf howl. After I had knocked down the stick the people all sat down. Then a man filled a pipe, offered it to the cardinal points, to the sky, and to the earth, and gave it to me and my companion. He did this four times, and then we smoked awhile together.

At length the man who had offered the pipe asked: "What have you done? Have you looked across the prairie or climbed a butte? Did you see a four-legged animal [meaning a wolf]? Do not deceive me, but tell the truth."

I said: "I went on a butte, looked over and saw nothing. Then I went farther, and what did I see but buffalo coming toward me. I looked again, and it was a Crow village which I saw. There were many horses. I beg that you give us something to eat, for we must start at once and travel far. We must reach there at night and take the horses in the dark."

They hastened and brought us food. We kept our blankets tied down as we ate and only waited to put on dry moccasins. As we journeyed toward the Crow village we hung food in trees, so that we would find it on our return. We could see our tracks in the snow when we started, and we came in sight of the Crow village at daybreak. All that day we stayed on the butte. We had no food that day. When night came we went in and out of a creek, and so reached a second butte, from which we had a full view of the Crow camp. The smoke was thick above the tipis. We put on fresh moccasins and tied them very firmly. We fastened our belts tight and arranged our buffalo-hair lariats so they could be let out most freely. As we started for the Crow camp I said: "Don't take too many horses, or they will make a wide track in the snow and we shall be followed. Whoever first reaches the trees where the food is stored must wait for the others."

Although the snow was deep we secured 21 horses. I had 6 horses and no colts, so I could travel rapidly. The man with me rode 1 horse and led 4. I heard a sound, and looking back, I saw a mule following us. The mule came up and joined us, as he had probably been raised with the horses. Mules were highly valued by the Sioux, and I claimed this mule as mine.

A few of our men reached the meeting place before I and my companion arrived. We waited for the rest, but two men did not come. We fastened our moccasins and were about to go back for them when they came in sight. "Hurry!" they cried; there is excitement in the Crow camp. They have seen us and are jumping on their horses." Some of us were eating when the alarm came, but we made ready to start at once. Four went ahead so the horses would follow, and the rest of us drove the herd. The cold was intense. We traveled all that night, and I often went back to see if we were being pursued. The next morning we made a fire and put on dry moccasins. We were afraid that if we traveled slowly we would be caught and killed, so we hastened. That day we let the horses trot awhile and then walk awhile, but we did not dare stop to rest. The second night a man who had been on the lookout said, "The Crows are after us; they are right on our trail."

I said: "We are not cowards. We must stand our ground and not run away." My companions cried, "What shall we do?" I said, "We will go to that little rough ravine and take the horses down there." It was a "draw" in the prairie, and at the end of it there were some great rocks. It was a moonlight night, and bright as day. We got the horses into the ravine and could hear the voices of the Crows. Evidently there were many of them. I made up my mind that we had a hard time before us, but we had good guns and plenty of bullets. I said: "We will crawl up on top of the ridge of land and lie flat in a line, far apart. We can see them on the prairie, and as soon as they are in range we will fire." We threw off our blankets and were clad only in our calf-skin shirts. So we lay in a row watching for the Crows. I said, "Be ready with your guns."

There was a great crowd of the Crows. They were following the horses' tracks, and when they came near us we sprang up, yelled, and fired at random. The Crows turned and ran, leaving one man dead whose horse had run away, and one horse whose rider was going on foot. We all got together and ran a little way after them, firing as fast as we could reload our guns. We shot from above their heads so they could not tell where to shoot at us, and only once in awhile they shot in our direction. I said to my companions: "The Crows are too many for us. If we go out on the prairie to run away they will see how few of us there are. We will keep on shooting and stay out of sight. Then they will think there are a great many of us."

We could see the Crows. They were still there, like a big burned spot on the prairie. Once in awhile one of our men went toward them and shouted: "Come and fight. It is good to fight." [Cf. song No. 157.] This continued all day, and the Crows thought there were a great many of us because we called them to come back and fight. At last our scouts reported that the Crows had given up and gone away. I said, "Hurry; let us start for home." We rode our fastest horses, drove the herd before us, and went as fast as we could across the prairie. We camped three nights before we reached home with our horses.

The Sioux occasionally sent a man ahead of a returning war party, who gave a false report to the village. Thus when an old man came forward to receive his report, the man might say, "All were killed except me." Then would follow great wailing on the

ONE BUFFALO

ONE FEATHER

HEADDRESS OF WOLF HIDE

part of those who were easily deceived, but most of the people understood the trick. The war party came immediately after, so the people were not left long in uncertainty.

On the expedition of which I have told you my brother-in-law was the one to make the report, and he said, "Eagle Shield was the very first one killed."

I suspected that he would do this, so I said to my companions, "Hurry, before my friends harm themselves with grief." So we fired guns, whipped up our horses, and came dashing into the village with not even one man wounded, and driving before us a fine herd of captured horses.

Eagle Shield said that on one of his war expeditions he and his companions were five days without food, except a few roots which they gathered. He said, further, "We were all so very *sleepy.*" When they secured food they ate only a little at a time, and even that caused them great distress.

The singer of the following group of songs is Wi'yaka-waŋźi'la (One Feather), plate 57, well known as one of the old warriors of the Standing Rock Reservation. He was 57 years old when giving these songs in 1913. On the warpath in the old days he wore on his head the skin of a wolf (pl. 58). Attention is called to the upright feathers on the head of the wolf, which were said to resemble the ears of the animal. A man lying in the grass on a rise of ground could lift his head to spy the enemy, and the feathers would look like the ears of a prowling wolf. The quills are very light, and the feathers tremble with every motion of the wearer.

The narrative concerning the first song of the group is as follows: When One Feather was 18 years of age he went with a war party against the Crows. It was winter, and they traveled as far as the Rocky Mountains. There were 22 Sioux in the party, three of whom were sent in advance as scouts. He was one of these scouts, and when coming near the Crow country, he saw a Crow butchering a buffalo. Pursuing the man, he killed him close to the Crow camp. One Feather said that he sang the following song as he ran back to his comrades after killing the Crow. It was said to be a dancing song of the Miwa'tani society. (See p. 326.)

No. 156. "May I Be There"   (Catalogue No. 623)

Sung by ONE FEATHER

WORDS

kola'pila...................... friends
ta'ku yaku'wapi kiŋhaŋ'....... whenever you pursue anything (see p. 349,
                              footnote 2)
kola'........................ friend
hema'tu nuŋwe'.............. may I be there

Analysis.—This melody has a compass of an octave and contains all the tones of the octave except the sixth and seventh. The progression is principally by whole tones, about 60 per cent of the intervals being major seconds. A change of time occurs with the introduction of the words. (See song No. 5.) The song is rhythmic throughout, but the rhythmic unit is found only in the first part of the melody.

The following song refers to the fire which a war party sometimes kindled on the prairie as a signal of defiance to the enemy:

No. 157. "A Prairie Fire"   (Catalogue No. 624)

Sung by ONE FEATHER

na wa - ye ćiŋ - haŋ   wi - i - ħa - kta śi - ća waŋ -la - ka   so   e - ća

he mi-ye he-ća-moŋ we

WORDS

ona'	a prairie fire
wa'ye	I started
ćiŋhaŋ'	when
wi'iħakta śića'	you were intent on women and hindered by them
waŋla'ka so	did you see it?
eća' he	well
miye'	it was I
he'ćamoŋ we	who did it

Analysis.—This melody is an example of interval formation rather than of key relationship of tones. All the tones of the octave are present in the song, which is transcribed and analyzed in the key of D major, though D is not entirely satisfactory as a keynote. The progressions are chiefly by small intervals, about 54 per cent of the intervals being minor thirds and 36 per cent major seconds. The other intervals are an ascending ninth and four fourths. The triad of A major is prominent in the melody. It is interesting to compare this with songs Nos. 108 and 166, in which the final interval is also a descending fourth. These songs are classified as "irregular."

The death of a brave man is commemorated in the next song. His name was Sitting Crow (Kaŋġi' iyo'take), a cousin of One Feather, who was in the war party. Many Crows were killed in the fight, but even that fact did not make the Sioux happy. They all were sad because they had to leave Sitting Crow where he fell. A lament for a warrior of this name occurs in the chapter on the Sun dance (see song No. 23). It is possible that both songs refer to the same man. This melody is a praise song of the Kaŋġi'yuha society, as Sitting Crow was a member of that organization.

No. 158. Song Concerning Sitting Crow   (Catalogue No. 625)

Sung by ONE FEATHER

VOICE ♩ = 76
DRUM not recorded

Ko - la Kaŋ-ġi - i - yo- ta-ke ko - la   ku - śni

ye - lo

WORDS

kola'............................. friends
Kaŋġi'-iyo'take................ Sitting Crow
kola'............................. friends
ku'śni yelo'.................... returned not

Analysis.—Three renditions of this song were recorded, in all of which the intonation was wavering. The song has a compass of 12 tones, is melodic in structure, and contains the tones of the second five-toned scale. Only four intervals larger than a minor third are found in the melody, a fact which may account in part for the uncertainty of intonation, the Indian usually finding it difficult to sing a long succession of small intervals with correctness. The total number of minor thirds and major seconds in this song is 32.

One Feather said the following song was sung in connection with a fight with the Assiniboin, in which he took part. The "spotted horses," strongly mottled with black and white, were greatly prized by the Sioux, and a few of these are seen among them at the present time.

No. 159. "A Spotted Horse"   (Catalogue No. 626)

Sung by ONE FEATHER

VOICE ♩ = 96
DRUM not recorded

Ko - la -pi - la

hi - ya - ya - pi - ye   yo   śuŋ - gle - śka   ċa   hi - yo

wa - u   we

WORDS [1]

kola′pila	....	friends
hiya′yapiye yo	....	come with me
śuŋgle′śka	....	a spotted horse
ċa	....	it is
hiyo′ waü′ we	....	I am coming after

Analysis.—This is a pleasing rhythmic melody on the fourth five-toned scale. The song is based on the tonic triad, but the second is twice accented, classifying the song as melodic with harmonic framework. The eighth rest in the third measure from the close was clearly given in the three renditions. The intonation was good on all except the highest tones. As frequently occurs in songs on the fourth five-toned scale, the minor third is prominent, in this instance forming one-third of the number of intervals. An ascending minor sixth is found in the early part of the melody. It is interesting to note that the minor sixth appears much oftener than the major sixth in the Sioux songs under analysis. (See Tables 11, 12, pp. 16, 17.)

---

[1] The first part of this song is addressed to friends, the remainder to the enemy.

No. 160. "Owls Hoot At Me"   (Catalogue No. 627)

Sung by ONE FEATHER

VOICE ♩ = 96

DRUM not recorded

WORDS[1]

(*First rendition*)

hiŋhaŋ′	owls
ama′ hotoŋ′ po	hoot at me (see p. 180, footnote)
hiŋhaŋ′	owls
ama′ hotoŋ′ po	hoot at me
he′ća	that is what
nahoŋ′ waöŋ′ welo	I hear in my life

(*Second rendition*)

śuŋ′ka	wolves
ama′ hopiye	howl at me
śuŋ′ka	wolves
ama′ hopiye	howl at me
he′ća	that is what
nahoŋ′ waöŋ′ welo	I hear in my life

Analysis.—This melody progresses chiefly by whole tones, 62 per cent of the intervals being major seconds. The minor third is also prominent, constituting about 22 per cent of the intervals. The song

---

[1] The idea of the song is, "owls may hoot and wolves howl at me. To these I am accustomed in all my life."

JAW

contains all the tones of the octave except the second and has a compass of an octave. The second count of the rhythmic unit is divided in three different ways, giving variety to the rhythm of the song as a whole. Three renditions were recorded, which are identical.

Songs Accompanied by Native Drawings

Four men contributed their drawings to this section of the work. Their names are Jaw, Eagle Shield, Swift Dog (Suŋ'ka-lu'zahaŋ), and Old Buffalo. The work of each man has certain characteristics apart from the peculiar outlines of his sketches of men or horses. Thus in the drawings of Jaw, most of the incidents concern the capture of horses and the numbers of the enemy are not shown, while in those of Eagle Shield the latter feature is clearly indicated, the work including more detail than the drawings of any other native artist except perhaps Old Buffalo. Several rescues are shown in Eagle Shield's work and none in that of any others. The coup stick appears frequently in Swift Dog's drawings, but in none of the others.

There is a difference in the part of the sheet on which the drawing "begins." This is determined by the narrative, as an observer would not know which sketch the artist regarded as the opening of the series.

The manner of delineating the Crows and the Assiniboin is similar in all the drawings, they being distinguished by the upright hair on top of the head.

The man who gave the material in the next succeeding pages is commonly known as Jaw (Ćehu'pa), plate 59, a name which he received from a white brother-in-law. His childhood name was Ma'za-ho'waśte (Loud-sounding Metal), and at the age of 17 he was given the name of Oki'ćize-ta'wa (His Battle), which is his true name at the present time. He was given this name after taking part in a fight for the first time. He had been out with a war party once before and had stolen horses, but this was his first experience in actual warfare. On being asked his connection in the tribe, he replied: "I am of two bands. My mother was a Gi'gilaś'ka, a division of the Hunkpa'pa band, and my father was a Sans Arc, of the Te'toŋwaŋ." He said that he was 63 years of age at that time (1913), and when asked the year of his birth, he said that he was born in the year known as *Ke woyu'spa ta wani'yetu*, 'winter that Turtle Catcher died.' On consulting the picture calendar (see p. 69) this year was found to be 1850.

As a further test of his memory Jaw was asked to name several succeeding years of the picture calendar of the Standing Rock Sioux. He did this with accuracy except for a different naming of one year. On reaching the name of his seventh year he added, "that was the year I killed the bird." In explanation of this he said that the people were moving camp and he was with his grandmother, who had taken care of him since his infancy, when his mother died. He said, "I killed the bird and took it to my grandmother." (See pl. 60, *B.*) "If I killed many she would carry them all, and when we camped at night she would eat my hunting, and I would eat some too." He said that his father first called him Ma′za-ho′waśte when he killed the bird. His name before that time is not recorded.

In his young manhood Jaw was known especially for his success in stealing horses from the enemy. In addition to his narratives of expeditions for this purpose he gave general information concerning war customs. Among other things he recalled that in the old days each warrior carried his own wooden bowl (pl. 61), hung by a cord from his belt. It is said that "A man on the warpath always ate and drank from his own dish. When he returned home the dish was put away with other articles which he used on the warpath and sweet grass was put with it." [1]

Jaw's manner of painting himself and his horse when going on the warpath was as follows: He painted a red crescent over his mouth, the points of the crescent extending upward halfway to his cheek-bones. His hands were painted red from the wrists and his feet from the ankles. A large crescent like that on his face was painted on his horse's chest, and a smaller one on the animal's left hip, while the entire end of the horse's nose was painted yellow. If a horse succeeded in some difficult undertaking it was his custom to reward the animal by putting a feather in its mane or tail, or a band of red list-cloth around its neck. (See p. 298.)

Jaw had two medicine bags containing the same 'medicine,' one for his horse and one for himself. The horse's medicine bag was tied to the bit of its bridle. He said that if his horse "had a headache" he chewed a certain herb and put it into the horse's mouth, where-upon the trouble was relieved at once. This was probably the herb numbered 4 in the component parts of his war 'medicine.' Jaw said that when going to steal horses he often went to windward of them and chewed this herb, at which the horses at once "pricked up their ears," being attracted by it.

When on the warpath, Jaw carried a leather pouch containing vermilion paint mixed with grease, for applying to his face and body. This pouch is shown in plate 61, together with Jaw's war whistle and a warrior's bowl. On his shoulder he wore a wolf skin, to the nose of which was tied his war whistle [2] and to this whistle was

---

[1] Regulations for protecting the health of a Chippewa war party are given in Bull. 53, p. 85.

[2] The dimensions and description of this whistle are the same as those of the undecorated Sun-dance whistle illustrated on p. 98 except that the sound hole in this whistle bears the marks of having been cut with a saw. Mr. E. H. Hawley of the U. S. National Museum states this to be the first instance of such cutting which has come under his observation.

A. THE HUNT (DRAWING BY JAW)

B. SCENES FROM JAW'S CHILDHOOD (DRAWING BY HIMSELF)

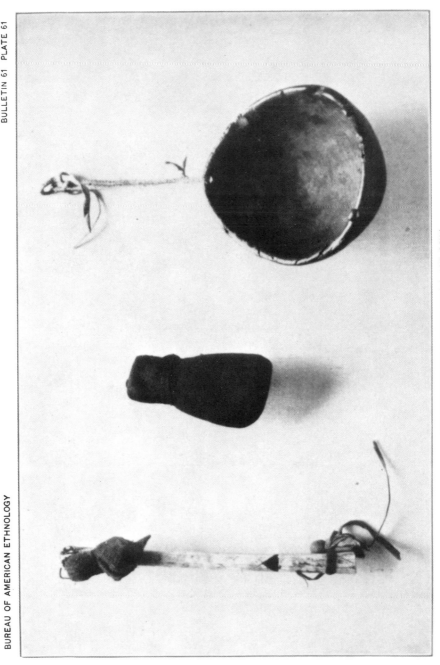

WARRIOR'S WHISTLE, PAINT POUCH, AND BOWL

INCIDENT IN THE LIFE OF JAW (DRAWING BY HIMSELF)

fastened the medicine bag, which he tied to his horse's bridle when
on the warpath. According to Jaw, these medicine bags contained
a mixture of four herbs, dried and powdered. It was said that they
could be used singly, as indicated, or in combination, as in his war
medicine, which had power as a charm in addition to its efficacy as
a curative agency. He secured fresh specimens of the herbs, which
were identified as follows:

(1) *Echinacea angustifolia* DC. (nigger head). Jaw said: "The
root of this plant when dried is good for toothache. The person
should chew it. The top also is good, but not so strong."

(2) *Cheirinia aspera* (DC.) Britton (western wall flower). This
was said to be "bitter and good for stomach trouble. The whole
plant is dried and chewed, or a tea may be made if preferred."

(3) *Erigeron pumilus* Nutt. (daisy). A decoction of this was used
for rheumatism and lameness, and it was used also for disorders of the
stomach.

(4) *Laciniaria punctata* (Hook.) Kuntze (blazing star). A decoction of this was given to persons with pain in the heart, the entire
plant being used for this purpose. The root was also dried and powdered. This medicine, either in a dry powder or in the form of a
decoction, was given also to horses.

An herb used by Jaw in the treatment of rheumatism is included
in the list of medicinal herbs on page 270.

A successful war expedition by Jaw is shown in a drawing by
himself (pl. 62), the same drawing appearing in the background of
his portrait (pl. 59). Jaw said that before any important undertaking he smoked a certain pipe in a ceremonial manner and "offered
prayers to Wakaŋ'taŋka." Instead of attempting to describe this,
he enacted it for the writer as follows:

(1) With the bowl of the pipe in his left hand and the stem in his
right hand he held the pipe upright in front of and close to his body,
saying rapidly in a low tone: "Wakaŋ'taŋka, behold this pipe,
behold it. I ask you to smoke it. I do not want to kill anybody, I
want only to get good horses. I ask you to help me. That is why
I speak to you with this pipe." (See p. 66.)

(2) Changing the position of his hands, placing his left hand on the
stem of the pipe and holding the bowl in his right hand, he pointed the
stem toward his left shoulder, saying: "Now, wolf, behold this
pipe. Smoke it and bring me many horses."

(3) He then placed his right hand once more on the stem of the
pipe and his left hand on the bowl, and pointing the stem upward and
forward holding the pipe level with his face, he said: "Wakaŋ'-
taŋka, behold this pipe. I ask you to smoke it. I am holding it for
you. Look also at me."

(4) After placing the stem of the unlighted pipe in his mouth (still holding the bowl in his left hand) again he said, "Wakaŋ'-taŋka, I will now smoke this pipe in your honor. I ask that no bullet may harm me when I am in battle. I ask that I may get many horses."

(5) Having elevated the pipe as in section 3, he lighted and smoked it, holding it firmly in both hands. Then he said (referring to his participation in the Sun dance):[1] "Wakaŋ'taŋka, behold this pipe and behold me. I have let my breast be pierced. I have shed much blood. I ask you to protect me from shedding more blood and to give me long life."

When this ceremonial act was completed Jaw filled another pipe, which was one that he commonly used, and smoked it. He said: "It is the office of a certain pipe that it be smoked in making a request of Wakaŋ'taŋka. I always did what I have now enacted for you, and my blood was never shed after I took part in the Sun dance. This was because I asked Wakaŋ'taŋka to give me success."

At that time the following song was sung:

No. 161. "I Wish to Roam"   (Catalogue No. 651)

Sung by JAW

VOICE ♩ = 92

DRUM ♩ = 88

Drum-rhythm similar to No. 5

Ko-la wa - ya-kte-pi kiŋ -

na to-kel wa - ćiŋ-ka o - - ma-wa-ni kte-lo *he* śuŋ - ka-wa-kaŋ

o - wa-le   kte-lo

---

[1] Jaw bore scars on his chest and back, also small scars the entire length of his arms, showing that he fulfilled his Sun-dance vow.

WORDS

kola′	friend
waya′ktepi kiŋ′na	be alert
tokel′	any way
waćiŋ′ka	I wish
oma′wani ktelo′	to roam about
śuŋ′kawakaŋ	horses
owa′le ktelo′	I will seek

Analysis.—The character of this melody would seem to indicate that it is an old song and is correctly sung. The rhythmic unit is well defined and has an evident influence on the rhythm of the song as a whole. More than half the intervals are minor thirds, and only four intervals larger than a minor third appear in the song. The ascent of a seventh is somewhat unusual. This ascending interval is found only 9 times in the 2,864 intervals of Chippewa songs and 13 times in the present series. This song is melodic in structure, has a range of nine tones, and contains all tones of the complete octave.

See plot of this melody on page 419.

When the war party came near the camp of the enemy they waited for night in order to make their attack under cover of darkness. At that time the following song is said to have been sung:

No. 162. "A Night Is Different"   (Catalogue No. 652)

Sung by JAW

VOICE ♩ = 88
DRUM ♩ = 88
Drum-rhythm similar to No. 19

Ko - la haŋ- he - pi waŋ   to - ke-ća   ća mi - ta - śuŋ - ke

o - ta *ya* nuŋ we

WORDS

kola′	friend
haŋhe′pi waŋ	a night
toke′ća	is different (from the day)
ća	so
mita′śuŋke o′ta nuŋwe′	may my horses be many

Analysis.—The second part of this song, containing the words, is an exact repetition of the first part, a somewhat unusual condition. The form of the song is simple. It has a compass of an octave and ends on the tonic. The melody tones are those of the minor triad and fourth, but only the tones of the tonic triad are accented. The size of interval varies more than in many of the songs, one-third of the intervals being larger than a minor third. The song contains no rhythmic unit, but the rhythm of the song as a whole is interesting and distinctive.

When night came the object of the expedition was carried out. Under cover of darkness Jaw succeeded in capturing on this occasion 70 horses. (See pl. 62.) In referring to this exploit he said: "I did not waken nor kill any of the Crows; I just took their horses. No Sioux ever took more horses than that in one night."

As Jaw and his party approached their village they gave the long wolf howl, at which the people came out to meet them. The following song celebrated the victory, the women singing with the men:

No. 163. "I Am Bringing Horses"   (Catalogue No. 653)

Sung by JAW

WORDS

śuŋ ka′wakaŋ	horses
owa′le	I seek
ća	so
awa′ku we	I am bringing them

INCIDENTS IN THE LIFE OF JAW (DRAWING BY HIMSELF)

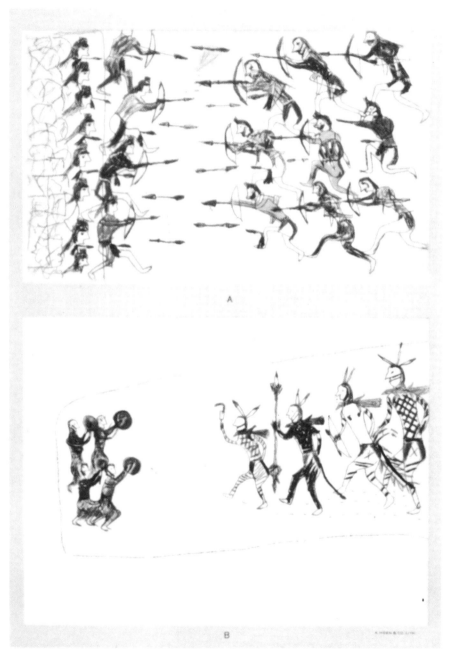

INCIDENTS IN THE LIFE OF EAGLE SHIELD (DRAWINGS BY HIMSELF)

A. HIS FIRST FIGHT
B. DANCE OF THE KAŊǴIŸUHA

Analysis.—Four renditions of this song were recorded. In all the renditions the accidental G flat appears, though the pitch of the tone varies slightly, the interval between G flat and F being usually sung too small. The song is based on the fourth five-toned scale and is melodic in structure. Though the song is major in tonality, 44 per cent of the intervals are minor thirds.

Events similar to those of the preceding narrative are depicted in plate 63, but no songs were recorded concerning them.

The following pages contain narratives of personal experiences on the warpath by Eagle Shield, illustrated by his own drawings. With few exceptions a song is associated with each drawing. Plate 64, *A*, depicts his first fight, which took place when he was 14 years of age. As he was so young he had no song to sing in this fight, neither did he commemorate it in a song, as he might have done had it occurred in his later life. His second drawing (pl. 64, *B*) represents the members of the Kaŋġi'yuha society (see p. 318 et seq.). The customs of this society among the Teton Sioux are described by Wissler. Thus Eagle Shield said, "I am leader of the dancers, and when I rise to dance the singers begin to beat their drums," while Wissler states that "the two rattle-bearers gave the signal for the dancing," and, further, that "the four drummers each carry a small hand-drum." (See pl. 64.)

The following was said to be a characteristic song of the Kaŋġi'yuha. The words express reproof.

No. 164. "Even the Eagle Dies"   (Catalogue No. 507)

Sung by EAGLE SHIELD

VOICE ♩ = 88
DRUM not recorded

A - ki - ći - ta na - ya - pa - pi   kiŋ   waŋ - bli ka-yeś

te ye - lo

WORDS

aki'ćita........................ soldiers
naya'papi...................... you fled
kiŋ waŋbli' kayeś' te yelo'..... even the eagle dies

Analysis.—The upward and downward progressions are more nearly equal in this than in many songs, as it contains 25 ascending and 28 descending intervals. The principal progressions are major seconds (48 per cent), and fourths (22 per cent). The intonation was somewhat wavering throughout the renditions, but the tones transcribed as C sharp and C natural were clearly distinguished. This was the first song recorded by Eagle Shield, and his voice grew steadier when he became accustomed to singing into the phonograph. This song is melodic in structure and contains all the tones of the octave except the seventh. Shrill war cries were given during the rest which precedes the words of the song.

Plate 65, *A*, depicts an incident in a Sioux expedition against the Crows which took place in midsummer. The Sioux were away from their village only 16 days, yet they returned with 100 Crow scalps. Approaching the Crow village, the Sioux sent forward a few men, who went around the camp and captured some horses. The Crows, supposing this to be the entire Sioux force, came out of the camp

INCIDENTS IN THE LIFE OF EAGLE SHIELD (DRAWINGS BY HIMSELF)

A. EAGLE SHIELD KILLS A CROW INDIAN

B. EAGLE SHIELD CAPTURES AN ASSINIBOIN WOMAN

and pursued them. Immediately the Crows were surrounded and most of them were killed.

Eagle Shield said that he sang the following song when he killed one of the Crows, and that it is a song of the Miwa'tani society:

No. 165. "I Took Courage"   (Catalogue No. 508)

Sung by EAGLE SHIELD

VOICE ♩ = 92
DRUM not recorded

Kaŋ-ġi wi - ća - śa kiŋ na-
taŋ hi - yu - ki - na   Mi - wa - ta - ni kiŋ - haŋ bli -
he - mi - ći ye - lo

WORDS

Kaŋġi' wića'śa kiŋ .... the Crow Indians
nataŋ' hiyu'kina .... rushing to fight
Miwa'tani kiŋhaŋ' .... I a Miwa'tani
blihe'mići yelo' .... took courage

Analysis.—The rhythmic structure of this song is interesting. The two rhythmic units are almost alike, yet their difference gives variety to the rhythm of the song as a whole. With the exception of the ascent of an octave with the entrance of the words there are only three intervals in the song—the fourth, the minor third, and the major second, the last-named forming 60 per cent of the entire number of intervals. The song is major in tonality, yet 28 per cent of the intervals are minor thirds. The only tones in the melody are those of the major triad and second. This would suggest that the song might be harmonic in form, but the second is frequently accented, causing the song to be classified as melodic with harmonic framework. The melody has a range of eight tones, extending from the dominant above the tonic to the dominant below the tonic.

In the time of ripe cherries [1] a party of Sioux were in the country of the Assiniboin. There they found a little group of cherry pickers and attacked them. This act was seen by the Assiniboin in the camp, who charged the Sioux in a vain attempt to save the cherry pickers. All the men were killed, but the women escaped with the exception of one whom Eagle Shield captured, carrying her away on his horse, as shown in plate 65, B. Eagle Shield took the captured woman to the Sioux camp, but the next autumn she ran away and returned to her own people.

The following song celebrates this victory:

No. 166. "Captives I Am Bringing"   (Catalogue No. 510)

Sung by EAGLE SHIELD

WORDS

kola'............................. friend
naya'honpi huwo'.............. do you hear?
waya'ka........................ captives
ko............................. also
awa'kuwe..................... I am bringing home

---

[1] The month of July is called by the Sioux Ćanpa' sa'pa wi, 'black-cherry moon.'

INCIDENTS IN THE LIFE OF EAGLE SHIELD (DRAWINGS BY HIMSELF)

A. EAGLE SHIELD CAPTURES HORSES

B. EAGLE SHIELD RESCUES A WOUNDED FRIEND

Analysis.—In regard to a keynote, this melody is classified as irregular. (See analysis of No. 108.) For this reason the signature should be understood as indicating only the pitch of the tones. Of the intervals, 45 per cent are minor thirds, and the minor second appears six times. The descending fourth at the close of each part of the song is peculiar and was clearly given in every rendition of the song. The song contains a change of tempo. (See No. 5.)

A memorable incident is depicted in plate 66, *A*. The Sioux attacked a Crow camp, capturing 80 horses. This was not the entire number of horses owned by the Crows, but the expedition was considered a successful one. The Sioux killed three Crows. On their way home they sang this song, the melody being the same as that of the preceding song.

WORDS

kola'............................ friend
naya'honpi huwo'............... do you hear?
tasuŋ'ke....................... their (the enemy's) horses
ko............................. also
awa'kuwe..................... I am bringing home

The narrative of the exploit illustrated by plate 66, *B*, runs thus: Eagle Shield said that the advance section of the war party deserted their leader, who was wounded in the knee, leaving him to the mercy of the enemy. Eagle Shield was a member of the second section of the war party. When he saw the leader's plight he went to him and succeeded in carrying him to a place of safety. In connection with the event he sang the following song, the words of which express derision for warriors who would desert their wounded leader.

No. 167. "They Deserted Their Leader"   (Catalogue No. 520)

Sung by EAGLE SHIELD

VOICE ♩ = 96
DRUM ♩ = 96
Drum-rhythm similar to No. 8

Psa-lo-ka kiŋ na-taŋ   a-hi-ye-lo blo-taŋ-huŋ-ka uŋ-yaŋ

na-pa-pi ye-lo

WORDS

Psa'loka[1] kiŋ................... the Crow Indians
nataŋ'.......................... came
ahi'yelo....................... attacking,
blotaŋ'huŋka.................. their leader
uŋ'yaŋ napa'pi yelo'........... was left behind

Analysis.—Several renditions of this song were recorded, in every one of which E flat was sung. This suggests the key of B flat, but the melody progressions are along the lines of the minor triad on D, and the song is accordingly analyzed as being in the key of D minor. The song has a compass of nine tones and lacks the sixth and seventh tones of the complete octave. Two rhythmic units are found in the song, the division of the last count being the same in each.

Eight of Eagle Shield's companions made a litter of poles and placed the wounded man upon it. They were 50 miles from home and were obliged to cross the Missouri River with their burden. After traveling about 25 miles they made a camp and also killed a buffalo. Food for a war party was obtained from the country through which it passed. Mention is frequently made of the killing of buffalo, the flesh being used for food and the hide for robes or for making

---

[1] See p. 337, footnote.

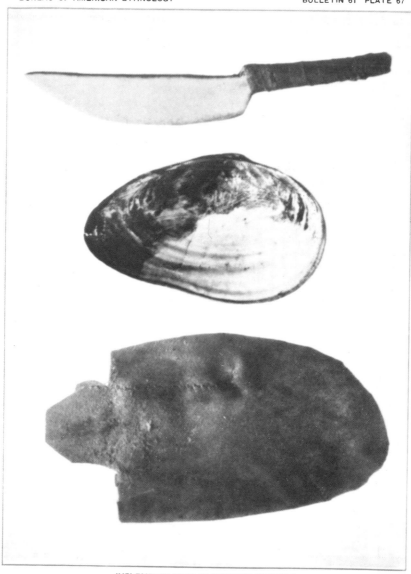

IMPLEMENTS USED IN SKINNING BUFFALO

moccasins. The use of the clamshell as an implement for skinning buffalo may have had its origin in some emergency. Plate 67 shows a clamshell which was said to have been used for that purpose, with the case in which it was carried. The size of the shell indicates that it was found at some distance from the territory of the Sioux, while the slits at the top of the case show that it was attached to the belt of the owner. This specimen was purchased from the mother of Eagle

FIG. 32. Apparatus for cooking meat without a kettle.

Shield, who was a very old woman. Plate 67 shows also a skinning knife made of the shoulder blade of a buffalo, the handle being wound with buffalo hide. The wounded man wanted soup, but the party carried no utensil large enough for boiling meat. Eagle Shield, remembering, however, that his grandfather told him how the warriors of his day cooked meat in the stomach casing of the slain animal, resolved to try the experiment. The casing, suspended on a tripod, was filled with water in which heated stones were placed. (See fig. 32.)

When the water was boiling the meat was put into it, and the process of cooking was accomplished without difficulty.[1]

The wounded man was refreshed by the broth, and after making him comfortable and cooking a quantity of meat, the war party left him in charge of a young man. Eight days later another war party passing that way found the wounded man able to travel. He and his companion joined this war party and reached home in safety.

As Eagle Shield, who gave this narrative, is a medicine-man who makes a specialty of treating wounds and fractures, his account of the man's injury was somewhat professional. He said the injury was so severe that at first the bones protruded and buckshot came from the wound for some time, after which the flesh began to heal, and that in one moon and the first quarter of the next moon the leg was entirely well.

Eagle Shield said that on one occasion he was pursued by Crow Indians as he was carrying with him a friend whose horse had been shot. This incident is depicted in plate 68, A.

The following song was said to have been sung at this time, but the meaning of the words in this connection is not clear:

No. 168. "One of Them Will Be Killed"   (Catalogue No. 521)

Sung by EAGLE SHIELD

VOICE ♩ = 104

DRUM not recorded

lo - ka kiŋ   na - taŋ hi - ye - lo ki - ći yaŋ-ka yo ki -

ći yaŋ-ka - yo ki - ći yaŋ-ka - yo waŋ-źi kte - pi   kte - lo he   yo

---

[1] The writer saw a cooking outfit of this kind prepared and used in a Sioux camp at Bull Head, S. Dak., on July 5, 1913. The stones were heated in a fire near the tripod, each stone being lifted on a forked stick and placed in the water. A blunt stick was used in pushing the heated stones on the forked sticks, and a short stick was used for stirring the boiling meat. All these articles (shown in fig. 32) are now in the U. S. National Museum, at Washington.

INCIDENTS IN THE LIFE OF EAGLE SHIELD (DRAWINGS BY HIMSELF)

A. EAGLE SHIELD IS PURSUED BY CROW INDIANS

B. EAGLE SHIELD CAPTURES HORSES IN CROW CAMP

WORDS

Psa'loka kiŋ	the Crow Indians
nataŋ 'hi'yelo	come attacking
kići' yaŋka' yo	sit you with them
waŋźi'	one of them
kte'pi ktelo'	will be killed

Analysis.—The rhythmic form of this song is interesting. Two rhythmic units appear, which in the middle of the song are used alternately. In the second complete measure containing words the rhythmic unit begins on the second count of the measure, the first count being clearly accented by the singer. The progressions of the melody are chiefly by whole tones, 60 per cent of the intervals being major seconds. The other intervals are varied and range from a minor third to a tenth. The song is based on the second five-toned scale and has a compass of 12 tones. In structure the song is melodic, with harmonic framework.

On one occasion when Eagle Shield led a war party against the Crows they found that the latter had picketed their horses within the circle of tents. Eagle Shield and a companion, having entered the village as scouts, saw these horses. (Pl. 68, *B*.) Eagle Shield said to his companion, "Let us go and get some of the horses." His companion replied, "No; if we do that the rest of the party will be angry." Eagle Shield then said, "Let us each take *one* horse." His companion replied, " *You* do it." Thereupon Eagle Shield, creeping into the circle of tents, took two horses, a black and a brown, and escaped without detection. Each mounting a horse, he and his companion reached their camp about daybreak.

The loss of the horses was soon discovered by the Crows, who increased their watchfulness, so that the other members of the Sioux war party were unable to secure any horses. So it happened that Eagle Shield and his companion were the only ones who returned on horseback, the rest being obliged to walk.

Eagle Shield said that he sang the following song when he went to steal the Crow horses:

No. 169. "I Intend to Take His Horses"   (Catalogue No. 522)

Sung by EAGLE SHIELD

VOICE ♩=80 (or ♪=160)
DRUM not recorded

Kaŋ-ġi to-ka kiŋ

waŋ - bla-ke ći - na - haŋ   ta - śuŋ-ke kiŋ-haŋ   - ću wa - ćaŋ -mi

ye he - ća- moŋ kiŋ-haŋ   o - ma - tiŋ - iŋ kte

WORDS

Kaŋġi' to'ka kiŋ	the Crow enemy
waŋbla'ke ći'nahaŋ	if I see him
taśuŋ'ke kiŋhaŋ' iću' waćaŋ'mi	
ye	it is my intention to take his horses
he'ćamoŋ kiŋhaŋ'	if I do this
oma'taŋiŋ kte	it will be widely known

Analysis.—The tempo of this song is slightly hastened in the first measure containing words, but the change is not steadily maintained. The 5–8 measures, however, are clearly given and are accurate in time. (See song No. 64.) The triad of D major is strongly suggested by the melody progressions; but F, the third of that chord, does not appear. The song, however, is analyzed as in the key of D major. The third is absent from 12 songs in the series of 340 Chippewa songs, this peculiarity being considered in the analysis of song No. 53 in Bulletin 53 (p. 140). In the present work the third is absent from only five songs. (See p. 135.) The interval of the fourth is remarkably prominent in this song, constituting more than half the entire number of intervals.

Swift Dog (Śuŋ'ka-lu'zahaŋ) was one of the oldest informants among the Sioux, being 68 years of age in 1913, when giving his information. Before beginning his narrative Swift Dog (pl. 69) said: "I am the son of an Hunkpati chief and it is from him that I

SWIFT DOG

INCIDENTS IN THE LIFE OF SWIFT DOG (DRAWING BY HIMSELF)

get my fame. My father's name was Running Fearlessly (Kaǵi'-śni-iŋ'yaŋka). When he went to Washington, long ago, he was given one of the first medals that ever were made. It is now in my possession. I belonged to Sitting Bull's band, known as the Band of the Bad Bow. In his portrait Swift Dog is shown wearing a headdress known as a "four-horned bonnet." He said that the Sioux once killed an enemy who wore a headdress similar to this and imitated the design for their own use. This incident occurred in the year 1852, designated in the Sioux picture calendar *Heto'pa uŋ'waŋ kte'pi*, 'winter of the killing of the four-horned enemy.'

Several of Swift Dog's war exploits are shown in his own drawing (pl. 70), and the songs accompanying these exploits are given herewith. In this drawing (*A*) Swift Dog has shown the first encounter in which he killed a man. He was then 24 years of age and had been to war several times. This expedition was to the country of the Assiniboin, and the man whom he killed was a member of that tribe. In describing the event he said that the enemy was on foot, while he was on horseback, on higher ground. On this expedition he sang the following song:

No. 170. "It is I, Myself"　　　　(Catalogue No. 583)

Sung by SWIFT DOG

VOICE ♩ = 80
DRUM not recorded

Ko - la-pi-la tu- wa ćaŋ-te ka-ćaś mi-ćaŋ-

te mi - ye o-ma-wa-ni ye

WORDS

kola'pila	friends
tu'wa	no one's
ćaŋte'	heart (cf. song No. 177)
kaćaś'	it is
mićaŋ'te	my own heart
miye'	I, myself
oma'wani ye	I am wondering

Analysis.—Progressions of a semitone characterize this melody, 55 per cent of the intervals being minor seconds. Strange to say, the major third is next in point of frequency, constituting one-fourth of the intervals, though the song is minor in tonality, and the minor triad on F forms the framework of the melody. The trend of the melody is such that F is considered to be the keynote, and the song is analyzed as in the key of F minor, though E and B are always sung natural instead of flat. This is one of many instances in which the term "key" is used for convenience, not as indicating a system of tones, all of which have an established relation to a keynote. In every rendition of this song the tempo began as indicated and after 10 or 12 measures began to retard, the words being sung in the indicated time. A dotted eighth and sixteenth note division of the count characterizes the rhythm of the song, and forms part of both rhythmic units. The upward and downward progressions are more nearly equal than usual, the ascending progressions being 20 and the descending intervals being 25. A change of tempo occurs in the song. (See No. 5.)

While Swift Dog was chasing the Assiniboin they ran and hid in a white man's house. Those who came near the window of the house were fired at by the Sioux. Meantime he stole one of the Assiniboin horses and rode away. He took a white horse with a saddle on it. (See pl. 70, *B*.) He said that he had a bow and arrows and shot as fast as he could, but did not know whether he hit anyone. At that time he sang the following song:

No. 171. "Horses I Seek"   (Catalogue No. 584)

Sung by SWIFT DOG

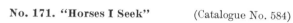

le ćaŋ-na he-ća - moŋ we

śuŋ'kawakaŋ................. horses
owa'le....................... I seek
ćaŋ'na....................... whenever
he'ćamoŋ we................ I do this

Analysis.—This melody contains little that is of special interest. It is based on the second five-toned scale and has only one interval larger than a major third. Two rhythmic units appear, each having the same division of the first two counts. A slight increase of tempo was made as indicated, with a return to the original tempo at the close of the song. This was uniform in the two renditions of the melody. (See No. 5.)

Swift Dog said that he once struck a woman with a coup stick. (See p. 359.) Later he struck a young man with the coup stick and took away his quiver. (See pl. 70, *C*.) He was a handsome young man. Afterward two others struck the young man, and he was killed by the last man who struck him.

The melody of this song is the same as that of the song next preceding, hence only the words are given.

WORDS

ite' isa'bye.................... black face paint (see p. 359.)
aö'pazaŋ...................... (and a) feather
owa'le........................ I seek
ća........................... so
he'ćamoŋ ye.................. I have done this

Concerning *D* of this drawing Swift Dog said: "I once struck an Assiniboin with a sword given me by a soldier. The man's name was Short Bull. He is still alive though I gave him a terrible wound on his temple."

4840°—Bull. 61—18——28

The following song is said to have been sung at this time:

No. 172. "When I Came You Cried"   (Catalogue No. 585)

Sung by SWIFT DOG

WORDS

taku′ owe′	why
hilu′huwo	do you come
hel ito′heya	toward here?
he	when
hibu′ we	I came
yaće′ yelo	you cried (cf. words of song No. 12)

Analysis.—The minor third and major second comprise all except four of the intervals in this melody. The final tone is low but audible in the phonograph record. As in many of these songs, the rhythmic unit appears in the first and last parts, but not in the middle part, which contains the words. This shows a rhythmic form, which is interesting. This song contains all the tones of the octave except the second, has a compass of 10 tones, and is melodic in form.

In explanation of *E*, Swift Dog said that he chased a number of Crow Indians, but they escaped. This song relates to the expedition:

No. 173. "I Struck the Enemy" (Catalogue No. 586)

Sung by SWIFT DOG

VOICE ♩ = 60
DRUM not recorded

E -haŋ-na he-ċa - mon

kte ċuŋ nom - la - la keś a - wa - pe - lo   he

ho na-ya - ħoŋ - pi hu - wo

WORDS

ehaŋ′na	a long time ago
he′ċamoŋ kte ċuŋ	I would have done this
nom′lala keś	only twice again
awa′pelo	I struck (the enemy)
ho	now
naya′ħoŋpi huwo′	do you hear it?

Analysis.—This song was recorded twice, the duplication being accidental. Both records were transcribed and are given herewith. The first was by Swift Dog, the second by Kills-at-Night (Haŋhe′pikte) and his wife Wita′hu (Woman's Neck), women being accustomed to join in these songs. The melody tones in both instances are the major triad and sixth, but it will be seen that the note values differ slightly with the difference in the words, and that in the second rendition the words are so placed as to repeat the rhythmic phrase of the previous measures. This seems to indicate a feeling for a rhythmic unit. The first rendition is by an old singer, the second by a comparatively young man, who usually "sits at the drum" at tribal gatherings of the present time. His wife is considered one of the best among the younger singers. The first rendition is the more complete, as it gives a considerable part of the song before the introduction of the words. In both renditions about 28 per cent of the intervals are minor thirds. The song has a range of 12 tones and is melodic in form.

Duplication of preceding

Sung by KILLS-AT-NIGHT

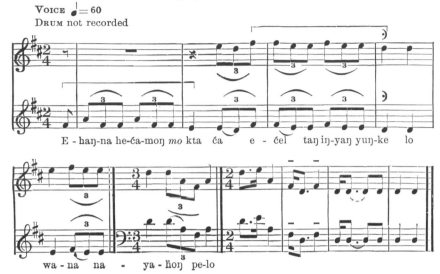

VOICE ♩=60
DRUM not recorded

E - haŋ-na he-ća-moŋ *mo* kta ća   e - ćel   taŋ iŋ-yaŋ yuŋ-ke   lo

wa - na   na - ya - ħoŋ pe-lo

WORDS

ehaŋ'na he'ćamoŋ........... a long time ago
kta ća..................... I would have done this
ećel'...................... well
taŋ iŋ'yaŋ yuŋke' lo........ it is widely known
wana'..................... now
naya'ħoŋ pelo'............. you have heard it

Analysis.—This is a duplication of the preceding, and its structure is considered in the analysis of that song. The renditions by
Kills-at-Night and his wife were recorded on two cylinders, each
containing four renditions of the song. In every instance her voice
was silent during the opening measures, the point of entrance varying
one or two measures. The transcription shows the earliest point of
entrance. The words, of course, are the same in both parts.

The reason for twice recording this song by Kills-at-Night and his
wife was that in the first performance there was a suggestion of "part
singing," the wife holding a tone during the length of several tones
in his part and then singing the delayed words rapidly in order to
overtake him. The writer questioned the singers concerning this
and asked whether they could repeat it. The woman said it was
unintentional on her part, as she had a "catch in her throat," and
the seven other renditions showed no trace of it. Much concerted
singing has been heard by the writer. In this the women invariably
sing an octave above the men, the note values being identical.

F of plate 70 was said to represent animals killed by Swift Dog on the hunt. Depicting war exploits is resumed in *G*, concerning which Swift Dog said:

It was almost winter when we went to the Crow country. It was very cold, but the river had not yet frozen. We made a corral near the river; then we jumped into the water and swam across to the side where the Crows were camped. The splash of the water was like that of great falls when we swam across. We drove all the Crow horses into the river and made them swim over. Then we put them into the corral until we were ready to start for home.

No. 174. "I Come After Your Horses"   (Catalogue No. 587)

Sung by Swift Dog

WORDS

Kangi′ to′ka	Crow enemies
nita′śuŋke	your horses
hiyo′ waü′ welo′	I come after
bluha′kta	I want to own them
ća	so
hiyo′ waü′ welo′	I come after them

Analysis.—In this melody will be noted what is often referred to as "the influence of the rhythmic unit on parts of the song in which it does not occur in entirety." Thus in the measure following the third occurrence of the rhythmic unit we have one quarter note followed by a group of four sixteenth notes, a reversal of count divisions appearing in the unit. The time quickens with the introduction of the words, a peculiarity often found in Sioux war songs, but not noted among the Chippewa. The song is major in tonality and progresses largely by whole tones, the major second constituting 46 per cent of the entire number of intervals. With the exception of three ascending fourths all the remaining intervals are major and minor thirds. The melody tones are those of the fourth five-toned scale, but the tonic is not prominent, the song beginning and ending on the third. The melody is harmonic in structure. Three renditions were recorded; these show no points of difference. Concerning a change in tempo see song No. 5.

See plot of this melody on page 419.

No narrative was given regarding *H* of this drawing (pl. 70), Swift Dog simply stating that he and his brother-in-law went after horses and each secured three, the following song being sung:

No. 175. "Two War Parties"   (Catalogue No. 588)

Sung by SWIFT DOG

WORDS

zuya′ nom′lala............... two war parties
oma′wani yelo′............... I roam with
miye′....................... I, myself
śuŋki′ću................... to capture horses
waćiŋ′ħći................. was my desire
oma′wani yelo′............. in roaming about

Analysis.—The proportion of minor thirds in this major song is larger than usual, the minor third forming about 60 per cent of the entire number of intervals. The major second is the only other interval used in descending progression. The song is based on the fourth five-toned scale, has a compass of 10 tones, and is melodic in structure. No rhythmic unit appears in the melody, and the time was not strictly maintained.

The incident depicted in *I* is connected with the song which appears below. Swift Dog said: "When the railroad first passed through the Black Hills we went on the warpath as far as the end of the road. We went through Shell River. I do not remember what tribe we went after, but I think it was the Omaha." Swift Dog captured a horse which he gave to his sister with the following song:

No. 176. "Sister, I Bring You a Horse"   (Catalogue No. 589)

Sung by SWIFT DOG

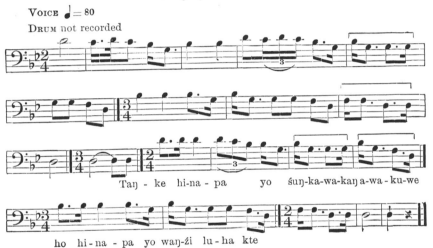

VOICE ♩ = 80

DRUM not recorded

Taŋ - ke hi-na - pa   yo   śuŋ-ka-wa-kaŋ a-wa - ku-we

ho hi - na - pa yo waŋ-źi lu - ha kte

WORDS

tanke′	older sister
hina′pa yo..................	come out
śuŋ′kawakaŋ.................	horses
awa′kuwe ho................	I bring
hina′pa yo............	come out
waŋźi′......................	one (of them)
luha′ kte................	you may have (cf. words of No. 145)

Analysis.—Three renditions of this song were recorded, in each of which a short pause was made after the third and sixth measures, and also after the fourth measure containing the words. These pauses were not such as are indicated by rests, but appeared to be merely breathing spaces. Such pauses are unusual in the singing of Indians and were probably due to the fact that Swift Dog recorded his songs during a period of intense heat, in a small, close building.

Considering B flat the keynote implied by the trend of this melody we find the melody tones to be those of the fourth five-toned scale.

This scale is major in tonality, yet about 55 per cent of the intervals in the song are minor thirds.   Only four intervals occur which are larger than a minor third, all of these being in ascending progression.

OLD BUFFALO'S WAR NARRATIVE

In August, 1913, Old Buffalo (Tataŋk'-ehaŋ'ni) (see pl. 41), with Swift Dog came to McLaughlin, S. Dak., to confer with the writer. They regarded this conference very seriously.   Old Buffalo said, "We come to you as from the dead.   The things about which you ask us have been dead to us for many years.   In bringing them to our minds we are calling them from the dead, and when we have told you about them they will go back to the dead, to remain forever."

Old Buffalo was born in the year 1845, designated in the Sioux picture calendar *Titaŋ'ka oble'ća kaha'pi kiŋ wani'yetu*, 'Winter in which lodges with roofs were built.'   When he was 28 years old he

FIG. 33.   Incident in the life of Old Buffalo (drawing by himself).

led a war party against the Crows.   On this expedition he and his comrades were entirely surrounded by the Crows, an event which Old Buffalo depicted in a drawing.   (Fig. 33.)   Old Buffalo said that at the time of this expedition his band of the Sioux were living in the "Queen's Land" (Canada), but had come down to the United States on a buffalo hunt.   From this temporary camp the expedition started under his leadership.

Old Buffalo said further: [1]

One night the Crows came and stole our horses.   I had an older sister of whom I was very fond.   The Crows stole her horse, and she cried a long time.   This made my heart very bad.   I said, "I will go and pay them back."   A friend said that he would go with me.   I said to my friend, "We will go and look for the Crows.   Wherever their horses are corralled we will find them."   Eleven others went with us, so there were 13 in the party, and I was the leader.   It was in the coldest part of the winter, the moon called by the Sioux *Caŋ napo'pa wi*, 'Wood-cracking moon'.   The

---

[1] This narrative was interpreted by Mrs. Hattie Lawrence (see p. 365), and is given as nearly as possible in her words.   Another narrative by Old Buffalo appears on p. 274.

snow was deep, and I am lame in one leg, but I was angry, and I went. I thought, "Even if I die, I will be content." The women made warm clothing and moccasins for us to wear, and we started away. We carried no shelter. When night came we shoveled aside the snow and laid down brush, on which we slept. At the fork of the Missouri River we took the eastern branch and followed its course. It was 11 nights from the fork of the river to the enemy's camp, and every night we sang this song. It is one of the "wolf songs." (See p. 333.)

No. 177. Song of Self-reliance   (Catalogue No. 636)

Sung by OLD BUFFALO

VOICE ♩ = 76

DRUM ♩ = 76

Drum-rhythm similar to No. 5

E - ya miś - e - ya tu - wa ćaŋ - te   ka - ćaś e - ćiŋ śuŋk

o - wa-le

WORDS

eya′......................... well

miśeya′ tuwa′ ćaŋte′........ I depend upon no one's heart (or courage) but my own (cf. song No. 170)

kaćaś′......................... so

ećiŋ′......................... thinking this

śuŋk owa′le................. I look for horses

Analysis.—Like many other melodies on the fourth five-toned scale, this song contains a large proportion of minor thirds, in this instance 58 per cent of the intervals, while the major third does not appear. The song has a compass of an octave, extending from the dominant above to the dominant below the tonic. Two-thirds of the progressions are downward. The chord of B major is prominent in the melody, which, however, is not harmonic in structure but is classified as melodic with harmonic framework. Three renditions were recorded; these are uniform in every respect.

See plot of this melody on page 419.

Old Buffalo continued:

As we neared the end of our journey, we were overtaken by a fearful blizzard. There was a butte in which we found a sheltered place and stayed for two days, as my leg was very painful. After the storm subsided we looked around and could see the enemy's village. Night came again, but my leg was so painful that we rested another day. The next afternoon, as the sun was getting low, I tightened my belt and made ready for whatever might befall. We walked toward the enemy's village and entered a rocky country, like the Bad Lands. Then it was dark.

A great number of Crows were camped at this place, and there was dancing in two parts of the village. We were close to the village, but no one saw us. Only the dogs barked. We went up to the edge of the village and got in where there were many horses in a bunch. We drove the herd before us, and they trotted quietly along. After getting a safe distance from the camp we mounted some of the horses and drove the rest before us. We did not stop, but kept the horses trotting fast all night. When daylight came we counted the horses and found that there were 53. All that day we traveled, and as the sun sank we rested. We were tired, as we had no saddles, and that night we slept.

The next morning there came another terrible blizzard. My eyelashes were frozen so that I could scarcely see. I went back a little distance to see if we were being followed, then I returned to my companions. I had realized that the tracks of the horses made a trail and I saw that the enemy were pursuing us. This was my war party and I felt a great responsibility for its safety.

The Crows overtook us and secured most of the horses which we had captured from them. We jumped down a steep rocky place, and soon we were entirely surrounded by the Crows. A Sioux boy, about 15 years old was with us, and he was shot in the back. We fought as long as the sun moved in the sky. It was a hard struggle. Every time we fired a gun it turned white with frost. During this fight I sang a very powerful song of the Fox society, to which I belong. [Concerning the Fox society, see p. 314 et seq.]

No. 178. "I Am the Fox" (Catalogue No. 637)

Sung by OLD BUFFALO

VOICE ♩ = 66

DRUM not recorded

To - ka - la ḳoŋ mi - ye ye - lo ta - ku o - te -

ḣi - ka o - wa - le ye - lo

toka′la ḳoŋ.................... the fox
miye′ yelo′.................... I am
ta′ku........................ something
ote′ḣika..................... difficult
owa′le yelo′.................. I seek

Analysis.—This is a particularly interesting melody. It contains only the tones A, B, C, and E, these being the tonic triad and second in the key of A minor, and the song is analyzed as being in that key. The melody is framed on the interval of a fourth, almost half the entire number of intervals being fourths. The major third occurs four times, but the minor third does not appear; there are, however, four minor seconds, or semitone progressions. In structure the song would be harmonic except for the accented B near the close; it is therefore classified as melodic with harmonic framework. Songs containing only one accented nonharmonic tone are frequently noted in both Chippewa and Sioux music. At the opening of the song there is a repeated phrase, which is not considered a rhythmic unit because it has seemingly no influence on the rhythm of the song as a whole. Its repetition on the same tone suggests that it may be simply an introductory phrase. The final tone is immediately preceded by a tone a major third lower, this close being somewhat unusual in the songs under analysis.

The account of his exploit was resumed by Old Buffalo as follows:

The Crows took the saddles from their horses and charged back at us, but our fire was more than they could stand, and they finally retreated, leaving their saddles on the ground. We captured these saddles and took them back to the place where we were first overtaken by the Crows. There we found only four horses alive. We put one of the captured saddles on a horse and lifted the wounded boy to the horse's back. I held the reins and walked beside the horse all that night. When daylight came we rested. The boy had no pillow, so I lay down and he laid his head on my body. There was timber near the place, and the next day we made a travois for the boy, and I rode the horse that dragged it. That night we traveled on, and about midnight we reached a certain place and made a camp. We had occasionally killed a buffalo for food, and as the men on foot had worn out their moccasins, we took fresh buffalo hide and tied it on their feet. The three horses ran away, but we caught them.

All the following night we traveled, and the next day we were at the fork of the Missouri River, where we stayed two nights.

While we were on the warpath our friends had finished their buffalo hunt and returned to Canada. I kept four men with me and the sick boy, and sent the others home to make a report of the expedition. We kept the horses with us and followed slowly. The boy was thirsty, and as there was no cup I took the hide of a buffalo head, put snow in it and then put a hot stone in the snow. Thus the boy had hot water to drink. He wanted soup, so I took the buffalo tripe and boiled meat in it. So the boy had soup. (See p. 399.)

We camped for a time beside a creek, and as we came near the "Queen's Land" we camped again. There the father and mother of the boy met us. They had heard the news from the other members of the party and started at once to meet us. After we had given the boy to his parents we went on with the horses, leaving them to travel more slowly. It was dark when we reached home, and we fired our guns to let the people know of our coming. The next day the boy arrived. For two days and nights I stayed with him constantly. I did this because I felt myself to be the cause of his misfortune. The boy had come to call me "father," and at the end of this time he said, "Father, you can go home now to your own lodge." I went to my own lodge and slept that night. The next morning the boy died. He is always spoken of as Wana'gli ya'ku, 'Brings the arrow,' because he brought home the arrow in his body.

I did not keep any of the horses for myself, because I was the leader of the war party.

FIG. 34. Incident in the life of Old Buffalo (drawing by himself).

Another expedition was described by Old Buffalo and illustrated by a drawing (fig. 34). Concerning this expedition he said:

A large number of Sioux were once moving camp, and five men left the party to steal horses. They were successful, and brought back 30 horses. The enemy were also moving camp. I made up my mind that I would go and see if I could get some horses, too. So I sent for a young man and talked with him about it. Then I said, "We will go;" and he replied, "I will go with you." One man asked to go with us, making three in the party. I said, "We will start without telling anyone and travel in the creek, so they will not know how we went." The one whom I invited gave up going at the last moment, but the man who had volunteered to go left camp with me while everyone was asleep.

On our expedition we sang this song, hoping that we would capture many horses:

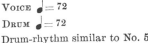

No. 179. **"I Look for Them"**   (Catalogue No. 638)

Sung by OLD BUFFALO

Kaŋ-ġi wi-ċa - śa kiŋ o-wi - ċa-wa-le *i ya e i ya* i-

ye - wa-ya *ċa i ya* ta - śuŋ-ke kiŋ a-wa-ku - we

WORDS

Kaŋġi′ wiċa′śa kiŋ...........	the Crow Indians
owi′ċawale...................	I look for them
iye′waya....................	I found them
ċa.........................	so
taśuŋ′ke kiŋ...............	their horses
awa′kuwe..................	I brought home

Analysis.—This song contains only the tones of the minor triad and fourth. Unlike the preceding song, from which the minor third was entirely absent, that interval constitutes about one-third of the intervals in this song. The fourth is also prominent in the melody. Exactly two-thirds of the intervals are downward. Except for the accented B the song would be classified as harmonic in structure. The form of the melody is simple, the song beginning on the octave and twice descending to the tonic along the intervals of the tonic chord.

In conclusion Old Buffalo said:

We found the direction in which the Crows were traveling, went around, and headed them off. It was almost dark when we approached their village. They were camped in a circle. The afterglow was still in the sky and this light was back of us as we went up a little creek from that direction toward the village. We could see the cooking fires. We were on horseback, and we lay flat on our horses, leaning close to the horses' heads. So we crept near to their horses.

When we stepped among the horses, one of them snorted at a stranger. Then the Crows came with their guns. They had seen us, though we did not know it. My eyes were only for the horses. They began firing, and before I had a chance to get away my horse was shot. I snatched the reins and pulled, but the horse's jaw was broken. I went on. They shot again, and he fell. I jumped as he went down. The man who went with me ran away at the first attack and left me alone. I ran ahead, and as the Crows were loading their guns, I dodged from one shelter to another. They kept firing in the direction I had started to go.

The young man who ran away saw me. He was in a safe place, and he shouted, "Come this way." He was on horseback, and we sat double on his horse. We traveled some distance and came to the creek by which we had approached the Crow camp. We staid at the creek that night. The Crows broke camp, and late the next day we went back to the deserted ground. There lay my horse, dead. We examined the horse and found that his shoulder was broken. My oldest sister had raised that horse.

We went back to the creek and staid that night. The Sioux were moving to their last camp of the year, and there we joined them.

PLOTS OF SONGS OF WAR

The songs of war, as already noted, are called "wolf songs." Many of them make reference to the wolf and many pertain to horses, hence we find among the plots of these songs (fig. 35) numerous examples of Class D (see p. 54). Song No. 120, however, is an example of Class A; No. 101 has the same general trend; and No. 136 is a good example of Class B. These types, as already stated, appear throughout the series. The interval of a fourth is prominent in songs concerning animals and implying motion, and this appears in the plots of the songs. Songs Nos. 111, 127, 145, and 174, as reference to their respective titles will show, are songs concerning horses, and the plots of the songs are seen to resemble one another. Songs 146 and 161 concern man and contain the idea of motion; their titles are, respectively, "He is returning," and "I wish to roam." These plots show the characteristics of Class D. No. 177 is called "A song of self-reliance," and we note in the plot of the song the emphasis and dwelling on the lowest, or keynote, which characterizes Class C and appears to be coincident with firmness of purpose and self-confidence. The interval of a fourth characterizes songs Nos. 99 and 100, the first of which is a song concerning the buffalo, and the second, the personal song of a man named Brave Buffalo, the words being "Brave Buffalo I am, I come." Such a song as the latter would undoubtedly be received in a dream of buffalo. The ascending interval at the opening of song No. 99 suggests Class E (see p. 519), and on reference to the words of the song we find in them the idea of suffering on the part of the buffalo, who are being driven in such a way that the wind strikes their faces like a lance.

ANALYSIS OF WAR SONGS

The songs of the military societies and the songs of war are divided into two analysis groups, the first comprising songs a majority of which are believed to be more than 50 years old and the second comprising songs believed to be of more recent origin.

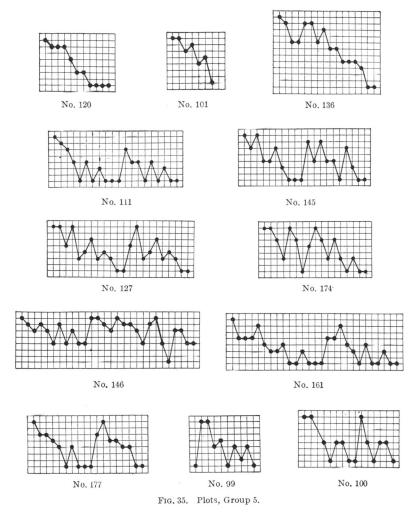

No. 120   No. 101   No. 136

No. 111   No. 145

No. 127   No. 174

No. 146   No. 161

No. 177   No. 99   No. 100

FIG. 35.   Plots, Group 5.

In the first group are the songs of the Miwa'tani and Kaŋġi'yuha, the older of the military societies, together with the older war songs. This group comprises songs Nos. 122, 125–177, and No. 179.   In the second group are those of the military societies more recently organized among the Teton—that is, the Fox, Badger, and Strong Heart societies, and the White Horse Riders—together with war songs found in the description of the Sun dance, and in the section on war customs; also such songs in honor of an individual as were sung to the melodies of these war societies. This group comprises songs Nos. 6, 7, 8, 9, 10, 22, 23, 26, 27, 28, 29, 30, 31, 32, 33, 34, 35, 114, 115, 116, 117, 118, 119, 120, 121, 123, 124, 178, 223, 224, 225, 231. The age of many war songs can not be stated with exactness, but the division between these two classes has been made as nearly accurate as possible.

The first of these analysis groups marks the end of the older songs contained in this volume, and with the second analysis group we enter on a consideration of musical material which is comparatively modern.

Old Songs—(6) War Songs (section 1)

MELODIC ANALYSIS

TONALITY

	Number of songs.	Serial Nos. of songs.
Major	23	128, 131, 132, 134, 137, 144, 151, 153, 155, 156, 157, 159, 160, 163, 164, 165, 169, 171, 173, 174, 175, 176, 177
Minor	31	122, 125, 126, 127, 129, 130, 133, 135, 136, 138, 139, 140, 141, 142, 143, 145, 146, 147, 148, 149, 150, 152, 154, 158, 161, 162, 167, 168, 170, 172, 179
Irregular	1	166
Total	55	

FIRST NOTE OF SONG—ITS RELATION TO KEYNOTE

	Number of songs.	Serial Nos. of songs.
Beginning on the—		
Twelfth	7	122, 130, 136, 139, 143, 158, 168
Eleventh	1	150
Tenth	3	142, 172, 173
Ninth	2	138, 157
Octave	14	129, 133, 134, 135, 141, 145, 148, 152, 154, 159, 160, 161, 162, 179
Fifth	16	126, 131, 140, 144, 146, 147, 151, 153, 155, 156, 164, 165, 166, 170, 175, 177
Third	6	128, 137, 163, 171, 174, 176
Keynote	5	125, 127, 132, 149, 169
Irregular	1	166
Total	55	

Old Songs—(6) War Songs (section 1)—Continued

MELODIC ANALYSIS—Continued

LAST NOTE OF SONG—ITS RELATION TO KEYNOTE

	Number of songs.	Serial Nos. of songs.
Ending on the—		
Fifth	16	126, 129, 131, 138, 140, 147, 151, 153, 155,
Third	8	156, 164, 165, 166, 169, 170, 177
Keynote	30	128, 132, 137, 163, 171, 174, 175, 176, 122,
		125, 127, 130, 133, 134, 135, 136, 139,
		141, 142, 143, 144, 145, 146, 148, 149, 150,
		152, 154, 157, 158, 159, 160, 161, 162, 168,
		172, 173, 179
Irregular	1	166
Total	55	

LAST NOTE OF SONG—ITS RELATION TO COMPASS OF SONG

	Number of songs.	Serial Nos. of songs.
Songs in which final tone is—		
Lowest tone in song	53	122, 125, 126, 127, 128, 129, 130, 131, 132,
		133, 134, 135, 136, 137, 138, 139, 140, 141,
		142, 143, 144, 145, 146, 147, 148, 149, 150,
		151, 152, 153, 154, 155, 156, 157, 158, 159,
		160, 161, 162, 163, 165, 167, 168, 169, 170,
		171, 172, 173, 174, 175, 176, 177, 179
Immediately preceded by whole tone below	1	164
Irregular	1	166
Total	55	

NUMBER OF TONES COMPRISING COMPASS OF SONG

	Number of songs.	Serial Nos. of songs.
Compass of—		
Thirteen tones	4	129, 148, 149, 154
Twelve tones	14	122, 125, 130, 133, 136, 138, 139, 142, 143,
		145, 152, 158, 168, 173
Eleven tones	2	150, 169
Ten tones	4	126, 166, 172, 175
Nine tones	7	128, 153, 157, 159, 161, 164, 167
Eight tones	23	127, 131, 132, 134, 135, 137, 140, 141, 144,
		147, 151, 155, 156, 160, 162, 163, 165, 170,
		171, 174, 176, 177, 179
Six tones	1	146
Total	55	

Old Songs—(6) War Songs (section 1)—Continued

MELODIC ANALYSIS—Continued

TONE MATERIAL

	Number of songs.	Serial Nos. of songs.
First five-toned scale	1	131
Second five-toned scale	11	122, 125, 126, 129, 133, 136, 137, 150, 152, 158, 168
Fourth five-toned scale	11	130, 132, 151, 153, 159, 163, 171, 174, 175, 176, 177
Major triad	1	155
Major triad and second	3	144, 165, 173
Minor triad and fourth	5	135, 139, 142, 162, 179
Octave complete	3	138, 157, 161
Octave complete except seventh	5	128, 146, 154, 160, 164
Octave complete except seventh and sixth	2	156, 167
Octave complete except seventh and second	2	127, 134
Octave complete except sixth	2	140, 170
Octave complete except sixth and third	1	169
Octave complete except fourth	1	147
Octave complete except second	6	141, 143, 145, 148, 149, 172
Other combinations of tones	1	166
Total	55	

ACCIDENTALS

	Number of songs.	Serial Nos. of songs.
Songs containing—		
No accidentals	47	125, 126, 127, 128, 129, 130, 131, 132, 133, 134, 135, 136, 137, 138, 139, 140, 141, 142, 143, 144, 145, 146, 148, 149, 150, 151, 152, 154, 155, 156, 157, 158, 159, 160, 161, 162, 165, 168, 169, 171, 172, 173, 174, 175, 176, 177, 179
Seventh raised a semitone	2	122, 147
Seventh and fourth lowered a semitone	1	170
Sixth lowered a semitone	1	163
Third lowered a semitone	2	153, 164
Second lowered a semitone	1	167
Irregular	1	166
Total	55	

Old Songs—(6) War Songs (section 1)—Continued

MELODIC ANALYSIS—Continued

STRUCTURE

	Number of songs.	Serial Nos. of songs.
Melodic	36	126, 127, 128, 129, 131, 134, 135, 137, 138, 139, 145, 146, 147, 148, 149, 150, 151, 152, 153, 154, 156, 157, 158, 160, 161, 163, 164, 165, 167, 169, 170, 171, 172, 173, 175, 176
Melodic with harmonic framework	10	125, 132, 136, 141, 143, 144, 159, 168, 177, 179
Harmonic	8	122, 130, 133, 140, 142, 155, 162, 174
Irregular	1	166
Total	55	

FIRST PROGRESSION—DOWNWARD AND UPWARD

	Number of songs.	Serial Nos. of songs.
Downward	37	122, 129, 130, 131, 134, 135, 136, 137, 138, 139, 140, 141, 143, 145, 147, 150, 151, 154, 155, 156, 157, 158, 160, 162, 163, 165, 166, 168, 169, 170, 171, 172, 174, 175, 176, 177, 179
Upward	18	125, 126, 127, 128, 132, 133, 142, 144, 146, 148, 149, 152, 153, 159, 161, 164, 167, 173
Total	55	

TOTAL NUMBER OF PROGRESSIONS—DOWNWARD AND UPWARD

Downward	1,251	
Upward	757	
Total	2,008	

INTERVALS IN DOWNWARD PROGRESSION

Interval of a—	
Major sixth	1
Fifth	3
Fourth	118
Major third	102
Minor third	409
Major second	559
Minor second	59
Total	1,251

Old Songs—(6) War Songs (section 1)—Continued

MELODIC ANALYSIS—Continued

INTERVALS IN UPWARD PROGRESSION

	Number of songs.	
Interval of a—		
Tenth	2	
Ninth	1	
Octave	24	
Seventh	2	
Major sixth	3	
Minor sixth	12	
Fifth	39	
Fourth	99	
Major third	103	
Minor third	223	
Major second	209	
Minor second	40	
Total	757	

AVERAGE NUMBER OF SEMITONES IN EACH INTERVAL

Total number of intervals	2,008	
Total number of semitones	5,465	
Average number of semitones in an interval	2.7	

KEY

	Number of songs.	Serial Nos. of songs.
Key of—		
A major	3	131, 155, 164
A minor	6	125, 133, 136, 142, 143, 168
B flat major	7	128, 130, 151, 156, 163, 174, 176
B flat minor	2	140, 152
B major	1	177
B minor	2	139, 158
C major	2	132, 137
C minor	1	150
C sharp minor	2	146, 147
D major	2	157, 169
D minor	3	138, 161, 167
E flat minor	1	162
F major	3	144, 159, 160
F minor	5	127, 129, 135, 170, 179
F sharp major	1	153
F sharp minor	5	126, 145, 148, 149, 172
G major	3	134, 165, 175
G minor	2	141, 154
A flat major	2	171, 173
G sharp minor	1	122
Irregular	1	166
Total	55	

Old Songs—(6) *War Songs* (*section 1*)—Continued

RHYTHMIC ANALYSIS

PART OF MEASURE ON WHICH SONG BEGINS

	Number of songs.	Serial Nos. of songs.
Beginning on unaccented part of measure.............	22	122, 125, 126, 127, 132, 135, 136, 138, 142, 144, 147, 150, 152, 154, 161, 165, 166, 167, 168, 173, 177, 179
Beginning on accented part of measure................	33	128, 129, 130, 131, 133, 134, 137, 139, 140, 141, 143, 145, 146, 148, 149, 151, 153, 155, 156, 157, 158, 159, 160, 162, 163, 164, 169, 170, 171, 172, 174, 175, 176
Total...	55	

RHYTHM OF FIRST MEASURE

	Number of songs.	Serial Nos. of songs.
First measure in—		
2–4 time...	27	122, 127, 129, 130, 133, 134, 138, 139, 140, 142, 144, 145, 146, 148, 149, 153, 156, 158, 161, 164, 167, 168, 172, 174, 175, 176, 179
3–4 time...	28	125, 126, 128, 131, 132, 135, 136, 137, 141, 143, 147, 150, 151, 152, 154, 155, 157, 159, 160, 162, 163, 165, 166, 169, 170, 171, 173, 177
Total...	55	

CHANGE OF TIME, MEASURE LENGTHS

	Number of songs.	Serial Nos. of songs.
Songs containing no change of time................	1	155
Songs containing a change of time....................	54	122, 125, 126, 127, 128, 129, 130, 131, 132, 133, 134, 135, 136, 137, 138, 139, 140, 141, 142, 143, 144, 145, 146, 147, 148, 149, 150, 151, 152, 153, 154, 156, 157, 158, 159, 160, 161, 162, 163, 164, 165, 166, 167, 168, 169, 170, 171, 172, 173, 174, 175, 176, 177, 179
Total...	55	

Old Songs—(6) War Songs (section 1)—Continued

RHYTHMIC ANALYSIS—Continued

RHYTHM OF DRUM

	Number of songs.	Serial Nos. of songs.
Eighth notes unaccented............................	3	130, 133, 162
Quarter notes unaccented...........................	2	142, 143
Eighth notes accented in groups of two..............	2	129, 167
Each beat preceded by an unaccented beat corresponding to third count of a triplet.	10	125, 127, 128, 132, 135, 151, 154, 161, 177, 179
Drum not recorded.................................	38	122, 126, 131, 134, 136, 137, 138, 139, 140, 141, 144, 145, 146, 147, 148, 149, 150, 152, 153, 155, 156, 157, 158, 159, 160, 163, 164, 165, 166, 168, 169, 170, 171, 172, 173, 174, 175, 176
Total...............................	55	

RHYTHMIC UNIT OF SONG

	Number of songs.	Serial Nos. of songs.
Songs containing—		
No rhythmic unit................................	22	122, 125, 126, 127, 130, 135, 140, 143, 146, 147, 148, 149, 152, 157, 158, 159, 162, 163, 169, 173 175, 179
One rhythmic unit..............................	27	128, 131, 132, 133, 134, 136, 137, 138, 139, 141, 142, 144, 145, 150, 151, 153, 154, 155, 156, 160, 161, 164, 166, 172, 174, 176, 177.
Two rhythmic units	5	165, 167, 168, 170, 171
Three rhythmic units............................	1	129
Total..........................	55	

METRIC UNIT OF VOICE (TEMPO)

	Number of songs.	Serial Nos. of songs.
Metronome—		
48...	1	141
54...	1	175
56...	2	146, 147
58...	2	131, 174
60...	1	173
63...	2	142, 156
66...	2	122, 148
69...	3	138, 144, 155
72...	3	140, 157, 179
76...	4	143, 150, 158, 177
80...	6	126, 134, 135, 169, 170, 176
84...	5	137, 145, 153, 171, 172
88...	2	162, 164

Old Songs—*(6) War Songs (section 1)*—Continued

RHYTHMIC ANALYSIS—Continued

METRIC UNIT OF VOICE (TEMPO)—Continued

	Number of songs.	Serial Nos. of songs.
Metronome—Continued.		
92	8	127, 128, 132, 151, 152, 159, 161, 165
96	7	125, 130, 133, 160, 163, 166, 167
104	2	129, 168
112	1	136
116	2	149, 154
144	1	139
Total	55	

METRIC UNIT OF DRUM (TEMPO)

	Number of songs.	Serial Nos. of songs.
Metronome—		
63	1	142
72	1	179
76	2	143, 177
80	1	135
88	2	161, 162
92	4	127, 128, 132, 151
96	4	125, 130, 133, 167
104	1	129
116	1	154
Drum not recorded	38	122, 126, 131, 134, 136, 137, 138, 139, 140, 141, 144, 145, 146, 147, 148, 149, 150, 152, 153, 155, 156, 157, 158, 159, 160, 163, 164, 165, 166, 168, 169, 170, 171, 172, 173, 174, 175, 176
Total	55	

COMPARISON OF METRIC UNIT OF VOICE AND DRUM

	Number of songs.	Serial Nos. of songs.
Drum and voice having same metric unit	16	125, 127, 128, 129, 130, 132, 133, 135, 142, 143, 151, 154, 162, 167, 177, 179
Drum faster than voice		
Drum slower than voice	1	161
Drum not recorded	38	122, 126, 131, 134, 136, 137, 138, 139, 140, 141, 144, 145, 146, 147, 148, 149, 150, 152, 153, 155, 156, 157, 158, 159, 160, 163, 164, 165, 166, 168, 169, 170, 171, 172, 173, 174, 175, 176
Total	55	

COMPARATIVELY MODERN SONGS [1]

(1) War Songs (Section 2)

Melodic Analysis

TONALITY

	Number of songs.	Serial Nos. of songs.
Major tonality	14	8, 9, 10, 27, 29, 30, 32, 35, 114, 116, 121, 123, 124, 225
Minor tonality	18	6, 7, 22, 23, 26, 28, 31, 33, 34, 115, 117, 118, 119, 120, 178, 223, 224, 231
Total	32	

FIRST NOTE OF SONG—ITS RELATION TO KEYNOTE

	Number of songs.	Serial Nos. of songs.
Beginning on the—		
Twelfth	7	6, 30, 34, 35, 117, 118, 224
Eleventh	1	23
Tenth	5	27, 28, 32, 33, 119
Ninth	3	26, 116, 124
Octave	6	22, 114, 120, 123, 223, 225
Fifth	6	9, 29, 31, 115, 121, 231
Third	1	8
Second	1	7
Keynote	2	10, 178
Total	32	

LAST NOTE OF SONG—ITS RELATION TO KEYNOTE

	Number of songs.	Serial Nos. of songs.
Ending on the—		
Fifth	12	7, 9, 10, 26, 31, 32, 114, 115, 116, 124, 178, 231
Third	5	8, 29, 33, 119, 121
Keynote	15	6, 22, 23, 27, 28, 30, 34, 35, 117, 118, 120, 123, 223, 224, 225
Total	32	

[1] This group comprises songs a majority of which are believed to be less than 50 years old.

Comparatively Modern Songs—(1) War Songs (sec. 2)—Continued

MELODIC ANALYSIS—Continued

LAST NOTE OF SONG—ITS RELATION TO COMPASS OF SONG

	Number of songs.	Serial Nos. of songs.
Songs in which final tone is—		
Lowest tone in song	27	6, 7, 8, 9, 22, 23, 26, 27, 29, 31, 32, 34, 35, 114, 115, 116, 117, 118, 119, 120, 121, 123, 124, 223, 224, 225, 231
Immediately preceded by major third below	1	178
Immediately preceded by whole tone below	1	28
Immediately preceded by semitone below	1	30
Songs containing a minor third below the final tone	2	10, 33
Total	32	

NUMBER OF TONES COMPRISING COMPASS OF SONG

	Number of songs.	Serial Nos. of songs.
Compass of—		
Thirteen tones	5	32, 34, 35, 124, 178
Twelve tones	10	6, 7, 26, 27, 30, 114, 116, 117, 118, 224
Eleven tones	1	23
Ten tones	6	8, 28, 29, 33, 120, 121
Nine tones	2	123, 223
Eight tones	7	9, 22, 31, 115, 119, 225, 231
Six tones	1	6
Total	32	

TONE MATERIAL

	Number of songs.	Serial Nos. of songs.
Second five-toned scale	2	23, 120
Fourth five-toned scale	3	8, 29, 225
Major triad and seventh	1	9
Major triad and second	1	124
Minor triad and fourth	3	118, 119, 231
Minor triad and second	1	178
Octave complete	4	34, 114, 117, 224
Octave complete except seventh	4	27, 32, 35, 123
Octave complete except seventh and sixth	3	7, 31, 223
Octave complete except seventh and fourth	2	26, 115
Octave complete except seventh and second	1	10
Octave complete except sixth	1	28
Octave complete except sixth, fifth, and second	1	33
Octave complete except sixth and second	1	6
Octave complete except fourth	2	30, 116
Octave complete except third and second	1	22
Octave complete except second	1	121
Total	32	

Comparatively Modern Songs—(1) War Songs (sec. 2)—Continued

MELODIC ANALYSIS—Continued

ACCIDENTALS

	Number of songs.	Serial Nos. of songs.
Songs containing—		
No accidentals..................................	23	7, 8, 10, 23, 26, 27, 28, 29, 30, 31, 32, 33, 34, 35, 115, 116, 117, 118, 119, 121, 178, 223, 231
Seventh raised a semitone.........................	2	6, 120
Sixth raised a semitone...........................	1	224
Second raised a semitone..........................	1	225
Seventh lowered a semitone........................	1	9
Sixth lowered a semitone..........................	1	123
Fourth lowered a semitone.........................	1	22
Third and second lowered a semitone, and fourth raised a semitone.	1	114
Third lowered a semitone..........................	1	124
Total..	32	

STRUCTURE

	Number of songs.	Serial Nos. of songs.
Melodic..	16	7, 22, 23, 26, 28, 29, 30, 33, 35, 114, 117, 120, 124, 224, 225, 231
Melodic with harmonic framework....................	10	31, 32, 34, 115, 116, 119, 121, 123, 178, 223
Harmonic..	6	6, 8, 9, 10, 27, 118
Total..	32	

FIRST PROGRESSION—DOWNWARD AND UPWARD

	Number of songs.	Serial Nos. of songs.
Downward..	26	6, 7, 9, 10, 22, 23, 26, 27, 28, 29, 30, 31, 32, 33, 35, 114, 115, 116, 117, 118, 119, 121, 178, 224, 225, 231
Upward..	6	8, 34, 120, 123, 124, 223
Total..	32	

TOTAL NUMBER OF PROGRESSIONS—DOWNWARD AND UPWARD

	Number of songs.	Serial Nos. of songs.
Downward..	707	
Upward..	390	
Total..	1,097	

Comparatively Modern Songs—(1) War Songs (sec. 2)—Continued

MELODIC ANALYSIS—Continued

INTERVALS IN DOWNWARD PROGRESSION

	Number of songs.	
Interval of a—		
Minor sixth	1	
Fifth	2	
Fourth	98	
Major third	49	
Minor third	186	
Augmented second	3	
Major second	316	
Minor second	52	
Total	707	

INTERVALS IN UPWARD PROGRESSION

Interval of a—		
Ninth	1	
Octave	12	
Major sixth	4	
Fifth	28	
Fourth	63	
Major third	44	
Minor third	90	
Major second	116	
Minor second	32	
Total	390	

AVERAGE NUMBER OF SEMITONES IN AN INTERVAL

Total number of intervals	1,097	
Total number of semitones	3,374	
Average number of semitones in an interval	3.07	

Comparatively Modern Songs—(1) War Songs (sec. 2)—Continued

MELODIC ANALYSIS—Continued

KEY

	Number of songs.	Serial Nos. of songs.
Key of—		
A major	2	22, 29
A minor	2	31, 178
B flat minor	1	34
B major	1	35
B minor	2	117, 231
C major	2	8, 121
C minor	5	6, 23, 115, 119, 224
D major	2	27, 30
D minor	3	26, 33, 120
E flat major	2	116, 124
E flat minor	1	28
E major	4	10, 32, 114, 123
E minor	1	7
G major	1	225
G minor	1	223
A flat major	1	9
G sharp minor	1	118
Total	32	

RHYTHMIC ANALYSIS

PART OF MEASURE ON WHICH SONG BEGINS

	Number of songs.	Serial Nos. of songs.
Beginning on unaccented part of measure	7	7, 8, 26, 27, 117, 119, 178
Beginning on accented part of measure	25	6, 9, 10, 22, 23, 28, 29, 30, 31, 32, 33, 34, 35, 114, 115, 116, 118, 120, 121, 123, 124, 223, 224, 225, 231
Total	32	

RHYTHM OF FIRST MEASURE

	Number of songs.	Serial Nos. of songs.
First measure in—		
2–4 time	27	6, 7, 8, 9, 22, 23, 26, 27, 29, 30, 31, 32, 33, 34, 35, 115, 116, 117, 118, 119, 120, 121, 123, 178, 224, 225, 231
3–4 time	5	10, 28, 114, 124, 223
Total	32	

Comparatively Modern Songs—(1) War Songs (sec. 2)—Continued

RHYTHMIC ANALYSIS—Continued

CHANGE OF TIME, MEASURE LENGTHS

	Number of songs.	Serial Nos. of songs.
Songs containing no change of time....................	4	31, 32, 34, 121
Songs containing a change of time.....................	28	6, 7, 8, 9, 10, 22, 23, 26, 27, 28, 29, 30, 33, 35, 114, 115, 116, 117, 118, 119, 120, 123, 124, 178, 223, 224, 225, 231
Total...	32	

RHYTHM OF DRUM

	Number of songs.	Serial Nos. of songs.
Eighth notes unaccented.............................	6	28, 32, 35, 117, 121, 231
Quarter notes unaccented............................	11	6, 26, 27, 29, 31, 33, 34, 114, 120, 123, 124
Eighth notes accented in groups of two...............	3	8, 30, 118
Each beat preceded by an unaccented beat corresponding to third count of a triplet.	4	9, 10, 115, 119
Drum not recorded...................................	8	7, 22, 23, 116, 178, 223, 224, 225,
Total...	32	

RHYTHMIC UNIT OF SONG

	Number of songs.	Serial Nos. of songs.
Songs containing—		
No rhythmic unit................................	5	22, 23, 178, 223, 231
One rhythmic unit...............................	19	9, 10, 27, 28, 29, 31, 32, 35, 114, 115, 116, 117, 119, 120, 121, 123, 124, 224, 225
Two rhythmic units.............................	6	6, 8, 26, 33, 34, 118
Three rhythmic units...........................	1	7
Five rhythmic units.............................	1	30
Total...	32	

*Comparatively Modern Songs—(1) War Songs (sec. 2)—*Continued

RHYTHMIC ANALYSIS—Continued

METRIC UNIT OF VOICE (TEMPO)

	Number of songs.	Serial Nos. of songs.
Metronome—		
56	1	23
63	1	22
66	3	123, 178, 225
69	1	224
72	1	223
76	2	27, 124
80	6	6, 29, 30, 115, 120, 231
84	3	31, 35, 116
88	4	26, 114, 117, 119
92	1	28
96	2	7, 9
104	3	8, 118, 121
112	1	10
176	3	32, 33, 34
Total	32	

METRIC UNIT OF DRUM (TEMPO)

	Number of songs.	Serial Nos. of songs.
Metronome—		
56	1	114
60	1	29
63	1	124
66	1	123
76	1	27
80	4	6, 30, 115, 120
84	2	31, 35
88	3	26, 117, 231
92	1	28
96	2	8, 119
104	4	9, 10, 118, 121
176	3	32, 33, 34
Drum not recorded	8	7, 22, 23, 116, 178, 223, 224, 225
Total	32	

Comparatively Modern Songs—(1) War Songs (sec. 2)—Continued

RHYTHMIC ANALYSIS—Continued

COMPARISON OF METRIC UNIT OF VOICE AND DRUM

	Number of songs.	Serial Nos. of songs.
Drum and voice having same metric unit.............	16	6, 26, 27, 28, 30, 31, 32, 33, 34, 35, 115, 117, 118, 120, 121, 123
Drum faster than voice..............................	3	9, 119, 231
Drum slower than voice.............................	5	8, 10, 29, 114, 124
Drum not recorded.................................	8	7, 22, 23, 116, 178, 223, 224, 225
Total..	32	

A majority of the remaining songs in this work are comparatively modern, their analyses, together with section 2 of the war songs, comprising Group 2 in the collective analyses shown on pages 12–21.

THE BUFFALO HUNT (WANA'SAPI[1])

The buffalo may be said to have been the essential element in the life of the Plains Indians, as it supplied them with material for their tents, clothing, and moccasins; with food and containers for food, and household articles; with tools for their handicraft, and even with fuel for their fires. Every part of the animal was utilized. Among the less familiar articles made from parts of the buffalo were handles for small tools. These were fashioned from a certain heavy sinew of the neck, sharp needles of bone or metal, and knife blades, being inserted in pieces of the "green" sinew. When dry the sinew served as a firm and servicable handle for the tool. It is said also that a heavy sinew of the buffalo's hind leg was dried and cut into arrowpoints.

The tribal life of the Sioux passed away with the herds of buffalo. The last great buffalo hunt on the Standing Rock Reservation took place in 1882, under the supervision of Maj. James McLaughlin, then Indian agent on that reservation. During this hunt 5,000 buffalo were killed, the hunting party comprising about 600 mounted Sioux.[2] Major McLaughlin became agent at Standing Rock in 1881, that year being designated in the Sioux picture calendar *Wable'za Tatan'ka-iyo'take wana' nape'yuza wani'yetu*, "Winter in which Major McLaughlin shook hands with Sitting Bull." The following year is called *wable'za Lako'ta ob wana'sa ipi' wani'yetu*, "Winter in which Major McLaughlin with the Sioux went on a buffalo hunt." The drawing which marks this year is shown in figure 36.

A graphic account of buffalo hunting is given by Catlin, who took part in the buffalo hunts of the Indians in the same part of the country, many years ago.[3]

In studying the customs of the buffalo hunt among the Teton Sioux the writer interviewed many old men, later reading the unfinished narrative to them so they might discuss it and make corrections or additions. The completed material comprises an account of the making of buffalo bows and arrows, and the cutting up of the buffalo, by White Hawk, a narrative of the searching party by Śiya'ka, and an account of the hunt consisting chiefly of information given by Swift Dog and Gray Hawk.

---

[1] This word means "hunt," the name of the animal to be hunted being understood. (Cf. use of the word *itan'čan*, footnote, p. 70.)

[2] McLaughlin, James, My Friend the Indian, pp. 97–116, Boston and New York, 1910.

[3] Catlin, George, The Manners, Customs, and Condition of the North American Indians, vol. 1, pp. 251–261, London, 1841. Cf. also a description of the hunting customs of the Omaha in The Omaha Tribe, Fletcher and La Flesche, op. cit., p. 275.

The usual time for a buffalo hunt was the early fall, when the buffalo came down from the north, but a few could be found at almost any season of the year. The medicine-men had an important part in maintaining the food supply for the camp. They sometimes gave warning of times of scarcity and advised the procuring of a liberal supply of food. This advice was heeded and a special hunt was made. There were times when it was not permissible for a man to hunt independently. At such a time, if a man were found with a supply of fresh meat which he could not satisfactorily account for, it was the duty of the aki'cita to seize it. Further, they might beat the man with clubs and tear down his tipi. (See p. 313.)

The making of bows and arrows for the buffalo hunt was described by White Hawk (Ćetaŋ'ska), a Sioux from the Cheyenne River

FIG. 36. Drawing from picture calendar—the year of the last buffalo hunt.

Reservation (Mr. Edward Swan interpreting). Although these were said to be "buffalo bows and arrows," it is probable that they were similar in design to those used in war. White Hawk said:

The buffalo bows of two men were seldom exactly alike, either in pattern or in strength, but one characteristic which all had in common was that the place for fitting the arrow was nearer the upper than the lower end of the bow, the lower section being longer and thicker than the upper. Some men used the wood of the cherry or plum tree for their bows, while others preferred the crab apple or some other hardwood. The back of the bow was covered with sinew which had been made flexible by rubbing and then dried. When this was ready the back of the bow was cut in numerous places and covered with glue made from the hide of the buffalo, the part used for this purpose being a strip between the horns, back of the eyes; the sinew was then applied and became part of the bow. The string of the bow was of the sinew of the buffalo bull, twisted and dried.

White Hawk said further he knew of three kinds of arrow points: (1) His great grandfather used arrow points of cut flint; he had seen these as a boy, but had never used them. (2) His father used arrow points of bone, made from the outer thickness of ribs or marrow bones. (3) He himself used arrow points of steel. It was the custom in his hunting days to cut arrow points from the thin frying pans sold by traders or used by the soldiers. Feathers used on the arrows were not confined to any one kind. Some used feathers of the prairie hen, owl, or chicken hawk that were large enough to split, while others used the smaller feathers of the eagle or buzzard. White Hawk said that after splitting a feather he held one end in his mouth and "scratched it carefully with a knife to smooth it." Three feathers were fastened to each arrow. Glue was placed under the feathers and under the arrow point, both being fastened by wrappings of deer sinew.

It was said that a *good* bow would send an arrow into a buffalo so that the arrow point was imbedded in the flesh, an *excellent* bow would drive it in almost to the feather, while a *fine* bow would send the same arrow clear through the animal.

The proper length for a man's buffalo arrow was the distance on the outside of his arm from the elbow to the end of the third finger, plus the length of his hand from the wrist to the large knuckle of the third finger. It was the intention to make the arrow as light as possible, therefore the woods preferred for the shaft were juneberry (*wi'paźukahu*) and wild currant (*wića'ganaśkahu*). These were so flexible that if a buffalo fell on an arrow, the latter bent without breaking. Thus the arrow could be recovered and used again by its owner.

Certain lines were cut in the shaft of an arrow "to make it go straight." A straight line about an inch long was cut in the shaft, extending downward from the point of attachment of the feather. Then the graving tool was held firmly in the hand while the shaft was moved sidewise, so that the line became wavy. At a distance of about 3 inches from the arrow point the shaft was held still so that a straight line was again secured. White Hawk said that the proper manner of cutting these lines was "the result of long experience," and that an arrow would not move in a direct course without them.

After fastening the arrow point and the feathers, and cutting the lines, the maker used a pair of small whetstones in polishing the shaft. These were said to be composed of a certain kind of stone found in the Black Hills, which was rather soft. A groove was cut in each whetstone, the grooves being of such size that when the stones were fitted together, the opening formed by the two grooves was the diameter of the arrow shaft, which was polished by moving the stones to and fro. In order that the surface of the arrow shaft might be kept clean the whetstones were brushed with buckskin after being used and were then carefully wrapped in the same material.

Each man had a special mark for his arrows. Bear Face (p. 78) said that he considered pelican feathers as best for arrows, and that he always used one pelican feather on his arrows, the other feathers being taken from some other bird. Others are said to have painted their arrows red, or with a blue section in the middle, or to have made "dents" in the shaft, each man using his own device.

As a final process the shaft of the arrow was smeared with buffalo blood, White Hawk saying this made the arrow go more smoothly through the tissues of the animal.

Most quivers held 10 arrows. A man might make his own quiver, although he usually ordered arrows from an arrow maker, a hundred at a time. Red Fox (pp. 90, 375, et seq.) was known as a skillful arrow-maker in the old days.

A buffalo hunt frequently took place when the tribe was about to move to a new camping place. In describing such a hunt Śiya'ka said:

When the tribe was about to move to a new camp the old men met to decide whether there was enough food to last for a considerable time. If it was decided that a hunt was advisable these old men consulted the leaders in the various societies (as the Strong Heart or White Horse societies), and together they decided on the young men who were to go and search for the buffalo. This task required young men who were known to be truthful and faithful to duty, as well as possessed of the necessary physical ability and general equipment. Only men were selected who were known to be ready, as there was not sufficient time to prepare after they were notified. This was one of the greatest honors which could be conferred on a man, as it indicated that the tribe depended upon him for help in the food supply, without which it could not exist. It was necessary that these men know the topography of the country and understand the ways of the buffalo.

These young men were notified, and as soon as they could make the arrangements which of necessity must be left till the last moment, they went to the center of the tribal circle, with their equipment of food and extra moccasins, each man carrying also a drinking cup and perhaps some cooking utensil. The man who was first selected was the leader of the searching party.[1] Their relatives were so gratified that the young men were thus honored that they gave away many presents when the party started out, these presents being valuable and including horses and blankets.

The departure of the searching party was a great event.[2] They were gathered in the midst of the camp circle, surrounded by rejoicing and gifts. A man recognized for high standing in the tribe was chosen to "start them off." A stick was placed upright in the ground, and he led them as they marched single file around this stick. The stick signified an enemy or a buffalo, and no one was allowed to strike it unless he had killed either an enemy or a buffalo. The man chosen to start off the party was usually a man who had done both these. People on horseback were ready to escort the party from the camp. The direction in which the buffalo were probably located was pointed out, and the party started in that direction. They moved with a dancing step, and no drum or rattle was carried. The following song was sung at this time.

---

[1] Śiya'ka was once appointed leader of a searching party, and six times was a member of such a party. Bows and arrows were used on those hunts.

[2] Compare description of departure of those who went to select the Sun-dance pole, p. 107.

No. 180. Song of the Buffalo Hunt (a)   (Catalogue No. 475)

Sung by ŚIYA′KA

VOICE ♩ = 92

DRUM ♩ = 92

Drum-rhythm similar to No. 6

Analysis.—The tones in this song are E flat–G–B flat and C. By the test of the ear E flat seems the most satisfactory keynote; the song is therefore classified as major in tonality, and its tone material is considered to be the major triad and sixth. The tonic is found only in the upper octave and in connection with C, forming the interval of a minor third, which comprises 69 per cent of the entire number of intervals. In this, as in many other Indian songs, the fact that a certain tone seems the keynote of the song does not imply that the corresponding "key" is fully established. Six renditions were recorded; these are uniform throughout. The song as a whole has an interesting completeness of rhythm, though there is no repeated phrase which can be regarded as a rhythmic unit.

Śiya′ka continued:

After the escorting party had returned to the camp, the searchers were entirely under the control of their leader. Sometimes he assigned a territory to each of his men and scattered them over the prairie, directing them to meet at a certain time and place. When the men made their report to him, they were expected to be definite and sure in their statements. If they reported that they had seen buffalo they must be able to give an estimate of the number in the herd. It occasionally happened that a searching party was unsuccessful. In that event they straggled back to the main camp, attracting as little attention as possible. The longest absence of a party remembered by Śiya′ka was 12 days.

As soon as the searching party had started, the tribe broke camp and began its journey to the place designated for the next camp, where the searchers were expected to make their report. Having reached this place and made their camp, they began an anxious watch for the return of the searchers. Men were stationed to watch for them, and if these men saw them coming they returned to the camp, and the crier announced to the people that the searching party was in sight. The searching party gave certain signals to indicate the result of their search, running back and forth if the buffalo were close at hand, or waving a blanket at its full width and then laying it flat on the ground if they had seen a particularly large herd. Some went on horseback to meet them, and the entire tribe assembled in the middle of the circle to hear their report. The following song was sung as they returned.

No. 181. Song of the Buffalo Hunt (b)   (Catalogue No. 476)

Sung by ŚIYA′KA

VOICE ♩ = 80
DRUM ♩ = 80
Drum-rhythm similar to No. 6

Analysis.—Five renditions of this song were recorded. The time was not strictly maintained, and the rhythm of the opening measures was difficult to discern; however, as in all such songs, when the correct note values are determined it is found that all the renditions are alike, and that the rhythm is in reality quite simple. The only ascending intervals in this song are the major second and fourth, and the only descending intervals are the major second and minor third. The song is based on the fourth five-toned scale, has a compass of nine tones, and is melodic in structure.

The party entered the tribal circle with the leader in advance.[1] The stick was again placed upright in the ground, and they circled around it, many striking it. In the middle of the council tent a small space of bare ground had been made ready. This was hard and smooth, not pulverized as in the Alo′waŋpi ceremony, the Spirit-keeping lodge, and the Sun-dance ceremony. [See pp. 71, 82, 122.] A buffalo chip was placed on this bare ground, and beside it were placed a little sweet grass and a pipe filled and ready to smoke. The searcher who was first to see the buffalo entered the lodge in advance of his companions. As they entered the lodge many of the people stood with hands upraised, then saying *Hi, hi!* they stooped and placed the palms of their hands on the ground.

Beside the spot of bare ground stood a man whose record was above reproach, and who had been selected to act as itaŋ′ćaŋ, master of ceremonies. [See footnote, p. 70.] His entire body was painted red. Lifting the pipe from the ground, he took a little of the buffalo chip and sprinkled it on the tobacco in the pipe. He then took flint and steel, lit the chip on the ground and laid the sweet grass upon it. After passing the pipe over the smoke of the sweet grass four times, he pretended to light it, holding the bowl first to one side and then to another side of the chip. This was done three times, and the fourth time he lit the pipe. The itaŋ′ćaŋ then swung the pipe in a circle over the chip, holding the bowl in the center, after which he offered it to the man who first saw the buffalo. He puffed it four times. The itaŋ′ćaŋ swung it again four times above the buffalo chip, and offered it to the other searchers, who also puffed it four times. It was necessary that this be done four times, and therefore if there were only two searchers the pipe was offered to each of them twice in order that the proper number be observed. After the searchers had puffed the pipe it was offered to all those sitting in the lodge, and they touched their lips to the pipe, even though it had gone out. When this was finished, the itaŋ′ćaŋ emptied the pipe, and the people in the front row of listeners sat with the palms of their hands on the ground as the searchers were

---

[1] From this point the narrative is chiefly that of Swift Dog, interpreted by Mrs. McLaughlin.

asked for their report. The itaŋ'ćaŋ did not ask a direct question but said to the man who first saw the buffalo, "You are not a child. You must tell me truthfully what you have seen, and where you saw it." The man might reply thus: "I mounted a certain butte and looked down where I have seen buffalo before, and there I saw two herds, near the butte on which I was standing." [It was the custom when speaking of buffalo to point with the thumb, not with the finger, and this custom was followed by Swift Dog when describing the event.]

"You say that you have seen the wallows and those who make the wallows. I am sure you have spoken truly, and you have made my heart good," said the itaŋ'ćaŋ, while the listeners cried *Hi'*, and touched the ground again with the palms of their hands.

Then the itaŋ'caŋ said, "If you saw anything beyond this which is worth reporting, tell it to me." The searcher might reply, "Beyond the two herds I saw the plain black with buffalo." And the people would say *Hi'* once more.

Thus far the people had remained very quiet, but when the report was completed there was great excitement. The crier shouted, "Put saddles on your horses! Put saddles on your horses! We go now to hunt the buffalo!" As soon as this announcement was made to the whole village, the horses were brought in, and men and horses were painted. Whetstones were brought out and knives were sharpened. The scene was one of busy preparation for the great event.

Five or more men were selected from among the aki'cita to keep order during the hunt. These men went to the council tent and received their final instructions from the chiefs, who told them to be sure to secure beeves for the helpless, the old and cripples, as well as for women who had no one to provide for them. These aki'cita were men of executive ability, and were men to whose authority the people were accustomed. They directed the people on their journey and required them to move quietly so that the buffalo would not become alarmed. When nearly in sight of the buffalo other aki'cita were selected. The method of approaching the herd was of course not always the same, but in an ordinary hunt the party was divided into two sections, each led by about five aki'cita, under whose direction they surrounded the herd, and at whose command they plunged into the chase. Those who were to chase the buffalo took the saddles from their horses. Every man had his arrows ready, with the special mark so he could claim the animals he killed. It was like a horse race. As soon as the man shouted "Ready!" they were off, and you could see nothing but dust. The men who had fast horses tried to get the fattest buffalo. Each man tried to get the best possible animals as his trophies of the hunt.

The following is a song of the chase, sung by Gray Hawk (pl. 71), a successful buffalo hunter in the old days, who contributed interesting details to the foregoing narrative.

No. 182. Song of the Buffalo Hunt (c)   (Catalogue No. 545)

Sung by GRAY HAWK

VOICE ♩ = 92
DRUM ♩ = 92
Drum-rhythm similar to No. 6

GRAY HAWK

Analysis.—In many respects this song is like No. 181. E flat appears to be most satisfactory as its keynote, and analyzing it in the key of E flat major, we find the tone material to be the tonic triad and sixth, yet 73 per cent of the intervals are minor thirds. The remaining intervals are two major seconds and one ascending fourth. The song is so short that the phonograph cylinder contains a large number of renditions, in which there are no points of difference. The song was usually sung twice with no break in the time, then shrill cries were given, after which the song was resumed, the drum continuing a steady beat throughout the entire performance.

When the killing of the buffalo was finished the meat was dressed and prepared for transportation to the camp. White Hawk gave a description of the cutting up of a buffalo, which was read to Heḣa′ka-wa′-kita (Looking Elk), who pronounced it correct. These two men were said to be especially proficient in this phase of the buffalo hunt. The description, which follows (interpreted by Edward Swan), is that of the cutting up of a buffalo cow:

If the hide were to be used for a tent it was removed whole instead of being cut along the back. In this process the animal was turned on its back, the head being turned to the left so it came under the shoulder, and the horns stuck in the ground so that the head formed a brace. In old days a clamshell was used as a skinning knife; such a tool with its case was carried by the mother of Eagle Shield. [See pl. 67.] When steel knives became available they were used instead of the shells.

In removing a hide to be used for a tent they began on the under side of a front leg, cut to the center of the breast, to the lip, then up to a point between the horns, and then from one horn to the other. A cut was made down the belly and the inside of the hind legs; the tail was also split. When removing a hide for use as a robe, they laid the animal on its belly with legs extended front and back. In this case the cut began on the upper lip and extended along the backbone to the tip of the tail. The hide of one side was folded back and spread on the ground, and the carcass was laid on that while the cuts were made along the belly as described above.

When removing a hide they did not cut all the meat from the inner surface, but left a layer of meat on the hide of the back and a still thicker piece along the belly. This was later removed by the women and was said to be very good to eat. After removing the hide it was the custom to take out the tongue, which was the part of the animal considered most delicate by the Sioux.

Beyond this point there were no established rules. White Hawk said, however, that the front quarters were usually removed first. He said there was a "blanket of flesh" on the back and sides of the animal which was removed in one piece, but that before taking this off they "worked up under it" and detached the front quarters. The hind quarters were removed at the hip joints. The hump was underneath the outer "blanket of flesh." It was composed of fat and was cut off at the backbone. Below the outer "blanket of flesh" is the inner "blanket," which was removed in two parts. One side of it was turned down, exposing the ribs and the entrails. The carcass was then cut along the belly, up the shoulder, and along the backbone. A fresh hoof was used as a hatchet, and in the old days a knife made of the shoulder blade was used in cutting up the animal. [See pl. 67.] The ribs were removed in the form of a slab, and the kidneys, liver, and fat also were taken out, as were the brains. White Hawk said: "In the intestines there is a pocket-shaped piece about the size of a man's arm. This was turned wrong side out, fastened with a stick, and tied at one end. The brains were put into it, and the liver and hump were tied in a bundle with it. The paunch was turned wrong side out and the heart, kidneys, and fat were put into it. The lower backbone was split and later would be chopped for boiling to extract the grease."

Each hunter usually provided two horses for bringing home the meat of one buffalo. This meat was divided into eight portions, as follows: (1) The outer "blanket of flesh."; (2) the hump, brains, and liver; (3) the intestines and small split bones; (4) the inner "blanket of flesh"; (5) the slabs of ribs; (6) the front quarters; (7) the hind quarters; (8) the hip bones and backbone.

If the hide had been split for a robe it was customary to put half the hide on each horse, then to lay the "outer blanket of flesh," which is in one piece, on the horse, and the inner "blanket of flesh," which is in two pieces, on the other horse, then to pile on the other bundles of meat but not tie them, as the ends of the hide were folded over and held them in place. If the hide had been removed in one piece for a tent, it was made into an additional bundle, and the hunter packed it separately.

A few women who were good riders usually went with a hunting party to help herd the pack horses until the men had the meat ready to load. After the hunting party returned to their camp the women finished cutting up the meat, the long strips for drying being cut with the grain of the meat. These long strips were hung in the open air and when thoroughly dried were pounded and mixed with wild cherries, or with the fat of the animal. Meat prepared in this way was kept for an indefinite length of time and constituted a staple article of food among the Sioux.

The following song is a medicine-man's song to secure buffalo in time of famine. Śiya'ka said that he had known of its successful use in this connection.

The medicine-man painted a buffalo skull with red and blue stripes and laid beside it a filled pipe on a bed of fresh sage.[1] It was believed that "the skull turned into a real buffalo and called others." This song was sung in the dark. In the song it is the buffalo who speaks. Śiya'ka said that in the old days, after this ceremony on the part of the medicine-man and the singing of this song, the buffalo came near the camp and thus the famine was relieved.

---

[1] See p. 185, footnote.

No. 183. Song To Secure Buffalo in Time of Famine   (Catalogue No. 469)

Sung by ŚIYA'KA

VOICE ♩ = 76
DRUM not recorded

Ća-noŋ-pa waŋ ća-źe - yal

ma - ni - pi   o - ta e - ya - ḣpe - ya ma - wa - ni

WORDS

(*First rendition*)

ćanoŋ'pa waŋ...............	a pipe [1]
ćaze'yal....................	they mentioned
ma'nipi....................	as they walked
o'ta.......................	many times
eya'ḣpeya..................	I have offered this
mawa'ni...................	as I walked

(*Second rendition*)

maka' śa waŋ...............	a red earth
ćaze'yal....................	they mentioned
ma'nipi....................	as they walked
o'ta.......................	many times
ićaḣ'tak...................	it has been placed upon me
mawa'ni...................	as I walked

(*Third rendition*)

maka'to waŋ...............	a blue earth
ćaze'yal....................	they mentioned
ma'nipi....................	as they walked
o'ta.......................	many times
ićaḣ'tak...................	it has been placed upon me
mawa'ni...................	as I walked

---

[1] This was said to refer to the pipe brought to the Sioux by the White Buffalo Maiden. (See pp. 63–66.)

Analysis.—All the "verses" of this song were recorded, the repetitions of the melody showing no differences except in note values affected by the words. It is not a rhythmic melody. In structure the song is melodic. The tonality is minor, and all the tones of the octave are present except the second. Two-thirds of the progressions are downward, and about 57 per cent of the intervals are major seconds.

A white buffalo is said to have been particularly swift and wary; for this reason, as well as because of its rarity, it was very difficult to secure. It was a handsome animal, the rougher parts of the fur being soft and fine, and the smooth parts shiny and glossy. The horns were black and the hoofs pinkish, the end of its nose, too, being pink. The last white buffalo seen on the Standing Rock Reservation was killed near the Missouri River, in the vicinity of the present town of Pollock.

If a white buffalo were killed in a hunt the fatal arrow was purified in the smoke of burning sweet grass. A knife was similarly purified before the animal was skinned, and the hide was removed in such manner that no blood was shed on it. Only men who had dreamed of animals were allowed to eat any portion of the flesh of a white buffalo.

Although a large prize was offered for the killing of this animal, the hide was not disposed of while the tribe was on the hunt, but was held until the people reached home, so that all the requirements could be fulfilled. The skin was not treated like an ordinary buffalo hide. Only women noted for purity of life could touch or tan it, and after the tanning was finished certain important ceremonies were required. It was the custom for a medicine-man to purify the hide with sweet grass.

The tanned robe was always kept in a rawhide case. The owner of such a robe usually retained it to be buried with him. If, however, he was willing to dispose of it, he might call together men who had owned similar robes and make this known to them. Great honor was given a man who was willing to dispose of a white buffalo robe. A small piece was worth a horse; even the smallest portion of the robe was a "sacred article" to the person who secured it, and could be taken only by one who had owned part or all of a similar robe.

Jaw said that he killed a white buffalo when his band of the tribe were in Canada. He was only 13 years of age at the time, and the buffalo which he killed was the only white one in a herd of about a hundred. Not caring for the others, he killed only this one. It was a beautiful animal, only its horns being black. Jaw killed it in the fall and kept the hide all winter, selling it in the spring to a man named Bone Club (Hohu'-ćaŋ'lipi) for two horses, a big buffalo-hide tent, and many other articles. This exploit, as well as his killing of a bear and an elk with bow and arrows, is shown in one of his drawings. (See pl. 60, A.)

Jaw said that on three occasions he killed a bear with a gun, but that it was very hard to do so with bow and arrows. The circumstances under which he was successful in this are as follows.

One summer he and another man had been hunting deer and were returning with their horses loaded with meat. Jaw had a gun, while his companion carried a bow and arrows. They saw a mother bear and two cubs coming toward them. Giving the gun to his companion, Jaw took his bow and arrows. The bear tried to fight him, and as it turned he hit the beast with an arrow. Three times the bear renewed the attack, but each time he wounded it with an arrow, finally killing it.

The elk hunt (shown in pl. 60) took place in winter, when he was 22 years old. He had recently married a Yankton Sioux girl and was staying in her part of the country. There were two other families camping near them, making three tents in all. Early one morning Jaw's wife left the tent, but returned, saying: "Wake up! There are lots of elk. Come and see." Putting on moccasins and leggins, and taking his arrows and his best horse, he went after them. The snow was very deep. It was early in the morning when he shot the elk.

COUNCIL AND CHIEF SONGS

Council Songs

The following are known as "council songs"; these were sung when the chiefs met in the council tent to decide matters of tribal importance. This tent was placed inside the camp circle and was decorated in various ways. Plate 72 shows the council tent at the gathering at Bull Head, S. Dak., July 4, 1912.

The first song of this group was sung by Many Wounds (Wopo'-tapi), who preceded the singing by an announcement of the song, which was recorded by the phonograph and translated as follows: "Tribe, listen to me. I will sing a song of the dead chiefs. What are you saying? The chiefs have come to an end, and I sing their songs. I wish I could do as they have done, but I will try to sing their song."

No. 184. "I Sing of the Dead Chiefs" (Catalogue No. 669)

Sung by MANY WOUNDS

WORDS

kola' .... friend
ta'ku yaka' pelo' .... what you are saying (is true)
itaŋ'ćaŋ kiŋ .... the chiefs

448

DECORATED COUNCIL TENT

hena'pila.................... are gone
yelo' he.................... so
miye' kakeś' ećuŋ' uwa'tahe
we........................ I myself will try it

Analysis.—This song contains only the tones of the major triad and
second. Of the intervals 55 per cent are whole tones, and about 22
per cent minor thirds, the remaining intervals presenting a variety
of progressions, including fifths, fourths, and one major third. In
structure the song is melodic with harmonic framework.

Śiya'ka stated that the following song is very old, having been
used in the days when the entire tribe assembled for a council. It
is still sung before a council of the tribe.

No. 185. "I Fear Not" (Catalogue No. 455)

Sung by ŚIYA'KA

VOICE ♩= 76
DRUM ♩= 76
Drum-rhythm similar to No. 6

Ko- la   ta-ku
o - te - ḣi - ka   i - ma - ku - wa - pe   o   i   e
he - na   ko - wa - ki - pe   śni   le   wa-oŋ   we   he

WORDS

kola'....................... friends
ta'ku ote'ḣika............... with all manner of difficulties
ima'kuwape.................. I have been pursued
he'na....................... these
kowa'kipe śni............... I fear not
le.......................... still
waoŋ'....................... alive
we......................... am I

Analysis.—Three renditions of this song were recorded, and in every instance the difference between the tones transcribed as C natural and C sharp was clearly marked. This accidental is the sharped seventh, often present in songs of minor tonality, making a semitone between the seventh and eighth tones of the octave. This song contains the tones of the second five-toned scale and has a compass of 11 tones. Almost one-third of the intervals are minor thirds, a proportion which corresponds with the tonality of the song. Two-thirds of the intervals are downward progressions.

The following is a typical song of the chiefs in council:

No. 186. "I Wish To Do My Part"   (Catalogue No. 614)

Sung by USED-AS-A-SHIELD

WORDS

oya'te kiŋhaŋ' ta'ku aki'yapi
ćaŋ'na he................. whatever the tribe deçide upon in council
he'na oki'hi waćaŋ'mi yelo'.   that is what I wish to do my part in accomplishing

Analysis.—In prominence of the fourth and the minor second this song resembles No. 194. The proportion of fourths is about 22 per cent, and of minor seconds about 36 per cent. A combination of these two intervals is unusual. Next in number are the minor thirds. The intonation is not good, yet in both renditions the flatted fourth was clearly sung. The song is minor in tonality and lacks the seventh tone of the complete octave. It is melodic in structure and has a compass of an octave, extending from the dominant above to the dominant below the tonic.

This council song is similar in use to the preceding:

No. 187. "His Customs I Adopted"　　(Catalogue No. 615)

Sung by Used-as-a-Shield

VOICE ♩ = 66
DRUM ♩ = 66
Drum-rhythm similar to No. 6

A - te　ta - wi - ćo - ḣaŋ - pi kiŋ

o - wa - piŋ　na he *ya* i - yo - ti - ye　wa - ki ye - lo

WORDS

ate′	father (referring to the old men, his ancestors)
tawi′ćoḣaŋ′pi kiŋ	his customs
owa′piŋ	I adopted
na	and
he	hence
iyo′tiye	a hard time
waki′ yelo′	I am having

Analysis.—This song contains a large variety of intervals, there being seven kinds of upward, and six kinds of downward, progressions. Of the intervals 75 per cent are minor thirds and major seconds. The song is major in tonality, melodic in structure, and lacks the seventh tone of the complete octave. Three rhythmic units are found in the song, the second and third having one count division in common. The manner in which these units are used is particularly interesting.

CHIEF SONGS

There appear to be two kinds of Chief songs: Those which voice the thought of the chiefs, and those sung in honor of the chiefs. Thus the second song in the Sun-dance group was said to be a Chief song. It contains the words, "Friends take courage; right here we are coming; they see us." In explanation of this class of songs a Sioux said, "The chiefs do not sing these songs; the people sing them meaning 'the *chief says* so and so'." The following belongs to the second class of Chief songs and is said to be an old and particularly good example. Two Bears was the head chief of the Lower Yanktonais band of Sioux, the most numerous band on the Standing Rock Reservation, and was prominent in tribal councils. He died about the year 1886. An interesting record concerning this man is preserved in the report of the Indian agent for the year 1874.[1] This record is as follows:

On the 1st of July I was informed that a party of young men had left this agency to make war on Indians up the river. I asked the principal chiefs to stop these proceedings. They promptly responded by sending their soldiers out, who overtook the war party and brought them back. The conduct of Chief Two Bears and Chief Antelope on this occasion deserves particular credit. The defeat of the party is mainly attributable to the energetic action of these two chiefs.

---

[1] Palmer, Edmond, in *Indian Affairs Rep.* for 1874, p. 248, Washington, 1874.

No. 188. Song in Honor of Two Bears (Catalogue No. 454)

Sung by ŚIYA´KA

VOICE ♩ = 112
DRUM ♩ = 112
Drum-rhythm similar to No. 19

O - ya - te kiŋ　　ta - ku　a - ki - ya - pi

ćaŋ - na　Ma - to - noŋ - pa　wi - ća - la　śni　wa - ni - će

WORDS

oya´te kiŋ................... the tribe
ta´ku aki´yapi ćaŋ´na........ whenever they council
Mato´-noŋ´pa................ Two Bears
wića´la śni wani´će.......... never refuses

Analysis.—Like many other melodies on the fourth five-toned scale, this song has a large proportion of minor thirds, that interval forming more than 55 per cent of the entire number. The major third and the fourth each appears three times. The indicated change of tempo occurs in all three renditions, the metronome speed of each part of the song being accurate. The tempo of the drum remains the same throughout the song. (See song No. 5.) The song has a compass of an octave and was sung with good intonation.

The two songs next following are in honor of Gabriel Renville, chief of the Sisseton Sioux, and were recorded at Sisseton by his son, Moses Renville. The following information concerning him has been published by the South Dakota Historical Society:[1]

Gabriel Renville, chief of the Sissetons, was a representative of one of the most noted families of the frontier. . . . The first representative of the Renville family in the Northwest was Joseph Raenville, or Renville, a French Canadian voyageur and fur hunter, who married into the Kaposia, or Little Raven band of the Sioux. The

[1] Robinson, De Lorme W., in *South Dakota Historical Collections*, vol. 1, p. 126, Aberdeen, S. Dak., 1902.

result of this union was two half-breed sons, Joseph and Victor, father of Gabriel. The elder Joseph Renville died about 1790. . . . Gabriel, the subject of this sketch, was born at Sweet Corn's village on the west shore of Big Stone Lake, April, 1824, and died at Brown's Valley, within 10 miles of his birthplace, August 26, 1892. He became chief of the Sissetons through the aid of the military, after his band had been located on their reservation in the northeast part of South Dakota. Subsequent to the Minnesota massacre he became chief of scouts under Gen. Sibley and gained distinction for his ability.

No. 189. Song in Honor of Gabriel Renville (a)   (Catalogue No. 665)

Sung by MOSES RENVILLE (MAWIS)

VOICE ♩ = 92

DRUM ♩ = 84

Drum-rhythm similar to No. 19

WORDS

Ti'wakaŋ [1].................... Holy House (known as Gabriel Renville)
heye'do..................... has said
aki'ćita..................... a soldier
waöŋ' we.................... I am
naŋke' noŋ na de............ it is but a short life [2]
waöŋ' we.................... I have to live

Analysis.—This and the following song were recorded at Sisseton; the words are in the Santee dialect. The rhythmic form of this song is interesting. Three phrases comprise practically the entire melody, the first consisting of three measures, the second also consisting of three measures, and the third (after a connecting measure) of four measures, after which two unimportant measures close the song. Several renditions were recorded, in all of which the drum is slightly slower than the voice. The song has a distinctly minor quality, though fewer than one-fourth of the intervals are minor thirds. All the tones of the octave except the sixth are contained in the melody, which has a compass of nine tones.

See plot of this melody on page 461.

---

[1] Full form is Ti'piwakaŋ.   [2] Cf. words of songs Nos. 222 and 231.

No. 190. Song in Honor of Gabriel Renville (b)   (Catalogue No. 666)

Sung by MOSES RENVILLE

VOICE ♩= 92
DRUM ♩= 84
Drum-rhythm similar to No. 19

Ti - pi -

wa - kaŋ kiŋ he   to - ki   i- ya - ye ċa tu-we ni wa-ċiŋ wa-

ye śni a   he   Si- si - te-toŋ-waŋ kiŋ he e   ha - ya-pi do

WORDS

Ti′piwakaŋ.................	Holy House (known as Gabriel Renville)
kiŋ he.....................	even he
to′ki iya′ye..............	is departed (I know not where)
ċa.......................	therefore
tuwe′....................	upon
ni.......................	no one
waċiŋ′ waye′ śni he........	can I rely
Sisi′toŋwaŋ kiŋ...........	the Sisseton Sioux
heya′pi do...............	have said

Analysis.—In general character this song resembles the preceding, but it is longer and contains a rhythmic unit. The drum is persistently slower than the voice, as in the preceding song, throughout five renditions. Of the intervals 80 per cent are minor thirds and major seconds, the other intervals consisting of five fourths and one ascending fifth. The song has a range of an octave and is melodic in structure.

Songs Nos. 191 and 192 are in honor of men living at the present time who were chiefs of the Teton Sioux under the old tribal organization. While their actual authority has passed away, they are still regarded as chiefs and accorded some of their former honor.

This melody was recently composed and was said to be a grass-dance tune. During a gathering of Sioux at the Standing Rock Agency in the summer of 1912 this song was sung in honor of John

Grass (pl. 73), one of whose native names is Mato'-wata'kpe (Charging Bear). John Grass is the most prominent Sioux chief living at the present time (see p. 89).

No. 191. Song in Honor of John Grass   (Catalogue No. 643)

Sung by Shoots First (Toké'ya-wiéa'o)

1st rendition

Voice ♩ = 63

Drum ♩ = 63

Drum-rhythm similar to No. 6

WORDS

oya'te kiŋ....................	the tribe
waćiŋ'mayaŋ'pi..............	depend upon me
ćaŋ'na he....................	thence
teḣi'ḣiya....................	through difficulties
oma'wani yelo'..............	I have traveled
Mato'-wata'kpe..............	Charging Bear
heya'keya' pelo'............	said this (it is reported)

Analysis.—This modern melody contains a larger variety of intervals than most of the older songs. Thus we note five different ascending and four different descending intervals. The numbers of ascending and descending intervals are more nearly equal than in the older songs. All the tones of the octave except the sixth and seventh are found in the melody.

JOHN GRASS

RED FISH

No. 192. Song in Honor of Red Fish   (Catalogue No. 673)

Sung by RED FISH (pl. 74)

VOICE ♩= 80
DRUM ♩= 80
Drum-rhythm similar to No. 19

Ku - wa - a - pe e e ku - wa - a - pe e e ku - wa - a - pe e e

ku - wa - a - pe e e ku - wa - a - pe e   te - e - haŋ ku - wa - a - pe e

Psa - do - e - ka kiŋ   ku - wa - a - pe e do he   yo

Ho - ġa - aŋ - du - u - ta Psa - do - o - ka a kiŋ na - źiŋ yam - pi e e

na - źiŋ yam - pi e e   te - e - haŋ ku - wa - a pe e

Psa - do - o - ka kiŋ   ku - wa - a - pe e do

WORDS

kuwa'pe	pursued
te'haŋ	a long time
kuwa'pe	pursued
Psa'doka kiŋ	the Crow Indians
kuwa'pe do	pursued him
Hoġaŋ'-du'ta	Red Fish [1]
Psa'doka kiŋ	the Crow Indians
na'ziŋ yam'pi	surrounded him
te'haŋ	a long time
kuwa'pe	pursued
Psado'ka kiŋ	the Crow Indians
kuwa'pe do	pursued him

[1] As Red Fish is a Santee-Yanktonais Sioux, the words of his song are in the Santee dialect. Cf. the words of the songs recorded at Sisseton, among the Santee Sioux (Nos. 95, 96, 97, 189, 190, 235–240).

Analysis.—The triplet of eighth notes is so constantly repeated that it can scarcely be called a rhythmic unit. It resembles a vibrato, yet was evenly and distinctly sung in all the renditions of the song. With the exception of the octave, which occurs midway of the song, there are no intervals other than minor thirds and major seconds. There are 24 progressions in the song, 17 of which are downward. The melody tones are those of the second five-toned scale, and the song is melodic in structure.

Probably no Sioux chief is more famous than Sitting Bull (Tataŋ'ka-iyo'take, literally translated "Sitting Buffalo Bull"), plate 75, of whom the Handbook of the Indians (pt. 1, pp. 583–584) says:

Sitting Bull . . . a noted Sioux warrior and tribal leader of the Hunkpapa Teton division, born on Grand R., S. Dak., in 1834, his father being Sitting Bull, . . . a subchief. . . . He took an active part in the Plains wars of the sixties, and first became widely known to the whites in 1866, when he led a memorable raid against Ft. Duford. Sitting Bull was on the warpath with his band of followers from various tribes almost continuously from 1869 to 1876, either raiding the frontier posts or making war on the Crows or the Shoshoni, especially the former. . . . His refusal to go upon a reservation in 1876 led Gen. Sheridan to begin against him and his followers the campaign which resulted in the surprise and annihilation of Custer's troop on Little Bighorn R., Mont., in June. During this battle, in which 2,500 to 3,000 Indian warriors were engaged, Sitting Bull was in the hills "making medicine," and his accurate foretelling of the battle enabled him "to come out of the affair with higher honor than he possessed when he went into it." (McLaughlin.) Sitting Bull . . . escaped to Canada, where he remained until 1881, when he surrendered at Ft. Buford under promise of amnesty and was confined at Ft. Randall until 1883. Although he had surrendered and gone upon a reservation Sitting Bull continued unreconciled. It was through his influence that the Sioux refused to sell their land in 1888; and it was at his camp . . . that Kicking Bear organized the first ghost dance on the reservation. The demand for his arrest was followed by an attempt on the part of some of his people to rescue him, during which he was shot and killed by . . . the Indian police, Dec. 15, 1890.

Part of the writer's work was done near the site of Sitting Bull's camp, and a majority of her informants had known him in the days of his power. It was said that a striking feature of his every-day appearance was a bunch of shed buffalo hair painted red, fastened on the side of his head.[1] There is a large number of songs connected with his name, these being either songs which he sang or songs into which his name has been introduced. No attempt was made to collect many of these songs or to study the character of Sitting Bull. Two songs said to have been used by him in the practice of medicine appear as Nos. 191 and 192. Sitting Bull is also mentioned on pages 218 and 220.

The following two songs of Sitting Bull's are connected with the last years of his life.

---

[1] Shed buffalo hair was, and still is, greatly valued by the Sioux. It is said to "signify the times when the buffalo were plenty and also a remembrance of the coming of the White Buffalo Maiden." In the old days it was used as an ornament for the head, especially at a buffalo dance, and also as a charm by the Buffalo societies. (See p. 64.)

SITTING BULL

The following song was sung by Sitting Bull after he had surrendered to the United States authorities, some time after the Custer massacre.

No. 193. Song of Sitting Bull (a)   (Catalogue No. 612)

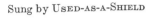

Sung by USED-AS-A-SHIELD

VOICE ♩ = 60
DRUM ♩ = 60
Drum-rhythm similar to No. 6

I - ki - ći - ze   wa - oŋ   ḳoŋ   *he*   wa - na he - na - la ye - lo

he   i - yo - ti - ye   ki - ya wa - oŋ

WORDS

iki'ćize...................... a warrior
waöŋ' ḳoŋ.................... I have been
wana'....................... now
hena'la yelo'................ it is all over
iyo'tiye kiya'.............. a hard time
waöŋ'...................... I have

Analysis.—There is an unusually large variety of intervals in this song, two renditions of which were recorded. It contains six kinds of upward and four of downward progressions. The song is characterized by the descending fourth, about one-fourth of the intervals being fourths, this number being exceeded only by the number of intervals of a major second. The tone material is the minor triad and fourth. The tonic chord is prominent in the melody, but the accents are so placed that the song is classified as melodic with harmonic framework.

See plot of this melody on page 461.

In explaining the following song Used-as-a-Shield said: "The last time that Sitting Bull was in a regular tribal camp was in the year

1889. The Sioux were camped together on the Standing Rock Reservation to consider ceding some land. Sitting Bull used to go around the camp circle every evening just before sunset on his favorite horse, singing this song." This gathering of the Sioux is mentioned on page 4.

No. 194. Song of Sitting Bull (b)   (Catalogue No. 613)

Sung by USED-AS-A-SHIELD

WORDS

oya'te kiŋhaŋ'............... the tribe
ćaźe' maya'tapi............. named me
ća......................... so
blihe'ićiya................. in courage
waöŋ' kte.................. I shall live
he heya' keya' pelo'........ it is reported
Tataŋ'ka- iyo'take.......... Sitting Bull
he heya' keya'pi lo......... said this.

Analysis.—The upward and downward progressions are more nearly equal in this than in many of the songs under analysis, the upward intervals being 18 and the downward intervals 22. The fourth is prominent, constituting 37 per cent of the intervals, while the minor second constitutes 31 per cent. Like the fourth five-toned scale, this song lacks the fourth and seventh tones of the complete octave, but the fourth five-toned scale is major in tonality (the first third being a major third), while this song is minor in tonality. This tone material is found in a few Chippewa songs and is considered in the analysis of No. 26 in this work. Syncopations occur in this melody, being clearly given in both renditions. These are unusual in Sioux and Chippewa songs. (See Songs Nos. 165 and 237, also Bull. 53, p. 130.)

PLOTS OF CHIEF SONGS

Although both Buffalo and Chief songs are included in the tabulated analysis, the plot of the hunt songs is considered with the war songs, the plot of song No. 177 appearing in figure 35, page 419.

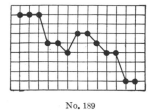
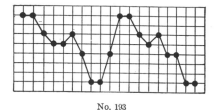

No. 189   No. 193

FIG. 37. Plots, Group 6.

An interesting peculiarity appears in the plots of the Chief songs. (Fig. 37.) Of the 8 songs constituting this group, 5 have a compass of an octave, beginning on the upper tonic and ending on the lower tonic, the note being repeatedly sounded in both octaves. It will be recalled that emphasis on the tonic is a characteristic of songs expressing self-reliance. The songs of the medicine-men and also certain war songs show this emphasis on the lower tonic. The placing of the emphasis on the upper as well as the lower tonic suggests a quality of character in the chiefs which was not in the medicine-men or the warriors. The two plots herewith shown are the songs of two men of radically different character. The first (No. 189) is a song concerning Gabriel Renville, whose stability of character won him an enduring place in history. His song, in addition to the emphasis on the tonic, shows the steadily descending trend which may be said to be the simplest as well as the most prevalent type of Indian melody. No. 193, a song of Sitting Bull's, shows as great a contrast as there was between the two men. Not only are the intervals wider and more irregular, but there appears an ascent from the lowest to the highest tone midway through the song. Such an interval at the opening of songs has been found associated with disappointment or distress. In this connection it is interesting to note that this song was associated with the last years of the life of Sitting Bull, and is said to have been sung by him during a gathering of the Sioux in 1889. This gathering was for the purpose of considering the ceding of a large portion of their land and was the preface to the breaking up of the tribe. Sitting Bull, who was a man of unusual discernment, may have foreseen what must inevitably follow. In this, as in other remarks concerning the form of these songs, the writer desires to be understood as offering only tentative observations.

The songs of this analysis group have neither origin nor use in common, the grouping being chiefly for convenience. The songs of the buffalo hunt (Nos. 180, 181) were favorite songs for that purpose, but the same songs could be used by those who went out to look for the enemy. These are followed by a song of the chase and a song to secure buffalo during a famine. (Nos. 182, 183.) Some of the council songs (Nos. 184–187) are undoubtedly very old, but it is impossible to determine their exact age. Some of the Chief songs (Nos. 5, 188–194) may also be old, as new names were often substituted for old names in songs of honor, but one of the songs (No. 191) was said to have been composed only three years ago.

Comparatively Modern Songs—(2) Songs of the Buffalo Hunt, also Council and Chief Songs

MELODIC ANALYSIS

TONALITY

	Number of songs.	Serial Nos. of songs.
Major tonality..	7	180, 181, 182, 184, 187, 188, 191
Minor tonality..	9	5, 183, 185, 186, 189, 190, 192, 193, 194
Total..	16	

FIRST NOTE OF SONG—ITS RELATION TO KEYNOTE

	Number of songs.	Serial Nos. of songs.
Beginning on the—		
Twelfth..	1	5
Tenth..	2	185, 192
Octave..	5	183, 187, 189, 190, 193
Sixth..	1	182
Fifth..	4	184, 186, 191, 194
Third..	1	188
Second..	1	181
Keynote..	1	180
Total..	16	

Comparatively Modern Songs—(2) Songs of the Buffalo Hunt, also Council and Chief Songs—Continued

MELODIC ANALYSIS—Continued

LAST NOTE OF SONG—ITS RELATION TO KEYNOTE

	Number of songs.	Serial Nos. of songs.
Ending on the—		
Fifth	5	181, 184, 186, 191, 194
Third	3	180, 182, 188
Keynote	8	5, 183, 185, 187, 190, 192, 193
Total	16	

LAST NOTE OF SONG—ITS RELATION TO COMPASS OF SONG

	Number of songs.	Serial Nos. of songs.
Songs in which final tone is lowest tone in song	15	5, 180, 182, 183, 184, 185, 186, 187, 188, 189, 190, 191, 192, 193, 194
Songs containing a minor third below the final tone	1	181
Total	16	

NUMBER OF TONES COMPRISING COMPASS OF SONG

	Number of songs.	Serial Nos. of songs.
Compass of—		
Twelve tones	1	5
Eleven tones	1	185
Ten tones	2	180, 192
Nine tones	3	181, 187, 189
Eight tones	8	183, 184, 186, 188, 190, 191, 193, 194
Six tones	1	182
Total	16	

TONE MATERIAL

	Number of songs.	Serial Nos. of songs.
Second five-toned scale	2	185, 192
Fourth five-toned scale	2	181, 188
Major triad and sixth	2	180, 182
Major triad and second	1	184
Minor triad and fourth	3	5, 190, 193
Octave complete except seventh	2	186, 187
Octave complete except seventh and sixth	1	191
Octave complete except seventh and fourth	1	194
Octave complete except sixth	1	189
Octave complete except second	1	183
Total	16	

Comparatively Modern Songs—(2) Songs of the Buffalo Hunt, also Council and Chief Songs—Continued

MELODIC ANALYSIS—Continued

ACCIDENTALS

	Number of songs.	Serial Nos. of songs
Songs containing—		
No accidentals	13	5, 180, 181, 182, 183, 184, 187, 188, 190, 191, 192, 193, 194
Seventh raised a semitone	2	185, 189
Fourth lowered a semitone	1	186
Total	16	

STRUCTURE

	Number of songs.	Serial Nos. of songs.
Melodic	11	181, 182, 183, 185, 186, 187, 189, 190, 191, 192, 194
Melodic with harmonic framework	5	5, 180, 184, 188, 193
Harmonic	None	
Total	16	

FIRST PROGRESSION—DOWNWARD AND UPWARD

	Number of songs.	Serial Nos. of songs.
Downward	11	5, 180, 181, 183, 184, 186, 188, 190, 192, 193, 194
Upward	5	182, 185, 187, 189, 191
Total	16	

TOTAL NUMBER OF PROGRESSIONS—DOWNWARD AND UPWARD

Downward	328
Upward	196
Total	524

INTERVALS IN DOWNWARD PROGRESSION

Interval of a—	
Fifth	2
Fourth	47
Major third	13
Minor third	106
Major second	139
Minor second	21
Total	328

Comparatively Modern Songs—(2) Songs of the Buffalo Hunt, also Council and Chief Songs—Continued

MELODIC ANALYSIS—Continued

INTERVALS IN UPWARD PROGRESSION

	Number of songs.	
Interval of a—		
Ninth	1	
Octave	5	
Seventh	1	
Major sixth	1	
Minor sixth	3	
Fifth	9	
Fourth	39	
Major third	15	
Minor third	57	
Major second	47	
Minor second	18	
Total	196	

AVERAGE NUMBER OF SEMITONES IN AN INTERVAL

Total number of intervals	524	
Total number of semitones	1,319	
Average number of semitones in an interval	2.5	

KEY

Key of—		
A minor	1	186
B flat minor	1	194
B major	1	191
B minor	1	5
D major	1	188
D minor	1	185
E flat major	1	182
E flat minor	1	193
E major	2	180, 181
E minor	1	183
F major	1	187
F minor	3	189, 190, 192
G major	1	184
Total	16	

Comparatively Modern Songs—(2) Songs of the Buffalo Hunt, also Council and Chief Songs—Continued

RHYTHMIC ANALYSIS

PART OF MEASURE ON WHICH SONG BEGINS

	Number of songs.	Serial Nos. of songs.
Beginning on unaccented part of measure.............	1	188
Beginning on accented part of measure................	15	5, 180, 181, 182, 183, 184, 185, 186, 187, 189, 190, 192, 193, 194
Total..	16	

RHYTHM OF FIRST MEASURE

	Number of songs.	Serial Nos. of songs.
First measure in—		
2–4 time...	10	5, 182, 183, 184, 187, 188, 189, 190, 192, 194
3–4 time...	6	180, 181, 185, 186, 191, 193
Total..	16	

CHANGE OF TIME, MEASURE-LENGTHS

	Number of songs.	Serial Nos. of songs.
Songs containing no change of time....................	None.	
Songs containing a change of time....................	16	5, 180, 181, 182, 183, 184, 185, 186, 187, 188, 189, 190, 191, 192, 193, 194
Total..	16	

RHYTHM OF DRUM

	Number of songs.	Serial Nos. of songs.
Eighth notes unaccented............................	4	188, 189, 190, 192
Quarter notes unaccented...........................	8	180, 185, 186, 187, 191, 193, 194
Each beat preceded by an unaccented beat corresponding to third count of a triplet.......................	1	5
Drum not recorded................................	3	181, 183, 184
Total..	16	

RHYTHMIC UNIT OF SONG

	Number of songs.	Serial Nos. of songs.
Songs containing—		
No rhythmic unit	6	180, 181, 183, 185, 189, 192.
One rhythmic unit	7	182, 184, 186, 188, 190, 191, 193
Two rhythmic units...........................	2	5, 194
Three rhythmic units	1	187
Total..	16	

Comparatively Modern Songs—(2) Songs of the Buffalo Hunt, also Council and Chief Songs—Continued

RHYTHMIC ANALYSIS—Continued

METRIC UNIT OF VOICE (TEMPO)

	Number of songs.	Serial Nos. of songs.
Metronome—		
60	2	193, 194
63	2	184, 191
66	2	186, 187
76	2	183, 185
80	2	181, 192
92	4	180, 182, 189, 190.
112	1	188
126	1	5
Total	16	

METRIC UNIT OF DRUM (TEMPO)

	Number of songs.	Serial Nos. of songs.
Metronome—		
60	2	193, 194
63	1	191
66	2	186, 187
76	1	185
80	1	192
84	2	189, 190
88	1	5
92	2	180, 182
112	1	188
Drum not recorded	3	181, 183, 184
Total	16	

COMPARISON OF METRIC UNIT OF VOICE AND DRUM

	Number of songs.	Serial Nos. of songs.
Drum and voice having same metric unit	10	180, 182, 185, 186, 187, 188, 191, 192, 193, 194
Drum slower than voice	3	5, 189, 190
Drum not recorded	3	181, 183, 184
Total	16	

SONGS CONNECTED WITH DANCES AND GAMES

DANCES

In every Sioux village there was a lodge of suitable size for social gatherings or dances. An old type of Sioux dance lodge is shown in plate 76, *A*, the walls being of logs and the roof of branches covered with earth, a large smoke-hole being left in the center. Plate 76, *B*, shows a lodge on the Standing Rock Reservation in which the writer witnessed a dance in 1912. The following summer she learned that it had been torn down, as the Government was enforcing more vigorously the restrictions on dancing among the Indians. In this lodge, as in the older type, the construction was of logs, branches, and earth, but the shape was rectangular, the logs were plastered with earth, and the roof was almost flat with projecting stovepipes, indicating that the lodge was heated by stoves instead of an open fire.

Concerning Indian dances it was said that—

In dancing the Indians imitate the actions of animals. In the grass dance the men imitate the motions of the eagle and graceful birds. In the buffalo dance they imitate the buffalo. The old-time dancing dress of the Indians imitated the animals, but there was always a charm or a headdress which indicated the personality of the wearer. The Indians imitate the cries of birds or animals when they dance. Some headdresses imitate the comb of a bird, and a man wearing such a headdress would imitate the actions of that bird. The actions of a dancer always correspond to his costume. This is a matter of choice and usually is not connected with a dream.

THE GRASS DANCE

The grass dance (peźi' waći'pi) may be said to exist at the present time among all the tribes of the northern plains, even to the Kutenai. The name Omaha identifies it with the Omaha tribe, from which it was received by many other tribes, but in transmission it has lost its significance, having become simply a social dance. According to Miss Fletcher, the dance originally was connected with the Hethu'shka society of the Omaha, a society whose object "was to stimulate an heroic spirit among the people and to keep alive the memory of historic and valorous acts." [1]

Miss Fletcher describes one of its meetings, stating that [2]—

No clothing except the breechcloth was worn by the members, and a long bunch of grass representing scalps the wearer had taken was fastened to the belt at the back. . . . When the dance became known to the Dakota tribes and the Winnebago, the significance of the bunch of long grass having been forgotten, they gave the

[1] Fletcher and La Flesche, The Omaha Tribe, op. cit., p. 459.　　[2] Ibid., p. 461.

A

B

SIOUX DANCE LODGES.

name "grass dance," or the "Omaha dance," the latter name in recognition of the tribe from which the dance had been obtained. Among the Omaha the leader had to be of sufficient rank to be able to wear "the crow," a decoration of the highest order.

The grass dance was noted among the Yankton Sioux by De Smet, who described it in a letter to Father Terwecoren, dated November, 1867, as follows: [1]

> The principal one [society] among the Yanktons is called the Grass band or *Peji-makinnanka*. All the braves, or men of heart, as the Indians express it, belong to this fraternity. . . . At the ceremonial dances each member carries a long bunch of grass, which is among them the emblem of abundance and charity. . . . The badge or distinctive mark of the society is the bunch of grass braided and attached to the waist of each member in the form and appearance of a long tail.

In this description we note the use of the grass, but a different symbolism is assigned to it.

Mr. La Flesche, who saw the Omaha and Yankton Sioux dance the grass dance together on the Yankton Reservation in the seventies is quoted as follows:

> The rhythm of the He-thu'-shka songs sung by the Yanktons was the same as that of the songs of the Omaha and the steps and bodily actions that were in accord with the rhythm of the music were the same as those of the Omaha. In fact the Yankton He-thu'-shka was and is now the same as the Omaha, except for certain preliminary ceremonies which the Omaha, also, have now omitted. Until within very recent times men only danced the He-thu'-shka, as it was strictly a warrior's dance.

The grass dance among the Sioux is briefly mentioned by George Bushotter, a Teton Sioux, in his "Texts," written in 1887–88. He includes it among the "intrusive dances" which took place in the camp while a Sun dance was in progress, and mentions the wearing of grass at the dancer's belt. [2]

In 1903–1912 Wissler found a society called the Omaha among the Oglala Sioux, [3] which he identifies with the grass dance. [4] "Crow belts" were worn in the ceremony of this society, but no mention is made of grass, either carried or hung from the belt. The grass dance among the Sisseton Sioux is described by Lowie, who says it was also called by them the Winnebago dance. [5] This widely distributed dance is noted by Wissler as existing at the present time among the Blackfoot, Piegan, Crow, Gros Ventre, and Assiniboin Indians. [6] A "feather-tail belt" seems to have been generally considered part of the dance regalia by these tribes.

[1] Life, Letters, and Travels of Father Pierre-Jean De Smet, S. J. 1801–1873 (edited by Hiram M. Chittenden and Alfred T. Richardson), III, pp. 1059, 1060, New York, 1905.

[2] The Bushotter Texts, translated by J. Owen Dorsey, A Study of Siouan Cults, *Eleventh Rep. Bur. Ethn.*, p. 463.

[3] Wissler, Clark, Societies and Ceremonial Associations of the Teton Dakota, op. cit., pp. 48–52.

[4] Ibid. (p. 49, footnote) "According to Mr. Nines *pezi mignaka* is another name for Omaha *kaiyotag*, which reached the Oglala through the Yankton."

[5] Lowie, Robt. H., Dance Associations of the Eastern Dakota, op. cit., p. 130.

[6] Wissler, Clark, Societies of the Blackfoot Indians, op. cit., pp. 451–456.

Many similarities may be traced between the accounts of the grass dance already cited and the descriptions of the dream dance, as practiced by the Menomini and the Chippewa. These resemblances touch, among other things, the custom of "presenting the pipe to the sky," the position of the drum in the dancing circle, the wearing of "crow belts," and the custom of divorce in connection with the ceremony of the society.[1]

Mr. Higheagle said that two kinds of grass dance are now danced on the Standing Rock Reservation—the old men's grass dance and the young men's. The former is shown in figure 38, reproduced

FIG. 38.   Grass dance.

from a photograph taken several years ago on that reservation and identified by Mr. Higheagle. This view undoubtedly presents some of the old features of the dance which have been changed by the present generation.

An instrument used in connection with this dance is called an elk whistle (*heĥa'ka ŝi'yotaŋka*). (Fig. 39.) Mr. Higheagle states that this instrument is called by the Santee and Yanktonais *ćo'taŋka* (*ćo*, 'pith'; *taŋ'ka*, 'large'). The whistle was made from the small, straight branches of a tree having a large pith, which could easily

[1] Cf. (1) Hoffman, Walter James, The Menomini Indians, *Fourteenth Rep. Bur. Ethn.*, pp. 157–161, Washington, 1896.

(2) Barrett, S. A., The Dream Dance of the Chippewa and Menomini Indians of Northern Wisconsin, *Bull. Pub. Mus. Milwaukee*, I, art. 4, Milwaukee, 1911.

(3) Skinner, Alanson, Social Life and Ceremonial Bundles of the Menomini Indians, *Anthr. Papers, Amer. Mus. Nat. Hist.*, XIII, pt. 1, p. 30, New York, 1913.

(4) *Bulletin 53, Bur. Amer. Ethn.*, pp. 142–180.

(5) Concerning the custom of divorce, see also Beckwith, Paul, Notes on Customs of the Dakotahs, *Smithson Rep.*, 1886, pt. 1, p. 256, Washington, 1889.

A

B

GRASS DANCE

be removed, a heated iron being commonly used for the purpose. Ash and box elder were woods frequently selected. The open end of the instrument was usually carved to represent the head of a bird. Mr. Higheagle stated further that the instrument was called *śi'yotaŋka* (*śi'yo*, 'prairie chicken'; *taŋ'ka*, 'large') by the Teton Sioux. The instrument is said to have had two uses: It was used in dances, especially in the grass dance, and also by young men as a "courting call." Plain bone whistles and bead-decorated whistles were similarly used in dances; these also were known as *śi'yotaŋka*. Three or four dancers might carry these whistles, but the signal was usually given by the recognized leader of the dancers. If the singers "came near the end of the tune," and he wished the dancing continued, he blew his whistle, whereupon they continued their repetitions of the melody.

In construction this instrument is a whistle, being an open pipe with the usual whistle or flageolet mouthpiece near one end. The pipe furnishes the series of harmonics obtained from a bugle or trumpet. The specimen illustrated [1] is old, having been in the possession of Mrs. James McLaughlin about 30 years, and could not be played, but a similar instrument, in perfect condition, was obtained among the Hidatsa at Fort Berthold, N. Dak., in 1915. The length of this instrument below the mouth is 22⅝ inches. The instrument was played by its Hidatsa owner, and a phonograph record of the performance was made. It was played also by Mr. E. H. Hawley, curator of musical instruments, United States National Museum. The following part of the long harmonic series could be produced on the Hidatsa whistle, the tones being named in ascending order: A flat (second space treble staff), D flat, F, A flat, C flat, D flat, E flat, F.

The grass dance of the Standing Rock Sioux at the present time (pl. 77, *A*) was thus described by Kills-at-Night (Haŋhe'pikte), a comparatively young man, who is a prominent singer at the drum whenever a dance is held:

This dance came to us from the Omaha and at first all the songs were Omaha. The melodies were repeated with care, and Sioux words were sung, but now we have many

FIG. 33. Grass-dance whistle.

[1] This instrument has been described as follows by Mr. Hawley, above mentioned: "Length, 25 inches; diameter, ⅜ inch. A straight stick of wood, its lower end carved to represent a crane with open beak, and its throat is the open end of the whistle. The bore appears to be from 7/16 to ¼ inch in diameter. A rectangular opening ¼ inch wide by 1 inch long, commencing 6½ inches below the upper end is made from the outside into the bore. A little above the middle of this opening a dam of wax or pitch is placed in the bore to deflect the current of air so as to impinge against the lip of the sound hole. The sound hole is about 7/16 inch square. Its cap is a piece of split quill, its lower edge a trifle above the crest of the dam of wax. The lip of the sound hole is also a split quill and is about ¼ inch below the lower edge of the cap. Both lip and cap are bound to the stick with red colored sinew. The instrument is a whistle."

grass-dance songs of our own, the melody and also the words being Sioux. There is always a feast at a grass dance. The men who have charge of the meeting decide who shall provide the feast, and the Crier notifies them. The same people are not asked to provide for two successive feasts. Each "cook" brings what she likes— dried berries or grapes, wild turnips, and sometimes sweet corn, prepared by boiling it with ashes until the husk drops off, then washing it thoroughly and boiling it with a bone which has fat on it. Dog is not insisted upon, but if one of the appointed "cooks" wishes to provide a dog it is greatly appreciated. The head and chest of the dog are cut into four pieces and put in a large dish. Four young men are selected to eat them, and after the young men have finished this the bones are put in a pile, and the four young men, one after another, dance four times around it. The pile is not in the center of the circle made by the young man as he dances; it is near one side, and as the young man passes near the pile of bones he extends his hand over it.[1]

In a grass dance the drum is outside the circle of dancers, near that side of the assembly where the men sit. A few women sing with the men at the drum.

One feature of this dance is that a lost article must be redeemed with a gift. Thus, if a feather falls to the ground the whole party dance around it, and one of the men goes forward and strikes it, afterwards giving a present to some old man, who is not expected to make any return. More than one may strike a feather, each being required to give a present to an old man. Sometimes four men do this, after which the feather is returned to its owner.

The men dance alone. The women also dance alone, but occasionally summon a few men, whom they call by various terms of relationship, as "brother" or "cousin." If a woman calls a married man into the dancing circle his wife regards it as an honor, which is correspondingly greater the longer he is required to dance. His wife always gives a present to the woman who asked him to dance. Sometimes a woman, rising, tells the brave deed of some relative, and all the women respond with the high, quavering cry which is their customary applause.

At the end of the men's dances the participants sit down, but the drum continues a moment or two, whereupon one of the men rises and dances around the circle, singing a short phrase. This is called "dancing the tail" (see pl. 77, B), and words are often used only in this part of the song. The tail dancer is selected by the other dancers, and it is considered an honor to be so chosen. Only a man who has done some brave deed may be chosen as a tail dancer. According to Mr. Higheagle, this feature of the grass dance had its origin in an honor dance, signifying that the dancer had acted as rear guard in a certain war expedition and been successful, or had been left behind on the warpath and had acted nobly. The same honor might be given to a man whose horse had been shot under him and who had

---

[1] Cf. the dog feast in the drum-presentation ceremony of the Chippewa (Bull. 53, pp. 173–189), which resembles the dream dance of the Menomini.

been rescued by a friend riding double in a fight.   The honor dance, in which also a man dances alone, is believed to be the origin of the tail dance.

This is the only recorded grass-dance song in which the words are continuous:

No. 195. "They Are Charging Them"   (Catalogue No. 593)

Sung by KILLS-AT-NIGHT

VOICE ♩ = 72
DRUM ♩ = 72
Drum-rhythm similar to **No. 19**

WORDS

awi′ća u pelo′	(they) are charging them
haki′kta yo	look back
nita′kola	your friends
awi′ća u pelo′	are charging them

Analysis.—This song has the remarkable compass of 17 tones, or 2 tones more than 2 octaves.   (See songs Nos. 55, 202.)   In order to observe this song the more closely it was recorded on two cylinders, thus securing six complete renditions.   These were uniform except that the last four measures were omitted from the fifth rendition.   The melody tones are those of the second five-toned scale.   The song appears to be a melody of much freedom, but on examination we find that only three intervals are used. All the ascending intervals are minor thirds. The descending intervals are as follows: 3 fourths, 14 minor thirds, and 3 major seconds. Minor thirds constitute 82 per cent of the intervals. The rhythmic unit is repeated throughout almost the entire song.

See plot of this melody on page 484.

In the following song the words were sung only during the "dancing of the tail of the song." Thus the principal part of the melody is found many times on the phonographic cylinder, while the part containing the words appears only at the close.

No. 196. Song of the Grass Dance (a)   (Catalogue N. 596o)

Sung by KILLS-AT-NIGHT

VOICE ♩ = 116
DRUM ♩ = 116
Drum-rhythm similar to No. 19

Śuŋ - ka- wit- ko ḳon he - ye - lo he- wa -

wo - ki- ya he wa- oŋ we he - e - ye - lo o a he yo

WORDS

Suŋ'ka-witko' ḳoŋ........... Crazy Dog himself
he'yelo..................... said
hewawo'kiya he............. "I helped"
waöŋ'..................... living
he'yelo.................... he said (this)

Analysis.—The accidental in the first measure of this song was clearly given in all the renditions. The words are found in what is called the tail of the song. The intervals in the first part of the song are larger than in a majority of these songs, but the intervals in the tail of the song are small. The time was not so strictly maintained in this as in many other songs. Thus in the first rendition the final tone in the third measure was sung as a half instead of a quarter note, and there was also a slight hastening of some measures in one or more of the renditions.

See plot of this melody on page 484.

No. 197. Song of the Grass Dance (b)   (Catalogue No. 594)

Sung by KILLS AT-NIGHT

Analysis.—The phonograph cylinder contains three complete renditions of this song, followed by four incomplete renditions from which the first and second measures, and also the sixth measure from the end, are occasionally omitted. The first tone in the transcription is not regarded as part of the melody, but seems to be a mannerism of the singer. The writer recorded the songs of an Hidatsa at Fort Berthold who sang the octave below the opening tone of a song in the same manner, but this is not a common custom among Indian singers. The progressions of this melody are such as to suggest either E or G as a possible keynote, placing the song in either the second or fourth five-toned scale, but as the only accented tones are G and D, the song is analyzed as having G as its keynote and being in the fourth five-toned scale. This indicates its tonality as major, yet the major third is not present, and about one-third of the intervals are minor thirds. This is one of many instances in which the term "key" can scarcely be applied to an Indian song with the full significance of the term as it is used by white musicians.

No. 198. Song of the Grass Dance (c)   (Catalogue No. 595)

Sung by KILLS-AT-NIGHT

Analysis.—This is typical of the songs heard at the present time on the reservation when the Indians are gathered for some social occasion. Like other modern Sioux songs, it contains a wide variety of progressions, there being five different ascending and the same number of different descending intervals. The minor second, an interval occurring infrequently in the older songs, is here found four times. The tone material of this song is peculiar. Considering G as the keynote of the entire song, the second, fifth, and seventh tones of the octave are not present. The drum was slightly slower than the voice in all the renditions.

No. 199. Song of the Grass Dance (d)   (Catalogue No. 597)

Sung by KILLS-AT-NIGHT

SHUFFLING-FEET DANCE.

Analysis.—Six renditions of this song were recorded, some beginning with an unaccented tone an octave below the opening tone, as in No. 197. All but 3 of the progressions are minor thirds and major seconds, the remaining 3 progressions being 2 fourths and 1 ascending ninth. The melody contains the tones of the fourth five-toned scale, has a compass of 13 tones, and is melodic in structure.

No. 200. Song of the Grass Dance (e)　　(Catalogue No. 526)

Sung by TWO SHIELDS

Analysis.—This is a simple melody, containing only the tones of the minor triad and fourth. It contains only 9 progressions, 6 of which are minor thirds. The melody has a range of 10 tones and is based on the tonic chord. The song was accurately repeated in many renditions, the drum and voice coinciding on each count.

When the gathering comes to a close the men and women stand in their places and dance. The men move more than the women, but none of them go toward the center of the circle.

No attempt to record songs of all the social dances has been made by the present writer. Two dances, in addition to the grass dance, serve to represent this phase of Sioux music, the two additional being the shuffling-feet dance (*naślo'haŋ waći'pi*) and the night dance (*haŋhe'pi waći'pi*).

SHUFFLING-FEET DANCE

The shuffling-feet dance is called also the Cheyenne, the glide, and the dragging-feet dance. (Pl. 78.) Lowie[1] noted this dance among the Sisseton and Santee, and Wissler[2] among the Oglala, who said they received it from a tribe living west of the Gros Ventre. Both men and women joined in the dance, whose step is indicated by its name.

Two songs of this dance are given herewith; a third song is No. 226.

---

[1] Lowie, Robt. H.. Dance Associations of the Eastern Dakota, op. cit., p. 130.
[2] Wissler, Clark, Societies and Ceremonial Associations of the Teton-Dakota, op. cit., p. 78.

No. 201. Song of the Shuffling-feet Dance (a)   (Catalogue No. 600)

Sung by KILLS-AT-NIGHT AND HIS WIFE

VOICE ♩ = 76
DRUM ♩ = 76
Drum-rhythm similar to No. 5

WORDS

waŋċi′ yaka................. I see (you)
waŋċa′ na.................... once
e′ ċi ya′ tahaŋ waöŋ′ .... (as) you stay on your side

Analysis.—The song, which is very rhythmic, is typical of the songs heard at gatherings on the reservation at the present time. The part sung by the woman is an octave above that of the man and is transcribed to show the manner of its entrance. The song has a range of 11 tones and progresses chiefly by whole tones.

No. 202. Song of the Shuffling-feet Dance (b)   (Catalogue No. 592)

Sung by KILLS-AT-NIGHT

Analysis.—This is typical of the songs heard at gatherings of the Sioux at the present time. It has a range of 17 tones, but a less proficient singer might omit the lowest tone. Two other songs with similar range are comprised in this series. (See Nos. 55, 195.) This song is harmonic in structure and contains only the tones of the major triad and second. Two rhythmic units occur, the division of the first count in the first unit being reversed in the second unit. The song was recorded twice, and the renditions on the two cylinders were exactly alike, showing that the two units and the rhythmic form of the song as a whole were clear in the mind of the singer. No interval larger than a fourth occurs in the melody.

See plot of this melody on page 484.

NIGHT DANCE

The night dance is mentioned by both Wissler and Lowie in connection with the shuffling-feet dance. It is also mentioned by Dorsey.[1] Both young men and women took part in this dance, which Wissler[2] describes as follows:

The young men sat on one side of the tipi, the young women on the other. As the songs for this dance were sung, a man would rise and dance with a present which he then presented to one of the young women. In the same way the young women danced with presents for the young men.[3] This was regarded as a kind of courting ceremony. Then all danced in a circle, holding hands. At the close a feast was made.

[1] Dorsey, J. Owen, Study of Siouan Cults, op. cit., p. 498.
[2] Op. cit., p. 79.
[3] [Cf. the giving of presents in the woman's dance of the Chippewa, Bull. 45, p. 192.]

No. 203. Song of the Night Dance   (Catalogue No. 601)

Sung by KILLS-AT-NIGHT AND HIS WIFE

VOICE ♩ = 100
DRUM ♩ = 100
Drum-rhythm similar to No. 6

Analysis.—This song has a compass of nine tones, the entire compass being attained in two progressions at the opening of the song. The rest in the fourth measure is somewhat unusual. The Indian does not seem to require "breathing spaces" in his songs, and when definite rests are found in a melody they are the more worthy of attention. (See song No. 79.) The rhythmic unit consists of a triplet of eighth notes on the accented part of a measure, followed by a quarter note. A similar triplet occurs on the unaccented part of the measure, showing the influence of the rhythmic unit on the rhythm of the song as a whole. The song is major in tonality and contains all the tones of the octave except the fourth. The seventh lowered a semitone is present as an accidental. The song is freely melodic in structure.

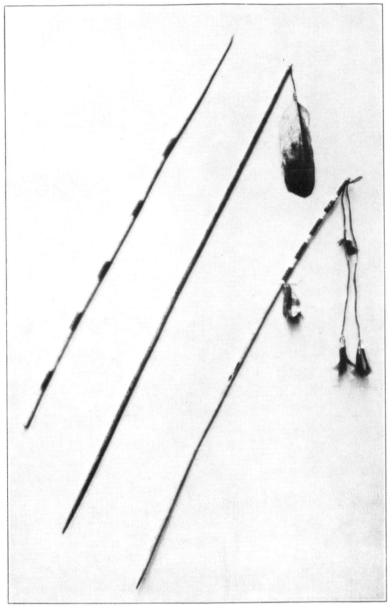

STICKS USED IN BEGGING

CAMP AT GRAND RIVER.

BEGGING DANCE

The begging dance is sometimes mentioned as though it were one of the social dances of the tribe, but it should rather be regarded as a custom, in which the dance step is merely incidental. The begging of food from tent to tent, which has been witnessed by the writer at tribal gatherings, was accompanied at times with merriment. Such a begging dance was seen among the Chippewa at Red Lake, Minn. (See Bull. 45, p. 171.) Certain songs are known from usage as begging-dance songs; most of these are very short. The songs originally used in begging food were "praise songs," the company standing in front of a tent and singing the praises of the occupant until he appeared with the desired donations. While this might be done for a social gathering it was more often done for the council tent or for some society. (See pp. 103, 320, 327.) When "praise songs" were used in this connection the time was gradually hastened, the begging party singing the song first in the usual tempo, after which the time was increased with each rendition until the gifts were received.

The council of chiefs might request contributions of food from three classes of men—those who had been successful leaders of war parties, those who had been victorious, but not as leaders, and those who had been wounded in battle. The request was made by means of sticks (pl. 79), appropriately decorated, which were placed in the ground before the tents. It was considered that the chiefs met in council for the benefit of the tribe, and therefore it was an honor for certain members of the tribe to provide them with food, while they were thus convened. One of the military societies usually decorated the sticks and "sang around the camp" to secure the food. A man was sent in advance to ascertain who occupied the various tents and to place the proper sticks in the ground. When the party collecting the food reached a tent they were ready to sing a song in honor of the occupant, who responded with a suitable contribution. Before the tent of a man who had been a successful leader of war parties they placed a stick covered with black paint and having a black feather suspended from it. For a man who had been victorious, but not as a leader, the stick was encircled with black bands, the number of which indicated the number of his victories, while for the man who had been wounded a stick was decorated in red. The elaborateness of the stick varied with the honor accorded the man. The sticks bearing the feather and the red tassels were used at a gathering of Sioux on the Standing Rock Reservation, July 4, 1911. The site of this gathering is shown in plate 80.

Distinct from the songs which were used when a party of people went from one tent to another is the following song of four old women.

It is called simply *wići'lowaŋ'pi*, 'begging song.' Yellow Hair said that she had a relative who went to war, and that the man's wife, with three other women relatives of the absent warrior, stood in the middle of the village and sang this song until donations were brought to them. The words are not transcribed, but are taunting in character, their general idea being, "If you have no buffalo chips in the tipi, go find some on the prairie for us," buffalo chips, used as fuel, being mentioned as the smallest gift which could be bestowed upon the poor.

No. 204. Begging Song of the Old Women   (Catalogue No. 682)

Sung by YELLOW HAIR

VOICE ♩ = 96
DRUM not recorded

Analysis.—In this song, as in No. 215 by the same singer, the only tones are those of the minor third and fourth, the song having a compass of four tones. (See song No. 217.) It is a wailing melody, well calculated to wear out the patience of listeners. The intonation was particularly unsteady, but the repetitions were so many that it was possible to determine the tones and make the transcription. The minor third and major second are the only progressions.

The following song is said to have been composed about the year 1870, being, therefore, comparatively modern. It came into use when the Indians first secured bread and coffee by trading with the white men. If it were known that an Indian had bread and coffee in his tent a party would go and sing this song, remaining in front of the tent and singing until he shared his luxuries with them.

No. 205. Begging Song   (Catalogue No. 619)

Sung by USED-AS-A-SHIELD

WORDS

wakal'yapi	. . . .	coffee
waćiŋ' ye	. . . .	I want
agu'yapi	. . . .	bread
waćiŋ' ye	. . . .	I want

Analysis.—The interval of the major third is prominent in this song, comprising 44 per cent of the intervals and occurring 9 times in upward and 12 times in downward progression. The song is based on the fourth five-toned scale, has a range of 10 tones, and is melodic in structure. The rhythmic unit appears 6 times, as well as in the first and second endings of the song where it is not indicated by the usual sign.

See plot of this melody on page 484.

PLOTS OF GRASS-DANCE SONGS

The four song plots here presented (fig. 40) are of two grass-dance songs (Nos. 195, 196), one shuffling-feet dance (No. 202), and a begging song (No. 205). As the first three contain no words, and as various kinds of songs could be sung in these dances, it is impossible to connect the idea of the song with its form. Songs Nos. 195 and 202 are of class A, which is a general type, and No. 196 is of class D, showing the characteristics of songs of motion or of animals.

In song No. 205, however, we have a plot which merits closer inspection. In this song the final interval between accented tones is an ascending interval, suggesting class E, in which the *first* such interval is ascending, and which was found to contain songs of distress. Songs similar to No. 205 can scarcely be said to constitute a class by themselves, yet on examining the plots of these songs in connection with their titles and words we find that many of them contain what might be called a "sense of indefiniteness." An exception to this is song No. 16, which was sung after the raising of the Sun-dance pole, though at this point in the ceremony there was an intense feeling of suspense and expectation. The only other songs having this interval between accented tones at the close are as follows: No. 47, "Owls were hooting in the passing of the night"—the song of a

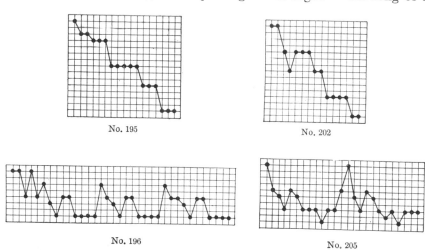

No. 195

No. 202

No. 196

No. 205

FIG. 40. Plots, Group 7.

medicine-man who anxiously watches a patient; No. 92, a medicine song of Sitting Bull's containing the words "No one is sacred, you said"; Nos. 95 and 97, concerning the buffalo walking in the north; No. 178, a war song with the words, "I am the fox, something difficult I seek"; No. 181, a song of the buffalo hunt; and Nos. 207 and 208, songs of the moccasin game, without words. In addition to these the only songs containing an accented tone lower than the final tone are as follows: No. 19, the opening song of the Sun dance, and No. 33, a dancing song used during that ceremony; Nos. 57 and 89, songs said to have been received from the bear, and No. 103 from the buffalo; No. 78, a song concerning the sacred stones, with the title "A voice I sent"; Nos. 147 and 149, songs concerning warriors slain on the warpath; and No. 218, the song of the maiden who leaped from the ledge.

GAMES

THE MOCCASIN GAME (HAŊ'PA APE'EĆUŊPI)

Guessing the location of a hidden object was the central idea in one distinct class of Indian games, the object varying in the different games.   The moccasin game is a familiar example of this class.   Culin says: "The moccasin game was played by the Algonquian tribes, and is found among the Dakota and Navajo.   Two, three, four, six, or eight moccasins are used, but four is the standard number.   The objects hidden vary from one to four, and consist either of bullets, stones, or little billets of wood." [1]   The game as played by the Santee Sioux in Minnesota is briefly described by Rev. E. D. Neill, as follows: "A bullet or plum stone is placed by one party in one of four moccasins or mittens and sought for by the opposite." [2]   In the usual manner of playing the game four bullets are hidden, one under each of four moccasins.   One of these bullets is marked, and the count is determined by the readiness with which the marked bullet is found by the "guessing side," and also by the position of the moccasin under which it was hidden, whether it were at the end or in the middle of the row.   The manner of playing the game among the Sioux is practically the same as among the Chippewa.   Illustrated accounts of this game among the Chippewa have been given by Culin,[3] and also by the present writer.[4]   The Sioux songs of the moccasin game are especially rhythmic, but the drum is not steadily maintained in one rhythm, as among the Chippewa.   Thus we find several drum rhythms occurring in this group of songs.   This is one of the instances which suggest a freer use of the drum among the Sioux than among the Chippewa.

---

[1] Culin, Stewart, Games of the North American Indians, *Twenty-fourth Rep. Bur. Amer. Ethn.*,p. 339, Washington, 1907.

[2] Dakota Land and Dakota Life (1853), *Minn. Hist. Colls.*, vol. 1, p. 280, St. Paul, 1872.

[3] Op. cit., pp. 340–344.

[4] Bulletin 53, pp. 210–213.

Cf. also The Menomini Indians, by Hoffman, W. J., *Fourteenth Rep. Bur. Ethn.*, pt. 1, pp. 242–244, Washington, 1896; and Skinner, Alanson, Social Life and Ceremonial Bundles of the Menomini Indians, op. cit., XIII, pt. 1, pp. 59–61, New York, 1913.

No. 206. Song of the Moccasin Game (a)   (Catalogue No. 551)

Sung by GRAY HAWK

VOICE ♩ = 92
DRUM ♩ = 108
Drum-rhythm similar to No. 6

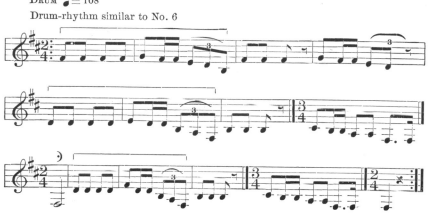

Analysis.—Three renditions of this song were recorded, the repetitions being without a break in the time. Throughout the renditions the drum was slightly faster than the voice, as indicated by the metronome tempo. The rhythmic unit, which is interesting, occurs three times. All the tones of the octave are found in the song, which is freely melodic in structure. The intonation was good. Intervals of an unusually large variety are present in the song, there being five kinds of ascending and five of descending intervals. The song contains two rests.   (See song No. 79.)

No. 207. Song of the Moccasin Game (b)   (Catalogue No. 552)

Sung by GRAY HAWK

VOICE ♩ = 76
DRUM ♩ = 108
Drum-rhythm similar to No. 19

Analysis.—This song begins and ends on the same tone.   (See No. 82.) The other instances of this kind in the present series with one exception begin with an ascent of an octave, returning to the original tone at the close. It will be noted that the first tone of this song is about midway of the compass. The tones in the melody are those of the minor triad and fourth. Five renditions were recorded, in all of which the peculiar rhythm was steadily maintained. The number of major thirds is twice that of minor thirds, though the song is minor in tonality. The song is harmonic in structure and contains a rhythmic unit which appears three times. Concerning rests in Sioux songs see No. 79.

No. 208. Song of the Moccasin Game (c)　(Catalogue No. 560)

Sung by GRAY HAWK

VOICE ♩ = 144
DRUM ♩ = 144
Drum-rhythm similar to No. 19

I - ći śni ya wi - lu - te

WORDS

ići' śni ya................ it is wrong
wi'lute.................... your signal ("you guessed wrong")

Analysis.—This melody is simple but has a taunting sound. It resembles song No. 211 in its brevity, its range of six tones, and its tone material, which is that of the second five-toned scale. A majority of the progressions are major seconds. Concerning songs which contain rests see No. 79.

No. 209. Song of the Moccasin Game (d)　(Catalogue No. 559)

Sung by GRAY HAWK

VOICE ♩ = 76
DRUM ♩ = 108
Drum-rhythm similar to No. 19

Analysis.—This song was recorded by Gray Hawk on two occasions, the duplication being accidental. On comparison it is found

that the two renditions are identical, even the pitch being the same.
The song contains the tones of the minor triad and fourth and has a
compass of an octave. It is a rhythmic melody, and the time of the
drum is slightly faster than that of the voice.

No. 210. Song of the Moccasin Game (e) (Catalogue No. 561)

Sung by GRAY HAWK

VOICE ♩ = 96
DRUM ♩ = 96
Drum-rhythm similar to No. 19

Analysis.—Sharply accented tones characterize this song. Eight
renditions were recorded without break in the time and in all the
accents were given as indicated. The major triad and sixth are the
only tones in the melody, which has a compass of seven tones. The
final tone is preceded by a lower tone. Table 4A (p. 27) shows that
in a large majority of both Chippewa and Sioux songs the final tone
is the lowest tone in the song.

No. 211. Song of the Moccasin Game (f) (Catalogue No. 525)

Sung by TWO SHIELDS

VOICE ♩ = 108
DRUM ♩ = 108
Principal drum-rhythm similar to No. 5

Analysis.—The drum rhythm of this song was not steadily maintained, the principal rhythm being often interrupted by beats separated by the value of a quarter note. (See song No. 125.) The song
is very rhythmic and is typical of the songs sung during a moccasin
game. The rhythmic unit is continuous, and the song was repeated
several times without break in the tempo. The latter part of the song
is characterized by a descending fourth followed by the ascent of a
whole tone. The melody tones are those of the second five-toned

scale, and two-thirds of the progressions are downward. The song is harmonic in structure and has a compass of only six tones.

The game of hiding a stick is called by the same name as that of hiding a moccasin (*haŋ'pa ape'ećuŋpi*). The implements used in the former are shown in figure 41. The rules of this game are given on the authority of Mr. Robert P. Higheagle, the writer's interpreter, who said:

Ten people play on each side, and 10 score sticks are used. One player from each side is chosen, these two competing to see which side shall first hide the stick. They sit on the ground opposite each other, and each has a little stick which he transfers rapidly from one hand to the other, his opponent watching and trying to determine which hand holds the stick. The player who conceals the stick most successfully

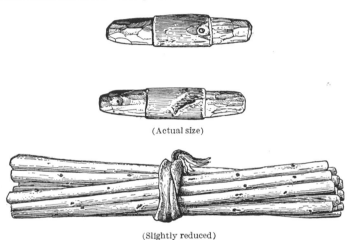

(Actual size)

(Slightly reduced)

FIG. 41. Implements used in the stick game.

thereby secures two score sticks for his side, in addition to the privilege of being the first side to hide the stick. The two lines of players are seated on the ground, and the leader of each side selects two players. These sit in front of the other players, facing each other, and each with a hiding-stick. The side whose representative won in the first contest is the side which first conceals the sticks, the opposing players being the guessers. If the location of one of the sticks is correctly guessed, the guessing side takes one score stick from the two acquired by their opponents in the first test. If the guessing side fails to locate the second hiding-stick, the rules require that the score stick be returned to the hiding side. If the guessing side succeeds in locating the second hiding-stick, they take the remaining score stick from the other side. The score sticks are taken from the opponent's pile as long as he has any, after which they are taken from the unappropriated pile on the ground. The leader of either side may at any time withdraw a player who is not successful and substitute one from the remaining players. The play of each side continues until the opponents have guessed the location of both sticks, and the game continues until one side has won all the score sticks.

The following signals are used to indicate guesses: Extending the first and second fingers and pointing toward the right indicates a guess that both players have the stick in their left hands. Similarly, pointing toward the left indicates a guess that both players have the stick in their right hands. Extending the right hand with the fingers spread means "the players have the sticks in the *outside* hands." The right arm descending with the hand cleaving the air like a knife means "the players have the sticks in the *inside* hands."

The writer witnessed a game as above described, at Bull Head, S. Dak., in 1912.

No. 212. Game Song   (Catalogue No. 598)

Sung by KILLS-AT-NIGHT

VOICE ♩ = 100
DRUM ♩ = 100
Drum-rhythm similar to No. 8

Analysis.—The compass of this song is nine tones, and this compass is accomplished in two intervals, at the opening of the song. More than half the progressions in this song are whole tones. The melody tones are those of the fourth five-toned scale. The rhythmic unit is interesting, and the song as a whole has a decided rhythmic quality

The following song was said to be used when a player was "on the verge of winning the game."

No. 213. Song When a Game Is Almost Won   (Catalogue No. 599)

Sung by KILLS-AT-NIGHT

VOICE ♩ = 108
DRUM ♩ = 108
Drum-rhythm similar to No. 8

Analysis.—This song was recorded on two occasions, each of the records comprising several renditions. The transcription is from the first rendition in the second recording. In this rendition the song began clearly with the ascending ninth, which is a most unusual beginning. Other renditions began with F sung once in the lower and twice in the upper octave, making the first interval an ascending octave, or with the three first tones on F in the upper octave. The song is rhythmic, with exact repetitions of the rhythmic unit except in one instance, in which the second tone is a quarter instead of two eighth notes. The progressions are chiefly major seconds and minor thirds. The final tone is preceded by a tone a minor third lower, which occurs in comparatively few songs.

The song of victory most commonly used in this game is a war song, the name of the opposing player being inserted in place of the defeated enemy. Used-as-a-Shield sang the song, inserting the name Red Bear as that of a player, and One Feather sang the song, using the words "the Crow tribe" in place of the man's name. The rendition by Used-as-a-Shield is given herewith. The idea of the words is that of derision, a free translation being "Did you think to save your life by that sign?"

No. 214. Song of Victory (Catalogue No. 618)

Sung by Used-as-a-Shield

Voice ♩ = 160
Drum ♩ = 80
Drum-rhythm similar to No. 5

Ma-to-lu-ta to-ke-śke   wiǂ-lu-te so

ha ya ya-ni *ha* kta ća *ya* he-ća-noŋ so

WORDS

Mato′-lu′ta	Red Bear
toke′śke wi′lute so	how did you make that sign? (indicating your guess)
ya′ni kta ća	in order to be alive
he′ćanoŋ so	did you do that?

Analysis.—This song is without change of time, a feature which is somewhat unusual. The melody tones are those of the minor triad and fourth, and the song is harmonic in structure. The last tone is preceded by one a whole tone lower. It will be recalled that the final tone is usually the lowest tone in the song. The interval of a fourth characterizes this melody, comprising about one-third of the progressions. The major seconds are equal in number, but are often used as passing tones and therefore are less distinctive than the fourths.

MISCELLANEOUS SONGS

CHILDREN'S SONGS

The little girls of the camp had their plays, which could scarcely be called games. In one of these childish plays the girls stood one behind another, each with her hands on the shoulders of the girl in front of her. Then they went around the village in a wavering line singing the following song,.the words of which are not transcribed, but which mean "the deer follow each other."

No. 215. Song of Little Girls' Play (a)   (Catalogue No. 680)

Sung by YELLOW HAIR

VOICE ♩= 76
DRUM not recorded

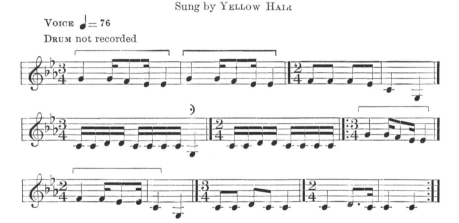

Analysis.—This is an example of a song in which the first part is sung only once, seeming to serve as an introduction to the musical performance. Thus the song was sung as transcribed and the last section was repeated four times. After a pause the song was recorded again, the singer beginning with the repeated part and singing it several times without a break in the tempo. The rhythmic unit is short but clearly given. The interval of a fourth occurs six times, forming about one-fourth of the entire number of intervals.

Another play which afforded much merriment was described by Yellow Hair, who said that the little girls sat in a circle and each girl, putting one hand over the hand of the girl who sat next to her, lightly pinched the hand near the wrist. The tickling sensation could be endured only a few seconds before the little girls all fell over in a state of helpless laughter. Almost immediately the play was resumed, and the song sung again, to be interrupted before it was half

492

finished.   It seems a foolish little play, yet war and ceremony were not all the life of the Indian; there were still the children, to whom life had not yet become serious.

No. 216. Song of Little Girls' Play (b)   (Catalogue No. 681)

Sung by YELLOW HAIR

Ho - śi - śi - pa   ho - śi - śi - pa   ho - śi - śi - pa   ho - śi

WORDS (FREE TRANSLATION)

hośiśi′pa.................... I catch but can not hold you

Analysis.—This melody seems almost too short and simple for analysis, yet it is marked by the steady downward trend and the emphasis on the descending minor third, which characterize many of the longer and more important songs.   It contains the tones of the minor triad and fourth, a tone material found in 12 per cent of the Sioux songs.

The following was said to be the only lullaby used among the Sioux:

No. 217. Lullaby   (Catalogue No. 679)

Sung by YELLOW HAIR

a · wa wa   wa   i - ni - na i - śti-ma - na a   a   wa wa

wa   i - ni - na i - śti-ma - na   a   a wa wa wa   wa   i-

ni - na i - śti-ma-na a   a wa wa wa wa   i - ni - na i - śti-ma-na a

WORDS

ini′la...................... be still
iśti′mana .... sleep

Analysis.—This song contains the tones of the minor third and fourth, the latter being sharped in three instances. The intonation of the song as a whole is wavering, yet in some renditions the descending semitones around the accidental were sung with reasonable accuracy. About 56 per cent of the intervals are major seconds. This and song No. 204 are the only songs in the present series having a compass of but four tones, a range occurring in only 2 of the 340 analyzed Chippewa songs. It is interesting to compare this with the Chippewa lullaby, which is in a major key. (See song No. 149, Bull. 45.)

Songs Connected with Legends

Legend of the Maiden's Leap

The legend of the maiden who killed herself by leaping from a rock is said to be found among many tribes of Indians. The writer first recorded the story and a song at Sisseton, S. Dak., among the eastern Sioux. The song was said to have been sung by the maiden before she leaped from the rock, but the record, being unsatisfactory, was not transcribed. The incident was said to have taken place at Lake Pepin, which is formed by a widening of the Mississippi River, on the eastern boundary of Minnesota. A promontory on the eastern shore of Lake Pepin is known as Maiden Rock, and tradition states that a Sioux maiden leaped thence and was killed on the rocks below.

A similar story was found by the writer at Standing Rock in North Dakota, among the Teton Sioux, who said they had been told that the rock was "somewhere in the west." Their version was as follows:

A young woman had promised to marry a man, but he wished to "make a name for himself" before the marriage took place. He had been on the warpath, but he wished to go again that he might distinguish himself by valor. When the war party returned they said that he had been killed by the Crows. Sometime afterward in the course of tribal wanderings a camp was made at the place where, according to the report of the war party, the young man had been killed. Dressing herself in her best attire, the maiden went to the edge of a cliff, and after singing the following song and giving the shrill "woman's tremolo," jumped into the river below.

No. 218. Song of the Maiden's Leap (Catalogue No. 620)

Sung by USED-AS-A-SHIELD

Zu-ya

i - ya - ye - lo e - ha - pi ḳoŋ he waś - te

wa - la - ke *ya* *he*   i - yo - ti - ye wa - ki ye

WORDS

zu′ya iya′yelo................ he is gone to war
eha′pi ḳoŋ.................... you said
he waś′te wala′ke............. I love him
iyo′tiye waki′ ye............ I am sad

Analysis.—The closing tone in this song is a fourth above the
lowest tone of the melody. This is somewhat unusual, the final
tone generally being also the lowest tone. The song is characterized
by the minor third, which forms more than half the number of intervals. The melody tones are those of the second five-toned scale.
The song has a compass of an octave and is melodic in structure.
Two renditions were recorded, which show no points of difference.

In connection with Type C, on page 53, it is noted that a recurrence
of accent on the lowest tone, usually the keynote, appears associated
with the idea of firmness and stability of character. A contrast to
this is afforded by the plot of this song (fig. 42).

LEGEND OF GHOST HILL

About 8 miles southeast of Fort Yates is a high butte known as Ghost Hill. (Pl. 81.) The following legend (given by Śiya'ka) and song (recorded by Two Shields) are connected with this butte:

When Sitting Bull and his band were brought from Canada they camped one winter on the lowland beside the Missouri River, a few miles below Fort Yates. It was a large camp, including many hostile Indians, who were afterward located at Pine Ridge and at Cherry Creek in the Cheyenne River Reservation. Among these Indians was a particularly handsome young man, who was very fascinating to the young women. One day he disappeared. As no trace of him could be found, his parents consulted a man who had some sacred stones, giving him a horse and asking that he would tell them of their son. This man said that during the next night the voice of the missing man would be heard passing through the camp, and that all must follow the voice. On the night designated all the camp was on the alert; just before dawn they heard the voice of the young man approaching. His parents and friends, recognizing the voice, began to lament, and the dogs barked as at the approach of a person. The voice passed through the camp, singing a love song, then turned and came back, retracing its way toward this hill. The people followed, but could not go as fast as the voice, which gradually became more distant until it was lost in the darkness.

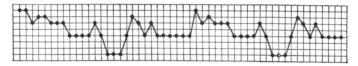

FIG. 42. Plot of song No. 218.

This incident seemed to make the grief of the young man's parents more acute, and they went again to the owner of the stones, to whom they gave another horse, asking him to tell who had killed their son. The man said he had been murdered by 10 men, who were jealous of him, and that one of these men would die in 10 days, another in 10 days after the first, and so on until all were dead. This came to pass as he predicted. The parents of the missing man then went again to the owner of the sacred stones and begged to know where they could find the body of their son. The man said that their son had been chased a long distance by his enemies and finally had been killed far from home, and that his body had been devoured by wolves. He also told the parents to follow the voice (which was still heard at intervals singing the same song) and to keep following it until they reached the place where the voice disappeared, where they would see their son. The next time they heard the voice they hastened toward the place whence it came and saw at some distance before them a figure wrapped in a gray Army blanket. They followed it but never could quite overtake it. Sometimes they would feel its presence behind them, and on looking back, would see it, but it never quite overtook them. It always followed the path toward Ghost Hill, and the parents thought it disappeared in the side of the hill. Accordingly they dug into the side of the hill and made diligent search, but the body of the young man was never found. A man named Walking Elk lived at the foot of Ghost Hill. He had a large family, the members of which died one after another. He laid their deaths to the ghost and shot at it with his rifle. The last appearance of the ghost was about the year 1889. It is said that a similar figure wrapped in a gray Army blanket was later seen at Pine Ridge and on the Rosebud Reservation.

GHOST HILL

Great difficulty was experienced in securing the song which was sung by the ghost. Two Shields finally consented to record it, and as compensation the writer gave him a valuable pipe, both the stem and the bowl of which were carved out of red pipestone.

No. 219. Song of a Ghost   (Catalogue No. 542)

Sung by Two Shields

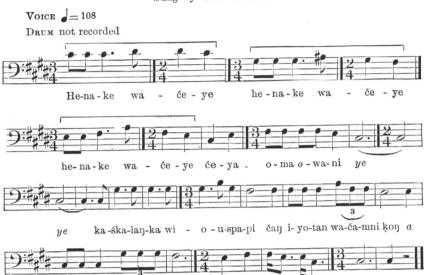

VOICE ♩= 108

DRUM not recorded

He-na-ke   wa - će - ye   he - na - ke   wa - će - ye

he - na - ke   wa - će - ye   će - ya .   o - ma o - wa - ni   *ye*

ye   ka -śka-laŋ-ka wi -   o - u-spa-pi   ćaŋ   i - yo-tan wa-ća-mni ḳoŋ   *a*

ı - yo-taŋ   wa-ća-mni ḳoŋ   će - ya   o-ma-wa-ni   *ye   yo*

WORDS

he′nake	finally
waće′ye	I weep
ćeya′	weeping
oma′wani	I roam
kaśka′laŋka	(among) young men
wiö′uspapi ćaŋ	courting
iyo′taŋ waća′mni ḳoŋ	(I was) most enthusiastic of all
ćeya′	weeping
oma′wani	I roam

Analysis.—This song is minor in tonality, contains all the tones of the octave, and has one accidental—the sixth raised a semitone. This accidental was clearly given in all the renditions. The song is melodic in structure and has a compass of nine tones. With the exception of three intervals of a fourth all the progressions are minor thirds and major seconds.

SONGS IN HONOR OF AN INDIVIDUAL

The following group of 12 songs illustrates the Sioux custom of introducing a new name in a praise song which has been used for other persons, and also of composing new words for songs. Three of these songs are melodies of distinct classes, No. 225 being a song of the White Horse Riders, No. 226 of the shuffling-feet dance, and No. 231 of the Strong Heart society. No. 222 is said to have been composed recently. The others are praise songs which have been used in the tribe. In many instances all the words of the song are new.

The person whose name appears in the songs is Two White Buffalo, whom Red Fox adopted in place of his deceased daughter and to whom he gave his daughter's name. Red Fox stated that he had a right to give this name as he had killed two white buffalo. Whenever these songs are sung it is expected that Red Fox will make, in behalf of Two White Buffalo, a gift to the singers or to any project for which donations are being solicited. Red Fox is a man who is highly respected in the tribe, and these songs have been widely sung.

No. 220. "The Poor Are Many"   (Catalogue No. 640)

Sung by SHOOTS FIRST

VOICE ♩ = 72
DRUM ♩ = 72
Drum-rhythm similar to No. 6

WORDS

Ptesaŋ'-noŋ'pawiŋ	Two White Buffalo
wakta' yaŋka' yo	watch
o'huŋke śni	the poor
o'taye	are many
heya'pi ćaŋ'na	whenever this is said
śuŋka'wakaŋ	horses
wećuŋ'we	I donated

Analysis.—This is the melody of an old praise song, used only for those who give freely. It opens with an ascending octave, a somewhat unusual feature. Aside from this interval and one ascending sixth, the melody progresses chiefly by minor thirds and major seconds, the former constituting 32 and the latter about 46 per cent of the entire number of intervals.

No. 221. "I Expect to Give Something" (Catalogue No. 641)

Sung by SHOOTS FIRST

1st rendition

VOICE ♩ = 56
DRUM ♩ = 56
Drum-rhythm similar to **No. 6**

2d rendition

VOICE ♩ = 84
DRUM ♩ = 84
Drum-rhythm as above

Ka-mi - te kiŋ-haŋ   wa-mna-yan-pi ćaŋ - na

o - ma - ki - ya - ka - po   *he*   Pte - saŋ - noŋ - pa - wiŋ

he - ya - ke - ya - pi ća ko-haŋ   wa-kta wa-oŋ ye - lo

WORDS

kami′te [1] kiŋhaŋ′ wamna′- tell me when the committee is raising funds
yaŋpi ćaŋ′ na oma′kiyaka po.
Ptesaŋ′-ȟoŋ′pawiŋ.......... Two White Buffalo
heyake′yapi ća.............. said (it is reported)
kohaŋ′ wakta′ waöŋ′ yelo′... so beforehand I expect to give something

---

[1] This is readily identified as the English word "committee" with the vowel sounds changed. Words are frequently added to Indian languages to express new ideas. An extended table of such words in the Omaha language is given by Miss Fletcher in The Omaha Tribe, op. cit., pp. 620, 621.

Analysis.—Like the preceding, this is a praise song in which words in honor of Two White Buffalo have been inserted. Like the preceding song, it opens with an ascending octave, and begins and ends on the same tone. (See song No. 82.) Almost one-third of the intervals are fourths, and the minor thirds are exactly equal in number. The song has a compass of an octave and contains all the tones of the octave except the second. Two rhythmic units occur in the second unit, the count divisions of the first unit being reversed in the second.

No. 222. "Two White Buffalo"   (Catalogue No. 642)

Sung by Shoots First

Voice $\downarrow$ = 60

Drum $\downarrow$ = 60

Drum-rhythm similar to No. 6

Pte-saŋ-noŋ-pa-wiŋ *he* bli-he - i - ći - ya uŋ - wo

o-ya - te o - kśaŋ *he*   wa-ćiŋ-ni-yaŋ a - u we - lo   *he*   na-ke - noŋ-la

ya-oŋ we - lo   To-ka - la - lu - ta *he* he-ya ke-ya pe - lo *he*   *he*

WORDS

Ptesaŋ'-noŋ'pawiŋ............	Two White Buffalo
blihe'ićiya uŋwo'............	take fresh courage
oya'te......................	the tribe
okśaŋ'......................	in general
waćiŋ'niyaŋ................	depend upon you
aü' welo'....................	when they come
nake'noŋla yaöⁿ' welo'.......	a short time you live[1]
Toka'la-lu'ta................	Red Fox
heya' keya' pelo'...........	said this, it is reported

[1] This is a common expression among the Sioux. (See songs Nos. 189 and 231.)

Analysis.—This song was sung by four singers, and was afterwards recorded by Shoots First alone, in order that it might be more easily transcribed. The structure of the song is interesting. There are two rhythmic units, having the same division of the first count; the first of these units appears nine times. There are also two similar phrases beginning on the unaccented instead of the accented beat. The second unit occurs twice, with a slight difference in the second measure due to the form of the words. The song has a compass of nine tones and lacks the sixth and seventh tones of the complete octave. Of the progressions 60 per cent are whole tones, the remaining intervals comprising 8 minor thirds, 7 fourths, and 1 ascending fifth.

No. 223. "Take Fresh Courage"   (Catalogue No. 478)

Sung by ŚIYA′KA

VOICE ♩ = 72
(or ♪ = 144)
DRUM not recorded

WORDS (NOT TRANSCRIBED)

Ptesaŋ′-noŋ′pawiŋ	Two White Buffalo
blihe′ićiya yo	take fresh courage
itaŋ′ćaŋ	(for) the chiefs
waŋwi′ćalaka će	you have seen

Analysis.—This song contains all the tones of the octave except the sixth and seventh. The principal intervals are the fourth and major second—an unusual melodic formation. The song is minor in tonality and has a compass of nine tones. The tonic chord is prominent in the melody, but the accents are so placed that the song is classified as melodic with harmonic framework.

No. 224. "The White Horse Riders Said This"   (Catalogue No. 477)

Sung by ŚIYA'KA

VOICE ♩ = 69
DRUM not recorded

E- ća Pte-saŋ - noŋ-pa - wiŋ

waŋ-bla - kiŋ   kte   h̓ćiŋ   na   i - yo - ti - ye   ki - ya   o - ma - wa - ni   ye - lo

Suŋk-ska A - kaŋ-yaŋ-ke ćiŋ   o   he-ya   a - u we - lo   he   yo

WORDS

eća'..........................	well
Ptesaŋ'-noŋ'pawiŋ...........	Two White Buffalo
waŋbla'kiŋ kte h̓ćiŋ.........	I am anxious to see
na...........................	and
iyo'tiye kiya' oma'wani yelo'.	I have traveled under difficulties
Suŋk'ska Akaŋ'yaŋke ćiŋ....	The White Horse Riders
heya' aü' welo'.............	said this as they are coming

Analysis.—This is a praise song, the structure of which suggests that the melody is old. It is probably a song of the White Horse Riders. With the exception of five progressions the intervals are minor thirds and major sixths, the first being about 36 and the latter 51 per cent of the entire number of intervals. An ascent of 11 tones occurs with the introduction of the words. The rhythmic unit occurs twice, and near the close of the song there is a phrase resembling the rhythmic unit, but having a different accent. All the tones of the octave are contained in the melody. The sixth occurs only twice, and in both instances is raised a semitone.

No. 225. "Two White Buffalo, Take Courage"   (Catalogue No. 671)

Sung by HAKA′LA (YOUNGEST CHILD)

Pte-saŋ-noŋ-pa - wiŋ   bli - he-i - ći - ya   yo

wa-wo - ki-ya - pi   kiŋ   he   waś-te   wa - la - ka   ke - lo

To-ka - la - lu - ta   he   he - ya   ke - ya   pe - lo   he   yo

WORDS

Ptesaŋ′-noŋ′pawiŋ...........	Two White Buffalo
blihe′ićiya yo...............	take courage
wawo′kiyapi kiŋ he..........	to give the assistance
waś′te wala′ka kelo′.........	I love
Toka′la-lu′ta...............	Red Fox
he heya′...................	has said
keya′ pelo′.................	so they say

Analysis.—This is a serenade song of the White Horse Riders, the present words being substituted for words formerly used. The man who recorded this song is a leader among the middle-aged singers of the tribe. The keynote appears to be G, and the tone-material is therefore that of the fourth five-toned scale, but the second is sharped in every occurrence. The interval of an augmented second occurs three times and was sung with good intonation. This interval is found also in two other songs. (See Nos. 63, 106.) The interval of a semitone appears seven times in this melody, and the minor third forms 47 per cent of the entire number of intervals. About two-thirds of the intervals are downward progressions.

No. 226. "The Tribe You Help"   (Catalogue No. 672)

Sung by HAKA'LA (YOUNGEST CHILD)

O-ya - te kiŋ-haŋ wa-wo-ki-ya - po Pte-saŋ-noŋ-pa-wiŋ

wa-na ig - la - so-te-a

WORDS

oya'te kiŋhaŋ'................ the tribe
wawo'kiyapo.................. (you) help
Ptesaŋ'-noŋ'pawiŋ.......... Two White Buffalo
wana'....................... now (by helping)
igla'sota.................... has consumed what she had [1]

Analysis.—This is a melody of the shuffling-feet dance. Two renditions of the song were recorded, one being sung by Haka'la as transcribed, and the other having the addition of the women's voices an octave higher. The song contains only the tones E flat–G–B flat–C. E flat seems the most satisfactory keynote, especially at the close of the song, though the tone is not prominent in the melody. Of the intervals 68 per cent are minor thirds, though with E flat as keynote the song is major in tonality. The submediant chord (C–E flat–G) forms the basis of a large part of the melody. The triplets of eighth notes suggest the song (No. 192) in honor of Red Fish and, though often repeated, have so little character that they can scarcely be considered a rhythmic unit of the song.

---

[1] Among the Sioux it is considered a particularly high compliment to say that a person has been so generous as to give away all his possessions.

No. 227. "Whenever the Tribe Assembles"   (Catalogue No. 684)

Sung by SILENT WOMAN (see pl. 54)

VOICE ♩ = 60
DRUM not recorded

O-ya - te kiŋ a - hi - mni-ći-ya ćaŋ - na *ha* mi-ta-śuŋ-ke

yu-ha pe   *he* Pte - saŋ - noŋ-pa-wiŋ he-ya ke-ya pe

WORDS

oya'te kiŋ ahi'mnićiya ćaŋ'na. whenever the tribe assembles
mita'śuŋke................. my horses
yuha' pe................... they receive
Ptesaŋ'-noŋ'pawiŋ .... Two White Buffalo
heya' keya' pe............. said this (it is said)

Analysis.—This is a praise-song melody. It is minor in tonality
and lacks the seventh and second tones of the complete octave.
Two accidentals occur, the sixth and third raised a semitone, both
of which are clearly given in the two recorded renditions of the song.
The intonation was good throughout the renditions, the semitone
progression, which appears six times, being well given. The tonic
chord is prominent in the formation of the melody, though the
accented tones are such that the song is classified as melodic in
structure.

No. 228. "They Depend Upon You"   (Catalogue No. 683)

Sung by SILENT WOMAN

VOICE ♩ = 58
DRUM not recorded

Pte-saŋ-noŋ-pa-wiŋ bli - he - i - ći - ya ye *he* kam-i - te kiŋ -

haŋ wa - ćiŋ - ni - yaŋ pe - lo he - ya-pi *he e*

e ćaŋ-na ma-zas - ka kiŋ-haŋ i - ɫipe-ya on-we *ne hu*

WORDS

Pteśaŋ'-noŋ'pawiŋ . . . . Two White Buffalo
blihe'ićiya ye . . . . take courage
kami'te kiŋhaŋ' . . . . (English word) the committee
waćiŋ'niyaŋ pelo' . . . . depend upón you
heya'pi . . . . they said
ćaŋ'na . . . . hence
ma'zaska kiŋhaŋ' . . . . the money (literally "white metal")
iɫipe'ya on'we . . . . you donated

Analysis.—This melody is one of the praise songs, or honor
songs, of the tribe. Three renditions were recorded. The first two
had no words, and the note values varied, but the third was as indicated, though the florid part of the first measure can not be transcribed
with absolute accuracy. The song is minor in tonality, harmonic in
structure, and contains all the tones of the octave. The upward and
downward progressions are more nearly equal than usual, there being
15 downward and 13 upward progressions.

No. 229. "I Donated a Horse"   (Catalogue No. 579)

Sung by SHOOTER

VOICE ♩ = 80
DRUM ♩ = 80
Drum-rhythm similar to No. 5

Pte-saŋ-noŋ-pa - wiŋ   ḳoŋ bli - hi - ća   ye *ya*   e - ha - pi

ća   he   śuŋ - ka - wa - kaŋ   *e*   we - ćoŋ we - lo

WORDS

Ptesaŋ'-noŋ'pawiŋ........... Two White Buffalo
ḳoŋ blihe'ićiya[1] ye........... take courage
eha'pi ća................... you said this
he......................... hence
śuŋka'wakaŋ................ a horse
we'ćoŋ welo'............... I donated

Analysis.—This, as well as the next preceding song, is a praise song in which new words have been inserted. It is based on the second five-toned scale and is minor in tonality, but the proportion of minor thirds is smaller than in many major songs, 44 per cent of the intervals being minor thirds. The rhythmic unit is the same as the first unit in the next preceding song.

---

[1] This word was shortened by the singer.

No. 230. "Hence They Come"   (Catalogue No. 578)

Sung by SHOOTER

VOICE ♩ = 66
DRUM ♩ = 66
Drum-rhythm similar to No. 6

O-ya - te kiŋ

hi - wi - ta - ya   ćan - na   o - huŋ - ke śni   mi - ta - śuŋ-ke   yu-ha   pe - lo

he   Pte-saŋ-noŋ-pa-wiŋ   he   he-ya - ća   he   a - u   we - lo

WORDS

oya'te kiŋ hiwi'taya ćaŋ'na..	whenever the tribe is gathered together
ohuŋ'ke śni..................	those without resources
mita'śuŋke yuha' pelo'.......	obtain my horses
Ptesaŋ'-noŋ'pawiŋ	Two White Buffalo
he heya'ća...................	has said this
he...........................	hence
aü' welo'....................	they come

Analysis.—Two rhythmic units are found in this song, the difference between them giving variety and character to the rhythm of the song as a whole. The melody tones are those of the fourth five-toned scale. The fourth is prominent, forming about 25 per cent of the intervals, while the minor thirds form 71 per cent of the entire number. The song is melodic in structure and has a compass of an octave. In addition to the recording of the song by Shooter it was, at the request of the Indians, recorded by several singers assisted by others who gave the sharp yells with which songs of this kind are punctuated.

Rests are considered in the analysis of song No. 79.

No. 231. "A Short Time"　　(Catalogue No. 558)

Sung by GRAY HAWK

VOICE ♩ = 80
DRUM ♩ = 88
Drum-rhythm similar to No. 19

Pte- saŋ - noŋ - pa - wiŋ

bli - i - he - i - ći - ya　yo　　na - ke - nuŋ - la　　ya - oŋ

WORDS

Ptesaŋ′-noŋ′pawiŋ............ Two White Buffalo
blihe′ićiya yo............... take courage
nake′nuŋla yaön′ .... a short time you live (see songs Nos. 189, 222)

Analysis.—This is a song of the Strong Heart society. It was considered a special honor to be praised in the songs of this society. This song contains only the tones of the minor triad and fourth and is melodic in structure. The progressions are interesting, as the ascending intervals are all larger than (and including) the minor third, while the descending intervals are smaller than (and including) the minor third. A majority of the descending intervals are whole tones. This is a particularly clear-cut and pleasing melody.

LOVE SONGS (WIÖ′WEŚTE OLO′WAŊ)

The three following songs are comparatively modern. The words of the first song only are transcribed. The words of the second are somewhat similar, being the expression of a maid whose parents object to the man of her choice. The third song was recorded at Sisseton, only the melody being taken.

The older form of love song is considered in connection with the war material on page 370.

No. 232. "Come"　　(Catalogue No. 659)

Sung by Dog Eagle

VOICE ♩= 88

DRUM not recorded

WORDS

wiċa′yaka heċi′na yaü′ śnï... if you are truthful, come
Taŋiŋ′yaŋ-ma′niwiŋ.......... Walks Visibly (woman's name)
he′ya helo′................. has said this

Analysis.—In several respects this melody resembles No. 234. Like that song, it has a range of 10 tones, lacks the sixth and seventh of the complete octave, and in structure is melodic with harmonic framework. About one-fifth of the intervals are fourths, the remaining intervals, with three exceptions, being minor thirds and major seconds. Two rhythmic units are present and a comparison of them as well as a study of their use is interesting. It will be noted that the first three and the last two counts of the two units are alike. · The triplets of eighth notes were distinctly given. Two renditions of the entire song were recorded, with a repetition of the part containing the words. These showed no points of difference.

No. 233. Love Song (a)   (Catalogue No. 590)

Sung by SWIFT DOG

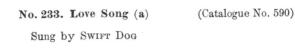

Analysis.—Two rhythmic units are found in this song, each appearing twice. The larger part of the second unit also appears at the close of the song, but a change of accent alters the phrase so materially that it is not marked as a repetition of the unit. One accidental occurs—the seventh raised a semitone—this being an accidental often found in songs of minor tonality. This melody is based on the second five-toned scale and is harmonic in structure. One-third of the intervals are minor thirds.

No. 234. Love Song (b)   (Catalogue No. 661)

Sung by BLUE CLOUD

Analysis.—This is an excellent example of the modern Sioux love song. Twenty-seven per cent of the intervals are minor thirds.

The remainder of the progressions show a greater variety than is found in a majority of the Sioux songs. This appears to be a characteristic of the more modern songs. All the tones of the octave except the sixth and seventh are present in the melody. The song begins and ends on the same tone, a somewhat unusual feature in both Chippewa and Sioux songs. (See song No. 82.) This song was recorded at Sisseton. (See below.)

SIOUX SONGS RECORDED AT SISSETON, S. DAK.

All the songs of this group were recorded among the Santee Sioux at Sisseton, S. Dak., at the opening of the writer's work among the Sioux. This place was selected because Sioux from this locality frequently visit the Chippewa, among whom the writer's previous work had been done, and it was thought that this acquaintance would facilitate the work. It was impossible, however, to secure a satisfactory interpreter at Sisseton, and most of the songs recorded there were translated from the phonograph record by Mr. Higheagle. Many of these songs were familiar to the Standing Rock Sioux and were identified by them when the records were played. In one instance a Standing Rock singer supplied words which were missing from the Sisseton rendition of a song. A few Sun-dance songs were recorded, but these were said to belong to the Santee ceremony and were accordingly discarded. It is, however, interesting to note Sioux material from more than one locality, and the songs are therefore included in the series. Other Sisseton songs are Nos. 95, 96, 97, 189, 190. The words of the songs recorded at Sisseton are in the Santee dialect. (See p. 2.)

On July 4, 1911, the writer attended a gathering of Indians on the Sisseton Reservation. The number of dancers was small compared with that at Standing Rock, and the striking contrast indicates the progress of the Sioux away from the old customs. A little group of dancers facing the setting sun is shown in plate 82. One of the mounted men was Good Thunder, the chief, who wore a gold-braided uniform and acted as "marshal of the day," and the other was a mounted Indian policeman. In the same plate is shown also the prairie on this reservation, which is more rolling than that at Standing Rock.

The three following songs are known at Standing Rock as songs of the Ticketless society. The term "society" is here a misnomer, being applied by the Sioux to those who were first dropped from the list of those receiving rations and accordingly had no "ration tickets." Such Indians were supposed to be able to provide for themselves, and for that reason were expected to show unlimited generosity toward their friends. The designation was used for only four or five years and

DANCERS ON SISSETON RESERVATION

PRAIRIE ON SISSETON RESERVATION

was in the nature of a jest, but many songs of the Ticketless society are still remembered by the Sioux.

The first of these songs was undoubtedly sung as a praise song in honor of Little Helper, who was expected to be inspired to still greater generosity by its words.

No. 235. "You Have Relied Upon Me"   (Catalogue No. 645)

Sung by HOLY-FACE BEAR (MATO′ITE′WAKAN)

VOICE ♩ = 96
DRUM ♩ = 96
Drum-rhythm similar to No. 8

O-śka-te caŋ-

na   wa-ćiŋ ma-ye   ya-pi   ke-ha-pi *a* bdi-he -   i-ći-ya wa-oŋ   *he ya*

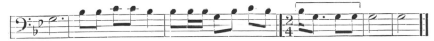

he   *e* Wo-wa-ćiŋ-ye-na   *o o* he-ya ćaŋ-na   taŋ-yaŋ

WORDS

ośka′te ćaŋ′na................ in dances and feasts
waćiŋ′ maye′ ya′pi......... you have relied upon me
ke′hapi........................ you have said
bdihe′ićiya waöŋ′........... so I have taken fresh courage
Wo′waćiŋ′ye-na .... Little Helper
heya′......................... said
ćaŋ′na........................ and
taŋyaŋ′...................... all is well

Analysis.—An unusually large variety of progressions is found in this song, there being 6 kinds of ascending and 5 of descending intervals. The number of major seconds is largest, though the intervals are more nearly equal in number than in most of the songs under analysis. The melody tones are those of the minor triad and fourth, the latter being sharped in one instance. This accidental was uniformly given in the several renditions. The song is melodic in structure and has a range of an octave.

No. 236. "I Have Been Helping"   (Catalogue No. 644)

Sung by HOLY-FACE BEAR

Voice ♩ = 72
Drum ♩ = 72
Drum-rhythm similar to No. 5

A - te he - ya ya *he* i - wa -

ho - ma - ya e - ća o - hoŋ - ke   śni *ke* wa - wo - ki - ya wa - oŋ

WORDS

ate′..........................	father
heya′ya......................	has advised me
iwa′homaya..................	by words
eća′.........................	so
o′hoŋke śni.................	the weak ones
wawo′kiya waöŋ′.............	I have been helping

Analysis.—This is a rhythmic melody. The rhythmic unit appears only twice, but its count-divisions appear frequently throughout the song. Of the progressions 79 per cent are either minor thirds or major seconds. The melody tones are those of the second five-toned scale, and the song has a compass of an octave.

No. 237. Song of the Ticketless Society (Catalogue No. 678)

Sung by **TWIN** (ĊEKPA′)

VOICE ♩ = 108

DRUM not recorded

Analysis.—This song contains all the tones of the octave, an unusual feature in a song of minor tonality. It has a range of 10 tones and is melodic in structure. Of the intervals 63 per cent are whole tones. The song is peculiar in that it contains only one tone less than an eighth note in value.

Rev. John Eastman [1] of Sisseton, S. Dak., told the story of the following song, saying that the incident occurred when his father was 15 or 16 years old, and was still remembered by many old people. The incident was as follows: A party of white men were driving cattle to one of the new settlements in the north. They lost their way and entered on territory along the Red River where the Sioux war parties were in the habit of going. They were seen by the Sioux, who, supposing them to be Cree half-breeds, fired on them, killing one or more of the number. These Sioux were under the white man's law, and when they found that they had killed a white man they knew that they were liable to arrest for murder. Accordingly they "lost themselves" among various bands of Indians. The chiefs tried to locate them, but could find only one man, whose name was Fierce Face (Ite′-hiŋyaŋ′za). In order to demonstrate the good faith of the Sioux toward the white men he traveled many miles without escort of any kind and voluntarily gave himself up to the authorities. He went from camp to camp down the Minnesota River, each camp encouraging him and praising him in the following song. His son, a boy of about 7 years, went with him to the edge of the

[1] Rev. Mr. Eastman's Sioux name is Maĥpi′ya-wakaŋ′-kidaŋ′ (Sacred Cloud Worshiper). See his biography in *Handbook of American Indians*, pt. 1, pp. 412–413.

Indian country.   After following the Minnesota River to its conflu-
ence with the Mississippi, Fierce Face went down the Mississippi
to Prairie du Chien, where he is said to have died in prison.

More than 70 years have passed since this took place, but through
a song the Indian who gave himself for the honor of his tribe now re-
ceives the reward which an Indian most desires—that his name and
deed shall be remembered.

No. 238. Song concerning Fierce Face   (Catalogue No. 662)

Sung by BLUE CLOUD

VOICE ♩= 76

DRUM not recorded

I - te - hiŋ - yaŋ - za *ga* na - ya - pe ćiŋ do   ni -

ta ko - da - pi ķoŋ o - ni do - ta - pi do

WORDS·

Ite′-hiŋyaŋ′za............... Fierce Face (man's name)
naya′pe ćiŋ do.............. you should not run away
nita′ ko′dapi ķoŋ........... your friends [1]
oni′ dota′p do.............. have borrowed you

Analysis.—This song is based on the second five-toned scale and
contains the seventh raised a semitone, this being an accidental
which frequently appears in songs of minor tonality.   The song
begins with an ascending octave (see song No. 220) and begins and
ends on the same tone (see song No. 82).   In common with many of the
modern Sioux songs, it has a variety of intervals, there being five sorts
of ascending and five of descending progressions.   The last count of
the rhythmic unit is not divided in the second as in the other
occurrences, this measure being sung the same in the four renditions
of the song.   In one rendition the first note of the song was sung
in the upper octave, avoiding the ascending octave.

See plot of this melody on page 519.

---

[1] Referring to the white men.

No. 239. Song Concerning a Message from Washington   (Catalogue No. 646)

Sung by HOLY-FACE BEAR

VOICE ♩ = 88
DRUM ♩ = 88
Drum-rhythm similar to No. 5

Tuŋ - ka - ŝi - na - na-ya-pɪ   he - ya   ke - ya - pi   *a*   *ha   i   a*

Da - ko - ta   kiŋ   wa - ŝi - ću   po   he - ya   ke - ya - pi   *hi*

tka   ta - moŋ-ka   ŝni   *e   he*   Da - ko - ta   kiŋ   te-wa - hiŋ - da

ye - do   *e   e   o*   *e* - pe   ća wa-wo wa - ki - ya

WORDS

Tuŋka´ŝinayapi...............	The great grandfather (the President)
heya´.......................	has said
ke´yapi....................	so they report
Dako´ta kiŋ.................	"Dakotas
waŝi´ću po..................	be citizens,"
heya´.......................	he said
ke´yapi....................	so they report
tka.........................	but
tamoŋ´ka ŝni...............	it will be impossible for me
Dako´ta kiŋ.................	the Dakota (ways)
tewa´hinda.................	them
ye´do......................	I love
epe´.......................	I said
ća.........................	therefore
wawo´ waki´ya	I have helped (to keep up the old ways)

Analysis.—This song is remarkable in its opening interval, which was uniformly given in three renditions, the fourth rendition beginning on the last part of the first measure. The song is melodic in structure, has a range of 10 tones, and lacks the sixth and seventh tones of the complete octave. This song was said to have been recently composed.

See plot of this melody on page 519.

4840°—Bull. 61—18——35

No. 240. Song of the Famine   (Catalogue No. 647)

Sung by HOLY-FACE BEAR

VOICE ♩ = 76
DRUM ♩ = 76
Drum-rhythm similar to No. 6

Wi-ća - ĺića-na kiŋ *he*

wa - na   he - na - ke - ća - pi   mi - ye   e - ha - ke

wa - oŋ   ća   *he*   i - yo - taŋ e   i - ye wa - ki - ye

WORDS

wića′ĺićana kiŋ . . . . the old men
wana′ . . . . now
hena′kećapi . . . . (are) so few that they are not worth counting
miye′ . . . . I myself (am)
eha′ke . . . . the last
waöŋ′ . . . . living
ća . . . . therefore
iyo′taŋ iye′ . . . . a hard time
wa′kiye . . . . I am having

Analysis.—This song is characterized by a sixteenth note followed by a dotted eighth, but this combination is used in so many connections that the song can scarcely be said to have a rhythmic unit. The melody progresses chiefly by whole tones, about 77 per cent of the intervals being major seconds. The song is melodic in structure and contains the tones of the second five-toned scale.

PLOTS OF SONGS OF SADNESS

Only 13 of the 240 songs under observation contain an ascending relation between the first two accented tones.   On examining these songs with reference to their titles it was found that those which begin with a large ascending interval are songs which have an idea, more or less evident, associated with sadness, disappointment, or suffering.   This type of plot, appearing to be distinct from others and to be connected with the content of the song, was accordingly designated Class E.   The plots of songs Nos. 238 and 239 (fig. 43) resemble each other, both being Sisseton songs, the former associated with a tragic incident and the latter expressing dissatisfaction. Similar to these is the plot of song No. 99, concerning the driving of buffalo against wind which cut their faces like a lance.   (See p. 419.)

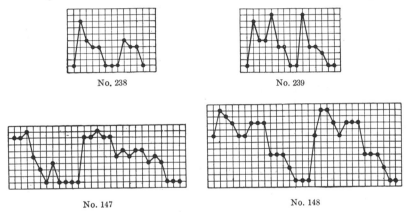

No. 238   No. 239

No. 147   No. 148

FIG. 43.   Plots, Group 8.

Songs Nos. 147 and 148 are songs concerning slain warriors.   The initial ascent is not so large in these, the large ascent occurring later in the song.   Song No. 149 begins with an ascending fifth and is similar in content to those last mentioned.   Song No. 191 is an exception, as it begins with an ascending sixth and contains no trace of the ideas mentioned.   Other songs having an ascending relation between the first and second accented tones are as follows: No. 207 (ascent of a fifth), moccasin-game song; No. 200 (ascent of a third), grass-dance song; No. 35 (ascent of a whole tone), Sun-dance song; No. 105, Elk-society song; No. 206, moccasin-game song; No. 212, hiding-stick game song; and No. 219, song of a ghost.   The last-named is distinctly a song of sadness; with one exception the others have no words, and the origin of these songs is somewhat uncertain.

This final analysis group comprises several small groups of songs. First are three incidental songs (Nos. 18, 24, 25) used during the Sun dance, which can not properly be included in former classifications. Next are songs of the social dances—the grass, shuffling-feet, and night dances (Nos. 195–203); songs used in ordinary begging, distinct from requests for food accompanied with singing of praise songs (Nos. 204, 205); and songs of games (Nos. 206–213) together with songs used in children's play (Nos. 215–217), and songs connected with legends (Nos. 218, 219). In this group are also such songs in honor of the writer as were sung to modern tunes; these are Nos. 220, 221, 222, 226, 227, 228, 229, 230. There is a small group of modern love songs (Nos. 232–234). These are followed by a group of miscellaneous songs (Nos. 235–240) recorded at Sisseton, S. Dak., a majority of which were probably Santee rather than Teton Sioux in origin. Three songs recorded at Sisseton (Nos. 95–97) are analyzed with the Teton songs, as they are general in character and may have been used by both branches of the tribe.

Comparatively Modern Songs—(3) Miscellaneous Songs

MELODIC ANALYSIS

TONALITY

	Number of songs.	Serial Nos. of songs.
Major tonality...	15	24, 25, 197, 198, 199, 201, 202, 203, 205, 20ĵ, 210, 212, 220, 226, 230
Minor tonality.......................................	30	18, 195, 196, 200, 204, 207, 208, 209, 211, 213, 214, 215, 216, 217, 218, 219, 221, 222, 227, 228, 229, 232, 233, 234, 235, 236, 237, 238, 239, 240
Total..	45	

FIRST NOTE OF SONG—ITS RELATION TO KEYNOTE

	Number of songs.	Serial Nos. of songs.
Beginning on the—		
Twelfth..	1	202
Tenth...	1	237
Ninth...	1	199
Octave..	16	25, 195, 197, 200, 209, 210, 219, 222, 227, 228, 229, 232, 233, 235, 236, 240
Fifth...	14	18, 24, 196, 201, 203, 208, 211, 212, 214, 215, 216, 218, 220, 230
Fourth...	1	217
Third...	6	198, 204, 205, 206, 213, 226
Keynote..	5	207, 221, 234, 238, 239
Total..	45	

Comparatively Modern Songs—(3) Miscellaneous Songs—Continued

MELODIC ANALYSIS—Continued

LAST NOTE OF SONG—ITS RELATION TO KEYNOTE

	Number of songs.	Serial Nos. of songs.
Ending on the—		
Fifth	12	18, 196, 199, 201, 202, 203, 206, 210, 212, 214, 220, 230
Third	6	24, 25, 198, 213, 226, 234
Keynote	27	195, 197, 200, 204, 205, 207, 208, 209, 211, 215, 216, 217, 218, 219, 221, 222, 227, 228, 229, 232, 233, 235, 236, 237, 238, 239, 240
Total		
	45	

LAST NOTE OF SONG—ITS RELATION TO COMPASS OF SONG

	Number of songs.	Serial Nos. of songs.
Songs in which final tone is—		
Lowest tone in song	34	18, 24, 25, 195, 196, 197, 199, 200, 203, 204, 205, 206, 209, 212, 215, 217, 219, 220, 221, 222, 226, 227, 228, 229, 230, 232, 233, 234, 235, 236, 237, 238, 239, 240
Immediately preceded by—		
Minor third below	2	202, 213
Whole tone below	4	208, 210, 211, 214
Songs containing a fourth below the final tone	3	207, 216, 218
Songs containing a major third below the final tone	1	198
Songs containing a minor third below the final tone	1	201
Total	45	

NUMBER OF TONES COMPRISING COMPASS OF SONG

	Number of songs.	Serial Nos. of songs.
Compass of—		
Seventeen tones	2	195, 202
Fourteen tones	1	25
Thirteen tones	1	198
Eleven tones	1	201
Ten tones	7	24, 200, 205, 232, 234, 237, 239
Nine tones	8	196, 198, 203, 206, 212, 214, 219, 222
Eight tones	19	18, 197, 207, 209, 213, 216, 218, 220, 221, 226, 227, 228, 229, 230, 233, 235, 236, 238, 240
Seven tones	1	210
Six tones	2	208, 211
Five tones	1	215
Four tones	2	204, 217
Total	45	

Comparatively Modern Songs—(3) Miscellaneous Songs—Continued

MELODIC ANALYSIS—Continued

TONE MATERIAL

	Number of songs.	Serial Nos. of songs.
Second five-toned scale	11	18, 195, 208, 211, 213, 218, 229, 233, 236, 238, 240
Fourth five-toned scale	8	24, 25, 197, 199, 201, 205, 212, 230
Major triad and sixth	2	210, 226
Major triad and second	1	202
Minor triad and fourth	7	200, 207, 209, 214, 215, 217, 235
Octave complete	3	206, 228, 237
Octave complete except seventh	1	219
Octave complete except seventh and sixth	5	216, 222, 232, 234, 239
Octave complete except seventh, fifth, and second	1	198
Octave complete except seventh and second	1	227
Octave complete except sixth	1	220
Octave complete except fourth	1	203
Octave complete except fourth and second	1	196
Octave complete except second	1	221
Minor third and fourth	1	204
Total	45	

ACCIDENTALS

	Number of songs.	Serial Nos. of songs.
Songs containing—		
No accidental	37	18, 24, 25, 195, 197, 198, 199, 200, 201, 202, 204, 205, 206, 207, 208, 209, 210, 211, 212, 213, 214, 215, 216, 218, 220, 221, 222, 226, 228, 229, 230, 232, 234, 236, 237, 239, 240
Seventh raised a semitone	2	233, 238
Sixth raised a semitone	2	196, 219
Fourth raised a semitone	2	217, 235
Third and sixth raised a semitone	1	227
Seventh lowered a semitone	1	203
Total	45	

STRUCTURE

	Number of songs.	Serial Nos. of songs.
Melodic	32	18, 24, 25, 195, 199, 201, 203, 204, 205, 206, 208, 209, 210, 212, 213, 215, 216, 217, 218, 219, 220, 221, 226, 227, 229, 230, 235, 236, 237, 238, 239, 240
Melodic with harmonic framework	4	200, 222, 232, 234
Harmonic	9	196, 197, 198, 202, 207, 211, 214, 228, 233
Total	45	

Comparatively Modern Songs—(3) Miscellaneous Songs—Continued

MELODIC ANALYSIS—Continued

FIRST PROGRESSION—DOWNWARD AND UPWARD

	Number of songs.	Serial Nos. of songs.
Downward..	22	18, 24, 197, 202, 208, 209 210, 211, 214, 215, 216, 217, 218, 226, 227, 229, 230, 233, 235, 236, 237, 240
Upward..	23	25, 195, 196, 198, 199, 200, 201, 203, 204, 205, 206, 207, 212, 213, 219, 220, 221, 222, 228, 232, 234, 238, 239
Total.............................	45	

TOTAL NUMBER OF PROGRESSIONS—DOWNWARD AND UPWARD

Downward...	795
Upward...	464
Total..	1,259

INTERVALS IN DOWNWARD PROGRESSION

Interval of a—	
Fifth...	4
Fourth...	80
Major third.......................................	43
Minor third.......................................	273
Major second......................................	376
Minor second......................................	19
Total..	795

INTERVALS IN UPWARD PROGRESSION

Interval of a—	
Tenth..	2
Ninth..	1
Octave...	14
Major sixth..	2
Minor sixth..	4
Fifth..	18
Fourth...	82
Major third..	38
Minor third..	130
Major second.......................................	160
Minor second.......................................	13
Total...	464

AVERAGE NUMBER OF SEMITONES IN AN INTERVAL

Total number of intervals.............................	1,259
Total number of semitones.............................	3,865
Average number of semitones in an interval............	3.07

Comparatively Modern Songs—(3) Miscellaneous Songs—Continued

MELODIC ANALYSIS—Continued

KEY

	Number of songs.	Serial Nos. of songs.
Key of—		
A minor	4	208, 214, 218, 222
B flat major	1	202
B major	3	201, 203, 212
B minor	4	18, 196, 215, 237
C minor	3	200, 207, 216
D flat major	1	205
C sharp minor	2	219, 233
D major	3	206, 220, 230
D minor	1	217
E flat major	2	210, 226
E flat minor	1	227
E minor	3	204, 232, 239
F minor	2	195, 240
G flat major	1	25
F sharp minor	1	238
G major	2	198, 199
G minor	8	197, 209, 211, 221, 228, 229, 235, 236
A flat major	1	24
G sharp minor	2	213, 234
Total	45	

RHYTHMIC ANALYSIS
PART OF MEASURE ON WHICH SONG BEGINS

	Number of songs.	Serial Nos. of songs.
Beginning on unaccented part of measure	16	18, 24, 195, 202, 203, 205, 209, 211, 212, 213, 217, 220, 221, 228, 232, 233
Beginning on accented part of measure	29	25, 196, 197, 198, 199, 200, 201, 204, 206, 207, 208, 210, 214, 215, 216, 218, 219, 222, 226, 227, 229, 230, 234, 235, 236, 237, 238, 239, 240
Total	45	

RHYTHM OF FIRST MEASURE

	Number of songs.	Serial Nos. of songs.
First measure in—		
2–4 time	22	25, 197, 198, 200, 201, 202, 204, 206, 208, 209, 214, 215, 217, 218, 220, 226, 229, 233, 234, 236, 237, 240
3–4 time	23	18, 24, 195, 196, 199, 203, 205, 207, 210, 211, 212, 213, 216, 219, 221, 222, 227, 228, 230, 232, 235, 238, 239
Total	45	

Comparatively Modern Songs—(3) Miscellaneous Songs—Continued

RHYTHMIC ANALYSIS—Continued

CHANGE OF TIME, MEASURE LENGTHS

	Number of songs.	Serial Nos. of songs.
Songs containing no change of time	5	208, 209, 213, 214, 215
Songs containing a change of time	40	18, 24, 25, 195, 196, 197, 198, 199, 200, 201, 202, 203, 204, 205, 206, 207, 210, 211, 212, 216, 217, 218, 219, 220, 221, 222, 226, 227, 228, 229, 230, 232, 233, 234, 235, 236, 237, 238, 239, 240
Total	45	

RHYTHM OF DRUM

	Number of songs.	Serial Nos. of songs.
Eighth notes unaccented	6	195, 196, 200, 207, 208, 209
Quarter notes unaccented	9	203, 205, 206, 210, 220, 221, 222, 230, 240
Eighth notes accented in groups of two	4	198, 212, 213, 235
Each beat preceded by an unaccented beat corresponding to third count of a triplet	6	201, 211, 214, 229, 236, 239
Drum not recorded	20	18, 24, 25, 197, 199, 202, 204, 215, 216, 217, 218, 219, 226, 227, 228, 232, 233 234, 237, 238
Total	45	

RHYTHMIC UNIT OF SONG

	Number of songs.	Serial Nos. of songs
Songs containing—		
No rhythmic unit	12	24, 196, 198, 201, 208, 214, 215, 218, 227, 228, 239, 240
Two rhythmic units	28	18, 25, 195, 197, 199, 200, 203, 204, 205, 206, 207, 209, 210, 211, 212, 213, 216, 217, 219, 220, 222, 226, 229, 234, 235, 236, 237, 238
One rhythmic unit	5	202, 221, 230, 232, 233
Total	45	

Comparatively Modern Songs—*(3) Miscellaneous Songs*—Continued

RHYTHMIC ANALYSIS—Continued

METRIC UNIT OF VOICE (TEMPO)

	Number of songs.	Serial Nos. of songs.
Metronome—		
56	1	221
58	2	25, 228
60	2	222, 227
63	3	18, 202, 234
66	6	24, 200, 217, 226, 230, 233
72	4	195, 220, 236, 238
76	6	201, 207, 209, 215, 216, 240
80	1	229
88	2	232, 239
92	1	206
96	3	204, 210, 235
100	3	197, 203, 212
108	5	211, 213, 218, 219, 237
112	1	199
116	1	196
120	1	205
144	2	198, 208
160	1	214
Total	45	

METRIC UNIT OF DRUM (TEMPO)

	Number of songs.	Serial Nos. of songs.
Metronome—		
56	1	221
60	1	222
66	2	220, 230
72	3	195, 220, 236
76	2	201, 240
80	2	214, 229
88	1	239
96	2	210, 235
100	3	203, 205, 212
108	5	206, 207, 209, 211, 213
116	2	196, 198
144	1	208
Drum not recorded	20	18, 24, 25, 197, 199, 202, 204, 215, 216, 217, 218, 219, 226, 227, 228, 232, 233, 234, 237, 238
Total	45	

Comparatively Modern Songs—(3) Miscellaneous Songs—Continued

RHYTHMIC ANALYSIS—Continued

COMPARISON OF METRIC UNIT OF VOICE AND DRUM

	Number of songs.	Serial Nos. of songs.
Drum and voice having same metric unit...............	20	195, 196, 200, 201, 203, 205, 208, 210, 211, 212, 213, 220, 221, 222, 229, 230, 235, 236, 239, 240
Drum faster than voice...............................	3	206, 207, 209
Drum slower than voice...............................	2	198, 214
Drum not recorded.........................	20	18, 24, 25, 197, 199, 202, 204, 215, 216, 217, 218, 219, 226, 227, 228, 232, 233, 234, 237, 238
Total.......	45	

RHYTHMIC UNITS

Old Songs[1]

1. CEREMONIAL SONGS

No. 1

No. 12

No. 13

No. 14

(1)

(2)

No. 15

(1)   (2)

No. 17

No. 19

[1] This group comprises songs a majority of which are believed to be 50 to 100 years old.

No. 20

No. 21

No. 36

2. SONGS OF PERSONAL DREAMS

No. 37

No. 39

No. 40

No. 41

No. 42

No. 43

No. 44

No. 47

No. 50

No. 51

No. 52

No, 54

(1)

(2)

No. 56

No. 57

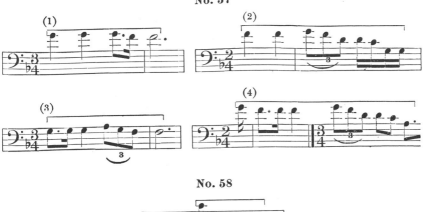

No. 58

3. SONGS CONCERNING THE SACRED STONES

No. 59

No. 60

No. 61

No. 64

No. 67

No. 68

No. 73

No. 74

No. 75

No. 76

No. 77

4. SONGS USED IN TREATMENT OF THE SICK

No. 79

No. 80

No. 81

No. 82

No. 83

No. 84

No. 85

No. 87

(1)   No. 88

(2)

No. 89

No. 90

No. 91

No. 92

No. 93

No. 94

5. SONGS OF DREAM SOCIETIES

No. 97

No. 98

No. 100

No. 101

No. 102

No. 103

No. 104

No. 105

No. 106

No. 107

No. 111

No. 112

No. 113

6. WAR SONGS (SEC. 1).

No. 128

No. 129

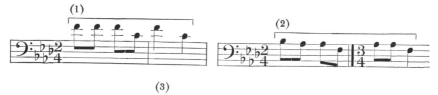

No. 131

No. 144

No. 145

No. 150

No. 151

No. 153

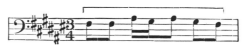

No. 154

No. 155

No. 156

No. 160

No. 132

No. 133

No. 134

No. 136

No. 137

No. 138

No. 139

No. 141

No. 142

No. 161

No. 164

No. 165

No. 166

No. 167

No. 168

No. 170

No. 171

No. 172

No. 174

No. 176

COMPARATIVELY MODERN SONGS [1]

1. WAR SONGS (SEC. 2)

No. 6

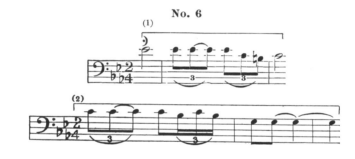

No. 7

No 8

No. 9

---

[1] This group comprises songs a majority of which are believed to be less than 50 years old.

No. 10

No. 23

No. 26

No. 27

No. 28

No. 29

No. 30

No. 31

No. 32

No. 33

No. 34

No. 35

No. 114

No. 115

No. 116

No. 117

No. 118

No. 119

No. 120

No. 121

No. 123

No. 124

No. 224

No. 225

No. 231

2. BUFFALO HUNT, COUNCIL, AND CHIEF SONGS

No. 182

No. 184

No. 186

No. 187

(1)   (2)   (3)

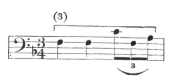

No. 188

No. 190

No. 191

No. 193

No. 194

3. MISCELLANEOUS SONGS

No. 18

No. 25

No. 195

No. 197

No. 199

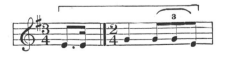

No. 200

No. 202

No. 204

No. 205

No. 206

No. 207

No. 209

No. 210

No. 211

No. 212

No. 213

No. 216

No. 217

No. 219

No. 220

No. 221

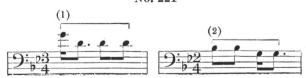

No. 222

No. 226

No. 229

No. 230

No. 231

No. 232

No. 233

No. 234

No. 235

No. 236

No. 237

No. 238

4840°—Bull. 61—18——37

BIBLIOGRAPHY

▸BARRETT, S. A. The dream dance of the Chippewa and Menomini Indians of northern Wisconsin. *Bull. Pub. Mus. Milwaukee*, vol. I, 1911.

BECKWITH, PAUL. Notes on customs of the Dakotahs. *Smithson. Rep. for 1886*, pt. 1, 1889.

BOAS, FRANZ, *and* SWANTON, JOHN R. Siouan Dakota (Teton and Santee dialects) with remarks on the Ponca and Winnebago. In Handbook of American Indian Languages (*Bull. 40, Bur. Amer. Ethn.*), pt. 1, 1911.

CATLIN, GEORGE. The manners, customs, and condition of the North American Indians. London, 1841.

CHITTENDEN, HIRAM M., *and* RICHARDSON, ALFRED T. Life, letters, and travels of Father Pierre-Jean de Smet, S. J., 1801–1873. Vols. I–IV. New York, 1905.

CLARK, W. P. The Indian sign language. Philadelphia, 1885.

CLARK, WM. *See* LEWIS.

COUES, ELLIOTT, *ed.* History of the expedition under the command of Lewis and Clark to the sources of the Missouri river, and to the Pacific ocean, in 1804-5-6. A new edition. Vols. I–IV. New York, 1893.

CROGHAN, GEORGE. Journal of Col. George Croghan. Reprinted from Featherstonhaugh, *Amer. Mo. Journ. Geol.*, Dec., 1831.

CULIN, STEWART. Games of the North American Indians. *Twenty-fourth Rep. Bur. Amer. Ethn.*, 1907.

DENSMORE, FRANCES. Chippewa music. *Bull. 45, Bur. Amer. Ethn.*. 1910.

—— Chippewa music—II. *Bull. 53, Bur. Amer. Ethn.*, 1913.

DOCUMENTS accompanying the President's message to Congress, at the commencement of the first session of the Nineteenth congress, 1825.

DORSEY, GEORGE A. The Arapaho Sun dance. *Pub. Field Col. Mus., Anthr. ser.*, vol. IV, 1903.

—— The Cheyenne. Pts. 1-2. Ibid., vol. IX, no. 2, 1905.

DORSEY, JAMES OWEN. Omaha sociology. *Third Rep. Bur. Amer. Ethn.*, 1884.

—— A study of Siouan cults. *Eleventh Rep. Bur. Amer. Ethn.*, 1894.

—— Siouan sociology. *Fifteenth Rep. Bur. Amer. Ethn.*, 1897.

FLETCHER, ALICE C. The Sun dance of the Ogallala Sioux. *Proc. Amer. Assoc. Adv. Sci.*, 1882 (1883).

—— The Elk mystery or festival. Ogallala Sioux. *Peabody Mus. Reps.*, vol. III, nos. 3 and 4, 1884.

—— The religious ceremony of the Four Winds or Quarters, as observed by the Santee Sioux. Ibid.

—— The White Buffalo festival of the Uncpapas. Ibid.

—— The "Wawan" or Pipe dance of the Omahas. Ibid.

—— The Shadow or ghost lodge: a ceremony of the Ogallala Sioux. Ibid.

—— The emblematic use of the tree in the Dakotan group. *Proc. Amer. Assoc. Adv. Sci.*, 1896 (1897).

—— The Hako; a Pawnee ceremony. *Twenty-second Rep. Bur. Amer. Ethn.*, pt. 2, 1904.

—— *and* LA FLESCHE, FRANCIS. The Omaha tribe. *Twenty-seventh Rep. Bur. Amer. Ethn.*, 1911.

FREIRE-MARRECO, BARBARA. *See* ROBBINS.

GRINNELL, GEORGE BIRD. Blackfoot lodge tales. New York, 1892.

HANDBOOK OF AMERICAN INDIANS NORTH OF MEXICO. *Bull. 30, Bur. Amer. Ethn.*, pts. 1-2, 1907–1910.

HARRINGTON, JOHN PEABODY. *See* ROBBINS.

HAYDEN, F. V. Contributions to the ethnography and philology of the Indian tribes of the Missouri valley. Philadelphia, 1862.

HELMHOLTZ, H. L. F. The sensations of tone as a physiological basis for the theory of music. Translated by A. J. Ellis. 2d ed., London, 1885.

HENNEPIN, LOUIS. A new discovery of a vast country in America. Reprinted from the second London issue of 1698. Reuben Gold Thwaites, *ed.* Vols. I–II. Chicago, 1903.

HOFFMAN, WALTER J. The Midē'wiwin or "Grand Medicine society" of the Ojibwa. *Seventh Rep. Bur. Amer. Ethn.*, 1891.

—— The Menomini Indians. *Fourteenth Rep. Bur. Amer. Ethn.*, 1896.

HOVEY, H. C. Eyay Shah: a sacrificial stone near St. Paul. *Amer. Antiquarian*, vol. IX, no. 1, Chicago, 1887.

INDIAN LAWS AND TREATIES. Vol. I (Laws), Vol. II (Treaties). Compiled and edited by Charles J. Kappler. Washington, 1903.

JAMES, EDWIN. Account of an expedition from Pittsburg to the Rocky mountains, under the command of Major Long. Vols. I–II. Philadelphia, 1823.

KAPPLER, CHARLES J. *See* INDIAN LAWS AND TREATIES.

KEATING, WILLIAM II. Narrative of an expedition to the source of St. Peter's river, under the command of Maj. Stephen H. Long. Vols. I–II. Philadelphia, 1824.

LA FLESCHE, FRANCIS. *See* FLETCHER.

LEWIS, MERIWETHER, *and* CLARK, WM. Original journals of the Lewis and Clark expedition, 1804–1806. Edited by Reuben Gold Thwaites. Vols. I–VIII. New York, 1904–1905.

—— *See* COUES.

LOWIE, ROBERT H. Dance associations of the Eastern Dakota. *Amer. Mus. Nat. Hist., Anthr. Papers*, vol. XI, pt. 2, 1913.

—— Societies of the Crow, Hidatsa, and Mandan Indians. Ibid., pt. 3.

—— The Sun dance of the Crow Indians. Ibid., vol. XVI, pt. 1, 1915.

LYND, JAMES W. Religion of the Dakotas. [Chap. VI of Lynd's Ms. "History of the Dakotas."] *Minn. Hist. Soc. Colls.* for 1864 [vol. II, pt. 2], 1865.

MCGEE, W J The Siouan Indians. *Fifteenth Rep. Bur. Amer. Ethn.*, 1897.

MCLAUGHLIN, JAMES. My friend the Indian. Boston and New York, 1910.

MATTHEWS, WASHINGTON. Ethnography and philology of the Hidatsa Indians. U. S. Geol. and Geogr. Surv., Misc. Pub., no. 7, 1877.

MAXIMILIAN, ALEX. P. Reise in das Innere Nord-America in den Jahren 1832 bis 1834. B. I–II. Coblenz, 1839–1841.

—— Travels in the interior of North America. Trans. from the German by H. Evans Lloyd. London, 1893.

MEYER, MAX. Experimental studies in the psychology of music. *Amer. Journ. Psychology*, vol. XIV, July–Oct., 1903.

MOONEY, JAMES. Siouan tribes of the East. *Bull. 22, Bur. Amer. Ethn.*, 1894.

—— The Ghost-dance religion and the Sioux outbreak of 1890. *Fourteenth Rep. Bur. Amer. Ethn.*, pt. 2, 1896.

—— Calendar history of the Kiowa Indians. *Seventeenth Rep. Bur. Amer. Ethn.*, pt. 1, 1898.

—— The Cheyenne Indians. *Mem. Amer. Anthr. Assoc.*, vol. I, 1905–1907.

NEILL, E. D. Dakota land and Dakota life. *Minn. Hist. Colls.*, vol. I. Reprint, 1872.

POND, G. H. Dakota superstitions. Ibid. for 1867 [vol. II, pt. 3] (1867).

RICHARDSON, ALFRED T. *See* CHITTENDEN.

Riggs, Stephen R. Tah'-koo Wah-kan; or, the gospel among the Dakotas. Boston [1869].

—— The theogony of the Sioux. *Amer. Antiquarian*, vol. ii, no. 4, 1880.

—— A Dakota-English dictionary. Edited by James Owen Dorsey. *Contr. N. Amer. Ethn.*, vol. vii, 1890.

—— Dakota grammar, texts, and ethnography. Edited by James Owen Dorsey. Ibid., vol. ix, 1893.

Robinson, DeLorme. Editorial notes on historical sketch of North and South Dakota. *South Dakota Hist. Colls.*, vol. i, 1902.

Robbins, Wilfred William, Harrington, John Peabody, *and* Freire-Marreco, Barbara. Ethnobotany of the Tewa Indians. *Bull. 55, Bur. Amer. Ethn.*, 1916.

Scott, Hugh Lenox. Notes on the Kado, or Sun dance of the Kiowa. *Amer. Anthropologist*, vol. xiii, no. 3, 1911.

Seashore, C. E. The measurement of pitch discrimination: a preliminary report. *Psychological Monographs*, vol. xiii, no. 1, 1910.

Skinner, Alanson. Social life and ceremonial bundles of the Menomini Indians. *Amer. Mus. Nat. Hist., Anthr. Papers*, vol. xiii, pt. 1, 1913.

—— War customs of the Menomini Indians. *Amer. Anthropologist*, vol. xiii, no. 2, 1911.

Stevenson, Matilda Coxe. Ethnobotany of the Zuñi Indians. *Thirtieth Rep. Bur. Amer. Ethn.*, 1915.

Swanton, John R. Indian tribes of the lower Mississippi valley and adjacent coast of the Gulf of Mexico. *Bull. 43, Bur. Amer. Ethn.*, 1911.

—— *See* Boas.

Warren, William W. History of the Ojibways. *Minn. Hist. Soc. Colls.*, vol. v, 1885.

Wilson, R. N. The sacrificial rite of the Blackfoot. *Proc. and Trans. Roy. Soc. Can.*, 1909, 3d ser., vol. iii, sec. ii, 1910.

Wissler, Clark. Societies and ceremonial associations in the Oglala division of the Teton-Dakota. *Amer. Mus. Nat. Hist., Anthr. Papers*, vol. xi, pt. 1, 1912.

—— Societies and dance associations of the Blackfoot Indians. Ibid., pt. 4, 1913.

United States Office of Indian Affairs. (Department of the Interior.) Reports of the Commissioners. For the years 1874, 1875, 1882, 1886.

INDEX

[For a list of the songs contained in this volume, see pages XIII-XXV, and of the authorities cited, pages 551-553.]